The Federal Income Taxation of Individuals

AN INTEGRATED APPROACH

JEFFREY L. KWALL

KATHLEEN AND BERNARD BEAZLEY PROFESSOR OF LAW
LOYOLA UNIVERSITY CHICAGO SCHOOL OF LAW

DOCTRINE AND PRACTICE SERIES™

FOUNDATION
PRESS

© 2020 LEG, Inc. d/b/a West Academic
    444 Cedar Street, Suite 700
    St. Paul, MN 55101
    1-877-888-1330

Printed in the United States of America

ISBN: 978-1-64020-751-6

To

My wife, Bobbi,

My daughters, Shanna, Rachel, and Nisa,

My sons(-in-law), Andrew, Jeremy, and Jordan, and

The next generation led by my grandson, Sander.

Preface

Law students typically approach the study of Federal Income Tax with some degree of trepidation. They have heard that tax is difficult and that it involves math. Some students believe that only those with a degree in accounting can succeed in a law school tax course. In spite of these concerns, almost all law students take the basic Federal Income Tax course because they have been told that all lawyers should know something about tax.

Contrary to popular belief, the vast majority of law students actually enjoy studying Federal Income Tax. The study of tax law is intellectually stimulating and appeals to students with a wide range of backgrounds. An analytical mind and a creative approach to problem solving are far more important than one's undergraduate major. Many students who dreaded taking their first tax course become motivated to take additional tax courses. Some of the most successful tax lawyers concentrated their undergraduate studies in the social sciences or the humanities. What about the math? Yes, you will need to do some basic addition, subtraction and multiplication but you can always use a calculator.

This casebook takes a more focused approach to the study of tax law than most introductory income tax casebooks. Although few students who enroll in the basic individual income tax course will become tax lawyers, tax issues pervade almost every area of law practice. It is critical for students to be equipped to recognize these issues regardless of their field of specialization. This book is therefore designed to enable students to appreciate the principal tax issues that might arise in any practice area.

A major goal of this casebook is to enable students to see the tax law as a cohesive whole, as opposed to a series of bits and pieces. To further this end, the casebook employs various unifying elements to facilitate a big picture perspective. Specifically, the book identifies and constantly reinforces four primary themes that pervade the study of income tax:

1. Economic considerations are more important than tax considerations. For example, it is preferable to receive a dollar and pay a tax, than not to receive the dollar and pay no tax.

2. The tax law imposes a "realization event" requirement that delays the tax on asset appreciation until property is sold.

3. The "time value of money" encourages individuals to defer income and accelerate deductions.

4. Our "progressive rate" system incentivizes individuals who are taxed at higher rates to shift income to relatives who are taxed at lower rates.

These four major themes are emphasized throughout the book and summarized in the Epilogue.

To enable students to easily categorize any income tax issue they might confront in practice, this casebook is organized into four principal parts:

1. Gross Income, which essentially represents any economic benefit an individual receives, unless Congress has provided an exception.

2. Deductions, which are payments that Congress specifically allows as a subtraction from gross income.

3. Timing of Income and Deductions, which is important because individuals normally wish to defer the payment of tax for as long as possible.

4. Impact of Multiple Tax Rates, which creates incentives for individuals to modify their behavior to cause their income to be taxed at the lowest possible rate.

In addition to offering unifying elements to facilitate a big picture perspective, this casebook endeavors to mitigate the foreign nature of tax law to most law students by focusing on familiar relationships. Most income tax casebooks begin by examining various types of gross income in a vacuum. By contrast, this casebook identifies a series of fundamental economic relationships with which all students are likely to have some familiarity (for example, the relationships between a business owner and an employee, a donor and a donee, and a lender and a borrower). The book then addresses the tax issues that apply to each party to the relationship.

This casebook also highlights certain simple, observable signals to help students identify when tax issues exist. For example, the observation of an individual receiving an economic benefit of any sort signals that gross income probably exists. Conversely, the observation of an individual making a payment signals that a deduction might be allowed. Moreover, the observation of one individual transferring property to another is normally indicative of a taxable realization event. In all three cases, the action observed is a necessary, though not sufficient, condition for an immediate tax consequence. By being attuned to these simple signals, students can increase the likelihood that they will not overlook basic tax issues in practice.

This casebook is not intended to serve as a comprehensive source of all the income tax rules that currently apply to individuals. Nor is it intended to analyze in great detail every rule it identifies. Instead, its goal is to examine existing law as a means to help students grasp fundamental income tax concepts and build confidence when working with complex rules. This approach is taken for two reasons. First, new tax legislation is frequently enacted and many of the current rules are likely to be changed or refined by the time students taking this course graduate from law school. In addition, even if the rules do not change, it is unlikely that students will remember in detail many of the rules explored in this course after the final exam. Consequently, a principal goal of this casebook is to cause the student to raise the right question, rather than to think that he or she knows the right answer.

A great deal of care has gone into the selection of cases for this casebook. I have endeavored to select provocative cases with fact patterns that will resonate with students. Many of the cases were chosen to expose students to practical tax problems and to heighten student awareness of quality of practice issues. These points are highlighted through "In Practice" text boxes appearing throughout the book. Other cases demonstrate how a lawyer who counsels a client in connection with a tax matter can create serious problems for the client if the lawyer is inadequately versed in the tax law. Hopefully, these cases will alert students who do not practice tax law to seek the assistance of a more knowledgeable professional whenever a tax issue might exist.

This casebook employs many examples and problems to aid student understanding. Most of the cases and rulings reproduced in this casebook have been heavily edited with the deletions indicated by asterisks. Many original footnotes in the cases have been deleted and each remaining footnote reflects the actual footnote number appearing in the case. All the other footnotes in each chapter are numbered consecutively.

I owe gratitude to many individuals. I thank my colleagues Anne-Marie Rhodes, Stuart Duhl, and Sam Brunson for adopting earlier drafts of this casebook and offering extremely helpful comments and suggestions. I thank Dean Michael Kaufman and my colleagues and friends at Loyola University Chicago School of Law for their interest and encouragement. Gratitude is also expressed to Loyola University Chicago School of Law for research support. I also thank Evelyn Brody, Katie Roskam, and Shanna Kwall Hill for their valuable input. For excellent research and editorial assistance, I thank Elizabeth Abramson, Emily Eggmann, Cote Klinefelter, Grace Luetkemeyer, Arthur Mitchell, David O'Donaghue, Katie O'Rourke, Benjamin Shaw, Jacalyn Smith, and Anthony Vander Kolk. Appreciation is also expressed to all the students who were taught from earlier drafts of this work. Thanks to Joyce Marvel for production assistance.

Finally, I encourage students not to be fearful of the road ahead. Students should anticipate finding the study of Federal Income Tax to be intellectually stimulating and highly practical. With this expectation, let us begin.

Jeffrey L. Kwall

CHICAGO, ILLINOIS
NOVEMBER, 2019

Summary of Contents

Table of Contents

Table of Cases

Principal cases are in bold.

Table of Code Sections

Table of Regulation Sections

The Federal Income Taxation of Individuals

of Individuals

AN INTEGRATED APPROACH

PART I

Introduction

Introduction to Federal Income Tax

Overview

Every law student should study Federal income tax in law school. Income tax issues exist in virtually all areas of practice. It is therefore critical for all attorneys to be capable of identifying potential tax issues. All lawyers need not have the expertise to resolve the tax issues raised by their practices. However, every lawyer must be capable of identifying these issues so she knows when to seek the input of tax counsel. Regardless of the area in which a lawyer practices, the failure to identify relevant tax issues can create serious problems for both the lawyer and her client.

Income tax is one of the most intellectually challenging areas of law. Students of all academic backgrounds typically enjoy studying tax law far more than they expected. The most successful students often have humanities and social science backgrounds. Students who previously studied accounting or business may be more familiar with the terminology of tax law, but the study of tax law is very different from the study of business and accounting. Thus, all students are pretty much on equal footing as they commence the study of tax law.

Chapter 1 of this book covers the following topics:

A. The Sources of Federal Tax Law

B. The Determination of Income Tax Liability

C. Economic Considerations Are More Important than Tax Considerations

A. Sources of Federal Tax Law

1. Legislative Sources

Unlike the common law courses that dominate the first year, law school curricula, the law of Federal income taxation is primarily statutory. The 16th Amendment to the Constitution sanctioned the enactment by Congress of an income tax. From 1913–1938, Congress enacted annual (sometimes bi-annual) tax laws. In 1939, Congress codified the Federal tax law in the Internal Revenue Code of 1939. From that point forward, Congress periodically amended an established body of tax law rather than reenacting an entire set of tax laws each year. Congress recodified the Internal Revenue Code in 1954 and again in 1986. The current primary source of Federal tax law is the Internal Revenue Code of 1986, as amended to date, hereinafter referred to simply as "the IRC" or "the Code."

The IRC is a vast body of law—two thick volumes of very small print. The statute is organized, however, in a manner that makes it readily accessible. The IRC is located at Title 26 of the U.S. Code. Title 26 is divided into approximately 100 Chapters but our study of Federal income tax will be almost exclusively confined to Chapter 1. Chapter 1 is divided into approximately 25 Subchapters. Our study will focus principally on Subchapters A (Determination of Tax Liability), B (Computation of Taxable Income), E (Accounting Periods and Methods of Accounting), O (Gain or Loss on Disposition of Property), and P (Capital Gains and Losses). Each Subchapter is then divided into Parts, each Part is divided into Subparts, and, finally, each Subpart is divided into Sections. For example, Section 1 of the Code imposes the Federal income tax.

Our study of tax law will focus on individual Code sections. Because the numerous Code sections are compiled by category (Subchapter, Part and Subpart), one normally knows the appropriate area of the Code to review to find the law relevant to the particular tax issue the lawyer is analyzing. You should spend some time reviewing the Table of Contents to the Code you are using in this course to familiarize yourself with its organizational structure.

2. Executive Sources

Although Congress plays the dominant role in Federal Tax law, the Executive Branch of the Federal government also plays a critical part. The Treasury

Department is authorized to issue regulations that interpret the Code (interpretive regulations). See IRC § 7805(a). These regulations offer helpful insights into the meaning of statutory rules and are easily found because the regulations are numbered to correspond to the Code section to which they apply. For example, Reg. § 1.61 interprets IRC § 61. Interpretive regulations are not law; however, they are accorded substantial deference by the courts.

In certain circumstances, Congress delegates to the Treasury lawmaking authority by authorizing the Treasury to promulgate legislative regulations (in contrast to interpretive regulations). For example, IRC § 132(*o*) authorizes "the Secretary [of the Treasury] to prescribe such regulations as may be necessary or appropriate to carry out the purposes of this section." Unlike interpretive regulations, legislative regulations have the force and effect of law.

In addition to regulations promulgated by the Treasury Department, the Internal Revenue Service (which is part of the Treasury Department) issues various forms of guidance with respect to Federal tax law. Historically, the I.R.S.'s most common form of guidance was the Revenue Ruling in which the I.R.S. delineates its view of how the tax issues raised by a particular fact pattern should be resolved. Although a Revenue Ruling merely reflects the I.R.S.'s position and does not constitute law, it will normally be accorded deference by the courts. In addition, any taxpayer may rely on the position advanced in a Revenue Ruling when reporting the tax consequences of an analogous transaction.

In contrast to a Revenue Ruling, the I.R.S. will sometimes issue a Private Letter Ruling to an individual taxpayer in advance of engaging in a transaction. Here, the taxpayer requests the I.R.S to confirm that if the facts delineated by the taxpayer with respect to the proposed transaction are indeed true, certain conclusions of law will follow. Unlike a Revenue Ruling, a Private Letter Ruling may be relied on only by the taxpayer to whom it is issued. Nevertheless, a private letter ruling may provide some indication of how the I.R.S. might rule in a similar situation. In recent years, the I.R.S. has released many other types of internal documents that can help educate taxpayers on the I.R.S.'s view of the tax law.

3. Judicial Sources

The judiciary also provides a significant source of tax law. When the I.R.S. alleges that a taxpayer owes additional taxes (i.e., asserts a deficiency) and the taxpayer disagrees, the taxpayer can seek to have the dispute resolved by one of three alternative courts of original jurisdiction. The taxpayer can refrain from paying the additional tax and sue for a redetermination of the deficiency in the U.S. Tax Court. Alternatively, the taxpayer can pay the deficiency and then sue for a refund in the Federal District Court with jurisdiction over the taxpayer, or in the U.S. Court of Federal Claims.

The court the taxpayer will select is often based on an assessment of which of the three alternative courts will likely be most sympathetic to the taxpayer, based on each court's past decisions. The vast majority of tax cases are litigated in the Tax Court.

IN PRACTICE From 2010–2015, <u>roughly 97% of pending tax cases</u> were in the Tax Court.

Tax decisions of the U.S. Tax Court or the Federal District Court are appealable to the U.S. Circuit Court of Appeals with jurisdiction over the taxpayer. Tax decisions of the U.S. Court of Federal Claims are appealable to the U.S. Court of Appeals for the Federal Circuit. The final arbiter of all tax decisions is, of course, the U.S. Supreme Court.

WORTH NOTING The Tax Court issues two types of decisions: "regular" decisions and memorandum decisions, the latter of which are issued with much greater frequency. Historically, memorandum decisions were regarded as less authoritative than regular decisions. In recent years, however, memorandum decisions have been cited with approval by courts and the Internal Revenue Service. This casebook incorporates many recent memorandum decisions illustrating the application of the tax law to present day situations.

B. Determination of Federal Income Tax Liability

The principal objective of this course is to understand how a taxpayer's Federal income tax liability is determined. Every tax consists of two elements:

(1) the base on which the tax is imposed, and

(2) the rate of tax.

The base is multiplied by the rate to determine the tax liability.

Section 1 of the Code states that the base on which the Federal income tax is imposed is "taxable income." Section 63(a) defines "taxable income" as "gross income minus the deductions allowed by this chapter * * *." Thus, the formula for computing an individual's Federal income tax liability is as follows:

Gross Income
– Deductions
Taxable Income
× Tax Rate
Federal Income Tax Liability

1. Income Tax Base

The principal purpose of any tax is to raise revenue. The wider the tax base, the more tax revenue will be generated. Congress has created a wide tax base for the income tax by broadly defining what goes into taxable income ("gross income") and severely limiting what comes out of taxable income ("deductions").

As you will see in Chapter 2, "gross income" is defined broadly. In over-simplified terms, gross income encompasses all economic benefits a taxpayer derives, unless Congress carves out a specific exception. See IRC § 61(a). By contrast, the "deductions" that are subtracted from gross income to arrive at taxable income are defined narrowly. In effect, no payment made by a taxpayer is allowed as a deduction, unless Congress specifically allows the payment in question to be deducted. Hence, the tax law presumes that any benefit is gross income but that no disbursement is deductible. By virtue of defining gross income broadly and deductions narrowly, the resulting tax base is maximized, thereby maximizing tax revenue.

2. Income Tax Rates

The base, of course, is only one part of the tax liability equation. The rate of tax must also be known to determine the taxpayer's Federal income tax liability. Tax rates can range from zero to 100%. If the tax rate were zero, the taxpayer's liability would also be zero and the tax would not raise any revenue. By contrast, if the tax rate were 100%, all taxable income would be confiscated by the government and, as a result, eliminate any incentive for an individual to earn income.

In the middle of the 20th century, the maximum individual income tax rate reached as high as 94%. In the last 35 years, however, the maximum individual tax rate has been below 50%. Under current law, individual income tax rates range from 10% to 37%. See IRC § 1(j)(2).

The United States does not have a "flat rate" income tax because not all income is taxed at a single, uniform tax rate. Rather, the United States has adopted a "progressive" or "graduated rate" income tax system. As such, multiple tax rates can apply to the income of a taxpayer, with higher rates applying to higher levels of income.

For example, under current law, an unmarried individual will pay a tax of 10% on *roughly* the first $10,000 of taxable income. See IRC § 1(j)(2)(C). However, the tax rate increases to 12% on *roughly* the next $29,000 of taxable income. A 22% rate applies to *roughly* the next $44,000 of taxable income. Higher amounts of income are taxed at 24%, then 32%, then 35%, and finally 37%, which applies to taxable income above *roughly* $500,000. Thus, an unmarried individual with $10,000 of taxable income would owe a Federal income tax of *roughly* $1,000 ($10,000 × 10% = $1,000). By contrast, an unmarried individual with twice as much income ($20,000) would pay a tax of *roughly* $2,200,[1] which is more than twice the tax of the taxpayer with half the income.

The justification for utilizing graduated tax rates (rather than a flat tax rate) is that higher income taxpayers can afford to pay a larger percentage of their incomes in tax relative to lower rate taxpayers. Thus, our progressive rate system furthers equitable goals. However, utilizing progressive rates augments the complexity of the tax system, as you will see later in the course.

---

[1]   A taxpayer with $20,000 of taxable income would pay the same tax on the first $10,000 of taxable income as the taxpayer with only $10,000 of taxable income ($1,000). But the taxpayer with $20,000 of taxable income would pay a tax of $1,200 on the second $10,000 of taxable income (12% × $10,000 = $1,200). Thus, a taxpayer with $20,000 of taxable income would owe a total tax of $2,200 ($1,000 + $1,200 = $2,200).

WORTH NOTING

The rate tables in IRC § 1(j)(2) show the range of taxable income to which each tax rate applies. The amounts of taxable income in each range are increased annually to account for inflation. The I.R.S. publishes updated rate tables each year reflecting these increased amounts of taxable income. Thus, to determine the tax liability of an individual in the current year, one must consult the I.R.S. publication delineating the rate tables that currently apply. To withstand the test of time, all examples and problems in this casebook will employ the rate tables appearing in IRC § 1(j)(2), rather than the tables that actually apply in the current year.

C. Economic Considerations Outweigh Tax Considerations

Taxes are an important consideration in every financial matter. However, the economic implications of a transaction are more important than the tax consequences. For example, assume you have the choice of receiving a dollar that will be included in gross income (and taxable income), or not receiving anything. If your primary goal were to minimize the taxes you pay, you would choose not to receive the dollar. Assume that if you take the dollar, it will be taxed at the highest current tax rate of 37%. As a result, you would owe a tax of $.37.[2] By contrast, if you chose to forego the dollar, you would owe no tax. Thus if your primary goal was to minimize taxes, you would choose not to receive the dollar (pay no tax) rather than taking the dollar (and paying a $.37 tax).

Quite clearly, though, you should choose to receive the dollar no matter how high the tax rate that applies to the dollar might be. If you take the dollar and pay a tax of $.37, you will keep $.63. By contrast, if you reject the dollar, you will have nothing. $.63 is clearly better than nothing. Thus, economic considerations, namely, the amount of money in your hands after all taxes have been paid, are always more important than the amount of tax that was imposed on your income.

Suppose you had a third option of receiving a dollar that could be excluded from gross income. Quite clearly, that option would yield the best result from both an economic standpoint (you keep the entire $1) and a tax standpoint (you pay no tax). But if that third option does not exist (it normally won't!) and your

---

[2] $1 × 37% = $.37.

choice is between receiving a dollar that is subject to tax or not receiving the dollar, it is always preferable to receive the dollar and pay the tax (provided the tax rate is less than 100%). Throughout this course and your professional career, it is important to elevate economic considerations above tax considerations.

WORTH NOTING

Tax considerations go beyond federal income taxes which are the focus of this casebook. In addition to federal income taxes, state income taxes, federal and state transfer taxes, and other federal, state and local taxes are all important tax considerations.

■ **PROBLEM 1-1.** *Applying progressive tax rates.* Using the tax table in IRC § 1(j)(2)(C), *estimate* the income tax liability of an unmarried individual with taxable income of—

a) $50,000.

b) $200,000.

c) $500,000.

■ **PROBLEM 1-2.** *Economics before taxes.* Assume your taxable income is high enough to be taxed at the maximum 37% rate.

a)   If you had a choice of receiving a dollar of gross income, or not receiving the dollar, which option would you choose and why would you choose that option?

b)   In addition to the two options in a), if you had a third option whereby you could receive a dollar that was excluded from gross income, which of the three options would you choose and why would you choose that option?

SYNTHESIS

The primary source of Federal income tax law is the Internal Revenue Code. The Code is interpreted by regulations promulgated by the Treasury Department. The Internal Revenue Service also issues rulings and other pronouncements providing guidance on tax issues. When a tax dispute reaches the courts, the litigation can originate in the U.S. Tax Court, Federal District court, or the U.S. Court of Federal Claims.

An individual's Federal income tax liability is determined annually by multiplying the individual's taxable income by the applicable tax rate. Taxable income is the amount by which the taxpayer's gross income exceeds any allowable deductions. Part II of this book will explore the scope of gross income and Part III will examine the deductions that might be allowed to an individual taxpayer. The United States employs a progressive rate system meaning that multiple tax rates can apply to the income of an individual, with higher rates applying to higher levels of income. The highest Federal income tax rate under current law is 37%. Part V of this book will explore tax rates.

 For an entertaining introduction to the history of the income tax, click here.

Perhaps the most critical message this book conveys is that **economic considerations are more important than tax considerations.** In its most basic iteration, if you have the choice of receiving $1 and paying tax on it, or not receiving the dollar, you are always better off choosing the former option, as long as the applicable tax rate is below 100%. If you receive $1 that is subject to tax, the maximum Federal income tax you will pay under current law is $.37 (37%). Thus, you will have at least $.63 left over after paying the tax. By contrast, you will have nothing if you do not receive the dollar. You should keep this maxim in mind at all times.

PART II

Gross Income

CHAPTER 2

Introduction to Gross Income

Overview

> **Primary Law:** IRC § 61(a)
>
> Except as otherwise provided in this subtitle, gross income means all income from whatever source derived, including (but not limited to) the following items:
>
> [The statute then lists fourteen examples of gross income.]

The first element in determining a taxpayer's federal income tax liability is "gross income." The Code defines "gross income" in § 61(a). The second clause of § 61(a) indicates that "gross income" means all "income." Unfortunately, the Code does not define the essence of "income." So we must resort to the common law for enlightenment on the meaning of this term. This Chapter will explore some common law interpretations of the meaning of income.

COMMISSIONER v. GLENSHAW GLASS COMPANY AND GOLDMAN THEATRES, INC.

Supreme Court of the United States, 1955
348 U.S. 426, 75 S. Ct. 473, 99 L. Ed. 483

MR. CHIEF JUSTICE WARREN delivered the opinion of the Court.

This litigation involves two cases with independent factual backgrounds yet presenting the identical issue. * * * The common question is whether money received as exemplary damages for fraud or as the punitive two-thirds portion of a treble-damage antitrust recovery must be reported by a taxpayer as gross income under § 22(a) of the Internal Revenue Code of 1939.[1] In a single opinion, the Court of Appeals affirmed the Tax Court's separate rulings in favor of the taxpayers. Because of the frequent recurrence of the question and differing interpretations by the lower courts of this Court's decisions bearing upon the problem, we granted the Commissioner of Internal Revenue's ensuing petition for certiorari.

The facts of the cases were largely stipulated and are not in dispute. So far as pertinent they are as follows:

> *Commissioner v. Glenshaw Glass Co.*—The Glenshaw Glass Company, a Pennsylvania corporation, manufactures glass bottles and containers. It was engaged in protracted litigation with the Hartford-Empire Company, which manufactures machinery of a character used by Glenshaw. Among the claims advanced by Glenshaw were demands for exemplary damages for fraud and treble damages for injury to its business by reason of Hartford's violation of the federal antitrust laws. In December, 1947, the parties concluded a settlement of all pending litigation, by which Hartford paid Glenshaw approximately $800,000. [I]t was ultimately determined that, of the total settlement, $324,529.94 represented payment of punitive damages for fraud and antitrust violations. Glenshaw did not report this portion of the settlement as income for the tax year involved. The Commissioner determined a deficiency claiming as taxable the entire sum less only

---

[1]   Editor's note: A statutory remedy for certain anti-trust law violations requires the perpetrator to pay the victim triple the amount of actual damages suffered ("treble damages") with the goal of deterring other potential offenders. Section 22(a) of the 1939 Code was the predecessor to § 61(a) of the current Code.

deductible legal fees. As previously noted, the Tax Court and the Court of Appeals upheld the taxpayer.

Commissioner v. William Goldman Theatres, Inc.—William Goldman Theatres, Inc., a Delaware corporation operating motion picture houses in Pennsylvania, sued Loew's, Inc., alleging a violation of the federal antitrust laws and seeking treble damages. After a holding that a violation had occurred, the case was remanded to the trial court for a determination of damages. It was found that Goldman had suffered a loss of profits equal to $125,000 and was entitled to treble damages in the sum of $375,000. Goldman reported only $125,000 of the recovery as gross income and claimed that the $250,000 balance constituted punitive damages and as such was not taxable. The Tax Court agreed and the Court of Appeals, hearing this with the Glenshaw case, affirmed.

It is conceded by the respondents that there is no constitutional barrier to the imposition of a tax on punitive damages. Our question is one of statutory construction: are these payments comprehended by § 22(a)?

The sweeping scope of the controverted statute is readily apparent:

§ 22. Gross income

(a) **General definition.** 'Gross income' includes gains, profits and income derived from salaries, wages, or compensation for personal service * * *, or from * * * trades, businesses, * * * or dealings in property * * *; also from interest, rent, dividends, * * * or the transaction of any business carried on for gain or profit, *or gains or profits and income derived from any source whatever.* * * * (Emphasis added.)

This Court has frequently stated that this language was used by Congress to exert in this field 'the full measure of its taxing power.' Respondents contend that punitive damages, characterized as 'windfalls' flowing from the culpable conduct of third parties, are not within the scope of the section. But Congress applied no limitations as to the source of taxable receipts, nor restrictive labels as to their nature. And the Court has given a liberal construction to this broad phraseology in recognition of the intention of Congress to tax all gains except those specifically exempted. [W]e cannot but ascribe content to the *catch-all* provision of § 22(a), 'gains or profits and income derived from any source whatever.' The importance of that phrase has been too frequently recognized since its first appearance in the Revenue Act of 1913 to say now that it adds nothing to the meaning of 'gross income.'

Nor can we accept respondents' contention that a narrower reading of § 22(a) is required by the Court's characterization of income in Eisner v. Macomber, 252 U.S. 189, 207, as "the gain derived from capital, from labor, or from both combined." The Court was there endeavoring to determine whether the distribution of a corporate stock dividend constituted a realized gain to the shareholder, or changed 'only the form, not the essence,' of his capital investment. It was held that the taxpayer had 'received nothing out of the company's assets for his separate use and benefit.' The distribution, therefore, was held not a taxable event. In that context distinguishing gain from capital—the definition served a useful purpose. But it was not meant to provide a touchstone to all future gross income questions.

Here we have instances of undeniable accessions to wealth, clearly realized, and over which the taxpayers have complete dominion. The mere fact that the payments were extracted from the wrongdoers as punishment for unlawful conduct cannot detract from their character as taxable income to the recipients. Respondents concede, as they must, that the recoveries are taxable to the extent that they compensate for damages actually incurred. It would be an anomaly that could not be justified in the absence of clear congressional intent to say that a recovery for actual damages is taxable but not the additional amount extracted as punishment for the same conduct which caused the injury. And we find no such evidence of intent to exempt these payments.

[N]or does the 1954 Code's legislative history, with its reiteration of the proposition that statutory gross income is 'all-inclusive,' give support to respondents' position. The definition of gross income has been simplified, but no effect upon its present broad scope was intended.[11] * * * We would do violence to the plain meaning of the statute and restrict a clear legislative attempt to bring the taxing power to bear upon all receipts constitutionally taxable were we to say that the payments in question here are not gross income.

---

[11]   In discussing § 61(a) of the 1954 Code, the House Report states:

> This section corresponds to section 22(a) of the 1939 Code. While the language in existing section 22(a) has been simplified, the all-inclusive nature of statutory gross income has not been affected thereby. Section 61(a) is as broad in scope as section 22(a). Section 61(a) provides that gross income includes 'all income from whatever source derived.' This definition is based upon the 16th Amendment and the word 'income' is used in its constitutional sense.

H.R. Rep.No.1337, at A18. A virtually identical statement appears in S.Rep.No.1622, at 168.

Reversed.

Mr. Justice Douglas dissents.

WORTH NOTING

Punitive damages vs. compensatory damages. In light of the Supreme Court's holding in Glenshaw Glass, it is clear that punitive damages are included in gross income. The Court implies that "actual damages" (i.e., compensatory damages) are also included in gross income. The compensatory damages received by Glenshaw Glass and Goldman Theatres substituted for profits that the businesses would have earned in the absence of interference by the defendants in those cases. As such, the compensatory damages would be included in gross income. See IRC § 61(a)(2). In certain cases, however, compensatory damages are excluded from gross income. These situations will be explored in Chapter 7.

The Glenshaw Glass opinion does not provide a detailed explanation of the term "income." The most pertinent language is "undeniable accessions to wealth, clearly realized, and over which the taxpayers have complete dominion." The meaning of "income" is further explored in the article excerpt that follows.

Defining Income

Alice G. Abreu and Richard K. Greenstein
11 Florida Tax Review 295, 296–97, 304–05 (2011)

More than half a century ago in *Commissioner v. Glenshaw Glass*, the Supreme Court defined "income," as used in section 61 of the Internal Revenue Code, as "undeniable accessions to wealth, clearly realized, and over which the taxpayers have complete dominion." The Code narrows the scope of income by providing for specific exclusions but, outside of those exclusions, the Code's own, self-referential definition—"gross income means income from whatever source derived"—seems to confirm the broad scope of the definition.

The breadth of the *Glenshaw Glass* definition appears to be nearly co-extensive with the Haig-Simons definition of income [defined in italics in the next paragraph], which is widely accepted as providing the theoretical foundation for the income tax.[4] Accordingly, many tax professionals interpret the language in section 61 and *Glenshaw Glass* solely in light of the economic principles reflected in the Haig-Simons definition. The analytical structure for determining what is income appears clear and is generally treated as immutable. The analysis begins with the broad mandate of section 61 and *Glenshaw Glass*. As long as there is a realized accession in the economic sense within the taxpayer's dominion, *Glenshaw Glass* would seem to provide that there is income unless, pursuant to the very first words of section 61, there is an exclusion in the statute. From the time they are introduced to the tax law, students are taught this analytical structure, and by the time they become practitioners and then judges or scholars, it is second nature.

* * *

[B]y the early 1950s, when *Glenshaw Glass* was making its way through the courts, the Haig-Simons definition of income had become the centerpiece of the scholarly lexicon, following Henry Simons's 1938 publication of the famous book in which he refined Robert Haig's definition of income. Simons wrote that *"[p]ersonal income may be defined as the algebraic sum of (1) the market value of rights exercised in consumption and (2) the change in the value of the store of property rights between the beginning and end of the period in question."* [Emphasis added.] This is an exceedingly broad definition, bringing within its grasp all accessions, whether consumed or saved. Its breadth allows it to serve the goal of raising maximum revenue while also being maximally equitable and efficient and therefore serving two important tax policy objectives. If all accessions are subject to tax then taxpayers who are similarly situated economically will be taxed similarly and the level of taxation can be adjusted to correspond to relative positions. This serves both horizontal and vertical equity.[2] In addition, because such a definition does not distinguish between sources of income, it does not privilege income from certain activities, which is efficient.

---

[4]   Henry C. Simons, Personal Income Taxation 50 (1938). * * *

[2]   Editor's note: "Horizontal equity" is the principle that all similarly situated individuals should bear the same tax burden irrespective of the sources of their incomes. "Vertical equity" is the principle that an individual's tax burden should increase as that individual's ability to pay increases. See R. Musgrave, The Theory of Public Finance, 160, 173 (1959).

Even Simons understood that his definition could not describe a workable tax base. One significant limitation on it comes from the absence of a realization requirement. Absent a realization requirement a taxpayer's property would have to be valued periodically and the difference between the beginning and ending values would have to be computed in order to determine the amount of a taxpayer's income. Even if the valuation were easy, as in the case of public traded securities, treating a positive difference as income would create persistent liquidity problems in the absence of cash. The realization requirement solves these problems.

The *Glenshaw Glass* definition, which is the Haig-Simons definition limited by realization, is faithful to all three major tax policy objectives: equity, efficiency and administrability. It is neither too broad, as Haig-Simons alone would be, nor too narrow * * *. By retaining realization while moving to embrace Haig-Simons, the Court may have gotten it just right. * * *

Notes

1. *Breadth of income.* The Supreme Court in Glenshaw Glass and the excerpt from Professor Abreu's article explain that Congress intended to define gross income as broadly as the Constitution permits. In effect, any economic benefit a taxpayer derives is presumed to be gross income unless an exception exists. It is not surprising that Congress defined that which goes into the tax base (gross income) broadly, because a large tax base furthers the primary objective of the income tax which is to raise revenue.

2. *Statutory exclusions and other exceptions to gross income.* The first clause of § 61(a) ("Except as otherwise provided by this Chapter") indicates that Congress reserved the right to carve out specific benefits from the broad definition of gross income. In addition, certain common law exceptions to gross income exist. The statutory and common law exceptions to gross income will be explored in Chapters 3–8.

3. *The realization requirement.* As Professor Abreu's article reveals, one of the most significant exceptions to gross income is the realization requirement. For example, if you purchased a parcel of land for $10,000 and, due to the commercial development of the surrounding area, the value of your land increased

to $18,000, the $8,000 increase in the value of the land represents an economic benefit to you, i.e., your wealth has increased by $8,000. That benefit, however, is not treated as gross income until a "realization event" occurs (e.g., you sell the property for $18,000). When a realization event occurs, your $8,000 profit constitutes gross income. See IRC § 61(a)(3). The realization requirement and § 61(a)(3) income will be examined in Chapter 6.

JAMES v. UNITED STATES

Supreme Court of the United States, 1961
366 U.S. 213, 81 S. Ct. 1052, 6 L.Ed.2d 246

MR. CHIEF JUSTICE WARREN announced the judgment of the Court and an opinion in which MR. JUSTICE BRENNAN, and MR. JUSTICE STEWART concur.

The issue before us in this case is whether embezzled funds are to be included in the "gross income" of the embezzler in the year in which the funds are misappropriated * * *.

The facts are not in dispute. The petitioner is a union official who, with another person, embezzled in excess of $738,000 during the years 1951 through 1954 from his employer union and from an insurance company with which the union was doing business. Petitioner failed to report these amounts in his gross income in those years and was convicted for willfully attempting to evade the federal income tax due for each of the years 1951 through 1954 in violation of * * * § 7201 of the Internal Revenue Code. He was sentenced to a total of three years' imprisonment. The Court of Appeals affirmed. Because of a conflict with this Court's decision in Commissioner of Internal Revenue v. Wilcox, 327 U.S. 404, a case whose relevant facts are concededly the same as those in the case now before us, we granted certiorari.

In Wilcox, the Court held that embezzled money does not constitute taxable income to the embezzler in the year of the embezzlement under § 22(a) of the Internal Revenue Code of 1939. * * *

The basis for the Wilcox decision was—

that a taxable gain is conditioned upon (1) the presence of a claim of right to the alleged gain and (2) the absence of a definite, unconditional obligation to repay or return that which would otherwise constitute a gain. Without some bona fide legal or equitable claim, even though it be contingent or contested in nature, the taxpayer cannot be said to have received any gain or profit within the reach of section 22(a).

Commissioner v. Wilcox, supra. Since Wilcox embezzled the money, held it "without any semblance of a bona fide claim of right," and therefore "was at all times under an unqualified duty and obligation to repay the money to his employer," the Court found that the money embezzled was not includible within "gross income." * * *

It had been a well-established principle, long before * * * Wilcox, that unlawful, as well as lawful, gains are comprehended within the term "gross income." Section II B of the Income Tax Act of 1913 provided that—

> the net income of a taxable person shall include gains, profits, and income * * * from * * * the transaction of any lawful business carried on for gain or profit, or gains or profits and income derived from any source whatever * * *. 38 Stat. 167.

When the statute was amended in 1916, the one word "lawful" was omitted. This revealed, we think, the obvious intent of that Congress to tax income derived from both legal and illegal sources, to remove the incongruity of having the gains of the honest laborer taxed and the gains of the dishonest immune. Thereafter, the Court held that gains from illicit traffic in liquor are includible within "gross income." And, the Court has pointed out, with approval, that there "has been a widespread and settled administrative and judicial recognition of the taxability of unlawful gains of many kinds." These include protection payments made to racketeers, ransom payments paid to kidnappers, bribes, money derived from the sale of unlawful insurance policies, graft, black market gains, funds obtained from the operation of lotteries, income from race track bookmaking and illegal prize fight pictures.

The starting point in all cases dealing with the question of the scope of what is included in "gross income" begins with the basic premise that the purpose of Congress was "to use the full measure of its taxing power." Helvering v. Clifford, 309 U.S. 331. And the Court has given a liberal construction to the broad phraseology of the "gross income" definition statutes in recognition of the intention of Congress to tax all gains except those specifically exempted. The language of * * * § 61(a) of the 1954 Code, "all income from whatever source derived," has been held to encompass all "accessions to wealth, clearly realized, and over which the taxpayers have complete dominion." Commissioner of Internal Revenue v. Glenshaw Glass Co., 348 U.S. 426, 431. A gain "constitutes taxable income when its recipient has such control over it that, as a practical matter, he derives readily realizable economic value from it." Under these broad principles, we believe that petitioner's contention, that all unlawful gains are taxable except those resulting from embezzlement, should fail.

When a taxpayer acquires earnings, lawfully or unlawfully, without the consensual recognition, express or implied, of an obligation to repay and without restriction as to their disposition, "he has received income which he is required to return, even though it may still be claimed that he is not entitled to retain the money, and even though he may still be adjudged liable to restore its equivalent." North American Oil Consolidated v. Burnet, 286 U.S. 417. In such case, the taxpayer has "actual command over the property taxed—the actual benefit for which the tax is paid," Corliss v. Bowers, 281 U.S. 376. This standard brings wrongful appropriations within the broad sweep of "gross income;" it excludes loans. When a law-abiding taxpayer mistakenly receives income in one year, which receipt is assailed and found to be invalid in a subsequent year, the taxpayer must nonetheless report the amount as "gross income" in the year received. United States v. Lewis, 340 U.S. 590. We do not believe that Congress intended to treat a law-breaking taxpayer differently. Just as the honest taxpayer may deduct any amount repaid in the year in which the repayment is made, the Government points out that, "If, when, and to the extent that the victim recovers back the misappropriated funds, there is of course a reduction in the embezzler's income." Brief for the United States.

Petitioner contends that the Wilcox rule has been in existence since 1946; that if Congress had intended to change the rule, it would have done so; that there was a general revision of the income tax laws in 1954 without mention of the rule; that a bill to change it was introduced in the Eighty-sixth Congress but was not acted upon; that, therefore, we may not change the rule now. But the fact that Congress has remained silent or has re-enacted a statute which we have construed, or that congressional attempts to amend a rule announced by this Court have failed, does not necessarily debar us from re-examining and correcting the Court's own errors. There may have been any number of reasons why Congress acted as it did. * * *

We believe that Wilcox was wrongly decided and we find nothing in congressional history since then to persuade us that Congress intended to legislate the rule. Thus, we believe that we should now correct the error and the confusion resulting from it * * *. We should not continue to confound confusion, particularly when the result would be to perpetuate the injustice of relieving embezzlers of the duty of paying income taxes on the money they enrich themselves with through theft while honest people pay their taxes on every conceivable type of income.

* * *

Since Mr. Justice Harlan, Mr. Justice Frankfurter, and Mr. Justice Clark agree with us concerning Wilcox, that case is overruled. * * *

Notes

1. *Control vs. entitlement.* The James Court stated—

> a gain constitutes taxable income when its recipient has such control over it that, as a practical matter, he derives readily realizable economic value from it * * * even though it may still be claimed that he is not entitled to retain the money, and even though he may still be adjudged liable to restore its equivalent.

Does taxing a person on misappropriated funds raise a fairness issue if, in a later year, the person is required to return the funds to the rightful owner?

2. *Wrongful appropriation vs. loan.* The James Court acknowledges that gross income does not occur when "consensual recognition of an obligation to repay" exists and states that "this standard brings wrongful appropriations within the broad sweep of gross income; it excludes loans." What justification exists for excluding loans from gross income?

> **LOOK ONLINE** **Tax evasion often captures the criminal.** The tendency of criminals not to report stolen funds as gross income often leads to tax evasion convictions that are easier to prove than the underlying criminal offenses. For example, Al Capone was convicted of tax evasion. See **Kelly Phillips Erb, "Al Capone Sentenced to Prison for Tax Evasion on this Day in 1931,"** *Forbes*, 10/17/2018.

The Cesarini case demonstrates that benefits constituting gross income can materialize from the most mundane events of daily life.

piano/buried treasure case

CESARINI v. UNITED STATES

United States District Court, Northern District of Ohio, 1969
296 F. Supp. 3

YOUNG, DISTRICT JUDGE.

This is an action by the plaintiffs as taxpayers for the recovery of income tax payments made in the calendar year 1964. Plaintiffs contend that the amount of $836.51 was erroneously overpaid by them in 1964, and that they are entitled to a refund in that amount * * *.

Plaintiffs and the United States have stipulated to the material facts in the case, and the matter is before the Court for final decision. * * * In 1957, the plaintiffs purchased a used piano at an auction sale for approximately $15.00, and the piano was used by their daughter for piano lessons. In 1964, while cleaning the piano, plaintiffs discovered the sum of $4,467.00 * * * [and] reported the sum of $4,467.00 on their 1964 joint income tax return as ordinary income from other sources. On October 18, 1965, plaintiffs filed an amended return with the District Director of Internal Revenue in Cleveland, Ohio, this second return eliminating the sum of $4,467.00 from the gross income computation, and requesting a refund in the amount of $836.51, the amount allegedly overpaid as a result of the former inclusion of $4,467.00 in the original return for the calendar year of 1964. On January 18, 1966, the Commissioner of Internal Revenue rejected taxpayers' refund claim in its entirety, and plaintiffs filed the instant action in March of 1967.

Plaintiffs make [two] alternative contentions in support of their claim that the sum of $836.51 should be refunded to them. First, that the $4,467.00 found in the piano is not includable in gross income under Section 61 of the Internal Revenue Code. (26 U.S.C. § 61) Secondly, even if the retention of the cash constitutes a realization of ordinary income under Section 61, it was due and owing in the year the piano was purchased, 1957, and by 1964, the statute of limitations provided by 26 U.S.C. § 6501 had elapsed. * * * The Government * * * asserts that the amount found in the piano is includable in gross income under Section 61(a) of Title 26, U.S.C. [and] that the money is taxable in the year it was actually found, 1964 * * *.

After a consideration of the pertinent provisions of the Internal Revenue Code, Treasury Regulations, Revenue Rulings, and decisional law in the area, this Court has concluded that the taxpayers are not entitled to a refund of the amount requested * * *.

The starting point in determining whether an item is to be included in gross income is, of course, Section 61(a) of Title 26 U.S.C., and that section provides in part:

> Except as otherwise provided in this subtitle, *gross income means all income from whatever source derived*, including (but not limited to) the following items: * * * (Emphasis added.)

Subsections (1) through (15) of Section 61(a) then go on to list fifteen items specifically included in the computation of the taxpayer's gross income, and Part II of Subchapter B of the 1954 Code (Sections 71 *et seq.*) deals with other items expressly included in gross income. While neither of these listings expressly includes the type of income which is at issue in the case at bar, Part III of Subchapter B (Sections 101 *et seq.*) deals with items specifically *excluded* from gross income, and found money is not listed in those sections either. This absence of express mention in any of the code sections necessitates a return to the "all income from whatever source" language of Section 61(a) of the code, and the express statement there that gross income is "not limited to" the following fifteen examples. Section 1.61–1(a) of the Treasury Regulations, the corresponding section to Section 61(a) in the 1954 Code, reiterates this broad construction of gross income, providing in part:

> Gross income means all income from whatever source derived, unless excluded by law. *Gross income includes income realized in any form,* whether in money, property, or services. * * * (Emphasis added.)

The decisions of the United States Supreme Court have frequently stated that this broad all-inclusive language was used by Congress to exert the full measure of its taxing power under the Sixteenth Amendment to the United States Constitution. Commissioner of Internal Revenue v. Glenshaw Glass Co., 348 U.S. 426, 429 (1955); Helvering v. Clifford, 309 U.S. 331, 334 (1940); Helvering v. Midland Mutual Life Ins. Co., 300 U.S. 216, 223 (1937); Douglas v. Willcuts, 296 U.S. 1, 9 (1935); Irwin v. Gavit, 268 U.S. 161, 166 (1925).

In addition, the Government in the instant case cites and relies upon an I.R.S. Revenue Ruling which is undeniably on point:

> The finder of treasure-trove is in receipt of taxable income, for Federal income tax purposes, to the extent of its value in United States currency, for the taxable year in which it is reduced to undisputed possession.

Rev. Rul. 61, 1953–1, Cum. Bull. 17.

The plaintiffs argue that the above ruling does not control this case * * *. [Their argument] overlooks the statutory scheme previously alluded to, whereby income from all sources is taxed unless the taxpayer can point to an express exemption. * * * While it is generally true that revenue rulings may be disregarded by the courts if in conflict with the code and the regulations, or with other judicial decisions, plaintiffs in the instant case have been unable to point to any inconsistency between the gross income sections of the code, the interpretation of them by the regulations and the courts, and the revenue ruling which they herein attack as inapplicable. On the other hand, the United States *has* shown a consistency in letter and spirit between the ruling and the code, regulations, and court decisions.

Although not cited by either party, and noticeably absent from the Government's brief, the following Treasury Regulation appears in the 1964 Regulations, the year of the return in dispute:

> § 1.61–14 Miscellaneous items of gross income.

> (a)   In general. In addition to the items enumerated in section 61(a), there are many other kinds of gross income * * *. *Treasure trove, to the extent of its value in United States currency, constitutes gross income for the taxable year in which it is reduced to undisputed possession."* (Emphasis added.)

Identical language appears in * * * all previous years back to 1958. This language is the same in all material respects as that found in Rev. Rul. 61–53 and is undoubtedly an attempt to codify that ruling into the Regulations which apply to the 1954 Code. This Court is of the opinion that Treas. Reg. § 1.61–14(a) is dispositive of the major issue in this case if the $4,467.00 found in the piano was "reduced to undisputed possession" in the year petitioners reported it, for this Regulation was applicable to returns filed in the calendar year of 1964.

This brings the Court to the second contention of the plaintiffs: that if any tax was due, it was in 1957 when the piano was purchased, and by 1964 the Government was blocked from collecting it by reason of the statute of limitations. Without reaching the question of whether the voluntary payment in 1964 constituted a *waiver* on the part of the taxpayers, this Court finds that the $4,467.00 sum was properly included in gross income for the calendar year of 1964. Problems of when title vests, or when possession is complete in the field of federal taxation, in the absence of definitive federal legislation on the subject, are ordinarily determined by reference to the law of the state in which the taxpayer resides, or where the property around which the dispute centers is located. Since both the taxpayers and the property in question are found within the State of Ohio, Ohio law must govern as to when the found money was "reduced to undisputed possession" within the meaning of Treas. Reg. § 1.61–14 and Rev. Rul. 61–53.

In Ohio, there is no statute specifically dealing with the rights of owners and finders of treasure trove, and in the absence of such a statute the common law rule of England applies, so that "title belongs to the finder as against all the world except the true owner." Niederlehner v. Weatherly, 69 N.E.2d 787 (1946). The *Niederlehner* case held that the owner of real estate upon which money is found does not have title as against the finder. Therefore, in the instant case if plaintiffs had resold the piano in 1958, not knowing of the money within it, they later would not be able to succeed in an action against the purchaser who *did* discover it. Under Ohio law, the plaintiffs must have actually *found* the money to have superior title over all but the true owner, and they did not discover the old currency until 1964. Unless there is present a specific state statute to the contrary, the

LOOK ONLINE **History repeats itself.** For a more a recent discovery of treasure trove in a piano, see "Shropshire Piano Gold Coin Hoard Declared Treasure."

majority of jurisdictions are in accord with the Ohio rule. Therefore, this Court finds that the $4,467.00 in old currency was not "reduced to undisputed possession" until its actual discovery in 1964, and thus the United States was not barred by the statute of limitations from collecting the $836.51 in tax during that year.

[S]ince it appears to the Court that the income tax on these taxpayers' gross income for the calendar year of 1964 has been properly assessed and paid, this taxpayers' suit for a refund in the amount of $836.51 must be dismissed, and judgment entered for the United States. An order will be entered accordingly.

NOTES

1.   *Order of authorities.* Notice how the Cesarini court analyzes the question of whether found money is gross income. It proceeds through the relevant authorities in order of authoritativeness; beginning its analysis with the Internal Revenue Code, then proceeding to the Treasury Regulations, and finally, considering a relevant Internal Revenue Service Revenue Ruling. You should follow this pattern when attempting to resolve a tax issue.

2.   *Rejection of "recurrence" element of income.* Early definitions of income suggested that for income to occur, it must be periodic or recurrent. For example, in 1924, one analyst defined income as follows: "Income is essentially wealth available for recurrent consumption, recurrently or periodically received. Its three essential characteristics are: receipt, recurrence and expendability." C. Plehn, "Income as Recurrent, Consumable Receipts," 14 American Economic Review 1, 5 (1924). All of the cases in this chapter involved isolated economic benefits thereby implicitly rejecting a recurrence element of income.

IN SIGHTS   **Specific categories of gross income vs. the "catch-all" provision.** Glenshaw Glass, James and Cesarini emphasize that the "all income from whatever source derived" language (the "catch-all" provision) of § 61(a) captures receipts not described in any of the fourteen specific categories of gross income delineated in §§ 61(a)(1)–(14). The fourteen categories listed in § 61(a) are merely non-exclusive examples of gross income (in the words of the statute;

"including (but not limited to) the following items"). The fact that the catch-all provision is broader than the fourteen categories delineated by the statute, however, does not diminish the significance of these fourteen categories. The vast majority of gross income items will fit into one or another of these specific categories. Rarely will a receipt fall outside of all fourteen categories and, therefore, be treated as gross income under the catch-all provision.

A compelling reason exists to determine whether a potential item of gross income falls into one of the fourteen specific categories before resorting to the catch-all provision. As your study of gross income progresses, you will discover that certain categories of gross income are taxed in less burdensome ways than other gross income. Hence, it can be beneficial to the taxpayer if an item of gross income fits into one of the fourteen categories rather than being captured by the catch-all provision, which should be regarded as a default rule.

In light of the above, whenever you confront a potential item of gross income, you should initially examine whether the item is described by any one of the fourteen categories listed in the statute. Only after determining that the item in question is outside the scope of all fourteen categories should you resort to the catch-all provision.

■ **PROBLEM 2-1.** *Scope of gross income.* How much gross income would you derive if you found the following on the street today? How much would you report on your tax return?

a) $1.   – 1

b) $10,000.   – 10,000

c)   A diamond with a value of $5,000.

d)   An antique vase with an uncertain value.

SYNTHESIS

Congress intended to define "gross income" as broadly as the Constitution permits. In effect, almost any benefit that an individual derives is presumed to be gross income, unless an exception applies. This Chapter revealed that benefits can be derived in the form of cash or property. You will soon see that benefits can also be derived in other forms.

The "all income from whatever source derived" language (the "catch-all" provision) of § 61(a) captures receipts not described in any of the fourteen specific categories of gross income delineated in §§ 61(a)(1)–(14). Under certain circumstances, it can be beneficial to the taxpayer if an item of gross income fits into one of the fourteen categories rather than being captured by the catch-all provision, which should be regarded as a default rule.

Whenever you confront a potential item of gross income, you should initially examine whether the item is described by any one of the fourteen categories listed in the statute. Only after determining that the item in question is outside the scope of all fourteen categories should you resort to the catch-all provision. The chapters that follow will explore the specific categories of gross income delineated in § 61(a) and reveal the beneficial tax treatment associated with certain of these categories.

Test Your Knowledge: To assess your understanding of the material in this chapter, **click here** to take a quiz.

Benefits Received by Business Owners and Employees

Overview

Gross income does not exist in a vacuum. It stems from a variety of capacities in which people live their daily lives. For example, most people are involved in business—they either own a business or are employed by a business. The principal economic objective of a business owner is to make a profit. The gross income of a business owner is captured by IRC § 61(a)(2) ("gross income derived from business"). The principal economic objective of an employee is to earn compensation for the services the employee performs. The gross income of an employee is captured by IRC § 61(a)(1) ("compensation for services"). Chapter 3 will explore "gross income derived from business" and "compensation for services," two of the most fundamental categories of gross income.

Primary Law: IRC § 61(a)

Except as otherwise provided in this subtitle, gross income means all income from whatever source derived, including (but not limited to) the following items:

(1) Compensation for services, including fees, commissions, fringe benefits, and similar items;

(2) Gross income derived from business;

* * *

A. Benefits Received by Business Owners—§ 61(a)(2)

A wide array of businesses exist. Most businesses, however, primarily either provide services or sell products. A law firm is an example of a business that primarily provides services. If, after graduating from law school, you open a law firm as a sole practitioner, you will hopefully collect fees from clients for the services you render. The fees you collect represent "gross income derived from business." IRC § 61(a)(2). You are also likely to incur many expenses in connection with your law business (e.g., rent, utility bills, licensing fees) and, accordingly, the profit you derive from practicing law will be far less than the fees you collect. These expenses, however, do not impact the calculation of your *gross income*. These expenses might be allowed as deductions that offset your gross income in arriving at *taxable income*, the base on which Federal income tax is imposed. See Chapter 1. But your gross income under § 61(a)(2) is measured by all the fees you collect. (The extent to which business expenses are allowed as deductions will be explored in Chapter 9.)

■ **EXAMPLE 3-A.** *Calculating gross income from a service business.* Jacalyn practices law as a sole practitioner and collects $25,000 of fees from her clients. Thus, her gross income from business is $25,000. Jacalyn is likely to incur additional expenses in connection with her law practice (e.g., rent, utility bills, license fees) in which case the profit derived from her business will be far less than $25,000. Some or all of these expenses might be allowed as deductions that offset her *gross income* in arriving at *taxable income*, the base on which Federal income tax is imposed. But Jacalyn's gross income under § 61(a)(2) is $25,000.

In contrast to a law firm, a seller of widgets is in the business of selling products. Instead of practicing law, if you decide to sell widgets after you graduate from law school, the income you derive from the sale of widgets would also be gross income derived from business. IRC § 61(a)(2). When a business sells products, its gross income is measured by subtracting the cost of the goods it sells from the sales revenue it derives.

■ **EXAMPLE 3-B.** *Calculating gross income from the sale of products.* David pays $10,000 to a widget manufacturer for 10,000 widgets. David sells these widgets to individual customers for a total of $25,000. As a result, David's gross income from business would be only $15,000 (the $25,000 in sales proceeds minus the $10,000 cost of the widgets). See Treas. Reg. 1.61–3(a) ("[G]ross income means the total sales, less the cost of goods sold.") David is likely to incur additional expenses in connection with the widget business (e.g., rent, utility bills, license fees) in which case the profit derived from his business will be far less than $15,000. Some or all of these expenses might be allowed as deductions that offset his *gross income* in arriving at *taxable income*, the base on which Federal income tax is imposed. But David's gross income under § 61(a)(2) is $15,000.

B. Benefits Received by Employees—§ 61(a)(1)

Rather than owning a business after you graduate from law school, you are more likely to be an employee; e.g., an associate in a law firm. In this case, the compensation you receive will be described in § 61(a)(1), "Compensation for services, including fees, commissions, fringe benefits, and similar items." Note that § 61(a)(1) income is not limited to conventional wages and salary. Rather, it includes all forms of compensation including fringe benefits.

1. Wages and Salary

Whether an individual is an hourly employee (paid for each hour worked) or receives an annual salary (without regard to the number of hours worked), the compensation she receives is included in gross income under § 61(a)(1). In the unlikely event that the employee is compensated with property rather than money, the value of the property received would be included in gross income under § 61(a)(1). Gross income is measured by the benefit the taxpayer receives, regardless of the form in which that benefit is conveyed.

IN SIGHTS **Impact of withholding from salary or wages.** When an employee receives a paycheck, the amount due the employee is reduced by a variety of items. For example, Federal income tax, state income tax, and various employment taxes are withheld from the employee's pay. These withheld amounts do *not* reduce the employee's gross income. Rather, they represent an advance payment of tax obligations imposed on all individuals—it is as if the employee is paid the gross amount and then pays the withheld amounts to the various federal and state authorities. By contrast, certain other withheld amounts are specifically excluded from the employee's gross income. For example, amounts withheld from an individual's salary or wages that are contributed to certain qualified retirement plans are specifically excluded from the employee's gross income.

■ **EXAMPLE 3-C.** *Impact of withholding on gross income.* Annie receives a salary of $5,000 per month. The monthly paycheck she receives from her employer is only $3,700. The following items are withheld from her monthly salary:

Federal Income Tax	$500
State Income Tax	$150
Social Security and Medicare Taxes	$350
Contribution to Qualified Retirement Plan	$300
Total Withholding	$1,300

Annie's gross income is $4,700. The $1,000 of withheld taxes do *not* reduce her gross income but are simply advance payments of her tax obligations. By contrast, the $300 contribution to the qualified retirement plan is excluded from her gross income.

OLD COLONY TRUST CO. et al. v. COMMISSIONER

Supreme Court of the United States, 1929
279 U.S. 716, 49 S.Ct. 499, 73 L.Ed. 918

Mr. Chief Justice Taft delivered the opinion of the Court.

[T]he petitioners are the executors of the will of William M. Wood, deceased. On June 27, 1925, before Mr. Wood's death, the Commissioner of Internal Revenue notified him by registered mail of the determination of a deficiency in income tax against him for the years 1919 and 1920, under the Revenue Act of 1918. [The Board of Tax Appeals] approved the action of the Commissioner, and found a deficiency in the federal income tax return of Mr. Wood for the year 1919 * * * and for the year 1920 * * *. [The decision was certified for appeal to the Supreme Court by the First Circuit Court of Appeals.]

The facts certified to us are substantially as follows:

William M. Wood was president of the American Woolen Company during the years 1918, 1919, and 1920. In 1918 he received as salary and commissions from the company $978,725, which he included in his federal income tax return for 1918. In 1919 he received as salary and commissions from the company $548,132.87, which he included in his return for 1919.

[On] August 3, 1916, the American Woolen Company adopted the following resolution, which was in effect in 1919 and 1920:

> 'Voted: That this company pay any and all income taxes, State and Federal, that may hereafter become due and payable upon the salaries of all the officers of the company, including the president, William M. Wood * * *, to the end that said persons and officers shall receive their salaries or other compensation in full without deduction on account of income taxes, State or Federal, which taxes are to be paid out of the treasury of this corporation.'

* * *

Pursuant to this resolution, the American Woolen Company paid to the collector of internal revenue Mr. Wood's federal income and surtaxes due to salary and commissions paid him by the company, as follows:

Taxes for 1918 paid in 1919 . . . .$681,169.88
Taxes for 1919 paid in 1920 . . . .$351,179.27

The decision of the Board of Tax Appeals here sought to be reviewed was that the income taxes of $681,169.88 and $351,179.27 paid by the American Woolen Company for Mr. Wood were additional income to him for the years 1919 and 1920.

The question certified by the Circuit Court of Appeals for answer by this Court is: 'Did the payment by the employer of the income taxes assessable against the employee constitute additional [gross] income to such employee?'

* * *

[W]e think the question presented is whether a taxpayer, having induced a third person to pay his income tax or having acquiesced in such payment * * * may avoid the making of a return thereof and the payment of a corresponding tax. We think he may not do so. The payment of the tax by the employer was in consideration of the services rendered by the employee, and was again derived by the employee from his labor. The form of the payment is expressly declared to make no difference. It is therefore immaterial that the taxes were directly paid over to the government. The discharge by a third person of an obligation to him is equivalent to receipt by the person taxed. The certificate shows that the taxes were imposed upon the employee, that the taxes were actually paid by the employer, and that the employee entered upon his duties in the years in question under the express agreement that his income taxes would be paid by his employer. This is evidenced by the terms of the resolution passed August 3, 1916, more than one year prior to the year in which the taxes were imposed. The taxes were paid upon a valuable consideration, namely, the services rendered by the employee and as part of the compensation therefor. We think, therefore, that the payment constituted income to the employee.

* * *

Nor can it be argued that the payment of the tax * * * was a gift. The payment for services, even though entirely voluntarily, was nevertheless compensation within the statute. * * *

It is next argued against the payment of this tax that, if these payments by the employer constitute income to the employee, the employee will be called upon to pay the tax imposed upon this additional income, and that the payment of the additional tax will create further income which will in turn be subject to tax, with the result that there would be a tax upon a tax. This, it is urged, is the result of the government's theory, when carried to its logical conclusion, and results in an absurdity which Congress could not have contemplated.

In the first place, no attempt has been made by the Treasury to collect further taxes, upon the theory that the payment of the additional taxes creates further income * * *. We can settle questions of that sort when an attempt to impose a tax upon a tax is undertaken, but not now. It is not, therefore, necessary to answer the argument based upon an algebraic formula to reach the amount of taxes due. The question in this case is, 'Did the payment by the employer of the income taxes assessable against the employee constitute additional taxable income to such employee?' The answer must be 'Yes.'

Notes

1.   *Discharge of obligation.* When the American Woolen Company paid Mr. Wood's tax, did Mr. Wood receive any cash or property? If not, what justification exists for treating the payment by American Woolen Company as gross income to Mr. Wood?

2.   *Tax on tax.* Assume Employee earned a salary of $150,000 in Year 1 and owed income tax on that salary of $30,000. If Employer paid Employee's $30,000 income tax obligation in Year 1, how much gross income would Employee have in Year 1? In these circumstances, will Employee's income tax liability be greater than $30,000, equal to $30,000, or less than $30,000?

■ **PROBLEM 3-1.** *Payment of employee's tax liability by employer.* How much gross income does Employee have in each of the following situations?

a)   Employee owes Bank $5,000 and Employer gives Employee a $5,000 bonus that Employee uses to repay Bank.   5,000

b)   Employee owes Bank $5,000 and Employer pays Bank $5,000 to satisfy Employee's debt.   5,000

c)   Employer gives Employee a $5,000 bonus that Employee uses to pay a part of his daughter's law school tuition. Employee has no legal obligation to pay his daughter's law school tuition. *5,000*

d)   Employer pays $5,000 of Employee's daughter's law school tuition directly to the law school. *5,000*

e)   Same as d), but Employee's daughter is also employed by Employer. *5,000 to daughter ✗ 5,000*

f)   How much gross income does Employee's daughter have in situations c), d) and e)? *0, 0, 0*

WORTH NOTING

Unemployment compensation and social security benefits. Unemployment compensation is included in the recipient's gross income. See IRC § 85. In addition, up to 85% of social security benefits are included in the recipient's gross income. See IRC § 86.

---

2. Common Fringe Benefits

In addition to wages and salary, section 61(a)(1) income includes other forms of compensation including fringe benefits. Fringe benefits can be defined broadly as any benefit an employee receives from an employer beyond conventional wages and salaries. Like wages and salary, fringe benefits are included in gross income unless Congress has specifically excluded the specific fringe benefit from gross income. As you will see, Congress has been very generous in this area by enacting statutory exclusions for several types of fringe benefits.

a.   Employer Provided Medical Coverage—§ 106; Reg. § 1.106–1

Primary Law: IRC § 106

[G]ross income of an employee does not include employer provided coverage under an accident or health plan.[1]

---

[1]   The first clause of this exclusion (acknowledging exceptions to this rule) is omitted because the exceptions are beyond the scope of this book.

One of the most common fringe benefits received by employees is the employer's payment of part or all of the premiums for medical insurance covering the employee and sometimes the employee's family. You might be familiar with this fringe benefit if you ever had a job where your employer provided you with medical insurance and paid part or all of the premiums. This benefit, like all benefits received by an employee, would be included in the employee's gross income except for the fact that Congress specifically excludes this benefit from gross income under IRC § 106.

Two different types of employer provided medical coverage exist. The first is where an employer purchases insurance from a third party (e.g., Blue Cross/Blue Shield) that covers its employees. Alternatively, the employer might "self-insure" by setting aside amounts for the benefit of its employees and paying claims out of the set aside funds. In both instances, the employee derives a benefit from the employer's coverage because she receives such coverage for free (or at a reduced cost). Regardless of whether the employer buys insurance or self-insures, the benefit derived by the employee of receiving such coverage without paying for it is excluded from the employee's gross income. See Reg. § 1.106–1.

IN SIGHTS **The exclusion for employer provided medical coverage is both costly and controversial.** Statutory exclusions and other tax relief provisions are referred to as "tax expenditures." The Joint Committee on Taxation makes an annual determination of the amount of tax revenue that is lost by virtue of each of the many "tax expenditures" in the Code. The exclusion of employer provided medical coverage has long been the most costly tax expenditure in the Code. This exclusion costs the government more than $150 billion annually and constitutes the largest tax expenditure.[2]

The exclusion for employer provided medical coverage is controversial both because of the magnitude of its cost and because the benefit is only available to individuals who are fortunate enough to have employers who provide this fringe benefit to their employees. Self-employed individuals and employees without employer provided medical coverage reap none of the tax savings resulting from this

---

[2]   Joint Committee on Taxation, Estimates of Federal Tax Expenditures for Fiscal Years 2017–2021 (May 25, 2018).

exclusion. Various proposals have been advanced in recent years to reduce or eliminate the favorable tax treatment of employer provided medical coverage but none have been adopted to date.

b.   Employer Provided Medical Benefits—§ 105

Primary Law: IRC § 105

(a)   Except as otherwise provided in this section, amounts received by an employee through accident or health insurance for personal injuries or sickness shall be included in gross income to the extent such amounts (1) are attributable to contributions by the employer which were not includible in the gross income of the employee, or (2) were paid by the employer.

(b)   Except in the case of amounts attributable to (and not in excess of) deductions allowed under section 213 (relating to medical, etc., expenses) for any prior taxable year, gross income does not include amounts referred to in subsection (a) if such amounts are paid, directly or indirectly, to the taxpayer to reimburse the taxpayer for expenses incurred by him for the medical care (as defined in section 213(d)) of the taxpayer, his spouse, his dependents * * *, and any child * * * of the taxpayer who as of the end of the taxable year has not attained age 27. * * *

As discussed above, IRC § 106 excludes from the employee's gross income the benefit derived from medical coverage that the employer provides. The employee derives a benefit from such coverage because it saves the employee the money he would have used to purchase medical insurance for himself. The employee derives a second benefit when the employer's insurance company (or the employer, if self-insured) pays the employee's actual medical expenses or reimburses the employee for such expenses. These payments made by the insurance company or the employer (if self-insured) would be gross income to the employee unless some other Code provision excludes such payments from the employee's gross income. IRC § 105(b) generally excludes the medical payments or reimbursements made under employer provided medical coverage from the employee's gross income.

IRC § 105 can be misleading because it initially indicates that amounts received by an employee from employer provided medical coverage are *included* in the employee's gross income. IRC § 105(a). However, § 105(b) provides that these amounts are excluded to the extent they reimburse the employee *for amounts expended for medical care.*[3] Hence, the employee can exclude all payments received from an employer provided medical plan to the extent of the actual medical expenses incurred by the employee (and his family if family coverage is provided).

If an employee works for an employer who does not provide medical coverage to its employees, the employee must purchase her own medical insurance. Because she must pay for her coverage, she does not derive the benefit of having medical coverage provided to her at no, or reduced, cost (i.e., she does not derive the benefit that the recipient of employer provided medical coverage can exclude under IRC § 106). The employee who purchases her own insurance derives a benefit when her medical insurance policy pays or reimburses her for medical expenses she incurs. An employee who receives benefits under a medical insurance policy that she purchased cannot exclude the benefits she receives under IRC § 105(b), which applies only to employer provided coverage. Instead, the employee can exclude the benefits under IRC § 104(a)(3). Moreover, IRC § 104(a)(3) allows the employee who purchases her own medical insurance to exclude the entire recovery, rather than limiting the exclusion to her actual medical expenses.

---

[3] The exclusion applies only if the employee does not deduct the medical expenses from gross income. See IRC § 105(b) (first clause). Deductions (including the deduction for medical expenses) are examined in Chapters 9 and 10.

Primary Law: IRC § 104

(a) [G]ross income does not include—

* * *

(3) amounts received through accident or health insurance
* * * for personal injuries or sickness (other than amounts
received by an employee, to the extent such amounts (A)
are attributable to contributions by the employer which
were not includible in the gross income of the employee,
or (B) are paid by the employer);

* * *

NOTES

1.   *Disability insurance.* Disability insurance pays benefits to an employee who
is unable to work. These benefits substitute for the income the employee otherwise would have earned while working. Some employers provide disability
coverage to their employees. Like the benefit derived by an employee whose
employer provides medical coverage, the benefit derived by an employee whose
employer provides disability insurance to the employee is excluded from the
employee's gross income under IRC § 106.

  a)   When an employee becomes disabled and collects benefits under an
employer provided disability plan, are the benefits excluded from the
employee's gross income? See IRC § 105(b).

  b)   If the employee purchases her own disability policy and she becomes
disabled and collects benefits, are the benefits excluded from the employee's gross income? See IRC § 104(a)(3).

2.   *Life insurance.* Life insurance generally pays a lump sum benefit to an individual's named beneficiary at the time of the individual's death. The insurance
proceeds are normally intended to replace lost income for those who were dependent upon the income earned by the decedent (e.g., the decedent's spouse
and children). Some employers provide life insurance to their employees. IRC
§ 106 does *not* apply to the benefit an employee derives from employer provided

life insurance coverage. However, under certain circumstances, the cost of up to $50,000 of certain types of life insurance is excluded from the employee's gross income under IRC § 79. In addition, if the insured individual dies and her beneficiary collects the life insurance proceeds from an employer provided policy, those proceeds are excluded from the beneficiary's gross income in their entirety. See IRC § 101. Likewise, if an individual who purchases his own life insurance policy dies, the proceeds are excluded from the beneficiary's gross income. See IRC § 101.

■ **PROBLEM 3-2.** *Medical coverage.* In Year 1, Baldwin's employer pays Blue Cross/Blue Shield $12,000 for medical insurance for Baldwin and his family. In Year 1, Baldwin and his family incur $8,000 of medical expenses all of which are paid for or reimbursed by Blue Cross/Blue Shield.

a) Does the $12,000 that Baldwin's employer pays Blue Cross/Blue Shield in Year 1 represent a benefit to Baldwin? Is the $12,000 included in Baldwin's Year 1 gross income? See IRC § 106. *yes, no*

b) Does the reimbursement by Blue Cross/Blue Shield of the $8,000 of medical expenses that Baldwin and his family incurred in Year 1 represent a benefit to Baldwin? Is the $8,000 included in Baldwin's Year 1 gross income? See IRC § 105(b). *yes, no*

c) Rather than purchasing insurance from Blue Cross/Blue Shield, Baldwin's employer self-insures and provides coverage to Baldwin in that manner. Does the value of the employer provided coverage represent a benefit to Baldwin? Is the value of the employer provided coverage included in Baldwin's Year 1 gross income? See IRC § 106.

d) If Baldwin's employer self-insures and Baldwin receives $10,000 under the employer's plan in Year 1 (even though Baldwin only incurred $8,000 of medical expenses), would the $10,000 payment represent a benefit to Baldwin? How much, if any, of the $10,000 is included in Baldwin's Year 1 gross income? See IRC § 105(b).

yes, no

yes, 2k?

e) Baldwin's sister, Clara, does not have an employer who pays for her medical insurance. Instead, Clara pays $6,000 a year to Alliance Insurance for medical coverage for Clara and her family. In Year 1, Clara and her family incur $11,000 of medical expenses and her policy with Alliance pays (or reimburses) $9,000 of those expenses.

1) Does the reimbursement by Alliance Insurance of $9,000 of the medical expenses that Clara and her family incurred in Year 1 represent a benefit to Clara? Is the $9,000 included in Clara's Year 1 gross income? See IRC § 104(a)(3).

2) In the highly unlikely event that Alliance Insurance paid Clara $12,000 in Year 1 (even though Clara only incurred $11,000 of medical expenses), would the $12,000 payment represent a benefit to Clara? How much, if any, of the $12,000 is included in Clara's Year 1 gross income? See IRC § 104(a)(3).

■ **PROBLEM 3-3.** *Disability coverage.* In Year 1, Baldwin's employer purchases disability insurance for Baldwin from Calamity Insurance Co. for a $5,000 annual premium that will pay Baldwin an annual benefit of $60,000 (60% of his $100,000 salary) if he becomes disabled. (The disability insurance is in addition to the medical coverage that Baldwin's employer provides.) Baldwin becomes disabled in May of Year 1 and collects $35,000 under the disability policy in Year 1.

a) Does the $5,000 that Baldwin's employer pays Calamity Insurance in Year 1 represent a benefit to Baldwin? Is the $5,000 included in Baldwin's Year 1 gross income? See IRC § 106.

b) Does the $35,000 payment by Calamity Insurance to Baldwin in Year 1 represent a benefit to Baldwin? Is the $35,000 included in Baldwin's Year 1 gross income? See IRC § 105(b).

c) If, rather than purchasing disability insurance from Calamity Insurance, Baldwin's employer self-insures and provides disability coverage to Baldwin that would have cost Baldwin $5,000 to replicate, would the employer provided coverage represent a benefit to Baldwin? If so, would the $5,000 be included in Baldwin's Year 1 gross income? See IRC § 106.

d) If Baldwin's employer self-insures and provides disability benefits to Baldwin of $35,000 in Year 1, would the $35,000 payment represent a benefit to Baldwin? Is the $35,000 included in Baldwin's Year 1 gross income? See IRC § 105(b).

e) In Year 1, Baldwin's sister, Clara, purchases her own disability insurance for a $4,000 annual premium from Continental Casualty Co. that will pay Clara an annual benefit of $30,000 if she becomes disabled. Clara becomes disabled in August of Year 1 and collects $10,000 under the policy in Year 1. Does the $10,000 payment by Continental Casualty to Clara in Year 1 represent a benefit to Clara? Is the $10,000 included in Clara's Year 1 gross income? See IRC § 104(a)(3).

---

3.   Other Excluded Fringe Benefits

Section 61(a)(1) includes the value of all fringe benefits, other than those that are specifically excluded, in the employee's gross income. As discussed above, employer provided medical coverage and medical benefits are excluded from gross income. Certain other fringe benefits are also excluded from the gross income of the employees who receive these benefits. Among the excluded fringe benefits are "no additional cost services," "qualified employee discounts," "working condition" benefits," and certain "de minimis" benefits. See IRC § 132. The legislative history to section 132 describes the scope of these exclusions.

Supplemental Report of the Committee on Ways and Means, U.S. House of Representatives

H.R. 4170, 98th Cong. 2d Sess., Rept. 98–432, Pt. 2, 1593–1607
Mar. 5, 1984

Title V—Fringe Benefit Provisions

* * *

Explanation of Provisions

1.   Overview

Under the bill, certain fringe benefits provided by an employer are excluded from the recipient employee's gross income for Federal income tax purposes * * *.

The excluded fringe benefits are those benefits that qualify under one of the following * * * categories as defined in the bill: (1) a no-additional-cost service, (2) a qualified employee discount, (3) a working condition fringe, [and] (4) a de minimis fringe * * *.

In the case of a no-additional-cost service [or] a qualified employee discount * * *, the exclusion applies with respect to benefits provided to officers, owners, or highly compensated employees only if the benefit is made available to employees on a basis which does not discriminate in favor of officers, owners, or highly compensated employees.

Any fringe benefit that does not qualify for exclusion under the bill (for example, free or discounted goods or services which are limited to corporate officers) and that is not excluded under another statutory fringe benefit provision of the Code is taxable to the recipient under Code section 61 * * *.

2.   No-additional-cost Service ([N]ew Code sec. 132(b))

General rule

Under this category, the entire value of any no-additional-cost service provided by an employer to an employee for the use of the employee (or of the employee's spouse or dependent children) is excluded for income * * * tax purposes. However, the exclusion applies only if the service is available to employees on a nondiscriminatory basis (see description below of the nondiscrimination rules of the bill). The exclusion applies whether the service is provided directly for no charge or at a reduced price or whether the benefit is provided through a cash rebate of all or part of the amount paid for the service.

To qualify under this exclusion, the employer must incur no substantial additional cost in providing the service to the employee, computed without regard to any amounts paid by the employee for the service. For this purpose, the term cost includes any revenue forgone because the service is furnished to the employee rather than to a nonemployee. In addition, the service provided to the employee must be of the type which the employer offers for sale to nonemployee customers in the ordinary course of the line of business of the employer in which the employee is performing services.

Generally, situations in which employers incur no additional cost in providing services to employees are those in which the employees receive, at no substantial additional cost to the employer, the benefit of excess capacity which otherwise would have remained unused because nonemployee customers would not have purchased it. Thus, employers that furnish airline, railroad, or subway seats or hotel rooms to employees working in those lines of business in such a way that nonemployee customers are not displaced, and telephone companies that provide telephone service to employees within existing capacity, incur no substantial additional cost in the provision of these services to employees, as this term is used in the bill.

* * *

Reciprocal arrangements

Under the bill, the employees of one employer are allowed the no-additional-cost service exclusion for services provided by an unrelated employer * * * only if the services provided to the employee are the same type of services as provided to nonemployee customers by both the line of business (of the first employer) in which the employee works and the line of business (of the other employer) in which the services are provided to the employee. In addition, both employers must be parties to a written reciprocal agreement under which the employees of such line of business may receive the service from the other employer, and neither employer may incur any substantial additional cost (including foregone revenue or payments to the other employer) in providing such service or pursuant to such agreement.

* * *

Examples

As an illustration of the no-additional-cost service category of excludable benefits, assume that a corporation which operates an airline as its only line of business provides all of its employees (and their spouses and dependent children) with free travel, on the same terms to all employees, as stand-by passengers on the employer airline if the space taken on the flight has not been sold to the public shortly before departure time. In such a case, the entire fair market value of the free travel is excluded under the no-additional-cost service rule in the bill. This conclusion follows because the service provided by the employer to its employees who work in the employer's airline line of business is the same as that sold to the general public (airline flights), the service is provided at no substantial additional cost to the employer (the seat would have been unsold to nonemployees if the employee had not taken the trip), and the eligibility terms satisfy the nondiscrimination rules of [IRC § 132(j)(1)] since all employees are eligible for the benefit on the same terms.

3.   *Qualified Employee Discount ([N]ew Code sec. 132(c))*

General rule

Under the bill, certain employee discounts allowed from the selling price of qualified goods or services of the employer are excluded for income * * * tax purposes, but only if the discounts are available to employees on a nondiscriminatory basis (see description below of the nondiscrimination rules of the bill). The exclusion applies whether the qualified employee discount is provided through a reduction in price or through a cash rebate from a third party.

* * *

Amount of exclusion

General rule.—Under the bill, an employee discount is excluded only up to a specified limit. In the case of merchandise, the excludable amount of the discount is limited to the selling price of the merchandise, multiplied by the employer's gross profit percentage. The discount exclusion for a service may not exceed 20 percent of the selling price, regardless of the actual gross profit percentage.

Merchandise.—In the case of merchandise, the excludable amount of the discount may not exceed the selling price of the merchandise, multiplied by the employer's gross profit percentage. For this purpose, the employer's gross profit percentage for a period means the excess of the aggregate sales price for the period of merchandise sold by the employer in the relevant line of business over the aggregate cost of such merchandise to the employer, then divided by the aggregate sales price.

For example, if total sales of such merchandise during a year were $1,000,000 and the employer's cost for the merchandise was $600,000, then the gross profit percentage for the year is 40 percent ($1,000,000 minus $600,000 equals 40 percent of $1,000,000). Thus, an employee discount with respect to such merchandise is excluded from income to the extent it does not exceed 40 percent of the selling price of the merchandise to nonemployee customers. If in this case the discount allowed to the employee exceeds 40 percent (for example, 50 percent), the excess discount on a purchase (10 percent in the example) is included in the employee's gross income.

* * *

Services.—The discount exclusion for a service is limited to 20 percent of the selling price of the service; there is no profit percentage limitation. The selling price is the price at which the service is provided in the ordinary course of business to customers who are not employees.

* * *

4.   *Working Condition Fringe ([N]ew Code sec. 132(d))*

General rules

Under the bill, the fair market value of any property or services provided to an employee of the employer is excluded for income * * * tax purposes to the extent that the costs of the property or services would be deductible as ordinary and necessary business expenses * * * if the employee had paid for such property or services. The nondiscrimination provisions applicable to certain other provisions * * * of the bill do not apply as a condition for exclusion as a working condition fringe * * *.

* * *

5.   *De Minimis Fringe ([N]ew Code sec. 132(e))*

General rules

Under the bill, if the fair market value of any property or a service that otherwise would be a fringe benefit includible in gross income is so small that accounting for the property or service would be unreasonable or administratively impracticable, the value is excluded for income * * * tax purposes. The nondiscrimination rules applicable to certain other provisions of the bill do not apply as a condition for exclusion of property or a service as a de minimis fringe * * *.

In determining whether the de minimis exclusion applies, the fair market values of all property or services provided to an individual during a calendar year are to be aggregated, except for (1) property or services that are excluded from taxation under another specific statutory exclusion provision of the Code, as amended by this bill (such as health benefits or qualified employee discounts) and (2) any nonexcluded property or service provided to the employee that (without regard to the aggregation rule) does not qualify as a de minimis fringe because the value of the individual item is too large.

To illustrate, benefits which generally are excluded from income * * * taxes as de minimis fringes (without regard to the aggregation rule) include the typing of personal letters by a company secretary, occasional personal use of the company copying ma-chine, monthly transit passes provided at a discount not exceeding $15, occasional company cocktail parties or picnics for employees, occasional supper money or taxi fare because of overtime work, traditional holiday gifts of property with a low fair market value, occasional theatre or sporting event tickets, and coffee and doughnuts furnished to employees.

* * *

8.   *Nondiscrimination Rules*

To qualify under the bill for the exclusions for no-additional-cost services [and] qualified employee discounts * * *, the benefit must be available on substantially the same terms to each member of a group of employees which is defined under a reasonable classification set up by the employer that does not discriminate in favor of officers, owners, or highly compensated employees (the "highly compensated group"). If the availability of the fringe benefit does not satisfy this nondiscrimination test, the exclusion applies only to those employees (if any) who receive the benefit and who are not members of the highly compensated group. For example, if an employer offers a 20-percent discount (which otherwise satisfies the requirements for a qualified employee discount) to rank-and-file employees and a 35-percent discount to the highly compensated group, the entire value of the 35-percent discount (not just the excess over 20 percent) is includible in gross income and wages of the members of the highly compensated group who make purchases at a discount.

The determination of whether a particular classification is reasonable depends on the facts and circumstances involved. A classification that, on its face, makes benefits available only to officers, owners, or highly compensated employees is per se discriminatory, and no exclusion is available to the highly compensated group members for the value of such benefits. On the other hand, an employer could establish a classification that is based on certain appropriate factors, such as seniority, full-time vs. part-time employment, or job description, provided that the effect of the classification is nondiscriminatory. * * *

[An] example of a fringe benefit to which the nondiscrimination requirement applies is the provision by retail stores of discounts to employees and their families. Suppose that a store makes this benefit available only to executives and salespersons, but not to employees in other categories, such as clerical and maintenance. To determine whether such a classification would be discriminatory in this particular case, all employees of the store would be divided into categories according to their level of compensation. If the number of the most highly compensated employees to whom the benefit is available, as a proportion of all employees in that category, were not substantially higher than the corresponding proportions for the remaining categories of employees, then the classification would not be considered to be one that discriminated in favor of the highly compensated.

* * *

The nondiscrimination rules [IRC § 132(j)(1)] do not apply to a working condition fringe * * * or a de minimis fringe * * *.

a.   No Additional Cost Service—§§ 132(a)(1), (b), (j)

Primary Law: IRC § 132

(a)   Gross income shall not include any fringe benefit which qualifies as a—

   (1)   no additional-cost service,

   * * *

(b)   For purposes of this section, the term "no-additional-cost service" means any service provided by an employer to an employee for use by such employee if—

   (1)   such service is offered for sale to customers in the ordinary course of the line of business of the employer in which the employee is performing services, and

   (2)   the employer incurs no substantial additional cost (including forgone revenue) in providing such service to the employee (determined without regard to any amount paid by the employee for such service).

   * * *

(j)

   (1)   Paragraphs (1) and (2) of subsection (a) shall apply with respect to any fringe benefit described therein provided with respect to any highly compensated employee only if such fringe benefit is available on substantially the same terms to each member of a group of employees which is defined under a reasonable classification set up by the employer which does not discriminate in favor of highly compensated employees.

* * *

I.R.S. Technical Advice Memorandum 8741007

June 5, 1987

ISSUE

Whether the value of free or discounted flights offered to employees of a company engaged in the business of transporting goods and information may be excluded from the employees' gross income as a no-additional-cost service pursuant to section 132(a)(1) of the Internal Revenue Code.

FACTS

The taxpayer (Company) is a corporation principally engaged in the transportation of freight. The Company utilizes * * * aircraft * * * in this process. The Company does not offer passenger flights for sale to the public. The Company makes available free or discounted passenger flights to its employees. * * *

The Company provides * * * air travel for the personal use of its employees. [T]he Company permits employees to occupy jumpseats in its airplanes. Regulations of the Federal Aviation Administration (FAA) require all commercial aircraft to have jumpseats. Such seats must be made available for FAA inspectors and U.S. Secret Service Agents. * * * If the jumpseats are unoccupied, then Company employees may use the seats for personal travel.

* * *

LAW AND RATIONALE

Section 132(a)(1) of the Code provides that certain services an employer provides to its employees, termed 'no-additional-cost services' are excluded from the employees' gross income.

Section 132(b) of the Code provides that the term 'no-additional-cost service' means any service provided by any employer to an employee for use by such employee if—

(1) such service is offered for sale to customers in the ordinary course of the line of business of the employer in which the employee is performing services, and

(2) the employer incurs no substantial additional cost (including forgone revenue) in providing such service to the employee (determined without regard to any amount paid by the employee for such service).

* * *

At issue is whether the service provided to an employee must, in addition to being in the same line of business in which the employee works, also be the same as the service sold to customers in the ordinary course of business. The Company does not offer passenger travel for sale, rather, it offers freight transportation. Thus, if the Code requires that the service provided be the same as the service sold to customers, the exclusion is not available to the employees of the Company.

* * *

We believe that in order to qualify as no-additional-cost services the language in section 132(b)(1) of the Code requires that the flights made available to the Company's employees must actually be offered for sale to the Company's customers in the ordinary course of the Company's business. * * *

[S]ection 132(b)(1) of the Code is more than a line of business limitation. This is evident from the portion of the Supplemental Report [of the Committee on Ways and Means on the Tax Reform Act of 1984] discussing the 'Line of business limitation' at page 1594 which contains the following:

To be excluded under this category, a service must be the same type of service which is sold to the public in the ordinary course of the line of business of the employer in which the employee works. (Thus, types of services most of the employer's production of which are provided or sold to the employer's employees do not qualify for this exclusion.)

The parenthetical demonstrates that the phrase 'offered for sale to customers' in section 132(b)(1) of the Code has application apart from the line of business requirement because a service made available to an employee may be within the line of business in which the employee works and still fail to satisfy section 132(b)(1). [S]ection 132(b)(1) requires more than that the benefit satisfy the line of business limitation * * *.

* * *

HOLDING

The value of free or discounted flights offered to employees of the Company may not be excluded from the employees' gross income as a no-additional-cost service pursuant to section 132(a)(1) of the Code.

FOR DISCUSSION

Impact of IRC § 132(j)(7). How does IRC § 132(j)(7) impact the conclusion reached in Technical Advice Memorandum 8741007?

■ **PROBLEM 3-4.** *No additional cost service.* Excelsior Airlines is in the business of transporting passengers between mid-size towns throughout the United States. Excelsior allows certain employees to ride for free as a passenger on flights when the employee is not working. Bree is a pilot for Excelsior and flies as a passenger on Excelsior to a vacation spot for a one-week vacation. The fair market value of Bree's round trip flights is $1,000.

a) In the absence of IRC § 132, how much gross income would Bree derive as a result of the free flights? See IRC § 61(a)(1).

b)   In light of IRC § 132, how much gross income does Bree derive if the vacation flights Bree took had empty seats and Bree occupied the empty seats? See IRC § 132(b)(2); Reg. § 1.132–2(a)(5). How does your answer change under each of the following alternatives:

1)   Bree paid $1,000 for the flights and the airline subsequently reimbursed the $1,000 to her. See Reg. § 1.132–2(a)(3).

2)   All the passengers, including Bree, were given a complimentary bag of peanuts that cost Excelsior $.59. See IRC § 132(b)(2); Reg. § 1.132–2(a)(5).

3)   Bree is a "highly compensated" employee and only highly compensated employees were permitted to fly for free. See IRC § 132(j)(1).

4)   Bree is a "highly compensated" employee and non-highly compensated employees are required to pay $600 for the flights that Bree took for free. See Reg. § 1.132–8(a)(2)(i).

5)   Bree is not a "highly compensated" employee but she is the only non-highly compensated employee who is permitted to fly for free? See IRC § 132(j)(1).

c)   How much gross income does Bree derive if the vacation flights Bree took were full and a paying passenger was removed from each flight so Bree could have a seat? See IRC § 132(b)(2); Reg. § 1.132–2(a)(5).

1)   Would your answer change if the per passenger cost of the flights to the airline (cost of crew, gasoline, etc.) was $250 and Bree reimbursed that $250 cost to the airline? See IRC § 132(b)(2); Reg. § 1.132–2(a)(5).

d)   How much gross income does Bree derive if Excelsior also allowed Bree to take her spouse, two children, two parents, and two in-laws on the flights? Assume sufficient empty seats existed so that no paying passengers were displaced from the flights. Since eight people were traveling, the fair market value of the flights totaled $8,000. See IRC § 132(h).

e)   How much gross income does Bree derive if Excelsior Airlines and Belvidere Airlines agreed that employees of one airline may fly for free on the other airline and Bree flies to the vacation spot on a Belvidere flight, rather than an Excelsior flight? See IRC § 132(i). Does it matter whether Excelsior reimburses Belvidere for the cost of the flight?

---

b.   **Qualified Employee Discount**—§§ 132(a)(2), (c), (j)

Primary Law: IRC § 132

(a)   Gross income shall not include any fringe benefit which qualifies as a—

* * *

(2)   qualified employee discount,

* * *

(c)   For purposes of this section—

(1)   The term "qualified employee discount" means any employee discount with respect to qualified property or services to the extent such discount does not exceed—

(A)   in the case of property, the gross profit percentage of the price at which the property is being offered by the employer to customers, or

(B)   in the case of services, 20 percent of the price at which the services are being offered by the employer to customers.

* * *

(3)   The term "employee discount" means the amount by which—

(A)   the price at which the property or services are provided by the employer to the employee for use by such employee, is less than

(B)   the price at which such property or services are being offered by the employer to customers.

(4) The term "qualified property or services" means any property * * * or services which are offered for sale to customers in the ordinary course of the line of business of the employer in which the employee is providing services.

* * *

(j)

(1) Paragraphs (1) and (2) of subsection (a) shall apply with respect to any fringe benefit described therein provided with respect to any highly compensated employee only if such fringe benefit is available on substantially the same terms to each member of a group of employees which is defined under a reasonable classification set up by the employer which does not discriminate in favor of highly compensated employees.

* * *

WORTH NOTING

A **Field Attorney Advice** is legal advice prepared by field attorneys of the Internal Revenue Service's Office of Chief Counsel at the request of Internal Revenue Service agents during the conduct of an audit.

Field Attorney Advice 20171202F

Office of Chief Counsel, Internal Revenue Service
March 24, 2017

MEMORANDUM

To: * * *, Internal Revenue Agent

From: Area Counsel * * *

This memorandum responds to your request for assistance. This advice may not be used or cited as precedent.

ISSUES

* * *

[W]hether [a discount program offered by employer] qualifies as a qualified employee discount under I.R.C. § 132(a)(2) where such program allows employee to sign up a total of [x] people [some of whom] may not meet the definition of employee under Treas. Reg. § 1.132–1(b)(1).

* * *

CONCLUSIONS

* * *

[O]nly employees, as defined in I.R.C. § 132(h) and Treas. Reg. § 1.132–1(b)(1), can qualify for a nontaxable fringe benefit under I.R.C. § 132(a), and therefore, [program], as it applies to nonemployees, is a taxable fringe benefit.

* * *

FACTS

The facts are based upon information you provided. * * *

[Employer] provides its employees a discount program * * *. Under the [program], employees may designate up to [z] individuals, including themselves, to receive a [15%] discount off published rates for * * * services from [employer]. [T]hese individuals can be spouses or domestic partners, family members and friends of the employee. * * *

In order to participate in the [program], the employee and each of his or her designated individuals must become members. * * *

After becoming a member, employees must log into the [program] and register themselves, as well as each of the other individuals they have designated to participate in the [program] using the [member] numbers provided by those individuals. Employees and their designated individuals book in the same manner as the general public * * *. The [members] must use their [membership] numbers in order to obtain the discount.

* * *

LAW AND ANALYSIS

* * *

I.R.C. § 61(a) provides that gross income includes all income, from whatever source derived, including fringe benefits. Treas. Reg. § 1.61–21(a)(4) provides that a taxable fringe benefit is included in the income of the person performing the services in connection with which the fringe benefit is furnished. Thus, a fringe benefit may be taxable to a person even though that person did not actually receive the fringe benefit. * * *

I.R.C. § 132(a)(2) excludes from gross income the fringe benefit of qualified employee discounts. For purposes of I.R.C. § 132(a), an employee is defined as an individual currently employed by the employer, an individual who retired from the employer, or became disabled while working for the employer, or a widow or widower of any of these. I.R.C. § 132(h), Treas. Reg. § 1.132–1(b)(1). Spouses and dependent children of the above mentioned groups are also treated as "employees" for purposes of I.R.C. § 132(a)(2). I.R.C. § 132(h)(2). * * *

Only individuals meeting the definition of employee under I.R.C. § 132(h) and Treas. Reg. § 1.132–1(b)(1) qualify for a nontaxable fringe benefit of a qualified employee discount. [Employer] allows employees to designate up to [z] other individuals for the [15%] discount. These individuals do not have to meet the definition of "employee" as defined by I.R.C. § 132(h) and Treas. Reg. § 1.132–1(b)(1). * * * Basically, the employee can designate any person to participate, regardless of the employee's relationship with that person.

The value of any discount given to an individual through the [program] who is not an "employee" as defined by I.R.C. § 132(h) and Treas. Reg. § 1.132–1(b)(1) is taxable as income *to the employee* who designated such individual. Treas. Reg. § 1.61–21(a)(4). (emphasis added)

* * *

PROBLEM 3-5. *Qualified employee discount.* Employer owns a hair salon and charges customers $100 for certain basic services. Employer permits certain employees to purchase those same services for $75.

a) How much *potential* gross income does an employee who purchases the services have? *value of the discount*

b) How much *actual* gross income does the employee have? See IRC § 132(c).

c) How much gross income does the employee have under each of the following alternative scenarios:

   1) Employee pays $100 for the services and Employer subsequently reimburses $25 to her. See Reg. § 1.132–3(a)(4).

   2) Employee is a "highly compensated" employee and only highly compensated employees are eligible for the discount. See IRC § 132(j)(1).

   3) Employee is a "highly compensated" employee and non-highly compensated employees are required to pay $90 for the services. See Reg. § 1.132–8(a)(2)(i).

   4) Employee is not a "highly compensated" employee. Employee and "highly compensated" employees are permitted to purchase the service for $75.

   5) Employer extends the discount to a list of employee's friends (compiled by employee) and 10 of employee's friends take advantage of the offer.

c.   Employer Provided Lodging and Meals—§ 119(a)

Primary Law: IRC § 119

(a)   There shall be excluded from the gross income of an employee the value of any meals or lodging furnished to him, his spouse, or any of his dependents by or on behalf of his employer for the convenience of the employer, but only if—

    (1)   in the case of meals, the meals are furnished on the business premises of the employer, or

    (2)   in the case of lodging, the employee is required to accept such lodging on the business premises of his employer as a condition of his employment.

* * *

VANICEK v. COMMISSIONER; MODEN v. COMMISSIONER

United States Tax Court, 1985
85 T.C. 731

Nims, Judge:

* * *

FINDINGS OF FACT

[P]etitioners Edward Vanicek and John Moden were employed by the Forest Preserve District of Cook County, Illinois (hereinafter sometimes referred to as the District). The District, an incorporated political unit of the State of Illinois, was created by state statute in 1915—

> (t)o acquire * * * and hold lands * * * containing * * * natural forests * * * for the purpose of protecting and preserving the flora, fauna and scenic beauties within such district, and to restore, protect and preserve the natural forests * * * for the purpose of the education, pleasure, and recreation of the public.

Since 1915, the District has systematically acquired property to return the land to its natural state as well as to develop golf courses, swimming pools, nature centers and picnic areas on and throughout the District property. * * *

[R]esident watchmen are selected from employees of the District * * * to protect designated areas within the District from fire, hunting, vandalism or other encroachment. * * *

As a condition of being a resident watchman, people performing this function were required to live in residences strategically located within the areas they were assigned to patrol. * * * Although participants in the resident watchman program were not paid additional compensation for their services as resident watchmen, they were allowed to live in the residences rent-free.

A prospective resident watchman must file an application for permit in which he agrees to (1) maintain a telephone in his residence at his own expense; (2) answer emergency and fire calls at all times; (3) remain on areas, in fire season, at all times; and (4) maintain his residence at his own expense. Once accepted as a resident watchman, he receives a document listing his specific duties as follows:

1. You must be thoroughly familiar with District boundaries within your assigned area and make periodic inspections to make certain that District property is protected.

2. Check for encroachments especially by home owners living adjacent to District lands.

3. Be on constant watch for fires. During times of extreme fire dangers, all residents must remain on his respective area at all times. * * *

4. Check your area frequently during the hunting season. Report all hunters to your Division Superintendent immediately. * * *

5. You are expected to clean all minor debris dumping incidents. Report all major dumpings at once.

6. Check all water bodies for picnic tables and other objects and report same to the Division Superintendent.

7. Check all facilities for vandalism. Do not apprehend vandals, but try to obtain positive identification for authorities. (i.e. make, model, and license number of car if available).

8.   Complete and submit resident watchman reports on a monthly basis.

[D]uring the years in issue, Edward Vanicek (Edward) was employed as a Maintenance Supervisor II by the District. As a maintenance supervisor, Edward was in charge of the central equipment garage located in downtown Chicago, several miles from the District's general headquarters. Edward generally worked at the garage on weekdays from 8 a.m. until 4 p.m.

In addition to his employment as a maintenance supervisor, Edward also served as a resident watchman during the years in issue. As a resident watchman, Edward, with his wife, Sara resided in District Property No. 115 and District Property No. 525 rent-free from 1972 through May 15, 1973, and from May 15, 1973 through 1974, respectively. For purposes of this Opinion, the parties agree that during the years in issue, the monthly fair rental value of District Property No. 115 and District Property No. 525 was $275 and $475, respectively.

As a resident watchman of District Property No. 115 and District Property No. 525, Edward was responsible for an area consisting of approximately 365 acres and 824 acres, respectively. The designated area surrounding Property No. 115 included reforestation beds, an overflow parking lot, a boat launch and a shelter. The minimum value of this property during the years in issue was $313,200. The designated area surrounding Property No. 525 included several picnic groves and a nature preserve. The minimum value of this property during the years in issue was $950,625. A substantial portion of the designated areas surrounding Edward's residences at Property No. 115 and Property No. 525 was visible from those residences.

During the years in issue, Edward patrolled his designated area two to three times per week on foot and in his automobile. * * *

On their Federal income tax returns for the years in issue, petitioners did not report as income the fair rental value of lodging furnished to them rent-free as participants in the District's resident watchman program. In the statutory notice of deficiency, respondent determined that petitioners should have reported this amount as income.

OPINION

The * * * issue for decision is whether petitioners are entitled to exclude from gross income the fair rental value of lodging furnished to them by their employer.

Gross income is defined in section 61 to include all income from whatever source derived, including compensation for services. It includes income realized in any form, i.e., money, property or services. If compensation for services is paid in the form of property, the fair market value of the property must be included in income. In the instant case, although Edward was not required to live in his lodgings to perform his duties as maintenance supervisor, the parties agree that the lodgings were furnished to him because of his employment as a resident watchman. * * * Consequently, the value of such lodgings is includable in petitioners' gross income for the years in issue unless specifically excludable under another provision of the Code. Petitioners contend that the value of their lodgings is excludable under section 119.

Section 119 grants an exclusion for lodging furnished to an employee by his employer if three conditions are met:

(1)   the lodging is furnished for the convenience of the employer;

(2)   the lodging is on the business premises of the employer; and

(3)   the employee is required to accept the lodging as a condition of his employment.

The failure of petitioners to meet any one of these requirements will cause the value of their lodgings to be included in gross income. Respondent contends that petitioners failed to meet all three of the statutorily imposed conditions. His determination is presumptively correct and petitioners have the burden of proving error in this determination. On the facts before us, we believe that petitioners have satisfied their burden of proof.

We must first determine whether petitioners were required to accept their lodging as a condition of their employment. According to the relevant regulations, the 'condition of employment' test is satisfied if an

> employee is required to accept the lodging in order to enable him properly to perform the duties of his employment. Lodging will be regarded as furnished to enable the employee properly to perform the duties of his employment when, for example, the lodging is furnished because the employee is required to be available for duty at all times OR because the employee could not perform the services required of him unless he is furnished such lodging. * * *

Section 1.119–1(b), Income Tax Regs. (Emphasis supplied.)

We observe that the conditions stated in the last sentence of the above-quoted regulation are stated in the disjunctive. Admittedly, * * * Edward, was [not] required to be available for duty at all times. Nevertheless, the requirements of the regulation can be met if performance of the watchmen services required that the lodging be furnished to the employee. Respondent contends that petitioners' duties as resident watchmen did not require their occupancy of the lodging. We disagree.

Petitioners, as resident watchmen, were required to be on call to respond to fires and other emergencies which might develop in their designated areas at night. The strategic location of petitioners' residences within their designated areas enabled the District to rely on petitioners' prompt response to any emergency that might arise. We therefore find that petitioners were required to accept their lodging as a condition of their employment.

We also find that petitioners' lodgings were furnished for the convenience of the District. The 'convenience of employer' test is essentially the same as the 'condition of employment' test. Thus, for the reasons stated above, we also find that petitioners have satisfied the 'convenience of employer' test.

To exclude the value of their lodgings from income under section 119, petitioners must also satisfy their burden of proving that their lodgings were located on the business premises of the District.

The regulations provide that "the term 'business premises of the employer' generally means the place of employment of the employee." Section 1.119–1(c)(1), Income Tax Regs. Since Edward performed all of [his] watchmen services on the District's property where the houses were located, the short answer would seem to be that the lodgings were located on the business premises of the employer. The reported cases support the conclusion that the short answer is the right answer.

Lodging is considered located 'on the business premises of the employer' if such lodging is furnished at a place where the employee performs a significant portion of his duties or on the premises where the employer conducts a significant portion of his business. We have also held that lodging is located on the business premises of the employer if (1) the living quarters constitute an integral part of the business property or (2) the company carries on some of its business activities there. The extent or boundaries of the business premises in each case is a factual question whose resolution follows a consideration of the employee's duties as well as the nature of the employer's business. * * *

Respondent does not dispute that petitioners' residences were located on land owned by their employer, the District. Respondent argues, however, that petitioners' lodgings were not integrally related to the business activity of the District. We disagree.

The parties stipulated * * * that the legislation which created the Federal Preserve District described the nature of the District's business as follows:

> To acquire * * * and hold lands * * * containing * * * natural forests * * * for the purpose of protecting and preserving the flora, fauna and scenic beauties within such district, and to restore, protect and preserve the natural forests * * * for the purpose of the education, pleasure, and recreation of the public.

Thus, during the years in issue, a major business activity of the District was to protect and preserve approximately 64,000 acres of land for the public's education, pleasure and recreation.

Petitioners' appointment as resident watchmen and their occupancy of strategically located residences were an integral part of the District's efforts to protect and preserve the District's more than 64,000 acres of land. * * *

[T]he strategic location of Edward's seriatim residences within his designated areas enabled him to perform his resident watchman duties at Properties Nos. 115 and 525 during each of the periods during which he resided on these respective properties. From these residences Edward was able to observe a substantial portion of his designated areas and therefore was able to continuously monitor those areas for fire, hunting and vandalism. The strategic location of Edward's residences also allowed him to quickly respond to any problem he might discover. The District's ability to rely on Edward's quick response problems to was especially important during the hours from 1 a.m. to 9 a.m. when the rangers were off-duty. During this period of time, the resident watchmen were often the first people called by the District's general headquarters to respond to emergencies in their designated areas.

[T]he District's primary reason for providing these residences to petitioners was to enable them to protect their designated areas from fire, vandalism, hunting and other encroachments. Indeed, we are convinced that petitioners' location at these residences was integral and essential to the performance of their duties as resident watchmen. Consequently, we must conclude that petitioners' residences were integrally related to a major business activity of the District.

Respondent * * * argues that in the absence of petitioners' performance of significant employer activities at their residences, we cannot find that petitioners' residences were located on the District's business premises. * * *

Without doubt the performance of significant employer activities at the taxpayer's residence is often an important factor to consider in determining whether lodgings are located on the business premises of an employer; nevertheless, we do not believe that the absence of this factor is determinative in every case. To argue, as respondent seems to be arguing, that the conditions of Treas. Reg. section 1.119–1(b) can only be met by the performance of services within the four walls of a structure strikes us as illogical. Edward [was] required to be [a watchman from within his] strategically located residences and by 'walking the territory.' Thus, while we agree with respondent that 'business premises' is not an infinitely elastic concept, we do not believe that its parameters are to be as severely circumscribed as respondent contends. Accordingly, we find that petitioners are entitled to exclude from gross income under section 119 the fair rental value of their residences. * * *

FOR DISCUSSION

Exclusion of employer provided meals. What are the statutory requirements for excluding employer provided meals? See IRC § 119(a). What differences exist between the requirements for excluding employer provided lodging and the requirements for excluding employer provided meals?

Note

Convenience of the employer. The standard for determining whether meals are furnished for the convenience of the employer stems from Kowalski v. Commissioner, 434 U.S. 77 (1977). The "Kowalski test" entails the application of a "business necessity theory." Under that theory, the value of employer provided meals may be excluded from the employee's gross income when the employee receives the meals "in order to properly perform his or her duties." See Boyd Gaming Corp. v. Commissioner, 177 F.3d 1096 (9th Cir., 1999). In Boyd Gaming, meals were provided to the employees of a casino operator who were required to remain on the property during their shifts. The court concluded that the convenience of the employer test was satisfied because—

> Boyd has adopted a 'stay-on-premises' requirement and, as a consequence, furnishes meals to its employees because they cannot leave the casino properties during their shifts. Common sense dictates that once the policy was embraced, the 'captive' employees had no choice but to eat on the premises. [T]he furnished meals here were, in effect, 'indispensable to the proper discharge' of the employees' duties. 177 F.3d at 1100.

The Internal Revenue Service has acknowledged that employees need not be compelled to accept the meals for the convenience of the employer test to be satisfied.

> If the employer's particular business policies are such that employer-provided meals are necessary for the employee to properly discharge the duties of a particular job position, then meals provided to employees with such duties in the job position are provided for the convenience of the employer, even if certain employees in that position decline the meals.

Internal Revenue Service, Technical Advice Memorandum 201903017 (1/18/2019).

■ **PROBLEM 3-6.** *Employer provided lodging and meals.* Rachel serves as a medical resident in a small town hospital. Her employer requires her to live within a one mile radius of the hospital and pays her rent at the only hotel within that area. Her employer also provides meals to Rachel in the hospital cafeteria when she is on call but she is not required to eat those meals. Do the payments made by the hospital for Rachel's lodging and meals constitute gross income to Rachel?

SYNTHESIS

The gross income of an individual who owns a business involving the performance of services is measured by the fees the owner collects. By contrast, the gross income of an individual who sells goods to customers is measured by the difference between—1) the amount of sales revenue received and, 2) the costs incurred by the owner to produce or purchase the goods that were sold. In both cases, the business owner's gross income is captured by IRC § 61(a)(2).

The gross income of an employee is captured by IRC § 61(a)(1). The employee's gross income is measured by the total amount of the employee's salary or wages and is not reduced by any taxes withheld from the employee's paycheck. In addition, employer provided fringe benefits are also included in the employee's gross income under IRC § 61(a)(1) unless the fringe benefit is within the scope of a statutory exclusion. For example, the benefit an employee derives from employer provided medical insurance or disability insurance is excluded from the employee's gross income under IRC § 106. In addition, payments received by an employee for unreimbursed medical expenses under an employer provided plan are excluded from the employee's gross income under IRC § 105(b). By contrast, benefits received by an employee under an employer provided disability plan are included in the employee's gross income because no exclusion applies.

The benefits derived by employees from certain "no additional cost services" and "qualified employee discounts" are excluded from the employee's gross income under IRC § 132. In addition, the benefits an employee derives from employer provided housing and/or meals are excluded from the employee's gross income under IRC § 119 when its conditions are satisfied. Other fringe benefits received by an employee that are not within the scope of a specific statutory exclusion add to the employee's § 61(a)(1) income.

 Test Your Knowledge: To assess your understanding of the material in this chapter, **click here** to take a quiz.

Benefits Received by Donors and Donees

Overview

Chapter 3 focused on the benefits arising in a business context both to the business owner and to the employee. By contrast, Chapter 4 will focus on the benefits derived when a personal relationship causes one person to make a gift to the other. When a gift is made, both the donor and the donee derive benefits. The donor's benefits are intangible—it simply feels good to give a gift. By contrast, the donee's benefit takes the form of tangible property or money received from the donor.

Neither the benefits derived by a donor, nor the benefits derived by a donee, are listed among the categories of gross income in IRC § 61(a). Nevertheless, unless Congress specifically excludes these benefits from gross income, one would expect the benefits derived by both a donor and a donee to be included in gross income under the "all income from whatever source derived" language of IRC § 61(a). Although no statutory exclusion applies to the donor's benefit, the "feel good" benefit derived by a donor does not constitute gross income. As to the donee, IRC § 102 excludes the benefit the donee derives from gross income.

A. Benefits Received by Donors

The notion that a donor derives a benefit when making a gift might not be obvious to you. Some might argue that the donor derives no benefit when a gift is made. After all, the donor receives nothing tangible in return for the gift. But concluding that the donor derives no benefit ignores the fact that the donor receives emotional satisfaction from giving a gift. The act of giving causes the donor to feel happy or triggers some other positive emotion. Thus, it is wrong to regard a donor as deriving no benefit from giving a gift.

Others might argue that the donor derives a benefit equivalent to the amount of the gift in which case the gift does not result in an increase in the donor's wealth. For example, if a donor who makes a gift of $500 derives psychic pleasure equal to $500, the net increase in her wealth would be zero.[1] In many cases, however, the benefit derived by a donor will not be equal to the amount of the gift. Particularly when gifts take the form of property, such as a family keepsake, it is highly unlikely that the amount of pleasure derived by the donor will be exactly equivalent to the value of the keepsake. Thus, the question of whether a donor derives gross income cannot be avoided by assuming that the benefit derived by a donor is necessarily equivalent to the amount of the gift.

The benefit derived by a donor from making a gift is difficult, if not impossible, to quantify. As you will learn, the fact that a benefit may be difficult to value normally does not preclude the benefit from constituting gross income. Moreover, the question of whether the benefit derived by a donor constitutes gross income cannot be disposed of by pointing to a statutory exclusion. Congress has not specifically excluded the psychic benefits derived by a donor from gross income. Nevertheless, it is widely accepted that the "feel good" benefit derived by a donor from giving a gift is *not* within the scope of gross income, presumably because the income tax was not intended to capture this type of amorphous benefit.[2]

B. Benefits Received by Donees—§ 102

Primary Law: IRC § 102(a)

Gross income does not include the value of property acquired by gift, bequest, devise or inheritance.

Quite clearly, the receipt of a gift could constitute income. As Judge Posner has written: "The broadest definition of income would be all pecuniary and

---

[1]   Recall that the Supreme Court in Commissioner v. Glenshaw Glass tied gross income to "undeniable accessions to wealth." See p. 16.

[2]   Other types of benefits that the income tax fails to capture will be discussed in Chapter 8.

non-pecuniary receipts, including leisure and gifts."[3] Nevertheless, IRC § 102 excludes gifts, bequests, devises, and inheritances from the gross income of the recipient.

WORTH NOTING

Gifts, bequests, devises and inheritances. A "gift" is a gratuitous transfer from a living donor. A "bequest" is a transfer of personalty (as opposed to real estate) under a decedent's will. A "devise" is a transfer of real estate under a decedent's will. An "inheritance" is a transfer of property from a decedent who dies intestate and, as a result, whose property is distributed pursuant to state law.

---

1. Exclusion of Gifts (Intervivos Gratuitous Transfers)

The recipient of a gift may exclude the gift from gross income. IRC § 102(a). Normally, it is easy to identify when a gift is made. For example, if your aunt sends you $50 for your birthday, the benefit you receive is a gift that is excluded from gross income. It is easy to determine that the $50 from your aunt is a gift if the only relationship that exists between the two of you is a personal relationship. In certain cases, however, both business and personal relationships may exist between the same parties. Under those circumstances, it is far less clear whether the transfer was motivated by a personal relationship, in which case it is a gift, or by a business relationship, in which case it is gross income.

COMMISSIONER v. DUBERSTEIN et al.; STANTON et al. v. UNITED STATES

United States Supreme Court, 1960
363 U.S. 278, 80 S. Ct. 1190, 4 L.Ed.2d 1218

MR. JUSTICE BRENNAN delivered the opinion of the Court.

These two cases concern the provision of the Internal Revenue Code which excludes from gross income * * * 'the value of property acquired by gift.' [IRC § 102(a).] They pose the frequently recurrent question whether a specific

---

[3]   R. Posner, Economic Analysis of Law, 231–32 (1973).

transfer to a taxpayer in fact amounted to a 'gift' to him within the meaning of the statute. The importance to decision of the facts of the cases requires that we state them in some detail.

No. 376, Commissioner v. Duberstein. The taxpayer, Duberstein, was president of the Duberstein Iron & Metal Company, a corporation with headquarters in Dayton, Ohio. For some years the taxpayer's company had done business with Mohawk Metal Corporation, whose headquarters were in New York City. The president of Mohawk was one Berman. The taxpayer and Berman had generally used the telephone to transact their companies' business with each other, which consisted of buying and selling metals. The taxpayer testified, without elaboration, that he knew Berman 'personally' and had known him for about seven years. From time to time in their telephone conversations, Berman would ask Duberstein whether the latter knew of potential customers for some of Mohawk's products in which Duberstein's company itself was not interested. Duberstein provided the names of potential customers for these items.

One day in 1951 Berman telephoned Duberstein and said that the information Duberstein had given him had proved so helpful that he wanted to give the latter a present. Duberstein stated that Berman owed him nothing. Berman said that he had a Cadillac as a gift for Duberstein, and that the latter should send to New York for it; Berman insisted that Duberstein accept the car, and the latter finally did so, protesting however that he had not intended to be compensated for the information. At the time Duberstein already had a Cadillac and an Oldsmobile, and felt that he did not need another car. Duberstein testified that he did not think Berman would have sent him the Cadillac if he had not furnished him with information about the customers. * * *

Duberstein did not include the value of the Cadillac in gross income for 1951, deeming it a gift. The Commissioner asserted a deficiency for the car's value against him, and in proceedings to review the deficiency the Tax Court affirmed the Commissioner's determination. It said that 'The record is significantly barren of evidence revealing any intention on the part of the payor to make a gift. * * * The only justifiable inference is that the automobile was intended by the payor to be remuneration for services rendered to it by Duberstein.' The Court of Appeals for the Sixth Circuit reversed.

No. 546, Stanton v. United States. The taxpayer, Stanton, had been for approximately 10 years in the employ of Trinity Church in New York City. He was comptroller of the Church corporation, and president of a corporation * * * the church set up * * * to manage its real estate holdings * * *. His salary by the end of his employment there in 1942 amounted to $22,500 a year. Effective November 30, 1942, he resigned from both positions to go into business for himself. The Operating Company's directors, who seem to have included the rector and vestrymen of the church, passed the following resolution upon his resignation:

> Be it resolved that in appreciation of the services rendered by Mr. Stanton * * * a gratuity is hereby awarded to him of Twenty Thousand Dollars, payable to him in equal instalments of Two Thousand Dollars at the end of each and every month commencing with the month of December, 1942; provided that, with the discontinuance of his services, the Corporation of Trinity Church is released from all rights and claims to pension and retirement benefits not already accrued up to November 30, 1942.

The Operating Company's action was later explained by one of its directors as based on the fact that, 'Mr. Stanton was liked by all of the Vestry personally. He had a pleasing personality. He had come in when Trinity's affairs were in a difficult situation. He did a splendid piece of work, we felt. * * * '

On the other hand, there was a suggestion of some ill-feeling between Stanton and the directors, arising out of the recent termination of the services of one Watkins, the Operating Company's treasurer, whose departure was evidently attended by some acrimony. * * *

The 'gratuity' was duly paid. * * * There was undisputed testimony that there were in fact no enforceable rights or claims to pension and retirement benefits which had not accrued at the time of the taxpayer's resignation, and that the last proviso of the resolution was inserted simply out of an abundance of caution. The taxpayer * * * was required to perform no further services for Trinity after his resignation.

The Commissioner asserted a deficiency against the taxpayer after the latter had failed to include the payments in question in gross income. After payment of the deficiency and administrative rejection of a refund claim, the taxpayer sued the United States for a refund in the District Court for the Eastern District of New York. The trial judge, sitting without a jury, made the simple finding that the payments were a 'gift,' and judgment was entered for the taxpayer. The Court of Appeals for the Second Circuit reversed.

The Government, urging that clarification of the problem typified by these two cases was necessary, and that the approaches taken by the Courts of Appeals for the Second and the Sixth Circuits were in conflict, petitioned for certiorari in No. 376, and acquiesced in the taxpayer's petition in No. 546. On this basis, and because of the importance of the question in the administration of the income tax laws, we granted certiorari in both cases.

The exclusion of property acquired by gift from gross income under the federal income tax laws was made in the first income tax statute passed under the authority of the Sixteenth Amendment, and has been a feature of the income tax statutes ever since. The meaning of the term 'gift' as applied to particular transfers has always been a matter of contention. Specific and illuminating legislative history on the point does not appear to exist. * * * The meaning of the statutory term has been shaped largely by the decisional law. With this, we turn to the contentions made by the Government in these cases.

First. The Government suggests that we promulgate a new 'test' in this area to serve as a standard to be applied by the lower courts and by the Tax Court in dealing with the numerous cases that arise.[6] We reject this invitation. We are of opinion that the governing principles are necessarily general and have already been spelled out in the opinions of this Court, and that the problem is one which, under the present statutory framework, does not lend itself to any more definitive statement that would produce a talisman for the solution of concrete cases. The cases at bar are fair examples of the settings in which the problem usually arises. They present situations in which payments have been made in a context with business overtones—an employer making a payment to a retiring employee; a businessman giving something of value to another businessman who has been of advantage to him in his business. In this context, we review the law as established by the prior cases here.

The course of decision here makes it plain that the statute does not use the term 'gift' in the common-law sense, but in a more colloquial sense. This Court has indicated that a voluntarily executed transfer of his property by one to another, without any consideration or compensation therefor, though a common-law gift, is not necessarily a 'gift' within the meaning of the statute. For the Court has shown that the mere absence of a legal or moral obligation to make such a payment does not establish that it is a gift. Old Colony Trust Co.

---

[6]   The Government's proposed test is stated: 'Gifts should be defined as transfers of property made for personal [reasons] as distinguished from business reasons.'

v. Commissioner, 279 U.S. 716, 730. And, importantly, if the payment proceeds primarily from 'the constraining force of any moral or legal duty,' or from 'the incentive of anticipated benefit' of an economic nature, it is not a gift. And, conversely, '(w)here the payment is in return for services rendered, it is irrelevant that the donor derives no economic benefit from it.' A gift in the statutory sense, on the other hand, proceeds from a 'detached and disinterested generosity,' 'out of affection, respect, admiration, charity or like impulses.' And in this regard, the most critical consideration * * * is the transferor's 'intention.' 'What controls is the intention with which payment, however voluntary, has been made.'

[T]he donor's characterization of his action is not determinative—there must be an objective inquiry as to whether what is called a gift amounts to it in reality. It scarcely needs adding that the parties' expectations or hopes as to the tax treatment of their conduct in themselves have nothing to do with the matter.

[W]e take it that the proper criterion, established by decision here, is one that inquires what the basic reason for his conduct was in fact—the dominant reason that explains his action in making the transfer. * * *

Second. The Government's proposed 'test,' while apparently simple and precise in its formulation, depends frankly on a set of 'principles' or 'presumptions' derived from the decided cases, and concededly subject to various exceptions; and it involves various corollaries, which add to its detail. Were we to promulgate this test as a matter of law * * *, we would be passing far beyond the requirements of the cases before us, and would be painting on a large canvas with indeed a broad brush. The Government derives its test from such propositions as the following: That payments by an employer to an employee, even though voluntary, ought, by and large, to be taxable; * * *; that a gift involves 'personal' elements; that a business corporation cannot properly make a gift of its assets. The Government admits that there are exceptions and qualifications to these propositions. We think, to the extent they are correct, that these propositions are not principles of law but rather maxims of experience that the tribunals which have tried the facts of cases in this area have enunciated in explaining their factual determinations. * * * The conclusion whether a transfer amounts to a 'gift' is one that must be reached on consideration of all the factors.

Third. Decision of the issue presented in these cases must be based ultimately on the application of the fact-finding tribunal's experience with the mainsprings of human conduct to the totality of the facts of each case. The nontechnical nature of the statutory standard, the close relationship of it to the date of practical human experience, and the multiplicity of relevant factual elements, with their various combinations, creating the necessity of ascribing the proper force to each, confirm us in our conclusion that primary weight in this area must be given to the conclusions of the trier of fact.

This conclusion may not satisfy an academic desire for tidiness, symmetry and precision in this area, any more than a system based on the determinations of various fact-finders ordinarily does. But we see it as implicit in the present statutory treatment of the exclusion for gifts, and in the variety of forums in which federal income tax cases can be tried. If there is fear of undue uncertainty or overmuch litigation, Congress may make more precise its treatment of the matter by singling out certain factors and making them determinative of the matters * * *. But the question here remains basically one of fact, for determination on a case-by-case basis.

One consequence of this is that appellate review of determinations in this field must be quite restricted. Where a jury has tried the matter upon correct instructions, the only inquiry is whether it cannot be said that reasonable men could reach differing conclusions on the issue. Where the trial has been by a judge without a jury, the judge's findings must stand unless 'clearly erroneous.' Fed.Rules Civ.Proc. 52(a), 28 U.S.C.A. 'A finding is 'clearly erroneous' when although there is evidence to support it, the reviewing court on the entire evidence is left with the definite and firm conviction that a mistake has been committed.' * * *

Fourth. A majority of the Court is in accord with the principles just outlined. And, applying them to the Duberstein case, we are in agreement, on the evidence we have set forth, that it cannot be said that the conclusion of the Tax Court was 'clearly erroneous.' It seems to us plain that as trier of the facts it was warranted in concluding that despite the characterization of the transfer of the Cadillac by the parties and the absence of any obligation, even of a moral nature, to make it, it was at bottom a recompense for Duberstein's past services, or an inducement for him to be of further service in the future. We cannot say with the Court of Appeals that such a conclusion was 'mere suspicion' on the Tax Court's part. To us it appears based in the sort of informed experience with human affairs that fact-finding tribunals should bring to this task.

As to Stanton, we are in disagreement. To four of us, it is critical here that the District Court as trier of fact made only the simple and unelaborated finding that the transfer in question was a 'gift.' To be sure, conciseness is to be strived for, and prolixity avoided, in findings; but, to the four of us, there comes a point where findings become so sparse and conclusory as to give no revelation of what the District Court's concept of the determining facts and legal standard may be. * * * While the standard of law in this area is not a complex one, we four think the unelaborated finding of ultimate fact here cannot stand as a fulfillment of these requirements. It affords the reviewing court not the semblance of an indication of the legal standard with which the trier of fact has approached his task. * * * While the judgment of the Court of Appeals cannot stand, the four of us think there must be further proceedings in the District Court looking toward new and adequate findings of fact. In this, we are joined by Mr. Justice Whittaker, who agrees that the findings were inadequate, although he does not concur generally in this opinion.

Accordingly, in No. 376, the judgment of this Court is that the judgment of the Court of Appeals is reversed, and in No. 546, that the judgment of the Court of Appeals is vacated, and the case is remanded to the District Court for further proceedings not inconsistent with this opinion. It is so ordered.

 LOOK ONLINE For a link to the oral arguments in the Duberstein case, click here.

[Concurring and dissenting opinions are omitted.]

Notes

1.   *Donor's intent is determinative.* The determination of whether a transfer constitutes a gift for income tax purposes depends solely on the donor's intent; the donee's intent is irrelevant.

2.   *Fact based standard.* In determining the donor's intent, it is necessary to examine the facts and circumstances of each case. What systemic problems does such a standard pose?

3.   *Government's proposed test.* Footnote 6 of Duberstein delineates the government's proposed test for ascertaining whether a transfer constitutes a gift. The Duberstein Court declined to adopt the government's test. What are the pros and cons of utilizing such a test?

LISA B. WILLIAMS v. COMMISSIONER

United States Tax Court, 2003
T.C. Memo. 2003–97

MEMORANDUM FINDINGS OF FACT AND OPINION

GERBER, JUDGE:

[T]he controversy between the parties presents the following issue for our consideration: Whether the amounts of $25,000, $35,000, and $35,000, received from her employer for 1993, 1994, and 1995, respectively, were gifts or income that petitioner failed to report * * *.

FINDINGS OF FACT

Petitioner Lisa B. Williams * * * began her career as a staff radiation therapist with Deland and Noell, a corporate entity with its place of business in Lafayette, Louisiana. The corporation, which provided treatment to cancer patients was owned and operated by Thomas Noell and Maitland Deland, two doctors, who were also husband and wife.

Petitioner was 21 when she began working on the staff of the corporation, and in * * * 1993, petitioner was promoted to the position of corporate chief therapist. As the corporate chief therapist, petitioner supervised all of the corporation's radiation therapists. During 1991 through 1995, the corporation was in a period of expansion and opening cancer treatment centers in multiple geographical locations. Petitioner was instrumental in the successful expansion and operation of the radiation therapy aspect of the corporate business. Corporate management was grooming petitioner to become part of administration and management, rather than limiting her focus to clinical operations.

During her employment with the corporation, a personal friendship developed between petitioner and Dr. Maitland Deland, who was the president and a shareholder of the corporation. Dr. Deland and petitioner spent time together during and after work, and their relationship developed into a close and personal one. Their families, including the children, were also involved in the personal relationship.

During the years in issue, Marvin K. Sullivan was the corporation's chief operating officer, and procedures were in place for evaluating employee compensation. Each department head would evaluate the employees under him and send his evaluations of them, along with salary and bonus recommendations to Mr. Sullivan. He would then meet with Drs. Deland and Noell to discuss salary and bonus adjustments for the corporation's employees. Mr. Sullivan personally supervised petitioner and evaluated her performance in the same manner as other employees of the corporation. Mr. Sullivan considered petitioner to be one of the "finest clinical therapists in the country". Mr. Sullivan evaluated petitioner's performance for 1993, 1994, and 1995, and he recommended the amounts of her bonuses for those years, which were approved by Drs. Deland and Noell.

Petitioner received the following annual salary and bonuses for [1993] through 1995:

Year	Salary	Bonus	Total
1993	56,292.61	25,000	81,292.61
1994	59,242.70	35,000	94,242.70
1995	62,856.81	35,000	97,856.81

With respect to 1993, 1994, and 1995, petitioner received Forms W-2, Wage and Tax Statement, from the corporation that reflected her base salary. The Forms W-2, however, did not include the amount of the bonus that she had received during the taxable year. * * * The corporation did not withhold income or employment taxes from petitioner's bonus checks. * * *

* * *

During 1996, the corporation's in-house counsel hired certified public accountants to examine or audit the corporation's books because of discrepancies on the corporation's Federal tax returns. * * *

Petitioner's friendship with Dr. Deland ended during 1996, after petitioner's sister, who also worked for the corporation, was dismissed from her position. Petitioner did not receive a bonus during and for the 1996 year, and she resigned from the employ of the corporation.

During the spring of 1997, the corporation sent petitioner Forms W-2c, Statement of Corrected Income and Tax Amounts, for 1993, 1994 and 1995, which reflected the bonuses (additional compensation) in the amounts of $25,000, $35,000, and $35,000, respectively. After receiving the Forms W-2c, petitioner did not amend her 1993, 1994, or 1995 income tax returns to report the increased amounts reflected on the Forms W-2c. During December 1997, petitioner was advised that she was under criminal investigation by the

Internal Revenue Service. Ultimately, there was no prosecution of petitioner in connection with her tax matters.

* * *

OPINION

The factual focus of this case concerns annual lump-sum payments to petitioner in the amounts of $25,000, $35,000, and $35,000 during 1993, 1994, and 1995, respectively. The amounts were not reported to respondent or petitioner on Forms W-2, and no withholding was effected by petitioner's employer. Key to petitioner's position is that the $25,000 and $35,000 payments were gifts from Dr. Deland, who, during those years, was a personal friend of petitioner. In that regard, "Gross income does not include the value of property acquired by gift". Sec. 102(a).

Section 102(c)(1), however, denies section 102 exclusion treatment for "any amount transferred by or for an employer to, or for the benefit of, an employee." * * * Accordingly, under section 102(c)(1), petitioner would not be entitled to treat the amounts received as excludable from gross income.

Furthermore, the record does not support a finding that Dr. Deland, based on detached and disinterested generosity and out of affection, respect, and admiration, intended to make gifts to petitioner. Commissioner v. Duberstein, 363 U.S. 278 (1960). The facts in this case reflect that the amounts paid to petitioner were in exchange for her high-quality performance as an employee. The amounts were paid as bonuses after evaluation of her performance by the corporation's chief operating officer and his recommendation of the bonus amounts. The recommended amounts were approved by Dr. Deland, the person who petitioner alleges made the alleged gifts.

It is clear from this record that petitioner was a key employee and that the amount she received in each of the 3 years was earned and commensurate with the bonuses paid to other employees. Petitioner has placed much emphasis on the fact that Dr. Deland was a personal friend, and she contends that the friendship was the source of disinterested generosity to support a gift. Dr. Deland's approval and payment of the amounts in question, however, were not out of disinterested generosity. The bonuses were set by a third person and based on petitioner's quality performance and approved by Drs. Deland and Noell. The facts in this record do not support a finding that the payments to petitioner were intended as gifts. See also sec. 102(c). Accordingly, we hold that the

$25,000, $35,000, and $35,000 payments of bonuses constituted gross income that petitioner failed to report.

* * *

Notes

1.   *Relevance of Duberstein.* IRC § 102(c) was enacted subsequent to Duberstein. Is IRC § 102(c) dispositive of Williams? If so, why does the court address the Duberstein decision in its opinion?

2.   *Government's proposed test in Duberstein.* To what extent does IRC § 102(c) adopt the test proposed by the IRS in footnote 6 of Duberstein?

 IN PRACTICE

Criminal investigation. The Williams opinion indicates that the IRS had considered prosecuting Williams criminally. When the government discovers that a taxpayer has omitted income from her tax return, a serious threat exists that the government will assert a criminal tax fraud claim against the taxpayer. The hidden nature of an income omission can support a tax fraud claim because the government will normally be unable to detect the omission unless it happens to audit the taxpayer or a related party. Note that the fact that Williams' employer failed to include her bonus on her W-2 form would not eliminate the threat of a fraud prosecution. Thus, the threat of criminal exposure should deter taxpayers from failing to report any item that is clearly income and, in the case of an uncertain item, should generally cause the taxpayer to disclose the position she is taking on her tax return so that the issue is not hidden from the government.

■   **PROBLEM 4-1.** *Gift vs. compensation.* Donna Eggbert has served as a key employee of Eggbert Tool and Die, a small business owned by her father, Frank, since she graduated from college. On Donna's 30th birthday, Frank gave her $3,000. Shortly before Donna's birthday,

Frank announced that his business had just completed its most profitable year ever.

a) Is the $3,000 gross income to Donna? See IRC § 102(c), Proposed Reg. § 1.102–1(f)(2). *gut says no.*

b) How would each of the following alternative factors impact your conclusion?

1) On every one of Donna's birthdays since she turned 18, Frank gave Donna an amount of money equal to $100 for every year of her life. *supports*

2) Frank gave every key employee of the company $3,000 on Donna's 30th birthday. None of the other key employees were related to Frank. *challenges it - change it → this would be income then*

2. Exclusion of Bequests, Devises and Inheritances (Testamentary Transfers)

Normally if a decedent's will includes a specific bequest to a beneficiary, the bequest is excluded from the beneficiary's gross income under IRC § 102(a). What facts of the following case complicated that analysis and led the court to conclude that the bequest in question was not excludable from gross income?

WOLDER v. COMMISSIONER

United States Court of Appeals, Second Circuit, 1974
493 F.2d 608

Before FRIENDLY, MANSFIELD and OAKES, CIRCUIT JUDGES.

OAKES, CIRCUIT JUDGE:

[This case] essentially turns on one question: whether an attorney contracting to and performing lifetime legal services for a client receives income when the client, pursuant to the contract, bequeaths a substantial sum to the attorney in lieu of the payment of fees during the client's lifetime. [T]he Tax Court held that the fair market value of the stock and cash received under the client's will [by the taxpayer, Victor R. Wolder, the attorney who drafted the will,] constituted [gross] income under § 61, Int.Rev. Code of 1954, and was not exempt from taxation as a bequest under § 102 of the Code. From this ruling the individual taxpayer [appeals]. * * *

* * *

There is no basic disagreement as to the facts. On or about October 3, 1947, Victor R. Wolder, as attorney, and Marguerite K. Boyce, as client, entered into a written agreement which, after reciting Mr. Wolder's past services on her behalf in an action against her ex-husband for which he had made no charge, consisted of mutual promises, first on the part of Wolder to render to Mrs. Boyce "such legal services as she shall in her opinion personally require from time to time as long as both . . . shall live and not to bill her for such services," and second on the part of Mrs. Boyce to make a codicil to her last will and testament giving and bequeathing to Mr. Wolder or to his estate * * * [my] 750 shares of Schering common and * * * $15,845. In a revised will dated April 23, 1965, Mrs. Boyce, true to the agreement with Mr. Wolder, bequeathed to him or his estate the sum of $15,845 and the 750 shares of common stock of Schering Corp. There is no dispute but that Victor R. Wolder had rendered legal services to Mrs. Boyce over her lifetime (though apparently these consisted largely of revising her will) and had not billed her therefor * * *.

* * *

Wolder argues that the legacy he received under Mrs. Boyce's will is specifically excluded from income by virtue of § 102(a), Int.Rev.Code of 1954, which provides that "Gross Income does not include the value of property acquired by gift, bequest, devise or inheritance . . . ." See also Treas.Reg. 1.102–1(a). * * *

[T]here is no dispute but that the parties did contract for services and—while the services were limited in nature—there was also no question but that they were actually rendered. Thus the provisions of Mrs. Boyce's will, at least for federal tax purposes, went to satisfy her obligation under the contract. The contract in effect was one for the postponed payment of legal services, i.e., by a legacy under the will for services rendered during the decedent's life.

[I]n Commissioner v. Duberstein, 363 U.S. 278 (1960), the Court held that the true test is whether in actuality the gift is a bona fide gift or simply a method for paying compensation. This question is resolved by an examination of the intent of the parties, the reasons for the transfer, and the parties' performance in accordance with their intentions—"what the basic reason for the

handwritten marginal note: disagree b/c your estate still had to pay bills ; this is income to the vendor

donor's conduct was in fact—the dominant reason that explains his action in making the transfer." 363 U. S. at 286. * * *

Indeed, it is to be recollected that § 102 is, after all, an exception to the basic provision in § 61(a) that "Except as otherwise provided in this subtitle, gross income means all income from whatever source derived . . . ." The congressional purpose is to tax income comprehensively. A transfer in the form of a bequest was the method that the parties chose to compensate Mr. Wolder for his legal services, and that transfer is therefore subject to taxation, whatever its label whether by federal or by local law may be.

Taxpayer's argument that he received the stock and cash as a "bequest" under New York law * * * is thus beside the point. New York law does, of course, control as to the extent of the taxpayer's legal rights to the property in question, but it does not control as to the characterization of the property for federal income tax purposes. New York law cannot be decisive on the question whether any given transfer is income under § 61(a) or is exempt under § 102(a) of the Code. We repeat, we see no difference between the transfer here made in the form of a bequest and the transfer under Commissioner v. Duberstein, *supra*, which was made without consideration, with no legal or moral obligation, and which was indeed a "common-law gift," but which was nevertheless held not to be a gift excludable under § 102(a).

* * *

Judgment in the appeal of Victor R. Wolder and Marjorie Wolder affirmed.

Note

State law vs. tax law. Note the distinction the Wolder court draws between the state law definition of a bequest and the tax treatment of the transfer in the case. The state law treatment of a particular item will often deviate from its Federal income tax treatment.

IN PRACTICE **Substance over form.** The doctrine of substance over form is frequently applied in Federal tax law. In form, Wolder received value from the widow's estate as a bequest. But in substance, Wolder received value from the widow's estate to compensate him for the services he performed for the widow during her lifetime. Form is important for Federal tax law purposes but may not be dispositive when the form is inconsistent with the substance of a transaction.

■ **PROBLEM 4-2.** *Modified facts of Wolder.* In each of the following situations, assume that Ms. Boyce was under no obligation to transfer the Schering stock to Mr. Wolder.

a) If Mr. Wolder had been unaware that Ms. Boyce had substantial wealth and he took her on as a pro bono client, would Mr. Wolder have had gross income if Ms. Boyce left him the Schering stock in her Will? yes b/c its donor intent

b) Would your answer to a) change if Mr. Wolder had known Ms. Boyce was a wealthy individual but nevertheless took her on as a pro bono client? no - b/c donor intent

c) Would your answer to a) change if Mr. Wolder had known Ms. Boyce was a wealthy individual but took her on as a pro bono client and, during the course of his representation, he said to her "I hope you will take care of me under your Will"? no ?

In class
■ **PROBLEM 4-3.** *Employer bequest.* If Employer dies and leaves a bequest of $100,000 to Employee, is the $100,000 gross income to Employee? See IRC § 102(c). Does it matter if Employer and Employee had agreed during Employer's lifetime that Employer would make the bequest to Employee?

in class

■ **PROBLEM 4-4.** *Death of employee.* If Employee dies and Employer pays a death benefit of $25,000 to Employee's family, is the $25,000 gross income? See IRC § 102(c). Does it matter if Employer and Employee had agreed during Employee's lifetime that Employer would provide the death benefit at Employee's death?

SYNTHESIS

A donor derives a benefit from the good feelings that motivate a donor to make a gift. The donor's benefit is not within the scope of gross income, however, because the income tax was not intended to capture such an amorphous benefit.

In contrast to the donor, a donee derives a tangible benefit equal to the amount of money or the value of the property received. However, IRC § 102 excludes gifts, bequests, devises and inheritances from the recipient's gross income. Thus, the benefit received by a donee is not gross income because a specific statutory exclusion applies.

In certain cases, it may be unclear whether a transfer of money or property constitutes a gift or some form of gross income. In these cases, a factual inquiry must normally be undertaken to determine whether the transfer was made with the "detached and disinterested generosity" that must exist for the transfer to constitute a gift. When property is transferred from an employer to an employee, however, the statute treats the recipient as receiving compensation for services, rather than a gift, regardless of the employer's motivation for the transfer.

Test Your Knowledge: To assess your understanding of the material in this chapter, **click here** to take a quiz.

CHAPTER 5

Benefits Received by Lenders and Borrowers

Overview

Chapter 4 focused on the benefits derived when a personal relationship causes one person to make a gift to another. By contrast, Chapter 5 will focus on the benefits derived when a lender permits a borrower to use the lender's money or property. A lender will normally expect a borrower to compensate the lender by paying interest, rent or royalties. Not surprisingly, interest, rent and royalties constitute gross income. See IRC §§ 61(a)(4), (5), (6).

Turning to the borrower, a borrower derives a potential benefit equal to the amount borrowed. However, the receipt of borrowed money does not augment the borrower's wealth due to the borrower's obligation to repay the loan. The borrower's obligation to repay the loan offsets the potential benefit to the borrower and, therefore, the borrower does not derive an accession to wealth. Thus, borrowed money or property is not included in the borrower's gross income. However, if a borrower's debt is discharged before repayment occurs, the amount of the discharged debt normally constitutes gross income to the borrower. See IRC § 61(a)(11).

A. Benefits Received by Lenders—§§ 61(a)(4), (5), (6)

> **Primary Law:** IRC § 61(a)
>
> Except as otherwise provided in this subtitle, gross income means all income from whatever source derived, including (but not limited to) the following items:
>
> * * *
>
> (4) Interest;
>
> (5) Rents;
>
> (6) Royalties
>
> * * *

A lender will expect to be compensated for the use of the money or property that is lent by requiring the borrower to pay interest, rent or royalties. When a bank lends money, the bank expects to be paid interest to compensate the bank for the use of its money. When a car rental company allows you to use a car, the company expects to be paid rent to compensate it for the use of its property. When an owner of intangible property (i.e., a copyright, trademark or patent) allows you to use that property, the owner expects to be paid a royalty to compensate the owner for the use of the property. Interest, rent and royalties constitute gross income to the lender. See IRC §§ 61(a)(4), (5), (6).

A lender does not derive gross income when the borrowed money or property is returned to the lender. The return of money or property to the lender does not increase the lender's wealth; it simply restores the lender to her original position.

Notes

1. *Interest on state and local bonds.* Not all interest is included in gross income. Specifically, interest paid on debt instruments issued by state and local governments is normally excluded from gross income. See IRC § 103.

2. *Return of property improved by tenant to landlord.* The owner of leased property has no gross income when the property reverts at the end of the lease even if the tenant makes improvements during the leasehold that increase the value of the property. See IRC § 109.

B. Benefits Received by Borrowers

1. Exclusion of Borrowed Funds from Gross Income

The Internal Revenue Code does not address the tax treatment of borrowed money. Thus, one must examine the common law to determine whether borrowed money is included in, or excluded from, gross income. As a starting point, consider the arguments for and against treating borrowed money as gross income.

Argument for Including Borrowed Money in Gross Income: If Andrew borrows $1,000, he will have an immediate "accession to wealth"[1] *if* the tax system assumes that Andrew will not repay the loan. Under these circumstances, he will have $1,000 in hand that he will never repay resulting in a $1,000 benefit to him that would normally constitute gross income. Quite clearly, the assumption that a borrower will not repay the loan is erroneous in most cases because the vast majority of borrowers repay their loans. However, some borrowers will undoubtedly default on their obligations and in those cases, the assumption that a borrower will not repay would appropriately cause the borrower to be taxed on receipt of the loan proceeds.

Argument Against Including Borrowed Money from Gross Income: If Andrew borrows $1,000, he will *not* have an accession to wealth *if* the tax system assumes that Andrew will satisfy his obligation to repay. Under these circumstances, the $1,000 of cash he receives is offset by the $1,000 obligation to repay resulting in no net increase in wealth at the time of the borrowing. The assumption that borrowers will repay their loans will be correct most of the time. However, that assumption will be wrong in the case of those borrowers who fail to satisfy their repayment obligations.

U.S. Tax System Excludes Borrowed Money from Gross Income: When a loan is made, it is impossible at the outset to know with certainty whether the borrower

---

[1]   See Commissioner v. Glenshaw Glass, 348 U.S. 426 (1955) (defining income as "undeniable accessions to wealth, clearly realized, and over which the taxpayers have complete dominion."), reprinted at p. 16.

will repay or default. Yet, a decision must be made at the time of the borrowing whether to include loan proceeds in gross income. Hence, the tax system is compelled to make an assumption about repayment that will undoubtedly be wrong in some cases. The U.S. tax system has adopted the assumption that the borrower will repay the loan.[2] As a result, when Andrew borrows $1,000, he does *not* have an accession to wealth because the tax system assumes he will repay the loan. Therefore, he does not have gross income when the borrowing occurs.

■ **EXAMPLE 5-A.** *Tax treatment of loan.* Andrew borrows $1,000 on July 14 of Year 1. Andrew does not have gross income in Year 1 because the tax system assumes that borrowed funds will be repaid. Therefore, the $1,000 repayment obligation offsets the $1,000 of loan proceeds resulting in no net increase in Andrew's wealth. Thus, Andrew does not have gross income in Year 1.

---

a.   Determining Whether a Loan Exists

It is established law that loan proceeds are not included in the borrower's gross income because of the obligation to repay the loan. It is not always clear, however, whether a purported borrowing actually constitutes a loan.

STANLEY v. COMMISSIONER

United States Tax Court
T.C. Memo. 2016–196

Pugh, Judge: * * *

FINDINGS OF FACT

[Clifton Stanley and his wife ("petitioners") filed joint tax returns during the years in issue.] Mr. Stanley owned and operated Stanley & Associates, a

---

[2]   See Dilks, 15 BTA 1294 (1929); Slayton, 32 BTA 940 (1935); Indianapolis Power, 493 US 203, 207–208 (1990) ("It is settled that receipt of a loan is not income to the borrower."); Tufts, 461 US 300, 307 (1983) ("When a taxpayer receives a loan, he incurs an obligation to repay that loan at some future date. Because of this obligation, the loan proceeds do not qualify as income to the taxpayer.").

sole proprietorship engaged in the insurance business. Mr. Stanley worked for Stanley & Associates as an insurance agent selling annuities and providing retirement advice to clients. He also invested in real estate.

In 2010 and 2011 Mr. Stanley received what petitioners claim to be loan proceeds from clients and friends, and he made periodic payments to some of those clients and friends (and in some cases returned the amounts provided). Respondent argues that the amounts are income (identified through a bank deposits analysis by respondent). * * *

Mr. Stanley believed that lenders made funds available to him because he offered an attractive return on their investment. During the years in issue Mr. Stanley was trying to grow his insurance business. He had a general idea that he would repay lenders from his real estate investment income and his insurance business. Generally, Mr. Stanley used the loan proceeds: (1) to expand Stanley & Associates; (2) to invest in real estate; (3) to cover some personal and business expenses; and (4) occasionally to repay loans that became due. * * *

Mr. Stanley issued promissory notes to lenders for 22 loans during the years in issue. The promissory notes totaled $302,000 and $399,000 for 2010 and 2011, respectively. * * *

The promissory notes included the following: (1) the amount and date of the loan; (2) the lender's name and address; (3) the interest rate; (4) the length of the loan period; (5) the due date of interest payments and unpaid principal; (6) the signatures of the parties; and (7) a covenant that the "promisor agrees to remain fully bound until the note shall be paid in full." All but one of the promissory notes were unsecured. Repayment periods ranged from 6 to 24 months, and interest rates ranged from 7% to 25% * * *.

Mr. Stanley made interest payments on the loans. Some of the interest payments were made in accordance with the terms of the corresponding promissory note while other interest payments were untimely. Mr. Stanley recorded the amounts of interest paid on some of the corresponding promissory notes. For other payments the only record was the check itself.

When the loans became due, some were paid in full while others were renewed. With respect to the loans that were renewed, the repayment period of each loan was extended and interest continued to accrue. Mr. Stanley indicated in writing on most (but not all) of the promissory notes whether the loans were paid in full or were renewed. In some cases loans were renewed without any documentation of the renewal; the only indication of renewal was that Mr. Stanley paid interest or in some cases made a partial loan repayment. * * *

[T]he disputed loan proceeds that petitioners received in 2010 and 2011 were not included in income on their [2010 and 2011 Federal income tax returns.]

In the notice of deficiency respondent * * * increased petitioners' taxable income by [the disputed loan proceeds.]

Petitioners timely petitioned the Court for redetermination.

OPINION

* * *

The * * * issue is whether the amounts Mr. Stanley received were nontaxable loan proceeds. Section 61 defines gross income as "all income from whatever source derived". It is well settled that loan proceeds are not included in gross income because of the obligation to repay the loan. Whether a particular transaction constitutes a loan is a question of fact to be determined by considering all of the pertinent facts in the case.

A bona fide loan requires both parties to have an actual, good-faith intent to establish a debtor-creditor relationship when the funds are advanced. An intent to establish a debtor-creditor relationship exists if the debtor intends to repay the loan, and the creditor intends to enforce the repayment.

Courts consider various factors in determining whether the parties intended a bona fide loan, such as: (1) the ability of the borrower to repay; (2) the existence or nonexistence of a debt instrument; (3) security, interest, a fixed repayment date, and a repayment schedule; (4) how the parties' records and conduct reflect the transaction; (5) whether the borrower had made repayments; (6) whether the lender had demanded repayment; (7) the likelihood that the loan was disguised compensation for services; and (8) the testimony of the purported borrower and lender. The factors are "non-exclusive" and provide a "general basis upon which courts may analyze a transaction".

Courts assess the borrower's ability to repay by evaluating whether there was a reasonable expectation of repayment in the light of the economic realities of the situation. An expectation at the time the funds were advanced that the borrower would be unable to repay suggests that the parties did not intend a bona fide loan. Security, interest, a fixed repayment date, and a repayment schedule suggest that the parties intended a bona fide loan. A lack of security, a low interest rate, and an open-ended repayment period suggest otherwise.

Mr. Stanley credibly testified that the lenders provided him funds because he offered an attractive return on their investment and that he intended to repay the outstanding loans in full and intended to pay any interest that had accumulated. While Mr. Stanley did not have a specific plan for repayment, he intended to use the proceeds from his insurance business and his real estate investments. Although Mr. Stanley did not offer testimony of any lenders, we found his testimony credible, as noted above, and respondent offered no evidence to contradict his testimony save the fact that certain loans had been renewed.

Mr. Stanley's records, although not complete, generally support loan characterization. The record contains 22 promissory notes between Mr. Stanley and the lenders for 2010 and 2011. The promissory notes included: (1) the amount and date of the loan; (2) the lender's name and address; (3) the interest rate; (4) the length of the loan period; (5) the due date of interest payments and the unpaid principal; and (6) the signatures of the parties. The promissory notes included repayment periods ranging from 6 to 24 months and interest rates ranging from 7% to 25% * * *.

Mr. Stanley's actions on balance support loan characterization as well. He paid the interest for the corresponding promissory notes although he was not always timely. He made repayments on some of the loans while other loans were renewed. The record is insufficient, however, to allow us to find that any lenders demanded repayment and if so whether the demand was honored.

 FOR DISCUSSION **Evidence of a loan.** When a purported loan is made, what actions should the parties take to establish that the transaction is indeed a loan?

After carefully reviewing the record and considering the factors, we find that [the amounts Mr. Stanley received] were proceeds from bona fide loans and properly excluded from petitioners' 2010 and 2011 income. * * *

b.   Recourse and Nonrecourse Debt Treated Alike

When money is loaned, the borrower is normally required to execute a promissory note that permits the lender to recover the amount the lender is owed from any and all of the borrower's assets in the event of a default. This type of debt is referred to as a "recourse" liability. For example, when money is borrowed to buy a house, the lender will normally require the buyer to execute a promissory note that enables the lender to recover from all the borrower's personal assets in the event the borrower defaults. In addition, the lender will require the borrower to *give* the lender a mortgage in the house that enables the lender to take the house in the event the borrower defaults. With a recourse liability, therefore, the lender has two remedies; i.e., it can foreclose on the house and/or make a claim against the borrower's other assets or both. The lender's total recovery, however, is limited to the amount of the outstanding loan.

WORTH NOTING

Mortgage vs. loan. Although laypeople often equate a mortgage to a loan, a mortgage is actually an interest in property that secures a loan. When a home is purchased, the bank gives the buyer a loan, and the buyer gives the bank a mortgage (lien) against the home.

In a commercial context, particularly with respect to real estate, it is not unusual for a lender to require the borrower merely to give the lender a mortgage in the financed property. Under these circumstances, the lender would forego the right to recover from the borrower's other assets in the event of default often because the borrower does not have significant other assets. Here, the underlying debt is referred to as a "nonrecourse" liability. In the event of a default by the borrower, the lender's remedy is limited to foreclosing on the property that secures the loan. The lender cannot recover from the borrower's other assets to satisfy a nonrecourse loan.

■ **EXAMPLE 5-B.** *Recourse liability.* Bobbi borrows $500,000 to purchase a residence. The lender requires Bobbi to give the lender a mortgage in the residence and to execute a note that enables the lender to collect any other assets she owns in the event of a default. If Bobbi defaults, the lender has the option of foreclosing and/or collecting Bobbi's other assets. The lender, however, cannot recover more than $500,000.

■   EXAMPLE 5-C. *Nonrecourse liability.* Clara borrows $5,000,000 to acquire an apartment building. The lender requires Clara to give the lender a mortgage in the apartment building. However, because Clara does not have substantial personal assets, the lender does not require her to give the lender the right to recover from her personal assets in the event of a default. If Clara defaults, the lender can foreclose on the apartment building. Even if the value of the apartment building is less than $5,000,000, the lender cannot recover from Clara's personal assets. If the value of the building exceeds $5,000,000 when the lender forecloses, the lender must return the excess value to the borrower.

WORTH NOTING

Recourse and nonrecourse debt treated alike.
Regardless of whether a loan is recourse or nonrecourse, the borrower may exclude the loan proceeds from gross income. In the case of both recourse and nonrecourse debt, the borrower is obligated to repay the loan. In both cases, the borrower's obligation to repay offsets the receipt of the loan proceeds.

2.   Income from Discharge of Indebtedness—§ 61(a)(11)

Primary Law: IRC § 61(a)

Except as otherwise provided in this subtitle, gross income means all income from whatever source derived, including (but not limited to) the following items:

* * *

(11) Income from discharge of indebtedness;

* * *

Borrowed money is excluded from gross income because the U.S. tax system assumes that a debtor will repay the loan. It is sensible for the tax system to assume repayment will occur, rather than that repayment will not occur, because most loans will in fact be repaid. However, when a lender discharges a borrower's debt (normally because the lender has given up hope of being repaid), the assumption made by our tax system turns out to be erroneous and the borrower is normally deemed to have gross income when the debt is discharged.

WORTH NOTING

Corporate bond issuance. When a corporation borrows money, it often evidences the debt with "bonds" issued to the lenders that delineate the corporation's obligations to the lenders, including the date the corporation must repay the loan (the maturity date). The market value of the bonds may fluctuate over time, generally due to changes in market interest rates. In the Kirby Lumber case that follows, the corporation had issued bonds that it repurchased before the maturity date at their then current market value.

UNITED STATES v. KIRBY LUMBER CO.

Supreme Court of the United States, 1931
284 U.S. 1, 52 S. Ct. 4, 76 L. Ed. 131

MR. JUSTICE HOLMES delivered the opinion of the court.

In July, 1923, the plaintiff, the Kirby Lumber Company, issued its own bonds for $12,126,800. Later in the same year it purchased in the open market the same bonds [for $12,000,000], the difference of price being [$126,800]. The question is whether this difference is a taxable gain or income of the plaintiff for the year 1923. By the Revenue Act of 1921, gross income includes "gains or profits and income derived from any source whatever," and by the Treasury Regulations, "If the corporation purchases and retires any of such bonds at a price less than the issuing price, the excess of the issuing price over the purchase price is gain or income for the taxable year." We see no reason why the Regulations should not be accepted as a correct statement of the law.

In Bowers v. Kerbaugh-Empire Co., 271 U. S. 170, the defendant in error * * * had borrowed money repayable in marks [to purchase] an enterprise that failed. At the time of [repayment of the loan], the marks had fallen in value, which so far as it went was a gain for the defendant in error, and it was contended by the plaintiff in error that the gain was taxable income. But the transaction as a whole was a loss [because the purchased enterprise failed], and the contention [that the defendant in error had taxable income] was denied. [By contrast, in the case at bar,] there was no shrinkage of assets and the taxpayer made a clear gain. As a result of its dealings it made available [$126,800 of] assets previously offset by the obligation of bonds. The defendant in error has realized within the year an accession to income, if we take words in their plain popular meaning, as they should be taken here.

NOTES

1. *Income triggered when discharge occurs.* When a lender discharges a borrower's debt, the assumption made by the tax system when the loan arose that the borrower would repay the loan turns out to be erroneous. The mistake could have been rectified in either of two ways. First, the borrower could have been compelled to go back to the year in which the loan was made and include the loan proceeds in gross income for that earlier year. Alternatively, the exclusion of the borrowed money could be sanctioned until the year of the discharge, at which time the borrower would be compelled to include the borrowed money in gross income. Although the first option (including the loan in gross income when the proceeds were received) might be seen as more fully rectifying the tax system's erroneous assumption that the loan would be repaid, it presents difficult practical problems because the discharge might occur many years after the loan was made. Moreover, until the discharge actually occurs, the tax system's assumption that the loan will be repaid is not erroneous so it would be inappropriate to include the loan in gross income prior to the discharge. Thus, a defaulting borrower does not have gross income until the year in which the debt is discharged.

2. *Default vs. discharge.* Normally, a debtor will default months or years before a creditor discharges the debt. Income is triggered under IRC § 61(a)(11) when the debt is discharged, not when the debtor defaults.

---

3.   Exceptions to Discharge of Indebtedness Income—§ 108

As a general rule, the cancellation of a debt triggers gross income to the borrower when the discharge occurs. However, several significant exceptions to discharge of indebtedness income exist.

a.   Exceptions for Bankruptcy and Insolvency

Primary Law: IRC § 108(a)(1)

Gross income does not include any amount which (but for this subsection) would be includible in gross income by reason of the discharge (in whole or in part) of indebtedness to the taxpayer if—

(A)   the discharge occurs in a title 11 case,

(B)   the discharge occurs when the taxpayer is insolvent,

* * *.

i.   Bankruptcy Exception—§ 108(a)(1)(A)

When debt is discharged "in a title 11 case," the amount discharged is excluded from gross income. A "title 11 case" means a case under title 11 of the United State Code relating to bankruptcy and entails certain additional requirements. See IRC § 108(d)(2). The title 11 case exclusion takes priority over the other exclusions under section 108, all of which are less generous to the taxpayer than the title 11 exclusion. See IRC § 108(a)(2)(A).

ii.   Insolvency Exception—§ 108(a)(1)(B)

A taxpayer may be in financial distress without being immersed in a bankruptcy proceeding. If the taxpayer is "insolvent" when the taxpayer's debt is discharged, the taxpayer may exclude part or all of the discharged debt from gross income. The statute defines "insolvency" as the amount by which the taxpayer's liabilities exceed the fair market value of the taxpayer's assets. See IRC § 108(d)(3). The amount of the taxpayer's insolvency is determined immediately *before* the discharge occurs; hence, the amount of the liability that is discharged is included in the calculation. The amount of the taxpayer's insolvency is significant because the exclusion is limited to that amount. See IRC § 108(a)(3).

■ **EXAMPLE 5-D.** *Insolvency exception.* David owes the bank $100,000. The total value of his assets is $400,000 and his total liabilities (including the amount he owes the bank) is $440,000. The bank discharges David's debt and he is not in a title 11 case. David potentially has $100,000 of § 61(a)(11) income. However, he is insolvent by $40,000 ($400,000 of assets less $440,000 of liabilities *before* the discharge). Hence, he may exclude $40,000 of the $100,000 discharged debt. Therefore, David must only report $60,000 of § 61(a)(11) income ($100,000 − $40,000 = $60,000).

NEWMAN v. COMMISSIONER

United States Tax Court, 2016
T.C. Memo 2016–125

Vasquez, Judge:

Respondent issued a notice of deficiency * * * in petitioner's 2011 Federal income tax. After concessions, the remaining issues for decision are: (1) whether petitioner received $7,875 in cancellation of debt income (COD income) during 2011 and (2) whether petitioner is entitled to exclude any COD income received during 2011 under the insolvency exception provided in section 108(a)(1)(B).

FINDINGS OF FACT

[I]n July 2008 petitioner opened a checking account at Bank of America. Between July and August petitioner made deposits totaling [$8,625] into the bank account. Of the total deposits, $8,500 was attributable to a single check drawn from another bank account petitioner maintained at Wells Fargo. Shortly after making the initial deposits petitioner withdrew $8,000 in cash from the Bank of America account. However, the initial $8,500 check petitioner deposited into the Bank of America account did not clear and was later returned to Wells Fargo. This caused the Bank of America account to be overdrawn. Petitioner did not deposit funds in the Bank of America account to correct the negative balance. Consequently, Bank of America closed the account in August 2008.

In 2011 petitioner owned various items of personal property including furniture, clothes, and electronics of marginal value; he owned two watches valued at $500; and he owned a car valued at $35,000. Petitioner also had several liabilities in 2011—he owed $35,000 on a car loan, and he owed $15,000 in student loans.

In December 2011 Bank of America issued to petitioner a Form 1099-C, Cancellation of Debt, for 2011 reporting COD income of $7,875. Petitioner did not report the $7,875 as income on his 2011 Federal income tax return. On November 12, 2013, the IRS issued petitioner the notice of deficiency determining that the $7,875 of COD income constituted unreported gross income. Petitioner timely filed a petition with this Court for redetermination.

OPINION

I.   Cancellation of Debt Income

The first issue to resolve is whether petitioner received $7,875 of COD income for 2011.

Gross income generally includes income from the discharge of indebtedness. Sec. 61(a)(11). The rationale of this principle is that the cancellation of indebtedness provides the debtor with an economic benefit that is equivalent to income. See United States v. Kirby Lumber Co., 284 U.S. 1 (1931) * * *.

The year for which a taxpayer realizes COD income is a question of fact to be determined on the basis of the evidence. A debt is deemed discharged the moment it becomes clear that the debt will never be repaid. "Any 'identifiable event' which fixes the loss with certainty may be taken into consideration." [Citations omitted]; see also sec. 1.6050P–1(b)(2)(i), (iv), Income Tax Regs. (providing an exclusive list of eight "identifiable events" under which debt is discharged for information reporting purposes, including the expiration of a 36-month nonpayment testing period).

A bookkeeping entry by a creditor does not result in COD income. The issuance of a Form 1099-C is an identifiable event, but it is not dispositive of an intent to cancel indebtedness. There is a rebuttable presumption that an identifiable event occurred in a calendar year if, during a testing period (generally 36 months) ending at the close of the year, the creditor has received no payments from the debtor. Sec. 1.6050P–1(b)(2)(iv), Income Tax Regs.

The bank records reflect that all account activity leading to the overdrawn account occurred within a one-month period in 2008. Bank of America did not receive any payments from petitioner after August 2008. Therefore, the 36-month nonpayment testing period under section 1.6050P–1(b)(2)(iv), Income Tax Regs., began in August 2008 and ended at the close of 2011. Because Bank of America did not receive any payments during this testing period, a rebuttable presumption has arisen that the debt was discharged in 2011.

Petitioner has not rebutted the presumption that the debt was discharged in 2011. Therefore, because he has not rebutted the presumption of discharge of indebtedness, and because the Form 1099-C was issued in 2011, we find that petitioner had COD income of $7,875 for 2011.

II.   Insolvency Exception

Now that we have found that petitioner had COD income for 2011, we must determine whether the COD income is excludable from his gross income under the insolvency exception provided in section 108(a)(1)(B).

Section 108(a)(1)(B) excludes COD income from gross income if the discharge of indebtedness occurs when the taxpayer is insolvent. The amount by which the taxpayer is insolvent is defined as the excess of the taxpayer's liabilities over the fair market value of the taxpayer's assets. Sec. 108(d)(3). Whether a taxpayer is insolvent and by what amount is "determined on the basis of the taxpayer's assets and liabilities immediately before the discharge." *Id.* The amount of income excluded under section 108(a)(1)(B) cannot exceed the amount by which the taxpayer is insolvent. Sec. 108(a)(3).

As stated earlier, petitioner owned assets in 2011 valued at a total of $35,500. Petitioner was also liable for debts totaling $50,000. Therefore, after netting assets and liabilities, petitioner's claimed amount of insolvency is $14,500.

Insolvency is a question of fact. Petitioner has the burden of proving his claim that he was insolvent. At trial petitioner provided credible testimony that his assets and liabilities were what he claimed they were. Therefore, we accept petitioner's claimed amount of insolvency and find that his liabilities at the end of 2011 exceeded his assets by $14,500. We also find that section 108(a)(1)(B) allows petitioner to exclude all $7,875 of COD income from his 2011 gross income because the amount of his insolvency in 2011 exceeded his COD income for 2011.

FOR DISCUSSION

When insolvency is determined. Section 108 states that the taxpayer's insolvency is to be determined immediately *before* the discharge. Sec. 108(d)(3). In light of this rule, did the Newman court correctly calculate the taxpayer's insolvency? If not, did the court's error impact the outcome of the case?

Notes

1. *Pension rights.* Pension rights of a debtor are treated as assets for purposes of computing the debtor's insolvency. See Shepherd v. Commissioner, TC Memo 2012–212.

2. *Contingent liabilities.* A debtor may have potential liabilities that may or may not evolve into actual liabilities. Contingent liabilities existing at the time of the discharge do not count as liabilities for purposes of computing the debtor's insolvency. See Merkel v. Commissioner, 192 F.3d 844 (9th Cir. 1999) (when determining the discharge of indebtedness income of a taxpayer who guarantees the debt of another, the guaranty is not regarded as a liability of the guarantor for purposes of measuring the guarantor's insolvency unless and until the primary obligor defaults on the debt).

PROBLEM 5-1. *Discharge of indebtedness.* Elaine borrowed $100,000 from Frank in Year 1. The loan was a recourse liability (i.e., if Elaine defaulted, Frank had recourse to all of Elaine's assets). Elaine never made any payments to Frank. In Year 3, Elaine paid Frank $60,000 and Frank discharged the remaining $40,000 of Elaine's debt. Assume the discharge did not occur in a title 11 (bankruptcy) case unless otherwise indicated.

a)   What are the tax consequences to Elaine in Year 1?

b)   What are the tax consequences to Elaine in Year 3 if, immediately before the discharge, Elaine had assets with a value of $1,000,000 and—

1) $1,000,000 of liabilities? See § 61(a)(11).

2) $2,000,000 of liabilities? See §§ 108(a)(1)(B), 108(d)(3).

3) $1,025,000 of liabilities? See § 108(a)(3).

c)   How do your answers to b) change if the discharge occurred in a title 11 case? See §§ 108(a)(1)(A), (a)(2)(A), (d)(2).

d)   How do your answers to a) and b) change if the liability had been a nonrecourse liability (secured only by a specific property owned by Elaine)?

NOTES

1.   *Surrender of tax attributes.* Under certain circumstances, taxpayers who exclude potential discharge of indebtedness income under § 108(a) must surrender certain "tax attributes." See IRC § 108(b). The surrender of these attributes will often cause the debtor to derive greater taxable income in future years than would otherwise be the case. When tax attributes must be surrendered, § 108 effectively *defers* tax liability, rather than eliminating it. A practical reason exists for sanctioning deferral in these circumstances. A taxpayer who is bankrupt or insolvent normally does not have the wherewithal to pay taxes. Deferring the tax liability to a future time when the taxpayer is more likely to have the means to pay the tax augments the likelihood that the government will actually collect the tax.

2.   *Other exceptions.* In addition to the bankruptcy and insolvency exceptions to discharge of indebtedness income, exceptions also exist for qualified farm indebtedness and qualified real property business indebtedness. See IRC §§ 108(a)(1)(C), (D).

b.   Purchase Money Debt Exception for Solvent Debtors— § 108(e)(5)

When a buyer purchases goods on credit extended by the seller and the creditor-seller subsequently reduces the amount owed by the debtor-buyer, it is generally unclear, as a factual matter, as to the capacity in which the creditor-seller is reducing the debt. Specifically, it is unclear whether the creditor-seller is reducing the amount owed—1) in his capacity as a creditor (i.e., reducing the amount of the debtor-buyer's debt), or 2) in his capacity as a seller (i.e., reducing the amount of the purchase price of the property). If the creditor-seller reduced the amount owed to him in his capacity as a creditor, discharge of indebtedness income should result to the debtor-buyer. By contrast, if the creditor-seller reduced the amount owed to him in his capacity as a seller, the change in terms would constitute a purchase price reduction and not result in gross income to the debtor-buyer.[3] Section 108(e)(5) eliminates the need to undertake a factual inquiry to determine the capacity in which the creditor-seller reduces the debt by mandating that the reduction be treated as a purchase price adjustment, rather than as discharge of indebtedness income.

Primary Law: IRC § 108(e)(5)

If—

   (A) the debt of a purchaser of property to the seller of such property which arose out of the purchase of such property is reduced,

   (B) such reduction does not occur–

      (i) in a title 11 case, or

      (ii) when the purchaser is insolvent, and

   (C) but for this paragraph, such reduction would be treated as income to the purchaser from the discharge of indebtedness,

then such reduction shall be treated as a purchase price adjustment.

Under IRC § 108(e)(5), solvent debtors who purchase goods on credit extended by the seller can generally avoid discharge of indebtedness income if the creditor-seller reduces the amount owed by the debtor-buyer.

---

[3]   The tax consequences of purchase price reductions are examined in detail in Chapter 8.

■ **EXAMPLE 5-E.** *Purchase money exception for solvent debtors.* In Year 1, Felipe agrees to purchase a car from Gail for $10,000. Felipe pays Gail $4,000 in Year 1 and agrees to make additional payments of $3,000 in Year 2 and $3,000 in Year 3. Before Felipe makes the Year 2 payment, Gail agrees to reduce Felipe's Year 2 payment from $3,000 to $1,000, notwithstanding that Felipe is solvent. In the absence of IRC § 108(e)(5), a factual question would exist as to whether Gail reduced the Year 2 payment from $3,000 to $1,000 in her capacity as a lender (in which case Felipe would have $2,000 of discharge of indebtedness income) or in her capacity as a seller (in which case Gail would be regarded as reducing the purchase price of the car from $10,000 to $8,000 which would not trigger gross income to Felipe). By virtue of IRC § 108(e)(5), the factual issue is avoided because the statute mandates that the change in terms be treated as a purchase price adjustment. Therefore, Gail is treated as reducing the purchase price of the car and Felipe would not have gross income.

creditor   *seller*

■ **PROBLEM 5-2.** *Modified facts of Example 5-E.* If, in Example 5-E, Felipe had borrowed money from Harry to purchase the car from Gail, what tax consequences would result to Felipe if—

a)   Harry reduced Felipe's obligation to him by $2,000?

b)   Gail reduced Felipe's obligation to her by $2,000?

Why does IRC § 108(e)(5) apply only when the seller finances the purchase and not when a third-party lender finances the purchase?

c.   **Gift Exception**

PLOTINSKY v. COMMISSIONER

United States Tax Court, 2008
T.C. Memo. 2008–244

Chiechi, Judge.

* * *

FINDINGS OF FACT

[D]uring 1993 through [2000], petitioner financed a portion of his college [and law school] education through * * * Federal student loans.

As part of its business, Key Bank USA/American Education Services (AES) offered to consolidate student loans like petitioner's Federal student loans. As an incentive designed to induce individuals with student loans to consolidate those loans with AES, AES offered an on-time payment incentive program (AES's incentive program). Pursuant to AES's incentive program, if an individual were to consolidate the individual's student loans by taking out a loan from AES (AES loan) and the individual were to make 36 consecutive on-time monthly payments on the AES loan, AES would discharge a portion of that loan.

Petitioner was aware of AES's incentive program when in August 2001, after graduating from law school, he consolidated petitioner's Federal student loans through AES (petitioner's consolidated student loan). * * *

* * *

In 2004, pursuant to AES's incentive program and as a result of 36 consecutive on-time payments having been made on petitioner's consolidated student loan, AES discharged $3,043 of that loan.

AES issued Form 1099-C, Cancellation of Debt (2004 Form 1099-C), to petitioner for his taxable year 2004. That form showed $3,043.28 as the amount of debt canceled. The instructions to the 2004 Form 1099-C that AES sent to petitioner stated in pertinent part:

Generally, if you are an individual, you must include the canceled amount on the 'Other Income' line of Form 1040. * * * However, some canceled debts are not includible in your income.

Petitioner timely filed Form 1040, U.S. Individual Income Tax Return, for his taxable year 2004 (petitioner's 2004 return). In that return, petitioner reported gross income of $76,917 that did not include the $3,043.28 of petitioner's consolidated student loan that AES discharged.

Petitioner attached to petitioner's 2004 return a document (petitioner's attachment to petitioner's 2004 return) that stated in pertinent part:

> I received a Form 1099-C from AES Graduate & Professional Loan Services ('AES'), which stated a cancellation of debt in the amount of $3043.28. I am not reporting this amount as income because it is my reading of Internal Revenue Service Pub. 525, at 17–18, that this cancellation constitutes a gift rather than income. AES is the lender with which I consolidated my law school loans approximately three years ago. As an incentive to select AES as my lender, AES offered a reduction in the total amount of my loans, and it is this offer that forms the entire basis for the debt cancellation of $3043.28. The offer was contingent upon my making 36 consecutive on-time monthly payments, and now that this has been achieved the debt cancellation is locked in.

On November 13, 2006, respondent issued a notice of deficiency to petitioner for his taxable year 2004. In that notice, respondent determined to include in gross income the $3,043 of petitioner's consolidated student loan that AES discharged.

OPINION

* * *

It is petitioner's position that he is entitled for his taxable year 2004 to exclude from gross income under section 102(a) $3,043 of petitioner's consolidated student loan that AES discharged in that year.

Section 61(a) defines the term "gross income" broadly to mean all income from whatever source derived. Generally, income from the discharge of indebtedness is includible in gross income. Sec. 61(a)(11). There are, however, certain exceptions to that general rule. One of those exceptions on which petitioner relies is found in section 102(a). As pertinent here, section 102(a) excludes from gross income the value of property acquired by gift. If the discharge of a loan constitutes a gift from the creditor to the debtor, the debtor has no income as a result of that discharge.

* * *

[T]he Supreme Court in Commissioner v. Duberstein, 363 U.S. 278, 292–293, requires us to consider AES's intention in discharging $3,043 of petitioner's consolidated student loan. We shall do so now.

We have found that AES offered AES's incentive program in order to induce individuals like petitioner to consolidate their student loans with AES. We have also found that in 2004, pursuant to AES's incentive program, AES discharged $3,043 of petitioner's consolidated student loan because 36 consecutive on-time payments had been made on that loan. On the record before us, we find that AES did not intend to discharge $3,043 of petitioner's consolidated student loan out of "detached and disinterested generosity", Commissioner v. LoBue, 351 U.S. 243, 246 (1956), or "out of affection, respect, admiration, charity or like impulses", Robertson v. United States, 343 U.S. 711, 714 (1952). See Commissioner v. Duberstein, supra at 285. On that record, we further find that petitioner has failed to carry his burden of establishing that, in discharging $3,043 of petitioner's consolidated student loan, AES intended to make a gift to him.

Based upon our examination of the entire record before us, we find that the $3,043 of petitioner's consolidated student loan that AES discharged is not excludable for his taxable year 2004 from his gross income under section 102(a). On that record, we further find that petitioner must include for that year that amount in his gross income.

* * *

IN PRACTICE

Wisdom of disclosure. The Plotinsky opinion reveals that the taxpayer disclosed on his tax return that he was not reporting a potential income item. Disclosure is normally prudent in these circumstances because the hidden nature of an income omission normally makes it difficult for the government to detect the item unless it audits the taxpayer or a related party for some other reason. As a result, a taxpayer who omits income can be subject to serious civil and criminal penalties. Disclosure is unlikely to mitigate exposure to these penalties, however, unless the taxpayer has a defensible position for not reporting the income.

■ **PROBLEM 5-3.** *Discharge of debt as a gift.* Aaron lends Betty, a close friend, $1,000. A few months later, on Betty's birthday, Aaron tells Betty that as a birthday present, Aaron will cancel the loan. Does Betty have gross income when Aaron cancels the loan? Does it matter whether Aaron is Betty's employer? See IRC § 102(c).

NOTE

Exclusion for certain student loans. IRC § 108(f) provides an exclusion from gross income for the discharge of certain student loans. The exclusion applies to loans made to students with terms that provide for cancellation of the debt if the student provides certain types of services in certain disadvantaged geographical areas, and to certain other types of student loans.

d.   Recourse and Nonrecourse Debt Treated Alike—§ 108(d)(1)

When debt is discharged, the same tax consequences occur regardless of whether the discharged debt is a recourse liability or a nonrecourse liability. In both cases, the discharged debt triggers § 61(a)(11) income unless the discharge occurs in a title 11 case, when the taxpayer is insolvent or where some other exception applies. Thus, recourse and nonrecourse debts are treated alike both at the time of the borrowing (the proceeds are excluded from gross income) and when a discharge occurs (discharge of indebtedness income is triggered unless an exception applies).

SYNTHESIS

A lender of money or property normally expects to be compensated for the borrower's use of the money or property. Compensation for the use of money constitutes interest which is gross income to the lender under IRC § 61(a)(4). Compensation for the use of property constitutes rent or royalties which are gross income to the lender under IRC §§ 61(a)(5), (6).

A borrower does not derive gross income when loan proceeds are received because the proceeds are offset by the borrower's obligation to repay. Consequently, the loan does not increase the borrower's wealth. Borrowed amounts are excluded from gross income regardless of whether the loan is recourse or nonrecourse.

If the borrower fails to repay the loan and the debt is discharged, the borrower derives gross income under IRC § 61(a)(11) when the discharge occurs. This is the case regardless of whether the debt is recourse or nonrecourse. But if the discharge occurs in a title 11 case (bankruptcy) or when the borrower is insolvent, the debtor may exclude all or part of the gross income under IRC § 108. Additional exclusions exist for debtors who purchase goods on credit extended by the seller, and for debtors whose creditors discharge debt in the form of a gift.

 Test Your Knowledge: To assess your understanding of the material in this chapter, **click here** to take a quiz.

CHAPTER 6

Benefits Received by Transferor of Property—§ 61(a)(3)

Overview

This Chapter continues our exploration of gross income by examining the benefits individuals receive in various different capacities. Prior chapters explored the benefits received by a business owner (IRC § 61(a)(2)), an employee (IRC § 61(a)(1)), a donor, a donee (IRC § 102), a lender (IRC §§ 61(a)(4), (5), (6)) and a borrower (IRC § 61(a)(11)). This chapter focuses on the benefits derived by an individual who transfers property (IRC § 61(a)(3)).

> **Primary Law:** IRC § 61(a)
>
> Except as otherwise provided in this subtitle, gross income means all income from whatever source derived, including (but not limited to) the following items:
>
>   * * *
>
> (3)   Gains derived from dealings in property;
>
>   * * *

Unlike other types of gross income, § 61(a)(3) income has four unique features, the first two of which will be examined in this chapter. First, a "realization event" (normally, a sale of the property) must occur before the owner is taxed on any increase in the value of her property. Second, when a realization event occurs, § 61(a)(3) income is quantified by reducing what the seller receives by her "adjusted basis" in the property she transferred. The other two unique features of § 61(a)(3) income are explored in later chapters ("recognition" in Chapter 12, and "characterization" in Chapter 16).

A. The Realization Event Requirement

When property owned by a taxpayer increases in value (i.e., appreciates), the taxpayer's wealth increases. For example, assume a taxpayer owns nothing but a parcel of land she purchased for $1,000. If the area surrounding the parcel of land is subsequently improved, the value of the taxpayer's land might increase to $3,000. Correspondingly, the taxpayer's wealth will have increased from $1,000 to $3,000 because her wealth is measured by the value of her property (less any liabilities, which are assumed to be zero for this taxpayer). As we have seen, gross income normally results when the taxpayer's wealth increases. However, an increase in wealth resulting from asset appreciation does *not* trigger gross income to the owner of the property until the owner transfers the property to another person. Specifically, a "realization event" must occur before asset appreciation is treated as gross income.

The origin of the realization event requirement has been traced to the Supreme Court decision in Eisner v. Macomber, 252 U.S. 189, 207 (1920), where the Court embraced a definition of income adopted by earlier courts: " 'Income may be defined as the gain derived from capital, from labor, or from both combined,' provided it be understood to include profit gained through a sale or conversion of capital assets." The Macomber Court found that the "derived from capital" language was indicative of a realization requirement:

> Here we have the essential matter: *not* a gain *accruing* to capital, not a *growth* or *increment* of value *in* the investment; but a gain, a profit, something of exchangeable value *proceeding from* the property, *severed from* the capital however invested or employed, and *coming in*, being '*derived*,' that is, *received* or *drawn by* the recipient (the taxpayer) for his *separate* use, benefit and disposal;—*that* is income derived from property. * * *

The Code does not define a realization event. The only evidence of the realization requirement in the Code is Congress's use of the term "dealings" in IRC § 61(a)(3). In addition, the nature of the requirement can be inferred from IRC § 1001(a) (discussed below) which makes reference to gain from "the sale or other disposition of property." The following law review article excerpt explores the justification for the realization event requirement.

When Should Asset Appreciation Be Taxed? The Case for a Disposition Standard of Realization

Jeffrey L. Kwall
86 Indiana Law Journal 77, 78–80 (2011)

From an economist's perspective, an income tax should tax any increase in a taxpayer's wealth when it occurs.[2] Accordingly, asset appreciation should be taxed as it occurs. The U.S. income tax, however, has always embraced a realization requirement, thereby deferring the taxation of asset appreciation until the occurrence of a realization event (normally, a sale or exchange of the property). * * *

Initially, the realization requirement was seen as a constitutional mandate. The jurisprudence that emerged from this view regarded realization as requiring the transfer of property in exchange for a tangible benefit (normally money or other property). By conditioning realization on the contemporaneous receipt of a tangible benefit, the courts treated asset appreciation in the same manner as other forms of income (e.g., salary, rents), which normally occur when a person receives money or property. Unlike other forms of income, however, asset appreciation confers a benefit on the property owner as the appreciation occurs by increasing the taxpayer's wealth. Hence, the benefit from the appreciation is derived *before* the asset is transferred and is *independent* of the transfer. Indeed, the timing of the benefit is precisely why economists have argued that asset appreciation should be taxed as it occurs.

 To access the entire law review article, click here.

---

[2]   See Henry Simons, PERSONAL INCOME TAXATION 50 (1938) ("Personal income may be defined as the algebraic sum of (1) the market value of rights exercised in consumption and (2) the change in the value of the store of property rights between the beginning and end of the period in question."); Roswell Magill, TAXABLE INCOME (rev. ed. 1945) ("Income is the money value of the net accretion to economic power between two points in time.").

The view that realization is constitutionally mandated has dissipated over the past century. Now the realization requirement is generally regarded as a concession to the administrative burdens of, and political opposition to, a system taxing asset appreciation as it occurs. Nevertheless, the common law requirement that a contemporaneous benefit must be received for realization to occur still exists.

As the article excerpt suggests, the principal justification for the realization event requirement is that taxing increases in the value of property before the property is transferred would impose heavy administrative burdens on the tax system. If there were no realization requirement, every piece of property owned by the taxpayer would need to be valued annually to measure the taxpayer's gross income from asset appreciation. Many types of property are difficult to value and annual valuations would likely lead to frequent disputes between taxpayers and the government. Deferring the taxation of asset appreciation until property is sold normally eliminates the valuation issue because the purchase price the parties agree to will typically reflect the true value of the property. In most cases, the buyer will wish to pay as little as possible, and the seller will wish to extract as much as possible. Hence, the negotiated price will normally establish the true value of the property.

Although a sale, where property is transferred in exchange for money, is the classic realization event, certain other transfers of property also trigger realization events. For example, an exchange of property for other property constitutes a realization event. An exchange triggers a realization event even though such a transaction requires that the property received by each taxpayer be valued to measure each taxpayer's gross income.

5-1   C

While a transfer of property is a *necessary* condition for a realization event, it is *not* a *sufficient* condition. In addition to a transfer of property, a realization event normally requires the receipt of a quantifiable benefit.[1] The receipt of money or other property clearly constitutes such a benefit. By contrast, as discussed in Chapter 3, the "feel good" benefit derived by one who makes a gift is too amorphous to constitute "income" under IRC § 61(a) and, from a practical

---

[1]   As discussed below, when property is received in exchange for services, a realization event occurs. Hence, the receipt of an intangible benefit, like services, can trigger a realization event. Thus, it is more accurate to describe the nature of the benefit that must be received for a realization event to occur as "quantifiable," rather than as "tangible."

standpoint, impossible to quantify. Hence, a gift of appreciated property is *not* treated as a realization event to the donor. See Taft v. Bowers, 278 U.S. 470 (1929) (reprinted at p. 128).

WORTH NOTING

Meaning of "other disposition." IRC § 1001(a) (discussed below) makes reference to gain from the "sale or other disposition" of property. One might infer from the "other disposition" terminology that *any* transfer of property triggers a realization event. It is well established, however, that a gratuitous transfer of property is *not* a realization event.[2] Under current law, an increase in the value of property owned by a taxpayer is not taxed until: 1) the property is transferred, *and* 2) a quantifiable benefit is received in exchange for the transferred property.

■ **PROBLEM 6-1.** *Realization event.* Francine purchases an antique car for $10,000. Demand for antique cars increases dramatically and, as a result, the value of Francine's car increases to $25,000. Does Francine have a realization event—

a)   when the value of the car increases?

b)   if she sells the car for $25,000?

c)   if she exchanges the car for some diamonds with a value of $25,000?

d)   if she makes a gift of the car to her nephew?

e)   if she borrows $15,000 and the lender requires her to secure the loan by giving the lender a security interest in the car (so that if she fails to repay the loan, the lender can repossess the car)?

f)   if she transfers the car to her spouse as part of a divorce settlement? See United States v. Davis, below.

---

[2]   "Congress's use of the term 'disposition' appears to have been a matter of happenstance, rather than being indicative of an intention to treat every transfer of property as a realization event." Kwall, "When Should Asset Appreciation Be Taxed?: The Case for a Disposition Standard of Realization," 86 IND. L.J. 77, 81 (2011).

UNITED STATES v. DAVIS

Supreme Court of the United States, 1962
370 U.S. 65, 82 S. Ct. 1190, 8 L.Ed.2d 335

Mr. Justice Clark delivered the opinion of the Court.

These cases involve the tax consequences of a transfer of appreciated property by Thomas Crawley Davis ["the taxpayer"] to his former wife pursuant to a property settlement agreement executed prior to divorce * * *. The Court of Claims [reversed] the Commissioner's determination that there was taxable gain on the transfer * * *. We granted certiorari on a conflict in the Courts of Appeals * * * on the taxability of such transfers. * * *

In 1954 the taxpayer and his then wife made a voluntary property settlement and separation agreement calling for * * * the transfer of certain personal property to the wife. Under Delaware law all the property transferred was that of the taxpayer, subject to certain statutory marital rights of the wife including a right of intestate succession and a right upon divorce to a share of the husband's property. Specifically as a 'division in settlement of their property' the taxpayer agreed to transfer to his wife, inter alia, 1,000 shares of stock in the E. I. du Pont de Nemours & Co. The then Mrs. Davis agreed to accept this division 'in full settlement and satisfaction of any and all claims and rights against the husband whatsoever (including but not by way of limitation, dower and all rights under the laws of testacy and intestacy) * * *.' Pursuant to the above agreement which had been incorporated into the divorce decree, * * * this stock was delivered in the tax year involved, 1955 * * *. [The taxpayer had originally purchased the stock for $70,000] and the fair market value of the * * * shares [at the time they were] transferred was $82,250. * * *

I.

* * *

II.

We now turn to the threshold question of whether the transfer in issue was an appropriate occasion for taxing the accretion to the stock. There can be no doubt that Congress, as evidenced by its inclusive definition of income subject to taxation, i.e., 'all income from whatever source derived, including * * * (g)ains derived from dealings in property,' intended that the economic growth of this stock be taxed. The problem confronting us is simply when is such accretion to be taxed. Should the economic gain be presently assessed against taxpayer, or should this assessment await a subsequent transfer of the property by the wife? The controlling statutory language, which provides that gains from dealings in property are to be taxed upon 'sale or other disposition,' is too general to include or exclude conclusively the transaction presently in issue. Recognizing this, the Government and the taxpayer argue by analogy with transactions more easily classified as within or without the ambient of taxable events. The taxpayer asserts that the present disposition is comparable to a nontaxable division of property between two co-owners,[6] while the Government contends it more resembles a taxable transfer of property in exchange for the release of an independent legal obligation. * * *

[T]he taxpayer's analogy * * * stumbles on its own premise, for the inchoate rights granted a wife in her husband's property by the Delaware law do not even remotely reach the dignity of co-ownership. The wife has no interest—passive or active—over the management or disposition of her husband's personal property. Her rights are not descendable, and she must survive him to share in his intestate estate. * * *

This is not to say it would be completely illogical to consider the shearing off of the wife's rights in her husband's property as a division of that property, but we believe the contrary to be the more reasonable construction. Regardless of the tags, Delaware seems only to place a burden on the husband's property rather than to make the wife a part owner thereof. In the present context the rights of succession and reasonable share do not differ significantly from the husband's obligations of support and alimony. They all partake more of a personal liability of the husband than a property interest of the wife. The effectuation of these marital rights may ultimately result in the ownership of some of the husband's property as it did here, but certainly this happenstance does not equate the transaction with a division of property by co-owners. * * *

* * *

[We therefore find that a realization event occurred.]

---

[6]   Any suggestion that the transaction in question was a gift is completely unrealistic. Property transferred pursuant to a negotiated settlement in return for the release of admittedly valuable rights is not a gift in any sense of the term. * * *

WORTH NOTING

Congress neutralizes the holding in Davis. In Davis, the Supreme Court held that the transfer of property pursuant to a divorce settlement constitutes a realization event. Congress, however, subsequently enacted a "nonrecognition" provision to defer the tax on these transactions. See IRC § 1041. Several nonrecognition provisions (including IRC § 1041) will be examined in Chapter 12.

B. Quantifying Gain or Loss When a Realization Event Occurs—§ 1001(a)

When a realization event occurs, the potential § 61(a)(3) income ("gains derived from dealings in property") must be quantified. IRC § 1001(a) delineates the formula for quantifying such income.

Primary Law: IRC § 1001(a)

The gain from the sale or other disposition of property shall be the excess of the amount realized over the adjusted basis of the property.

IN SIGHTS

The excess of A over B. The statutory formula delineated by IRC § 1001(a) ("the excess of the amount realized over the adjusted basis") is a subtraction problem. The Code frequently uses this "excess of A over B" convention. That convention is not describing a fraction (i.e., a division problem). Rather, the convention requires the subtraction of "B" from "A." Thus the formula for computing the gain or loss when a realization event occurs is as follows:

Amount Realized

– Adjusted Basis

Realized Gain (Loss)[3]

---

[3]   A loss will be realized if the adjusted basis of the transferred property exceeds the amount realized. The tax treatment of losses will be explored in Chapter 10.

When a realization event occurs, the taxpayer's gain is quantified by determining the taxpayer's "amount realized" and then subtracting the "adjusted basis" of the transferred property. IRC § 1001(a). The statute defines the amount realized in IRC § 1001(b).

Primary Law: IRC § 1001(b)

The amount realized from the sale or other disposition of property shall be the sum of any money received plus the fair market value of the property (other than money) received.

The amount realized is essentially "what you get" for the property transferred and is analogous to how all other forms of gross income under § 61(a) are quantified (e.g., compensation for services rendered under § 61(a)(1) is measured by the amount of money and the fair market value of property received for the services). The amount realized will be explored later in this Chapter.

Unlike other forms of gross income, § 61(a)(3) income is quantified by offsetting the amount realized ("what you get") by the "adjusted basis" of the transferred property. The statute defines the adjusted basis in IRC § 1011.

Primary Law: IRC § 1011

The adjusted basis for determining the gain or loss from the sale or other disposition of property, whenever acquired, shall be the basis * * *, adjusted as provided in section 1016.

Thus, the meaning of "basis" must be understood before one can master the meaning of "adjusted basis."

1. Basis

Basis in property is determined when the taxpayer acquires the property. The way in which basis is determined varies depending upon whether property is acquired by purchase, as an inter vivos gift, or as a testamentary transfer.

a. Basis of Property Is Its "Cost"—§ 1012

Purchase of property. When a taxpayer purchases property, the price paid by the taxpayer establishes her basis in the property. The basis represents the amount of dollars invested by the taxpayer in the property that were previously subject to the income tax when they were earned. When the taxpayer later sells the property, she is not taxed on the return of the dollars she invested because those dollars were subject to income tax before she purchased the property. If she were not permitted to recover the amount of dollars she invested in the property tax-free, she could effectively be taxed twice on the same amount.

■ **EXAMPLE 6-A.** *Basis of purchased property.* Greg buys a parcel of land for $1,000. Therefore, Greg's cost basis in the land is $1,000. If the value of the land increases to $3,000 and Greg sells the land for $3,000, the sale is a realization event. His $2,000 realized gain is computed as follows:

Amount Realized:	$3,000
– Adjusted Basis:	–1,000
Realized Gain	$2,000

Greg is taxed on only $2,000 of the $3,000 selling price because he had invested $1,000 on which he had previously paid tax when he purchased the land.

Purchase of property with borrowed funds. When a taxpayer purchases property, the price paid establishes her basis in the property regardless of whether she invests her own money or borrows the money she invests. If she invests borrowed funds, she is treated as if she used her own money to make the purchase and receives a basis equal to the purchase price. This result is consistent with the assumption the tax system makes that borrowed funds will be repaid. Because of that assumption, borrowed funds are not included in gross income (see Chapter 5). Correspondingly, borrowed funds are treated as the borrower's own money when used to purchase property and, therefore, the borrower gets basis in the property for the borrowed funds.

It is perfectly appropriate to award the borrower basis for borrowed funds if the loan is ultimately repaid because, in this situation, the borrower effectively uses her own money to purchase the property. Granting the borrower basis in property purchased with borrowed funds is also appropriate if the borrower's debt is ultimately discharged. If the debt is discharged, the borrower will be taxed on the borrowed funds (see Chapter 5), resulting in her having invested dollars in the property on which she paid tax.[4]

■ **EXAMPLE 6-B.** *Basis of property purchased with borrowed funds.* Same facts as Example 6-A, but Greg borrows the $1,000 used to purchase the land, rather than investing his own money. Greg's basis in the land is still $1,000. Greg was not taxed on the borrowed funds he invested in the land. However, when he repays the loan, he will have effectively invested his own money on which he previously paid tax. By repaying the loan, he will have earned the basis he was awarded at the time of the purchase. By contrast, if Greg's debt is discharged, Greg will be taxed on the borrowed funds under IRC § 61(a)(11) (see Chapter 5) which effectively causes him to pay tax on the dollars invested in the land. In both cases, he is investing dollars that were subject to tax and this fact justifies awarding him basis in the property purchased with borrowed funds.

Recourse and nonrecourse debt treated alike. When property is purchased with recourse debt (i.e., in the event of default, the lender can recover from the property securing the debt *and* all the borrower's personal assets—see Chapter 5), basis includes the amount of the debt.[5] Basis also includes the amount of the debt when property is purchased with nonrecourse debt (i.e., in the event of default, the lender can recover *only* from the property securing the debt—see

---

[4] If the borrower can exclude the discharge of indebtedness income due to bankruptcy or insolvency, she will normally be required to surrender basis or other tax attributes. See IRC § 108(b).

[5] Brons Hotel, Inc. v. Commissioner, 34 BTA 376 (1936) (when property purchased with recourse debt, basis includes amount of debt).

Chapter 5).[6] In this situation, the tax system treats recourse debt and nonrecourse debt alike.

■ **PROBLEM 6-2.** *Basis.* What is Hernando's basis if he purchases property—

a)   with $100,000 of his own money?

b)   with $20,000 of his own money and an $80,000 loan from a bank? The loan is a recourse liability (the lender can recover from Hernando's personal assets as well as the property in the event of a default).

c)   Same as b), but the loan is a nonrecourse liability (secured only by specific property)?

Receipt of property as compensation for services. The term "cost" in section 1012 means "cost" in a tax sense. Specifically, "cost" focuses on the amount of dollars the taxpayer has invested in the property that were previously subject to tax. The taxpayer can invest after-tax dollars by taking money out of his pocket to purchase the property. Alternatively, the taxpayer will be treated as investing after-tax dollars in the property if the taxpayer is taxed on the value of the property on receipt (e.g., the property is received as compensation for the taxpayer's services). In this situation, the taxpayer will establish a basis in the property equal to the value of the property at the time of receipt.

■ **EXAMPLE 6-C.** *Basis when taxpayer is taxed on the value of property received.* Josh employs Iris and compensates her for her services by transferring to her a parcel of land with a value of $1,000. As a result, Iris has § 61(a)(1) income of $1,000 because her gross income is measured by the value of the property she receives for her services. Iris also takes a basis in the land of $1,000 because she included the value of the

---

6   Blackstone Theatre Co. v. Commissioner, 12 TC 801 (1949) (when property purchased with nonrecourse debt, basis includes amount of debt). See Crane v. Commissioner, 331 U.S. 1 (1947) (explaining the rationale for awarding basis for nonrecourse debt).

land in gross income and, therefore, paid tax on the value of the land at the time of receipt.

If Iris sells the land after it increases in value for $3,000, the sale is a realization event and Iris realizes a $2,000 gain ($3,000 amount realized minus $1,000 basis). This result is sensible because she was previously taxed on the $1,000 value of the land at the time of receipt. Thus, the value of the land on receipt is treated as a "cost" in a tax sense. As a result, Iris receives a basis of $1,000 and, at the time of sale, is only taxed on the $2,000 increase in the value of the land while she held the land. If she did not receive a basis of $1,000 on receipt of the land, she would be taxed on $3,000 when the sale occurred which would cause her to be taxed twice on the portion of the value of the land that existed at the time of receipt.

IN SIGHTS   Another way of understanding the result of Example 6-C is to consider the following substantively equivalent situation. Assume Josh paid Iris $1,000 for her services and that Iris used the $1,000 to purchase land that she ultimately sells for $3,000. Here, she clearly establishes a cost basis of $1,000 when she purchases the land and realizes a $2,000 gain when she sells the land ($3,000 amount realized minus $1,000 basis). Thus, the result is identical to Example 6-C. The only difference between the two fact patterns is that here, Iris receives money for her services and uses the money to purchase the land. By contrast, in Example 6-C, Iris simply receives the land for her services. The omission of cash from the transaction does not change the tax consequences.

■ **PROBLEM 6-3.** *Receipt of property for services.* James leases an apartment to Karen and the lease provides that Karen will pay $10,000 of rent to James. How much gross income does James derive in each of the following alternative situations if Karen transfers—

a) $10,000 to James?

b)   a diamond with a value of $10,000 to James? What is James's basis in the diamond?

c)   a diamond with a value of $12,000 to James? What is James's basis in the diamond?

Might the amount of James's gross income in c) change if Karen is James's mother? See IRC § 102(a).

---

b.   Basis to Donee for Intervivos Gratuitous Transfers—§ 1015

When a donor makes a gift of property, the donor does not derive a quantifiable benefit. Therefore, a gift is *not* a realization event. Hence, if a donor makes a gift of appreciated property, the donor is not taxed on the appreciation (i.e., the extent to which the value exceeds the basis) in the transferred property. Under these circumstances, the donee's basis is governed by IRC § 1015(a).

> **Primary Law:** IRC § 1015(a)
>
> If the property was acquired by gift * * *, the basis shall be the same as it would be in the hands of the donor or the last preceding owner from whom it was not acquired by gift * * *.

TAFT v. BOWERS, COLLECTOR OF INTERNAL REVENUE

Supreme Court of the United States, 1929
278 U.S. 470, 49 S. Ct. 199, 73 L.Ed. 460

Mr. Justice McReynolds delivered the opinion of the Court.

Petitioners, who are donees of stocks, seek to recover income taxes exacted because of advancement in the market value of those stocks while owned by the donors. The facts are not in dispute. Both causes must turn upon the effect of [the predecessor to IRC § 1015(a)] which prescribes the basis for estimating taxable gain when one disposes of property which came to him by gift. * * *

During the calendar years 1921 and 1922 the father of petitioner, Elizabeth C. Taft, gave her certain shares of Nash Motors Company stock, then more valuable than when acquired by him. She sold them during 1923 for more than their market value when the gift was made.

The United States demanded an income tax reckoned upon the difference between cost to the donor and price received by the donee. She paid accordingly and sued to recover the portion imposed because of the advance in value while the donor owned the stock. The right to tax the increase in value after the gift is not denied.

Abstractly stated, this is the problem:

> In 1916 A purchased 100 shares of stock for $1,000, which he held until 1923 when their fair market value had become $2,000. He then gave them to B who sold them during the year 1923 for $5,000. The United States claim that under the Revenue Act of 1921 B must pay income tax upon $4,000, as realized profits. B maintains that only $3,000—the appreciation during her ownership—can be regarded as income; that the increase during the donor's ownership is not income assessable against her within intendment of the Sixteenth Amendment.

The District Court ruled against the United States; the Circuit Court of Appeals held with [the United States].

* * *

We think the manifest purpose of Congress expressed in [the predecessor to IRC § 1015(a)] was to require the petitioner to pay the enacted tax.

The only question subject to serious controversy is whether Congress had power to authorize the exaction.

* * *

The Sixteenth Amendment provides:

> The Congress shall have power to lay and collect taxes on incomes, from whatever source derived, without apportionment among the several states, and without regard to any census or enumeration.

Income is the thing which may be taxed-income from any source. The amendment does not attempt to define income or to designate how taxes may be laid thereon, or how they may be enforced.

Under former decisions here the settled doctrine is that the Sixteenth Amendment confers no power upon Congress to define and tax as income without apportionment something which theretofore could not have been properly regarded as income.

Also, this court has declared: "Income may be defined as the gain derived from capital, from labor, or from both combined,' provided it be understood to include profit gained through a sale or conversion of capital assets.' Eisner v. Macomber, 252 U. S. 189, 207. The 'gain derived from capital,' within the definition, is 'not a gain accruing to capital, nor a growth or increment of value in the investment, but a gain, a profit, something of exchangeable value proceeding from the property, severed from the capital however invested, and coming in, that is, received or drawn by the claimant for his separate use, benefit and disposal.' United States v. Phellis, 257 U. S. 156, 169.

If, instead of giving the stock to petitioner, the donor had sold it at market value, the excess over the capital he invested (cost) would have been income therefrom and subject to taxation under the Sixteenth Amendment. He would have been obliged to share the realized gain with the United States. He held the stock-the investment-subject to the right of the sovereign to take part of any increase in its value when separated through sale or conversion and reduced to his possession. Could he, contrary to the express will of Congress, by mere gift enable another to hold this stock free from such right, deprive the sovereign of the possibility of taxing the appreciation when actually severed, and convert the entire property into a capital asset of the donee, who invested nothing, as though the latter had purchased at the market price? And after a still further enhancement of the property, could the donee make a second gift with like effect, etc.? We think not.

In truth the stock represented only a single investment of capital-that made by the donor. And when through sale or conversion the increase was separated therefrom, it became income from that investment in the hands of the recipient subject to taxation according to the very words of the Sixteenth Amendment. By requiring the recipient of the entire increase to pay a part into the public treasury, Congress deprived her of no right and subjected her to no hardship. She accepted the gift with knowledge of the statute and, as to the property received, voluntarily assumed the position of her donor. When she sold the stock she actually got the original sum invested, plus the entire appreciation and out of the latter only was she called on to pay the tax demanded.

The provision of the statute under consideration seems entirely appropriate for enforcing a general scheme of lawful taxation. To accept the view urged in behalf of petitioner undoubtedly would defeat, to some extent, the purpose of Congress to take part of all gain derived from capital investments. To prevent that result and insure enforcement of its proper policy, Congress had power to require that for purposes of taxation the donee should accept the position of the donor in respect of the thing received. And in so doing, it acted neither unreasonably nor arbitrarily.

* * *

There is nothing in the Constitution which lends support to the theory that gain actually resulting from the increased value of capital can be treated as taxable income in the hands of the recipient only so far as the increase occurred while he owned the property. * * *

The judgment below is affirmed.

Notes

1. *Shifting of gain from donor to donee.* Pursuant to IRC § 1015(a), the donor's basis in the transferred property normally becomes the basis of the donee. As a result, the potential gain in the transferred property is preserved, but the gift causes that gain to be shifted from the donor to the donee.

■ EXAMPLE 6-D. *Gift of appreciated property.* Max purchases a parcel of land for $10,000 that increases in value to $100,000. Max makes a gift of the land to Nisa. The gift is not a realization event to Max because he does not receive a quantifiable benefit in return for the property. Thus, the potential $90,000 gain in the land is not taxed to Max when he transfers the land to Nisa. As to Nisa, the $100,000 gift is excluded from her gross income. IRC § 102(a). Nisa takes a basis in the land equal to Max's basis; namely, $10,000. IRC § 1015(a). Thus, if Nisa were to sell the land for $100,000, a $90,000 gain would be triggered but it will be taxed to Nisa, not to Max.

2.   *Transferred basis property.* When property is governed by a statutory provision that causes a transferee of the property to take a basis equal to that of the transferor, the property is referred to as "transferred basis property." See IRC § 7701(a)(43). IRC § 1015(a) is an example of such a provision. You will see other provisions establishing transferred basis property in later chapters.

3.   *Gift of loss property.* If a donor transfers property with a basis in excess of value ("loss property"), the transferred basis rule of IRC § 1015(a) applies only if a sale of the transferred property by the donee would result in a realized gain. For purposes of determining loss on a subsequent sale of the property, the donee's basis is limited to the value of the property at the time of the gift. See § 1015(a). Thus, when a donor makes a gift of property with a basis in excess of value, the unrealized loss will not be preserved.

■ **EXAMPLE 6-E.** *Gift of loss property.* Jordan owns a parcel of land with a basis of $15,000 and a value of only $10,000. Thus, an unrealized loss of $5,000 exists in the property. Jordan makes a gift of the property to Mindy. If the value of the land then falls to $9,000 and Mindy sells the land for $9,000, her basis would be only $10,000 (the value of the land at the time of the gift). Thus, she would realize a loss of only $1,000. By contrast, if, after the gift is made, the value of the land increases to $20,000 and Mindy sells the land for $20,000, her basis would be $15,000 (i.e., the donor's basis) and her realized gain would be $5,000.

---

c.   Basis to Beneficiary for Testamentary Transfers—§ 1014

All the property owned by a decedent on the date of death is transferred pursuant to the terms of the decedent's will, trust(s), or state law. Under current law, however, death is *not* a realization event because the decedent does not receive a quantifiable benefit in exchange for the property. Hence, if an individual dies owning property with a value in excess of basis, the appreciation is not taxed to the decedent.

As discussed in Chapter 4, a beneficiary who receives property from a decedent can exclude the value of the property from gross income (IRC § 102(a)). The beneficiary's basis in the property is determined by IRC § 1014.

Primary Law: IRC § 1014(a)

Except as otherwise provided in this section, the basis of property in the hands of a person acquiring the property from a decedent or to whom the property passed from a decedent shall, * * *, be—(1) the fair market value of the property at the date of the decedent's death, * * *.

When a taxpayer who owns appreciated property dies, the gain that existed in the property will disappear because the basis is "stepped-up" to fair market value when death occurs. As a result, IRC § 1014 creates an incentive for taxpayers to hold appreciated property until death, rather than selling such property prior to death and paying tax on the gain.

NOTES

1. *Economic considerations are more important than tax considerations.* If a taxpayer owns property with a value in excess of basis, a tax incentive exists to hold the property until death. Holding the property until death avoids tax liability for both the taxpayer (no realization event) and the taxpayer's successor (IRC § 1014 "step-up" in basis eliminates the gain). However, as Example 6-F reveals, this strategy would backfire if the value of the property declined before the taxpayer died.

■ **EXAMPLE 6-F.** Olivia purchases corporate stock for $5,000 that increases in value to $105,000. To avoid paying tax on the $100,000 of appreciation, she decides to hold the stock until she dies. Before Olivia dies, the value of the stock declines to $5,000. Olivia achieved her goal of avoiding tax on the $100,000 gain but, unfortunately, the gain disappeared. If she had sold the stock when it had a value of $105,000, she would have realized a $100,000 gain on which she would have paid a maximum tax of $37,000 (37%). The sale would have enabled her to enjoy an after-tax profit of at least $63,000 ($105,000 proceeds minus $5,000 investment minus $37,000 tax). Instead, by holding the stock until death, her successor can only sell the stock for its then value of $5,000, and neither Olivia nor her successor reaps any economic benefit from the investment.

---

2.   *Decedent's loss property.* The basis rule of IRC § 1014 is a two-way street. If a taxpayer owns property with a basis in excess of value, the unrealized loss will also disappear at the time of death because the decedent's successor will take a basis in the property equal to the value of the property on the date of the decedent's death. Thus, in contrast to the incentive that exists for a taxpayer to hold appreciated property until death, an incentive exists for a taxpayer to sell loss property before death so that a tax loss can be triggered.[7]

3.   *Federal estate tax.* When an individual dies, a federal estate tax is sometimes imposed on the value of the decedent's property. The estate tax is independent of the income tax. When the estate tax was originally enacted, some commentators regarded the imposition of an estate tax as justifying the step-up in the basis of the decedent's property to fair market value on the date of death. The estate tax, however, applies to very few taxpayers because the value of a decedent's property must exceed $11,400,000 (in 2019)[8]   before the estate tax is imposed. Moreover, the magnitude of the estate tax when it is imposed bears no relation to the income tax. Therefore, the argument that the estate tax justifies the basis rule of IRC § 1014 is not compelling.

---

[7]   A tax loss may be allowed as a deduction from gross income which can reduce a taxpayer's income tax liability. Tax losses will be explored in Chapter 10.

[8]   This amount is adjusted annually for inflation.

■ **PROBLEM 6-4.** *Basis before and after death.* Peter purchased land many years ago for $100,000. The land now has a value of $300,000. Peter wants his niece, Rachel, to have the land. What are the income tax consequences to Peter and Rachel if Peter transfers the land to Rachel—

a)   during Peter's lifetime?

b)   when Peter dies?

c)   Would you advise Peter to transfer the land to Rachel during his lifetime or upon his death?

2.   Adjusted Basis—§§ 1011, 1016

A taxpayer's "basis" is determined when property is acquired. If property is purchased, the buyer's basis is the amount paid for the property. IRC § 1012. If property is received as a gift, the donee's basis is normally the same as that of the donor. IRC § 1015(a). If property is received from a decedent, the recipient's basis is the fair market value of the property on the date of the decedent's death. IRC § 1014.

The basis determined when property is acquired can change during the period of time the taxpayer owns the property. IRC § 1016 delineates several adjustments that can change the original basis of the property during the ownership period. The term "basis" is utilized only at the moment property is acquired. During the remainder of the ownership period, the term "adjusted basis" is utilized. IRC § 1011(a) defines "adjusted basis" as "the basis (determined under section 1012 or other applicable sections * * *), adjusted as provided in section 1016." Property is deemed to have an adjusted basis at all times after the moment the property is acquired, even if IRC § 1016 does not cause the amount of the original basis to change.

This section will focus on one important adjustment to basis described in § 1016(a)(2).

Primary Law: IRC § 1016(a)

Proper adjustment in respect of the [basis of] property shall in all cases be made—

* * *

(2)   in respect of any period since February 28, 1913, for exhaustion, wear and tear, obsolescence, * * *, to the extent of the amount—

(A)   allowed as a deduction in computing taxable income under this subtitle or prior income tax laws * * *

but not less than the amount allowable under this subtitle or prior income tax laws. * * *

The adjustment to basis delineated in IRC § 1016(a)(2) is commonly referred to as an adjustment for "depreciation." To understand the nature of the basis adjustment for depreciation, we must digress from our examination of gross income and explore certain statutory provisions that allow taxpayers to claim an annual deduction for depreciation with respect to certain types of property.

a.   Depreciation Deduction—§§ 167, 168

Chapter 1 introduced the base on which the income tax is imposed. That base, taxable income, is defined as gross income minus the deductions allowed to the taxpayer. See IRC § 63(a). A deduction is any payment or disbursement made by a taxpayer that Congress permits the taxpayer to subtract from gross income. A deduction may be claimed only when a specific statutory provision authorizes the deduction. See IRC § 161(a).

IRC § 167(a) allows an annual depreciation deduction with respect to certain types of property.

Primary Law: IRC § 167(a)

There shall be allowed as a depreciation deduction a reasonable allowance for the exhaustion, wear and tear (including a reasonable allowance for obsolescence)—

(1)   of property used in the trade or business, or

(2)   of property held for the production of income.

IRC § 167 responds to the fact that most property used in a business deteriorates with the passage of time. For example, Widget Company purchases a widget manufacturing machine for $100,000. The machine will wear out and decline in value as it produces widgets. Assume that the widget machine will serve its productive purpose for only ten years. At the end of the ten years, it will constitute a worthless piece of scrap.

If the deterioration of the machine is ignored, the annual profits of the business will be overstated. Assume the business sells $1,000,000 of widgets each year and incurs cash expenses of $800,000 to produce those widgets. If the deterioration of the machine is ignored, one might conclude that the business has a $200,000 annual profit.

Sales Revenue	$1,000,000
Less: Cash Expenses	$800,000
Annual Profit	$200,000

This conclusion *overstates* the profit because it ignores that the $100,000 invested in the widget machine dissipates as the machine deteriorates with the passage of time.

A more accurate measure of Widget Company's economic profit would treat a portion of the $100,000 purchase price of the widget machine as an additional cost of producing the widgets sold each year. Because the widget machine is productive for ten years, one-tenth of the cost of the machine (1/10 × $100,000 = $10,000) might be regarded as an additional annual expense. This treatment reduces the business's annual profit from $200,000 to $190,000.

Sales Revenue	$1,000,000
Less: Cash Expenses	$800,000
Less: Depreciation Expense	$10,000
Annual Profit	$190,000

The $100,000 cost might be allocated equally to each year of the 10-year period or it might be allocated over that period in some other manner. But regardless of how much of the $100,000 cost is allocated to each year, the annual profits over the ten-year period should be reduced to reflect that nothing remains of the original $100,000 investment at the end of the machine's functional ten-year period.

IRC § 167 acknowledges the economic reality that the widget machine deteriorates with the passage of time by allowing an annual tax deduction for a portion of the basis of the machine. While IRC § 167 allows the depreciation deduction, the mechanics of computing the deduction are delineated in IRC § 168, the accelerated cost recovery system ("ACRS"). Two important elements of the depreciation deduction must be grasped at the outset. First, depreciation deductions stem from the basis of eligible property. Each year the taxpayer owns the property, a portion of the basis is allowed as a depreciation deduction under IRC § 167 and the taxpayer's basis in the property is adjusted downward by the allowable deduction under IRC § 1016(a)(2). Second, the amount of the annual depreciation deduction is dictated by statute; it bears no relation to the actual annual decline in the value of the property.

WORTH NOTING The annual depreciation deduction permitted for income tax purposes bears no relationship to the actual change in the value of the property with respect to which the deduction is allowed.

The Simon case, below, illustrates that depreciation deductions may be allowed even with respect to property that increases in value over time.

SIMON v. COMMISSIONER

United States Court of Appeals, Second Circuit, 1995
68 F.3d 41, *nonacq.* 1996–29 IRB 4[9]

Winter, Circuit Judge:

This appeal from the Tax Court raises the question whether professional musicians may take a depreciation deduction for wear and tear on antique violin bows under [IRC Secs. 167 and 168].

* * *

BACKGROUND

The facts are essentially undisputed. Richard and Fiona Simon are highly skilled professional violinists. Richard Simon began to play and study the violin at the age of 7. He received a bachelor of music degree from the Manhattan School of Music in 1956 and subsequently pursued his master's degree in music at the Manhattan School of Music and Columbia University. In 1965, Mr. Simon joined the New York Philharmonic Orchestra ("Philharmonic") as a member of its first violin section. Since then, he has also been a soloist, chamber music player, and teacher. Mr. Simon was a full-time performer with the Philharmonic throughout the relevant tax year.

Fiona Simon has played and studied the violin since the age of 4. She studied at the Purcell School in London from 1963 to 1971 and at the Guildhall School of Music from 1971 to 1973. Ms. Simon joined the first violin section of the Philharmonic in 1985. She, too, has been a soloist, chamber music player, teacher, and free-lance performer. Ms. Simon was a full-time performer with the Philharmonic throughout the pertinent tax year.

The business property at issue consists of two violin bows ("the Tourte bows") made in the nineteenth century by Francois Tourte, a bowmaker renowned for technical improvements in bow design. These bows were purchased by the Simons in 1985 and were in a largely unused condition at the time. The Tax Court found that "[o]ld violins played with old bows produce exceptional sounds that are superior to sounds produced by newer violins played with newer bows." The Tax Court also found that violin bows suffer wear and tear when

---

[9]   Editor's note: By non-acquiescing in the decision, the Internal Revenue Service puts taxpayers on notice that it will continue to challenge fact patterns analogous to *Simon* arising outside the Second Circuit.

used regularly by performing musicians. With use, a violin bow will eventually become "played out," producing an inferior sound. However, a "played out" Tourte bow retains value as a collector's item notwithstanding its diminished utility. The Simons' Tourte bows, for example, were appraised in 1990 at $45,000 and $35,000, even though they had physically deteriorated since their purchase by the Simons in 1985 for $30,000 and $21,500, respectively.

The Simons use the Tourte bows regularly in their trade. In 1989, the tax year in question, the Simons performed in four concerts per week as well as numerous rehearsals with the Philharmonic. Their use of the Tourte bows during the tax year at issue subjected the bows to substantial wear and tear. Believing that they were entitled to depreciate the bows under the [Accelerated Cost Recovery System of IRC sec. 168 ("ACRS")], the Simons claimed depreciation deductions for the two bows on their 1989 Form 1040 in the amount of $6,300 and $4,515. The parties stipulated that these amounts represent the appropriate ACRS deductions if deductions are allowable.

The Tax Court agreed with the Simons and allowed the depreciation deductions. The Commissioner brought the present appeal.

DISCUSSION

This appeal turns on the interpretation of the ACRS provisions of I.R.C. § 168, which provide a depreciation deduction for "recovery property" placed into service after 1980. Recovery property is tangible property of a character subject to the allowance for depreciation when used in a trade or business or held for the production of income. The record establishes that the Simons' Tourte bows were tangible property placed in service after 1980 and used in the taxpayers' trade or business. The Commissioner contends, however, that the bows are not "property of a character subject to the allowance for depreciation."

The parties agree that Section 168's phrase "of a character subject to depreciation" must be interpreted in light of the I.R.C. Sec. 167(a) allowances for "exhaustion, wear and tear, and * * * obsolescence." The Simons and the Tax Court maintain that, when read in conjunction with the plain language of Section 167, Section 168 requires only that the Tourte bows suffer wear and tear in the Simons' trade to qualify as "recovery property." The Commissioner, on the other hand, argues that because all property used in a trade or business is necessarily subject to wear and tear, the Simons' construction of Section 168 would effectively render Section 168's phrase "of a character subject to the allowance for depreciation" superfluous, a result that Congress presumably could not have intended. * * *

We do not agree with the Commissioner's premise [that all property used in a trade or business is necessarily subject to wear and tear] because some tangible assets used in business do not suffer wear and tear. For example, paintings that hang on the wall of a law firm merely to be looked at, to please connoisseur clients or to give the appearance of dignity to combative professionals, do not generally suffer wear or tear. More to the point, the Simons' Tourte bows were playable for a time precisely because they had been kept in a private collection and were relatively unused since their manufacture. Indeed, it appears that one had never been played at all. Had that collection been displayed at a for-profit museum, the museum could not have depreciated the bows * * * because, although the bows were being used in a trade or business, they were not subject to wear and tear. The Tourte bows are not unlike numerous kinds of museum pieces or collectors' items. The Commissioner's textual argument thus fails because there are tangible items not subject to wear and tear.

The Commissioner next argues that Congressional intent and the notion of depreciation itself require that Section 168's statutory language be supplemented by reading into the word "character" a requirement that tangible property have a demonstrable useful life. To address that issue, we must briefly examine the history of the depreciation allowance.

The tax laws have long permitted deductions for depreciation on certain income-producing assets used in a trade or business. The original rationale for the depreciation deduction was to allow taxpayers to match accurately, for tax accounting purposes, the cost of an asset to the income stream that the asset produced. In its traditional incarnation, therefore, the pace of depreciation deductions was determined by the period of time that the asset would produce income in the taxpayer's business. * * *

To implement this accurate tax accounting, the concept of a determinable useful life was necessary because, without such a determination, one could not calculate the proper annual allowance—"the sum which should be set aside for the taxable year, in order that, at the end of the useful life of the [property], the aggregate of the sums set aside will suffice to provide an amount equal to the original cost." United States v. Ludey, 274 U.S. 295, 300–01 (1927). * * *

[The Economic Recovery Tax Act of 1981 ("ERTA") created ACRS which] altered the depreciation scheme for two reasons (other than sound accounting practice) that are not consistent with the Commissioner's argument [that tangible property must have a determinable useful life to be eligible for depreciation deductions]. First, the ACRS introduced accelerated depreciation periods as a stimulus for economic growth. *Under ACRS, the cost of an asset is recovered over a predetermined period unrelated to—and usually shorter than—the useful life of the asset* (editor's emphasis). Moreover, the depreciation deductions do not assume consistent use throughout the asset's life, instead assigning inflated deductions to the earlier years of use. See I.R.C. Sec. 168(b). Therefore, the purpose served by the determinable useful life requirement of the pre-ERTA scheme—allowing taxpayers to depreciate property over its actual use in the business—no longer exists under the ACRS. Because the ACRS is different by design, there is no logic in the Commissioner's suggestion that depreciation practice under the old Section 167 calls for the imposition of a determinable useful life requirement after ERTA.

A second congressional purpose embodied in ERTA also militates against reading a determinable useful life prerequisite into Section 168. In addition to stimulating investment, Congress sought to simplify the depreciation rules by eliminating the need to adjudicate matters such as useful life which are inherently uncertain and result in unproductive disagreements between taxpayers and the Internal Revenue Service. Indeed, the legislation specifically sought to "de-emphasize" the concept of useful life. On this point, we agree with the Tax Court that:

> [The Commissioner's] argument that a taxpayer must first prove the useful life of personal property before he or she may depreciate it * * * would bring the Court back to pre-ERTA law and reintroduce the disagreements that the Congress intended to eliminate by its enactment of ERTA.

> * * *

> [W]e thus hold that, for the purposes of the "recovery property" provisions of Section 168, "property subject to the allowance for depreciation" means property that is subject to exhaustion, wear and tear, or obsolescence.

> * * *

We acknowledge that the result of our holding may give favorable treatment to past investment decisions that some regard as wasteful, such as a law firm's purchase of expensive antique desks, the cost of which could have been quickly depreciated under our current ruling. However, Congress wanted to stimulate investment in business property generally, and it is not our function to draw subjective lines between the wasteful and the productive. Moreover, courts should take care that the Commissioner's role as revenue maximizer does not vitiate Congress's intent to sacrifice revenue to generate economic activity. If taxpayers cannot trust that such tax measures will be fully honored, some or all of the hoped-for activity will not occur.

One should not exaggerate the extent to which our holding is a license to hoard and depreciate valuable property that a taxpayer expects to appreciate in real economic value. The test is whether property will suffer exhaustion, wear and tear, or obsolescence in its use by a business. Even without a determinable useful life requirement, a business that displayed antique automobiles, for example, and kept them under near-ideal, humidity-controlled conditions, would still have difficulty demonstrating the requisite exhaustion, wear and tear, or obsolescence necessary to depreciate the automobiles as recovery property. Nor is valuable artwork purchased as office ornamentation apt to suffer anything more damaging than occasional criticism from the tutored or untutored, and it too would probably fail to qualify as recovery property. Indeed, even a noted artwork that serves as a day-to-day model for another artist's work cannot be depreciated as recovery property if it does not face exhaustion, wear and tear, or obsolescence in the pertinent business.

LOOK ONLINE

An article on the Simon case that appeared in the New York Times Arts section can be accessed here.

For the foregoing reasons, we affirm.

OAKES, SENIOR CIRCUIT JUDGE, dissenting: [Omitted]

NOTES

1. *Wasting property.* IRC § 167(a) requires that property be—1) used in a trade or business, or 2) held for the production of income, to be eligible for depreciation deductions. IRC § 167(a). In addition to the statutory requirement, the property must be "wasting" property; i.e., property that deteriorates with the passage of time. For example, land is not eligible for depreciation deductions

because it normally does not deteriorate over time. By contrast, equipment and buildings used in a trade or business are eligible for depreciation deductions because they deteriorate over time. Property may be wasting even if it does not actually decline in value during the period when depreciation deductions are allowed, as evidenced by the *Simon* case. As long as the property will eventually deteriorate, it will satisfy the wasting requirement.

2.   *Personal use property.* IRC § 167(a) allows depreciation deductions only with respect to property used in a trade or business or held for the production of income. Depreciation deductions may not be claimed for property used for personal purposes. For example, if Tom purchases a car for $30,000 that he uses for personal purposes, he is not allowed depreciation deductions with respect to the car, notwithstanding that the car is a wasting asset (i.e., will deteriorate with the passage of time).

3.   *Section 1016(a)(2) ensures that basis offsets income not more than once.* When a taxpayer purchases property, the taxpayer takes a basis in the property equal to its cost. IRC § 1012. If the property does not qualify for depreciation deductions, the entire basis will offset the amount realized when the property is sold, thereby reducing gain from the sale. If the property qualifies for depreciation deductions, the depreciation deductions will offset gross income earned while the taxpayer owns the property and, pursuant to IRC § 1016(a)(2), the basis is reduced by the allowable depreciation deductions. This downward adjustment to the basis of depreciable property is necessary to avoid allowing the taxpayer's basis to offset income twice.

■   **EXAMPLE 6-G.**   *Section 1016(a)(2) precludes double benefit.* On January 1 of Year 1, Shanna purchases a piece of property for $100,000. Assume Shanna is entitled to a depreciation deduction in Year 1 of $7,000, if the property is wasting property used in a trade or business. In this case, she would be allowed a $7,000 deduction in Year 1 that would offset her Year 1 gross income. Correspondingly, her basis in the property would be reduced by $7,000 (from $100,000 to $93,000).

On January 1 of Year 2, Shanna sells the property for $110,000. In Year 2, Shanna would realize a $17,000 gain on the sale ($110,000 amount realized less $93,000 adjusted basis). By contrast, if the property were not eligible for depreciation deductions, Shanna would not be allowed a depreciation deduction in Year 1 and she would realize only a $10,000 gain on the sale ($110,000 amount realized less $100,000 adjusted basis).

---

4. *Depreciation deduction must be claimed to obtain even a single tax benefit.* Pursuant to IRC § 1016(a)(2), the basis of property is adjusted downward to the extent depreciation deductions are allowed, "but not less than the amount allowable." Thus, regardless of whether a taxpayer claims depreciation deductions with respect to eligible property, the basis of the property will be reduced by the "allowable deduction."

WORTH NOTING The basis of depreciable property will be reduced by the allowable depreciation deduction regardless of whether the owner of the property actually claims the deduction.

■ **EXAMPLE 6-H.** *Basis of depreciable property is reduced even if taxpayer fails to claim depreciation deduction.* Same facts as Example 6-G. In that Example, Shanna is allowed to claim a $7,000 depreciation deduction that would offset her Year 1 gross income. If, however, Shanna fails to claim the $7,000 depreciation deduction, her basis is still reduced by the amount of the allowable deduction. Thus, if Shanna fails to claim the $7,000 depreciation deduction, her basis in the property is still reduced from $100,000 to $93,000 and she will realize a $17,000 gain on the sale of the property ($110,000 sale price less $93,000 adjusted basis). In this situation, neither the income she earns in Year 1, nor the amount realized on the sale of the property in Year 2, is offset by the $7,000 of basis she could have claimed as a depreciation deduction in Year 1.

---

5. *Applicable recovery periods (IRC § 168(c)).* The period of time over which depreciation deductions may be claimed depends on the nature of the property. Most personalty, including an automobile or small truck, is classified as "5-year property" which means that the basis of the property can be recovered through

depreciation deductions over a five-year period. See IRC § 168(e)(3)(B). By contrast, basis in residential rental property can be recovered through depreciation deductions over 27.5 years, and basis in nonresidential real property can be recovered over 39 years. See IRC § 168(e)(2). As explained in *Simon*, these recovery periods are generally shorter than the actual useful life of the property.

6.   *Bonus depreciation allowed until 2026.* In lieu of the recovery periods for *personalty* discussed in Note 5, the Tax Cuts and Jobs Act of 2017 permits taxpayers to deduct 100% of the adjusted basis of most new *and used* depreciable personalty (e.g., vehicles, machinery and equipment) placed in service before 2023. See IRC § 168(k). The deduction allowed by section 168(k) is referred to as "bonus depreciation." After 2022, the percentage of the adjusted basis that may be deducted in the year the property is placed in service is reduced by 20% each year (i.e., 80% of the adjusted basis of property placed in service in 2023 may be deducted as bonus depreciation, 60% of the adjusted basis of property placed in service in 2024 may be deducted as bonus depreciation, 40% of the adjusted basis of property placed in service in 2025 may be deducted as bonus depreciation, and 20% of the adjusted basis of property placed in service in 2026 may be deducted as bonus depreciation). See IRC § 168(k)(6). Property placed in service after 2026 is not eligible for bonus depreciation. See IRC § 168(k)(2)(A)(iii).

7.   *Applicable depreciation methods (IRC § 168(b)).* Two principal methods of depreciation exist: straight-line depreciation and accelerated depreciation.

Straight-line depreciation. Under the straight-line method, an equal amount of depreciation is claimed during each year of the recovery period. The statute mandates the straight-line method for real property. IRC §§ 168(b)(3)(A), (B).

WORTH NOTING   The purchase of real property often entails the acquisition of both a building and the underlying land. Only the basis allocable to the building can be recovered through depreciation deductions. The basis allocable to the land is not eligible for tax depreciation because land is not a wasting asset.

■ **EXAMPLE 6-I.** *Straight-line depreciation of building.* A business purchases a factory for $5,000,000 with $1,100,000 of the purchase price allocated to the land and $3,900,000 allocated to the building. No depreciation deductions may be claimed with respect to the land. The basis in the building may be recovered through depreciation deductions over 39 years, the applicable recovery period for nonresidential real property. See IRC § 168(e)(2). Thus, an annual depreciation deduction of $100,000 is allowable to the taxpayer ($3,900,000 basis ÷ 39 years = $100,000). If the factory were sold after four years, the adjusted basis in the building would be $3,500,000; the original basis ($3,900,000) less the allowable depreciation deductions (4 × $100,000).

WORTH NOTING Under the **straight-line method**, the amount of the depreciation deduction allowed during each year of the recovery period remains the same.

Accelerated depreciation. When personalty qualifies for depreciation deductions, the statute sanctions accelerated depreciation. IRC §§ 168(b)(1), (2). Accelerated depreciation permits depreciation deductions to be claimed at a faster rate than the straight-line method would permit. If property is held for the entire recovery period, the total depreciation deductions allowed under both methods is equal to the basis of the property. However, when accelerated depreciation applies, larger depreciation deductions are allowed in the early years and, correspondingly, smaller deductions are allowed in the later years.

■ **EXAMPLE 6-J.** *Accelerated depreciation of personalty.* A business purchases depreciable personalty for $30,000. The property qualifies as "5-year property" (§ 168(e)(3)(B)) and, until 2022, the entire basis can be deducted as "bonus depreciation" in the year the property is placed in service. See Note 6, above. If the property is placed in service after

2026,[10] the basis can be recovered through depreciation deductions over a five-year period. The following table compares the annual depreciation deductions allowed under the accelerated method, which normally applies to "5-year property," to the deductions that would be allowed under the straight-line method:

Year	Accelerated depreciation	Straight-line depreciation
1	$12,000	$6,000
2	9,000	6,000
3	6,000	6,000
4	1,500	6,000
5	1,500	6,000
Total	$30,000	$30,000

WORTH NOTING When accelerated depreciation applies, larger depreciation deductions are allowed in the early years and, correspondingly, smaller deductions are allowed in the later years.

3.   Amount Realized—§ 1001(b)

When a realization event occurs, the taxpayer's gain is quantified by subtracting the "adjusted basis" of the transferred property from the "amount realized." IRC § 1001(a).[11] The statute defines the amount realized in IRC § 1001(b).

Primary Law: IRC § 1001(b)

The amount realized from the sale or other disposition of property shall be the sum of any money received plus the fair market value of the property (other than money).

---

[10]   For property placed in service in 2023 through 2026, a portion of the basis can be immediately deducted as bonus depreciation and the remainder of the basis would be recovered over the normal five-year recovery period. See Note 6, above.

[11]   If the adjusted basis of the property exceeds the amount realized, a realized loss will occur. The treatment of losses will be explored in Chapter 10.

IN SIGHTS The amount realized is essentially "what you get" for the property transferred and is analogous to how all other kinds of gross income are quantified (e.g., compensation for services is measured by the amount of money and the fair market value of any property received for the services).

a. Sale of Property for Money

A sale of property, i.e., the transfer of property in exchange for money, is the classic realization event. When a sale occurs, gain is quantified by subtracting the adjusted basis in the transferred property from the amount of money received. IRC § 1001(a). This "realized" gain is normally "recognized," i.e., immediately included in gross income. IRC § 1001(c). However, Congress has enacted a variety of nonrecognition provisions pursuant to which a realized gain may be deferred. Some of these nonrecognition provisions will be explored in Chapter 12. For now, you may assume that all realized gains are recognized.

■ **EXAMPLE 6-K.** *Sale of property.* Abby purchased a parcel of land several years ago for $10,000. The current value of the parcel of land is $50,000. Abby transfers the parcel of land to Boris for $50,000. Abby has an amount realized of $50,000 (the cash she received from Boris) and realizes a gain of $40,000 on the exchange (amount realized of $50,000 less adjusted basis in the land of $10,000). The realized gain is recognized, unless a nonrecognition provision applies.

b. Exchange of Property for Other Property

An exchange of property for other property is also a realization event. When an exchange occurs, gain is quantified by subtracting the adjusted basis of the transferred property from the fair market value of the property received. IRC §§ 1001(a), (b). The resulting gain is recognized unless a nonrecognition provision applies. IRC § 1001(c).

■ **EXAMPLE 6-L.** *Exchange of properties of equal value.* Same facts as Example 6-K except that Abby transfers the land to Boris in exchange for an antique car with a value of $50,000 (instead of cash). Abby has an amount realized of $50,000 (the value of the car) and realizes a gain of $40,000 on the exchange (amount realized of $50,000 less adjusted basis in land of $10,000). The realized gain is recognized, unless a non-recognition provision applies.

■ **PROBLEM 6-5.** *Exchange of properties with unequal values.* The facts are the same as Example 6-L, except that the value of the antique car transferred to Abby is only $40,000. Although the value of the land Abby transfers exceeds the value of the antique car, she agrees to the exchange because the car was formerly owned by her uncle and Abby has a strong emotional attachment to the car. What are the tax consequences of the exchange to Abby?

c.   **Exchange of Property for Services**

INTERNATIONAL FREIGHTING CORPORATION v. COMMISSIONER

United States Court of Appeals, Second Circuit, 1943
135 F.2d 310

[D]uring the years 1933 to 1936, taxpayer informally adopted [a] bonus plan * * *. Bonuses were [awarded to employees of taxpayer] in the form of common stock of the duPont Company * * *.

* * *

Pursuant to the bonus plan, taxpayer's board of directors made * * * bonus awards to certain of its employees in common stock of the duPont Company * * *. During the calendar year 1936 taxpayer paid over and distributed to [its employees] 150 shares of the common stock of the duPont Company, whose cost to taxpayer * * * was $16,153 and whose market value was then $24,858. Each of the employees receiving those shares in 1936 paid a tax thereon, computing the market value at the time of delivery as taxable income. [Taxpayer did not report any taxable gain when it transferred the duPont stock to its employees.]

[T]he Commissioner * * * alleged that * * * taxpayer realized a taxable profit of $8,705 on the disposition of the shares, and taxpayer's net taxable income otherwise determined should be increased accordingly.

[T]he Tax Court decided for the Commissioner * * * holding that taxpayer realized a gain of $8,705 in 1936 by paying the * * * bonus in stock which had cost taxpayer $8,705 less than its market value when taxpayer transferred the stock to its employees. * * * From that decision taxpayer seeks review.

Frank, Circuit Judge.

[W]e turn to the question whether the transaction resulted in taxable gain to taxpayer. We think that the Tax Court correctly held that it did. The delivery of those shares was not a gift * * *. It was not a gift precisely because it was "compensation for services actually rendered," i. e., because the taxpayer received a full quid pro quo. Accordingly, cases holding that one is not liable for an income tax when he makes a gift of shares are not in point. * * *

But, as the delivery of the shares here constituted a disposition for a valid consideration, it resulted in a closed transaction with a consequent realized gain. It is of no relevance that here the taxpayer had not been legally obligated to award any shares * * * to the employees; bonus payments by corporations are recognized as proper even if there was no previous obligation to make them * * *. [T]he bonuses would be invalid to the extent that what was delivered to the employees exceeded what the services of the employees were worth * * *. [It therefore] follows that the consideration received by the taxpayer from the employees must be deemed to be equal at least to the value of the shares in 1936. Here then, as there was no gift but a disposition of shares for a valid consideration equal at least to the market value of the shares when delivered, there was a taxable gain equal to the difference between the cost of the shares and that market value.

[The predecessor to IRC § 1001(a)] provides that the gain from "the sale or other disposition of property" shall be the excess of "the amount realized therefrom" over "the adjusted basis" * * *. True, [the predecessor to IRC § 1001(b)] provides that "the amount realized" is the sum of "any money received plus the fair market value of the property (other than money) received." Literally, where there is a disposition of stock for services, no "property" or "money" is received by the person who thus disposes of the stock. But, in similar circumstances, it has been held that "money's worth" is received and that such a receipt comes within [the predecessor to IRC § 1001(b)].

The taxpayer properly asks us to treat this case "as if there had been no formal bonus plan" and as if taxpayer "had simply paid outright 150 shares of duPont stock to selected employees as additional compensation." On that basis, surely there was a taxable gain. For to shift the equation once more, the case supposed is the equivalent of one in which the taxpayer in the year 1936, without entering into a previous contract fixing the amount of compensation, had employed a transposition expert for one day and, when he completed his work, had paid him 5 shares of duPont stock having market value at that time of $500 but which it had bought in a previous year for $100. There can be no doubt that, from such a transaction, taxpayer would have a [$400] taxable gain. And so here.

The order of the Tax Court is affirmed.

■ **EXAMPLE 6-M.** *Exchange of property for services.* Chuck purchased a

7,000 appreciation painting several years ago for $5,000. The painting has a current value of $12,000. Chuck hires Donna to perform medical services with a value of $12,000. Chuck transfers the painting to Donna as compensation for the services she performed. The transfer of the painting for Donna's services is a realization event to Chuck. His amount realized is the value of the services received ($12,000). He realizes a gain of $7,000 ($12,000 amount realized minus $5,000 adjusted basis in the painting). The realized gain is recognized, unless a nonrecognition provision applies.

■ **PROBLEM 6-6.** *Tax consequences to service performer.* What are the tax consequences to Donna in Example 6-M?

Chuc

d. Gift of Property (Intervivos or Testamentary)

As discussed earlier in this Chapter, a gift of property, during one's lifetime or at death, is not a realization event. Even if a gift were regarded as a realization event, it would be impossible to determine the donor's amount realized. When a gift is made, the donor derives emotional benefits but these benefits are not within the scope of gross income and their value is not quantifiable. The quagmire of ascertaining the amount realized to a donor is avoided, however, because it is generally understood that a gratuitous transfer of appreciated property does not trigger a realization event.

■ **EXAMPLE 6-N.** *Gift of appreciated property.* Jonathan purchases a parcel of land for $10,000 that increases in value to $100,000. Jonathan makes a gift of the land to Rachel. The gift is not a realization event to Jonathan because he does not receive a quantifiable benefit in return for the property. Thus, the potential $90,000 gain in the land is not taxed to Jonathan when he transfers the land to Rachel.

[handwritten margin note: gd t apprec.]

---

e. Sale of Leveraged Property with Value in Excess of Debt— Recourse and Nonrecourse Debt Treated Alike

Often times, a taxpayer will sell property that secures a liability of the taxpayer. The liability the property secures might be a recourse liability (i.e., in the event of default, the lender can recover from both the property securing the debt and all of the borrower's other assets) or a nonrecourse liability (i.e., in the event of default, the lender's sole remedy is to foreclose on the property securing the debt).[12]   If the value of the transferred property is greater than the amount of debt the property secures, the tax consequences to the debtor will be the same, regardless of whether the debt the property secures is recourse debt or nonrecourse debt.[13]

---

[12]   See Chapter 5 for further discussion of recourse liabilities and nonrecourse liabilities.

[13]   Even if the value of the transferred property is *equal* to the amount of the debt the property secures, the same tax consequences result regardless of whether the debt is recourse or nonrecourse. See Crane v. Commissioner, reprinted below.

i.   Recourse Debt

When a taxpayer sells property securing a recourse liability and the value of the property exceeds the amount of debt the property secures, the buyer will normally agree to—

1) satisfy the seller's debt (i.e., "assume" the liability), and

Pay difference

2) pay the seller an amount equal to the difference between the value of the property and the amount of debt the property secures.

When a buyer assumes a liability of the seller, the buyer becomes contractually obligated to the seller to pay the seller's debt. If the buyer does not meet its obligation to the seller, the seller has a cause of action against the buyer. In these circumstances, the lender can still hold the seller accountable unless the lender releases the seller from its repayment obligation when the buyer assumes the seller's liability (i.e., the lender gives the seller a "novation").

■ **EXAMPLE 6-O.** *Sale of property with a value in excess of the recourse liability the property secures.* Eric sells real estate to Buyer. The real estate has a value of $1,000,000 and secures a $300,000 recourse debt. Buyer pays Eric $700,000 and also contractually agrees to satisfy Eric's $300,000 debt (i.e., Buyer "assumes" the liability). Furthermore, the lender releases Eric from any claims the lender would have against Eric's personal assets if Buyer breached her agreement with Eric to satisfy the debt (i.e., the lender gives Eric a "novation"). Assume Eric has an adjusted basis in the property of $600,000.

b/c seller rec. less cash, proceeds are still 1M

The sale is a realization event. Eric's amount realized is $1,000,000 ($700,000 cash plus the $300,000 benefit Eric derives from Buyer's assumption of the debt and the lender's novation). Eric realizes a gain of $400,000 ($1,000,000 amount realized less $600,000 adjusted basis). The realized gain is recognized, unless a nonrecognition provision applies.

Secondary Law: Reg. § 1.1001–2(a)

(1)   [T]he amount realized from a sale or other disposition of property includes the amount of liabilities from which the transferor is discharged as a result of the sale or disposition.

* * *

(4)   For purposes of this section—

* * *

(ii)   The sale or other disposition of property that secures a recourse liability discharges the transferor from the liability if another person agrees to pay the liability (whether or not the transferor is in fact released from liability);

* * *

■   **PROBLEM 6-7.** *Impact of novation.* Do the tax consequences to Eric in Example 6-O change if Buyer assumes Eric's liability but the lender does not give Eric a novation? See Reg § 1.1001–2(a)(4)(ii).

Lets him off the hook

ii.   Nonrecourse Debt

When a taxpayer sells property securing nonrecourse debt, the lender has no residual claims against the seller. Unlike a recourse debt assumed by the buyer, where the lender can still recover from the seller's personal assets after the property is transferred (unless the lender gives the seller a novation), the lender cannot recover from any of the seller's assets after the seller transfers property securing nonrecourse debt. When a buyer acquires property securing nonrecourse debt, the property remains encumbered by the debt after it is in the buyer's hands. Thus, if the buyer does not make the payments required by the debt instrument, the lender can foreclose on the property.

What is the amount realized of a taxpayer who sells property securing nonrecourse debt when the value of the property is greater than (or equal to) the amount of the nonrecourse debt it secures? The Crane case answers this question.

(there paid at the difference?

CRANE v. COMMISSIONER

United States Supreme Court, 1947
331 U.S. 1, 67 S. Ct. 1047, 91 L.Ed. 1301

Mr. Chief Justice Vinson delivered the opinion of the Court.

The question here is how a taxpayer who acquires depreciable property subject to [a nonrecourse liability], holds it for a period, and finally sells it still so encumbered, must compute her taxable gain.

Petitioner was the sole beneficiary and the executrix of the will of her husband, who died January 11, 1932. He then owned an apartment building and lot subject to a mortgage, which secured a principal debt of [$262,000.00] ***. As of that date, the property was appraised for federal estate tax purposes at a value exactly equal to the total amount of this encumbrance. Shortly after her husband's death, petitioner entered into an agreement with the mortgagee whereby she was to continue to operate the property—collecting the rents, paying for necessary repairs, labor, and other operating expenses, and reserving $200.00 monthly for taxes—and was to remit the net rentals to the mortgagee. This plan was followed for nearly seven years, during which period petitioner reported the gross rentals as income, and claimed and was allowed deductions for taxes and operating expenses paid on the property, for interest paid on the mortgage, and for the physical exhaustion of the building. *** On November 29, 1938, with the mortgagee threatening foreclosure, petitioner sold to a third party for [$2,500.00] cash, subject to the [$262,000 nonrecourse debt].

Petitioner reported a taxable gain of [$2,500.00]. Her theory was that the "property" which she had acquired in 1932 and sold in 1938 was only the equity, or the excess in the value of the apartment building and lot over the amount of the mortgage. This equity was of zero value when she acquired it. No depreciation could be taken on a zero value.[2] Neither she nor her vendee ever assumed the mortgage, so, when she sold the equity, the amount she realized on the sale was the net cash received, or $2,500.00. This sum less the zero basis constituted her gain ***.

The Commissioner, however, determined that petitioner realized a taxable gain of [$30,500]. His theory was that the "property" acquired and sold

---

[2] This position is, of course, inconsistent with her practice in claiming such deductions in each of the years the property was held. The deductions so claimed and allowed by the Commissioner were in the total amount of $25,500.00.

was not the equity, as petitioner claimed, but rather the physical property itself, or the owner's rights to possess, use, and dispose of it, undiminished by the mortgage. The original basis thereof was [$262,000], its appraised value in 1932. *** During the period that petitioner held the property, there was an allowable depreciation of [$28,000] on the building, so that the adjusted basis of the [property] at the time of sale was [$234,000]. The amount realized on the sale was said to include not only the $2,500.00 net cash receipts, but also the principal amount of the mortgage subject to which the property was sold, both totaling [$264,500. Thus, the realized gain, according to the Commissioner, was $30,500 (amount realized of $264,500 less adjusted basis of $234,000).]

The Tax Court *** adopted petitioner's contentions, and expunged the deficiency.[9] [O]n the Commissioner's appeal, the Circuit Court of Appeals reversed. We granted certiorari because of the importance of the questions raised as to the proper construction of the gain and loss provisions of the Internal Revenue Code.

The 1938 Act defines the gain from "the sale or other disposition of property" as "the excess of the amount realized therefrom over the adjusted basis ***." [Current Code § 1001(a).] It proceeds, to define "the amount realized from the sale or other disposition of property" as "the sum of any money received plus the fair market value of the property (other than money) received." [Current Code § 1001(b).] Further, the "adjusted basis for determining the gain or loss from the sale or other disposition of property" is declared to be "the basis as adjusted for exhaustion, wear and tear *** to the extent allowed (but not less than the amount allowable) ***." [Current Code § 1016(a)(2).] The basis "if the property was acquired by *** devise *** or by the decedent's estate from the decedent," is "the fair market value of such property at the time of such acquisition." [Current Code § 1014(a).]

Logically, the first step under this scheme is to determine the unadjusted basis of the property and the dispute in this case is as to the construction to be given the term "property". If "property" means the same thing as "equity", it would necessarily follow that the basis of petitioner's property was zero, as she contends. If, on the contrary, it means the land and building themselves,

---

[9]   [B]ecause the Court accepted petitioner's theory that the entire property had a zero basis, it held that she was not entitled to the 1938 depreciation deduction on the building which she had inconsistently claimed. For these reasons, it did not expunge the deficiency in its entirety.

or the owner's legal rights in them, undiminished by the mortgage, the basis was [$262,000].

We think that the reasons for favoring * * * the latter construction are of overwhelming weight. In the first place, the words of statutes—including revenue acts—should be interpreted where possible in their ordinary, everyday senses. The only relevant definitions of "property" to be found in the principal standard dictionaries[14] are the two favored by the Commissioner, i.e., either that "property" is the physical thing which is a subject of ownership, or that it is the aggregate of the owner's rights to control and dispose of that thing. "Equity" is not given as a synonym, nor do either of the foregoing definitions suggest that it could be correctly so used. Indeed, "equity" is defined as "the value of a property * * * above the total of the liens. * * * " The contradistinction could hardly be more pointed. Strong countervailing considerations would be required to support a contention that Congress, in using the word "property", meant "equity", or that we should impute to it the intent to convey that meaning.

In the second place, the Commissioner's position has the approval of the administrative construction [of the statute]. With respect to the valuation of property under that section, [a regulation] promulgated under the 1938 Act provided that "the value of property as of the date of the death of the decedent as appraised for the purpose of the federal estate tax * * * shall be deemed to be its fair market value. * * * " The land and building here involved were so appraised in 1932, and their appraised value—[$262,000]—was reported by petitioner as part of the gross estate. This was in accordance with the estate tax law and regulations, which had always required that the value of decedent's property, undiminished by liens, be so appraised and returned, and that mortgages be separately deducted in computing the net estate. As the quoted provision of the Regulations has been in effect since 1918, and as the relevant statutory provision has been repeatedly reenacted since then in substantially the same form, the former may itself now be considered to have the force of law.

Moreover, in the many instances in other parts of the Act in which Congress has used the word "property", or expressed the idea of "property" or "equity", we find no instances of a misuse of either word or of a confusion of the ideas. In some parts of the Act other than the gain and loss sections, we find "property" where it is unmistakably used in its ordinary sense. On the other

---

[14]   See Webster's New International Dictionary, Unabridged, 2d Ed.; Funk & Wagnalls' New Standard Dictionary; Oxford English Dictionary.

hand where either Congress or the Treasury intended to convey the meaning of "equity," it did so by the use of appropriate language.

A further reason why the word "property" in [the statute] should not be construed to mean "equity" is the bearing such construction would have on the allowance of deductions for depreciation and on the collateral adjustments of basis.

Section 23(*l*) permits deduction from gross income of "a reasonable allowance for the exhaustion, wear and tear of property * * *." Sections 23(n) and 114(a) declare that the "basis upon which exhaustion, wear and tear * * * are to be allowed" is the basis "provided in section 113(b) for the purpose of determining the gain upon the sale" of the property, which is the § 113(a) basis "adjusted * * * for exhaustion, wear and tear * * * to the extent allowed (but not less than the amount allowable) * * *."

Under these provisions, if the mortgagor's equity were * * * the original basis from which depreciation allowances are deducted * * * and if the amount of the annual allowances were to be computed on that value, as would then seem to be required, they will represent only a fraction of the cost of the corresponding physical exhaustion, and any recoupment by the mortgagor of the remainder of that cost can be effected only by the reduction of his taxable gain in the year of sale. If, however, the amount of the annual allowances were to be computed on the value of the property, and then deducted from an equity basis, we would in some instances have to accept deductions from a minus basis or deny deductions altogether. The Commissioner also argues that taking the mortgagor's equity as the § 113(a) basis would require the basis to be changed with each payment on the mortgage, and that the attendant problem of repeatedly recomputing basis and annual allowances would be a tremendous accounting burden on both the Commissioner and the taxpayer. Moreover, the mortgagor would acquire control over the timing of his depreciation allowances.

Thus it appears that the applicable provisions of the Act expressly preclude an equity basis, and the use of it is contrary to certain implicit principles of income tax depreciation, and entails very great administrative difficulties. It may be added that the Treasury has never furnished a guide through the maze of problems that arise in connection with depreciating an equity basis, but, on the contrary, has consistently permitted the amount of depreciation allowances to be computed on the full value of the property, and subtracted from it as a basis. Surely, Congress' long-continued acceptance of this situation gives it full legislative endorsement.

We conclude that the proper basis * * * is the value of the property, undiminished by mortgages thereon, and that the correct basis here was [$262,000]. The next step is to ascertain what adjustments are required under § 113(b) [current Code sec. 1016(a)(2)]. As the depreciation rate was stipulated, the only question at this point is whether the Commissioner was warranted in making any depreciation adjustments whatsoever.

Section 113(b)(1)(B) provides that "proper adjustment in respect of the property shall in all cases be made * * * for exhaustion, wear and tear * * * to the extent allowed (but not less than the amount allowable)." The Tax Court found on adequate evidence that the apartment house was property of a kind subject to physical exhaustion, that it was used in taxpayer's trade or business, and consequently that the taxpayer would have been entitled to a depreciation allowance, except that, in the opinion of that Court, the basis of the property was zero, and it was thought that depreciation could not be taken on a zero basis. As we have just decided that the correct basis of the property was not zero, but [$262,000], we avoid this difficulty, and conclude that an adjustment should be made as the Commissioner determined.

Petitioner urges to the contrary that she was not entitled to depreciation deductions, whatever the basis of the property, because the law allows them only to one who actually bears the loss, and here the loss was not hers but the mortgagee's. We do not see, however, that she has established her factual premise. There was no finding of the Tax Court to that effect, nor to the effect that the value of the property was ever less than the amount of the lien. Nor was there evidence in the record, or any indication that petitioner could produce evidence, that this was so. The facts that the value of the property was only equal to the lien in 1932 and that during the next six and one-half years the physical condition of the building deteriorated * * *, are entirely inconclusive, particularly in the light of the buyer's willingness in 1938 to take subject to the increased lien and pay a substantial amount of cash to boot. Whatever may be the rule as to allowing depreciation to a mortgagor on property in his possession which is subject to an unassumed mortgage and clearly worth less than the lien, we are not faced with that problem and see no reason to decide it now.

At last we come to the problem of determining the "amount realized" on the 1938 sale. [The statute] defines the "amount realized" from "the sale * * * of property" as "the sum of any money received plus the fair market value of the property (other than money) received," and defines the gain on "the sale * * * of property" as the excess of the amount realized over the basis. Quite obviously, the word "property", used here with reference to a sale, must mean "property" in the same ordinary sense intended by the use of the word with reference to acquisition and depreciation * * * because the functional relation of the two sections requires that the word mean the same in one section that it does in the other. If the "property" to be valued on the date of acquisition is the property free of liens, the "property" to be priced on a subsequent sale must be the same thing.

Starting from this point, we could not accept petitioner's contention that the $2,500.00 net cash was all she realized on the sale * * *. She argues that because only $2,500.00 was realized on the sale, the "property" sold must have been the equity only, and that consequently we are forced to accept her contention as to the meaning of "property" in [the statute]. We adhere, however, to what we have already said on the meaning of "property", and *we find that the absurdity is avoided by our conclusion that the amount of the mortgage is properly included in the "amount realized" on the sale.* [Emphasis added.]

Petitioner concedes that if she had been personally liable on the mortgage and the purchaser had either paid or assumed it, the amount so paid or assumed would be considered a part of the "amount realized". The cases so deciding have already repudiated the notion that there must be an actual receipt by the seller himself of "money" or "other property", in their narrowest senses. It was thought to be decisive that one section of the Act must be construed so as not to defeat the intention of another or to frustrate the Act as a whole, and that the taxpayer was the "beneficiary" of the payment in "as real and substantial (a sense) as if the money had been paid it and then paid over by it to its creditors."

Both these points apply to this case. The first has been mentioned already. As for the second, we think that a mortgagor, not personally liable on the debt, who sells the property subject to the mortgage and for additional consideration, realizes a benefit in the amount of the mortgage as well as the boot.[37] If a purchaser pays boot, it is immaterial as to our problem whether the mortgagor is also to receive money from the purchaser to discharge the mortgage prior to sale, or whether he is merely to transfer subject to the mortgage—it may make

---

[37]   Obviously, if the value of the property is less than the amount of the mortgage, a mortgagor who is not personally liable cannot realize a benefit equal to the mortgage. Consequently, a different problem might be encountered where a mortgagor abandoned the property or transferred it subject to the mortgage without receiving boot. That is not this case.

a difference to the purchaser and to the mortgagee, but not to the mortgagor. Or put in another way, we are no more concerned with whether the mortgagor is, strictly speaking, a debtor on the mortgage, than we are with whether the benefit to him is, strictly speaking, a receipt of money or property. We are rather concerned with the reality that an owner of property, mortgaged at a figure less than that at which the property will sell, must and will treat the conditions of the mortgage exactly as if they were his personal obligations. If he transfers subject to the mortgage, the benefit to him is as real and substantial as if the mortgage were discharged, or as if a personal debt in an equal amount had been assumed by another.

Therefore we conclude that the Commissioner was right in determining that petitioner realized [$264,500] on the sale of this property [($2,500 cash plus $262,000 liability secured by the property). Her allowable depreciation deduction was $28,000 so her adjusted basis was $234,000 ($262,000 original basis less $28,000). Hence, she realized a gain of $30,500 ($264,500 amount realized less $234,000 adjusted basis).]

* * *

Petitioner * * * was entitled to depreciation deductions for a period of nearly seven years, and she actually took them * * *. The crux of this case, really, is whether the law permits her to exclude allowable deductions from consideration in computing gain. We have already showed that, if it does, the taxpayer can enjoy a double deduction, in effect, on the same loss of assets. * * *

Affirmed.

Mr. Justice Jackson, dissenting.

The Tax Court concluded that this taxpayer acquired only an equity worth nothing. The mortgage was in default, the mortgage debt was equal to the value of the property, and possession by the taxpayer was forfeited and terminable immediately by foreclosure. Arguments can be advanced to support the theory that the taxpayer received the whole property and thereupon came to owe the whole debt. Likewise it is argued that when she sold she transferred the entire value of the property and received release from the whole debt. But we think these arguments are not so conclusive that it was not within the province of the Tax Court to find that she received an equity which at that time had a zero value. The taxpayer never became personally liable for the debt, and hence when she sold she was released from no debt. The mortgage debt was simply a subtraction from the value of what she did receive, and from what she sold. The subtraction left her nothing when she acquired it and a small margin when she sold it. She acquired a property right equivalent to an equity of redemption and sold the same thing. It was the "property" bought and sold as the Tax Court considered it to be under the Revenue Laws. We are not required in this case to decide whether depreciation was properly taken, for there is no issue about it here.

We would reverse the Court of Appeals and sustain the decision of the Tax Court.

Mr. Justice Frankfurter and Mr. Justice Douglas join in this opinion.

Decades after the Crane case, the Treasury Department promulgated the following regulation:

Secondary Law: Reg. § 1.1001–2(a)

(1)   [T]he amount realized from a sale or other disposition of property includes the amount of liabilities from which the transferor is discharged as a result of the sale or disposition.

* * *

(4)   For purposes of this section—

(i)   The sale or other disposition of property that secures a nonrecourse liability discharges the transferor from the liability;

* * *

■ **PROBLEM 6-8.** *Recourse vs. nonrecourse debt.* Lizzie owns property with a value of $300,000 that secures $155,000 of debt.

a)   What is Lizzie's amount realized if—

1)   the debt secured by the property is recourse, Manny pays Lizzie $145,000 for the property and assumes the debt, and the lender releases Lizzie from any claims the lender would otherwise have against Lizzie's personal assets? See Reg. § 1.1001–2(a)(4)(ii).

2)   the debt secured by the property is recourse and Manny pays Lizzie $145,000 for the property and assumes the debt, but the lender does not release Lizzie from her liability to the lender? See Reg. § 1.1001–2(a)(4)(ii).

3)   the debt is secured only by the property Lizzie is transferring and Manny pays Lizzie $145,000 for the property and takes the property subject to the liability? See Reg § 1.1001–2(a)(4)(i).

b)   In all three situations in a), why is Manny willing to pay Lizzie only $145,000 when the property has a value of $300,000?

IN SIGHTS   **Three situations in which nonrecourse debt and recourse debt are treated alike.** When property with a value in excess of the debt it secures is sold, the unpaid debt is included in the seller's amount realized, regardless of whether the debt is nonrecourse or recourse (provided any recourse debt is assumed by the buyer). Thus, recourse debt and nonrecourse debt are taxed alike—

i)   when the borrowing occurs (see Chapter 5);

ii)   if the lender discharges the debt (see Chapter 5); and

iii)   when property securing the debt is sold, provided the value of the property is greater than or equal to the debt it secures.

Notes

1.   *Inconsistent reporting positions.* Footnote 2 of the Crane case indicates that Mrs. Crane took inconsistent positions on her tax returns with respect to depreciation deductions. In the year she sold the property, she claimed that her initial basis in the property was zero and therefore, that she was not entitled to depreciation deductions in prior years. However, she had actually claimed $25,500 of depreciation deductions on prior years' tax returns. It is never prudent for a taxpayer to take inconsistent reporting positions because it is impossible to successfully defend both positions if they are challenged, i.e., one of the two positions is necessarily wrong. In Mrs. Crane's case, it is very possible that the government would never have even challenged her tax reporting in the year of sale had she not (inconsistently) claimed depreciation deductions on prior years' tax returns.

2.   *Nonrecourse debt in excess of value of property.* Footnote 37 of the Crane case distinguished the transfer of property securing nonrecourse debt that does *not* exceed the value of the property (the facts of Crane) from a transfer of property securing nonrecourse debt that exceeds the value of the property. The tax consequences of the latter situation are explored in Commissioner v. Tufts, reprinted at p. 170.

---

f.   Sale of Leveraged Property with Debt in Excess of Value— Recourse and Nonrecourse Debt Treated Differently

Unfortunately, a taxpayer may own property that secures a liability in excess of the value of the property. In these circumstances, the liability the property secures might be a recourse liability or a nonrecourse liability. If the taxpayer transfers the property and the amount of debt the property secures exceeds the value of the transferred property, the tax consequences to the debtor will differ, depending on whether the debt the property secures is a recourse debt or a nonrecourse debt.

WORTH NOTING   Property securing an amount of debt in excess of the fair market value of the property is commonly referred to as "underwater" property.

i.   Recourse Debt   *when property is under water*

When a taxpayer owns property securing a recourse debt that exceeds the value of the property and the owner defaults on the debt, the lender can foreclose on the property and continue to hold the owner responsible for the amount of the debt that exceeds the value of the property. The Aizawa case illustrates the tax consequences to the owner of the property in these circumstances.

AIZAWA v. COMMISSIONER

United States Tax Court, 1992
99 T.C. 197

Tannenwald, Judge:

Respondent determined deficiencies in petitioners' Federal income tax * * *.

As a result of concessions of the parties, the only issue remaining for decision is the proper amount of petitioners' loss in 1987, resulting from a foreclosure sale. * * *

Petitioners owned rental property which they purchased in 1981 for $120,000. At the time of purchase, they gave the sellers a $90,000 recourse mortgage note with interest only payable at the rate of $750 monthly, and the entire principal due and payable in June 1985. * * * Petitioners did not make any payment on the principal when due.

In 1987, the sellers obtained a judgment of [$90,000] against petitioners in a foreclosure action, consisting of $90,000 mortgage principal * * *. Also in 1987, the property was sold to the sellers at a foreclosure sale for $72,700 which was applied to petitioners' obligation under such judgment, leaving a deficiency judgment of [$17,300].

There is no dispute between the parties that the foreclosure sale constituted a sale for tax purposes, Helvering v. Hammel, 311 U.S. 504 (1941), that petitioners suffered a loss thereon in 1987, and that petitioners' basis in the property at the time of the foreclosure sale was [$100,000]. Their dispute is with respect to the calculation of the "amount realized" on the foreclosure sale which should be applied against petitioners' basis, under section 1001(a), in order to determine the amount of their loss.

Surprisingly, as far as we can determine, this is the first time a court has confronted this issue directly. Petitioners contend that the deficiency judgment should be deducted from the unpaid mortgage principal and that the difference of [$72,700 ($90,000 minus $17,300)] constitutes the amount realized on the foreclosure sale which, when deducted from their basis, produces a loss of [$27,300 ($100,000 minus $72,700)]. Respondent counters that the $90,000.00 unpaid mortgage principal constitutes the amount realized on the foreclosure sale which, when deducted from petitioners' basis, produces a loss of [$10,000 ($100,000 minus $90,000.00)].

[R]espondent's position does not present an acceptable resolution of the issue before us. It requires petitioners to treat as money received an amount of their unpaid mortgage principal obligation *from which they have not yet been discharged* * * * [emphasis added].

* * *

The key to the resolution of the issue before us lies in the recognition that, in this case, there is a clear separation between the foreclosure sale and the unpaid recourse liability for mortgage principal which survives as part of a deficiency judgment. * * *

Where, as in this case, such separateness exists, the significance of the amount of the proceeds of the foreclosure sale becomes apparent. It cannot be [denied] that the property was sold for $72,700 (an amount which we have no reason to conclude did not represent the fair market value of the property) and that petitioners received, by way of a reduction in the judgment of foreclosure, that amount and nothing more. That is the "amount realized" under section 1001(a) [from] which petitioners' basis [is subtracted] in order to determine the amount of their loss.

We are aware of the fact that this approach enables petitioners to increase their loss by $17,300 [(from $10,000 to $27,300)] representing borrowed funds which they might not repay and on which they have not yet paid a tax. But this is nothing more than the logical consequence of Crane v. Commissioner, 331 U.S. 1 (1947), which has been treated as sanctioning the right of a cash-basis taxpayer to include the amount of an unpaid mortgage liability in his or her basis. * * *

Our conclusion that the proceeds of the foreclosure sale is the "amount realized" under section 1001(a) is further supported by the following analogy. Assume that, prior to the foreclosure, petitioners had an opportunity to sell the property for $72,700 to a third party who wanted to acquire the property free and clear. Petitioners asked their mortgagee to release the mortgage as security for their recourse obligation, and the mortgagee was willing to do so because petitioners were then persons of substantial means so that their unsecured obligation, which would continue, involved little or no risk. The mortgage was released (a nontaxable event, see Lutz & Schramm Co. v. Commissioner, 1 T.C. 682, 689 (1943)), and the property was then sold to the third party. There can be no doubt that, under these circumstances, petitioners' loss would be [$27,300 ($72,700 amount realized less $100,000 adjusted basis)]. This scenario is, in substance, the same as exists herein; in both situations, the mortgage disappears as security and *the personal obligation of the petitioners to pay the balance of their recourse obligation survives.* [Emphasis added.]

In sum, we conclude that the $72,700 proceeds of the foreclosure sale constitute the "amount realized" under section 1001(a) and that consequently petitioners' loss was [$27,300 (the foreclosure sale proceeds of $72,700 less petitioners' basis of $100,000)].

NOTE

Hope springs eternal—pursuit of a deficiency judgment. In *Aizawa*, property with a value of $72,700 secured $90,000 of recourse debt. The lender foreclosed, sold the property for $72,700, and held Aizawa responsible for the $17,300 deficiency. As a result, the court held that Aizawa's amount realized on the foreclosure sale was only $72,700. In spite of Aizawa's financial problems, the lender secured a deficiency judgment, apparently believing that it could recover additional amounts from Aizawa. If the lender could not collect the deficiency from Aizawa and ultimately discharged the remaining debt, what would be the tax consequences to Aizawa? See IRC §§ 61(a)(11), 108 (discussed in Chapter 5).

IN PRACTICE

Deed in lieu of foreclosure. When property secures recourse debt that exceeds the value of the property, a lender will often conclude that it cannot extract additional funds from the borrower because of the borrower's weak financial position. In these circumstances, the lender might persuade the borrower to transfer the property voluntarily to the lender (in lieu of making the lender go through the cost and inconvenience of foreclosure proceedings) by agreeing to forego any deficiency; i.e., the lender will take the property in full satisfaction of the debt. As Example 6-P will demonstrate, the tax consequences to the borrower differ from those in *Aizawa* if the lender accepts the property in full satisfaction of the borrower's obligations.

■ **EXAMPLE 6-P.** *Transfer of property to lender in full satisfaction of recourse debt.* If the borrower in *Aizawa* had transferred the property to the lender in full satisfaction of the debt, the borrower still would have had an amount realized equal to the value of the property ($72,700) because that portion of the debt is being satisfied by the $72,700 value of the property. In addition, however, the borrower would be compelled to report discharge of indebtedness income of $17,300, the extent the amount of the debt ($90,000) exceeded the value of the transferred property ($72,700). See Reg §§ 1.1001–2(a)(2); –2(c) Example 8. If the borrower were bankrupt or insolvent (which is not unusual in these situations), the borrower could exclude all or part of the $17,300 of discharge of indebtedness income. See Chapter 5 (IRC § 108).

ii.   Nonrecourse Debt

When a debtor transfers underwater property securing *recourse* debt to the lender, the debtor's amount realized is limited to the value of the underwater property. This is the case regardless of whether the lender pursues a deficiency judgment (see Aizawa, above) or accepts the property in full satisfaction of the debt (see Example 6-P, above). By contrast, when a debtor transfers underwater property securing *nonrecourse* debt, the debtor's amount realized includes the full amount of the nonrecourse debt. The Tufts case addresses the tax consequences of a transfer of underwater property securing nonrecourse debt.

COMMISSIONER v. TUFTS

United States Supreme Court, 1983
461 U.S. 300, 103 S. Ct. 1826, 75 L.Ed.2d 863

JUSTICE BLACKMUN delivered the opinion of the Court.

Over 35 years ago, in Crane, this Court ruled that a taxpayer, who sold property encumbered by a nonrecourse mortgage (the amount of the mortgage being less than the property's value), must include the unpaid balance of the mortgage in the computation of the amount the taxpayer realized on the sale. The case now before us presents the question whether the same rule applies when the unpaid amount of the nonrecourse mortgage exceeds the fair market value of the property sold.

I

[John Tufts was an investor in a project] to construct a 120-unit apartment complex in Duncanville, Tex., a Dallas suburb. [Project financing was effectuated under] a mortgage loan agreement with the Farm & Home Savings Association (F & H). Under the agreement, F & H was committed for a $1,851,500 loan for the complex. [The loan was obtained] on a nonrecourse basis: neither [Tufts nor any of the other investors] assumed any personal liability for repayment of the loan.

The construction of the complex was completed in August 1971. During 1971, [Tufts and the other investors contributed $44,212 to the project and] claimed as income tax deductions * * * depreciation * * * in 1971 and 1972 [which] totaled $439,972. Due to these contributions and deductions, the adjusted basis in the property in August 1972 was $1,455,740.[14]

In 1971 and 1972, major employers in the Duncanville area laid off significant numbers of workers. As a result, the [project's] rental income was less than expected, and it was unable to make the payments due on the mortgage. [The project was sold] to an unrelated third party, Fred Bayles. As consideration, Bayles agreed to reimburse * * * sale expenses up to $250 * * *.

---

[14]   Editor's note: The adjusted basis of the property is calculated as follows:

Investor contributions	$44,212
+ Loan from F & H	1,851,500
Total cost	$1,895,712
– Depreciation	439,972
Adjusted basis	$1,455,740

On the date of transfer, the fair market value of the property did not exceed $1,400,000. [The taxpayers were of the view that a] loss of $55,740 had been sustained.[1] The Commissioner of Internal Revenue, on audit, determined that the sale resulted in a capital gain of approximately $400,000. His theory was that the [sellers] had realized the full amount of the nonrecourse obligation.[2]

[T]he United States Tax Court, in an unreviewed decision, upheld the asserted deficiencies. 70 T.C. 756 (1978). The United States Court of Appeals for the Fifth Circuit reversed. 651 F.2d 1058 (1981). * * * We granted certiorari to resolve [a conflict among the Circuits].

II

[S]ection 1001 governs the determination of gains and losses on the disposition of property. Under § 1001(a), the gain or loss from a sale or other disposition of property is defined as the difference between "the amount realized" on the disposition and the property's adjusted basis. Subsection (b) of § 1001 defines "amount realized": "The amount realized from the sale or other disposition of property shall be the sum of any money received plus the fair market value of the property (other than money) received." At issue is the application of the latter provision to the disposition of property encumbered by a nonrecourse mortgage of an amount in excess of the property's fair market value.

A

In Crane, this Court took the first and controlling step toward the resolution of this issue. [The Crane] Court concluded that [Crane's amount realized included the amount of the nonrecourse debt secured by the transferred property because] Crane obtained an economic benefit * * * identical to the benefit conferred by the cancellation of personal debt. Because the value of the property in that case exceeded the amount of the mortgage, it was in Crane's economic interest to treat the mortgage as a personal obligation; only by so doing could she realize upon sale the appreciation in her equity represented by the $2,500 boot. The [transfer of the property to the purchaser subject to] the liability thus resulted in a taxable economic benefit to her, just as if she had been given, in addition to the boot, a sum of cash sufficient to satisfy the mortgage.

---

[1]   The loss was the difference between the adjusted basis, $1,455,740, and the fair market value of the property, $1,400,000. On their individual tax returns, the [taxpayers] did not claim deductions for their respective shares of this loss. In their petitions to the Tax Court, however, the [taxpayers] did claim the loss.

[2]   The Commissioner determined the [approximately $400,000] gain on the sale by subtracting the adjusted basis, $1,455,740, from the liability [the property secured], $1,851,500. * * *

In [footnote 37, the Crane] Court observed:

Obviously, if the value of the property is less than the amount of the mortgage, a mortgagor who is not personally liable cannot realize a benefit equal to the mortgage. Consequently, a different problem might be encountered where a mortgagor abandoned the property or transferred it subject to the mortgage without receiving boot. That is not this case.

B

This case presents that unresolved issue. We are disinclined to overrule *Crane*, and we conclude that the same rule applies when the unpaid amount of the nonrecourse mortgage exceeds the value of the property transferred. Crane ultimately does not rest on its limited theory of economic benefit; instead, we read Crane to have approved the Commissioner's decision to treat a nonrecourse mortgage in this context as a true loan. This approval underlies *Crane*'s holdings that the amount of the nonrecourse liability is to be included in calculating both the basis and the amount realized on disposition. That the amount of the loan exceeds the fair market value of the property thus becomes irrelevant.

When a taxpayer receives a loan, he incurs an obligation to repay that loan at some future date. Because of this obligation, the loan proceeds do not qualify as income to the taxpayer. When he fulfills the obligation, the repayment of the loan likewise has no effect on his tax liability.

Another consequence to the taxpayer from this obligation occurs when the taxpayer applies the loan proceeds to the purchase price of property used to secure the loan. Because of the obligation to repay, the taxpayer is entitled to include the amount of the loan in computing his basis in the property; the loan, under § 1012, is part of the taxpayer's cost of the property. Although a different approach might have been taken with respect to a nonrecourse mortgage loan, the Commissioner has chosen to accord it the same treatment he gives to a recourse mortgage loan. The Court approved that choice in Crane, and the respondents do not challenge it here. The choice and its resultant benefits to the taxpayer are predicated on the assumption that the mortgage will be repaid in full.

When [property] encumbered [by nonrecourse debt] is sold or otherwise disposed of***, the associated extinguishment of the mortgagor's obligation to repay is accounted for in the computation of the amount realized. Because no difference between recourse and nonrecourse obligations is recognized in calculating basis, Crane teaches that the Commissioner may ignore the nonrecourse nature of the obligation in determining the amount realized upon disposition of the encumbered property. He thus may include in the amount realized the amount of the nonrecourse [loan secured by the transferred property]. The rationale for this treatment is that the original inclusion of the amount of the mortgage in basis rested on the assumption that the mortgagor incurred an obligation to repay. Moreover, this treatment balances the fact that the mortgagor originally received the proceeds of the nonrecourse loan tax-free on the same assumption. Unless the outstanding amount of the mortgage is deemed to be realized, the mortgagor effectively will have received untaxed income at the time the loan was extended and will have received an unwarranted increase in the basis of his property. The Commissioner's interpretation of § 1001(b) in this fashion cannot be said to be unreasonable.

<h2 style="text-align:center">C</h2>

[R]espondents received a mortgage loan with the concomitant obligation to repay by the year 2012. The only difference between that mortgage and one on which the borrower is personally liable is that the mortgagee's remedy is limited to foreclosing on the securing property. This difference does not alter the nature of the obligation; its only effect is to shift from the borrower to the lender any potential loss caused by devaluation of the property. If the fair market value of the property falls below the amount of the outstanding obligation, the mortgagee's ability to protect its interests is impaired, for the mortgagor is free to abandon the property to the mortgagee and be relieved of his obligation.

This, however, does not erase the fact that the mortgagor received the loan proceeds tax-free and included them in his basis on the understanding that he had an obligation to repay the full amount. When the obligation is canceled, the mortgagor is relieved of his responsibility to repay the sum he originally received and thus realizes value to that extent within the meaning of § 1001(b). * * *

[I]n the specific circumstances of Crane, the economic benefit theory did support the Commissioner's treatment of the nonrecourse mortgage as a personal obligation. The footnote in *Crane* acknowledged the limitations of that theory when applied to a different set of facts. Crane also stands for the broader proposition, however, that a nonrecourse loan should be treated as a true loan. We therefore hold that a taxpayer must account for the proceeds of obligations he has received tax-free and included in basis. Nothing in either § 1001(b) or in the Court's prior decisions requires the Commissioner to permit a taxpayer to treat a sale of encumbered property asymmetrically, by including the proceeds of the nonrecourse obligation in basis but not accounting for the proceeds upon transfer of the encumbered property.

* * *

IV

When a taxpayer sells or disposes of property encumbered by a nonrecourse obligation, the Commissioner properly requires him to include among the assets realized the outstanding amount of the obligation. The fair market value of the property is irrelevant to this calculation. We find this interpretation to be consistent with Crane * * *.

The judgment of the Court of Appeals is therefore reversed.

Justice O'Connor, concurring.

I concur in the opinion of the Court, accepting the view of the Commissioner. I do not, however, endorse the Commissioner's view. Indeed, were we writing on a slate clean except for the *Crane* decision, I would take quite a different approach * * *.

Crane established that a taxpayer could treat property as entirely his own, in spite of the "co-investment" provided by his mortgagee in the form of a nonrecourse loan. That is, the full basis of the property, with all its tax consequences, belongs to the mortgagor. That rule alone, though, does not in any way tie nonrecourse debt to the cost of property or to the proceeds upon disposition. I see no reason to treat the purchase, ownership, and eventual disposition of property differently because the taxpayer also takes out a mortgage, an independent transaction. In this case, the taxpayer purchased property, using nonrecourse financing, and sold it after it declined in value to a buyer who assumed the mortgage. There is no economic difference between the events in this case and a case in which the taxpayer buys property with cash; later obtains a nonrecourse loan by pledging the property as security; still later, using cash on hand, buys off the mortgage for the market value of the devalued property; and finally sells the property to a third party for its market value.

The logical way to treat both this case and the hypothesized case is to separate the two aspects of these events and to consider, first, the ownership and sale of the property, and, second, the arrangement and retirement of the loan.

Under Crane, the fair market value of the property on the date of acquisition the purchase price—represents the taxpayer's basis in the property, and the fair market value on the date of disposition represents the proceeds on sale. The benefit received by the taxpayer in return for the property is the cancellation of a mortgage that is worth no more than the fair market value of the property, for that is all the mortgagee can expect to collect on the mortgage. His gain or loss on the disposition of the property equals the difference between the proceeds and the cost of acquisition. Thus, the taxation of the transaction *in property* reflects the economic fate of the *property*. If the property has declined in value, as was the case here, the taxpayer recognizes a loss on the disposition of the property. The new purchaser then takes as his basis the fair market value as of the date of the sale.

In the separate borrowing transaction, the taxpayer acquires cash from the mortgagee. He need not recognize income at that time, of course, because he also incurs an obligation to repay the money. Later, though, when he is able to satisfy the debt by surrendering property that is worth less than the face amount of the debt, we have a classic situation of cancellation of indebtedness, requiring the taxpayer to recognize income in the amount of the difference between the proceeds of the loan and the amount for which he is able to satisfy his creditor. The taxation of the financing transaction then reflects the economic fate of the loan.

The reason that separation of the two aspects of the events in this case is important is, of course, that the Code treats different sorts of income differently. A gain on the sale of the property may qualify for capital gains treatment, §§ 1202, 1221, while the cancellation of indebtedness is ordinary income, but income that the taxpayer may be able to defer. §§ 108, 1017. * * *

Persuaded though I am by the logical coherence and internal consistency of [the approach I delineated above], I agree with the Court's decision not to adopt it judicially. We do not write on a slate marked only by Crane. The Commissioner's longstanding position is now reflected in the regulations. Treas.Reg. § 1.1001–2, 26 CFR § 1.1001–2 (1982). * * * As the Court's opinion demonstrates, [the Commissioner's] interpretation is defensible. One can reasonably read § 1001(b)'s reference to "the amount realized *from* the sale or other disposition of property" (emphasis added) to permit the Commissioner to collapse the two aspects of the transaction. As long as his view is a reasonable reading of § 1001(b), we should defer to the regulations promulgated by the agency charged with interpretation of the statute. Accordingly, I concur.

■ **EXAMPLE 6-Q.** *Transfer of property securing nonrecourse debt in excess of the value of the property.* If the property in the Aizawa case (p. 166) had secured nonrecourse debt (rather than recourse debt) and the borrower transferred the property, the entire debt ($90,000) would be included in the borrower's amount realized (and result in § 61(a)(3) income, to the extent the amount realized exceeded the borrower's adjusted basis in the property). Tufts; Reg. §§ 1.1001–2(a)(1), –2(a)(4)(i), –2(b). Moreover, the borrower would *not* have discharge of indebtedness income in this situation. Thus, the borrower cannot exclude any part of the $90,000 amount realized (potential § 61(a)(3) income) even if the borrower is bankrupt or insolvent because only discharge of indebtedness income (§ 61(a)(11) income) can be excluded under § 108. Compare Example 6-P.

IN SIGHTS **Recourse and nonrecourse debt treated differently when underwater property is transferred.** In light of the Tufts case, when property securing *nonrecourse debt* in excess of the value of the property is transferred, the full amount of the debt is included in the transferor's amount realized and the transferor has no discharge of indebtedness income. By contrast, when property securing *recourse* debt in excess of the value of the property is transferred, the transferor's amount realized is limited to the value of the property. In addition, the difference between the amount of the debt and the value of the property is taxed as discharge of indebtedness income (if the excess amount of the debt is extinguished). See Example 6-P. Thus, the *only* situation we have seen where the tax law treats recourse debt and nonrecourse debt differently is the transfer of property securing *debt in excess of the value of the property.* By contrast, we have seen several situations where recourse debt and nonrecourse debt are treated alike, namely,

 i)   at the time of the borrowing (see Chapter 5),

 ii)   when a debt is discharged (see Chapter 5), and

 iii) when *property with a value in excess of the debt* it secures is transferred (see pp. 153–165).

NOTES

1.   *Magnitude of depreciation deductions.* In the third paragraph of the Tufts opinion, the Court states: "During 1971, [Tufts and the other investors contributed $44,212 to the project and] claimed as income tax deductions * * * depreciation * * * in 1971 and 1972 [which] totaled $439,972." How could the investors claim $440,000 of depreciation deductions when they only invested $44,000?

2.   *No loss claimed.* The tax position taken by the investors in Tufts led to a realized loss of $55,470 on the sale of the property ($1,400,000 amount realized less $1,455,740 adjusted basis). Footnote 1 of the case indicates that the investors did not claim a deduction for this loss on their tax returns. Assuming that the loss was a permissible deduction (an issue examined in Chapter 10), it is worth contemplating why the investors refrained from deducting the loss. Note that the investors were taking a very aggressive tax position in claiming that the nonrecourse debt in excess of the value of the property had no tax effect (i.e., did not trigger any form of income to them) when they disposed of the property. Claiming a tax loss on the sale of the property would probably have highlighted their aggressive position. Thus, they might have refrained from claiming the relatively small loss in the hope that not claiming the loss would reduce the likelihood of an audit. Nevertheless, an audit occurred and the rest is history.

■ **EXAMPLE 6-R.** *Comparison of transfer of underwater property securing recourse debt with transfer of underwater property securing nonrecourse debt.* Sander purchased a parcel of land for $20,000 that has a current fair market value of $70,000. The land secures $80,000 of debt. What are the tax consequences to Sander if he transfers the land to the lender in full satisfaction of the debt?

Debt is a Recourse Liability		Debt is a Nonrecourse Liability	
Section 61(a)(3) Income		Section 61(a)(3) Income	
Realization Event		Realization Event	
Amount Realized:	$70,000 *	Amount Realized:	$80,000 **
– Adjusted Basis:	20,000	– Adjusted Basis:	20,000
Realized Gain:	$50,000	Realized Gain:	$60,000
Section 61(a)(11) Income		Section 61(a)(11) Income	
$10,000 (Debt – Value of Property)		None	

    * Value of property   ** Amount of debt

[handwritten note in margin:]
300 Value
500 debt
200 ₪

■ **PROBLEM 6-9.** *Recourse debt vs. nonrecourse debt.* Nicole owns property with a value of $300,000 that secures $500,000 of debt. What is Nicole's amount realized and how much discharge of indebtedness income does she have if—

a) the debt secured by the property is recourse, the lender forecloses on the property, and the lender secures a deficiency judgment? See *Aizawa.*

b) the debt secured by the property is recourse and Nicole voluntarily transfers the property to the lender in full satisfaction of her obligations to the lender (i.e., the lender does not seek a deficiency judgment)? See Example 6-P; Reg §§ 1.1001–2(a)(2), –2(c) Example 8.

c)   the debt secured by the property is nonrecourse and—

  1)   Nicole transfers the property to a third party who pays her
       $1,000? See *Tufts*, Example 6-Q.

  2)   the lender forecloses on the property? See Reg. §§ 1.1001–2(a)(1),
       –2(a)(4)(i), –2(b).

d)   How does the answer to c)1) change if—

  1)   Nicole receives no payment from the transferee?

  2)   Nicole pays the transferee $1,000 to take the property off her
       hands?

SYNTHESIS

Unlike all other types of gross income, which are triggered when the taxpayer's wealth increases, IRC § 61(a)(3) income is not triggered until a realization event occurs. A realization event cannot occur until property is transferred. In addition, the transferor must receive a quantifiable benefit (e.g., money, other property or services) in return for the property.

Unlike all other types of gross income, which are measured by the amount of money or the fair market value of any property received, IRC § 61(a)(3) income is quantified by reducing the consideration received (amount realized) by the adjusted basis of the transferred property. A taxpayer's initial basis is determined when property is acquired. Generally, the property's initial basis is its "cost" (i.e., the dollars invested in the property that were previously subject to income tax when they were earned). A "cost" basis ensures that the taxpayer is not taxed a second time on dollars that were previously subject to tax.

When wasting property is used in a trade or business, or held for the production of income, a portion of the basis is allowed as a depreciation deduction each year and, correspondingly, the basis is adjusted downward by the allowable deduction. The remaining adjusted basis (or all the basis if the property is not eligible for depreciation) offsets the taxpayer's amount realized to quantify gain or loss when a realization event occurs.

If property securing recourse debt is sold when the value of the property exceeds the amount of the debt and the buyer assumes the debt, the seller includes the entire debt (along with any additional consideration) in the seller's amount realized. The same result occurs when property securing nonrecourse debt with a value in excess of the debt is sold.

When property with a value that is less than the recourse debt it secures ("underwater property") is transferred to the lender in satisfaction of the debt, the seller's amount realized is limited to the value of the underwater property. In this situation, the difference between the amount of the recourse debt and the value of the property is treated as discharge of indebtedness income (§ 61(a)(11) income). By contrast, if underwater property securing nonrecourse debt is transferred, the entire debt is included in the amount realized (the same result as when the value of property securing nonrecourse debt is greater than the amount of the debt). No discharge of indebtedness income is triggered when property securing nonrecourse debt is transferred.

Two other unique features of § 61(a)(3) income are explored in later chapters ("recognition" in Chapter 12, and "characterization" in Chapter 16).

Test Your Knowledge: To assess your understanding of the material in this chapter, **click here** to take a quiz.

CHAPTER 7

Benefits Received by a Physically Injured Party—§ 104(a)(2)

Overview

In the first year of law school, students read many torts cases where plaintiffs recover damages for their injuries. At that time, students normally do not consider whether the recoveries by these plaintiffs constitute gross income. In this course, however, students should be thinking that any recovery in a personal injury case is a benefit and, therefore, constitutes gross income, unless an exclusion applies. By virtue of IRC § 104(a)(2), personal injury recoveries are often, but not always excluded, from gross income.

Primary Law: IRC § 104(a)

[G]ross income does not include—

* * *

(2)   the amount of any damages (other than punitive damages) received (whether by suit or agreement and whether as lump sums or as periodic payments) on account of personal physical injury or physical sickness;

* * *

A. Physical Injury vs. Emotional Distress

STEPP v. COMMISSIONER

United States Tax Court, 2017
T.C. Memo. 2017–191

Paris, Judge: * * *

FINDINGS OF FACT

* * *

From 2004 through the year in issue, Mrs. Stepp worked for the Transportation Security Administration (TSA). She performed duties as a baggage screener until January 2006 when she tore her left rotator cuff in an on-the-job incident. Mrs. Stepp requested and received compensation for this injury under the worker's compensation program and returned to her baggage screening position in November of 2006.

During 2006 and 2007 TSA management at the airport where Mrs. Stepp worked began to involuntarily reassign female baggage screeners to passenger screening. Mrs. Stepp was informed on June 23, 2007, that she was among those reassigned. She contacted an EEO counselor on several occasions, protesting the gender-based reassignment, and raised the issue with her managers. She also made numerous requests to remain in baggage screening because of her shoulder injury and the resulting mobility difficulties she experienced. These requests were denied.

Mrs. Stepp requested that reasonable accommodations be made because the limited mobility from her prior injury affected her ability to properly perform some of the passenger screening duties. Before TSA denied her request, however, she became the target of reprisal for engaging in protected EEO activities and opposing discriminatory practices. Her supervisors created a hostile work environment that subjected Mrs. Stepp to emotional harm and undue stress.

On January 5, 2008, Mrs. Stepp filed a formal EEO complaint against TSA and the U.S. Department of Homeland Security under the administrative guidelines of the U.S. Equal Employment Opportunity Commission (EEOC). She supplemented her initial complaint on January 12, 2010, adding claims of gender discrimination, disability discrimination, harassment, retaliation, and hostile work environment against TSA. [M]rs. Stepp did not allege that she had suffered any physical injury.

On March 24, 2011, the EEOC issued its decision. The decision described each of Mrs. Stepp's claims as "broad claims of retaliation, gender discrimination, and disability discrimination in connection with * * * [her] involuntary reassignment in July 2007 from baggage screener to passenger screener." None of the issues framed in the issues section included a claim for physical injury or personal sickness-related damages.

The decision concluded that TSA had subjected Mrs. Stepp to "a hostile work environment based on reprisal for engaging in protected EEO activities and/or opposing discriminatory practices." It also found TSA's misclassification of Mrs. Stepp's medical status and failure to timely process her request for reasonable accommodations to be part of a hostile work environment, which caused her emotional harm and stress. * * * But other than finding that Mrs. Stepp had already received worker's compensation for her torn rotator cuff and that she alleged that she injured her other shoulder, the decision made no finding concerning any type of physical injury.

After the EEOC issued its decision, Mrs. Stepp reached a monetary settlement with TSA. The settlement agreement stated that she would withdraw with prejudice her EEOC complaint that was the subject of the EEOC decision as well as "any other pending informal or formal complaints filed with * * * [TSA] and allegations of hostile work environment, harassment, retaliatory harassment, gender and disability discrimination, and retaliation." In return, TSA would (among other things) pay Mrs. Stepp a lump sum of $121,500. The agreement recited her understanding that she bore sole responsibility for "compliance with all federal, state and local tax requirements" and "any federal or state income taxes she may owe as the result of her receipt of the lump sum settlement amount."

Mrs. Stepp and TSA executed this settlement agreement in early August 2011, resolving all issues between them, and she filed a motion to dismiss the EEOC complaint. * * * The settlement agreement made no reference to "physical injury" or "personal illness".

Petitioners timely filed their Form 1040, U.S. Individual Income Tax Return, for 2011. Before preparing this return, they received from the U.S. Department of Homeland Security a Form 1099-MISC, Miscellaneous Income, reporting a $121,500 payment from the litigation settlement. Petitioners reported the settlement income on their return but deducted [$121,500] as "PERSONAL INJURY REIMBURSEMENT", effectively excluding the settlement proceeds from their gross income. After a document-matching examination revealed this discrepancy, the IRS issued petitioners a timely notice of deficiency for 2011, determining that the $121,500 payment should have been included in gross income. Petitioners timely petitioned this Court, contending that the $121,500 payment was excludable from gross income under section 104(a)(2).

OPINION

* * *

Section 61(a) defines "gross income" as "all income from whatever source derived". This definition has broad scope, and exclusions from gross income must be narrowly construed. Commissioner v. Glenshaw Glass Co., 348 U.S. 426, 429 (1955). Litigation settlement proceeds constitute gross income unless the taxpayer proves that the proceeds fall within a specific statutory exclusion.

The exclusion from gross income upon which petitioners rely appears in section 104(a)(2). It provides that gross income does not include "the amount of any damages * * * received (whether by suit or agreement * * *) on account of personal physical injuries or physical sickness." Congress intended this exclusion to cover damages that flow from a physical injury or physical sickness. For this purpose, "emotional distress shall not be treated as a physical injury or physical sickness," sec. 104(a) (penultimate sentence), nor shall "mental anguish, humiliation and embarrassment" (citation omitted).

When damages are received under a settlement agreement, the nature of the claim that was the actual basis for the settlement determines whether the damages are excludable under section 104(a)(2). "The nature of the claim" is typically determined by reference to the terms of the agreement. The "key question" is: "In lieu of what were the damages awarded?". (citations omitted). If the agreement does not explicitly state which claims the payment was made to settle, the "dominant reason for [the payor's] making the payment" is critical. (citation omitted).

The intent of the payor is determined by taking into consideration all of the facts and circumstances, including the amount paid, the circumstances leading to the settlement, and the allegations in the injured party's complaint. "[T]he nature of underlying claims cannot be determined from a general release that is broad and inclusive." (citation omitted). And where there is a general release but no allocation of settlement proceeds among various claims, this Court has held that all settlement proceeds are includible in gross income.

Mrs. Stepp's complaints against TSA were expressed in a variety of formats over several years from 2007 to 2011. These included informal counseling with TSA EEO counselors, formal and informal internal complaints, a formal EEOC proceeding that entailed extensive discovery, and a settlement offer from TSA that Mrs. Stepp accepted. At every stage of these proceedings, Mrs. Stepp uniformly alleged as the bases for her complaints some combination of disability- or gender-based discrimination and reprisal for protected EEO activity. Mrs. Stepp points to the EEOC decision discussing her shoulder injuries as proof that the nature of her claims involved personal physical injury. But the EEOC opinion's discussion of her left shoulder injury—and her alleged right shoulder injury—was included to establish that she was "disabled" and therefore entitled to recover under the standards of the ADA Amendments Act of 2008.

The settlement agreement states that it is "in full and final satisfaction of all claims against the Agency." The nonpecuniary relief she secured was employment related and responded directly to her claims of discrimination. TSA promised to reassign Mrs. Stepp to baggage screening for a certain period, expunge any disciplinary marks relating to the EEOC case, and approve a certain quantity of leave that Mrs. Stepp would request. The settlement agreement mentions no personal injury or physical sickness and provides her no relief for such an injury or sickness.

* * *

The settlement agreement executed by the parties in August 2011 stated quite clearly what claims the payment was made to settle—namely, the claims of discrimination, harassment, retaliation, and hostile work environment that were the subject of the EEOC litigation. Looking more broadly at the dominant intent of the payor, the Court finds it clear from the record that TSA's dominant reason behind this agreement was to settle the EEOC litigation. The settlement documents nowhere refer to physical injury of any kind. And there is no suggestion in the broad and inclusive, general release clause that she had made, or was releasing the defendants from, any claim for damages on account of physical injury or physical sickness.[12]

---

[12]   Even assuming arguendo that some portion of TSA's settlement payment was intended by TSA to compensate Mrs. Stepp for her shoulder injuries, she has not shown the extent to which the settlement proceeds were allocated among her many claims.

This Court has considerable sympathy for Mrs. Stepp's position. She endured great indignities in her workplace and undoubtedly suffered consequential emotional distress for a very long period. But Congress has limited the section 104(a)(2) exclusion from gross income to damages received "on account of personal physical injuries or physical sickness", and Congress explicitly provided that "emotional distress shall not be treated as a physical injury or physical sickness." "Damages received on account of emotional stress, even when resultant physical symptoms occur, are not excluded from income under section 104(a)(2)." (citation omitted). Petitioners have not carried their burden of proving that any portion of the settlement proceeds was paid on account of "physical injury" thus defined. The Court accordingly has no alternative but to conclude that the $121,500 payment reported on the Form 1099-MISC was includible in full in petitioners' gross income for 2012.

Notes

1. *Stating the claim.* If a taxpayer files a complaint against a party whom she believes caused her physical injury or physical sickness, how important is it, from an income tax standpoint, to explicitly state that claim in the complaint? How likely is it that the plaintiff will be successful in attributing payments made by a defendant to a physical injury if the defendant was not even made aware of the alleged harm?

2. *Securing the evidence.* What evidence might a taxpayer secure to persuade a court that a physical injury had occurred?

3. *Drafting the settlement agreement.* In a case involving both emotional distress and physical harm, what advice would you offer a personal injury lawyer in connection with drafting the settlement agreement?

4. *Language of release.* In a case involving an alleged physical injury, what advice would you offer the personal injury lawyer with regard to the language used in the release?

5. *Why did taxpayer claim a deduction rather than an exclusion?* Rather than excluding the recovery from her gross income, taxpayer reported the recovery and then claimed an offsetting deduction to eliminate her tax liability. As you

will see in future chapters, no grounds existed for the taxpayer to claim a deduction. Why did she not simply exclude the recovery from her gross income?

6.   *Physical manifestations resulting from emotional distress.* In Sanford v. Commissioner, T.C. Memo 2008–158, a U.S. postal service employee who had been the victim of sexual harassment attempted to exclude a settlement payment on the ground that the damages were for physical sickness. The court stated:

> The EEOC decision noted, and we acknowledge, that the sexual harassment petitioner suffered caused her emotional distress. We further acknowledge, as did the EEOC, that the emotional distress manifested itself in physical symptoms such as asthma, sleep deprivation, skin irritation, appetite loss, severe headaches, and depression. These physical symptoms were not the basis of the award petitioner received, however. Petitioner sought, and was awarded, relief for sexual harassment, discrimination based on sex, and the failure of the USPS to take appropriate corrective action.

> The EEOC and USPS decisions and orders compensated petitioner for the emotional distress she suffered because of the sexual harassment she experienced at work and her employer's failure to take appropriate corrective action. Despite her argument to the contrary, petitioner was not compensated for the physical symptoms she experienced as a result. *Damages received on account of emotional distress, even when resultant physical symptoms occur, are not excludable from income under section 104(a)(2).* (Emphasis added.)

As the Sanford case illustrates, unless a taxpayer suffering both emotional distress and physical harm can demonstrate that some portion of the damages she receives are compensation for physical harm, the taxpayer cannot exclude any part of the recovery.

■   **PROBLEM 7-1.**   *Physical injury vs. emotional distress.* Sharon was bullied at her place of employment for several years and underwent extensive therapy to help her cope with a stressful work environment. Sharon eventually developed an ulcer presumably from the stress in her work life. The medicine she took for the ulcer made her groggy and, as a result, she tripped and broke her leg. Sharon sued her employer for damages.

a)   A jury awarded Sharon $50,000 for the stress caused by her hostile work environment, $50,000 for the ulcer, and $50,000 for her broken leg. What are the tax consequences of the award to Sharon?

b)   If, instead of allowing the case to reach the jury, Sharon's employer settled the case for a lump sum payment of $100,000, what are the tax consequences of the settlement to Sharon?

B.   Allocation of Damages

AMOS v. COMMISSIONER

United States Tax Court, 2003
T.C. Memo. 2003–329

MEMORANDUM FINDINGS OF FACT AND OPINION

CHIECHI, JUDGE:

* * *

FINDINGS OF FACT

* * *

During 1997, petitioner was employed as a television camera man. In that capacity, on January 15, 1997, petitioner was operating a handheld camera during a basketball game between the Minnesota Timberwolves and the Chicago Bulls. At some point during that game, Dennis Keith Rodman, who was playing for the Chicago Bulls, landed on a group of photographers, including petitioner, and twisted his ankle. Mr. Rodman then kicked petitioner. (We shall refer to the foregoing incident involving Mr. Rodman and petitioner as the incident.)

On January 15, 1997, shortly after the incident, petitioner was taken by ambulance for treatment at Hennepin County Medical Center. Petitioner informed the medical personnel at that medical center that he had experienced shooting pain to his neck immediately after having been kicked in the groin, but that such pain was subsiding. The Hennepin County medical personnel observed that petitioner was able to walk, but that he was limping and complained of experiencing pain. * * *

While petitioner was seeking treatment at Hennepin County Medical Center, he contacted Gale Pearson about representing him with respect to the incident. Ms. Pearson was an attorney who had experience in representing plaintiffs in personal injury lawsuits. After subsequent conversations and a meeting with petitioner, Ms. Pearson agreed to represent him with respect to the incident.

On January 15, 1997, after the incident and petitioner's visit to the Hennepin County Medical Center, petitioner filed a report with the Minneapolis Police Department. In the police report, petitioner claimed that Mr. Rodman had assaulted him.

* * *

Very shortly after the incident on a date not disclosed by the record, Andrew Luger, an attorney representing Mr. Rodman with respect to the incident, contacted Ms. Pearson. Several discussions and a few meetings took place between Ms. Pearson and Mr. Luger. Petitioner accompanied Ms. Pearson to one of the meetings between her and Mr. Luger, at which time Mr. Luger noticed that petitioner was limping. Shortly after those discussions and meetings, petitioner and Mr. Rodman reached a settlement.

On January 21, 1997, Mr. Rodman and petitioner executed a document entitled "CONFIDENTIAL SETTLEMENT AGREEMENT AND RELEASE". The settlement agreement provided in pertinent part:

> For and in consideration of TWO HUNDRED THOUSAND DOLLARS ($200,000), the mutual waiver of costs, attorneys' fees and legal expenses, if any, and other good and valuable consideration, the receipt and sufficiency of which is hereby acknowledged, Eugene Amos [petitioner], on behalf of himself, his agents, representatives, attorneys, assignees, heirs, executors and administrators, hereby releases and forever discharges Dennis Rodman, the Chicago Bulls, the National Basketball Association and all other persons, firms and corporations together with their subsidiaries, divisions and affiliates, past and present officers, directors, employees, insurers, agents, personal representatives and legal counsel, from any and all claims and

causes of action of any type, known and unknown, upon and by reason of any damage, loss or injury which heretofore have been or heretoafter may be sustained by Amos arising, or which could have arisen, out of or in connection with an incident occurring between Rodman and Amos at a game between the Chicago Bulls and the Minnesota Timberwolves on January 15, 1997 during which Rodman allegedly kicked Amos ("the Incident"), including but not limited to any statements made after the Incident or subsequent conduct relating to the Incident by Amos, Rodman, the Chicago Bulls, the National Basketball Association, or any other person, firm or corporation, or any of their subsidiaries, divisions, affiliates, officers, directors, employees, insurers, agents, personal representatives and legal counsel. This Agreement and Release includes, but is not limited to claims, demands, or actions arising under the common law and under any state, federal or local statute, ordinance, regulation or order, including claims known or unknown at this time, concerning any physical, mental or emotional injuries that may arise in the future allegedly resulting from the Incident.

* * *

It is further understood and agreed that the payment of the sum described herein is not to be construed as an admission of liability and is a compromise of a disputed claim. It is further understood that part of the consideration for this Agreement and Release includes an agreement that Rodman and Amos shall not at any time from the date of this Agreement and Release forward disparage or defame each other.

It is further understood and agreed that, as part of the consideration for this Agreement and Release, the terms of this Agreement and Release shall forever be kept confidential and not released to any news media personnel or representatives thereof or to any other person, entity, company, government agency, publication or judicial authority for any reason whatsoever except to the extent necessary to report the sum paid to appropriate taxing authorities or in response to any subpoena issued by a state or federal governmental agency or court of competent jurisdiction * * * Any court reviewing a subpoena concerning this Agreement and Release should be aware that part of the consideration for the Agreement and Release is the agreement of Amos and his attorneys not to testify regarding the existence of the Agreement and Release or any of its terms.

* * *

It is further understood and agreed that Amos and his representatives, agents, legal counsel or other advisers shall not, from the date of this Agreement and Release, disclose, disseminate, publicize or instigate or solicit any others to disclose, disseminate or publicize, any of the allegations or facts relating to the Incident, including but not limited to any allegations or facts or opinions relating to Amos' potential claims against Rodman or any allegations, facts or opinions relating to Rodman's conduct on the night of January 15, 1997 or thereafter concerning Amos. In this regard, Amos agrees not to make any further public statement relating to Rodman or the Incident or to grant any interviews relating to Rodman or the Incident. * * *

* * *

Amos further represents, promises and agrees that no administrative charge or claim or legal action of any kind has been asserted by him or on his behalf in any way relating to the Incident with the exception of a statement given by Amos to the Minneapolis Police Department. Amos further represents, promises and agrees that, as part of the consideration for this Agreement and Release, he has communicated to the Minneapolis Police Department that he does not wish to pursue a criminal charge against Rodman, and that he has communicated that he will not cooperate in any criminal investigation concerning the Incident. Amos further represents, promises and agrees that he will not pursue any criminal action against Rodman concerning the Incident, that he will not cooperate should any such action or investigation ensue, and that he will not encourage, incite or solicit others to pursue a criminal investigation or charge against Rodman concerning the Incident.

Petitioner filed a tax return for his taxable year 1997. In that return, petitioner excluded from his gross income the $200,000 that he received from Mr. Rodman under the settlement agreement.

In the notice that respondent issued to petitioner with respect to 1997, respondent determined that petitioner is not entitled to exclude from his gross income the settlement amount at issue.

OPINION

We must determine whether the settlement amount at issue may be excluded from petitioner's gross income for 1997. Petitioner bears the burden of proving that the determination in the notice to include the settlement amount at issue in petitioner's gross income is erroneous.

Section 61(a) provides the following sweeping definition of the term "gross income":

> Except as otherwise provided in this subtitle, gross income means all income from whatever source derived.

Not only is section 61(a) broad in its scope, exclusions from gross income must be narrowly construed.

Section 104(a)(2) on which petitioner relies provides that gross income does not include:

> (2)   the amount of any damages (other than punitive damages) received (whether by suit or agreement and whether as lump sums or as periodic payments) on account of personal physical injuries or physical sickness;
>
> * * *

Where damages are received pursuant to a settlement agreement, such as is the case here, the nature of the claim that was the actual basis for settlement controls whether such damages are excludable under section 104(a)(2). The determination of the nature of the claim is factual. Where there is a settlement agreement, that determination is usually made by reference to it. If the settlement agreement lacks express language stating what the amount paid pursuant to that agreement was to settle, the intent of the payor is critical to that determination. Although the belief of the payee is relevant to that inquiry, the character of the settlement payment hinges ultimately on the dominant reason of the payor in making the payment. Whether the settlement payment is excludable from gross income under section 104(a)(2) depends on the nature and character of the claim asserted, and not upon the validity of that claim.

The dispute between the parties in the instant case relates to how much of the settlement amount at issue Mr. Rodman paid to petitioner on account of physical injuries. It is petitioner's position that the entire $200,000 settlement amount at issue is excludable from his gross income under section 104(a)(2). In support of that position, petitioner contends that Mr. Rodman paid him the entire amount on account of the physical injuries that he claimed he sustained as a result of the incident.

Respondent counters that, except for a nominal amount (i.e., $1), the settlement amount at issue is includable in petitioner's gross income. In support of that position, respondent contends that petitioner has failed to introduce any evidence regarding, and that Mr. Rodman was skeptical about, the extent of petitioner's physical injuries as a result of the incident. Consequently, according to respondent, the Court should infer that petitioner's physical injuries were minimal. * * *

On the instant record, we reject respondent's position. With respect to respondent's contentions that petitioner has failed to introduce evidence regarding, and that Mr. Rodman was skeptical about, the extent of petitioner's physical injuries as a result of the incident, those contentions appear to ignore the well-established principle under section 104(a)(2) that it is the nature and character of the claim settled, and not its validity, that determines whether the settlement payment is excludable from gross income under section 104(a)(2). * * *

On the record before us, we find that Mr. Rodman's dominant reason in paying the settlement amount at issue was to compensate petitioner for his claimed physical injuries relating to the incident. Our finding is supported by the settlement agreement [and] a declaration by Mr. Rodman.[6] * * *

The settlement agreement expressly provided that Mr. Rodman's payment of the settlement amount at issue—

> releases and forever discharges * * * [Mr.] Rodman * * * from any and all claims and causes of action of any type, known and unknown, upon and by reason of any damage, loss or injury * * * sustained by Amos [petitioner] arising, or which could have arisen, out of or in connection with * * * [the incident].

---

[6]   The parties introduced into evidence a declaration by Mr. Rodman, who did not appear as a witness at trial. The parties stipulated the accuracy and truthfulness of Mr. Rodman's statements in that declaration.

Mr. Rodman stated in Mr. Rodman's declaration that he entered into the settlement agreement "to resolve any potential claims" and that the settlement agreement was intended to resolve petitioner's "claim without having to expend additional defense costs." The only potential claims of petitioner that are disclosed by the record are the potential claims that petitioner had for the physical injuries that he claimed he sustained as a result of the incident. * * *

We have found that Mr. Rodman's dominant reason in paying petitioner the settlement amount at issue was to compensate him for his claimed physical injuries relating to the incident. However, the settlement agreement expressly provided that Mr. Rodman paid petitioner a portion of the settlement amount at issue in return for petitioner's agreement not to: (1) Defame Mr. Rodman, (2) disclose the existence or the terms of the settlement agreement, (3) publicize facts relating to the incident, or (4) assist in any criminal prosecution against Mr. Rodman with respect to the incident (collectively, the nonphysical injury provisions).

The settlement agreement does not specify the portion of the settlement amount at issue that Mr. Rodman paid petitioner on account of his claimed physical injuries and the portion of such amount that Mr. Rodman paid petitioner on account of the nonphysical injury provisions in the settlement agreement. Nonetheless, based upon our review of the entire record before us, and bearing in mind that petitioner has the burden of proving the amount of the settlement amount at issue that Mr. Rodman paid him on account of physical injuries, we find that Mr. Rodman paid petitioner $120,000

LOOK ONLINE For a video of the Amos incident, click here.

of the settlement amount at issue on account of petitioner's claimed physical injuries and $80,000 of that amount on account of the nonphysical injury provisions in the settlement agreement. On that record, we further find that for the year at issue petitioner is entitled under section 104(a)(2) to exclude from his gross income $120,000 of the settlement amount at issue and is required under section 61(a) to include in his gross income $80,000 of that amount. * * *

agreement becomes very critical

Notes

1. *Impact of allocation in settlement agreement between physical injuries and non-physical injuries.* The settlement agreement in Amos did not explicitly state how much of the $200,000 settlement was attributable to physical injuries and how much was attributable to non-physical injuries. As a result, the court made the determination. If the parties in Amos had made an explicit allocation of damages in the settlement agreement, how likely is it that the allocation made by the parties would have been respected for tax purposes? See Forest v. Commissioner, T.C. Memo 1995–397 (1995) ("In cases involving a settlement agreement which contains an express allocation, such allocation is generally the most important factor in deciding whether a payment was made on account of a [physical] personal injury for purposes of the exclusion under section 104(a)(2). It is well settled that express allocations in a settlement agreement will be respected to the extent that the agreement is entered into by the parties at arm's length and in good faith.").

2. *Relevance of plaintiff's tax consequences to defendant.* For what *economic* reason might a defendant in a personal injury case be inclined to agree to an allocation of a settlement amount in a manner that would minimize the tax liability of a plaintiff? *publicity, insurance doesn't cover punitive, plaintiff might settle for less if they can get it tax free*

C. Punitive Damages

IRC § 104(a)(2) does not permit the exclusion of punitive damages. In a case that might result in the award of punitive damages, how likely is it that a settlement agreement that allocates nothing to punitive damages will be respected? See Bagley v. Commissioner, 121 F.3d 393, 396 (8th Cir. 1997), where the court stated as follows:

> [T]he language of a negotiated settlement agreement that allocates nothing to punitive damages should not be lightly disregarded. Initially, however, we note that while the agreement in this case does not expressly allocate anything to punitive damages, it does not explicitly say that punitive damages are not part of the settlement. More importantly, the language of a settlement agreement cannot always be dispositive. It will almost never be to a defendant's advantage to allocate part of a lump-sum settlement to punitive damages, and it

will often be disadvantageous. Often, insurance policies will not cover such awards, and punitive-damage awards result in worse publicity than compensatory awards. Most plaintiffs will not want specific allocations to punitive damages in their settlement agreements, because punitive damages are taxable. Therefore, when the time comes to settle a case, no matter how adversarial the proceedings have been to that point, the parties will almost always be in agreement that no part of a settlement agreement should be explicitly allocated to punitive damages.

The Bagley court highlighted the facts of another case (McKay v. Commissioner, 102 T.C. 465 (1994)), vacated on other grounds, 84 F.3d 433 (5th Cir. 1996), in which a court upheld a settlement agreement that allocated nothing to punitive damages where—

1) evidence existed that the plaintiff desired a portion of the settlement proceeds to be allocated to punitive damages to publicize the defendant's unlawful activity (suggesting that the parties were truly adverse with respect to the issue of how to allocate the settlement proceeds),

2) the settlement agreement explicitly stated that none of the settlement was allocable to punitive damages (and that the parties' reached that conclusion based on their attorneys' estimates of the probability of appellate success on the punitive claims), and

3) the amount of the settlement (less the amount allocated to attorneys' fees) was less than the jury had awarded in compensatory damages, thus making it plausible that the defendant had agreed to pay only compensatory damages.

bc its non dedt to def.
? taxable to plaintiff

penative damages aren't excludable

■ **PROBLEM 7-2.** *Tax consequences of settlement to plaintiff.* How does IRC § 104(a)(2) impact the tax consequences *to Plaintiff* if Plaintiff and Defendant allocate $150,000 of a $200,000 settlement to compensatory damages and the other $50,000 of the settlement to punitive damages in a—

a)   breach of contract case?

b)   defamation case?

c)   "slip and fall" case?

d)   In which of the above cases would Plaintiff care about the allocation between compensatory and punitive damages? In this (these) case(s), what allocation would minimize Plaintiff's tax burden?

e)   What would determine whether an allocation that minimized Plaintiff's tax burden would be respected for tax purposes?

■ **PROBLEM 7-3.** *Tax consequences of settlement to defendant (reviews topics from prior chapters).* What are the tax consequences in Problem 7-2 *to Defendant* if, instead of transferring cash in settlement of Plaintiff's claim, Defendant—

a)   transferred property to Plaintiff with a value of $200,000 and an adjusted basis of $40,000? *basis ?*

b)   performed $200,000 worth of services for Plaintiff?

c)   allowed Plaintiff to occupy a building owned by Defendant rent-free for a year when the annual rent paid by the most recent tenant was $200,000?

SYNTHESIS

Like other benefits a taxpayer derives, damages received as compensation for a personal injury constitute gross income unless an exclusion applies. IRC § 104(a)(2) allows taxpayers to exclude recoveries for *physical* injury or *physical* sickness. Only compensation for physical harms may be excluded; damages received for *emotional* distress are included in gross income. When damages are received in a case where both emotional distress and physical harm exists, the taxpayer bears the burden of demonstrating the amount of the recovery intended to compensate the taxpayer for the physical harm. The taxpayer's case will be strongest when the complaint addresses the physical harm and the settlement agreement allocates a specific part of the recovery to the physical harm.

Punitive damages are never excludable. Thus, if any part of the damages received for a physical harm is punitive damages, that portion of the recovery will be included in gross income. Here again, when a settlement is reached in a case involving punitive damages, the settlement agreement should state what portion of the damages are intended to compensate the taxpayer for physical harm and what portion, if any, represents punitive damages.

Test Your Knowledge: To assess your understanding of the material in this chapter, <u>click here</u> to take a quiz.

CHAPTER 8

Benefits Not Constituting Gross Income

Overview

At this point in your study of gross income, you have probably developed a pattern of thinking that any benefit a taxpayer derives is gross income, unless a specific statutory exclusion applies. However, you have already seen two exceptions to the principle that a statutory exclusion is a necessary condition for negating gross income. In Chapter 4, you saw that the psychic benefits derived by a donor when making a gift are not within the scope of gross income because the income tax was not intended to capture this type of amorphous benefit. In Chapter 5, you saw that the receipt of borrowed funds does not constitute gross income. This result transpired because the tax law assumes a borrower will satisfy her repayment obligation and that obligation therefore offsets any benefit derived when borrowed funds are received. This Chapter will explore several additional non-statutory exceptions to gross income.

A. Return of Capital/Purchase Price Reduction

1.   Return of Capital

RAYTHEON PRODUCTION CORPORATION
v. COMMISSIONER

United States Court of Appeals, First Circuit, 1944
144 F.2d 110

MAHONEY, CIRCUIT JUDGE.

This case presents the question whether an amount received by the taxpayer in a compromise settlement of a suit for damages under the Federal Anti-Trust Laws is a * * * return of capital or income. * * *

[In] 1931, the petitioner [Raytheon Production Corporation brought] suit against [Radio Corporation of America, R.C.A.,] alleging that the plaintiff had by 1926 created and then possessed * * * a large and profitable established business [that manufactured and sold "rectifying tubes" making it possible for a radio to operate on alternating current rather than batteries;] that the business had an established prospect of large increases and that the business and good will[1] thereof was of a value of exceeding $3,000,000; that by the beginning of 1927 the plaintiff was doing approximately 80% of the business of rectifying tubes of the entire United States; that the defendant conspired to destroy the business of the plaintiff and others by a monopoly of such business and did suppress and destroy the existing companies; that the manufacturers of radio sets and others ceased to purchase tubes from the plaintiffs; that by the end of 1927 the conspiracy had completely destroyed the profitable business and that by the early part of 1928 the tube business of the plaintiff and its property and good will had been totally destroyed * * *.

[In 1938, Raytheon] began negotiations for the settlement of the litigation with R.C.A. * * * R.C.A. and the petitioner finally agreed on the payment by R.C.A. of $410,000 in settlement of the anti-trust action. * * *

---

[1]   Editor's note: The "good will" of a business is an intangible asset that arises when a business establishes a good reputation in the community and/or a history of profitability. In these circumstances, the value of the business exceeds the value of its tangible assets. The excess value ("premium") is attributable to good will and other intangible assets.

Damages recovered in an anti-trust action are not necessarily *** a return of capital. As in other types of tort damage suits, recoveries which represent a reimbursement for lost profits are income. The reasoning is that since the profits would be taxable income, the proceeds of litigation which are their substitute are taxable in like manner. [Thus,] damages for violation of the anti-trust acts are treated as ordinary income where they represent compensation for loss of profits.

[T]he question to be asked is "In lieu of what were the damages awarded?" Where the suit is not to recover lost profits but is for injury to good will, the recovery represents a return of capital and, with certain limitations to be set forth below, is not taxable.

Upon examination of Raytheon's declaration in its anti-trust suit we find nothing to indicate that the suit was for the recovery of lost profits. The allegations were that the illegal conduct of R.C.A.

> completely destroyed the profitable interstate and foreign commerce of the plaintiff and thereby, by the early part of 1928, the said tube business of the plaintiff and the property good will of the plaintiff therein had been totally destroyed * * *. [Citation omitted]

This was not the sort of antitrust suit where the plaintiff's business still exists and where the injury was merely for loss of profits. * * * Since the suit was to recover damages for the destruction of the business and good will, the recovery represents a return of capital. Nor does the fact that the suit ended in a compromise settlement change the nature of the recovery; "the determining factor is the nature of the basic claim from which the compromised amount was realized." Paul Selected Studies in Federal Taxation.

But, to say that the recovery represents a return of capital in that it takes the place of the business good will is not to conclude that it may not contain a taxable benefit. Although the injured party may not be deriving a profit as a result of the damage suit itself, the conversion thereby of his property into cash is a realization of any gain made over the cost or other basis of the good will prior to the illegal interference. Thus A buys Blackacre for $5,000. It appreciates in value to $50,000. B tortiously destroys it by fire. A sues and recovers $50,000 tort damages from B. Although no gain was derived by A from the suit, his prior gain due to the appreciation in value of Blackacre is realized when it is turned into cash by the money damages. [Thus, A realizes a gain of $45,000 with respect to the $50,000 of damages received.]

Compensation for the loss of Raytheon's good will in excess of its cost is gross income. * * *

The decision of the Tax Court is affirmed.

FOR DISCUSSION

Return of capital vs. compensation for lost profits. As a general rule, good will that arises in connection with the operation of a successful business (i.e., self-created good will) has a basis of zero.

a) If Raytheon had a basis of zero in the good will, how much gain would it have realized when it received the $416,000 settlement? *all of it*

b) If the court had found that the settlement represented the recovery of lost profits (rather than a payment for good will), how much income would Raytheon have derived from the settlement? *416k of income*

If you concluded that Raytheon would have had $416,000 of income in either case, it may not be apparent why the parties were at odds with one another. As you will learn in Chapter 16, gain derived from the sale of self-created goodwill is normally taxed at lower rates than gross income derived from business (section 61(a)(2)) because gain from the sale of self-created goodwill is characterized as capital gain.

---

2.   Purchase Price Reduction

Another context in which the return of capital principle applies is when the purchase price of goods is reduced. Undoubtedly, you have all purchased goods at a sale price. Assume you liked a pair of shoes being sold online for $100 but you did not want to pay that price. Suddenly, the website has a 30% off flash sale and you can now purchase the shoes for $70. If you purchase the shoes for $70, is the $30 discount you enjoyed gross income?

Fortunately for you, discounts are not treated as gross income. The discount simply reduces the purchase price (and the tax basis) of the product. If the discount were a discrete benefit independent of the purchase, it would constitute gross income. But the discount is directly connected to the purchase and its effect is merely to reduce the purchase price paid.

Are frequent flyer miles gross income or do they merely reduce the purchase price of a plane ticket? See IRS Announcement 2002–18 which follows.

IRS Announcement 2002–18

2002–10 I.R.B. 621
March 11, 2002

Most major airlines offer frequent flyer programs under which passengers accumulate miles for each flight. Individuals may also earn frequent flyer miles or other promotional benefits, for example, through rental cars or hotels. These promotional benefits may generally be exchanged for upgraded seating, free travel, discounted travel, travel-related services, or other services or benefits.

Questions have been raised concerning the taxability of frequent flyer miles or other promotional items that are received *as the result of business travel and used for personal purposes*. [Emphasis added.] There are numerous technical and administrative issues relating to these benefits on which no official guidance has been provided, including issues relating to the timing and valuation of income inclusions and the [manner of] identifying personal use benefits attributable to business (or official) expenditures versus those attributable to personal expenditures. Because of these unresolved issues, the IRS has not pursued a tax enforcement program with respect to promotional benefits such as frequent flyer miles.

Consistent with prior practice, the IRS will not assert that any taxpayer has understated his federal tax liability by reason of the receipts or personal use of frequent flyer miles or other in-kind promotional benefits attributable to the taxpayer's business or official travel. Any future guidance on the taxability of these benefits will be applied prospectively.

This relief does not apply to travel or other promotional benefits that are converted to cash, to compensation that is paid in the form of travel or other promotional benefits, or in other circumstances where these benefits are used for tax avoidance purposes.

* * *

NOTES

1.   *Frequent flier miles for business travel.* IRS Announcement 2002–18 address-es frequent flier miles from business travel that are used for personal purposes. The justification for not taxing the benefit a business owner or employee derives in these circumstances is unclear. It may be difficult to put a value on the miles and onerous to keep records of these awards. However, no conceptual justifi-cation exists for excluding this benefit from the gross income of an owner or employee.

2.   *Exceptions to general rule.* Why does IRS Announcement 2002–18 not apply to frequent flyer miles that are converted to cash? Why does the Announcement not apply to compensation that is paid in the form of travel? *tax avoidance*

3.   *Frequent flier miles for personal travel.* Announcement 2002–18 does not address frequent flyer miles earned from personal travel. Unlike miles received by an owner or employee for business travel, miles received by an individual who purchases travel with personal funds can be regarded as a reduction in the purchase price of the ticket. If you purchase a plane ticket for $420 and receive miles with a value of $20 as a result of that purchase, the miles, in substance, represent a reduction in your purchase price to $400. The purchase price paid and the miles awarded are not discrete; they are directly connected and reduce the purchase price of the ticket, rather than triggering gross income.

■ **PROBLEM 8-1.** *Auto incentives.* Mindy currently drives a six-year old Honda and she would like to move up to a new Acura. When she researched the purchase, she discovered the following incentives:

1)   Anyone who tests drives a new Acura will be given a $100 gift card. *purchase price adjustment*
      $100 income

2) Anyone who purchases a new Acura will qualify for a $2,000 rebate. PP ∽

3) Any current Honda owner who purchases a new Acura will qualify for an additional $1,000 rebate. PP∽

Mindy test drives an Acura and decides to purchase the car. The manufacturer's suggested retail price ("sticker price") of the car is $45,000, but Mindy pays the dealer only $28,000 due to the adjustments listed below. What are the tax consequences to Mindy of each adjustment?

a) Mindy negotiated a $4,000 discount from the sticker price, thereby reducing the amount she owed the dealer from $45,000 to $41,000.

b) Mindy negotiated a trade-in allowance of $10,000 for her Honda, thereby reducing the amount she owed the dealer from $41,000 to $31,000.

c) Mindy qualified for the $2,000 rebate available to any Acura purchaser (see 2), above) and the dealer credited her for that rebate, reducing the amount she owed the dealer from $31,000 to $29,000.

d) Mindy also qualified for the $1,000 rebate available only to current Honda owners (see 3), above) and the dealer credited her for that rebate, reducing the amount she owed the dealer from $29,000 to $28,000.

e) In addition, Mindy received the $100 gift card for test driving the new car (see 1), above).

f) If, instead of the dealer crediting Mindy for the rebates in c) and d), Mindy had paid the dealer $31,000 ($45,000, minus the $4,000 discount and the $10,000 trade-in allowance) and Mindy later received the rebates in the form of a $3,000 payment directly from Acura, would that $3,000 payment be gross income to her?

B. Imputed Income

As discussed in Chapter 5, when you use someone else's property or money, you normally must pay rent (in the case of property) or interest (in the case of money) for such use. The reason you must pay rent or interest is that the owner loses the opportunity to occupy her property or invest her money. Therefore, the owner expects to be compensated for losing the potential benefits she could otherwise derive from possessing the property or money.

When you use someone else's house or condominium, you derive a benefit from having a place to live but you pay rent which offsets that benefit and thereby precludes you from having gross income. If you occupy a house or condominium that you yourself own, you derive the same benefit of having a place to live that you derive when you use a house or condominium that someone else owns. But you do not pay rent for the use of your own house or condominium. Thus, the benefit derived from using your own house or condominium is not offset by a rent payment because you do not pay rent to yourself. Hence, a benefit is derived from the rent free use of a house you own or any other property that you own. This benefit is referred to as "imputed income."

As you might imagine, it would be administratively difficult, if not impossible, to tax imputed income. How would you quantify the daily benefits an individual derives from all the property she owns? Fortunately, although a taxpayer derives benefits from property she owns (because she does not pay herself rent), imputed income is *not* within the scope of gross income. Almost a century ago, the Supreme Court ruled that the rental value of property owned by a taxpayer does not constitute income within the meaning of the 16th amendment to the Constitution. Helvering v. Independent Life Insurance Co., 292 U.S. 371, 54 S. Ct. 758 (1934).

■ **PROBLEM 8-2.** *Imputed income.* Nisa repurposes old furniture into custom dining room tables that she sells to customers through a retail store and online.

a) Does Nisa derive gross income if she places one of the custom tables in the dining room of her home and she, her husband and her two young children eat their meals at the table? Do the husband and children derive gross income?

b) If Nisa makes a gift of one of the custom tables to her parents and they use the table in their home, does Nisa derive gross income? Do her parents derive gross income from using the table?

c) If Nisa places one of the custom tables in a stranger's home and the stranger eats his meals at the table, does the stranger derive gross income from using the table?

d) If Nisa purchased one of the old tables for $2,000 and, after repurposing the table, sells it for $20,000, does she derive § 61(a)(2) income or § 61(a)(3) income and how much?   *income derived from biz*

income derived from dealings w/ property

C. The General Welfare Exception

IRS Letter Ruling 201001013

Jan. 8, 2010

Dear _____:

This is in reply to your letter requesting a private letter ruling concerning whether certain housing benefits provided to employees of County C are excludable from gross income * * *.

FACTS

According to the facts submitted, County C and the Authority are political subdivisions of the State. The Authority is charged * * * with regulating the provision of safe, decent, and sanitary housing accommodations to County C residents of low and moderate income levels, in part through its Program B. Under this program, * * * affordable housing accommodations are made available to low and moderate income level individuals living or working in County C. In addition to Program B, the Authority has also established Program A to provide safe, decent and affordable short-term rental housing of modest standards to low and moderate income individuals who are enrolled in an employer-sponsored training program within County C, and who will likely succeed if given some additional supports, such as affordable housing assistance.

* * *

The housing/training assistance benefits provided under Program B and Program A to low and moderate income level County C trainees are made available to such employees on the same basis and for the same purposes as such benefits are extended to other county employee/trainees generally, and no benefits have been set aside specifically for County C employee/trainees. Benefits are awarded on a nondiscriminatory and nonpreferential selection basis among the class of eligible participants that includes both County C employees/trainees and employees of other county employers.

You have requested a ruling concerning whether the value of the housing benefits provided to individuals who are employees of County C governmental functions, under the Authority's Program A * * * and under Program B under the circumstances described above are excludable from the recipients' gross incomes for federal income tax purposes * * *.

LAW & ANALYSIS

Section 61(a) of the Internal Revenue Code provides that, except as otherwise provided by law, gross income means all income from whatever source derived. Under section 61, Congress intends to tax all gains or undeniable accessions to wealth, clearly realized, over which taxpayers have complete dominion. Commissioner v. Glenshaw Glass Co., 348 U.S. 426 (1955).

Although section 61 provides for broad includibility in gross income, the Internal Revenue Service (IRS) has consistently held that payments to individuals by governmental units under legislatively provided social benefit programs for promotion of the general welfare, that do not represent compensation for services, are excludable from the recipient's gross income ("general welfare exclusion").

The general welfare exclusion applies only to governmental payments out of a welfare fund based upon the recipients' identified need and not where made as compensation for services. See, e.g., Rev. Rul. 57–102, 1957–1 C.B. 26 (payments to the blind); Rev. Rul. 74–74, 1974–1 C.B. 18 (awards to crime victims or their dependents); Rev. Rul. 74–205, 1974–1 C.B. 20 (replacement housing payments under the Housing and Urban Development Act of 1968 to aid displaced individuals and families); Rev. Rul. 75–271, 1975–2 C.B. 23 (assistance payments for lower income families to acquire homes); Rev. Rul. 76–395, 1976–2 C.B. 16 (home rehabilitation grants to low-income recipients); Rev. Rul. 77–77, 1977–1 C.B. 11 (payments to Indians to stimulate and expand Indian-owned economic enterprises); and Rev. Rul. 98–19, 1998–15 I.R.B. 5 (relocation payments made to flood victims).

Rev. Rul. 98–19 and Rev. Rul. 76–373 concern the taxation of relocation payments under Title I of the Housing and Community Development Act of 1974 ("1974 Act"), which has the primary objective of developing viable urban communities by providing decent housing and a suitable living environment and expanding economic opportunities, principally for persons of low and moderate income. Rev. Rul. 98–19 holds that the payments authorized by the 1974 Act and made by a local government to individuals moving from flood-damaged areas to other residences, are in the nature of 'general welfare' and therefore are not includible in gross income. Similarly, Rev. Rul. 76–373 holds that relocation payments (e.g., for reasonable expenses in moving a person's family or personal property) made to individuals displaced by activities assisted under Title I of the 1974 Act, are in the nature of 'general welfare' and therefore are not includible in gross income.

In Rev. Rul. 75–271, the IRS held that mortgage assistance payments to lower income individuals provided under a governmental housing program designed to assist lower income families in acquiring home ownership and that were based on a consideration of financial need determined under Department of Housing and Urban Development guidelines, were in the nature of general welfare payments, and were excludable from recipients' gross incomes under the general welfare exclusion.

Similarly, amounts provided by governmental units to low and moderate-income level individuals for training, retraining, and the development of productive job skills, to assist such individuals in obtaining gainful employment, are also in the nature of general welfare. See, Rev. Rul. 63–136, Rev. Rul. 75–246, Rev. Rul. 71–425.

Under County C's Program A and Program B, affordable housing assistance and job training benefits are provided to county employees and trainees, including County C employees/trainees, on the basis of low and moderate-income level qualification, without regard to the employees' status as the employee of a particular county employer, municipal, state or local governmental employer.

Rev. Rul. 75–246, states that the determination as to whether payments under work-training programs are includable in a participant's gross income rests on whether the activity for which the payments are received is basically the performance of services, or is only participation in the training program that promotes the general welfare. In the case of County C's Program B and Program A, benefits flow from a recipient's general eligibility as a low or moderate-income level county trainee, and not by reason of any County C or governmental employee relationship; any County C-employer relationship is merely coincidental. * * *

Based on the information submitted and representations made, and assuming Program B and Program A are operated substantially as described, the benefits provided to low and moderate-income level county employees/trainees, including County C employees/trainees, to assist them in securing safe, affordable, and reasonably proximate housing and acquiring new job skills, are substantially similar to those benefits previously considered by the IRS in the authorities addressed above, are similarly within the scope of the "general welfare exclusion," and are thus excludable from the gross incomes of recipients for federal income tax purposes. The subject benefits are made by a governmental body, from a governmental welfare fund, pursuant to a legislative enactment, not as compensation for services, and for the promotion of the general welfare.

* * *

RULINGS

Assuming Program B and Program A are operated as described, with no particular preference or prejudice shown to County C employees or their governmental employers over the employees of other eligible county employers in the selection of benefit recipients, we conclude that the value of the described housing assistance benefits provided under Program B and Program A to employees of County C, including the Workers, is excludable from the gross incomes of such recipients for federal income tax purposes because the payments or benefits are in the nature of general welfare, and do not represent compensation for services within the contemplation of section 61(a) of the Code. * * *

This ruling is directed only to the taxpayer requesting it. Section 6110(k)(3) of the Code provides that it may not be used or cited as precedent.

* * *

The rulings contained in this letter are based upon information and representations submitted by the taxpayer and accompanied by a penalty of perjury statement executed by an appropriate party. While this office has not verified any of the material submitted in support of the request for rulings, it is subject to verification on examination.

Note

Limitation on general welfare exception. At several points in the Letter Ruling, the IRS emphasizes that the general welfare exclusion applies only if the payments "do not represent compensation for services." Why is this limitation imposed?

IN SIGHTS

Limitation on private letter rulings. Note that the IRS conditions its rulings on the assumption that the programs "are operated as described." In addition, the final paragraph states that the rulings "are based on information and representations submitted by the taxpayer" and that the IRS "has not verified any of the material submitted" but such material is "subject to verification on examination." These statements demonstrate that the validity of the ruling is entirely dependent on the accuracy of the representations made by the taxpayer. If it is subsequently determined that any representation made by the taxpayer is inaccurate, the ruling will be retroactively withdrawn. Thus, a taxpayer can only take comfort in securing a ruling if the taxpayer is confident that all representations made during the ruling process are accurate.

SYNTHESIS

As a general rule, any benefit derived by an individual constitutes gross income, unless a statutory exclusion applies. This Chapter has identified a few narrow exceptions to that general rule. First, a return of capital does not constitute gross income except to the extent it exceeds the basis of the underlying property. Similarly, discounts do not constitute gross income. Because a discount is directly connected to the purchase of a good or service, no discrete benefit is derived when a discount is granted. Rather, the purchase price of the good or service is simply being reduced. Second, the benefits derived from the use of property one owns are not gross income. The Supreme Court has ruled that "imputed income" does not constitute income within the meaning of the Constitution. Finally, certain general welfare benefits are not gross income even though no statutory exclusion applies to these benefits.

This Chapter reveals that a few non-statutory exclusions to gross income exist. Nevertheless, students should emerge from the study of gross income with the general understanding that any economic benefit a taxpayer derives is gross income, unless a statutory exclusion applies.

Test Your Knowledge: To assess your understanding of the material in this chapter, click here to take a quiz.

PART III

Deductions

CHAPTER 9

Disbursements for Business and Income-Producing Activities

Overview

Chapter 1 introduced the base on which the income tax is imposed. That base, taxable income, is defined as gross income minus the deductions allowed to the taxpayer. See IRC § 63(a). A deduction is any payment or disbursement made by a taxpayer that Congress permits the taxpayer to subtract from gross income. A deduction may be claimed only when a specific statutory provision authorizes the deduction. See IRC § 161(a). As the Supreme Court explained more than eighty years ago in New Colonial Ice Co., Inc. v. Helvering, 292 U.S. 435, 440, 54 S. Ct. 788, 790 (1934),

> The power to tax income * * * is plain and extends to gross income. Whether and to what extent deductions shall be allowed depends upon legislative grace; and only as there is clear provision therefor can any particular deduction be allowed. * * * Obviously, therefore, a taxpayer seeking a deduction must be able to point to an applicable statute and show that he comes within its terms.

The analysis of whether a disbursement is deductible is the converse of the analysis of whether a benefit constitutes gross income. As you learned in Part II, almost any economic benefit is gross income, unless a specific statutory provision excludes the benefit from gross income. By contrast, *no* disbursement is deductible, unless a specific statutory provision states that the disbursement may be claimed as a deduction. In other words, the burden is on the taxpayer to demonstrate that a benefit *is not* gross income. Conversely, the burden is on the taxpayer to demonstrate that a particular disbursement *is* allowed as a deduction.

Whenever a taxpayer makes a disbursement, a question arises as to whether that disbursement may be deducted from gross income. To answer that question in the affirmative, you must find a substantive Code provision allowing the disbursement in question to be deducted. The deductibility or non-deductibility of a disbursement normally depends upon the activity in which the disbursement is made. If the disbursement is made in connection with a trade or business, it will normally be allowed as a deduction. See IRC § 162. By contrast, if the disbursement is made for personal purposes, it normally will not be allowed as a deduction. See IRC § 262. This Chapter will explore disbursements in connection with a trade or business, and other income-producing activities. Chapter 10 will explore disbursements made for personal purposes and identify several exceptions to the general disallowance rule of IRC § 262.

A. Disbursements for Business Activities—§ 162

Primary Law: IRC § 162

(a)   There shall be allowed as a deduction all the ordinary and necessary expenses paid or incurred during the taxable year in carrying on any trade or business * * *

IRC § 162(a) is a broad deduction allowance provision for business expenses. The fact that expenses incurred in a business are generally allowed as a deduction should not surprise you. The principal objective of a business is to make a profit; i.e., to generate revenue in excess of expenses. For the business to generate revenue, expenses must be incurred (i.e., you must spend money to make money). It would be unfair for a business to be taxed on all the revenue it generates. To avoid this result, IRC § 162(a) allows a deduction for expenses incurred by the business and, therefore, only the profit is taxed. The meaning of each of the following elements of IRC § 162(a) will be explored in turn: 1) "trade or business;" 2) "ordinary and necessary;" 3) "expense;" and 4) "carrying on."

1.   Meaning of "Trade or Business"

To deduct expenses under § 162, the taxpayer must be engaged in a "trade or business." Unfortunately, neither Congress nor the courts have defined the phrase "trade or business." The Supreme Court, in Commissioner v. Groetzinger, 480 U.S. 23, 107 S. Ct. 980 (1987), summed up the situation as follows:

> The phrase "trade or business" has been in § 162(a) and in that section's predecessors for many years. Indeed, the phrase is common in the Code, for it appears in over 50 sections and 800 subsections and in hundreds of places in proposed and final income tax regulations. * * * The concept thus has a well-known and almost constant presence on our tax-law terrain. Despite this, the Code has never contained a definition of the words "trade or business" for general application, and no regulation has been issued expounding its meaning for all purposes. Neither has a broadly applicable authoritative judicial definition emerged. * * *

> In one of its early tax cases, *Flint v. Stone Tracy Co.,* 220 U.S. 107, 31 S.Ct. 342, 55 L.Ed. 389 (1911), the Court was concerned with * * * the status of being engaged in business. It said: " 'Business' is a very comprehensive term and embraces everything about which a person can be employed." 220 U.S., at 171, 31 S.Ct., at 357. It embraced the Bouvier Dictionary definition: "That which occupies the time, attention and labor of men for the purpose of a livelihood or profit." *Ibid.* * * *

> * * *

> [W]e accept the fact that to be engaged in a trade or business, the taxpayer must be involved in the activity with continuity and regularity and that the taxpayer's primary purpose for engaging in the activity must be for income or profit. A sporadic activity, a hobby, or an amusement diversion does not qualify.

> * * *

> We * * * adhere to the general position * * * that resolution of [whether a trade or business exists] "requires an examination of the facts in each case." This may be thought by some to be a less-than-satisfactory solution, for facts vary. But the difficulty rests in the Code's wide

utilization in various contexts of the term "trade or business," in the absence of an all-purpose definition by statute or regulation, and in our concern that an attempt judicially to formulate and impose a test for all situations would be counterproductive, unhelpful, and even somewhat precarious for the overall integrity of the Code. We leave repair or revision, if any be needed, which we doubt, to the Congress where we feel, at this late date, the ultimate responsibility rests.

WORTH NOTING

Subsequent developments. Not surprisingly, Congress has not accepted the Court's invitation to clarify the meaning of "trade or business" in the 30+ years since the Groetzinger decision was rendered.

The case that follows involves a taxpayer who operated a community center for severely ill individuals. As part of that operation, the taxpayer distributed medical marijuana in a state where such distribution was legal. Regardless of state law, Federal tax law prohibits a taxpayer from deducting expenses incurred in connection with the distribution of marijuana. See IRC § 280E (discussed in the case that follows). Hence, the taxpayer endeavored to segregate the marijuana business from the other activities of the community center and argued that those other activities constituted a separate trade or business. If the non-marijuana activities constituted a separate trade or business, any expenses attributable to that separate business would be deductible under IRC § 162(a).

CALIFORNIANS HELPING TO ALLEVIATE MEDICAL PROBLEMS, INC. v. COMMISSIONER

United States Tax Court, 2007
128 T.C. 173

Laro, Judge. * * *

FINDINGS OF FACT

* * *

Petitioner was organized on December 24, 1996 * * *. Petitioner * * * operated as an approximately break-even (i.e., the amount of its income approximated the amount of its expenses) community center for members with debilitating diseases. Approximately 47 percent of petitioner's members suffered from Acquired Immune Deficiency Syndrome (AIDS); the remainder suffered from cancer, multiple sclerosis, and other serious illnesses. * * *

Petitioner operated with a dual purpose. Its primary purpose was to provide caregiving services to its members. Its secondary purpose was to provide its members with medical marijuana pursuant to the California Compassionate Use Act of 1996 and to instruct those individuals on how to use medical marijuana to benefit their health. Petitioner required that each member have a doctor's letter recommending marijuana as part of his or her therapy * * *.

Each of petitioner's members paid petitioner a membership fee in consideration for the right to receive caregiving services and medical marijuana from petitioner. Petitioner's caregiving services were extensive. First, petitioner's staff held various weekly or biweekly support group sessions that could be attended only by petitioner's members. * * * Second, petitioner provided its low-income members with daily lunches * * *. Third, petitioner allowed its members to consult one-on-one with a counselor about benefits, health, housing, safety, and legal issues. * * * Fourth, petitioner coordinated for its members' weekend social events * * *. Fifth, petitioner instructed its members on yoga * * *. Sixth, petitioner provided its members with online computer access and delivered to them informational services through its Web site. * * *

Petitioner furnished its services at its main facility in San Francisco, California, and at an office in a community church in San Francisco. * * * The main facility was approximately 1,350 square feet and was the site of the daily lunches, distribution of hygiene supplies, benefits counseling, Friday and Saturday night social events and dinners, and computer access. This location also was the site where petitioner's members received their distribution of medical marijuana; the medical marijuana was dispensed at a counter of the main room of the facility, taking up approximately 10 percent of the main facility. The peer group meetings and yoga classes were usually held at the church, where petitioner rented space. * * *

Petitioner paid for the services it provided to its members by charging a membership fee that covered, and in the judgment of petitioner's management approximated, both the cost of petitioner's caregiving services and the cost of the medical marijuana that petitioner supplied to its members. Petitioner notified its members that the membership fee covered both of these costs, and petitioner charged its members no additional fee. Members received from petitioner a set amount of medical marijuana; they were not entitled to unlimited supplies.

On May 6, 2002, petitioner's board of directors decided that petitioner would henceforth discontinue all of its activities. Petitioner thus ceased conducting any activity and filed a "Final Return" (Form 1120, U.S. Corporation Income Tax Return) for 2002. This return reported the following items on the basis of an accrual method of accounting:

Gross receipts or sales		$1,056,833
Less returns and allowances		8,802
Balance		1,048,031
[Less] Cost of goods sold * * *		835,312
Gross profit		212,719
Deductions:		
Compensation of officers	14,914	
Salaries and wages	44,799	
Repairs and Maintenance	1,456	
Rents	25,161	
Taxes and Licenses	28,201	
Depreciation	8,409	
Advertising	200	
Employee Benefit Programs	24,453	
Other Deductions * * *	65,365	
Total deductions	212,958	212,958
Taxable loss		(239)

In a notice of deficiency * * *, respondent disallowed all of petitioner's deductions and costs of goods sold, determining that those items were "Expenditures in Connection with the Illegal Sale of Drugs" within the meaning of section 280E. Respondent has since conceded [that the taxpayer may subtract "Cost of goods sold" of $835,312 in calculating taxable income but may not subtract] the "Total deductions" of $212,958.[4] * * *

The "Total deductions" were ordinary, necessary, and reasonable expenses petitioner incurred in running its operations during the subject year. * * *

---

[4]   In other words, respondent concedes that the disallowance of sec. 280E does not apply to costs of goods sold, a concession that is consistent with the caselaw on that subject and the legislative history underlying sec. 280E. * * *

OPINION

The parties agree that during the subject year petitioner had at least one trade or business for purposes of section 280E. According to respondent, petitioner had a single trade or business of trafficking in medical marijuana. Petitioner argues that it engaged in two trades or businesses. Petitioner asserts that its primary trade or business was the provision of caregiving services. Petitioner asserts that its secondary trade or business was the supplying of medical marijuana to its members. * * * Respondent argues that section 280E precludes petitioner from benefiting from any of its deductions.

[T]axpayers such as petitioner may generally deduct the ordinary and necessary expenses incurred in carrying on a trade or business. See sec. 162(a). Items specified in section 162(a) are allowed as deductions, subject to exceptions listed in section 261. See sec. 161. Section 261 provides that "no deduction shall in any case be allowed in respect of the items specified in this part." The phrase "this part" refers to part IX of subchapter B of chapter 1, entitled "Items Not Deductible". "Expenditures in Connection With the Illegal Sale of Drugs" is an item specified in part IX. Section 280E provides:

> No deduction or credit shall be allowed for any amount paid or incurred during the taxable year in carrying on any trade or business if such trade or business (or the activities which comprise such trade or business) consists of trafficking in controlled substances (within the meaning of schedule I and II of the Controlled Substances Act) which is prohibited by Federal law or the law of any State in which such trade or business is conducted.

In the context of section 280E, marijuana is a schedule I controlled substance. Such is so even when the marijuana is medical marijuana recommended by a physician as appropriate to benefit the health of the user.

Respondent argues that petitioner, because it trafficked in a controlled substance, is not permitted by section 280E to deduct any of its expenses. We disagree. * * *

Section 280E and its legislative history express a congressional intent to disallow deductions attributable to a trade or business of trafficking in controlled substances. They do not express an intent to deny the deduction of all of a taxpayer's business expenses simply because the taxpayer was involved in trafficking in a controlled substance. We hold that section 280E does not preclude petitioner from deducting expenses attributable to a trade or business other than that of illegal trafficking in controlled substances simply because petitioner also is involved in the trafficking in a controlled substance.

* * *

We now turn to analyze whether petitioner's furnishing of its caregiving services is a trade or business that is separate from its trade or business of providing medical marijuana. Taxpayers may be involved in more than one trade or business and whether an activity is a trade or business separate from another trade or business is a question of fact that depends on (among other things) the degree of economic interrelationship between the two undertakings. The Commissioner generally accepts a taxpayer's characterization of two or more undertakings as separate activities unless the characterization is artificial or unreasonable.

We do not believe it to have been artificial or unreasonable for petitioner to have characterized as separate activities its provision of caregiving services and its provision of medical marijuana. Petitioner was regularly and extensively involved in the provision of caregiving services, and those services are substantially different from petitioner's provision of medical marijuana. By conducting its recurring discussion groups, regularly distributing food and hygiene supplies, advertising and making available the services of personal counselors, coordinating social events and field trips, hosting educational classes, and providing other social services, petitioner's caregiving business stood on its own, separate and apart from petitioner's provision of medical marijuana. On the basis of all of the facts and circumstances of this case, we hold that petitioner's provision of caregiving services was a trade or business separate and apart from its provision of medical marijuana.

Respondent argues that the "evidence indicates that petitioner's principal purpose was to provide access to marijuana, that petitioner's principal activity was providing access to marijuana, and that the principal service that petitioner provided was access to marijuana * * * and that all of petitioner's activities were merely incidental to petitioner's activity of trafficking in marijuana." We disagree. Petitioner's executive director testified credibly and without contradiction that petitioner's primary purpose was to provide caregiving services for terminally ill patients. * * * The evidence suggests that petitioner's operations were conducted with that primary function in mind, not with the principal purpose of providing marijuana to members.

* * *

Respondent relies heavily on his assertion that "Petitioner's only income was from marijuana-related matters, except for a couple of small donations". The record does not support that assertion, and we decline to find it as a fact. Indeed, the record leads us to make the contrary finding that petitioner's caregiving services generated income attributable to those services. In making this finding, we rely on the testimony of petitioner's executive director, whom we had an opportunity to hear and view at trial. We found his testimony to be coherent and credible, as well as supported by the record. He testified that petitioner's members paid their membership fees as consideration for both caregiving services and medical marijuana, and respondent opted not to challenge the substance of that testimony. While a member may have acquired, in return for his or her payment of a membership fee, access to all of petitioner's goods and services without further charge and without explicit differentiation as to the portion of the fee that was paid for goods versus services, we do not believe that such a fact establishes that petitioner's operations were simply one trade or business. As the record reveals, and as we find as a fact, petitioner's management set the total amount of the membership fees as the amount that management consciously and reasonably judged equaled petitioner's costs of the caregiving services and the costs of the medical marijuana.

Given petitioner's separate trades or businesses, we are required to apportion its overall expenses accordingly. Respondent argues that "petitioner failed to justify any particular allocation and failed to present evidence as to how * * * [petitioner's expenses] should be allocated between marijuana trafficking and other activities." We disagree. Respondent concedes that many of petitioner's activities are legal and unrelated to petitioner's provision of medical marijuana. The evidence at hand permits an allocation of expenses to those activities. Although the record may not lend itself to a perfect allocation with pinpoint accuracy, the record permits us with sufficient confidence to allocate petitioner's expenses between its two trades or businesses on the basis of the number of petitioner's employees and the portion of its facilities devoted to each business. Accordingly, in a manner that is most consistent with petitioner's breakdown of the disputed expenses, we allocate to petitioner's caregiving services 18/25 of the expenses for salaries, wages, payroll taxes, employee benefits, employee development training, meals and entertainment, and parking and tolls (18 of petitioner's 25 employees did not work directly in petitioner's provision of medical marijuana), all expenses incurred in renting facilities at the church (petitioner did not use the church to any extent to provide medical marijuana), all expenses incurred for "truck and auto" and "laundry and cleaning" (those expenses did not relate to any extent to petitioner's provision of medical marijuana), and 9/10 of the remaining expenses (90 percent of the square footage of petitioner's main facility was not used in petitioner's provision of medical marijuana).[6] We disagree with respondent that petitioner must further justify the allocation of its expenses, reluctant to substitute our judgment for the judgment of petitioner's management as to its understanding of the expenses that petitioner incurred as to each of its trades or businesses. * * *

Notes

1.   *Distinguishing cost of goods sold from deductions.* As the foregoing opinion reveals, the taxpayer subtracted from its Gross Receipts both Cost of Goods Sold ($835,312) and Deductions ($212,958) on its 2002 tax return. The IRS initially disallowed both of the subtractions under IRC § 280E.

    a)   Why did the IRS concede that the taxpayer could subtract Cost of Goods Sold? See fn. 4 of the case and Reg. § 1.61–3(a).

    b)   How significant was the IRS's concession that cost of goods sold were outside the scope of IRC § 280E?

    c)   To what extent did the IRS's concession enable the taxpayer effectively to deduct costs attributable to the marijuana business? See fn. 6 of the case.

    d)   Might the IRS have been better off questioning the validity of including certain expenses of the marijuana business in cost of good sold, rather than attempting to disallow the subtraction of cost of goods sold in its entirety?

2.   *Allocating deductions between multiple businesses.* Although the taxpayer persuaded the court that it was conducting two businesses, rather than one,

---

[6]   While we apportion most of the $212,958 in "Total deductions" to petitioner's caregiving services, we note that the costs of petitioner's medical marijuana business included the $203,661 in labor and $43,783 in other costs respondent conceded to have been properly reported on petitioner's tax return as attributable to cost of goods sold in the medical marijuana business.

the court bore the burden of allocating the claimed deductions between the caregiving business (allowed under § 162) and the medical marijuana business (disallowed under § 280E). Thus, the taxpayer was at the mercy of the court to allocate the expenses between the two businesses. The court's allocation was generous to the taxpayer in this case but that may have just been a matter of luck. If you represented a client like the taxpayer at the outset of its business, what steps would you advise your client to take to exercise greater control over the allocation of expenses?

2.   Meaning of "Ordinary and Necessary"

A business expense must be "ordinary and necessary" to be allowed as a deduction under IRC § 162(a). The cases that follow reveal the meaning of "ordinary" and "necessary."

WELCH v. HELVERING

United States Supreme Court, 1933
290 U.S. 111, 54 S.Ct. 8, 78 L.Ed. 212

Mr. Justice Cardozo delivered the opinion of the Court.

The question to be determined is whether payments by a taxpayer, who is in business as a commission agent, are allowable deductions in the computation of his income if made to the creditors of a bankrupt corporation in an endeavor to strengthen his own standing and credit.

In 1922 petitioner was the secretary of the E. L. Welch Company, a Minnesota corporation, engaged in the grain business. The company was adjudged an involuntary bankrupt, and had a discharge from its debts. Thereafter the petitioner made a contract with the Kellogg Company to purchase grain for it on a commission. In order to re-establish his relations with customers whom he had known when acting for the Welch Company and to solidify his credit and standing, he decided to pay the debts of the Welch business so far as he was able. In fulfillment of that resolve, he made payments of substantial amounts during five successive years. In 1924, the commissions were $18,028.20, the payments $3,975.97; in 1925, the commissions $31,377.07, the payments $11,968.20; in 1926, the commissions $20,925.25, the payments $12,815.72; in 1927, the commissions $22,119.61, the payments $7,379.72; and in 1928, the commissions $26,177.56, the payments $11,068.25. The Commissioner ruled that these payments were not deductible from income as ordinary and necessary expenses, but were rather in the nature of capital expenditures, an outlay for the development of reputation and good will. The Board of Tax Appeals sustained the action of the Commissioner and the Court of Appeals for the Eighth Circuit affirmed. The case is here on certiorari.

> In computing net income there shall be allowed as deductions * * * all the ordinary and necessary expenses paid or incurred during the taxable year in carrying on any trade or business. [Predecessor to IRC § 162(a).]

We may assume that the payments to creditors of the Welch Company were necessary for the development of the petitioner's business, at least in the sense that they were appropriate and helpful. He certainly thought they were, and we should be slow to override his judgment. But the problem is not solved when the payments are characterized as necessary. Many necessary payments are charges upon capital. There is need to determine whether they are both necessary and ordinary. Now, what is ordinary, though there must always be a strain of constancy within it, is none the less a variable affected by time and place and circumstance. Ordinary in this context does not mean that the payments must be habitual or normal in the sense that the same taxpayer will have to make them often. A lawsuit affecting the safety of a business may happen once in a lifetime. The counsel fees may be so heavy that repetition is unlikely. None the less, the expense is an ordinary one because we know from experience that payments for such a purpose, whether the amount is large or small, are the common and accepted means of defense against attack. The situation is unique in the life of the individual affected, but not in the life of the group, the community, of which he is a part. At such times there are norms of conduct that help to stabilize our judgment, and make it certain and objective. The instance is not erratic, but is brought within a known type.

The line of demarcation is now visible between the case that is here and the one supposed for illustration. We try to classify this act as ordinary or the opposite, and the norms of conduct fail us. No longer can we have recourse to any fund of business experience, to any known business practice. Men do at times pay the debts of others without legal obligation or the lighter obligation imposed by the usages of trade or by neighborly amenities, but they do not do so ordinarily, not even though the result might be to heighten their reputation for generosity and opulence. Indeed, if language is to be read in its natural and common meaning, we should have to say that payment in such circumstances, instead of being ordinary is in a high degree extraordinary. There is nothing ordinary in the stimulus evoking it, and none in the response. Here, indeed, as so often in other branches of the law, the decisive distinctions are those of degree and not of kind. One struggles in vain for any verbal formula that will supply a ready touchstone. The standard set up by the statute is not a rule of law; it is rather a way of life. Life in all its fullness must supply the answer to the riddle.

The Commissioner of Internal Revenue resorted to that standard in assessing the petitioner's income, and found that the payments in controversy came closer to capital outlays than to ordinary and necessary expenses in the operation of a business. His ruling has the support of a presumption of correctness, and the petitioner has the burden of proving it to be wrong. Unless we can say from facts within our knowledge that these are ordinary and necessary expenses according to the ways of conduct and the forms of speech prevailing in the business world, the tax must be confirmed. But nothing told us by this record or within the sphere of our judicial notice permits us to give that extension to what is ordinary and necessary. Indeed, to do so would open the door to many bizarre analogies. One man has a family name that is clouded by thefts committed by an ancestor. To add to this own standing he repays the stolen money, wiping off, it may be, his income for the year. The payments figure in his tax return as ordinary expenses. Another man conceives the notion that he will be able to practice his vocation with greater ease and profit if he has an opportunity to enrich his culture. Forthwith the price of his education becomes an expense of the business, reducing the income subject to taxation. There is little difference between these expenses and those in controversy here. Reputation and learning are akin to capital assets, like the good will of an old partnership. For many, they are the only tools with which to hew a pathway to success. The money spent in acquiring them is well and wisely spent. It is not an ordinary expense of the operation of a business.

Many cases in the federal courts deal with phases of the problem presented in the case at bar. To attempt to harmonize them would be a futile task. They involve the appreciation of particular situations, at times with border-line conclusions. * * *

The decree should be Affirmed.

UNITED TITLE INSURANCE CO. v. COMMISSIONER

United States Tax Court, 1988
T.C. Memo. 1988–38

Parker, Judge:

* * *

Petitioner is a North Carolina real estate title insurance company organized in 1975. During 1977 through 1979, the years before the Court, petitioner was not only a newcomer to the business, it was substantially smaller than most of its principal competitors.

The North Carolina real estate title insurance industry is intensely competitive. Because of its competitive disadvantages, petitioner focused its marketing efforts on establishing and maintaining close business relationships with carefully selected real estate attorneys and other real estate professionals who could directly refer business to petitioner. Petitioner also sought to educate these individuals about, among other things, petitioner's conservative underwriting philosophy and restrictive practices.

During the years in issue, petitioner held three out-of-state board meetings and an out-of-state planning conference. Petitioner invited selected eastern North Carolina real estate attorneys, developers, realtors, and lenders on these four trips. Spouses and friends were also invited on the board meeting trips. Respondent argues that petitioner's trip expenses were not ordinary and necessary within the meaning of section 162 * * *.

Section 162(a) allows as a deduction all the ordinary and necessary expenses paid or incurred during the taxable year in carrying on any trade or business. Whether an expense is ordinary and necessary is a question of fact.

Although this issue necessitates a facts and circumstances inquiry and is a peculiarly factual matter, respondent seems to try to impose a legal test on the Court. Respondent argues that petitioner's expenses for the out-of-state board meetings and conference were not "ordinary" within the meaning of section 162(a), relying on the following language from *Deputy v. du Pont*, 308 U.S. 488, 495 (1940):

> Ordinary has the connotation of normal, usual, or customary. To be sure, an expense may be ordinary though it happen but once in the

taxpayer's lifetime. Yet the transaction which gives rise to it must be of common or frequent occurrence in the type of business involved.

Respondent says the trips were not transactions "of common or frequent occurrence in the type of business involved" because "no other title company in the history of North Carolina had ever engaged in the practice of offering resort trips to real estate attorneys and others." Respondent chooses to focus on what he calls "resort trips" and to close his eyes to the business meetings and conferences that occurred at those locations, which will be discussed below. Respondent's argument is based on a sweeping generalization that is not really borne out by the record, but which would not necessarily be determinative even if the factual predicate existed. In making his argument, respondent relies on general testimony by representatives of three competing companies stating that they did not sponsor similar trips and that they knew of no title insurance company other than petitioner that did. This testimony does not establish, and we decline to find as a fact, that "no other title company in the history of North Carolina" engaged in this practice. No witness claimed such all encompassing knowledge. Moreover, since the years in issue, at least one competitor has offered overseas trips to its insurance agents. Again it is a matter of whether one labels petitioner's "practice" as "offering resort trips" or as holding out-of-state board meetings and conferences. Out-of-state business meetings and conferences are not unknown in the business world.

Moreover, even if petitioner were the only North Carolina title insurance company to hold out-of-state board meetings and planning conferences, that in itself would not mean the expenses were not ordinary within the meaning of section 162(a). "One should not be penalized taxwise for his business ingenuity in utilizing advertising techniques which do not conform to the practices of one whom he is naturally trying to surpass in profits." *Poletti v. Commissioner*, 330 F.2d 818, 822 (8th Cir. 1964). In any event, we reject respondent's attempt to convert the above-quoted language from *Deputy v. du Pont* into a narrow legal test of what constitutes an "ordinary" expense. Respondent, ignoring that this issue requires a facts and circumstances inquiry, tried and argued this case as if there existed some simple talismanic definition of the term ordinary, which the Court must apply by rote. The Supreme Court, in *Welch v. Helvering*, 290 U.S. 111 (1933), long ago disabused us of such a simplistic notion. Discussing the concept of "ordinary" expense, Justice Cardozo cogently explained the problem facing the fact finder:

One struggles in vain for any verbal formula that will supply a ready touchstone. The standard set up by the statute is not a rule of law; it is rather a way of life. Life in all its fullness must supply the answer to the riddle. 290 U.S. at 115.

Respondent's effort to transmute the *Deputy v. du Pont* language into such a "ready touchstone" is misdirected. Instead we must consider the record as a whole to make our determination.

The record is clear that petitioner and its competitors routinely entertained real estate attorneys and others in the field. Petitioner, as a very small and new company, focused its marketing efforts even more narrowly and invited "the cream of the crop" of the eastern North Carolina real estate industry to three out-of-state board meetings and an out-of-state planning conference. Petitioner's selected real estate guests actively participated in the board meetings and the planning conference. These trips served petitioner's marketing and other business purposes at that point in its young corporate life. Entertaining attorneys and other real estate professionals was necessary in the North Carolina title insurance business because they were the principal source of business referrals and such activities were actively engaged in by petitioner's competitors. In *Deputy v. du Pont, supra*, the problem was that the expenditures did not arise out of the taxpayer's trade or business. Here the expenditures for petitioner's out-of-state board meetings and planning conference clearly arose out of its conduct of its trade or business.

* * *

Respondent argues that the trip expenses were not "necessary" because "all other companies found alternative and acceptable methods of competition and business practices." Respondent has not cited and we have not found any authority stating that expenses are necessary only if everyone else in the industry incurs them. The word "necessary" as used in section 162(a) imposes only the minimal requirement that an expense be appropriate and helpful to the development of the taxpayer's business. *Commissioner v. Tellier*, 383 U.S. at 689; *Welch v. Helvering*, 290 U.S. at 113. Petitioner has amply demonstrated that the trip expenses were appropriate and helpful and therefore "necessary" to its title insurance business. Based on the record as a whole, we find as a fact that petitioner's trip expenses, except as specifically otherwise noted below, were both "ordinary and necessary" as that term is used in section 162(a).

Respondent argues that even if the board meeting trip expenses for petitioner's directors and real estate guests were ordinary and necessary, the expenses for the * * * spouses and friends were not, because there was no business purpose for their attendance. Here we agree. Section 1.162–2(c), Income Tax Regs., provides that where a spouse is included on a business trip, the spouse's expenses are not deductible unless the spouse's presence serves a bona fide business purpose, and performance of incidental services is insufficient. The spouse must provide substantial services directly and primarily related to the business. * * *

[T]here is no evidence that the spouses or friends provided any services whatsoever related to petitioner's business. Their presence and their activities were purely social. Thus, trip expenses attributable to the spouses and friends are not deductible under section 162(a). * * *

In sum, the reasonable trip expenses attributable to petitioner's officers, directors, and real estate guests were ordinary and necessary business expenses and therefore deductible under section 162(a).

    * * *

Notes

1. *Factual determinations.* As you have seen, various elements of IRC § 162(a) are dependent on the specific facts and circumstances. Both the existence of a trade or business and the question of whether an expense is ordinary and necessary are fact dependent. Additional fact dependent elements exist in other aspects of the provision. As a result, the provision absorbs a great deal of judicial resources.

2. *Tax consequences to beneficiaries of United Title Insurance Co.'s hospitality.* Did the real estate professionals whose travel expenses were paid by United Title Insurance Co. derive gross income? See IRC § 61(a). Could those real estate professionals also deduct the expenses of their attendance at the board meetings and planning conferences? See IRC § 162(a)(2).

3.   Meaning of "Expense" (vs. Capital Expenditure)

A disbursement made by a business must constitute an "expense," not a "capital expenditure," to be allowed as a deduction under IRC § 162(a). The Midland Empire cases sheds light on how that distinction is drawn.

MIDLAND EMPIRE PACKING COMPANY
v. COMMISSIONER

Tax Court of the United States, 1950
14 T.C. 635

FINDINGS OF FACT.

The petitioner, herein sometimes referred to as Midland, is a Montana corporation and the owner of a meat-packing plant which is located adjacent to the city of Billings * * *.

The basement rooms of petitioner's plant were used by it in its business for the curing of hams and bacon and for the storage of meat and hides. These rooms have been used for such purposes since the plant was constructed in about 1917. The original walls and floors, which were of concrete, were not sealed against water. There had been seepage for many years and this condition became worse around 1943. At certain seasons of the year, when the water in the Yellowstone River was high, the underground water caused increased seepage in the plant. Such water did not interfere with petitioner's use of the basement rooms. They were satisfactory for their purpose until 1943.

The Yale Oil Corporation, sometimes referred to herein as Yale, was the owner of an oil-refining plant and storage area located some 300 yards upgrade from petitioner's meat-packing plant. The oil plant was constructed some years after petitioner had been in business in its present location. Yale expanded its plant and storage from year to year and oil escaping from the plant and storage facilities was carried to the ground surrounding the plant of petitioner. In 1943 petitioner found that oil was seeping into its water wells and into water which came through the concrete walls of the basement of its packing plant. The water would soon drain out through the sump, leaving a thick scum of oil on the basement floor. Such oil gave off a strong odor, which permeated the air of the entire plant. The oil in the basement and fumes therefrom created a fire hazard. The Federal meat inspectors advised petitioner to oilproof the basement and discontinue the use of the water wells or shut down the plant.

* * *

The original walls and floor of petitioner's plant were of concrete construction. For the purpose of preventing oil from entering its basement, petitioner added concrete lining to the walls from the floor to a height of about four feet, and also added concrete to the floor of the basement. Since the walls and floor had been thickened, petitioner now had less space in which to operate. Petitioner had this work done by independent contractors, supervised by Jacoby, in the fiscal year ended November 30, 1943, at a cost of $4,868.81. Petitioner paid for this work during that year.

The oilproofing work was effective in sealing out the oil. While it has served the purposes for which it was intended down to the present time, it did not increase the useful life of the building or make the building more valuable for any purpose than it had been before the oil had come into the basement. The primary object of the oilproofing operation was to prevent the seepage of oil into the basement so that the petitioner could use the basement as before in preparing and packing meat for commercial consumption.

* * *

Midland charted the $4,868.81 to repair expense on its regular books and deducted that amount on its tax returns as an ordinary and necessary business expense for the fiscal year 1943. The Commissioner, in his notice of deficiency, determined that the cost of oilproofing was not deductible * * * in 1943.

OPINION.

Arundell, Judge:

The issue in this case is whether an expenditure for a concrete lining in petitioner's basement to oilproof it against an oil nuisance created by a neighboring refinery is deductible as an ordinary and necessary expense under [the predecessor of section 162(a)] of the Internal Revenue Code, on the theory it was an expenditure for a repair * * *.

The respondent has contended that the expenditure is for a capital improvement and should be recovered through depreciation charges and is, therefore, not deductible as an ordinary and necessary business expense * * *.

It is none too easy to determine on which side of the line certain expenditures fall so that they may be accorded their proper treatment for tax purposes. * * * In Illinois Merchants Trust Co., Executor, 4 B.T.A. 103, at page 106, we discussed this subject in some detail and in our opinion said:

> [I]n determining whether an expenditure is a capital one or is chargeable against operating income, it is necessary to bear in mind that purpose for which the expenditure was made. To repair is to restore to a sound state or to mend, while a replacement connotes a substitution. A repair is an expenditure for the purpose of keeping the property in an ordinarily efficient operating condition. It does not add to the value of the property nor does it appreciably prolong its life. It merely keeps the property in an operating condition over its probable useful life for the uses for which it was acquired. Expenditures for that purpose are distinguishable from those for replacements, alterations, improvements, or additions which prolong the life of the property, increase its value, or make it adaptable to a different use. The one is a maintenance charge, while the others are additions to capital investment which should not be applied against current earnings.

[As described in the Findings of Fact, the taxpayer was advised by Federal meat inspectors] that it must discontinue the use of the water from the wells and oilproof the basement, or else shut down its plant.

To meet this situation, petitioner during the taxable year undertook steps to oilproof the basement by adding a concrete lining to the walls from the floor to a height of about four feet and also added concrete to the floor of the basement. It is the cost of this work which it seeks to deduct as a repair. The basement was not enlarged by this work, nor did the oilproofing serve to make it more desirable for the purpose for which it had been used through the years prior to the time that the oil nuisance had occurred. The evidence is that the expenditure did not add to the value or prolong the expected life of the property over what they were before the event occurred which made the repairs necessary. It is true that after the work was done the seepage of water, as well as oil, was stopped, but, as already stated, the presence of the water had never been found objectionable. The repairs merely served to keep the property in an operating condition over its probable useful life for the purpose for which it was used.

While it is conceded on brief that the expenditure was 'necessary,' respondent contends that the encroachment of the oil nuisance on petitioner's property was not an 'ordinary' expense in petitioner's particular business. But the fact that petitioner had not theretofore been called upon to make a similar expenditure to prevent damage and disaster to its property does not remove that expense from the classification of 'ordinary' for, as stated in Welch v. Helvering, 290 U.S. 111, 'ordinary in this context does not mean that the payments must be habitual or normal in the sense that the same taxpayer will have to make them often. * * * the expense is an ordinary one because we know from experience that payments for such a purpose, whether the amount is large or small, are the common and accepted means of defense against attack. The situation is unique in the life of the individual affected, but not in the life of the group, the community, of which he is a part.' Steps to protect a business building from the seepage of oil from a nearby refinery, which had been erected long subsequent to the time petitioner started to operate its plant, would seem to us to be a normal thing to do, and in certain sections of the country it must be a common experience to protect one's property from the seepage of oil. Expenditures to accomplish this result are likewise normal.

In American Bemberg Corporation, 10 T.C. 361, we allowed as deductions, on the ground that they were ordinary and necessary expenses, extensive expenditures made to prevent disaster, although the repairs were of a type which had never been needed before and were unlikely to recur. In that case the taxpayer, to stop cave-ins of soil which were threatening destruction of its manufacturing plant, hired an engineering firm which drilled to the bedrock and injected grout to fill the cavities where practicable, and made incidental replacements and repairs, including tightening of the fluid carriers. In two successive years the taxpayer expended $734,316.76 and $199,154.33, respectively, for such drilling and grouting * * *. We [allowed the taxpayer to deduct these costs] and stated in our opinion:

> In connection with the purpose of the work, the Proctor program was intended to avert a plant-wide disaster and avoid forced abandonment of the plant. The purpose was not to improve, better, extend, or increase the original plant, nor to prolong its original useful life. Its continued operation was endangered; the purpose of the expenditures was to enable petitioner to continue the plant in operation not on any new or better scale, but on the same scale and, so far as possible, as efficiently as it had operated before. The purpose was not to rebuild

or replace the plant in whole or in part, but to keep the same plant as it was and where it was.

The petitioner here made the repairs in question in order that it might continue to operate its plant. Not only was there danger of fire from the oil and fumes, but the presence of the oil led the Federal meat inspectors to declare the basement an unsuitable place for the purpose for which it had been used for a quarter of a century. After the expenditures were made, the plant did not operate on a changed or larger scale, nor was it thereafter suitable for new or additional uses. The expenditure served only to permit petitioner to continue the use of the plant, and particularly the basement for its normal operations.

In our opinion, the expenditure of $4,868.81 for lining the basement walls and floor was essentially a repair and, as such, it is deductible as an ordinary and necessary business expense. * * *

Notes

1.   *Deduction vs. capital expenditure.* What difference does it make to a taxpayer conducting a trade or business if a disbursement is treated as an expense or a capital expenditure? Is any tax benefit derived from a capital expenditure? See IRC §§ 167, 168, 1016(a)(1).

2.   *Current law.* IRC § 263, entitled "Capital Expenditures" provides as follows:

> No deduction shall be allowed for new buildings or for permanent improvements or betterments made to increase the value of any property or estate.

The Treasury has promulgated detailed and voluminous regulations under this Code provision that attempt to draw the line between business expenses and capital expenditures. See Reg. § 1.263(a). These regulations are a relatively recent installment (2013) in a long and tortured history of attempting to resolve an intractable issue. Whether these regulations represent the final destination for this journey remains to be seen.

4. Meaning of "Carrying on"

An ordinary and necessary expense must be incurred "in carrying on" a trade or business to be allowed as a deduction under IRC § 162(a). The Bennett Paper case examines the "carrying on" requirement.

BENNETT PAPER CORPORATION v. COMMISSIONER

United States Tax Court, 1982
78 T.C. 458, *aff'd* 699 F.2d 450 (8th Cir. 1983)

WILES, JUDGE:

Respondent determined a deficiency * * * in petitioners' 1974 Federal income tax. After concessions, the issues for decision are:

(1)   Whether certain preopening expenditures claimed on petitioners' consolidated return were incurred in the course of a trade or business under section 162(a).

(2)   * * *

FINDINGS OF FACT

Some of the facts have been stipulated and are found accordingly.

* * *

Bennett Paper Corp. (hereinafter petitioner) * * * manufactures corrugated boxes and various paper packaging products. * * *

[O]n August 27, 1974, [petitioner] created a wholly owned subsidiary, the Commodores International Yacht Club, Inc. (hereinafter CIYC), * * * to establish a marina and yacht club.

In September and October 1974, CIYC entered into leases of certain raw unimproved land with water rights. CIYC originally planned to operate a marina and yacht club on the leased premises, and it set up a temporary office thereon to sell memberships in the proposed yacht club. CIYC soon realized, however, that it would be less costly to purchase an existing marina facility rather than to build one on the unimproved leased property. As a result, CIYC decided to attempt to purchase an existing marina facility, and it never established a marina or yacht club on the leased premises.

By the end of 1974, CIYC had not yet purchased a marina; however, it had collected approximately $5,000 in application fees from persons interested in becoming members of its proposed yacht club. On CIYC's books, it recorded these application fees as liabilities because it was obligated to refund the moneys if the yacht club never began operation. As of December 31, 1974, CIYC recorded no gross receipts of any kind; it had neither yacht club members nor the facilities, boats, and other equipment needed to operate a yacht club; it neither owned nor operated a marina facility; it did not own any depreciable property; and it did not have reciprocal membership privileges with other marinas or yacht clubs.

In March 1975, CIYC purchased an existing marina facility known as the Caladesi Cay Marina (hereinafter Caladesi Cay), which was adjacent to the property that CIYC had leased in September and October of 1974. CIYC immediately began operating the marina at Caladesi Cay. On June 1, 1975, CIYC held the grand opening of its yacht club at Caladesi Cay, and first made boats available for rental on June 16, 1975.

On petitioners' consolidated return for 1974, a deduction of $57,870 was claimed for business expenses incurred by CIYC during such year. In the notice of deficiency, respondent determined that the claimed $57,870 business deduction represented nondeductible preopening expenses, which were required to be capitalized.

* * *

OPINION

Issue 1. Carrying on a Trade or Business

Section 162(a) provides that a taxpayer may deduct ordinary and necessary expenses paid or incurred during the taxable year "in carrying on any trade or business." This trade or business requirement denies a taxpayer deductions for preopening costs until actual business operations are commenced and the taxpayer performs those activities for which it was organized. * * * In the instant case, respondent maintains that he disallowed the claimed deduction for preopening expenses because CIYC was not carrying on a trade or business at the time such expenses were incurred.

* * *

Petitioners argue that * * * CIYC was carrying on a trade or business when it incurred the preopening expenses in 1974. We disagree. The leading case of Richmond Television Corp. v. United States, 345 F.2d 901, 907 (4th Cir. 1965), vacated and remanded on other issues 382 U.S. 68 (1965), after reviewing many of the cases which considered the carrying on requirement, stated:

> The uniform teaching of these several cases is that, even though a taxpayer has made a firm decision to enter into business and over a considerable period of time spent money in preparation for entering that business, he still has not "engaged in carrying on any trade or business" within the intendment of section 162(a) until such time as the business has begun to function as a going concern and performed those activities for which it was organized. [Fn. ref. omitted.]

* * *

In light of the foregoing, we hold that CIYC was not carrying on a trade or business in 1974. Prior to CIYC's acquisition of Caladesi Cay in 1975, CIYC was in no position to carry out its intended business purpose, to operate a marina and yacht club. As of December 31, 1974, CIYC had none of the following: ownership or use of a marina facility; yacht club members or the boats and equipment to operate such a club; reported gross receipts or depreciable property of any kind; reciprocal membership privileges with other yacht clubs. During 1974, CIYC's only activities related to preparations for entering the marina and yacht club business. In fact, as late as December 31, 1974, CIYC was still uncertain as to when, if ever, it would be operating a marina and yacht club. Consequently, we uphold respondent's determination that the preopening expenses which CIYC incurred were not properly deductible on petitioners' consolidated return for 1974.

* * *

Note

Election to deduct pre-opening expenses after commencing a trade or business. As the Bennett Paper case demonstrates, ordinary and necessary expenses incurred *before* commencing a trade or business are not allowed as a deduction when these expenses are incurred. However, these pre-opening expenses may be allowed as a deduction *after* the taxpayer begins carrying on the trade or business. Pursuant to IRC § 195(b)(1), a taxpayer who elects to deduct "start-up expenditures" may deduct up to $5,000 of such expenditures in the year in which the business begins (if total start-up expenditures do not exceed $50,000). In addition, a taxpayer making this election may deduct the remainder of its "start-up expenditures" ratably over a 180-month period beginning with the month in which the business begins. For purposes of IRC § 195, "start-up expenditures" include payments made in connection with investigating the creation or acquisition of a trade or business. See IRC § 195(c). In light of IRC § 195, is a taxpayer who incurs start-up expenditures hurt by the fact that the payments may not be deducted when they are made?

5.   Reasonable Compensation (vs. Dividend)—§ 162(a)(1)

> **Primary Law:** IRC § 162
>
> (a)   There shall be allowed as a deduction all the ordinary and necessary expenses paid or incurred during the taxable year in carrying on any trade or business, including—
>
> (1)   a reasonable allowance for salaries and other compensation for personal services actually rendered;
>
> * * *

In addition to the general rule of IRC § 162(a) allowing the deduction of ordinary and necessary business expenses, the statute provides some specific examples of the types of expenses the provision contemplates. The most fundamental example of an ordinary and necessary business expense is salary and other compensation paid to employees. IRC § 162(a)(1). Note, however, that a payment of salary is deductible only to the extent that the amount is "reasonable." Why is this restriction necessary? Would not an employer normally wish to minimize the amount of salary it pays to an employee, and an employee wish to maximize what she receives from her employer? If so, it would seem that the marketplace would ensure that the employer would pay no more than it absolutely had to pay to secure the employee's services. The case that follows demonstrates why the reasonableness restriction exists.

ELLIOTTS, INC. v. COMMISSIONER

United States Court of Appeals, Ninth Circuit, 1983
716 F.2d 1241

Hug, Circuit Judge: * * *

I.   Background

Taxpayer is an Idaho corporation that sells equipment manufactured by John Deere Co. and services equipment made by Deere and several other manufacturers * * *.

Taxpayer was incorporated in 1952. During its first year, it grossed $500,000 in agricultural equipment sales in the Burley area. It employed about eight people at that time. By 1975, Taxpayer was employing 40 people, selling both agricultural and industrial equipment throughout southeast Idaho, and achieving gross annual sales in excess of $5 million.

Edward G. Elliott has been Taxpayer's chief executive officer since its incorporation and he has also been its sole shareholder since 1954. He has always had total managerial responsibility for Taxpayer's business. In addition to being Taxpayer's ultimate decision and policy maker, he has performed the functions usually delegated to sales and credit managers. It is undisputed that he works about 80 hours each week.

For several years, Taxpayer has paid Elliott a fixed salary of $2000 per month plus a bonus at year's end. Since Taxpayer's incorporation, Elliott's bonus has been fixed at 50% of net profits (before subtraction of taxes and management bonuses).

On its return for the fiscal year ending February 28, 1975, Taxpayer claimed a $181,074 deduction for total compensation paid Elliott. It claimed a similar $191,663 deduction on its return for the fiscal year ending February 28, 1976. The Commissioner of Internal Revenue ("Commissioner") found these deductions to be in excess of the amounts Taxpayer properly could deduct as reasonable salary under section 162(a)(1). On June 16, 1978, the Commissioner issued Taxpayer a notice of deficiency which limited deductions for Elliott's salary to $65,000 for each fiscal year.

Taxpayer petitioned the Tax Court for a redetermination of liability. The court * * * concluded that the payments to Elliott, in addition to providing compensation for personal services, were intended in part to distribute profits [and constituted non-deductible dividends]. Although the Tax Court acknowledged that it could not determine what amounts paid Elliott actually were dividends, it found that the total amounts paid him were in excess of reasonable compensation. It determined that $120,000 was reasonable compensation for the year 1975 and that $125,000 was reasonable for 1976. The deficiencies assessed to Taxpayer by the Commissioner were reduced accordingly. Taxpayer appeals the Tax Court's determination of reasonable compensation.

II.   The Shareholder-Employee Problem

The issue presented by this case concerns the deductibility by a corporation of payments ostensibly made as compensation for services to an employee who is also a shareholder. If the payments are reasonable compensation for services rendered, the corporation may deduct them. 26 U.S.C. § 162(a)(1). If, however, they are actually dividends, they are not deductible. Thus, it will normally be in a corporation's interest to characterize such payments as compensation rather than dividends.

The general problem is that of distinguishing between dividends and compensation for services received by a shareholder-employee of a closely held corporation. What makes this situation troublesome is that the shareholder-employee and the corporation are not dealing with each other at arm's length. It is likely to be in the interests of both the corporation and the shareholder-employee to characterize any payments to the shareholder-employee as compensation rather than dividends. For this reason, a taxpayer's characterization of such payments may warrant close scrutiny to ensure that a portion of the purported compensation payments is not a disguised dividend.

* * *

Section 162(a)(1) of the Internal Revenue Code permits a corporation to deduct "a reasonable allowance for salaries or other compensation for personal services actually rendered." There is a two-prong test for deductibility under section 162(a)(1): (1) the amount of the compensation must be reasonable and (2) the payments must in fact be purely for services.

Proof of the second prong, which requires a "compensatory purpose," can be difficult to establish because of its subjective nature * * *. By and large, the inquiry under section 162(a)(1) has turned on whether the amounts of the purported compensation payments were reasonable.

* * *

In evaluating the reasonableness of compensation paid to a shareholder-employee, particularly a sole shareholder it is helpful to consider the matter from the perspective of a hypothetical independent investor. A relevant inquiry is whether an inactive, independent investor would be willing to compensate the employee as he was compensated. The nature and quality of the services should be considered, as well as the effect of those services on the return the investor is seeing on his investment. The corporation's rate of return on equity would be relevant to the independent investor in assessing the reasonableness of compensation in a small corporation where excessive compensation would noticeably decrease the rate of return * * *.

III. Reasonableness Determination

Section 162(a)(1) provides that a taxpayer may deduct "all the ordinary and necessary expenses paid or incurred during the taxable year in carrying on any trade or business," including "a reasonable allowance for salaries or other compensation for personal services actually rendered." That Elliott actually rendered services as an employee of Taxpayer is not disputed. At issue is whether the payments made to Elliott are attributable to that employment relationship or to his role as Taxpayer's sole shareholder. Our inquiry focuses on whether the Tax Court, in finding that a part of the payments made to Elliott could not be attributed to his employment status, correctly defined and applied the factors that determine what is "reasonable compensation" under section 162(a)(1).

Although we accord deference to the Tax Court's special expertise, definition of the appropriate factors is reviewable by this court as a question of law. The Tax Court's findings of fact, derived from application of the appropriate factors, must be affirmed unless clearly erroneous.

Our cases have defined a number of factors that are relevant to this attribution determination, "with no single factor being decisive of the question." For analytical purposes, these factors may be divided into five broad categories.

A.   Role in Company

The first category of factors concerns the employee's role in the taxpaying company. Relevant considerations include the position held by the employee, hours worked, and duties performed, as well as the general importance of the employee to the success of the company. * * *

The Tax Court found that Elliott worked 80 hours per week, performed the functions of general manager, sales manager, and credit manager, and made all policy decisions concerning the parts and service department. These are all appropriate considerations. The Tax Court also considered Elliott's qualifications and found that although he was a "capable executive" he had no "special expertise." The Tax Court did not seem, however, to consider Elliott's extreme personal dedication and devotion to his work. To the extent that this benefited the corporation, it is surely something for which an independent shareholder would have been willing to compensate Elliott * * *.

B.   External Comparison

The second set of relevant factors is a comparison of the employee's salary with those paid by similar companies for similar services.

The Tax Court did compare Elliott's compensation to that of managers at other John Deere dealers. In making these comparisons, it appears that the Tax Court considered that Elliott was performing the functions that two or three people performed at other dealers. This was correct. Such comparisons should be made on the basis of services performed. If Elliott was performing the work of three people, the relevant comparison would be the combined salaries of those three people at another dealer.

C.   Character and Condition of Company

The third general category of factors concerns the character and condition of the company. The focus under this category may be on the company's size as indicated by its sales, net income, or capital value. Also relevant are the complexities of the business and general economic conditions. To the extent that they are relevant to this case, the Tax Court did adequately consider these factors.

D.   Conflict of Interest

The fourth category focuses on those factors that may indicate a conflict of interest. The primary issue within this category is whether some relationship exists between the taxpaying company and its employee which might permit the company to disguise nondeductible corporate distributions of income as salary expenditures deductible under section 162(a)(1). Such a potentially exploitable relationship may exist where, as in this case, the employee is the taxpaying company's sole or controlling shareholder, or where the existence of a family relationship indicates that the terms of the compensation plan may not have been the result of a free bargain. * * *

In this case, where Elliott was the sole shareholder, the sort of relationship existed that warrants scrutiny. The mere existence of such a relationship, however, when coupled with an absence of dividend payments, does not necessarily lead to the conclusion that the amount of compensation is unreasonably high. Further exploration of the situation is necessary.

In such a situation, as discussed earlier, it is appropriate to evaluate the compensation payments from the perspective of a hypothetical independent shareholder. If the bulk of the corporation's earnings are being paid out in the form of compensation, so that the corporate profits, after payment of the compensation, do not represent a reasonable return on the shareholder's equity in the corporation, then an independent shareholder would probably not approve of the compensation arrangement. If, however, that is not the case and the company's earnings on equity remain at a level that would satisfy an independent investor, there is a strong indication that management is providing compensable services and that profits are not being siphoned out of the company disguised as salary.

During the fiscal year ending February 28, 1975, Taxpayer reported equity of $415,133 and net profits (profits less taxes and compensation paid Elliott) of $88,969—a return of 21%. For fiscal year 1976, Taxpayer reported equity of $513,429 and net profits of $98,297—a return of 19%. Thus, the average rate of return on equity during these years was 20%. The Tax Court failed to consider the significance of this data. It seems clear, however, that this rate of return on equity would satisfy an independent investor and would indicate that Taxpayer and Elliott were not exploiting their relationship.

The Tax Court erred by limiting its analysis in this area to the facts that Elliott was Taxpayer's sole shareholder and Taxpayer paid no dividends. These are relevant factors, but they cannot be viewed in isolation * * *.

E.   Internal Consistency

Finally, evidence of an internal inconsistency in a company's treatment of payments to employees may indicate that the payments go beyond reasonable compensation. Bonuses that have not been awarded under a structured, formal, consistently applied program generally are suspect, as are bonuses consistently designated in amounts tracking either the percentage of the recipient's stock holdings, or some type of tax benefit. Similarly, salaries paid to controlling shareholders are open to question if, when compared to salaries paid non-owner management, they indicate that the level of compensation is a function of ownership, not corporate management responsibility. On the other hand, evidence of a reasonable, longstanding, consistently applied compensation plan is evidence that the compensation paid in the years in question was reasonable.

There was evidence in this case of a longstanding, consistently applied compensation plan. Since Taxpayer's incorporation, it had paid to Elliott an annual bonus equal to 50% of its net profits. Taxpayer contended before the Tax Court that because the yearly bonuses paid Elliott were derived from a prede-termined formula that had been in use for over 20 years, it could be inferred that the bonuses constituted compensation for services rather than a dividend distribution. It noted that under the bonus formula Elliott's salary in some prior years had been too low to compensate him for the services he had rendered to Taxpayer, so that the higher salaries in the years in issue "resulted in average reasonable compensation during the 10-year period * * * 1968 through 1978."

* * *

Incentive payment plans are designed to encourage and compensate that extra effort and dedication which can be so valuable to a corporation. There is no reason a shareholder-employee should not also be entitled to such compensation if his dedication and efforts are instrumental to the corporation's success. In this case, there is no doubt that Elliott's extreme dedication and hard work were valuable to Taxpayer. If an outside investor would approve of such a compensation plan, that plan is probably reasonable. The fact that the recipient is a shareholder-employee does not make the plan unreasonable.

IV. Conclusion

We reverse and remand to the Tax Court for reconsideration in light of this opinion * * *.

Notes

1. *Non-deductibility of dividends.* Why are dividends paid by a corporation not deductible to the corporation? See IRC § 161.

2. *Mutual preference for compensation.* The court in Elliotts states: "It is likely to be in the interests of both the corporation and the shareholder-employee to characterize any payments to the shareholder-employee as compensation rather than dividends." The corporation prefers payments it makes to shareholders to be treated as compensation, rather than dividends, because compensation is

deductible to the corporation and dividends are not. But why does the court suggest that the shareholder-employee also prefers payments from the corporation to be treated as compensation?

3. *Countervailing consideration.* When the Elliotts case was decided, both compensation and dividends received by an employee-shareholder were taxed at the same rates. Under current law, compensation is taxed at a maximum rate of 37% (see IRC § 1(a)) but dividends are taxed at a maximum rate of only 20% (see IRC §§ 1(h)(1)(D), (11)(A)). Thus, although compensation paid to an employee-shareholder is deductible to the corporation, compensation is taxed at a much higher rate to high-income employee-shareholders than dividends. As a result, little incentive exists under current law to treat payments made by a closely-held corporation to high-income employee-shareholders as compensation, rather than dividends.

4. *Tests employed by other Circuits.* The Ninth Circuit continues to apply the multi-factor test delineated in Elliotts when called on to determine whether compensation paid to an employee-shareholder is reasonable. See, e.g., E.J. Harrison & Sons v. Commissioner, 270 F. Appx. 667 (9th Cir. 2008). Most of the other Circuits also use a multi-factor test although the factors employed by other courts are not necessarily identical to the factors utilized by the Ninth Circuit. The Seventh Circuit, however, has abandoned the multi-factor test and, instead, focuses exclusively on whether a sufficient profit is earned by the corporation after purported compensation paid to shareholders has been deducted to satisfy a hypothetical independent investor. See Exacto Spring Corp. v. Commissioner, 196 F.3d 833 (7th Cir. 1999). The perspective of an independent investor was one of the factors considered by the Elliotts' court (Part III.D. of the court's opinion).

6. Travel Expenses While Away from Home—§ 162(a)(2)

Primary Law: IRC § 162

(a) There shall be allowed as a deduction all the ordinary and necessary expenses paid or incurred during the taxable year in carrying on any trade or business, including—

* * *

(2) traveling expenses (including amounts expended for meals and lodging other than amounts which are lavish or extravagant under the circumstances) while away from home in the pursuit of a trade or business; * * *

Expenses incurred for business travel are another example of an ordinary and necessary business expense. One of the most significant issues in connection with this deduction is determining whether the taxpayer is "away from home" when the expenses are incurred.

BARRETT v. COMMISSIONER

United States Tax Court
T.C. Memo. 2017–195

Cohen, Judge: * * *

FINDINGS OF FACT

[P]etitioners resided in Las Vegas, Nevada, at all material times. They purchased rental properties in the area of Las Vegas as investments toward retirement. Petitioner arranged for and supervised repairs on the rental properties. * * *

[Petitioner's] primary source of income for many years through early 2016, and the subject of the current dispute, was petitioner's business as a video producer for the American Israel Public Affairs Committee (AIPAC).

Petitioner has been in the video production business since the mid-1980s and began working with AIPAC in 1995. * * * Video production includes writing scripts and reviewing footage, much of which petitioner did out of an office in his Las Vegas home. Interviews relating to the videos were conducted in various locations around the world.

Before 2007 petitioner produced videos for AIPAC using studio facilities in Las Vegas. In 2007 AIPAC built a new building in DC. Petitioner advised AIPAC to include a recording studio with editing facilities and a library for videos and audios in order to save money. AIPAC agreed, and petitioner helped design and build the studio. Thereafter AIPAC required petitioner to travel to DC to use the editing facilities and the library at AIPAC's building to perform postproduction activities. Petitioner continued to write scripts and perform pre-production services in his Las Vegas home. The average duration of petitioner's stays in DC was two weeks. Initially he stayed at hotels, but from 2007 through June 2013 he rented a condominium apartment because he and AIPAC agreed that an apartment would be more cost efficient than hotel stays. * * *

   * * *

Petitioner reported his income from AIPAC on Schedules C, Profit or Loss From Business. His gross receipts from AIPAC were $132,810 for 2011, $121,328 for 2012, $75,695 for 2013, and $63,182 for 2014. [P]etitioners reported travel, meals, and entertainment expenses of $55,383 [in 2011], $49,882 [in 2012], and $26,363 [in 2013, and] $24,502 [in 2014].

In the notice of deficiency for 2011, 2012, and 2013 deductions for travel, meals, and entertainment expenses totaling $26,576, $23,969, and $12,284, respectively, were allowed. * * *

OPINION

The primary dispute identified by the parties is whether petitioner was "away from home in pursuit of a trade or business" when he performed services for AIPAC in DC. See sec. 162(a)(2). Petitioners contend that petitioner's "tax home" during the years in issue was in Las Vegas, where they maintained a residence and managed rental properties and where petitioner performed some of the services related to his video production business. Respondent argues that petitioner's tax home was in DC because his work for AIPAC over a period of 21 years was "permanent" rather than temporary and produced the bulk of petitioners' total income for the years in issue. * * *

Petitioners bear the burden of proving entitlement to the deductions claimed. * * *

Deciding whether transportation and travel expenses are deductible requires the determination of a taxpayer's tax home. See sec. 162(a). The word "home" for purposes of section 162(a)(2) generally refers to the area of a taxpayer's principal (if there is more than one regular) place of employment and not where his personal residence is located. When taxpayers have multiple jobs in different locations during the year, are married, and incur duplicate living expenses, identifying the location of the tax home requires review of multiple factors, including: (1) whether employment is permanent, temporary, or indefinite; (2) whether there is a business justification for incurring duplicate living expenses; (3) whether the spouses have separate tax homes; and (4) whether the taxpayers actually have multiple tax homes during one year because their principal places of business have changed.

In considering whether employment is permanent, temporary, or indefinite, the general rule is that if the location of the taxpayer's regular place of business changes, so does the taxpayer's tax home—from the old location to the new location. There is an exception to this rule if the employment is, or is reasonably expected to be, temporary. However, this exception does not apply if the employment away from home is indefinite. Unless termination within a short period is foreseeable, employment that merely lacks permanence is considered indefinite. A taxpayer will not be treated as being temporarily away from home during any period of employment exceeding one year. Sec. 162(a). Although petitioner's work with AIPAC was long term, his travel to DC was sporadic and for short periods totaling less than half a year.

The second factor for identifying the tax home is that the taxpayers must have some business justification beyond merely personal reasons for maintaining an alleged tax home remote from a place of employment. Petitioner performed some business services and had rental activities to justify maintaining a home in Las Vegas.

* * *

Last, when taxpayers have employment or business in multiple locations during one year, the principal place of business is generally used to determine the tax home. When a taxpayer accepts employment either permanently or for an indefinite time away from the place of his usual abode, the taxpayer's tax home will shift to the location of the taxpayer's new principal place of business. Determining the principal place of business includes review of the location where the taxpayer spends more of his time, engages in greater business activity, and derives a greater proportion of his income. * * *

Respondent relies heavily on the assumption that AIPAC's payments to petitioner were solely for work performed during his trips to DC, while petitioner testified that much of his work was performed in his home office in petitioners' Las Vegas residence. Petitioner testified that 75% of his time was spent outside of DC, interviewing on location and writing scripts and reviewing footage in Las Vegas. The record does not explain how his services were billed to AIPAC; thus we cannot determine whether, for example, he billed only for the time spent in DC or billed also for time spent in Las Vegas or elsewhere. But his testimony is uncontradicted and not improbable or unreasonable. Respondent's assumption is not supported by any evidence. We cannot conclude that petitioner's income from AIPAC is attributable solely or primarily to work in DC.

In Kroll v. Commissioner, 49 T.C. at 562, the Court explained:

The purpose of the "away from home" provision is to mitigate the burden of the taxpayer who, because of the exigencies of his trade or business, must maintain two places of abode and thereby incur additional and duplicate living expenses. The "tax home" doctrine is directed toward accomplishing this purpose. In effect, it asks the question whether in a particular case it is reasonable to expect the taxpayer to maintain a residence near his trade or business and thereby incur only one set of living expenses, which are of course nondeductible under section 262. * * *

On balance, because petitioner performed substantial services for AIPAC in Las Vegas, traveled to DC only to complete the production process, was required to be in DC only a few weeks at a time, and had other income-producing activities in the Las Vegas area, we accept petitioners' position that Las Vegas was petitioner's tax home. * * *

WORTH NOTING

Additional restrictions on deducting business meals.
Food and beverage expenses otherwise deductible under
IRC § 162 are subject to additional restrictions. As a general
matter, taxpayers may not deduct more than 50% of otherwise allowable food and beverage expenses (see IRC § 274(n)(1)), subject to certain exceptions (see IRC § 274(n)(2)). Moreover, no amount
of food and beverage expenses that constitute "entertainment" may
be deducted (see IRC § 274(a)(1)(A)), subject to certain exceptions
(see IRC § 274(e)). Thus, even when a meal constitutes an ordinary
and necessary business expense under IRC § 162, part or all of the expense is normally not deductible.

7.   Rental Expense (vs. Purchase)—§ 162(a)(3)

Primary Law: IRC § 162

(a)   There shall be allowed as a deduction all the ordinary and necessary expenses paid or incurred during the taxable year in
carrying on any trade or business, including—

* * *

(3)   rentals or other payments required to be made as a condition to the continued use or possession, for purposes of
the trade or business, of property to which the taxpayer
has not taken or is not taking title or in which he has no
equity.

Rental payments made by a business for the use of real estate or other
property are another common example of an ordinary and necessary business
expense. An issue that frequently arises in this area is whether purported payments of rent actually constitute payments for the use of another's property or,
instead, represent payments made to acquire ownership of the property.

CAL-MAINE FOODS, INC. v. COMMISSIONER

Tax Court of the United States, 1977
T.C. Memo. 1977–89

Goffe, Judge:

* * *

FINDINGS OF FACT

Petitioner Cal-Maine Foods, Inc. * * * is the successor to Adams Egg Farms, Inc. * * * (hereinafter Farms). * * *

The principal business activity of Farms is the production and sale of eggs. In 1963 and during the years in question, the commercial egg business was speculative, cyclical, and highly competitive. Since 1963, major egg producers have gone out of business as the result of bankruptcy or lack of working capital. Egg consumption per capita and the number of laying chickens in the United States have decreased.

* * *

In 1962, [Fred Adams, Jr., a principal shareholder and employee of Farms], prepared a "Plan for Producing Commercial Eggs" which he believed would result in a substantial decrease in production costs and increase profits. The facility contemplated by the plan was unique * * * in that it represented a new and unproven concept in at least two respects: (1) chickens were kept closely confined on wire rather than allowed to run loose on litter, and (2) a large number of chickens were concentrated in one area. Previously, the majority of eggs produced throughout the South were under contract egg-production arrangements whereby hens were "farmed out" to many independent farmers who provided the necessary buildings, equipment and care. The concentration of over 1,000,000 hens at one location, as proposed, was considered by many persons knowledgeable in the egg business to create a hazardous disease potential. The plan contemplated a lessor who would be willing to construct a specified egg production facility and lease it to Farms, for the financial condition of Farms would not have permitted it to construct the facility with borrowed funds. * * *

After learning that Cargill, Inc. * * * might be interested in the plan, Mr. Adams began negotiations with Cargill over the construction and leasing of the facility. An agreement entitled "Agreement of Lease" was subsequently executed

* * * by Cargill and Farms which provided for the construction and rental of the facilities envisioned in the proposed plan. The negotiations were devoted mainly to the primary term of the lease and rental payments. Little thought was given by the parties to the inclusion in the lease of an option to purchase.

The lease agreement required Cargill, the lessor, to acquire certain equipment and construct certain improvements on a particular parcel of land and to lease the land, equipment and improvements to Farms, the lessee. The improvements and equipment consist of a complete facility of specialized buildings and equipment designed specifically for the brooding, growing and caring of laying chickens, including 16 brooder houses, 32 cage growing houses, 178 cage laying houses and an egg processing plant. The land on which the leased facility was constructed consists of approximately 1,080 acres, and the buildings are spread over essentially all of the land. At the time the lease was executed the buildings, improvements and equipment could not have been removed from the land economically.

       * * *

The Agreement of Lease provides that rental payments during the [twelve year] primary term of the lease are to be based upon a monthly payment of $11.10 for each $1,000 of the "Lessor's total original cost." Cargill's total original cost for the land involved was $136,366, [its cost of "improvements" (i.e., buildings and equipment) was $2,368,885,] and its cost for the entire leased property was $2,505,251 [$136,366 land + $2,368,885 improvements]. Although rental payments under the lease agreement were not separately computed for the land, such payments attributable to the land were [approximately $18,000] per year based on the rental formula contained in the lease. [Rental payments attributable to the improvements were approximately $316,000 per year based on the rental formula contained in the lease.] * * * [The total annual rental payments were approximately $334,000 [$18,000 for land + $316,000 for improvements].]

Under the Agreement of Lease, Farms is given the option to renew the lease at the expiration of the primary term for up to ten years on a year-by-year basis with yearly rentals based on decreasing percentages of Cargill's "total original cost." Rental payments under the renewal option would be as follows:

Year of Extension	Percentage of Lessor's Total Original Cost	Approximate Rent Per Year
1	5%	$125,000
2	3%	75,000
3	2%	50,000
4 through 10	1%	25,000

Petitioner is given the option to purchase the leased premises at the end of the primary term, or at the end of any extension thereof, for 12 percent of Cargill's total original cost of $2,505,251, or $300,630.12. The option to purchase is not severable as to the various components of the leased premises and, therefore, cannot be exercised only as to improvements or only as to land.

The lease agreement provides that during the term of the lease, all taxes, assessments and charges are to be paid by Farms. In addition, it requires that any taxes payable by Cargill or its assigns by reason of sale or purchase of the leased premises be paid by Farms. Farms must also purchase and maintain a satisfactory comprehensive general liability insurance policy covering the premises and indemnify and save harmless Cargill from any claim resulting from injury or death to persons or damage to property occurring on such premises.

Farms is required by the lease to purchase fire insurance in favor of Cargill. * * *

Under the agreement the responsibility for repairing and maintaining the premises is placed upon Farms. Damage to or destruction of the premises does not relieve Farms of any obligation under the lease. Farms is required to replace any property damaged or destroyed by any casualty * * *.

The lease agreement prohibits the assignment of the lease or the leased premises without prior written consent of the lessor. * * *

Farms treated the payments made under the Agreement of Lease during the years in question as rental expense; Cargill treated the payments received from Farms as rental income and claimed depreciation on the improvements and equipment. The Commissioner, in his statutory notice of deficiency * * *, determined that the payments under the lease attributable to the land constituted capital expenditures under section 263 and were, therefore, not allowable deductions.

OPINION

The sole issue for decision is whether certain amounts paid by Farms under an "Agreement of Lease" constitute rental expense deductible under section 162(a)(3) or part of the sales price of the subject property. Petitioner contends that the agreement is in substance as well as in form a lease with an option to purchase, thus entitling Farms to a deduction for all payments made thereunder. Respondent, on the other hand, maintains that the transaction is in substance a sale of the property by Cargill to Farms. * * * Although respondent's position is that all payments made under the agreement were for the purchase of the subject property, he capitalized only those amounts attributable to the land involved after concluding that the capitalization of payments attributable to the improvements and equipment would be offset by depreciation thereon.

Section 162(a)(3) provides as follows:

SEC. 162. TRADE OR BUSINESS EXPENSES.

(a)   IN GENERAL.—There shall be allowed as a deduction all the ordinary and necessary expenses paid or incurred during the taxable year in carrying on any trade or business, including—

* * *

(3)   rentals or other payments required to be made as a condition to the continued use or possession, for purposes of the trade or business, of property to which the taxpayer has not taken or is not taking title or in which he has no equity.

Therefore, the payments in question are deductible as rent only if at the time they were made Farms had not taken title to the property, was not taking title to the property, and had no equity in the property.

The written agreement itself is in the form of a lease with an option to purchase. However, it is well settled that we are not bound by the form of the agreement or the characterization thereof by the parties. Even if the parties enter into an agreement which they believe to be a lease but which has all the characteristics of a sale, it will nevertheless be treated as a sale for tax purposes. * * *

The principle extending through the numerous cases in this area is that where the "lessee" as a result of "rental" payments acquires something of value in relation to the overall transaction, other than the mere use of property, he is building up an equity and the payments therefore do not come within the definition of rent. On the other hand, if the parties actually intended to enter into a lease contract containing an option to purchase, then the lessee, up until the time he exercises his option to purchase, acquires no equity in the property. What he has paid until that time is rent and will be treated as such for tax purposes.

Whether an agreement, which in form is a lease, is in substance a conditional sales contract depends upon the intent of the parties as evidenced by the provisions of the agreement, read in light of the attending facts and circumstances existing at the time the agreement was executed. In ascertaining such intent, no single test, or any special combination of tests, is absolutely determinative. Each case must be decided in light of its particular facts.

Petitioner relies upon the economic condition of Farms and the egg industry at the time of the execution of the contract and the absence of factors often contained in agreements found to constitute conditional sales contracts in maintaining that no sale was intended. Respondent points to the following terms and characteristics of the Agreement of Lease in support of his position that a sale of the property by Cargill to Farms was intended: (1) the numerous burdens and responsibilities placed upon Farms by the lease, such as its duty to pay all taxes, assessments and charges, its obligation to make all repairs and maintain the premises, and the requirement that it purchase fire and liability insurance and save harmless the lessor from claims arising from accidents occurring on the premises; (2) the fact that it bears the full risk of loss in the event of casualty or condemnation; (3) the relationship between the size of the payments to be made during the primary term of the lease to those required during any extension thereof; * * * and [(4)] the size of the option price in relation to the total cost of the premises.

In considering each of the above-mentioned characteristics of the agreement in our attempt to ascertain the true intent of the parties, we must be careful to view them in light of the facts and circumstances existing at the time of the execution of the agreement. Respondent first emphasizes the fact that the lease agreement imposes numerous risks and responsibilities upon Farms usually associated with ownership which some courts have found to be an important consideration in determining the intent of the parties. Indeed, the fact that the entire risk of loss in the event of casualty or condemnation is placed upon Farms might appear to raise a presumption of sale. However, most cases in this area have generally found that "such terms, being the subject of negotiation, are mere surplusage in determining whether in fact a lease was intended." Northwest Acceptance Corp. v. Commissioner, 58 T.C. 836, 850 (1972). When considered in light of Farms' poor financial condition, its inability to obtain adequate financing for the project, and Cargill's superior bargaining position at the time of the execution of the lease, it is hardly surprising that the risks and burdens were shifted to Farms to the greatest extent possible. * * * Although we recognize that it is uncommon for a lease agreement to require the lessee to pay any taxes due by reason of the sale of the leased premises, we do not consider that this provision, by itself, indicates the parties intended a sale.

The fact that the monthly payments made during the primary term of the lease are greater than those to be made in the event of an extension of the lease is also relied upon by respondent in support of his contention that the transaction constitutes a sale by Cargill to Farms. If payments are not uniform under a lease agreement, the failure of such payments to vary in accordance with changes in the rental value of the property may indicate that the parties intended a sale. However, we are satisfied that in the instant case the provision for decreasing payments after the primary term of the lease merely reflects the anticipated reduction in the rental value of the premises resulting from the depreciation of improvements and equipment.

* * *

Respondent's final argument is that the size of the option price when compared to the total payments to be made over the primary term of the lease and Cargill's total original costs strongly indicates that the parties intended for Farms to become the owner of the property at the end of the primary term of the lease. The size of the option price is also relied upon by petitioner in support of his contention that the parties did not contemplate a sale. The economic relationship of the value of the property to the option price is an important factor to be considered in attempting to ascertain whether what is in form a lease is in effect a conditional sales contract. In applying this important test, courts have examined the size of the option price both in relation to the subject property's original cost and to its anticipated value at the time the option may be exercised. Whether the option price is compared to the original cost of the property or to its anticipated value at the end of the primary term of the lease, it cannot be considered so insubstantial to raise a presumption of sale, when considered in light of the useful life of the property, Farms' economic condition at the time of the execution of the lease, and the great risks involved. Under the terms of the lease agreement, Farms is entitled to purchase the entire premises for 12 percent of Cargill's total original cost of $2,505,251, or $300,630.12. * * *

When the relationship of the option price to the property's original cost is considered in light of Farms' economic situation at the time of the execution of the contract and the novelty of the venture, we cannot conclude that the ultimate purchase of the property was an absolute certainty. In our opinion, of greater importance is the relationship between the option price and the anticipated value of the property at the end of the primary term of the lease. As evidenced by Mr. Adams' testimony and respondent's own determination, the improvements and equipment were subject to rapid depreciation and were expected to be substantially, if not fully, depreciated by the end of the primary term of the lease. In view of this fact, we are unable to conclude that the option price was substantially less than the anticipated value of the property at the end of the primary term. In fact, a substantial payment was required to make Farms the owner.

In addition to the factors discussed above, we consider a number of other facts to be significant in our attempt to ascertain the intent of the parties. First, there was apparently little concern during the negotiations over the ownership of the property after the primary term of the lease, or any extensions thereof. Mr. Adams testified that there was little discussion devoted to the option to purchase during the negotiations and that it "was somewhat of an afterthought." After having carefully observed his demeanor on the witness stand, we find his testimony worthy of belief. Second, there is no evidence that the tax motivation was a force in structuring the transaction. Third, the payments under the agreement do not appear to exceed the fair rental value of the property. Fourth, the expected life of the improvements was not materially greater, if at all, than the primary term of the lease. Finally, unlike many agreements which courts have found to have characteristics of a sale, there is no provision providing that a portion of the monthly payments will be credited against the option price.

In conclusion, we are convinced that there is no reasonable economic basis to infer that a sale of the subject property by Cargill to Farms was intended. * * *

Accordingly, after a careful review of the entire record, we conclude that the substance of the transaction was not a sale of the subject property by Cargill to Farms. * * * The lease agreement * * * is in substance what it purports to be in form. Accordingly, we hold that the payments made under the lease agreement * * * constitute rental payments within the meaning of section 162(a)(3).

NOTES

1.   *Difference between lease vs. purchase treatment.* How do the tax consequences of payments made by a lessee of business property differ from those made by a purchaser of such property? See IRC §§ 162(a)(3), 263. Does a purchaser of business property derive any tax benefit from the payments it makes to purchase the property? See IRC §§ 167, 168, 1001(a), 1012. If tax benefits are derived in both cases, why is the tax benefit derived from a rental payment potentially greater than the tax benefit derived from a payment of purchase price?

2.   *Magnitude of the issue.* The case indicates that the taxpayer's annual rental payment was approximately $334,000, with $18,000 attributable to the land and $316,000 attributable to the improvements (i.e., buildings and equipment). With this in mind, explain the meaning of the following statement near the beginning of the court's opinion:

> Although respondent's position is that all payments made under the agreement were for the purchase of the subject property, he capitalized only those amounts attributable to the land involved after concluding that the capitalization of payments attributable to the improvements and equipment would be offset by depreciation thereon.

3.   *Relevance of various factors.* Explain why the following factors were relevant to the outcome of the case. To what extent do you agree or disagree with the court's treatment of each factor?

a)   The entire risk of loss was placed upon the taxpayer.

b)   The taxpayer was required to pay any taxes due if the leased premises were sold.

c)   The monthly payments during the primary term of the lease were greater than those to be made in the event of an extension of the lease.

d)   The taxpayer had an option to purchase the property at the end of the lease.

e)   The price to exercise the purchase option was only 12% of the original cost of the property.

8.   Employment as a Trade or Business

An individual need not own a business to incur deductible business expenses under IRC § 162(a). One who works as an employee in a business owned by someone else is also regarded by the tax law as being engaged in a trade or business. See Reg. § 1.162–17(a). Thus, ordinary and necessary business expenses incurred by an employee are deductible under § 162(a).

PEVSNER v. COMMISSIONER

United States Court of Appeals, Fifth Circuit, 1980
628 F.2d 467

Before Ainsworth, Garza and Sam D. Johnson, Circuit Judges.

Sam D. Johnson, Circuit Judge:

* * *

Since June 1973 Sandra J. Pevsner, taxpayer, has been employed as the manager of the Sakowitz Yves St. Laurent Rive Gauche Boutique located in Dallas, Texas. The boutique sells only women's clothes and accessories designed by Yves St. Laurent (YSL), one of the leading designers of women's apparel. Although the clothing is ready to wear, it is highly fashionable and expensively priced. Some customers of the boutique purchase and wear the YSL apparel for their daily activities and spend as much as $20,000 per year for such apparel.

As manager of the boutique, the taxpayer is expected by her employer to wear YSL clothes while at work. In her appearance, she is expected to project the image of an exclusive lifestyle and to demonstrate to her customers that she is aware of the YSL current fashion trends as well as trends generally. Because the boutique sells YSL clothes exclusively, taxpayer must be able, when a customer compliments her on her clothes, to say that they are designed by YSL. In addition to wearing YSL apparel while at the boutique, she wears them while commuting to and from work, to fashion shows sponsored by the boutique, and to business luncheons at which she represents the boutique. During 1975, the taxpayer bought, at an employee's discount, the following items: four blouses, three skirts, one pair of slacks, one trench coat, two sweaters, one jacket, one tunic, five scarves, six belts, two pairs of shoes and four necklaces. The total cost of this apparel was $1,381.91. In addition, the sum of $240 was expended for maintenance of these items.

Although the clothing and accessories purchased by the taxpayer were the type used for general purposes by the regular customers of the boutique, the taxpayer is not a normal purchaser of these clothes. The taxpayer and her husband, who is partially disabled because of a severe heart attack suffered in 1971, lead a simple life and their social activities are very limited and informal. Although taxpayer's employer has no objection to her wearing the apparel away from work, taxpayer stated that she did not wear the clothes during off-work hours because she felt that they were too expensive for her simple everyday lifestyle. Another reason why she did not wear the YSL clothes apart from work was to make them last longer. Taxpayer did admit at trial, however, that a number of the articles were things she could have worn off the job and in which she would have looked "nice."

On her joint federal income tax return for 1975, taxpayer deducted $990 as an ordinary and necessary business expense with respect to her purchase of the YSL clothing and accessories. However, in the tax court, taxpayer claimed a deduction for the full $1381.91 cost of the apparel and for the $240 cost of maintaining the apparel. The tax court allowed the taxpayer to deduct both expenses in the total amount of $1621.91. The tax court reasoned that the apparel was not suitable to the private lifestyle maintained by the taxpayer. This appeal by the Commissioner followed.

The principal issue on appeal is whether the taxpayer is entitled to deduct as an ordinary and necessary business expense the cost of purchasing and maintaining the YSL clothes and accessories worn by the taxpayer in her employment as the manager of the boutique. This determination requires an examination of the relationship between Section 162(a) of the Internal Revenue Code of 1954, which allows a deduction for ordinary and necessary expenses incurred in the conduct of a trade or business, and Section 262 of the Code, which bars a deduction for all "personal, living, or family expenses." Although many expenses are helpful or essential to one's business activities—such as commuting expenses and the cost of meals while at work—these expenditures are considered inherently personal and are disallowed under Section 262.

The generally accepted rule governing the deductibility of clothing expenses is that the cost of clothing is deductible as a business expense only if: (1) the clothing is of a type specifically required as a condition of employment, (2) it is not adaptable to general usage as ordinary clothing, and (3) it is not so worn.

In the present case, the Commissioner stipulated that the taxpayer was required by her employer to wear YSL clothing and that she did not wear such apparel apart from work. The Commissioner maintained, however, that a deduction should be denied because the YSL clothes and accessories purchased by the taxpayer were adaptable for general usage as ordinary clothing and she was not prohibited from using them as such. The tax court, in rejecting the Commissioner's argument for the application of an objective test, recognized that the test for deductibility was whether the clothing was "suitable for general or personal wear" but determined that the matter of suitability was to be judged subjectively, in light of the taxpayer's lifestyle. Although the court recognized that the YSL apparel "might be used by some members of society for general purposes," it felt that because the "wearing of YSL apparel outside work would be inconsistent with . . . (taxpayer's) lifestyle," sufficient reason was shown for allowing a deduction for the clothing expenditures.

            * * *

[T]he Circuits that have addressed the issue have taken an objective, rather than subjective, approach. Stiner v. United States, 524 F.2d 640, 641 (10th Cir. 1975); Donnelly v. Commissioner, 262 F.2d 411, 412 (2d Cir. 1959). * * * Under an objective test, no reference is made to the individual taxpayer's lifestyle or personal taste. Instead, adaptability for personal or general use depends upon what is generally accepted for ordinary street wear.

The principal argument in support of an objective test is, of course, administrative necessity. The Commissioner argues that, as a practical matter, it is virtually impossible to determine at what point either price or style makes clothing inconsistent with or inappropriate to a taxpayer's lifestyle. Moreover, the Commissioner argues that the price one pays and the styles one selects are inherently personal choices governed by taste, fashion, and other unmeasurable values. * * * An objective test, although not perfect, provides a practical administrative approach that allows a taxpayer or revenue agent to look only to objective facts in determining whether clothing required as a condition of employment is adaptable to general use as ordinary streetwear. Conversely, the tax court's reliance on subjective factors provides no concrete guidelines in determining the deductibility of clothing purchased as a condition of employment.

In addition to achieving a practical administrative result, an objective test also tends to promote substantial fairness among the greatest number of taxpayers. As the Commissioner suggests, it apparently would be the tax court's position that two similarly situated YSL boutique managers with identical wardrobes would be subject to disparate tax consequences depending upon the particular manager's lifestyle and "socio-economic level." This result, however, is not consonant with a reasonable interpretation of Sections 162 and 262.

For the reasons stated above, the decision of the tax court upholding the deduction for taxpayer's purchase of YSL clothing is reversed.

Notes

1. *Reimbursed employee business expenses.* Quite often, an employer will reimburse the employee for any business expenses that the employee incurs. For example, a law firm might reimburse an associate for the cost of attending a continuing legal education seminar because furthering the education of its employees will improve the quality of the law firm's practice. What are the tax consequences to the employee of the reimbursement? See IRC § 61(a)(1).

2. *Unreimbursed employee business expenses.* An employee might sometimes be willing to incur a business expense even if the employer will not reimburse the employee for the expense. For example, an associate in a law firm might be willing to pay for a continuing legal education seminar even if the law firm that employs him will not reimburse him for the cost. The associate is willing to incur the cost of the seminar because the associate knows continuing education will enhance his career.

■ **PROBLEM 9-1.** *Employee business expenses.* What are the tax consequences to Law Firm and Associate in each of the following circumstances?

    a)   Associate pays $500 to attend a continuing legal education seminar and Law Firm reimburses Associate.

b)   Law Firm simply pays the $500 fee for Associate to attend the continuing legal education seminar directly to the sponsors of the seminar.

c)   Associate pays $500 to attend a continuing legal education seminar but Law Firm does *not* reimburse Associate. See the discussion that follows.

---

9.   Disallowance of Deduction for Unreimbursed Employee Business Expenses

As discussed at the beginning of this chapter, no disbursement is deductible unless a statutory provision allows the deduction. Section 162(a) is the substantive provision that allows the deduction of all trade or business expenses, including those of an employee. Section 162(a) allows an employee to deduct any ordinary and necessary trade or business expense incurred as an employee regardless of whether the employee business expense is, or is not, reimbursed by the employer. Although both reimbursed employee business expenses and unreimbursed employee business expenses are allowed as deductions under § 162(a), they are treated differently from one another when calculating a taxpayer's tax liability.

All trade or business expenses, other than *unreimbursed* employee business expenses, are generally subtracted from gross income in their entirety when calculating taxable income. Mechanically, trade or business expenses incurred by an employer (business owner), as well as *reimbursed* business expenses incurred by an employee, are subtracted from gross income in arriving at "adjusted gross income" as defined in IRC § 62(a). See IRC §§ 62(a)(1), (2)(A).

In contrast to reimbursed employee business expenses, unreimbursed employee business expenses are outside the scope of IRC § 62(a). Rather, unreimbursed employee business expenses are treated as "itemized deductions" (see IRC § 63(d)) and further delineated as "miscellaneous itemized deductions" (see IRC § 67(b)). As you will see in Chapter 10, miscellaneous itemized deductions are **not** allowed for any tax year beginning before 2026. See IRC § 67(g). **No unreimbursed employee business expenses may be deducted under current law.** Thus, in Problem 9-1(c), Associate cannot deduct the unreimbursed cost of attending the continuing legal education seminar.

At this point in the course, it is helpful to expand the formula for computing a taxpayer's tax liability to the following:

Gross Income
<u>– § 62 Deductions</u>   (i.e, allowed deductions listed in IRC § 62(a))
Adjusted Gross Income
<u>– Other Deductions</u>
Taxable Income
<u>× Tax Rates</u>
Federal Income Tax Liability

---

10. Business Bad Debts—§ 166

Primary Law: IRC § 166

(a) General rule—

    (1) There shall be allowed as a deduction any debt which becomes worthless within the taxable year.

    * * *

(b) For purposes of subsection (a), the basis for determining the amount of the deduction for any bad debt shall be the adjusted basis provided in section 1011 for determining the loss from the sale or other disposition of property.

    * * *

OWENS v. COMMISSIONER

United States Tax Court, 2017
T.C. Memo. 2017–157

Holmes, Judge:

William Owens has spent his career lending money for a profit * * *. One of his personal loans to a commercial laundry wound up mangled into a total loss. Owens claimed a bad-debt deduction, and the Commissioner objected. His primary argument is that Owens's private lending was not a trade or business. But he has a load of other contentions which we'll have to iron out here as well.

FINDINGS OF FACT

Owens lends money for a living now, but after he graduated from Westmount College in 1973 with a B.A. in literature he had hoped to pursue a career in property development. * * * But his father was in the moneylending business and it wasn't long before he answered his family's call to assume his own place in the firm.

A. Owens's Lending Career

[Owens] "reluctantly" went to work for his father. Whatever reluctance he might have felt in his youth couldn't mask his skill in the business. It didn't work out horribly in the end: He, and what is now *his* company, have made billions from loans over the last 35 years. Here are the entities he uses.

1. Owens Financial Group

[O]wens Financial Group, Inc. (OFG) is a * * * company that arranges commercial loans. Owens has been the president of OFG for more than 20 years and owns a majority interest in it. * * *

 * * *

[2.] Owens's Personal Lending

In addition to his responsibilities at OFG * * *, Owens also makes loans from his personal assets * * *. He explained during trial that the return on a personal loan was higher than any return that he'd see at a bank and that because his lack of experience made him uncomfortable investing in the stock market, he instead invested his assets by way of loans. Owens credibly explained that these personal loans typically were to borrowers too risky for OFG, and his willingness to make them depended less on the value of any assets they might be backed by than it did on his belief in the borrower and his business model.

* * *

Owens does not, and did not during the years at issue, keep a separate office for business related to his personal lending ventures. He instead conducted his personal business out of OFG. OFG staff handled all correspondence, documentation, and legal issues arising from Owens's personal lending. OFG staff also managed loan servicing throughout the duration of a loan. * * * At the end of the day, the only difference between Owens's loans and OFG's loans is that the money goes into a different "bucket". Owens believes that because he's been the president of OFG since 1996, there would have been "no point" in having a separate office. * * *

B.   Lohrey

In 2002 Owens began a series of loan transactions with a businessman named David Lohrey. Lohrey was in the laundry business. He'd started a laundry company in 1971 with his two older brothers called West Coast Linen, and together they grew it to become the largest commercial laundry in the San Francisco Bay Area. They serviced all the major hotel chains—Hyatt, Marriott, and even Hilton. They also serviced hospitals throughout northern California. But in the early '80s, Lohrey's brothers wanted to retire and he bought their shares of the company.

[Lohrey also owned Lohrey Investments, LLC, an entity that owned] a commercial site in Gilroy (the Garlic Capital of the World and a thriving town south of the Bay Area). [Lohrey Investments operated a giant commercial laundry on the Gilroy site (the "Gilroy laundry"). It was clear Lohrey Investments needed a lot more money to make the Gilroy laundry a success.]

1.   Owens's Loans to Lohrey Investments

Owens reviewed the Gilroy property as well as [the laundry equipment owned by] Lohrey Investments and determined that they were worth $20 million. [In August 2003,] Owens made a personal loan to Lohrey Investments for $2.75 million. * * * Owens credibly testified that he forecasted Lohrey Investments would be in "growth mode" for at least the next two years. [The Gilroy laundry] did begin to grow rapidly and won more contracts from the San Francisco hotel industry. Lohrey Investments soon needed more equipment, and Owens was happy to keep the funds flowing. Everything went as planned with the first several loans, and Lohrey Investments kept up with its monthly payments, but that changed when it fell behind. Owens's business relationship with Lohrey Investments was about to get a lot more personal.

* * *

Lohrey hit a point with [the Gilroy laundry] where he needed [to use all the cash that came into the business] to expand the business * * * and to pay creditors. Owens understood this, so when Lohrey Investments fell behind on its payments [on the loans Owens had made to Lohrey Investments], Owens remained patient [and] was willing to wait for payments on his personal loans * * *. The economy was stable, and Owens didn't think he had cause for concern. * * *

[Over the next several years, Owens loaned additional large amounts of money to Lohrey Investments.] The [Gilroy laundry] business started to grow. [The Gilroy laundry] then won other contracts and bought even more equipment. [Additional cash was generated by the business] but not as quickly as Lohrey had projected.

* * *

[Eventually, Lohrey Investments could not secure sufficient funding to satisfy the cash needs of the business.] Even though Lohrey Investments was processing about 150–175 *tons* of laundry a day, there's no making up on volume when one loses money on every sale, and the business couldn't make the $500,000 bi-weekly payroll for its 700 employees.

It was October 2008, the start of the Great Recession, and Lohrey was out of options. [From 2003–2008,] Owens had made many personal loans to Lohrey Investments, all memorialized in promissory notes. [By 2008, Lohrey Investments' outstanding debt to Owens was roughly $9.5 million.]

[2.]   The Three Bankruptcies

a.   West Coast Linen

West Coast Linen filed for chapter 11 bankruptcy [in November 2008 and] it ended in disaster. [Shortly after the bankruptcy filing], Lohrey woke in the early morning hours to find that West Coast Linen had new locks.

Lohrey solemnly described his memory of that morning. The trustee had padlocked the gate to West Coast Linen around midnight. By about 4 or 5 a.m. that morning, Lohrey's phone started ringing off the hook—hotels, hospitals, employees—no one could get in the building, and no one knew what was going on. This was devastating: Hospitals and hotels typically have only three to four sets of linens—one on the bed, one on the shelves, and at least one being washed. And both industries rely on their laundry services. Lohrey said that as a result of the padlock, "you now have thousands and thousands of sick people in hospitals literally laying on mattresses with no sheets, no gowns, no operating [room linens;] literally overnight you had 25,000 people with no towels, no sheets, and no surgeries."

This was the end of West Coast Linen. * * * [Owens recovered nothing from West Coast Linen when] the bankruptcy case closed in December 2010.

b.   Lohrey Investments

[In January 2009, Lohrey Investments] followed West Coast Linen into bankruptcy. * * * This bankruptcy closed in May 2012 and Owens recovered nothing.

c.   David Lohrey

For Lohrey, the end of the story came early in 2009. He had signed personal guaranties on all his loans, and he and his wife were forced into filing for bankruptcy themselves. * * * Owens recovered nothing from this bankruptcy either. He didn't recover a penny.

C.   The [Tax] Return

We return to Owens—despite having some interest in these three related bankruptcy cases, he recovered not a cent through them. But they did at least generate a deduction. [His] CPA advised Owens that his loss on the loan with Lohrey Investments entitled him to a bad-debt deduction under IRC section 166. Owens took this advice and claimed a $9.5 million bad-debt [deduction] on his 2008 tax return. * * * The Commissioner [denied] the bad-debt deduction * * * The total [deficiency] is more than $3 million.

* * *

OPINION

We have three issues:

- Was Owens's lending from his personal funds a trade or business?;

- Did the loans he made to Lohrey Investments constitute *bona fide* debt?; and

- Did that debt become worthless in 2008?

Owens argues that he has been in the business of making personal loans on a continual and regular basis for years. He also argues that the loans he made to Lohrey Investments created *bona fide* debts and that those debts then became wholly worthless in 2008 when West Coast Linen filed for bankruptcy * * *. The Commissioner doesn't think that Owens's lending activity amounted to a trade or business and even if it did, the Lohrey loans were more equity than debt. Even if they were debts, they didn't become worthless in the 2008 tax year.

These arguments all mirror section 166. That section allows a deduction for a *bona fide* debt that becomes worthless *within* a taxable year. Sec. 166(a); sec. 1.166–1(c), Income Tax Regs. It requires that:

- the debt be created or acquired in connection with the taxpayer's trade or business;

- a *bona fide* debt existed between the taxpayer and his debtor; and

- the debt became worthless in the year the bad debt deduction was claimed.

We will discuss each requirement in turn.

I. Trade or Business

For Owens's moneylending activity to be considered a trade or business he must have been involved in the activity with continuity and regularity—with the primary purpose of earning income or making a profit. This is a question of fact, of course, but one whose recurrence in a great many cases has triggered the natural prongification reflex of judges trying to fit the case before them into a larger matrix of precedent. We've developed a non-exhaustive list of facts and circumstances to consider in deciding whether a taxpayer is in the business of lending money:

- the total number of loans made;

- the time period over which the loans were made;

- the adequacy and nature of the taxpayer's records;

- whether the loan activities were kept separate and apart from the taxpayer's other activities;

- whether the taxpayer sought out the lending business;

- the amount of time and effort expended in the lending activity; and

- the relationship between the taxpayer and his debtors.

[I]t is clear from the record that from 1999 through 2013 Owens personally * * * made at least 66 loans (including the Lohrey loans) to a multitude of borrowers, easily exceeding $24 million. These figures are more than sufficient when compared to the benchmark we've set in other cases. Compare Serot v. Commissioner, T.C. Memo. 1994–532 (55 loans over 10 years totaling approximately $1.2 million shows business), Ruppel v. Commissioner, T.C. Memo. 1987–248 (1987) (27 loans over 4 years totaling just under $1.4 million shows business), and Jessup v. Commissioner, T.C. Memo. 1977–289 (31 loans over 10 years ranging from $315,000 to $2.7 million each year shows business), with Cooper v. Commissioner, T.C. Memo. 2015–191 (12 loans over 6 years not a business).

From 2003 through 2008—the most crucial years in this case—Owens made approximately 33 loans totaling over $21 million, including $17 million in Lohrey loans. This period was not unusual—money had been Owens's stock in trade since the first days of his career, and lending had long since become his vocation. We are convinced that, over the years, he had fallen into the understandable and prudent habit of lending money raised from the public through OFG to more secured and better risks; the riskier-but-still-promising loans he took on for himself.

The Commissioner reasonably points out that Owens did not personally maintain records regarding the loans he made—staff at OFG did that for him. OFG treated documentation related to Owens's lending the same as it did its own: It kept a file for each loan that included the underwriting documentation, legal documentation, and any security agreements. * * * OFG also kept records of existing loans reflecting the balances, summary of payments, and due dates.

Should any of this count against Owens? We don't think so. Remember that the question we're asking is whether his personal lending was a trade or business. The answer to this question is more probably "yes" the more his personal-lending activity looks like the activity of a traditional lender—in contrast, say, to the activity of someone who writes a personal check to his brother-in-law and then bugs him about repaying it every so often. That Owens kept good records of his loans in exactly the same way OFG kept records on its loans very much suggests that Owens was treating his personal lending as a continual and regular activity.

* * *

The Commissioner next asserts that Owens failed to prove how much time he spent making personal loans. Owens testified that he generally spent an average of 50 hours at work each week and did not distinguish the time he spent on lending from his personal funds from the time he spent on lending from OFG's funds. We recognize this as an officially approved factor-to-be-considered but also find that the toilsome drudgery of measuring out one's days in six-minute increments is rarely found among our more entrepreneurial countrymen—they are more inclined to focus on getting the chore in front of them done as efficiently as possible than on keeping detailed time sheets. And on the facts of this case, we find * * * that Owens had no need to bill specific hours on his personal lending while managing OFG. Just look at the number of loans Owens made and how much money he tied up in them—unless motivated by some hidden whimsy or charitable purpose, he spent a sufficient amount of time on them.

* * *

The Commissioner's final argument focuses on Owens's relationship with Lohrey. He claims that a reasonable businessman in the lending business would not [have continued lending money to a failing enterprise.] It's easy in hindsight to argue that a lender who kept lending more money to a borrower who ultimately failed was unreasonable. But we try to look at things as the lender saw them at the time, and here we find that Owens's advancing more and more money to a growing and capital-intensive business was reasonable under the circumstances. It turned out to be a bad business decision, but it was a *business* decision and not charity or lunacy or something else.

We find that Owens lent from his personal funds continuously and regularly and did so with the purpose of making a profit. He was therefore in the trade or business of lending money during the years at issue.

II.   *Bona Fide* Debt

That Owens was in the moneylending business is not by itself enough to make his failed loans to Lohrey deductible. He must also show that they were *bona fide* debt. A *bona fide* debt is one that "arises from a debtor-creditor relationship based upon a valid and enforceable obligation to pay a fixed or determinable sum of money." Sec. 1.166–1(c), Income Tax Regs. Whether a purported loan is a *bona fide* debt is determined by the facts and circumstances of each case. This is an even more hyperprongified inquiry than whether an activity is a trade or business. And it can be even harder to figure out because the line between debt (deductible as an ordinary loss) and equity * * * is clearly blurry. The Ninth Circuit has identified 11 factors to consider in a debt-equity analysis but strongly cautions us not to overemphasize any one of them. We consider:

- the names given to the certificates evidencing the indebtedness;

- the presence or absence of a maturity date;

- the source of the payments;

- the right to enforce the payment of principal and interest;

- participation and management;

- a status equal to or inferior to that of regular corporate creditors;

- the intent of the parties;

- "thin" or adequate capitalization;

- identity of interest between creditor and stock holder;

- payment of interest only out of "dividend" money; and

- the ability of the corporation to obtain loans from outside lending institutions.

[The court then engaged in a lengthy discussion of each of these factors.]

After looking at all these factors, we find that Owens's advances to Lohrey Investments created *bona fide* debts.

Owens has only one more hurdle to clear.

III. Worthless Debt

We've found that Owens was in the trade or business of lending money during the years at issue, and we've found that his advances to Lohrey Investments were *bona fide* debts. Owens may therefore deduct these as worthless debt, but for what year? Owens says 2008.

The Commissioner disagrees. This is also a question of fact. When a debt is worthless should be determined objectively:

> It is obvious that there is no precise test for determining worthlessness within the taxable year and neither the statutory enactment, its regulations, nor the decisions attempt such an all-inclusive definition.

* * * Furthermore, it is often impossible to select a single factor or "identifiable event" which clearly establishes the time at which a debt becomes worthless and thus deductible. * * *

(Citation omitted.) We are to consider all relevant evidence. Sec. 1.166–2(a), Income Tax Regs. A taxpayer must show "identifiable events that form the basis of reasonable grounds for abandoning any hope of recovery." (Citation omitted.) The Commissioner contends that there is only one good "identifiable event" here—Lohrey Investments' bankruptcy filing in 2009. While bankruptcy is certainly an indication that a debt is worthless, the absence of a bankruptcy filing does not mean a debt isn't worthless. We have identified a multitude of objective criteria that indicate a debt is worthless:

- a decline in the debtor's business;

- a decline in the value of the debtor's assets;

- overall business climate;

- serious financial hardship suffered by the debtor;

- the debtor's earning capacity;

- events of default;

- insolvency of the debtor;

- the debtor's refusal to pay;

- actions taken by the creditor to pursue collection; and

- subsequent dealings between the creditor and debtor.

Lohrey's laundry business had been struggling for many years despite promising opportunities. Once West Coast Linen filed for bankruptcy, * * * Owens knew Lohrey was doomed. The padlock on the door meant Lohrey was going to lose his primary client, and his reputation, with little hope for a comeback. Lohrey even told Owens that Lohrey Investments was going to file for bankruptcy in 2008. We find that this showed Lohrey Investments was not going to be able to repay its debt. * * *

The Commissioner asserts that *Lohrey* still *believed* in 2008 that Lohrey Investments' equipment and property were worth more than its liabilities, and that without proof that Lohrey's subjective belief was not true, Owens's belief that he would not recover anything on his loan to Lohrey Investments has no weight. We can think of no reason why we would give Lohrey's subjective belief at the time more merit than the facts and circumstances surrounding Owens's belief that the value of the property was "very small relative to the debt." In fact, we can take into consideration subsequent events to prove the reasonableness of this belief. And Owens indeed did not recover in the bankruptcies: Lohrey Investments' liabilities towered over what the Gilroy Property * * * and equipment sold for. Owens recovered nothing.

[L]ooking to all the facts and circumstances, we find that Lohrey Investments' debt to Owens became worthless in 2008.

IV. Conclusion

Because Owens was involved in the trade of business of lending money during the years at issue and his advances to Lohrey Investments during the years constitute *bona fide* debt that became worthless in 2008, he is entitled to the claimed bad-debt deduction. * * *

NOTES

1.   *Timing of deduction.* Why might Owens have preferred that the bad debt deduction be allowed in 2008, rather than 2009 (when Lohrey Investments filed for bankruptcy)?

2.   *Bona fide debt.* The Tax Court recently described attributes of a bona fide debt in Dickinson v. Commissioner, T.C. Memo. 2014–136, as follows:

> In order for a transfer of funds to constitute a loan and thus a bona fide debt for purposes of section 166, at the time the funds are transferred there must be an unconditional obligation (i.e., an obligation that is not subject to a condition precedent) on the part of the transferee to repay, and an unconditional intention on the part of the transferor to secure repayment of, such funds. Whether a transfer of funds constitutes a loan may be inferred from objective characteristics surrounding the transfer, including the presence or absence of a debt instrument, collateral securing the purported loan, interest accruing on the purported loan, repayments of the funds transferred, a fixed schedule for repayments of the funds transferred, and any other attributes indicative of an enforceable obligation to repay the funds transferred. Another factor to be considered is whether the alleged

borrower has the ability to repay the alleged loan at the time the alleged lender transfers the funds.

3.   *Deduction measured by basis.* Note that the taxpayer's deduction is measured
by the taxpayer's adjusted basis in the debt instrument. See IRC § 166(b).

WORTH NOTING

Non-business bad debts. IRC § 166(d) allows a deduction for a non-business bad debt that becomes wholly worthless within the taxable year. A non-business bad debt, however, is treated as an "itemized deduction" (see IRC § 63(d)) and further delineated as a "miscellaneous itemized deduction" (see IRC § 67(b)). As you will see in Chapter 10, miscellaneous itemized deductions are *not* allowed for any tax year beginning before 2026. See IRC § 67(g). **Thus, non-business bad debts may not be deducted under current law.**

[handwritten margin note: Blinka disagrees — its changed to cap. loss]

B.   Disbursements for Non-Business, Income Producing Activities—§ 212

Not all income producing activity rises to the level of a trade or business.
As the Supreme Court has stated in Commissioner v. Groetzinger, 480 U.S.
23, 107 S. Ct. 980 (1987):

> Of course, not every income-producing and profit-making endeavor
> constitutes a trade or business. The income tax law, almost from the
> beginning, has distinguished between a business or trade, on the one
> hand, and "transactions entered into for profit but not connected with
> . . . business or trade," on the other. See Revenue Act of 1916, § 5(a),
> Fifth, 39 Stat. 759. Congress "distinguished the broad range of in-
> come or profit producing activities from those satisfying the narrow
> category of trade or business." *Whipple v. Commissioner,* 373 U.S., at
> 197, 83 S.Ct., at 1171. * * *

The Higgins case that follows illustrates an income producing activity that
does not rise to the level of a trade or business.

HIGGINS v. COMMISSIONER

United States Supreme Court, 1941
312 U.S. 212, 61 S.Ct. 475, 85 L.Ed. 783

MR. JUSTICE REED delivered the opinion of the Court.

Petitioner, the taxpayer, with extensive investments in real estate, bonds and stocks, devoted a considerable portion of his time to the oversight of his interests and hired others to assist him in offices rented for that purpose. For the tax years in question, * * * he claimed the salaries and expenses incident to looking after his properties were deductible [as ordinary and necessary trade or business expenses under the predecessor to IRC § 162(a)]. The Commissioner [disallowed a portion of these] deductions. * * * There is no dispute over whether the claimed deductions are ordinary and necessary expenses. As the Commissioner also conceded * * * that the real estate activities of the petitioner in renting buildings constituted a business, [the Commissioner] allowed such portions of the claimed deductions as were fairly allocable to the handling of the real estate. The same offices and staff handled both real estate and security matters. After this adjustment there remained [over 36] thousand dollars expended for managing the stocks and bonds.

Petitioner's financial affairs were conducted through his New York office pursuant to his personal detailed instructions. His residence was in Paris, France, where he had a second office. By cable, telephone and mail, petitioner kept a watchful eye over his securities. While he sought permanent investments, changes, redemptions, maturities and accumulations caused limited shiftings in his portfolio. These were made under his own orders. The offices kept records, received securities, interest and dividend checks, made deposits, forwarded weekly and annual reports and undertook generally the care of the investments as instructed by the owner. Purchases were made by a financial institution. Petitioner did not participate directly or indirectly in the management of the corporations in which he held stock or bonds. The method of handling his affairs under examination had been employed by petitioner for more than thirty years. No objection to the deductions had previously been made by the Government.

The Board of Tax Appeals held that these activities did not constitute carrying on a business * * *. The Circuit Court of Appeals affirmed, and we granted certiorari because of conflict.

Petitioner urges that the "elements of continuity, constant repetition, regularity and extent" differentiate his activities from the occasional like actions of the small investor. His activity is, and the occasional action is not, "carrying on business." On the other hand, the respondent urges that "mere personal investment activities never constitute carrying on a trade or business, no matter how much of one's time or of one's employees' time they may occupy."

Since the first income tax act, the provisions authorizing business deductions have varied only slightly. The Revenue Act of 1913 allowed as a deduction "the necessary expenses actually paid in carrying on any business." By 1918 the present form was fixed and has so continued. No regulation has ever been promulgated which interprets the meaning of "carrying on a business," nor any rulings approved by the Secretary of the Treasury * * *.

　　* * *

To determine whether the activities of a taxpayer are "carrying on a business" requires an examination of the facts in each case. As the Circuit Court of Appeals observed, all expenses of every business transaction are not deductible. Only those are deductible which relate to carrying on a business. The Bureau of Internal Revenue has this duty of determining what is carrying on a business, subject to reexamination of the facts by the Board of Tax Appeals and ultimately to review on the law by the courts on which jurisdiction is conferred. The Commissioner and the Board appraised the evidence here as insufficient to establish petitioner's activities as those of carrying on a business. The petitioner merely kept records and collected interest and dividends from his securities, through managerial attention for his investments. No matter how large the estate or how continuous or extended the work required may be, such facts are not sufficient as a matter of law to permit the courts to reverse the decision of the Board. Its conclusion is adequately supported by this record * * *.

　　* * *

Affirmed.

NOTE

Investing for one's self versus investing for others. The Higgins case held that an investor who manages and monitors his or her own investments is not engaged in a trade or business. The Tax Court has recently elaborated on this conclusion in Lender Management LLC v. Commissioner, T.C. Memo 2017–246, 25–27, as follows:

> The taxpayer's activities as an investor may produce income or profit, but profit from investment is not taken as evidence that the taxpayer is engaged in a trade or business. Any profit so derived arises from the successful conduct of the trade or business of the * * * venture in which the taxpayer has taken a stake, rather than from the taxpayer's own activities.
>
> A common factor distinguishing the conduct of a trade or business from mere investment has been the receipt by the taxpayer of compensation other than the normal investor's return. Compensation other than the normal investor's return is income received by the taxpayer directly for his or her services rather than indirectly through the corporate enterprise. If the taxpayer receives not just a return on his or her own investment but compensation attributable to his or her services provided to others, then that fact tends to show that he or she is in a trade or business. The trade-or-business designation may apply even though the taxpayer invests his or her own funds alongside those that are managed for others, provided the facts otherwise support the conclusion that the taxpayer is actively engaged in providing services to others and is not just a passive investor.
>
> An activity that would otherwise be a business does not necessarily lose that status because it includes an investment function. Work that includes investing or facilitating the investing of others' funds may qualify as a trade or business. In Dagres [136 T.C. 263, 281 (2011)], we held that "[s]elling one's investment expertise to others is as much a business as selling one's legal expertise or medical expertise." Investment advisory, financial planning, and other asset management services provided to others may constitute a trade or business.

In response to the Supreme Court's decision in Higgins, Congress enacted IRC § 212, which allows the deduction of ordinary and necessary expenses incurred in profit seeking activities that do not rise to the level of a trade or business.

Primary Law: IRC § 212

In the case of an individual, there shall be allowed as a deduction all the ordinary and necessary expenses paid or incurred during the taxable year—

(1) for the production or collection of income;

(2) for the management, conservation, or maintenance of property held for the production of income; or

(3) in connection with the determination, collection or refund of any tax.[3]

REDISCH v. COMMISSIONER

United States Tax Court
T.C. Memo. 2015–95

MEMORANDUM FINDINGS OF FACT AND OPINION

Buch, Judge: * * *

FINDINGS OF FACT

Mr. and Mrs. Redisch were married during * * * the years in issue. Mr. Redisch is a veterinary doctor and has been in practice over 40 years.

Hammock Dunes is a private oceanfront community in Palm Coast, Florida. Hammock Dunes has two golf courses, two clubhouses, and a variety of housing options including condominiums, golf villas, and single-family homes. In 2002 Mr. Redisch rented a golf villa in Hammock Dunes. Mr. Redisch

---

[3]   Expenses that may be deducted under IRC § 212(3) include tax return preparation fees and accounting and legal fees incurred in a tax audit. The deductions allowed by § 212(3) bear no relation to the deductions allowed by § 212(1) and § 212(2).

enjoyed his stay at Hammock Dunes and decided to pursue purchasing real estate within the community.

* * *

The Redisches purchased an oceanfront condo (Porto Mar property) in April 2004 for $875,000. The Porto Mar property was a seasonal home, and the Redisches never intended that it be, nor did it become, their primary residence. After purchasing the Porto Mar property the Redisches made some cosmetic changes, such as painting the condo and installing track lighting, carpet, and custom closets, and they purchased furniture.

The Redisches purchased the Porto Mar property for their personal use and often spent time there with their daughter. Tragically, the Redisches' daughter passed away in 2006. After that, the Redisches decided that they could no longer stay in the Porto Mar property. Rather than selling it in 2008, the Redisches decided to rent it out because they believed that they could sell it later at a profit while generating cash in the short term.

Mr. Redisch contacted a realtor from Hammock Dunes Real Estate Co. (realty company) to assist him in renting out the Porto Mar property. Hammock Dunes was still under development, and the realty company showed potential purchasers properties within the community, including those that were newly constructed. Mr. Redisch selected this company because most of the realtors lived within the Hammock Dunes community and he believed they would be in the best position to rent out the Porto Mar property. The realty company also operated an information center within the community that was staffed with realtors who would provide information and tours to potential buyers. Mr. Redisch testified that he entered into a one-year contract with the realty company beginning around April 2008. The Redisches intended to rent out the furnished Porto Mar property under a one-year lease that included the option to assume Mr. Redisch's golf membership. Mr. Redisch determined the monthly rental price on the basis of discussions he had with realtors that he knew and his past experience renting in the community.

The Redisches stopped staying at the Porto Mar property after their daughter passed away. In April 2008 they removed most of their personal belongings, but they would visit to ensure the Porto Mar property was in suitable condition for showings. The Redisches did not return in part because of the memories of spending time in the Porto Mar property with their daughter and in part because they had agreed to keep it available to the realty company to show at any time. The realty company maintained an on-call agent at all times to be available to prospective clients. The Redisches were not paid to keep the Porto Mar property available as a model, but the agents would let prospective clients know that it was available to rent. * * * The Porto Mar property was also featured in a portfolio of rental properties in the realty company's office. The Redisches did not offer any evidence to show the efforts that the realtor took to market the Porto Mar property outside Hammock Dunes.

* * *

The Redisches received inquiries from two potential renters. However, neither rented the Porto Mar property because one wanted to rent it for only two months and one had a large dog, both of which situations conflicted with building restrictions.

Because of lackluster interest in renting the Porto Mar property, the Redisches listed it for sale with a different agent in June 2009. The Redisches still hoped to rent it out but were considering other options such as selling * * *.

The Redisches jointly filed Forms 1040, U.S. Individual Income Tax Return, for 2009 and 2010. Each return * * * claim[ed] deductions relating to the Porto Mar property. Respondent examined the returns and issued a notice of deficiency on November 15, 2012 * * *.

* * *

OPINION

* * *

Conversion to a Property Held for the Production of Income

Generally, no deduction is allowed for personal, living, or family expenses. [IRC § 262(a).] However, an individual can deduct all ordinary and necessary expenses paid or incurred during the taxable year "for the management, conservation, or maintenance of property held for the production of income". [IRC § 212(2).] The individual bears the burden of proving that a conversion to a profit-motivated purpose occurred. That burden cannot be satisfied if the profit-motivated purpose was secondary to another purpose not motivated by profit.

Whether an individual converted his personal property to one held for the production of income is a question of fact that "depends on the purpose or intention of the individual, as gleaned from all of the facts and circumstances". In the case of a converted residence, the Court often looks to five factors to determine the taxpayer's intent: "(1) the length of time the house was occupied by the individual as his residence before placing it on the market for sale; (2) whether the individual permanently abandoned all further personal use of the house; (3) the character of the property (recreational or otherwise); (4) offers to rent; and (5) offers to sell." No one factor is determinative, and we consider all of the facts and circumstances.

* * *

After considering all of the facts and circumstances, we find that the Porto Mar property was not converted to a rental property. The Redisches used the Porto Mar property for four years before abandoning personal use of it in April 2008. Although Mr. Redisch testified that he signed a one-year agreement with a realty company to rent the Porto Mar property, he did not provide any other evidence of such an agreement. Even if the Redisches had produced the contract, Mr. Redisch stated that the efforts of the realty company to rent out the Porto Mar property were limited to featuring it in a portfolio kept in the company's office and telling prospective buyers that it was available when showing it as a model. It is unsurprising that this minimal effort yielded only minimal interest. Mr. Redisch did not testify regarding any other tactics that he attempted to employ to rent out the Porto Mar property other than getting a new real estate agent. Mr. Redisch also did not provide any evidence, beyond a copy of a multiple listing service listing of the Porto Mar property, of the actions taken by the second agent to rent out the home. Accordingly, we find that the Redisches did not make a bona fide attempt to rent out the Porto Mar property and therefore did not convert it to one held for the production of income. Consequently, the Redisches are not entitled to deductions under section 212 * * * relating to the Porto Mar property.

* * *

Conclusion

On the basis of our examination of the record before us and the parties' arguments at trial, we find that the Redisches are not entitled to deductions under section 212 * * * for the Porto Mar property because they did not convert it to a property held for the production of income. * * *

FOR DISCUSSION

Additional actions. What additional actions might Redisch have taken to bolster the position that he had converted the Porto Mar property to property held for the production of income?

Notes

1. *Limitation on IRC § 212 deductions.* Certain IRC § 212 expenses are subtracted from gross income in their entirety when calculating taxable income. Specifically, deductions allowed by IRC § 212 which are attributable to property held for the production of rents or royalties are subtracted from gross income in arriving at "adjusted gross income" as defined in IRC § 62(a). See IRC § 62(a)(4). All other deductions allowed by IRC § 212 are treated as "itemized deductions" (see IRC § 63(d)) and further delineated as "miscellaneous itemized deductions" (see IRC § 67(b)). As you will see in Chapter 10, miscellaneous itemized deductions are *not* allowed for any tax year beginning before 2026. See IRC § 67(g). **Thus, only those § 212 deductions attributable to "property held for the production of rents or royalties" may be deducted under current law.**

   a) If the expenses in Redisch had been allowed as deductions under § 212 (i.e., if the court had found that the Redisches had converted the Porto Mar property to property held for the production of income), would they have been within the scope of § 62(a)(4) (and subtracted in their entirety when computing taxable income), or would they have been treated as miscellaneous itemized deductions (and not be allowed as deductions at the present time)?

   b) If the expenses in Higgins had been incurred after the enactment of § 212, would they have been within the scope of § 62(a)(4) (and subtracted in their entirety when computing taxable income), or would they have been treated as miscellaneous itemized deductions (and not be allowed as deductions at the present time)?

2. *No deduction for legal fees incurred to recover damages.* Legal fees incurred to recover damages are generally within the scope of IRC § 212 and classified

as non-deductible "miscellaneous itemized deductions" (see Note 1) unless the litigation involves—

1) a trade or business (in which case the legal fees are deductible under IRC § 162), or

2) property held for the production of rents or royalties (the only type of deductible IRC § 212 expenses under current law—see Note 1).

■ **EXAMPLE 9-A.** *Impact of non-deductibility of legal fees.* Melissa was defrauded with respect to a personal investment and recovers $300,000 in damages. Her attorney is entitled to a contingent fee of $100,000 (one-third of the recovery). The $100,000 legal fee is within the scope of IRC § 212 but is a non-deductible "miscellaneous itemized deduction." Because Melissa may not deduct the $100,000 of legal fees she paid, the $300,000 of damages augment her taxable income by $300,000. If Melissa's federal and state income tax rates total 50%, she will owe $150,000 of income taxes by virtue of the recovery (50% × $300,000 = $150,000). Thus, after Melissa pays the attorney $100,000 and her income taxes of $150,000, she retains only $50,000 of the $300,000 recovery.

---

3. *Distinguishing a profit-oriented activity from a hobby.* In certain cases, ambiguity may exist as to whether a taxpayer is engaging in a commercial activity to earn a profit or merely for personal enjoyment. For example, one individual might own a farm to make a living. By contrast, another individual might own a farm as a relaxing diversion from a demanding law practice and be indifferent as to whether the farming activities generate a profit. The same might be true of a racehorse. In these cases,

> The determination whether an activity is engaged in for profit is to be made by reference to objective standards, taking into account all of the facts and circumstances of each case.

Reg. § 1.183–2(a). The regulations contain a nonexclusive list of the following objective factors to be considered in deciding whether an activity is engaged in for profit:

(1)   the manner in which the taxpayer carries on the activity;

(2)   the expertise of the taxpayer or his advisors;

(3)   the time and effort expended by the taxpayer in carrying on the activity;

(4)   the expectation that assets used in the activity may appreciate in value;

(5)   the success of the taxpayer in carrying on other similar or dissimilar activities;

(6)   the taxpayer's history of income or losses with respect to the activity;

(7)   the amount of occasional profits, if any, which are earned;

(8)   the financial status of the taxpayer; and

(9)   elements of personal pleasure or recreation.

Reg. § 1.183–2(b).

When an activity is not engaged in for profit, IRC § 183 essentially allows the taxpayer to deduct expenses incurred in the activity only to the extent of the income generated by the activity.[4] However, the deductions allowed by IRC § 183 are generally treated as "itemized deductions" (see IRC § 63(d)) and further delineated as "miscellaneous itemized deductions" (see IRC § 67(b)). As you will see in Chapter 10, miscellaneous itemized deductions are *not* allowed for any tax year beginning before 2026. See IRC § 67(g). Thus, at the present time, the only deductions allowed with respect to an activity not engaged in for profit are certain deductions (discussed in Chapter 10) that are allowed irrespective of whether the taxpayer's objective is to make a profit. See IRC § 183(b)(1).

---

[4]   Technically, the taxpayer may claim (1) the deductions allowable without regard to a profit objective (examined in Chapter 10), and (2) those deductions which would be allowable if the activity were engaged in for profit, but only to the extent that gross income attributable to the activity exceeds the deductions allowable without regard to a profit objective (i.e., the deductions allowed by (1)). See IRC § 183(b).

C.   Deduction for Qualified Business Income—§ 199A

The Tax Cuts and Jobs Act of 2017 purportedly "deliver[ed] significant tax relief to Main Street job creators"[5] by allowing certain business owners to deduct an amount equal to as much as 20% of the taxpayer's "qualified business income." See IRC § 199A(b)(2)(A). Qualified business income is essentially the operating income of a business. Qualified business income excludes investment income (e.g., dividends and interest) and certain other items. See IRC § 199A(c).

If a business owner who pays tax at the maximum individual rate of 37% is allowed to claim a deduction equal to 20% of the business's income, the deduction will have the effect of reducing the tax burden on that income from 37% to 29.6%. See Example 9-B.

■ **EXAMPLE 9-B.** *Impact of IRC § 199A on effective tax rate of business owner.* Angela owns a business and pays tax at a marginal rate of 37%. In 2018, Angela's qualified business income is $100. In the absence of IRC § 199A, her tax liability on that $100 would be $37 [$100 gross income × 37% tax rate = $37.00]. Assume that Angela is allowed a deduction under IRC § 199A equal to 20% of her qualified business income because none of the constraints discussed below apply. Consequently, Angela reports $100 of business income and claims a $20 deduction under IRC § 199A. As a result, her tax liability is $29.60 [($100 gross income − $20 deduction) × 37% tax rate = $29.60]. Hence, the IRC § 199A deduction reduces the tax burden on her business income from 37% to 29.6%.

---

1.   Constraint on High-Income Taxpayer Conducting a Specified Service Business

The IRC § 199A deduction allowed to a business owner is subject to one of two alternative constraints in any year in which the taxpayer reports taxable income in excess of a threshold amount. For purposes of these constraints, the

---

[5]   House and Senate Conference Committee, Tax Cuts and Jobs Act Policy Highlights, at 2 (Dec. 15, 2017).

threshold amount of taxable income is $157,500 in 2018 ($315,000 for a joint return). See IRC § 199A(e)(2)(A).[6]

The first constraint on a business owner's IRC § 199A deduction applies when the taxpayer's taxable income exceeds the threshold amount *and* the taxpayer conducts a "specified service business." See IRC § 199A(d). A specified service business includes any business in the following fields: health, law, consulting, athletics, financial services, brokerage services, or a business whose principal asset is the reputation or skill of its employees or owners, or certain investment and investment related services. See IRC § 199A(d)(2).[7] If a business owner who conducts a specified service business reports taxable income in excess of $157,500 in 2018 ($315,000 in the case of a joint return), the 20% deduction will be curtailed, and the deduction will be eliminated entirely if the taxpayer's taxable income exceeds $207,500 ($415,000 on a joint return). See IRC § 199A(d)(3).

■ **EXAMPLE 9-C.** *Application of IRC § 199A to high-income taxpayer conducting a specified service business.* Ben conducts a specified service business. In 2018, Ben's qualified business income is $200,000 and he has taxable income in excess of $207,500 (and does not file a joint return). If Ben's taxable income were less than $157,500, Ben would be allowed a deduction under IRC § 199A equal to 20% of his $200,000 of business income; specifically a deduction of $40,000. However, because Ben conducts a specified service business *and* he has taxable income in excess of $207,500 (and does not file a joint return), Ben's potential $40,000 IRC § 199A deduction is reduced to zero.

2. Constraint on Other High-Income Taxpayers

If the taxpayer does not conduct a specified service business, an alternative constraint applies if the taxpayer reports taxable income above the threshold amount ($157,500 in 2018, or $315,000 if a joint return is filed). This

---

[6]   These threshold amounts are adjusted upward annually to compensate for inflation. See IRC § 199A(e)(2)(B). This casebook will utilize the threshold amounts in effect in 2018 because those amounts are currently reflected in the Code.

[7]   Architecture and engineering are excluded from the scope of a specified service business. See IRC § 199A(d)(2)(A).

constraint is phased-in for any taxpayer with taxable income between $157,500 and $207,500 (between $315,000 and $415,000 in the case of a joint return) and applies in full to any taxpayer with taxable income in excess of $207,500 ($415,000 for a joint return). See IRC § 199A(b)(3). When this constraint applies, it limits the taxpayer's IRC § 199A deduction to the *greater of*—

1) 50% of the wages paid by the business, or

2) 25% of the wages paid by the business plus 2.5% of the unadjusted basis (at the time of acquisition) of the "qualified property" of the business.

See IRC § 199A(b)(2)(B). "Qualified property" encompasses certain tangible property used in a trade or business eligible for depreciation deductions. See IRC § 199A(b)(6). Thus, land and intangible assets are not qualified property. To apply this constraint, both the wages paid by the business and the unadjusted basis of the business's qualified property must be determined.

■ **EXAMPLE 9-D.** *Application of IRC § 199A to taxpayer with taxable income in excess of $207,500 who does not file a joint return.* Same facts as Example 9-C, but the taxpayer does not conduct a specified services business. In 2018, Ben pays $20,000 of wages and has an unadjusted basis in qualified property of $100,000. If Ben's taxable income were less than $157,500, Ben would be allowed a deduction under IRC § 199A equal to 20% of his $200,000 of business income; specifically a deduction of $40,000. However, because Ben's taxable income exceeds $207,500, his IRC § 199A deduction is limited to the *greater of*—

1) 50% of the wages paid by the business = 50% × $20,000 = **$10,000**

OR

2) a) 25% of the wages paid by the business: 25% × $20,000 = **$5,000**

PLUS

b) 2.5% the unadjusted basis in qualified property: 2.5% × $100,000 = **$2,500**

Sum of a) and b): $5,000 + $2,500 = **$7,500**

Conclusion: As a result of the constraint imposed by IRC § 199A on a business owner with taxable income in excess of $207,500 who does not file a joint return, Ben's potential $40,000 IRC § 199A deduction is limited to $10,000 (the greater of 1), or 2), in this Example).

■   **PROBLEM 9-2.** *Application of IRC § 199A to business owner.* Clara is a physician who owns a medical practice. She and her spouse reported less than $315,000 of taxable income on their joint return for 2018. In 2018, Clara's qualified business income was $250,000.

a)   What is the amount of the IRC § 199A deduction that Clara and her spouse may claim on their 2018 tax return? *200 K → 40 deduction*

b)   How would your answer to a) change if Clara and her spouse reported more than $415,000 of taxable income on their 2018 tax return?

c)   How would your answers to a) and b) change if Clara owns a business that manufactures trinkets, rather than a medical practice? Assume Clara paid $80,000 of wages and had an unadjusted basis in qualified property of $400,000 in 2018.

d)   How would your answers a) and b) change if Clara owned an architecture firm, rather than a medical practice? As in c), assume Clara paid $80,000 of wages and had an unadjusted basis in qualified property of $400,000 in 2018.

Note

No disbursement requirement. Normally, the question of whether a taxpayer is allowed a deduction arises when the taxpayer makes a disbursement. For example,

Limited duration. IRC § 199A(e) applies only to taxable years beginning before January 1, 2026.

for a deduction to be allowed by IRC §§ 162 or 212, a taxpayer must first make a payment in connection with a business or an income-producing activity. By contrast, the deduction allowed by IRC § 199A is not contingent on the taxpayer making any payments. Rather, IRC § 199A allows a deduction equal in amount to a percentage of the taxpayer's qualified business income without regard to whether the taxpayer has disbursed any funds.

SYNTHESIS

No disbursement is deductible unless a specific statutory provision allows the deduction. IRC § 162 allows the deduction of all ordinary and necessary expenses incurred in a trade or business. Examples of these expenses include reasonable compensation, travel while away from home, and rental of business property. Employment constitutes a trade or business. However, unreimbursed employee business expenses incurred before 2026 may not be deducted.

Disbursements in connection with profit seeking activities that do not reach the level of a trade or business are allowed as deductions under IRC § 212. However, expenses incurred before 2026 in profit seeking activities may not be deducted, unless the expenses are attributable to property held for the production of rents or royalties.

IRC § 199A allows business owners to claim a deduction equal to 20% of their qualified business income. In the case of a business owner paying tax at the maximum 37% rate, the IRC § 199A deduction reduces the tax rate on the income to which it applies to 29.6%. No deduction is allowed, however, if the owner's total taxable income is above a certain threshold and the owner engages in certain service businesses. Even if an owner whose taxable income is above the threshold does not engage in such a service business, the amount of the deduction may be mitigated or even eliminated in certain cases.

Test Your Knowledge: To assess your understanding of the material in this chapter, click here to take a quiz.

CHAPTER 10

Disbursements for Personal Purposes—§ 262

Overview

Chapter 9 focused on disbursements made in connection with a business. It demonstrated that ordinary and necessary expenses incurred in a business are generally allowed as deductions from gross income. In a business context, expenses are incurred to generate revenue. Fairness dictates that the taxpayer should only be taxed on the difference between the revenue and the expenses incurred to generate that revenue; i.e., the taxpayer's profit. This result is achieved by allowing a deduction for ordinary and necessary business expenses (IRC § 162(a)).

Not all disbursements are made in connection with a business. Rather, many disbursements are made for personal purposes, such as meals and recreation. Unlike business expenses incurred to generate revenue, disbursements for personal purposes are incurred for enjoyment. Because the tax system does not tax personal enjoyment, no justification exists for allowing individuals to deduct expenses for personal matters. Accordingly, disbursements for personal purposes are generally *not* allowed as deductions. See IRC § 262(a).

Primary Law: IRC § 262

(a)   Except as otherwise expressly provided in this chapter, no deduction shall be allowed for personal, living, or family expenses.

* * *

Pursuant to the first clause of § 262(a), Congress has carved out several exceptions from the general prohibition on the deduction of personal expenses. The disbursements described by these statutory exceptions to § 262(a) are allowed as deductions in spite of their personal nature. Chapter 10 will explore some of these exceptions to the general prohibition on deducting personal expenses.

Almost all allowable deductions are categorized as either § 62 deductions or itemized deductions. For example, as discussed in Chapter 9, all trade or business expenses allowed as a deduction under § 162 are § 62 deductions (other than unreimbursed employee business expenses). See IRC §§ 62(a)(1), (2). By contrast, almost all non-business deductions are categorized as itemized deductions. See IRC § 63(d).

Itemized deductions are often not as beneficial to the taxpayer as § 62 deductions because various restrictions are imposed on itemized deductions that are not imposed on § 62 deductions. For example, certain itemized deductions are delineated as "miscellaneous itemized deductions." See IRC § 67(b). Miscellaneous itemized deductions do not currently offset a taxpayer's gross income because no miscellaneous itemized deductions may be claimed in any tax year before 2026. See IRC § 67(d). Even those itemized deductions that are not miscellaneous itemized deductions can be subject to restrictions that will be discussed later in this chapter.

As you learn about the types of personal expenses that are allowed as deductions, you should determine whether each allowed deduction is a § 62 deduction or an itemized deduction. In this regard, it is desirable to keep in mind the following formula introduced in Chapter 9 for computing a taxpayer's tax liability:

Gross Income
– § 62 Deductions   (i.e, allowed deductions listed in IRC § 62(a))
Adjusted Gross Income
– Other Deductions   (including certain itemized deductions)
Taxable Income
× Tax Rates
Federal Income Tax Liability

A. Borrowing for Personal Purposes—§ 163(h)

An individual might borrow money for various reasons. For example, money might be borrowed to purchase machinery or equipment for use in a trade or business. Alternatively, money might be borrowed to purchase stocks and bonds in a non-business, income producing activity. Finally, an individual might borrow money for personal purposes, perhaps to purchase a house or a car for her family.

When money is borrowed, the lender will expect the borrower to compensate the lender for the use of the lender's money by paying the lender interest. The lender must be compensated for the use of her money because she cannot invest and earn a return on her money when the money is in the borrower's possession. Interest, therefore, is an expense paid by the borrower to compensate the lender for the use of the lender's money. When borrowed money is used in a trade or business, we would expect the interest to be allowed as a deduction to the borrower because the interest cost is incurred to produce income. By contrast, if the borrowed money is used for personal purposes, we would expect that the interest paid by the borrower would *not* be allowed as a deduction by virtue of IRC § 262(a). IRC § 163(h) addresses the deductibility of interest.

Primary Law: IRC § 163(h)

(1)   In the case of a taxpayer other than a corporation, no deduction shall be allowed under this chapter for personal interest * * *.

(2)   For purposes of this subsection, the term "personal interest" means any interest allowable as a deduction under this chapter other than—

  (A)   interest * * * on indebtedness property allocable to a trade or business * * *,

  (B)   any investment interest (within the meaning of subsection (d)),

  * * *

  (D)   any qualified residence interest (within the meaning of paragraph (3)),

  * * *

(3) For purposes of this subsection—

 (A) The term "qualified residence interest" means any interest which is paid or incurred during the taxable year on—

  (i) acquisition indebtedness with respect to any qualified residence of the taxpayer * * *.

 (B) (i) The term "acquisition indebtedness" means any indebtedness which—

   (I) is incurred in acquiring, constructing, or substantially improving any qualified residence of the taxpayer, and

   (II) is secured by such residence.

  * * *

  (ii) The aggregate amount treated as acquisition indebtedness for any period shall not exceed $750,000 ($375,000 in the case of a married individual filing a separate return).[1]

 * * *

As expected, interest incurred in a trade or business and interest incurred in an investment activity is generally allowed as a deduction. See IRC §§ 163(h)(2)(A), (B). By contrast, interest incurred in a personal activity is generally *not* allowed as a deduction, unless it constitutes "qualified residence interest." See IRC §§ 163(h)(2)(D), (h)(3).

---

[1] See IRC § 163(h)(3)(F)(i)(II) indicating that the $1,000,000/$500,000 limits appearing in § 163(h)(3)(B)(ii) are reduced to $750,000/$375,000 for taxable years beginning before January 1, 2026.

1. Qualified Residence Interest

VOSS v. COMMISSIONER

United States Court of Appeals, Ninth Circuit, 2015
796 F.3d 1051, *acq.* AOD 2016–02, 2016–31 IRB 193[2]

Bybee, Circuit Judge:

* * *

I

Section 163 of the Internal Revenue Code governs the deductibility of interest on a taxpayer's indebtedness. This section of the Tax Code, like much of the Code, is complex—it requires attention to definitions within definitions and exceptions upon exceptions. To assist the reader, we begin with a brief overview of the section's relevant provisions.

Section 163 begins with the general rule that interest on indebtedness is deductible. *See* 26 U.S.C. § 163(a). Subsection (h), however, provides that, "[i]n the case of a taxpayer other than a corporation," personal interest is not deductible. *See id.* § 163(h)(1) ("In the case of a taxpayer other than a corporation, no deduction shall be allowed under this chapter for personal interest paid or accrued during the taxable year."). [Moreover,] "personal interest" is defined [expansively] as "*any* interest * * * other than" certain specified categories of interest. *See id.* § 163(h)(2). One of those carved-out categories [that is allowed as a deduction] is "any qualified residence interest." *Id.* § 163(h)(2)(D).

Section 163(h)(3) thus provides that interest on a "qualified residence" is not "personal interest" and, accordingly, may be deducted * * *. The Code defines "qualified residence" as the taxpayer's principal residence and "1 other residence of the taxpayer which is selected by the taxpayer * * * and which is used by the taxpayer as a residence." *Id.* § 163(h)(4)(A)(i).

"Qualified residence interest" encompasses interest payments on * * * acquisition indebtedness * * *. *Id.* § 163(h)(3)(A)[(i)]. "Acquisition indebtedness" generally means debt incurred in * * * "acquiring, constructing, or substantially

---

[2]   Editor's note: By acquiescing in the decision, the Internal Revenue Service puts taxpayers on notice that it will not challenge fact patterns analogous to Voss.

improving" a qualified residence. *Id.* § 163(h)(3)(B)(i). * * * So, for example, if a taxpayer has a purchase money mortgage * * * on both a primary home and a summer home, she can deduct interest payments on both mortgages. She may also deduct the interest on any home equity line of credit on both residences.

Significantly, the statute does not allow taxpayers to deduct interest payments on an unlimited amount of acquisition * * * indebtedness. Instead, the statute limits "[t]he aggregate amount treated as acquisition indebtedness for any period" to $1,000,000 * * *. *Id.* § 163(h)(3)(B)(ii).[3] * * *

If a taxpayer's total mortgage debt exceeds the debt limits, a Treasury regulation, 26 C.F.R. § 1.163–10T, provides the method for calculating qualified residence interest. Subsection (e) of that regulation sets out the usual method: qualified residence interest is calculated by multiplying the total interest paid by the ratio of the applicable debt limit over the total debt. *See id.* § 1.163–10T(e). For example, if a single individual has a $2 million mortgage * * *, the ratio is 50%: $1 million (the total applicable debt limit under the statute) over $2 million (the total debt). Thus, the taxpayer is entitled to deduct 50% of whatever interest is paid or accrued during her taxable year.

In sum, under § 163 and the applicable Treasury regulation, a taxpayer may deduct the interest paid on a mortgage * * * for a principal residence and a second home. [T]he deduction is limited to interest paid on $1 million of mortgage debt * * *. If the taxpayer's home indebtedness exceeds $1 million, then she is entitled to deduct a portion of her interest, determined by the ratio of the statutory debt limit divided by her total actual debt. * * *

[T]he Code does not specify whether, in the case of residence co-owners who are not married, the debt limits apply per residence or per taxpayer. That is, is the $1 million debt limit the limit on the qualified residence, irrespective of the number of owners, or is it the limit on the debt that can be claimed by any individual taxpayer? That gap in the Code is the source of the present controversy.

II

A

Bruce Voss and Charles Sophy are domestic partners registered with the State of California. They co-own two homes as joint tenants—one in Rancho

---

[3]   Editor's note: This limit has been reduced to $750,000 until 2026. See IRC § 163(h)(3)(F)(i)(II).

Mirage, California and the other, their primary residence, in Beverly Hills, California.

When Voss and Sophy purchased the Rancho Mirage home in 2000, they took out a [$500,000 loan and secured the loan by giving the lender a mortgage in the home]. * * * Voss and Sophy are jointly and severally liable for the Rancho Mirage mortgage.

Voss and Sophy purchased the Beverly Hills home in 2002. They financed the purchase of the Beverly Hills home with a [$2,000,000 loan and secured the loan by giving the lender a mortgage in the] Beverly Hills property. * * * Voss and Sophy are jointly and severally liable for the Beverly Hills mortgage, which * * * is secured by the Beverly Hills property. * * *

The total average balance of the two mortgages * * * in 2006 and 2007 (the two taxable years at issue) was about [$2.5 million]. Thus, whether § 163(h)(3)'s debt limit [is] interpreted as applying per taxpayer (such that Voss and Sophy can deduct interest on up to $2 million of debt) or per residence (such that Voss and Sophy can deduct interest on up to $1 million of debt), it is in either event clear that Voss and Sophy's debt exceeds the statutory debt limits.

B

Voss and Sophy each filed separate federal income tax returns for taxable years 2006 and 2007. In their respective returns, Voss and Sophy each claimed home mortgage interest deductions for interest paid on the two mortgages * * *. The total interest paid [by Voss and Sophy] was $180,660.63 in 2006 and $176,536.43 in 2007. [Voss and Sophy each claimed a deduction for half of these amounts on their 2006 and 2007 tax returns.]

* * *

The IRS audited the 2006 and 2007 returns and, in 2009, [issued] notices of deficiency to Voss and Sophy. The IRS [claimed that the taxpayers could deduct the interest on only $1 million of the $2.5 million of mortgage debt. Because Voss and Sophy deducted all the interest they paid on the $2.5 million of mortgage debt and the IRS claimed they could only deduct the interest on $1 million of mortgage debt, the IRS disallowed a substantial portion of the interest deductions claimed on Voss and Sophy's 2006 and 2007 tax returns.]

C

Voss and Sophy each filed a petition with the Tax Court, and the two cases were consolidated for joint consideration. * * *

Based on the stipulated facts, exhibits, and proposed computations submitted by the parties, the Tax Court reached a decision and issued an opinion in the IRS's favor. The Tax Court framed the question presented as "whether the statutory limitations on the amount of acquisition and home equity indebtedness with respect to which interest is deductible under section 163(h)(3) are properly applied on a per-residence or per-taxpayer basis when residence co-owners are not married to each other." *Sophy v. Comm'r*, 138 T.C. 204, 209 (2012).

* * *

Noting that nothing in the legislative history of § 163(h)(3) suggested any contrary intention, the Tax Court concluded that "the limitation in section 163(h)(3)(B)(ii) * * * on the amounts that may be treated as acquisition * * * indebtedness with respect to a qualified residence [is] properly applied on a per-residence basis." *Id.* at 213.

We have jurisdiction to review the decisions of the Tax Court "in the same manner and to the same extent as decisions of the district courts in civil actions tried without a jury." 26 U.S.C. § 7482(a)(1). Accordingly, we review the Tax Court's factual findings for clear error, and we review the Tax Court's conclusions of law—including its interpretation of the Internal Revenue Code—de novo.

III

We are asked to decide an issue of first impression: When multiple unmarried taxpayers co-own a qualifying residence, do the debt limit provisions found in 26 U.S.C. § 163(h)(3)(B)(ii) * * * apply per taxpayer or per residence? We conclude that § 163(h)'s debt limits apply per taxpayer.

A

We begin with the text of the key provisions at issue—§ 163(h)(3)'s debt limit provisions. They provide:

(B) Acquisition indebtedness.—

. . .

(ii) $1,000,000 Limitation.—The aggregate amount treated as acquisition indebtedness for any period shall not exceed $1,000,000 ($500,000 in the case of a married individual filing a separate return).

* * *

Id. § 163(h)(3)(B)(ii) * * *.

The parties dispute whether the $1 million * * * debt limit in [this provision applies] per taxpayer or per residence. If [it applies] per taxpayer, then Voss and Sophy are each entitled to a $1 million debt limit, such that together they can deduct interest payments on up to $2 million of acquisition * * * debt. If the debt limit [applies] per residence, as the Tax Court held, then the $1 million [debt limit] must be divided up in some way between Voss and Sophy.

Discerning an answer from § 163(h) requires considerable effort on our part because the statute is silent as to how the debt limit should apply in co-owner situations. [The provision limits] "[t]he aggregate amount treated" as acquisition * * * debt, but neither says to whom or what the limits apply. Had Congress wanted to make clear that the debt limit applies per taxpayer, it could have drafted the provision to limit "the aggregate amount *each taxpayer* may treat as" acquisition * * * debt. But it did not. Or, had Congress wanted to make clear that the debt limit applies per residence, it could have provided that the debt limit must be divided or allocated in the event that two or more unmarried individuals co-own a qualified residence. *Cf.* 26 U.S.C. § 36(a)(1)(C) * * * But, again, it did not.

* * *

[N]othing in the statute compels the Tax Court's per-residence reading * * * .

* * *

[T]he impracticality of applying the provision under a per-residence approach suggests that Congress never intended that approach. We thus conclude that a per-taxpayer reading of the statute's debt limit provision is most consistent with § 163(h)(3) as a whole.

* * *

VI

[We] hold that § 163(h)(3)'s debt limit [applies] on a per-taxpayer basis to unmarried co-owners of a qualified residence. We infer this conclusion from the text of the statute * * *. We accordingly reverse the Tax Court's decision and remand for the limited purpose of allowing the parties to determine, in a manner consistent with this opinion, the proper amount of qualified residence interest that petitioners are entitled to deduct, as well as the proper amount of any remaining deficiency.

Erroneous tax reporting. Voss and Sophy each filed a tax return deducting the interest on $1.25 million of debt (i.e., each taxpayer deducted half the interest on the $2.5 million of total mortgage debt). These reporting positions were indefensible because a taxpayer could not deduct interest on more than $1 million of home acquisition debt at the time the taxpayers incurred the debt. If each of Voss and Sophy had deducted the interest on only $1 million of debt, it is possible that their reporting positions would not even have been challenged. But the fact that the tax return filed by each taxpayer was clearly erroneous likely led to an examination of the returns by the Internal Revenue Service and the discovery of the issue that was ultimately litigated (i.e., whether each taxpayer was allowed to deduct the interest on $1 million of debt, or only $500,000 of debt). Although the taxpayers prevailed in the litigation, they undoubtedly spent significant amounts of money and time in the process, and could have incurred penalties for their improper tax reporting. Thus, it is never in the taxpayer's interest to advance an indefensible position on a tax return.

NOTES

1.   *Qualified residence interest.* Historically, taxpayers were allowed to deduct all interest paid even when the proceeds of the loan were used for personal purposes. See IRC § 163(a). The Tax Reform Act of 1986 effectively reversed that rule by enacting IRC § 163(h) which disallows the deduction of "personal interest" (IRC § 163(h)(1)). Personal interest is defined expansively as *all* interest, other than the exceptions listed in IRC § 163(h)(2). As a result, interest is deductible only if it is within the scope of the exceptions to non-deductibility listed in IRC § 163(h)(2). Thus, interest paid by a borrower with respect to a loan used for personal purposes will generally *not* be allowed as a deduction unless it constitutes "qualified residence interest." IRC § 163(h)(2)(D).[4] For interest to constitute qualified residence interest, the interest must be attributable to "acquisition indebtedness" (IRC § 163(h)(3)(A)(i)).[5]

2.   *Acquisition indebtedness.* For a loan to constitute "acquisition indebtedness," the following three requirements must be met:

a)   The borrowed money must be used to acquire, construct, or substantially improve a qualified residence of the taxpayer. See IRC § 163(h)(3)(B)(i)(I).

b)   The loan must be secured by the taxpayer's qualified residence (i.e., the borrower must give the lender a mortgage in the qualified residence). See IRC § 163(h)(3)(B)(i)(II).

c)   The maximum amount of debt that can qualify as acquisition indebtedness for a taxpayer and the taxpayer's spouse is $750,000 until 2026, when it is scheduled to revert back to $1,000,000. See IRC §§ 163(h)(3)(B)(ii), (F)(i)(II).

---

[4]   Certain interest paid on educational loans is also allowed as a deduction even though the loan proceeds are used for personal purposes. See IRC § 163(h)(2)(F).

[5]   Prior to 2018, "home equity indebtedness" was also within the scope of qualified residence interest. See IRC §§ 163(h)(3)(A)(ii), (C). Under current law, however, home equity indebtedness will not be treated as qualified residence interest in tax years beginning before January 1, 2026. See IRC § 163(h)(3)(F)(i)(I).

■ **EXAMPLE 10-A.** *Determining qualified residence interest.* Nathan and Nina are husband and wife. They purchased the house in which they live in Year 1 for $1,000,000. They financed the purchase with $250,000 of savings and a $750,000 loan from the Bank 1 ("Loan 1") secured by a mortgage in the house. By Year 6, they had reduced the balance owed on Loan 1 to $700,000. In Year 6, they borrowed $200,000 from Bank 2 ("Loan 2") and used the money to take a trip around the world. How much of the interest paid on Loans 1 and 2 can Nathan and Nina deduct?

Loan 1 satisfies the three requirements for acquisition indebtedness. First, the loan was used to acquire a qualified residence. Second, the loan was secured by a mortgage in the house. Third, the amount of the loan did not exceed $750,000. Thus, they can deduct all the interest paid on Loan 1.

Loan 2 does not qualify as acquisition indebtedness because the loan proceeds were not used to acquire a qualified residence. As a result, none of the interest paid on Loan 2 is allowed as a deduction. Even if Loan 2 had been used to acquire a qualified residence *and* was secured by a mortgage in a qualified residence, only $50,000 of Loan 2 would constitute acquisition indebtedness ($750,000 ceiling on acquisition indebtedness less $700,000 of principal remaining on Loan 1. In these circumstances, the taxpayers would be allowed to deduct only 25% of the interest paid on Loan 2 ($50,000/$200,000 = 25%).

remaining
b

■ **PROBLEM 10-1.** *Qualified residence interest.* Elizabeth and Robert are married and purchased a primary home in Year 1 for $470,000. They financed the purchase with $60,000 in savings and a $410,000 loan (Loan 1) from Bank 1. They secured the Loan by giving the lender a mortgage in their home.

a)   What portion of the interest paid on Loan 1 can they deduct?

By Year 3, they had reduced the principal amount of Loan 1 to $400,000 and the value of their home had increased to $480,000. Consider each of the following *alternatives:*

b) In Year 3, they borrowed $75,000 (Loan 2) from Bank 2 and used the money to build an addition onto their home.

   1) What portion of the interest paid on Loan 2 could they deduct?

   2) Does it matter whether they gave Bank 2 a mortgage in their house?

   3) Does it matter if Loan 2 had been borrowed from the same bank that made Loan 1?

   4) Does Loan 2 impact the amount of interest they can deduct on Loan 1?

c) In Year 3, they borrowed $75,000 (Loan 2) from Bank 2 and used the money for an exotic vacation.

   1) What portion of the interest paid on Loan 2 could they deduct?

   2) Does it matter whether they gave Bank 2 a mortgage in their house?

d) In Year 3, the couple purchased a vacation home for $800,000. They financed the purchase with $100,000 from savings and a $700,000 loan (Loan 2) from Bank 2. They secured the loan by giving Bank 2 a mortgage in the vacation home. Assume the vacation home is a "qualified residence." What portion of the interest on Loan 2 can they deduct?

2.   Investment Interest

Although IRC § 163(h)(2)(B) allows a deduction for investment interest, the deduction is limited by IRC § 163(d). Investment interest is defined as interest paid on a loan, the proceeds of which are used to purchase property for investment. See IRC § 163(d)(3)(A). The amount of investment interest that may be deducted in any year is limited to the taxpayer's "net investment income." See IRC § 163(d)(1). Net investment income is the difference between the taxpayer's investment income and the taxpayer's investment expenses. See IRC § 163(d)(4)(A). In effect, the taxpayer may only deduct investment interest to the extent the taxpayer makes a profit on her investments.[6]

---

[6]   Note that no deduction is allowed for interest paid on money borrowed to purchase certain government bonds generating interest that is excluded from gross income. See IRC § 265(a)(2).

When investment interest paid by the taxpayer exceeds the taxpayer's net investment income, the excess amount of investment interest is not lost. Rather, the excess investment interest is carried to the following tax year and may be deducted in that year to the extent of net investment income in that later year. See IRC § 163(d)(2). If the excess investment interest cannot be deducted in the following year (due to insufficient net investment income), the excess investment interest can be carried to future years until sufficient net investment income exists to claim the deduction.

■ **EXAMPLE 10-B.** *Limitation on investment interest deduction.* Charley borrows $500,000 and uses the money to purchase stocks and bonds. In Year 1, he pays $20,000 of interest on the loan. In Year 1, Charley earns $50,000 of investment income and incurs $35,000 of investment expenses (not including the interest he paid on the loan) In Year 2, Charley pays $18,000 of interest on the loan. In Year 2, Charley again earns $50,000 of investment income but only incurs $30,000 of investment expenses (not including the interest he paid on the loan).

The amount of investment interest Charley can deduct in each year and the amount of investment interest that must be carried to the following year is computed as follows:

	Year 1	Year 2
Investment Interest Paid	$20,000	$18,000
Investment Interest Carried from Prior Year	+ 0	+ 5,000
Total Investment Interest	$20,000	$23,000
Investment Income	$50,000	$50,000
Investment Expenses	− 35,000	− 30,000
Net Investment Income	$15,000	$20,000
Deductible Investment Interest	$15,000	$20,000
Investment Interest Carried to Next Year	$5,000	$3,000

In Year 1, Charley has net investment income of $15,000. As such, he may deduct only $15,000 of the $20,000 of investment interest he paid in Year 1. The other $5,000 of investment interest he paid in Year 1 is carried forward to Year 2.

In Year 2, Charley has $20,000 of net investment income and $23,000 of investment interest (the $18,000 he paid in Year 2 plus the $5,000 he paid, but could not deduct, in Year 1). Hence, Charley may deduct only $20,000 of the $23,000 of investment interest in Year 2 (because his net investment income in Year 2 is only $20,000). The remaining $3,000 of Year 2 investment interest is carried forward to Year 3.

■ **PROBLEM 10-2.** *Investment interest.* Dina borrows $200,000 and uses the money to purchase stocks and bonds. In Year 1, she pays $10,000 of interest on the loan. In Year 1, she earns $15,000 of investment income and incurs $12,000 of investment expenses.

a)   How much investment interest may Dina deduct in Year 1?

b)   When, if ever, may Dina deduct any remaining Year 1 investment interest?

Section 62 deduction or itemized deduction. IRC § 163(h) essentially allows the deduction of:

FOR DISCUSSION

1)   interest incurred in a trade or business, *above the line*

2)   interest incurred in a non-business, income-producing activity (investment interest), and *below/ itemized*

3)   qualified residence interest. *below/ itemized*

Which of the three types of deductible interest are § 62 deductions? See IRC § 62(a). Which are itemized deductions? See IRC § 63(d).

B. Losses Incurred with Respect to Personal Use Property—§ 165

Primary Law: IRC § 165

(a) There shall be allowed as a deduction any loss sustained during the taxable year and not compensated for by insurance or otherwise.

(b) For purposes of subsection (a), the basis for determining the amount of the deduction for any loss shall be the adjusted basis provided in section 1011 for determining the loss from the sale or other disposition of property.

(c) In the case of an individual, the deduction under subsection (a) shall be limited to—

   (1) losses incurred in a trade or business;

   (2) losses incurred in any transaction entered into for profit, though not connected with a trade or business; and

   (3) except as provide in subsection (h), losses of property not connected with a trade or business or a transaction entered into for profit, if such losses arise from fire, storm, shipwreck, or other casualty, or from theft.

* * *

(h)

   * * *

   (2)

      (A) If the personal casualty losses for any taxable year exceed the personal casualty gains for such taxable year, such losses shall be allowed for the taxable year only to the extent of—

         (i) the amount of the personal casualty gains for the taxable year, plus

         (ii) so much of the excess as exceeds 10 percent of the adjusted gross income of the individual.

   * * *

(5)   In the case of an individual, * * * any personal casualty loss
       which (but for this paragraph) would be deductible in a
       taxable year beginning * * * before January 1, 2026, shall
       be allowed as a deduction under subsection (a) only to the
       extent it is attributable to a Federally declared disaster * * *.

* * *

IRC § 165 allows taxpayers to deduct certain losses. Like § 163, § 165 begins with a broad allowance rule (see § 165(a)) and then dramatically limits the
types of losses an individual may deduct (see § 165(c)). Pursuant to § 165(c)(1),
an individual may deduct losses incurred in a trade or business. In addition, an
individual may deduct losses incurred in a transaction entered into for profit
but not connected to a trade or business pursuant to § 165(c)(2).[7] These deductions are justified because fairness dictates that revenue generating activities
should be taxed on the difference between the revenue they generate and the
costs incurred to generate such revenue.

AUSTIN v. COMMISSIONER

Tax Court of the United States 1960
35 T.C. 221

ARUNDELL, JUDGE:

* * *

FINDINGS OF FACT.

* * *

Petitioners are husband and wife * * *. Since August 1954 petitioners have
resided in Wilton, Connecticut, within commuting distance of New York City.

Attached to their return, petitioners claimed, under the heading of "Other Business Deductions," a "Loss upon sale of improved real property with 40
acres located in Millbrook, New York" of [$30,000]. * * * This amount was

---

[7]   Although an individual may also deduct certain casualty losses pursuant to § 165(c)(3), that deduction is
severely restricted until 2026. See § 165(h)(5).

disallowed by the respondent and, in a statement attached to the deficiency notice, the respondent said:

> It is determined that the deduction of [$30,000] claimed in your return for the taxable year ended December 31, 1955, as resulting from the sale of improved property located in Millbrook, New York, is not deductible for the reason that * * * such loss is personal in nature and deduction of same is prohibited by Section 262 of the Internal Revenue Code of 1954 * * *.

At all times pertinent hereto, petitioner James E. Austin was a director, an elected officer, and general counsel of the DeLaval Separator Company (hereinafter sometimes referred to as Separator) and DeLaval Steam Turbine Company (hereinafter sometimes referred to as Turbine).

Separator is a corporation with its plant at Poughkeepsie, New York. Turbine is a corporation with its plant at Trenton, New Jersey. In and prior to 1949, the DeLaval corporations occupied joint offices on three floors of the Chemical Bank Building in New York City. One of these offices was the office of petitioner.

In and prior to 1949, petitioners resided with their children in Riverside, Connecticut, within commuting distance of New York City.

Sometime during 1947 petitioner was advised by the then president of Separator and chairman of Turbine's board that petitioner would probably have to move his residence to the vicinity of Poughkeepsie, New York. At that time the board of directors of Separator was studying a plan to build an office building in Poughkeepsie to house its own employees and also the joint executive officers of the two companies. This plan was studied for a period of 2 years. In January 1949, the board appointed a committee to complete plans and [enter into] contracts for the construction of the building. Construction of the building was commenced during 1950 and completed in August 1951.

The decision to remove the executive offices of the DeLaval corporations to Poughkeepsie, although acquiesced in, was against the better judgment of some of the officers of those corporations. Because of this division of opinion among the management, petitioner realized that the move to Poughkeepsie might later be reversed if and when the minority should gain control of the management. In the meantime, petitioner felt that in order to hold his position with the companies he would have to move his residence temporarily to the vicinity of Poughkeepsie.

Petitioner determined that, in seeking a place near Poughkeepsie, he should select a property which would be a venture from which he could ultimately make a profit and which, in the meanwhile, could be used as a temporary residence for his family. He sought such a property for 18 months until he finally found what he thought was a very good bargain from a profit standpoint, consisting of approximately 220 acres, with a house, cottage, and some small buildings, about 17 miles from Poughkeepsie in the small town of Millbrook, New York.

In August 1950 petitioners contracted to purchase the Millbrook property for $28,000 * * *.

Upon purchasing the Millbrook property, petitioners made immediate arrangements for substantial capital improvements, renovations, and land additions of approximately 10 acres, costing altogether $44,250 * * *. Those improvements and additions were not completed until sometime in 1952 or 1953.

In November 1950, shortly after contracting to purchase the Millbrook property, petitioners sold the home in which they were then living in Riverside, Connecticut, and moved into a rented house in Riverside.

At the annual meetings of the DeLaval corporations held in April 1951, newly elected officers decided that the principal officers of the companies (including petitioner) must have their offices in New York City. Petitioner was thereupon advised to attend the New York office daily and to establish his residence convenient to New York City, close enough for him to commute. Petitioners moved to the Millbrook property on May 30, 1951. Petitioner's family continued to reside in the Millbrook property until August 1954 when the entire family moved to Wilton, Connecticut. During the period his family was in Millbrook, petitioner, except on such occasions as his duties took him to Poughkeepsie, rented accommodations at the University Club in New York City for 4 nights a week, Monday, through Thursday. He was with his family in Millbrook the other 3 nights. Within a week after moving to Millbrook petitioners put the Millbrook property up for immediate sale with the leading real estate agent in Millbrook. In April 1952, petitioners purchased the previously mentioned 10 adjoining acres to round out the Millbrook property. The entire Millbrook property was on the market for sale at all times after June 2, 1951, and for rent at all times after July 1952, when the alterations and repairs were substantially completed. Advertisements were placed in [many] newspapers * * *. While at the Millbrook property, petitioner Elizabeth G. Austin showed the house to approximately 50 prospective purchasers and tenants.

On March 18, 1955, petitioners sold a part of the Millbrook property consisting of the main house, adjacent buildings, and 40 acres for $31,500. The [adjusted basis of] the part sold was [$61,500].[8]

* * *

Petitioners sustained a loss of [$30,000] on the sale of a part of the Millbrook property on March 18, 1955. No part of this loss was compensated for by insurance or otherwise. [Petitioners deducted the loss on their 1955 tax return. The Commissioner disallowed the deduction.]

The balance of the Millbrook property (cottage, small buildings, and approximately 190 acres) * * * has been at all times and still is on the market for sale.

OPINION.

We are satisfied that petitioners have proven that they sustained a loss of [$30,000] on the sale in 1955 of a part of the Millbrook property. * * *

We are not satisfied, however, that the evidence, taken in its entirety, establishes that the loss was not 'personal in nature' and therefore prohibited by section 262 of the Internal Revenue Code of 1954. Thus, we approve respondent's * * * disallowing the loss.

In order for petitioners to have prevailed, it would have been necessary for them to have established that the loss was either 'incurred in a trade or business' or 'in any transaction entered into for profit' as those phrases are used in section 165(c), I.R.C. 1954. * * *

It is clear that petitioners' activity in buying and selling real estate did not amount to "a trade or business" as that term is used in section 165(c)(1). * * *

Petitioner did not hold himself out as being engaged in the real estate business. At all times pertinent hereto, he was a director, elected officer, and general counsel of the DeLaval corporations, and assistant to the chairman of the board of Turbine and to the president of Separator. These duties occupied his full time. * * *

In order to classify as being in the real estate 'trade or business' it was incumbent upon petitioners to establish that for the purpose of making a livelihood, they held themselves out as being in the real estate business, and that they also devoted a substantial portion of their time to such activity. The evidence

---

[8]   Editor's note: The adjusted basis for determining a loss realized on the sale of a personal residence converted to rental property is determined under Reg. § 1.165–9(b)(2).

does not point in that direction. We hold that the loss in question was not one incurred in a trade or business.

Whether the loss was "incurred in any transaction entered into for profit" depends upon whether our ultimate finding is (1) that the Millbrook property was purchased by petitioner primarily for the purpose of deriving a gain upon the sale thereof, or (2) whether it was purchased primarily for a residence. Petitioners contend that the predominating factor in the selection of the Millbrook property was the prospect of future profits * * *. On the other hand, respondent contends that petitioners bought the Millbrook property primarily for a residence in case petitioner's office with the DeLaval corporations was moved to Poughkeepsie, as was then under contemplation. The then president of Separator and chairman of Turbine's board had already bought a home in Poughkeepsie with such a move in mind.

[W]e do not question the good faith of petitioners' testimony that they fully expected to make a profit on any ultimate sale of the Millbrook property. But this was not the predominating factor. We doubt if petitioners would ever have considered purchasing property in the vicinity of Poughkeepsie if it were not for the contemplated move of the offices of the DeLaval corporations to that city. That was the predominating factor which caused petitioners to purchase the Millbrook property. Furthermore, the large amount of money (some $44,250) spent by petitioners in renovations after they purchased the property (for $28,550) tends to show that the primary reason for acquiring the property was to acquire a convenient home for themselves and their five children. In April 1951, when it became definitely known that the offices of the principal officers of the two corporations (including petitioner) would remain in New York City, petitioner told the contractor who was making the renovations 'to cut these repairs off immediately.' This is but another indication that the primary reason for acquiring the Millbrook property was to acquire a residence.

* * *

In the instant case, one of our ultimate findings is that petitioners purchased the Millbrook property primarily for a residence and secondarily to make a profit. In view of this and other findings, we sustain the respondent's determination.

Decision will be entered for the respondent.

Notes

1.   *Realized loss must be allowed to yield a deduction.* Any increase in the value of property owned by a taxpayer is not taxed until a realization event occurs. See Chapter 6. Similarly, a decrease in the value of property owned by a taxpayer does not create a potential deduction until a realization event occurs. See IRC § 1001(a) (addressing both gain and loss). When a taxpayer sells property for an amount that exceeds the taxpayer's adjusted basis in the property, the resulting realized gain constitutes gross income.[9] By contrast, when a taxpayer sells property for an amount that is less than the taxpayer's adjusted basis in the property, the resulting realized loss does *not* trigger a deduction unless a substantive Code provision allows the deduction.

2.   *Circumstances when realized loss is allowed.* If a loss is realized by an individual on the sale of property used in a trade or business, the loss is allowed as a deduction under IRC § 165(c)(1).[10] If a loss is realized by an individual on the sale of property used in a non-business, income-producing activity, the loss is allowed as a deduction under IRC § 165(c)(2).[11] If a loss is realized by an individual on the sale of property used for personal purposes, the realized loss is generally *not* allowed as a deduction. See IRC § 262.

WORTH NOTING   A gain must be realized to trigger gross income. A loss must be realized AND ALLOWED to trigger a deduction.

3.   *Casualty losses.* A casualty loss occurs when property is damaged, destroyed, or stolen, rather than sold. IRC § 165(c)(3). The loss is measured by the adjusted basis of the property, not its fair market value. IRC § 165(b).

A casualty loss incurred with respect to property held in a trade or business is allowed as a deduction under IRC § 165(c)(1), not IRC § 165(c)(3) which excludes trade or business property.

---

[9]   When a gain is realized, the resulting income may be deferred if a nonrecognition provision applies. See IRC § 1001(c). Nonrecognition will be explored in Chapter 12.

[10]   When a loss is realized and allowed, the resulting deduction may be deferred if a nonrecognition provision applies. See IRC § 1001(c). Nonrecognition will be explored in Chapter 12.

[11]   When a loss is realized and allowed, the resulting deduction may be deferred if a nonrecognition provision applies. See IRC § 1001(c). Nonrecognition will be explored in Chapter 12.

A casualty loss incurred with respect to property held for profit (but not in a trade or business) is allowed as a deduction under IRC § 165(c)(2), not IRC § 165(c)(3) which excludes property connected to a transaction entered into for profit.

A casualty loss incurred with respect to property held for personal purposes is allowed as a deduction under IRC § 165(c)(3). However, until 2026, a personal casualty loss is allowed as a deduction only if the loss is attributable to a Federally declared disaster. IRC § 165(h)(5). Moreover, personal casualty losses attributable to Federally declared disasters are deductible only to the extent the aggregate losses suffered by an individual in a taxable year exceed 10% of adjusted gross income. IRC § 165(h)(2).

■ **PROBLEM 10-3.** *Loss allowance.* Mark bought a new minivan in Year 1 for $30,000. By Year 6, the value of the minivan had fallen to $10,000. What are the tax consequences to Mark in each of the following alternatives?

1) The minivan was used by Mark and his wife for family purposes and—

   a) Mark sold the minivan for $10,000 in Year 6.

   b) In Year 6, a piano fell on the unoccupied minivan and demolished it.

2) Mark was a florist. He used the minivan exclusively as a delivery vehicle for his florist shop and—

   a) Mark sold the minivan for $10,000 in Year 6.

   b) In Year 6, a piano fell on the unoccupied minivan and demolished it.

■ **PROBLEM 10-4.** *Section 62 deduction or itemized deduction.* Determine whether each of the following is allowed as a deduction and, if so, whether it is a § 62 deduction or an itemized deduction.

1)   A loss realized from the sale of property held—

    a)   in a trade or business,

    b)   for profit (but not in a trade or business),

    c)   for personal purposes.

2)   A casualty loss of property held—

    a)   in a trade or business,

    b)   for profit (but not in a trade or business),

    c)   for personal purposes.

C. Other Personal Expenses

1. Medical Expenses—§ 213

Primary Law: IRC § 213

(a)   There shall be allowed as a deduction the expenses paid during the taxable year, not compensated for by insurance or otherwise, for medical care of the taxpayer, his spouse, or a dependent * * *, to the extent that such expenses exceed 10% of adjusted gross income.   7.5%

* * *

Medical expenses incurred by an individual are personal expenses and, as such, would normally not be allowed as a deduction. See IRC § 262(a). However, Congress allows taxpayers to deduct certain medical expenses by providing an exception to the general prohibition on deducting personal expenses. See IRC § 213(a).

MORRISSEY v. UNITED STATES

United States Court of Appeals, Eleventh Circuit, 2017
871 F. 3d 1260

Newsom, Circuit Judge:

This is a tax case. Fear not, keep reading. In determining whether the IRS properly denied a taxpayer's claimed deduction on his 2011 return, we must decide [an] important and (as it turns out) interesting [question.] Was the money that a homosexual man paid to father children through *in vitro* fertilization [IVF] spent "for the purpose of affecting" his body's reproductive "function" within the meaning of I.R.C. § 213? * * *

I

A

Plaintiff-Appellant Joseph F. Morrissey is a homosexual man. * * * Although Mr. Morrissey concedes that he is not medically infertile, he characterizes himself as "effectively" infertile because he is homosexual and because it is physiologically impossible for two men to conceive a child through sexual relations.

In 2010, Mr. Morrissey and his partner decided to try to have children through IVF, with Mr. Morrissey serving as the biological father. The IVF process involved collecting Mr. Morrissey's sperm, using that sperm to fertilize eggs donated by one woman, and then implanting the resulting embryos into the uterus of a second woman who served as a gestational surrogate. Between 2010 and 2014, Mr. Morrissey paid expenses related to (among other things) seven IVF procedures, three egg donors, three surrogates, and two fertility specialists. All told, the IVF process cost Mr. Morrissey more than $100,000. In 2011 alone—the tax year at issue in this case—Mr. Morrissey paid nearly $57,000 out of pocket for IVF-related expenses.

Of that total, only about [$2,000] went toward procedures performed directly on Mr. Morrissey's body—namely, blood tests and sperm collection. He spent the remaining $55,000 to identify and retain the women who served as the egg donor and the gestational surrogate, to compensate those women for their services, to reimburse their travel and other expenses, and to provide medical care for them.

B

[Mr. Morrissey deducted on his 2011 tax return the roughly $57,000 of IVF-related expenses he incurred in 2011.]

[A]fter examining Mr. Morrissey's [tax] return, the IRS disallowed his IVF-related deduction in its entirety. The agency's formal claim-disallowance letter explained that I.R.C. § 213, which governs deductions for "medical care" expenses, "states that Medical Care must be for Medical Services provided to the taxpayer, his spouse, or dependent"—which, overwhelmingly, the services underlying Mr. Morrissey's claimed deduction were not. Mr. Morrissey appealed to the IRS Office of Appeals, which upheld the disallowance.

C

Following the IRS's final determination, Mr. Morrissey filed this refund suit in the United States District Court for the Middle District of Florida. [M]r. Morrissey contended that "Tax Code Section 213, as plainly written, authorizes [his] requested deduction." [T]he parties filed competing summary judgment motions. In a written order, the district court granted summary judgment for the IRS.

* * *

II

On appeal, Mr. Morrissey renews his argument * * * that under I.R.C. § 213, all of the IVF-related costs that he paid in 2011 are deductible "medical care" expenses * * *.

A

In pertinent part, I.R.C. § 213(a) states as follows: "There shall be allowed as a deduction the expenses paid during the taxable year, not compensated by insurance or otherwise, for medical care of the taxpayer, his spouse, or a dependent . . . ." Particularly important to this appeal is Section 213(d)'s definition of the term "medical care" as it is used in Section 213(a)—as relevant here, "[t]he term 'medical care' means amounts paid . . . for the diagnosis, cure, mitigation, treatment, or prevention of disease, or for the purpose of affecting any structure or function of the body." I.R.C § 213(d).

Mr. Morrissey rests his statutory argument on a specific portion of Section 213(d)'s definition. [M]r. Morrissey asserts that all of the IVF-related expenses that he incurred in 2011 are deductible as "medical care" on the ground that they constitute amounts paid "for the purpose of affecting any . . . function of the body." Significantly, because (as applicable here) Section 213(a) allows a deduction for medical care "of the taxpayer," all agree that "the body" at issue in Section 213(d)'s definition is the taxpayer's own—not a third party's. Accordingly, the lone statutory question before us is whether the * * * IVF-related expenses for which Mr. Morrissey claims a deduction constitute amounts paid for the purpose of "affecting any . . . function of [Mr. Morrissey's] body."

In an effort to bring his case within Section 213(d)'s terms, Mr. Morrissey contends that all of the IVF-related expenses that he incurred—including the costs attributable to the identification, retention, compensation, and care of the women who served as the egg donor and the surrogate—were made for the purpose of affecting his body's *reproductive* function. In particular, Mr. Morrissey asserts that because he and his male partner are physiologically incapable of reproducing together, IVF was his only means of fathering his own biological children. Accordingly, Mr. Morrissey claims, it was medically necessary to involve third parties—a female egg donor and a female surrogate—in order to enable his own body to fulfill its reproductive function.

Section 213's plain language—and particularly the ordinary meaning of the statutory terms "affecting" and "function"—forecloses Mr. Morrissey's argument. First, "affecting." The word "affect" means to "produce an effect upon" or (less tautologically) "to produce a material influence upon or alteration in." *Webster's Third New International Dictionary* 35 (2002). Tracing Section 213(d)'s language, we must therefore determine whether the IVF expenses at issue were paid for the purpose of *materially influencing or altering* some function of Mr. Morrissey's body.

Now, to "function." The term "function" is defined as "the action for which a person or thing is specifically fitted, used, or responsible or for which a thing exists"; "the activity appropriate to the nature or position of a person or thing"; or "one of a group of related actions contributing to a larger action," such as "the normal and specific contribution of any bodily part (as a tissue, organ, or system) to the economy of a living organism." *Webster's Third New International Dictionary* 920–21 (2002). Stated less technically, it seems fair to summarize—and the parties don't disagree—that the term "function" denotes a person's or thing's unique task or role.

Statutory context yields an additional—and important—insight. In Section 213(d), the word "function" is followed by the prepositional phrase "of the body." That limiting modifier, referring as it does to one "body" rather than multiple "bodies," confirms what Section 213(d)'s plain language indicates—that at least in this context, "function" is an attribute of a singular thing and, accordingly, that the statutory definition should be understood to cover medical care that affects the function of one body, while excluding care that might be thought to affect some "function" achieved by the cooperation of multiple bodies.

* * *

[A]s a man, Mr. Morrissey's body's specific responsibility in the reproductive process—his particular reproductive "function"—was to produce and provide healthy sperm. The question here is whether the IVF-related expenses for which Mr. Morrissey claimed tax deductions were paid for care that materially influenced or altered—i.e., "affect[ed]"—that function. Overwhelmingly, they were not.

To be sure, the aspects of the IVF process that related specifically to Mr. Morrissey's provision of healthy sperm could be said to have affected his reproductive function. So, for instance, [the parties agree that] the [$2,000] that Mr. Morrissey spent on sperm collection and accompanying bloodwork [were potentially] deductible. * * *

Mr. Morrissey's * * * appeal turns on the far more significant sums (more than $55,000) that he paid to identify, retain, compensate, and care for the women who served as the egg donor and gestational surrogate. The question is whether *those* expenses were undertaken for treatment or care that materially influenced or altered—affected—Mr. Morrissey's own reproductive function. They weren't. Mr. Morrissey is capable of producing and providing healthy sperm with or without the involvement of an egg donor or a gestational surrogate. His body could perform those functions before he engaged his female counterparts in the IVF process, and he can do so—just the same—after the completion of that process. Because the costs attributable to the identification, retention, compensation, and care of the egg donor and the surrogate weren't incurred "for the purpose of affecting any . . . function of [Mr. Morrissey's] body," he can't deduct them as "medical care" expenses under I.R.C. § 213.

* * *

We are thus constrained by I.R.C. § 213's plain language to reject Mr. Morrissey's statutory claim. Because the human reproductive process entails distinct male and female functions, because Mr. Morrissey's body's own function within that process is to produce and provide healthy sperm, and because Mr. Morrissey was and remains capable of performing that function without the aid of IVF-related treatments, those treatments did not "affect[ ]" any "function of [his] body" within the meaning of Section 213(d)—and accordingly do not qualify as deductible "medical care" within the meaning of Section 213(a).

* * *

III

We hold * * * that the Internal Revenue Code does not permit Mr. Morrissey to deduct the expenses attributable to the identification, retention, compensation, and care of the women who served as the egg donor and the gestational surrogate in his IVF process * * *. Accordingly, we affirm the district court's order granting summary judgment and dismissing Mr. Morrissey's claims.

Notes

1. *Only unreimbursed expenses qualify for the deduction.* The medical expense deduction is allowed only for unreimbursed medical expenses. IRC § 213(a). Thus, if the taxpayer's insurer or employer reimburses the taxpayer for the medical expense, the expense is not deductible. Why does this restriction exist?

2. *Annual expenses must exceed 10% of adjusted gross income.* The taxpayer's total unreimbursed medical expenses for the year are allowed as a deduction only to the extent that total exceeds 10% of the taxpayer's adjusted gross income. As you may recall, adjusted gross income is the difference between the taxpayer's gross income for the taxable year and the deductions allowed to the taxpayer that are described in IRC § 62(a). Because unreimbursed medical expenses can only be deducted to the extent that total medical expenses exceed 10% of adjusted gross income, the medical expense deduction is essentially limited to catastrophic medical expenses.

■ **EXAMPLE 10-C.** *Deductible medical expenses.* Eric has adjusted gross income of $100,000 in Year 1. He incurs medical expenses of $12,000 in Year 1.

If none of Eric's medical expenses are reimbursed, he may deduct only ~~$2,000~~ of medical expenses in Year 1. (His unreimbursed medical expenses of $12,000 exceed ~~10%~~ of his adjusted gross income [~~10%~~ × $100,000 = ~~$10,000~~] by ~~$2,000~~.) *[handwritten: $4,500, 7.5%, 7.5%]*

By contrast, if as little as ~~$2,000~~ of Eric's $12,000 of medical expenses is reimbursed by insurance, he cannot deduct *any* of his remaining ~~$10,000~~ of unreimbursed medical expenses in Year 1. (If $2,000 of his medical expenses are reimbursed, his unreimbursed expenses of $10,000 do not exceed 10% of his adjusted gross income [10% × $100,000 = $10,000].) *[handwritten: $7,500, $4,500, $4,500, $7,500]*

Section 62 deduction or itemized deduction. If a taxpayer has unreimbursed medical expenses in excess of 10% of adjusted gross income in a given tax year, is the amount allowed as a deduction under IRC § 213(a) a § 62 deduction (see IRC § 62(a)) or an "itemized deduction" (see IRC § 63(d))?

2. Charitable Contributions—§ 170

Primary Law: IRC § 170

(a)

    (1)   There shall be allowed as a deduction any charitable contribution (as defined in subsection (c)) payment of which is made within the taxable year. A charitable contribution shall be allowable as a deduction only if verified under regulations prescribed by the Secretary.

    * * *

HERNANDEZ v. COMMISSIONER

United States Supreme Court, 1989
490 U.S. 680, 109 S.Ct. 2136, 104 L.Ed.2d 766

* * *

Justice Marshall delivered the opinion of the Court.

Section 170 of the Internal Revenue Code of 1954 (Code), 26 U.S.C. § 170, permits a taxpayer to deduct from gross income the amount of a "charitable contribution." The Code defines that term as a "contribution or gift" to certain eligible donees, including entities organized and operated exclusively for religious purposes. We granted certiorari to determine whether taxpayers may deduct as charitable contributions payments made to branch churches of the Church of Scientology (Church) in order to receive services known as "auditing" and "training." We hold that such payments are not deductible.

I

Scientology was founded in the 1950's by L. Ron Hubbard. It is propagated today by a "mother church" in California and by numerous branch churches around the world. The mother Church instructs laity, trains and ordains ministers, and creates new congregations. Branch churches, known as "franchises" or "missions," provide Scientology services at the local level, under the supervision of the mother Church.

Scientologists believe that an immortal spiritual being exists in every person. A person becomes aware of this spiritual dimension through a process known as "auditing." Auditing involves a one-to-one encounter between a participant (known as a "preclear") and a Church official (known as an "auditor"). An electronic device, the E-meter, helps the auditor identify the preclear's areas of spiritual difficulty by measuring skin responses during a question and answer session. Although auditing sessions are conducted one on one, the content of each session is not individually tailored. The preclear gains spiritual awareness by progressing through sequential levels of auditing, provided in short blocks of time known as "intensives."

The Church also offers members doctrinal courses known as "training." Participants in these sessions study the tenets of Scientology and seek to attain the qualifications necessary to serve as auditors. Training courses, like auditing sessions, are provided in sequential levels. Scientologists are taught that spiritual gains result from participation in such courses.

The Church charges a "fixed donation," also known as a "price" or a "fixed contribution," for participants to gain access to auditing and training sessions. These charges are set forth in schedules, and prices vary with a session's length and level of sophistication. In 1972, for example, the general rates for auditing ranged from $625 for a 12-1/2-hour auditing intensive, the shortest available, to $4,250 for a 100-hour intensive, the longest available. Specialized types of auditing required higher fixed donations * * *. This system of mandatory fixed charges is based on a central tenet of Scientology known as the "doctrine of exchange," according to which any time a person receives something he must pay something back. In so doing, a Scientologist maintains "inflow" and "outflow" and avoids spiritual decline.

The proceeds generated from auditing and training sessions are the Church's primary source of income. The Church promotes these sessions not only through newspaper, magazine, and radio advertisements, but also through free lectures, free personality tests, and leaflets. The Church also encourages, and indeed rewards with a 5% discount, advance payment for these sessions. The Church often refunds unused portions of prepaid auditing or training fees, less an administrative charge.

Petitioners in these consolidated cases each made payments to a branch church for auditing or training sessions. They sought to deduct these payments on their federal income tax returns as charitable contributions under § 170. Respondent Commissioner, the head of the Internal Revenue Service (IRS), disallowed these deductions, finding that the payments were not charitable contributions within the meaning of § 170.

Petitioners sought review of these determinations in the Tax Court. * * * Before trial, the Commissioner stipulated that the branch churches of Scientology are religious organizations entitled to receive tax-deductible charitable contributions under the relevant sections of the Code. This stipulation isolated as the sole statutory issue whether payments for auditing or training sessions constitute "contribution[s] or gift[s]" under § 170.

The Tax Court held a 3-day bench trial during which the taxpayers and others testified and submitted documentary exhibits describing the terms under which the Church promotes and provides auditing and training sessions. Based on this record, the court upheld the Commissioner's decision. It observed first that the term "charitable contribution" in § 170 is synonymous with the word "gift," which case law had defined "as a *voluntary transfer* of property by the owner to another *without consideration* therefor." It then determined that petitioners had received consideration for their payments, namely, "the benefit of various religious services provided by the Church of Scientology." * * *

The Courts of Appeals for the First Circuit in petitioner Hernandez's case * * * affirmed. The First Circuit rejected Hernandez's argument that under § 170, the IRS' ordinary inquiry into whether the taxpayer received consideration for his payment should not apply to "the return of a commensurate *religious* benefit, as opposed to an *economic or financial* benefit." The court found "no indication that Congress intended to distinguish the religious benefits sought by Hernandez from the medical, educational, scientific, literary, or other benefits that could likewise provide the *quid* for the *quo* of a nondeductible payment to a charitable organization." The court also rejected Hernandez's argument that it was impracticable to put a value on the services he had purchased, noting that the Church itself had "established and advertised monetary prices" for auditing and training sessions, and that Hernandez had not claimed that these prices misstated the cost of providing these sessions.

> * * *

We granted certiorari to resolve a Circuit conflict concerning the validity of charitable deductions for auditing and training payments. We now affirm.

II

For over 70 years, federal taxpayers have been allowed to deduct the amount of contributions or gifts to charitable, religious, and other eleemosynary institutions. Section 170, the present provision, was enacted in 1954; it requires a taxpayer claiming the deduction to satisfy a number of conditions.[6] The Commissioner's stipulation in this case, however, has narrowed the statutory inquiry to one such condition: whether petitioners' payments for auditing and training sessions are "contribution[s] or gift[s]" within the meaning of § 170.

The legislative history of the "contribution or gift" limitation, though sparse, reveals that Congress intended to differentiate between unrequited

---

[6]   The charitable transfer must be made to a qualified recipient, § 170(c), within the taxable year, § 170(a)(1), and consist of cash or qualified property, §§ 170(e)–(h), not exceeding a specified percentage of the taxpayer's income in the year of payment * * *. §§ 170(b), 170(d).

payments to qualified recipients and payments made to such recipients in return for goods or services. Only the former were deemed deductible. * * *

In ascertaining whether a given payment was made with "the expectation of any quid pro quo," the IRS has customarily examined the external features of the transaction in question. This practice has the advantage of obviating the need for the IRS to conduct imprecise inquiries into the motivations of individual taxpayers. The lower courts have generally embraced this structural analysis. * * *

In light of this understanding of § 170, it is readily apparent that petitioners' payments to the Church do not qualify as "contribution[s] or gift[s]." As the Tax Court found, these payments were part of a quintessential *quid pro quo* exchange: in return for their money, petitioners received an identifiable benefit, namely, auditing and training sessions. The Church established fixed price schedules for auditing and training sessions in each branch church; it calibrated particular prices to auditing or training sessions of particular lengths and levels of sophistication; it returned a refund if auditing and training services went unperformed; it distributed "account cards" on which persons who had paid money to the Church could monitor what prepaid services they had not yet claimed; and it categorically barred provision of auditing or training sessions for free. Each of these practices reveals the inherently reciprocal nature of the exchange.

Petitioners do not argue that such a structural analysis is inappropriate under § 170, or that the external features of the auditing and training transactions do not strongly suggest a *quid pro quo* exchange. * * * Petitioners argue instead that they are entitled to deductions because a *quid pro quo* analysis is inappropriate under § 170 when the benefit a taxpayer receives is purely religious in nature. Along the same lines, petitioners claim that payments made for the right to participate in a religious service should be automatically deductible under § 170.

We cannot accept this statutory argument for several reasons. First, it finds no support in the language of § 170. Whether or not Congress could * * * provide for the automatic deductibility of a payment made to a church that either generates religious benefits or guarantees access to a religious service, that is a choice Congress has thus far declined to make. Instead, Congress has specified that a payment to an organization operated exclusively for religious (or other eleemosynary) purposes is deductible *only* if such a payment is a "contribution or gift." The Code makes no special preference for payments made in the expectation of gaining religious benefits or access to a religious service. * * *

Second, petitioners' deductibility proposal would expand the charitable contribution deduction far beyond what Congress has provided. Numerous forms of payments to eligible donees plausibly could be categorized as providing a religious benefit or as securing access to a religious service. For example, some taxpayers might regard their tuition payments to parochial schools as generating a religious benefit or a securing access to a religious service; such payments, however, have long been held not to be charitable contributions under § 170. Taxpayers might make similar claims about payments for church-sponsored counseling sessions or for medical care at church-affiliated hospitals that otherwise might not be deductible. Given that, under the First Amendment, the IRS can reject otherwise valid claims of religious benefit only on the ground that a taxpayers' alleged beliefs are not sincerely held, but not on the ground that such beliefs are inherently irreligious, the resulting tax deductions would likely expand the charitable contribution provision far beyond its present size. We are loath to effect this result in the absence of supportive congressional intent.

Finally, the deduction petitioners seek might raise problems of entanglement between church and state. If framed as a deduction for those payments generating benefits of a religious nature for the payor, petitioners' proposal would inexorably force the IRS and reviewing courts to differentiate "religious" benefits from "secular" ones. If framed as a deduction for those payments made in connection with a religious service, petitioners' proposal would force the IRS and the judiciary into differentiating "religious" services from "secular" ones. * * *

Accordingly, we conclude that petitioners' payments to the Church for auditing and training sessions are not "contribution[s] or gift[s]" within the meaning of that statutory expression.

III

* * *

IV

We turn, finally, to petitioners' assertion that disallowing their claimed deduction is at odds with the IRS' longstanding practice of permitting taxpayers to deduct payments made to other religious institutions in connection with certain religious practices. * * *

[P]etitioners make two closely related claims. First, the IRS has accorded payments for auditing and training disparately harsh treatment compared to payments to other churches and synagogues for their religious services: Recognition of a comparable deduction for auditing and training payments is necessary to cure this administrative inconsistency. Second, Congress, in modifying § 170 over the years, has impliedly acquiesced in the deductibility of payments to these other faiths; because payments for auditing and training are indistinguishable from these other payments, they fall within the principle acquiesced in by Congress that payments for religious services are deductible under § 170.

[A]s to whether the IRS, in fact, permits taxpayers to deduct payments made to purchase services from other churches and synagogues, the Commissioner's periodic revenue rulings have stated the IRS' position rather clearly. A 1971 ruling, still in effect, states: "Pew rents, building fund assessments, and periodic dues paid to a church . . . are all methods of making contributions to the church, and such payments are deductible as charitable contributions within the limitations set out in section 170 of the Code." Rev.Rul. 70–47, 1970–1 Cum.Bull. 49. We also assume for purposes of argument that the IRS also allows taxpayers to deduct "specified payments for attendance at High Holy Day services, for tithes, for torah readings and for memorial plaques."

The development of the present litigation, however, makes it impossible for us to resolve petitioners' claim that they have received unjustifiably harsh treatment compared to adherents of other religions. The relevant inquiry in determining whether a payment is a "contribution or gift" under § 170 is, as we have noted, not whether the payment secures religious benefits or access to religious services, but whether the transaction in which the payment is involved is structured as a *quid pro quo* exchange. To make such a determination in this case, the Tax Court heard testimony and received documentary proof as to the terms and structure of the auditing and training transactions; from this evidence it made factual findings upon which it based its conclusion of nondeductibility, a conclusion we have held consonant with § 170 * * *.

Perhaps because the theory of administrative inconsistency emerged only on appeal, petitioners did not endeavor at trial to adduce from the IRS or other sources any specific evidence about other religious faiths' transactions. The IRS' revenue rulings, which merely state the agency's conclusions as to deductibility and which have apparently never been reviewed by the Tax Court or any other judicial body, also provide no specific facts about the nature of these other faiths' transactions. In the absence of such facts, we simply have no way (other than the wholly illegitimate one of relying on our personal experiences and observations) to appraise accurately whether the IRS' revenue rulings have correctly applied a *quid pro quo* analysis with respect to any or all of the religious practices in question. We do not know, for example, whether payments for other faiths' services are truly obligatory or whether any or all of these services are generally provided whether or not the encouraged "mandatory" payment is made.

The IRS' application of the "contribution or gift" standard may be right or wrong with respect to these other faiths, or it may be right with respect to some religious practices and wrong with respect to others. It may also be that some of these payments are appropriately classified as partially deductible "dual payments." With respect to those religions where the structure of transactions involving religious services is established not centrally but by individual congregations, the proper point of reference for a *quid pro quo* analysis might be the individual congregation, not the religion as a whole. Only upon a proper factual record could we make these determinations. Absent such a record, we must reject petitioners' administrative consistency argument.

Petitioners' congressional acquiescence claim fails for similar reasons. Even if one assumes that Congress has acquiesced in the IRS' ruling with respect to "[p]ew rents, building fund assessments, and periodic dues," Rev.Rul. 70–47, 1970–1 Cum.Bull. 49, the fact is that the IRS' 1971 ruling articulates no broad principle of deductibility, but instead merely identifies as deductible three discrete types of payments. Having before us no information about the nature or structure of these three payments, we have no way of discerning any possible unifying principle, let alone whether such a principle would embrace payments for auditing and training sessions.

V

For the reasons stated herein, the judgments of the Courts of Appeals are hereby

Affirmed.

Justice Brennan and Justice Kennedy took no part in the consideration or decision of these cases.

Justice O'Connor, with whom Justice Scalia joins, dissenting.

[Omitted]

LOOK ONLINE **Closing agreement.** In 1993, the Internal Revenue Service and the Church of Scientology reportedly entered into a "closing agreement." See IRC § 7121. Pursuant to that agreement, the Church paid more than $12 million "to extinguish any potential tax liability that may be due or unpaid" for all prior tax years. In exchange, the IRS conceded that anyone who made a donation to the Church of Scientology for "auditing and training" would now be allowed a deduction for the amount of that contribution. To view the closing agreement, **click here**.

NOTE

Substantiation requirements. The charitable contribution deduction is contingent upon satisfying stringent substantiation requirements. For example, the regulations provide as follows:

> No deduction is allowed under section 170(a) for all or part of any contribution of $250 or more unless the taxpayer substantiates the contribution with a contemporaneous written acknowledgment from the donee organization.

Reg. § 1.170A–13(f)(1). To be deductible in full, the written acknowledgment must provide that no goods or services were provided to the donor in exchange for the contribution. Reg. § 1.170A–13(f)(2). The written acknowledgment will meet the contemporaneous requirement only if it is obtained by the date the taxpayer files her tax return for the taxable year in which the contribution was made or, if earlier, the due date (including extensions) for filing the taxpayer's return for that year. Reg. § 1.170A–13(f)(3). Thus, if a taxpayer files her tax return before securing the requisite written acknowledgment, she will not be allowed a deduction for her contribution.

The substantiation rules are even more stringent with respect to certain contributions of property. In one case, a taxpayer was denied a multi-million dollar deduction for a contribution of property because the taxpayer failed to disclose its basis in the contributed property on the tax return on which it claimed the deduction. See RERI Holdings, LLC v. Commissioner, No. 17–1266 (D.C. Cir. 2019).

FOR DISCUSSION

Section 62 deduction or itemized deduction. Is the deduction allowed by § 170(a) for charitable contributions a § 62 deduction (see IRC § 62(a)) or an itemized deduction (see IRC § 63(d))?

---

3.   Taxes—§ 164

A principal goal of this casebook is to enable students to determine an individual's Federal income tax liability. To achieve that goal, we must compute the individual's gross income for the tax year and then subtract the allowable deductions to determine taxable income. The rates in IRC § 1 are then applied to taxable income to determine the individual's Federal income tax liability.

The amount of Federal income tax an individual pays is *not* allowed as a deduction because no provision of the Code authorizes the deduction of Federal income tax. See IRC § 161. However, certain other taxes paid by an individual, including state income taxes, and state and local taxes imposed on real and personal property, *are* allowed as a deduction. See IRC § 164(a). If an individual pays these taxes in connection with a trade or business, the taxes would be deductible even if § 164 did not exist. See IRC § 162. However, when these taxes are paid in connection with a personal matter (e.g., the real estate taxes imposed on one's residence), they are allowed as a deduction by virtue of IRC § 164.

WORTH NOTING

Until 2026, the maximum amount of taxes that may be deducted by an individual in any year under IRC § 164 is limited to $10,000. See IRC § 164(b)(6).

Primary Law: IRC § 164

(a)   Except as otherwise provided in this section, the following taxes shall be allowed as a deduction for the taxable year within which paid or accrued:

(1)   State and local * * * real property taxes.

(2)   State and local personal property taxes.

(3)   State and local, and foreign, income, war profits, and excess profits taxes.

* * *

(b)

* * *

(6)   In the case of an individual and a taxable year beginning * * * before January 1, 2026—

* * *

(B)   the aggregate amount of taxes taken into account under paragraphs (1), (2), and (3) of subsection (a) * * * for any taxable year shall not exceed $10,000 * * *.

* * *

■   **PROBLEM 10-5.** *Limitations on the deduction of taxes.*

a)   If Joanne pays $15,000 of real estate taxes to the county in which she lives, is she allowed a deduction for those taxes if—

1)   the real estate taxes are imposed on a factory used in Joanne's business?

2)   the real estate taxes are imposed on non-business, rental property Joanne owns?

3)   the real estate taxes are imposed on Joanne's personal residence?

b)   In each of the above alternatives, if Joanne is allowed a deduction for the real estate taxes, is the allowed deduction a § 62 deduction (see IRC §§ 62(a)(1), (4)) or an itemized deduction (see IRC § 63(d))?

Note

Circumventing the $10,000 limitation on the state and local tax deduction. The Tax Cuts and Jobs Act of 2017 imposed a $10,000 cap on the annual deduction for taxes allowed under IRC § 164 until tax years beginning in 2026. See IRC § 164(b)(6). In an effort to enable taxpayers to deduct more than $10,000 per year of state taxes, several states enacted legislation permitting a taxpayer to reduce her liability for state taxes by the amount she contributes to certain state-related, charitable organizations. This legislation was designed to transform non-deductible payments of state taxes (i.e., amounts in excess of $10,000) into deductible charitable contributions. In response, the Treasury Department proposed regulations in 2018 treating contributions to these state-related charitable organizations as payments of state taxes, rather than deductible charitable contributions. The regulations were adopted with minor modifications in 2019. The following excerpt explores the issue and its resolution:

Department of the Treasury, Internal Revenue Service, Notice of Proposed Rulemaking, Contributions in Exchange for State or Local Tax Credits

REG–112176–18
Aug. 27, 2018

[I]n recent years, it has become increasingly common for states and localities to provide state and local tax credits in return for contributions by taxpayers to or for the use of certain [state-related charitable organizations]. As the use of these tax credit programs * * * became more common, the IRS Office of Chief Counsel (IRS Chief Counsel) * * * considered whether the receipt of state tax credits under these programs were *quid pro quo* benefits that would affect the amounts of taxpayers' charitable contribution deductions under section 170(a).

* * *

[Until 2018, IRC] section 164 generally allowed an itemized deduction—unlimited in amount—for the payment of state and local taxes. Accordingly, the question of how to characterize transfers pursuant to state tax credit programs had little practical consequence from a federal income tax perspective because

* * * a deduction was likely to be available under either section 164 or section 170. Permitting a charitable contribution deduction for a transfer made in exchange for a state or local tax credit generally had no effect on federal income tax liability because any increased deduction under section 170 would be offset by a decreased deduction under section 164.

However, as a result of the new limit on the deductibility of state and local taxes under section 164(b)(6) (as added by the [2017 Tax Act]), treating a transfer pursuant to a state or local tax credit program as a charitable contribution for federal income tax purposes may reduce a taxpayer's federal income tax liability. When a charitable contribution is made in return for a state or local tax credit and the taxpayer has pre-credit state and local tax liabilities in excess of the $10,000 limitation in section 164(b)(6), a charitable contribution deduction under section 170 would no longer be offset by a reduction in the taxpayer's state and local tax deduction under section 164. Thus, as a consequence, state and local tax credit programs now give taxpayers a potential means to circumvent the $10,000 limitation in section 164(b)(6) by substituting an increased charitable contribution deduction for a disallowed state and local tax deduction. State legislatures are also now considering or have adopted proposals to enact new state and local tax credit programs with the aim of enabling taxpayers to characterize their transfers as fully deductible charitable contributions for federal income tax purposes, while using the same transfers to satisfy or offset their state or local tax liabilities.

In light of the tax consequences of section 164(b)(6) and the resulting increased interest in preexisting and new state tax credit programs, the Treasury Department and the IRS determined that it was appropriate to review the question of whether amounts paid or property transferred in exchange for state or local tax credits are fully deductible as charitable contributions under section 170.

* * *

After reviewing the issue, * * * the Treasury Department and the IRS believe that when a taxpayer receives * * * a state or local tax credit in return for a payment [to a state-related charitable organization], the receipt of this tax benefit constitutes a *quid pro quo* that may preclude a full deduction under section 170(a). * * * Thus, the Treasury Department and the IRS believe that the amount otherwise deductible as a charitable contribution must generally be reduced by the amount of the state or local tax credit received or expected to be received, just as it is reduced for many other benefits. * * *

Compelling policy considerations reinforce the interpretation and application of section 170 in this context. Disregarding the value of all state tax benefits received or expected to be received in return for charitable contributions would precipitate significant revenue losses that would undermine and be inconsistent with the limitation on the deduction for state and local taxes adopted by Congress in section 164(b)(6). Such an approach would incentivize and enable taxpayers to characterize payments as fully deductible charitable contributions for federal income tax purposes, while using the same payments to satisfy or offset their state or local tax liabilities. Disregarding the tax benefit would also undermine the intent of Congress in enacting section 170, that is, to provide a deduction for taxpayers' gratuitous payments to qualifying entities, not for transfers that result in economic returns. The Treasury Department and the IRS believe that appropriate application of the *quid pro quo* doctrine to substantial state or local tax benefits is consistent with the Code and sound tax administration.

* * *

WORTH NOTING

Impact of state or local tax credit on charitable contribution deduction. Under the regulations, if an individual receives a state or local tax credit for making a payment to a state-related charity, the individual's charitable contribution deduction is normally reduced by the amount of the tax credit. Reg. § 1.170A–(1)(h)(3)(i). However, if the tax credit does not exceed 15% of the payment to the charity, the individual's charitable contribution deduction is not reduced by the tax credit. Reg. § 1.170A–(1)(h)(3)(vi).

■ **EXAMPLE 10-D.** *Application of regulations.* Ben makes a $10,000 payment to a state-related charity described in IRC § 170(c). In exchange for the payment, Ben receives a state tax credit of 80% of his $10,000 payment (i.e., an $8,000 state tax credit). Under the regulations, Ben's charitable contribution deduction is reduced by $8,000, the amount of the state tax credit. Thus, Ben's charitable contribution deduction for the $10,000 payment is limited to $2,000. See Reg. § 1.170A–(1)(h)(3)(vii)(A) Example 1.

By contrast, if Ben receives a state tax credit of only 10% of his $10,000 payment (i.e., a $1,000 state tax credit), Ben's charitable contribution deduction is not reduced by the state tax credit because the credit is not more than 15% of the payment. As such, Ben may claim a $10,000 charitable contribution deduction. See Reg. § 1.170A–(1)(h)(3)(vii)(A) Example 2.

D. Limitations on Itemized Deductions

1.   Section 62 Deductions vs. Itemized Deductions

No disbursement is deductible unless a specific statutory provision allows the deduction. See IRC § 161. Chapters 9 and 10 have explored several statutory provisions that allow deductions. Specifically, we have examined, IRC §§ 162, 163, 164, 165, 166, 170, 199A, 212, and 213. Moreover, IRC §§ 167 and 168 were examined in Chapter 6.

In Chapter 9, we expanded the formula for computing a taxpayer's Federal income tax liability to the following:

Gross Income
– § 62 Deductions   (i.e, allowed deductions listed in IRC § 62(a))
Adjusted Gross Income
– Other Deductions (including certain itemized deductions)
Taxable Income
× Tax Rates
Federal Income Tax Liability

This formula reveals that identifying the Code provision that allows a deduction is only the first of two steps that must be taken to determine whether an allowed deduction will be subtracted in its entirety from gross income in arriving at taxable income. The second step is to determine whether the deduction in question is listed in IRC § 62(a) or, alternatively, constitutes an itemized deduction under IRC § 63(d).

Primary Law: IRC § 63

* * *

(d) For purposes of this subtitle, the term "itemized deductions" means the deductions allowable under this chapter other than—

(1) the deductions allowable in arriving at adjusted gross income [i.e., the deductions listed in IRC § 62(a)],

(2) * * *, and

(3) the deduction provided in section 199A.

Although this second step of determining whether an allowed deduction is listed in IRC § 62(a) or constitutes an itemized deduction under IRC § 63(d) is purely mechanical, it is important because deductions listed in IRC § 62(a) are subtracted in their entirety in arriving at taxable income.[13] By contrast, itemized deductions are subject to limitations that may eliminate some or even all of these deductions from the calculation of taxable income. As such, taxpayers normally prefer deductions listed in § 62(a) to itemized deductions. The next two parts of this Chapter will explore the limitations imposed on itemized deductions.

WORTH NOTING

Sections 62(a) and 63(d) do NOT allow deductions.
Rather, the substantive allowance provisions we previously explored *allow* deductions (e.g., IRC §§ 162, 163, 164). Sections 62(a) and 63(d) simply tell us whether a deduction allowed by one of the substantive allowance provisions is *classified* as a § 62 deduction or as an itemized deduction.

---

[13] If the deductions described in § 62(a) are attributable to a "passive activity," however, they may be deferred under IRC § 469. This topic will be explored in Chapter 13.

FOR DISCUSSION

Deductions described in § 62(a) vs. itemized deductions. The following deduction allowance provisions have been examined in this casebook: IRC §§ 162, 163, 164, 165, 166, 167, 168, 170, 199A, 212, and 213.

a) Which of the deduction allowance provisions yield § 62 deductions (see IRC § 62(a))?

b) Which of the deduction allowance provisions yield itemized deductions (see IRC § 63(d))?

c) Do any of the allowance provisions yield deductions that are neither § 62 deductions nor itemized deductions (see IRC § 63(d)(3))?

2. Temporary Disallowance of Miscellaneous Itemized Deductions—§ 67(g)

Not all itemized deductions are treated equally. Rather, a taxpayer's itemized deductions are divided into two categories: "miscellaneous itemized deductions" (a statutory term defined in IRC § 67(b)) and all other itemized deductions, which for convenience, will be referred to in this casebook as "non-miscellaneous itemized deductions" (a term that does not appear in the statute).

Primary Law: IRC § 67

* * *

(b) For purposes of this section, the term "miscellaneous itemized deductions" means the itemized deductions other than—

(1) the deduction under section 163 (relating to interest),

(2) the deduction under section 164 (relating to taxes),

(3) the deduction under section 165(a) for casualty and theft losses, described in paragraph (2) or (3) of section 165(c)
* * * ,

(4) the deduction under section 170 (relating to charitable, etc., contributions * * *) * * *,

(5) the deduction under section 213 (relating to medical, dental, etc., expenses),

* * *

* * *

(g) [N]o miscellaneous itemized deduction shall be allowed for any taxable year beginning * * * before January 1, 2026.

Impact of IRC § 67. Section 67 does *not* impact the taxpayer's non-miscellaneous itemized deductions (i.e., the deduction allowed under the statutory provisions listed in IRC § 67(b)). However, IRC § 67 disallows all of a taxpayer's miscellaneous itemized deductions in tax years beginning before 2026. IRC § 67(g).

Miscellaneous itemized deductions vs. non-miscellaneous itemized deductions. The following deduction allowance provisions have been examined in this casebook: IRC §§ 162, 163, 164, 165, 166, 167, 168, 170, 199A, 212, and 213.

a) Which of the deduction allowance provisions yield miscellaneous itemized deductions?

b) Which of the deduction allowance provisions yield non-miscellaneous itemized deductions?

3.   Itemized Deductions vs. the Standard Deduction—§ 63

Primary Law: IRC § 63

(a)   Except as provided in subsection (b), for purposes of this subtitle, the term "taxable income" means gross income minus the deductions allowed by this chapter (other than the standard deduction).

(b)   In the case of an individual who does not elect to itemize his deductions for the taxable year, for purposes of this subtitle, the term "taxable income" means adjusted gross income minus—

  (1)   the standard deduction,

  (2)   * * *, and

  (3)   the deduction provided in section 199A.

(c)   For purposes of this subtitle—

  (1)   [T]he term "standard deduction" means * * *—

     (A) the basic standard deduction * * *.

  (2)   For purposes of paragraph (1), the basic standard deduction is—

     (A) 200 percent of the dollar amount in effect under subparagraph (C) for the taxable year in the case of—

        (i)   a joint return * * *,

     (B) * * *

     (C) $3,000 in any other case.

  * * *

  (7)   In the case of a taxable year beginning * * * before January 1, 2026—

     (A) Paragraph (2) shall be applied—

        (i)   * * *

        (ii) by substituting "$12,000" for $3,000 in subparagraph (C).

  * * *

The vast majority of individuals do not claim any itemized deductions. Rather, they claim a standard deduction allowed to taxpayers who opt not to claim the itemized deductions to which they would otherwise be entitled. See IRC § 63(b). In effect, a taxpayer will claim whichever of the following amounts is *greater:* the taxpayer's total non-miscellaneous itemized deductions or the standard deduction.

For 2018, the standard deduction for most single individuals was $12,000 and the standard deduction for most married couples was $24,000.[14] Thus, unless the total non-miscellaneous itemized deductions to which a married couple is entitled exceed $24,000, the couple will simply claim the standard deduction and forgo their itemized deductions. In this event, the itemized deductions to which they would otherwise be entitled are effectively worthless.

Note that the deductions described in § 62(a) are subtracted from the taxpayer's gross income regardless of whether the taxpayer claims the standard deduction or the allowable itemized deductions. See IRC §§ 63(b) (beginning with adjusted gross income), (d)(1). Because the deductions described in § 62(a) are subtracted from gross income in all cases, taxpayers who claim the standard deduction clearly prefer those deductions to itemized deductions. Like the deductions described in § 62(a), the deduction provided in § 199A is allowed to all individuals regardless of whether they claim the standard deduction or their itemized deductions. See IRC §§ 63(b)(3), (d)(3).

The following refined formula yields an individual's federal income tax liability:

Gross Income
– § 62 Deductions　　　(i.e., allowed deductions listed in IRC § 62(a))
Adjusted Gross Income
– Non-Miscellaneous Itemized Deductions or Standard Deduction (the
– § 199A Deduction　　　　　　　　　　　　　　　　　　greater of the two)
Taxable Income
× Tax Rates
Federal Income Tax Liability

---

[14]　See IRC §§ 63(c)(2)(A), (C), (7)(A)(ii). These amounts are adjusted annually for inflation. See IRC § 63(c)(7)(B)(ii).

■ **PROBLEM 10-6.** *Itemized deductions or standard deduction.* Jimmy and Beth are married. In 2018, they derived gross income and were allowed deductions as set forth below:

Gross Income	$300,000
Deductions described in IRC § 62(a)	20,000
Adjusted Gross Income	$280,000
Non-Miscellaneous Itemized Deductions	30,000
Taxable Income	$250,000

a) Should Jimmy and Beth claim their itemized deductions or, instead, claim the standard deduction?

b) Would your answer change if Jimmy and Beth had only $10,000 of non-miscellaneous itemized deductions?

c) Is the amount of Jimmy and Beth's deductions described in IRC § 62(a) relevant to the question of whether they should claim their non-miscellaneous itemized deductions or the standard deduction?

d) If Jimmy and Beth had been allowed a deduction under IRC § 199A, would the amount of that deduction be relevant to the question of whether they should claim their non-miscellaneous itemized deductions or the standard deduction?

SYNTHESIS

No disbursement may be deducted from gross income unless a statutory provision allows the deduction. Chapter 9, focused on trade or business expenses that are normally allowed as a deduction. By contrast, Chapter 10 focused on personal expenses that are normally *not* allowed as a deduction. However, deductions are allowed for—

1) qualified residence interest,

2) certain casualty losses,

3) unreimbursed medical expenses in excess of 10% of adjusted gross income,

4) charitable contributions, and

5) up to $10,000 of certain state and local taxes.

Most of the trade or business deductions in Chapter 9 were described in IRC § 62(a) and subtracted from gross income to arrive at adjusted gross income. By contrast, the personal expenses allowed as deductions in Chapter 10 are non-miscellaneous itemized deductions that are subtracted from adjusted gross income to arrive at taxable income. In lieu of these non-miscellaneous itemized deductions, a single individual may claim a standard deduction of $12,000 (in 2018) and a married couple filing a joint return may claim a standard deduction of $24,000 (in 2018). Hence, if the standard deduction exceeds the taxpayer's non-miscellaneous itemized deductions, the taxpayer will claim the standard deduction (in lieu of the itemized deductions). In this situation, the itemized deductions have no impact on the taxpayer's tax liability.

Test Your Knowledge: To assess your understanding of the material in this chapter, click here to take a quiz.

PART IV

Timing of Income and Deductions

CHAPTER 11

Time Value and Tax Accounting

Overview

Parts II and III of this casebook focused on determining whether each benefit derived by an individual is gross income and each disbursement made by an individual is allowed as a deduction. Normally, an individual must calculate her Federal income tax liability for each calendar year. See IRC § 441. This Part of the casebook focuses on how an individual determines the proper year's tax return on which to report each item of gross income and deduction. That determination is governed by the tax accounting method utilized by the individual. See IRC § 446(a).

Most individuals use the cash method of accounting. Under this method, an item of gross income is reported in the year that cash, property or services are received. Correspondingly, an allowable deduction is claimed in the year that payment is made. However, some individuals who conduct business as sole proprietors use the accrual method of accounting. Under the accrual method, an item of gross income is reported in the year the right to receive payment occurs, regardless of when payment is actually received. Similarly, a deduction is allowed in the year the obligation to make payment arises, regardless of when the payment is actually made.[1]

This Chapter will examine the cash method of accounting and the accrual method of accounting. Before doing so, however, it is important to consider why the timing of income and deductions has economic significance. As long as the taxpayer reports an item of gross income and tax is paid, what difference

---

[1]   Additional restrictions discussed later in this Chapter are generally imposed on the timing of an accrual method taxpayer's deductions.

does it make whether the taxpayer reports the item in an earlier tax year or a later tax year if the same tax rate would apply in both years? To answer this question, the time value of money must be understood.

A. Introduction to the Time Value of Money

The ability of an individual to possess money for a period of time has economic value. If you possess $1,000 for one year, you can invest that money and earn a return on it. For example, if you deposited the $1,000 in a bank that paid 1% per-year interest on its deposits, you would have $1,010 at year-end.[2] The "time value of money" refers to the economic benefit that can be derived by investing money that you possess for as long as you possess the money.

The time value of money motivates individuals to defer paying their obligations as long as possible. By deferring payment, the individual can continue to invest the money she would otherwise use to make the payment and earn returns on that money for the longest possible time. The obligation to pay Federal income tax is among the largest obligations of many individuals. The time value of money motivates these individuals to defer Federal income tax to later tax years so that they can keep the dollars that would have been used to pay their taxes invested as long as possible and thereby maximize the returns they earn.

In light of the time value of money, individuals normally wish to defer gross income and to accelerate deductions. Both objectives result in reducing taxable income in the current year and augmenting taxable income in a later year. When taxable income is deferred, the taxpayer will pay the same amount of tax over time (assuming the same tax rates apply at all times[3]) but will enjoy greater investment returns by keeping the money used to pay the tax invested for a longer period.

■ **EXAMPLE 11-A.** *Benefit of deferring taxes.* Melinda preliminarily determines that she has gross income of $150,000 and deductions of $30,000 for each of Years 1 and 2. Assume, unrealistically, that her tax rate is a flat 25% in both years. Based on her preliminary determina-

---

[2] $1,000 + ($1,000 × 1%) = $1,010.

[3]   The impact of different tax rates will be explored in Part V.

tion, she would have $120,000 of taxable income in each year and pay a tax of $30,000 in each year (a total tax of $60,000 for Years 1 and 2).

Year 1		Year 2	
Gross Income	$150,000	Gross Income	$150,000
Less: Deductions	30,000	Less: Deductions	30,000
Taxable Income	$120,000	Taxable Income	$120,000
Tax (25%)	$30,000	Tax (25%)	$30,000

a) *Deferral of gross income.* Assume Melinda learns that she can defer $20,000 of Year 1 gross income to Year 2. Also assume that she can earn 2% per-year on her investments. As the table that follows illustrates, if Melinda defers the $20,000 of gross income to Year 2, her Year 1 Taxable Income will fall from $120,000 to $100,000 and her Year 1 Tax will fall from $30,000 to $25,000, a savings of $5,000 that she can invest until Year 2. Of course, by deferring $20,000 of gross income from Year 1 to Year 2, her Year 2 Taxable Income will increase from $120,000 to $140,000 and her Year 2 tax will increase by $5,000 (from $30,000 to $35,000). Melinda still pays the same total amount of tax over the two year period ($25,000 + $35,000 = $60,000). However, by deferring $5,000 of her Year 1 tax liability to Year 2, she can invest that $5,000 for one year and reap a $100 investment return (2% × $5,000 = $100) due to the time value of money.

Year 1		Year 2	
Gross Income	$130,000	Gross Income	$170,000[4]
Less: Deductions	30,000	Less: Deductions	30,000
Taxable Income	$100,000	Taxable Income	$140,000
Tax (25%)	$25,000	Tax (25%)	$35,000

b) *Acceleration of deductions.* Accelerating deductions offers the same time value of money benefit as deferring gross income. Assume that rather than being able to defer $20,000 of Year 1 gross income to Year 2, Melinda learns that she can accelerate $20,000 of Year 2 deductions to Year 1. As the table that follows illustrates, if Melinda accelerates the $20,000 of deductions to Year 1, her Year 1 Taxable Income will fall from $120,000 to

---

[4]   The $100 investment return would add to Melinda's gross income unless an exclusion applied.

$100,000 and her Year 1 Tax will fall from $30,000 to $25,000, a savings of $5,000 that she can invest until Year 2. Of course, by accelerating the $20,000 of Year 2 deductions to Year 1, her Year 2 Taxable Income will increase from $120,000 to $140,000 and her Year 2 tax will increase by $5,000 (from $30,000 to $35,000). Thus, she still pays the same amount of tax over the two year period ($25,000 + $35,000 = $60,000). However, by deferring $5,000 of her Year 1 tax liability to Year 2, she can invest that $5,000 for one year and reap a $100 investment return (2% × $5,000 = $100) due to the time value of money.

Year 1		Year 2	
Gross Income	$150,000	Gross Income	$150,000[5]
Less: Deductions	50,000	Less: Deductions	10,000
Taxable Income	$100,000	Taxable Income	$140,000
Tax (25%)	$25,000	Tax (25%)	$35,000

IN SIGHTS

Economic benefits vs. tax costs. Example 11-A illustrates that the time value of money will normally motivate taxpayers to defer taxes. However, this motivation exists *only if the economic benefit that triggers the tax is not also deferred.* For example, if Taxpayer has the choice of—

1) receiving $20,000 today that will trigger an immediate $5,000 tax, or

2) receiving $20,000 a year from today that will trigger a $5,000 tax a year from today,

Taxpayer will prefer to receive the $20,000 today and pay the immediate tax. If Taxpayer receives the $20,000 today and pays the $5,000 tax, Taxpayer will keep $15,000 that Taxpayer can invest starting today. By contrast, if Taxpayer opts to wait to receive the $20,000 until a year from today and pay the $5,000 tax at that later time, Taxpayer will not have the $15,000 to invest until a year from today. Hence, Taxpayer will have lost the opportunity to earn an extra year's return on the $15,000 by deferring both the economic benefit and the tax.

---

[5]   The $100 investment return would add to Melinda's gross income unless an exclusion applied.

By contrast, if Taxpayer can enjoy an economic benefit today but defer the tax on that benefit until a year from today, taxpayer will be motivated to defer the tax. Thus, if Taxpayer receives $20,000 today and has the choice of—

1) paying the $5,000 tax today, or

2) paying the $5,000 tax a year from today,

Taxpayer will prefer to defer the tax until a year from today. See Example 11-A. By deferring the tax until next year, Taxpayer can invest the entire $20,000 and earn a return on that amount for an entire year before paying the $5,000 tax. If Taxpayer opted instead to pay the tax today, Taxpayer would have only $15,000 to invest today.

An easier way to absorb this point is to recognize that one could indefinitely defer all income taxes by never deriving any economic benefits. Quite clearly, that would not be a prudent strategy to pursue. The lesson from this discussion is that the time value of money only encourages tax deferral when the corresponding economic benefit is not also being deferred.

■ **PROBLEM 11-1.** *Accelerating deductions.*

a) If you were required to make a $20,000 payment a year from today, which of the following two options would yield the greater economic benefit?

1) a $20,000 tax deduction today (resulting in $5,000 of immediate tax savings), or

2) a $20,000 tax deduction a year from today (resulting in $5,000 of tax savings a year from today).

b)   Which of the following two options would yield the greater economic benefit if you had the choice of making a $20,000 payment—

1)   today (resulting in an immediate $20,000 tax deduction that saved $5,000 of tax), or

2)   a year from today (resulting in a $20,000 deduction a year from today that saved $5,000 of taxes a year from today)?

ESTATE OF STRANAHAN v. COMMISSIONER

United States Court of Appeals, Sixth Circuit, 1973
472 F.2d 867

Before Celebrezze, Peck and Kent, Circuit Judges.

Peck, Circuit Judge.

[T]he facts before us are briefly recounted as follows: On March 11, 1964, the decedent, Frank D. Stranahan, entered into a closing agreement with the Commissioner of Internal Revenue Service (IRS) under which it was agreed that decedent owed the IRS $754,815.72 for interest due to deficiencies in federal income * * * taxes * * *. Decedent, a cash-basis taxpayer, paid the amount during his 1964 tax year. Because his personal income for the 1964 tax year would not normally have been high enough to fully absorb the large interest deduction, decedent accelerated his future income to avoid losing the tax benefit of the interest deduction. To accelerate the income, decedent executed an agreement dated December 22, 1964, under which he assigned to his son, Duane Stranahan, $122,820 in anticipated stock dividends from decedent's Champion Spark Plug Company common stock (12,500 shares). At the time both decedent and his son were employees and shareholders of Champion. As consideration for this assignment of future stock dividends, decedent's son paid the decedent $115,000 by check dated December 22, 1964. The decedent thereafter directed the transfer agent for Champion to issue all future dividend checks to his son, Duane, until the aggregate amount of $122,820 had been paid to him. Decedent reported this $115,000 payment as ordinary income for the 1964 tax year and thus was able to deduct the full interest payment from the sum of this payment and his other income. During decedent's taxable year in question, dividends * * * were paid to and received by decedent's son. No part of [these dividends] was reported as income in the return filed by decedent's estate for this period. Decedent's son reported this dividend income on his own return as ordinary income subject to the offset of his basis of $115,000, resulting in a net amount of [$7,820] of taxable income. [$122,820 of dividends less $115,000 adjusted basis equals $7,820.]

Subsequently, the Commissioner sent appellant (decedent's estate) a notice of deficiency claiming that the [dividends] received by the decedent's son was actually income attributable to the decedent. [T]he Tax Court upheld the deficiency * * *. The Tax Court concluded that decedent's assignment of future dividends in exchange for the present discounted cash value of those dividends "though conducted in the form of an assignment of a property right, was in reality a loan to decedent masquerading as a sale and so disguised lacked any business purpose; and, therefore, decedent realized taxable income in the year 1965 when the dividend was declared paid."

As pointed out by the Tax Court, several long-standing principles must be recognized. First, under Section 451(a) of the Internal Revenue Code of 1954, a cash basis taxpayer ordinarily realizes income in the year of receipt rather than the year when earned. Second, a taxpayer who assigns future income for consideration in a bona fide commercial transaction will ordinarily realize ordinary income in the year of receipt. Third, a taxpayer is free to arrange his financial affairs to minimize his tax liability;[2] thus, the presence of tax avoidance motives will not nullify an otherwise bona fide transaction.[3] We also note there are no claims that the transaction was a sham, the purchase price was inadequate or that decedent did not actually receive the full payment of $115,000 in tax year 1964. And it is agreed decedent had the right to enter into a binding contract to sell his right to future dividends.

The Commissioner's view regards the transaction as merely a temporary shift of funds, with an appropriate interest factor, within the family unit. He argues that no change in the beneficial ownership of the stock was effected and no real risks of ownership were assumed by the son. Therefore, the Commissioner

---

[2]   "Any one may so arrange his affairs that his taxes shall be as low as possible; he is not bound to choose that pattern which will best pay the Treasury; there is not even a patriotic duty to increase one's taxes." Helvering v. Gregory, 69 F.2d 809, 810 (2d Cir. 1934) (Hand, J. Learned), aff'd 293 U.S. 465 (1935).

[3]   "As to the astuteness of taxpayers in ordering their affairs so as to minimize taxes, we have said that 'the very meaning of a line in the law is that you intentionally may go as close to it as you can if you do not pass it.' Superior Oil Co. v. Mississippi, 280 U.S. 390, 395–396. This is so because 'nobody owes any public duty to pay more than the law demands: taxes are enforced exactions, not voluntary contributions.'" Atlantic Coast Line v. Phillips, 332 U.S. 168, 172-173 (1947) (Frankfurter, J.).

concludes, taxable income was realized not on the formal assignment but rather on the actual payment of the dividends.

It is conceded by taxpayer that the sole aim of the assignment was the acceleration of income so as to fully utilize the interest deduction. Gregory v. Helvering, 293 U.S. 465, 55 S.Ct. 266, 79 L.Ed. 596 (1935), established the landmark principle that the substance of a transaction, and not the form, determines the taxable consequences of that transaction. In the present transaction, however, it appears that both the form and the substance of the agreement assigned the right to receive future income. What was received by the decedent was the present value of that income the son could expect in the future. On the basis of the stock's past performance, the future income could have been (and was) estimated with reasonable accuracy. Essentially, decedent's son paid consideration to receive future income. Of course, the fact of a family transaction does not vitiate the transaction but merely subjects it to special scrutiny.

* * *

The Commissioner also argues that the possibility of not receiving the dividends was remote, and that since this was particularly known to the parties as shareholders and employees of the corporation, no risks inured to the son. * * * However, it seems clear that risks, however remote, did in fact exist. The fact that the risks did not materialize is irrelevant. Assessment of the risks is a matter of negotiation between the parties and is usually reflected in the terms of the agreement. Since we are not in a position to evaluate those terms, and since we are not aware of any terms which dilute the son's dependence on the dividends alone to return his investment, we cannot say he does not bear the risks of ownership.

Accordingly, we conclude the transaction to be economically realistic, with substance, and therefore should be recognized for tax purposes even though the consequences may be unfavorable to the Commissioner. The facts establish decedent did in fact receive payment. Decedent deposited his son's check for $115,000 to his personal account on December 23, 1964, the day after the agreement was signed. The agreement is unquestionably a complete and valid assignment to decedent's son of all dividends up to $122,820. The son acquired an independent right against the corporation since the latter was notified of the private agreement. Decedent completely divested himself of any interest in the dividends and vested the interest on the day of execution of the agreement with his son.

* * *

The judgment is reversed and the cause remanded for further proceedings consistent with this opinion.

Notes

1.   *Time value of money.* By selling the right to future dividends to his son, Stranahan *accelerated* more than $100,000 of gross income that would normally have been reported on his 1965 income tax return to his 1964 return. The time value of money normally encourages *deferral* of gross income. Can the strategy employed by Stranahan be reconciled with the time value of money?

2.   *Change in law.* What was the source of Stranahan's excess deductions on his 1964 tax return? If current law applied to Stranahan's 1964 tax year, would those excess deductions have existed? See IRC § 163(h).

IN PRACTICE

Tax consequences to son. Stranahan's son purchased a right to receive future dividends for $115,000 and established a basis of $115,000 in that right. IRC § 1012. The opinion states that Stranahan's son reported as gross income the dividend income the son collected "subject to the offset of his basis of $115,000, resulting in a net amount of $7,820 of taxable income." Had the son sold the right to future dividends for $122,820, he clearly would have had $7,820 of § 61(a)(3) income. But instead the son collected the dividends; no sale or exchange of the right occurred. Conceptually, he recovered $122,820 from an intangible asset he purchased for $115,000 so he should only be taxed on the difference. But the technical justification for allowing the son to offset the dividends he received by the basis in the right he purchased is not entirely clear.

When a taxpayer like Stranahan takes an aggressive position and prevails, the government is likely to challenge related parties involved in the transaction if their tax positions are at all vulnerable. Thus, it would have been prudent for Stranahan's son to have retained counsel to evaluate the risk of adverse tax consequences to him before proceeding with the transaction.

B. Tax Accounting

Notwithstanding the unusual circumstances in the Stranahan case, the time value of money normally motivates taxpayers to attempt to defer gross income and accelerate deductions. Conversely, the government is normally motivated to seek to accelerate the taxpayer's gross income and defer the taxpayer's deductions. The taxpayer's method of accounting normally dictates the proper time to report each item of gross income and deduction. As you examine the following materials, consider whether the rules that apply to each method of accounting further the taxpayer's goals or the government's goals with respect to the time value of money.

1. Cash Method of Accounting

Secondary Law: Reg. § 1.446–1(c)(1)(i)

Generally, under the cash receipts and disbursement method in the computation of taxable income, all items which constitute gross income (whether in the form of cash, property, or services) are to be included for the taxable year in which actually or constructively received. Expenditures are to be deducted for the taxable year in which actually made. * * *

The cash method of accounting is relatively straight-forward. A taxpayer using the cash method does not report gross income until he receives payment in cash, property or services. Normally, a taxpayer will be entitled to payment before payment is received. Nevertheless, it is not entitlement to payment that triggers income under the cash method of accounting. Because income is not triggered until payment is received, the cash method of accounting tends to defer income.

A taxpayer using the cash method of accounting may not claim a deduction until payment is made. Just as the income side of the cash method of accounting tends to defer income, the deduction side of the cash method of accounting tends to defer deductions. A taxpayer will normally be obligated to make a payment before the payment is actually made. However, it is not the obligation to make a payment that triggers the deduction under the cash method. Deductions may not be claimed until payment is made.

Revenue Ruling 76–135

1976–1 C.B. 114

An individual issued and delivered a negotiable promissory note [with a face amount of 50x dollars] to a lawyer who accepted the note in payment for legal services rendered to the individual as operator of a small business. The cost of the legal services was an ordinary and necessary business expense. Upon receipt of the note from the individual, the lawyer immediately [sold] the note at a local bank [for 47x dollars]. Both the lawyer and the client file their Federal income tax returns on a calendar year basis and use the cash receipts and disbursements method of accounting.

The note in the instant case was issued in 1973 in the face amount of 50x dollars, bearing interest at six percent per annum. By its terms the note called for payment of one-half of its face value plus interest in 1974 and the remaining one-half with interest in 1975. * * * The bank discounted the note, and the lawyer received 47x dollars for it in 1973. The client made payments to the bank in the years 1974 and 1975 as required by the note.

Held, for purposes of section 451 of the Internal Revenue Code of 1954, which relates to the taxable year for which items of gross income are included, the fair market value of the note (47x dollars) accepted by the lawyer in 1973 as payment for legal services and discounted at a bank for cash was income includible in the lawyer's 1973 Federal income tax return. Section 1.61–2(d)(4) of the Income Tax Regulations.

Held further, for purposes of section 461 of the Code, which relates to the taxable year for which deductions may be taken, the same note was not a "payment" deductible on the client's 1973 Federal income tax return.

However, the client's payment to the bank of one-half of the face value of the note plus interest in 1974, and the payment of the remaining one-half with interest in 1975, are the actual payments of cash required as a basis for any deductions allowable to the individual as a cash basis taxpayer. Accordingly, amounts paid by the client to the bank as principal and interest on the note are deductible by the individual as business expenses and as interest on the Federal income tax returns for 1974 and 1975, respectively.

* * *

NOTES

1.   *Receipt of cash, property or services.* In Rev. Rul. 76–135, a lawyer who used the cash method of accounting received a negotiable promissory note in 1973 and sold the note in 1973. As such, the lawyer had § 61(a)(2) income in 1973. Was the lawyer's income triggered by the receipt of the note or the sale of the note? If the lawyer had received the note in 1973 but had not sold the note until 1974, would the income have been reportable in 1973 or 1974? See Reg. § 1.61–2(d)(4) (second sentence).

2.   *Opposite sides of the same coin?* The lawyer in Rev. Rul. 76–135 who received the negotiable promissory note had gross income in 1973, the year of receipt. By contrast, the issuer of the negotiable promissory note was not allowed to claim a deduction until payments were made on the note in 1974 and 1975. Why was the issuer not allowed a deduction in the same year that the recipient had gross income (i.e., 1973)?

HORNUNG v. COMMISSIONER

Tax Court of the United States, 1967
47 T.C. 428

HOYT, JUDGE:

* * *

FINDINGS OF FACT

* * *

Petitioner is a cash basis taxpayer residing in Louisville, Ky. * * * Petitioner is a well-known professional football player who was employed by the Green Bay Packers in 1962. Prior to becoming a professional, petitioner attended the

University of Notre Dame and was an All-American quarterback on the university football team.

* * *

Sport Magazine is a publication of the McFadden-Bartell Corp., with business offices in New York City. Each year Sport Magazine * * * awards a new Corvette automobile to the player selected by its editors * * * as the outstanding player in the National Football League championship game. * * * The existence of the award is announced several days prior to the sporting event in question, and the selection and announcement of the winner is made immediately following the athletic contest. The Corvette automobiles are generally presented to the recipients at a luncheon or dinner several days subsequent to the sporting event * * *. The Corvette awards are intended to promote the sale of Sport Magazine and their cost is deducted by the publisher for Federal income tax purposes as promotion and advertising expense.

The Corvette which is to be awarded to the most valuable player in the National Football League championship game is generally purchased by the magazine several months prior to the date the game is played, and it is held by a New York area Chevrolet dealer until delivered to the recipient of the award. In some years when the game is played in New York the magazine has had the car on display at the stadium on the day of the game.

On December 31, 1961, petitioner played in the National Football League championship game between the Green Bay Packers and the New York Giants. The game was played in Green Bay, Wis. Petitioner scored a total of 19 points during this game and thereby established a new league record. At the end of this game petitioner was selected by the editors of Sport as the most valuable player and winner of the Corvette * * *. At approximately 4:30 on the afternoon of December 31, 1961, following the game, the editor in chief of Sport informed petitioner that he had been selected as the most valuable player of the game. The editor in chief did not have the key or the title to the Corvette with him in Green Bay and the petitioner did not request or demand immediate possession of the car at that time but he accepted the award.

The Corvette which was to be awarded in connection with this 1961 championship game had been purchased by Sport in September of 1961. However, since the game was played in Green Bay, Wis., the car was not on display at the stadium on the day of the game, but was in New York in the hands of a Chevrolet dealership. As far as Sport was concerned the car was 'available' to petitioner on December 31, 1961, as soon as the award was announced. However, December 31, 1961, was a Sunday and the New York dealership at which the car was located was closed. Although the National Football League championship game is always played on a Sunday, Sport is prepared to make prior arrangements to have the car available in New York for the recipient of the award on that Sunday afternoon if the circumstances appear to warrant such arrangements—particularly if the game is played in New York. Such arrangements were not made in 1961 because the game was played in Green Bay, and, in the words of Sport's editor in chief, 'it seemed a hundred-to-one that * * * (the recipient of the award) would want to come in (to New York) on New Year's Eve to take possession' of the prize.

On December 31, 1961, when petitioner was informed that he had won the Corvette, he was also informed that a luncheon was to be held for him in New York City on the following Wednesday by the publisher of Sport, at which luncheon his award would be presented. At that time petitioner consented to attend the luncheon in order to receive the Corvette. There was no discussion that he would obtain the car prior to the presentation ceremony previously announced. The lunch was held as scheduled on Wednesday, January 3, 1962, in a New York restaurant. Petitioner attended and was photographed during the course of the presentation of the automobile to him. * * *

[Petitioner sold his prize Corvette several months after he received it.]

The fair market value of the Corvette automobile received by petitioner was $3,331.04. Petitioner reported the sale of the Corvette in his 1962 Federal income tax return in Schedule D attached thereto * * * as follows:

Kind of Property	Date Acquired	Date Sold	Gross Sales Price	Depreciation Allowed	Cost	Gain
1962 Corvette gift—Sport Magazine	1962	1962	3,331.04	0.00	0.00	None

Petitioner did not include the fair market value of this car in his gross income for 1962, or for any other year. * * *

Respondent determined that petitioner's taxable income for 1962 was understated by reason of his failure to include therein ordinary income in the amount of [$3,331.04 as reflected by the fair market value of the 1962 Corvette].

* * *

OPINION

* * *

Petitioner alleged in his petition that the Corvette was received by him as a gift in 1962 [and was therefore excludable from gross income]. However, at trial and on brief, he argues that [he should have included the value of the Corvette in gross income in 1961 because he] constructively received [the car] in 1961. * * * [Petitioner's constructive receipt] argument is based upon the assertion that the announcement and acceptance of the award occurred at approximately 4:30 on the afternoon of December 31, 1961, following the game.

[Respondent claims that the Corvette did not constitute gross income until the petitioner actually received the car at the luncheon on January 3, 1962. Therefore, respondent claims the value of the car should have been included in petitioner's gross income for 1962, not 1961.]

It is undisputed that petitioner was selected as the most valuable player of the National Football League championship game in Green Bay on December 31, 1961. It is also undisputed that petitioner actually received the car on January 3, 1962, in New York. Petitioner relies upon the statement at the trial by the editor in chief of Sport that as far as Sport was concerned the car was 'available' to petitioner on December 31, 1961, as soon as the award was announced. It is therefore contended that the petitioner should be deemed to have received the value of the award in 1961 under the doctrine of constructive receipt.

The amount of any item of gross income is included in gross income for the taxable year in which received by the taxpayer unless such amount is properly accounted for as of a different period. Sec. 451(a). It is further provided in section 446(c) that the cash receipts method, which the petitioner utilized, is a permissible method of computing taxable income. The doctrine of constructive receipt is developed by regulations under section 446(c) which provides as follows:

> Generally, under the cash receipts and disbursements method * * * all items which constitute gross income (whether in the form of cash, property, or services) are to be included for the taxable year in which actually or constructively received. * * *

[Reg. § 1.446–1(c)(1)(i).]

The regulations under section 451 elaborate on the meaning of constructive receipt:

> Income although not actually reduced to a taxpayer's possession is constructively received by him in the taxable year during which it is credited to his account, set apart for him, or otherwise made available so that he may draw upon it at any time, or so that he could have drawn upon it during the taxable year if notice of intention to withdraw had been given. However, income is not constructively received if the taxpayer's control of its receipt is subject to substantial limitations or restrictions. * * *

[Reg. § 1.451–2(a).]

The probable purpose for development of the doctrine of constructive receipt was stated as follows in Ross v. Commissioner, 169 F.2d 483, 491 (C.A. 1, 1948):

> The doctrine of constructive receipt was, no doubt, conceived by the Treasury in order to prevent a taxpayer from choosing the year in which to return income merely by choosing the year in which to reduce it to possession. Thereby the Treasury may subject income to taxation when the only thing preventing its reduction to possession is the volition of the taxpayer. * * *

However, it was held in the Ross case that the doctrine of constructive receipt could be asserted by a taxpayer as a defense to a deficiency assessment even though the item in controversy had not been reported for the taxable year of the alleged constructive receipt:

> if these items were constructively received when earned they cannot be treated as income in any later year, * * * and in the absence of misstatement of fact, intentional or otherwise, the petitioner cannot be estopped from asserting that the items were taxable only in the years in which constructively received.

The basis of constructive receipt is essentially unfettered control by the recipient over the date of actual receipt. Petitioner has failed to convince us that he possessed such control on December 31, 1961, over the receipt of the Corvette. The evidence establishes that the Corvette which was presented to petitioner on January 3, 1962, was in the possession of a Chevrolet dealer in New York City on December 31, 1961. At the time the award was announced in Green Bay, the editor in chief of Sport had neither the title nor keys to the car, and nothing was given or presented to petitioner to evidence his ownership or right to possession of the car at that time.

Moreover, since December 31, was a Sunday, it is doubtful whether the car could have been transferred to petitioner before Monday even with the co-operation of the editor in chief of Sport. The New York dealership at which the car was located was closed. The car had not been set aside for petitioner's use and delivery was not dependent solely upon the volition of petitioner. The doctrine of constructive receipt is therefore inapplicable, and we hold that petitioner received the Corvette for income tax purposes in 1962 as he originally alleged in his petition and as he reported in his 1962 income tax return.

We now must tackle the more basic question involving the Corvette which is whether the value of the car should be included in petitioner's gross income for the taxable year of receipt. Petitioner * * * contends that the car was received as a gift and therefore properly excluded from gross income under section 102(a) * * *.

It is our opinion that certainly the donor's motive here precludes a determination that Sport made a gift of the Corvette to petitioner in 1962. It is clear that there was no detached and disinterested generosity. * * *

[W]e hold that the value of the Corvette should have been included in petitioner's gross income for 1962. * * *

Notes

1.   *Time value of money.* Once it was determined that the car in fact constituted gross income to Hornung, in what year did the government claim that gross income occurred? In what year did Hornung claim that gross income occurred? Can you reconcile these positions with the time value of money?

2.   *Reporting position on receipt.* What was the taxpayer's justification for not reporting the value of the car in gross income? How compelling was that position? See IRC § 74.

3.   *Reporting position at time of sale.* Can you make sense of the taxpayer's reporting on Schedule D of his 1962 tax return that no gain occurred on the sale of the car? In light of the court's holding, was any gain in fact realized on the sale of the car?

WORTH NOTING

No doctrine of constructive payment. Although the doctrine of constructive receipt can accelerate income to a cash method taxpayer, no doctrine of constructive payment exists to accelerate a deduction for a cash method taxpayer. Thus, if a cash method taxpayer attempts to make a deductible payment but the recipient refuses to accept the payment, the cash method taxpayer may not claim a current deduction.

■ **PROBLEM 11-2.** *Cash method of accounting.* Susan rents a factory to David for his business for a monthly rent of $5,000. Both Susan and David use the cash method of accounting. Determine whether Susan has gross income in Year 1 or Year 2, and whether David is allowed a deduction in Year 1 or Year 2, under each of the following alternative scenarios:

a) Susan receives a $5,000 cash payment of rent from David on January 1, Year 2.

    1) Does it make any difference whether the rent payment is a timely payment of rent for David's occupancy of the leased premises during the month of January of Year 2, or whether it is a late payment for David's occupancy of the leased premises during December of Year 1?

b) Susan receives a $5,000 cash payment of rent from David on December 31, Year 1.

c) Susan receives a $5,000 check for rent from David on December 31, Year 1, but she does not deposit or cash the check until January 2, Year 2.

d) David offers Susan a $5,000 check for rent on December 31, Year 1, but Susan refuses to accept the check and tells David to bring it back to her on January 1, Year 2.

e) David mails the $5,000 check to Susan on December 31, Year 1, but a post office employee does not deliver the check to Susan until January 2, Year 2.

f) David charges the $5,000 rent payment on his credit card on December 31, Year 1, but the payment is not credited to Susan's account until January 2, Year 2.

g) David transfers a car with a value of $5,000 to Susan on December 31, Year 1, as a payment of rent. Susan sells the car for $5,000 on January 2, Year 2.

1) Might David and Susan also derive gross income under IRC § 61(a)(3)?

h) David performs $5,000 of services for Susan during January of Year 2, as a payment of rent.

1) Might David also derive gross income under this alternative? See IRC § 61(a)(1). Might Susan also be allowed a deduction? See IRC § 162(a)(1).

Note

Prepaid expenses of a cash method taxpayer. A cash method taxpayer might make a payment in the current year for benefits that will be received in both the current tax year and future years. Under these circumstances, the taxpayer may not deduct the entire payment in the year in which the payment is made. Instead, the taxpayer must deduct a portion of the payment in each year in which benefits are derived. See Reg. § 1.461–1(a)(1). The Ninth Circuit, however, has allowed the taxpayer to deduct the payment in full in the year of payment provided all benefits are derived within one year of making the payment. See Zaninovich v. Commissioner, 616 F.2d 429 (9th Cir. 1980).

2.   Accrual Method of Accounting

Secondary Law: Reg. § 1.446–1(c)(1)(ii)

Generally, under an accrual method, income is to be included for the taxable year when all the events have occurred that fix the right to receive the income and the amount of the income can be determined with reasonable accuracy. Under such a method, a liability is incurred, and generally is taken into account for Federal income tax purposes, in the taxable year in which all the events have occurred that establish the fact of the liability, the amount of the liability can be determined with reasonable accuracy, and economic performance has occurred with respect to the liability. * * *

a.   Timing of Income

Under the cash method of accounting, gross income does not occur until cash, property, or services are received. By contrast, under the accrual method of accounting, gross income occurs when the right to payment arises. The right to payment normally arises before payment is received. Hence, some degree of uncertainty will exist as to whether an item of income reported by an accrual method taxpayer will ever in fact be received. Does the possibility of non-payment have any relevance to the timing of an accrual method taxpayer's gross income? See Rev. Rul. 83–106 which follows.

Revenue Ruling 83–106

1983–2 C.B. 77

ISSUE

Under the circumstances described below, when is a gambling casino that uses the accrual method of accounting required to include in income the amount of gambling revenue derived from customers who gamble on credit?

FACTS

Taxpayer owns and operates a licensed gambling casino and uses the accrual method of accounting for both financial and income tax reporting purposes.

In connection with its gambling operations, the taxpayer extends credit to its customers to promote gambling at the tables. Generally, taxpayer only authorizes credit to customers that have furnished information enabling taxpayer to verify the particular customer's credit worthiness. The credit proceeds consist of gambling chips or money and the credit is extended at a central cashier's cage or at the gambling tables. At the time credit is extended the customer remits to taxpayer a promissory note, commonly referred to as a "marker," as evidence of the customer's indebtedness to the taxpayer for the gambling chips or cash. The "marker" specifies the amount of the credit extended to the customer.

In most instances, the gambling chips or cash advanced to the customer pursuant to the credit extension are used by the customer to gamble at taxpayer's tables. If a customer with an outstanding "marker" finishes gambling and still possesses chips or cash, the customer, sometimes, at the request of the taxpayer, applies the chips or cash toward the customer's indebtedness to the taxpayer.

With respect to those customers that have completed gambling and are unable to satisfy their indebtedness to the taxpayer at such time, taxpayer asks the customers when they intend to pay the outstanding indebtedness. If a customer indicates a specific date, the taxpayer holds the customer's "marker" until such time and then pursues collection activities. If a customer does not indicate a specific date for payment of the "marker," taxpayer begins collection activities immediately.

A debt incurred for gambling purposes is not enforceable in the courts of the state in which the taxpayer operates and is licensed. However, in an action for collection, unenforceability is conditioned on the debtor raising the defense that the debt was incurred for gambling purposes. The courts of the state in which taxpayer operates have held that credit transactions analogous to taxpayer's credit practices represent debts incurred for gambling purposes and, thus, are not legally enforceable upon the debtor's pleading of such defense.

Despite the inability to legally enforce the gambling obligations under state law, taxpayer has a reasonable expectancy that these amounts will be paid and such expectancy is supported by taxpayer's collection experience, which is generally over 95 percent. Taxpayer's collection experience is attributable to customers paying the markers voluntarily and not asserting the defense that the debt was incurred for gambling purposes.

For federal income tax purposes, taxpayer includes in gross income the gambling revenue derived from credit transactions for the tax year the gambling obligations are actually collected. * * *

LAW AND ANALYSIS

Section 446(c) of the Internal Revenue Code provides that a taxpayer may compute taxable income under the accrual method of accounting subject to the provisions of sections 446(a) and (b). Section 446(a) of the Code states that taxable income shall be computed under the method of accounting on the basis of which the taxpayer regularly computes its income in keeping its books. Section 446(b) provides that if the method used by the taxpayer does not clearly reflect income, the computation of taxable income shall be made under a method that, in the opinion of the Secretary, does clearly reflect income.

Section 451(a) of the Code provides that the amount of any item of gross income shall be included in gross income for the tax year in which received by the taxpayer, unless under the method of accounting used in computing taxable income, this amount is to be properly accounted for as of a different period.

Sections 1.451–1(a) and 1.446–1(c)(1)(ii) of the Income Tax Regulations indicate that income is clearly reflected under the accrual method of accounting when income is included in gross income for the tax year in which all the events have occurred that fix the right to receive the income and the amount thereof can be determined with reasonable accuracy.

For a taxpayer using the accrual method of accounting, it is the right to receive an item of income and not the actual receipt that determines the inclusion of the amount in gross income. Spring City Foundry Co. v. Commissioner, 292 U.S. 182 (1934). [A]s indicated in sections 1.451–1(a) and 1.446–1(c)(1)(ii) of the regulations, the right to receive an item of income arises for the tax year the "all events" test is satisfied. The two-prong "all events" test is comprised of (1) all the events occurring that fix the right to receive the income and (2) the amount thereof being determinable with reasonable accuracy. With respect to the first prong of the "all events" test, a fixed right to receive income occurs when (a) the required performance takes place, or (b) payment is due, or (c) payment is made. Legal enforceability of a right to receive income is not a prerequisite for the occurrence of all events. * * *

An exception to the "all events" test is that a fixed right to a determinable amount does not require accrual if the income is uncollectible when the right to receive the income item arises. Stated differently, the accrual of income is not required when a fixed right to receive arises if there is not a reasonable expectancy that the claim will ever be paid. The "reasonable expectancy of payment" criterion is an exception to the fundamental rules of income accrual and as an exception is strictly construed. Uncertainty as to collection must be substantial and not simply technical in nature for the accrual of income to be prevented. Substantial evidence as to the financial instability or even the insolvency of the debtor must be presented for this exception to the accrual of income to apply. If this were not so, a taxpayer could shift at its own will the reporting of income from one year to another. * * *

In the instant case, the "all events" test is satisfied for the tax year the credit customers wager and lose the credit proceeds (chips or money) at the taxpayer's gambling tables. This is so because (1) the taxpayer's right to receive the income is fixed for this tax year as the required performance has taken place, the customer's use of the taxpayer's gambling tables, and (2) the amount of the obligation is determinable with reasonable accuracy for this tax year as the customer's promissory note (marker) specifies the amount of the credit extension. With respect to the reasonable expectancy of payment exception to the "all events" test, there is no substantial uncertainty that the gambling obligation will be paid at the time the credit customers wager and lose the credit proceeds. This results from the fact that the taxpayer, generally, only authorizes credit to customers that have furnished information enabling taxpayer to verify the particular customer's credit worthiness. Secondly, despite the availability to the customers of a valid defense to the legal enforceability of taxpayer's collection of the gambling obligations, the taxpayer, based on its collection experience, has a reasonable expectancy that these obligations will be paid. See, Desert Palace, Inc. v. Commissioner, No. 82–7091 (9th Cir., Dec. 30, 1982), rev'g and rem'g 72 T.C. 1033 (1979) and Flamingo Resort, Inc. v. United States, 664 F.2d 1387 (9th Cir. 1982), aff'g 485 F.Supp. 926 (D. Nev. 1980), in which the Ninth Circuit held that casinos using the accrual method of accounting must include in gross income gambling revenue from customers gambling on credit for the tax year the credit is extended and the gambling occurs, despite the lack of legal enforceability of the credit obligations under state law.

HOLDING

Under the circumstances described above, a gambling casino that uses the accrual method of accounting must include in income the amount of gambling revenue derived from customers who gamble on credit for the tax year the gambling obligations arise and the gambling occurs.

* * *

WORTH NOTING

"All events" test. The all events test determines when an accrual method taxpayer must report an item of income. Specifically, an accrual method taxpayer is to report an item of income when—(1) all events occur that fix the right to receive the income, and (2) the amount thereof is determinable with reasonable accuracy. As Rev. Rul. 83–106 indicates, the possibility that an accrual method taxpayer will not in fact receive payment when the right to such payment exists will rarely cause the reporting of an item of income to be deferred to a future tax year.

If an accrual method taxpayer receives a payment of cash *before* the all events test is satisfied, does the receipt of cash impact the timing of the accrual method taxpayer's income? See the North American Oil Consolidated case that follows.

NORTH AMERICAN OIL CONSOLIDATED v. BURNET

United States Supreme Court, 1932
286 U.S. 417, 52 S.Ct. 613, 76 L.Ed. 1197

MR. JUSTICE BRANDEIS delivered the opinion of the Court.

The question for decision is whether the sum of $171,979.22, received by the North American Oil Consolidated in 1917, was taxable to it as income of that year.

The money was paid to the company under the following circumstances: Among many properties operated by it in 1916 was a section of oil land, the legal title to which stood in the name of the United States. Prior to that year, the government, claiming also the beneficial ownership, had instituted a suit to oust the company from possession; and on February 2, 1916, it secured the appointment of a receiver to operate the property, or supervise its operations, and to hold the net income thereof. The money paid to the company in 1917 represented the net profits which had been earned from that property in 1916 during the receivership. The money was paid to the receiver as earned. After entry by the District Court in 1917 of the final decree dismissing the bill, the money was paid, in that year, by the receiver to the company. The government took an appeal * * * to the Circuit Court of Appeals. In 1920, that court affirmed the decree. In 1922, a further appeal to this Court was dismissed by stipulation.

The income earned from the property in 1916 had been entered on the books of the company as its income. It had not been included in its original return of income for 1916; but it was included in an amended return for that year which was filed in 1918. Upon auditing the company's income and profits tax returns for 1917, the Commissioner of Internal Revenue determined a deficiency based on other items. The company appealed to the Board of Tax Appeals. There, in 1927, the Commissioner prayed that the deficiency already claimed should be increased so as to include a tax on the amount paid by the receiver to the company in 1917. The Board held that the profits were taxable * * * as income of 1916 * * *. The Circuit Court of Appeals held that the profits were taxable to the company as income of 1917 * * *. This Court granted a writ of certiorari.

It is conceded that the net profits earned by the property during the receivership constituted income. The company contends that they should have been reported * * * for taxation in 1916 * * * because they constitute income of the company accrued in that year; and that, if not taxable as income of the company for 1916, they were taxable to it as income for 1922, since the litigation was not finally terminated in its favor until 1922.

　　　* * *

[T]he net profits were not taxable to the company as income of 1916. For the company was not required in 1916 to report as income an amount which it might never receive. There was no constructive receipt of the profits by the company in that year, because at no time during the year was there a right in the company to demand that the receiver pay over the money. Throughout 1916 it was uncertain who would be declared entitled to the profits. It was not until 1917, when the District Court entered a final decree vacating the receivership and dismissing the bill, that the company became entitled to receive the money. Nor is it material, for the purposes of this case, whether the company's return was filed on the cash receipts and disbursements basis, or on the accrual basis. In neither event was it taxable in 1916 on account of income which it had not yet received and which it might never receive.

[T]he net profits earned by the property in 1916 were not income of the year 1922—the year in which the litigation with the government was finally terminated. They became income of the company in 1917, when it first became entitled to them and when it actually received them. If a taxpayer receives earnings under a claim of right and without restriction as to its disposition, he has received income which he is required to return, even though it may still be claimed that he is not entitled to retain the money, and even though he may still be adjudged liable to restore its equivalent. If in 1922 the government had prevailed, and the company had been obliged to refund the profits received in 1917, it would have been entitled to a deduction from the profits of 1922 * * *.

Affirmed.

NOTES

1.   *Time value of money.* Normally the time value of money motivates the taxpayer to defer gross income and the government to accelerate gross income. However, in North American Oil Consolidated, the taxpayer reported gross income in 1916 while the government claimed that the income should have been reported in 1917. With the advent of World War I, Congress increased tax rates dramatically in 1917. In light of this action, how can you reconcile the positions of the parties with the time value of money?

2.   *"Claim of right" doctrine.* An accrual method taxpayer normally does not report gross income until "all events occur that fix the right to receive income." When an accrual method taxpayer receives payment in a tax year *before* the unrestricted right to income has been established, however, the claim of right doctrine accelerates income to the year in which payment is received. Can you think of a practical reason why the government would wish to accelerate an

accrual method taxpayer's income when the taxpayer receives a cash payment before the all events test has been satisfied?

3.   *Prepayments received for future services.* An accrual method taxpayer might receive a payment in the current year for services to be performed in both the current year and future years. By virtue of the claim of right doctrine, the government historically claimed these taxpayers must include the entire payment in gross income in the year of receipt. The courts, however, have sometimes allowed accrual method taxpayer to defer reporting part of the prepayment to a subsequent year when it is readily apparent how much of the payment is allocable to each year. See, e.g., Artnell Co. v. Commissioner, 400 F.2d 981 (7th Cir. 1968) (where an accrual method professional baseball team received season ticket fees for a season in which some of the games were played in the tax year in which the payment was received and the remainder of the games were played in the following tax year, the team was required to report as income in the year of receipt only the portion of the payment attributable to the games played in that year with the remainder of the payment reportable in the following year). In 2017, IRC § 451 was amended to allow accrual method taxpayers to elect to defer a portion of the income associated with certain advance payments to the year following the year of receipt. See IRC § 451(c)(1)(B). If the election is not made, the entire advance payment must be included in gross income in the year of receipt. See IRC § 451(c)(1)(A).

b.   Timing of Deductions

GIANT EAGLE, INC. v. COMMISSIONER

United States Court of Appeals, Third Circuit, 2016
822 F.3d 666, *nonacq.* IRB 2016–40, 424[8]

ROTH, CIRCUIT JUDGE:

        * * *

I.

Giant Eagle operates a chain of retail supermarkets, pharmacies, gas stations, and convenience stores in the Northeastern and Midwestern United

---

[8]   Editor's note: By non-acquiescing in the decision, the Internal Revenue Service puts taxpayers on notice that it will continue to challenge fact patterns analogous to Giant Eagle arising outside the Third Circuit.

States. Giant Eagle uses the accrual method of accounting to determine and report its income tax liability.

A.

Giant Eagle's fuel rewards program traces its origins to the supermarket chain's introduction in 1991 of a customer-loyalty program called Advantage Cards. Initially, customers who presented an Advantage Card at checkout received discounts on promotion items and/or entire purchases. * * *

In April 2004, Giant Eagle revised the Advantage Card program. The new program, called "fuelperks!", linked customers' rewards at the pump to prior grocery purchases, *i.e.,* for every $50 spent on qualifying groceries, an Advantage Cardholder earned a ten cents-per-gallon discount on gas. A brochure distributed to customers set out the program's ground rules, including that "discounts expire on the last day of the month, 3 months after they are earned," and that "[t]he promotion is valid for a limited time only and may end at any time without prior notice." Giant Eagle did not in fact end the promotion or revoke any accumulated discounts in 2006 or 2007, the tax years at issue. Moreover, fuelperks! led to a dramatic increase in Giant Eagle's supermarket sales.

B.

On its 2006 and 2007 corporate income tax returns, Giant Eagle claimed a deduction for the discounts its customers had accumulated but, at year's end, had not yet applied to fuel purchases. * * *

From the outset of the fuelperks! program, Giant Eagle tracked customers' redemption of accumulated discounts and used the historical averages to determine the amount of the claimed deductions. * * * The Commissioner of Internal Revenue disallowed the deductions for the 2006 and 2007 tax years, which totaled $3,358,226 and $313,490, respectively.

C.

Giant Eagle petitioned the U.S. Tax Court for redetermination of its 2006 and 2007 income tax liabilities * * *. [I]t argued that the discounts accumulated but not applied by year's end satisfied the "all events" test because Giant Eagle's liability became fixed upon issuance of the discounts.

The Tax Court * * * found that Giant Eagle's claimed deductions did not satisfy the "all events" test because the purchase of gasoline functioned as a condition precedent to customers' redemption of discounts earned at checkout.

Accordingly, the court reasoned, any fuelperks!-related liability became fixed only after customers applied the accumulated discounts to a fuel purchase, which, in the case of the disallowed deductions, occurred after the end of the tax year. * * * [T]he Tax Court sustained the Commissioner's deficiency determinations for both tax years.

Giant Eagle appealed.

II.

The "all events" test derives from dictum in a 1926 Supreme Court decision, explaining that a liability may accrue even "in advance of the assessment of a tax" if "all the events [ ] occur which fix the amount of the tax and determine the liability of the taxpayer to pay it." The test has since been refined, prescribed as a Treasury Regulation, and eventually codified. Today, 26 U.S.C. § 461 and its implementing regulations limit accrual method taxpayers' deductibility of liabilities as follows:

> Under an accrual method of accounting, a liability . . . is incurred, and generally is taken into account for Federal income tax purposes, in the taxable year in which all the events have occurred that establish the fact of the liability, the amount of the liability can be determined with reasonable accuracy, and economic performance has occurred with respect to the liability.[9]

The Treasury Secretary prescribed a supplementary regulation defining "economic performance" in the context of rebates and refunds:

> If the liability of a taxpayer is to pay a rebate, refund, or similar payment to another person (whether paid in property, money, or as a reduction in the price of goods or services to be provided in the future by the taxpayer), economic performance occurs as payment is made to the person to which the liability is owed.[10]

Nonetheless, "certain recurring items" are subject to a more relaxed version of the "all events" test:

> Notwithstanding [the general rule that "the all events test shall not be treated as met any earlier than when economic performance with

---

[9]   Treas. Reg. § 1.461–1(a)(2)(i).

[10]   *Id.* § 1.461–4(g)(3).

respect to such item occurs"][11] an item shall be treated as incurred during any taxable year if—

    (i)   the all events test with respect to such item is met during such taxable year (determined without regard to [26 U.S.C. § 461(h)(1)]),

    (ii) economic performance with respect to such item occurs within the shorter of—

        (I) a reasonable period after the close of such taxable year,[12] or

        (II) 8 ½ months after the close of such taxable year,

    (iii) such item is recurring in nature and the taxpayer consistently treats items of such kind as incurred in the taxable year in which the requirements of clause (i) are met, and

    (iv) either—

        (I) such item is not a material item, or

        (II) the accrual of such item in the taxable year in which the requirements of clause (i) are met results in a more proper match against income than accruing such item in the taxable year in which economic performance occurs.[13]

For purposes of the "recurring item" exception, "the all events test is met with respect to any item if all events have occurred which determine the fact of liability and the amount of such liability can be determined with reasonable accuracy."[14]

The Commissioner does not contest that fuelperks! rewards qualify as both "a rebate, refund, or similar payment" and a "recurring expense" subject to the less onerous "economic performance" requirement. Moreover, the Commissioner concedes that Giant Eagle calculated its anticipated fuelperks!-related liability "with reasonable accuracy," and that economic performance had occurred by

---

[11]   26 U.S.C. § 461(h)(1).

[12]   A Treasury Regulation defines a "reasonable period" as "[t]he date the taxpayer files a timely (including extensions) return for that taxable year." Treas. Reg. § 1.461–5(b)(1)(ii)(A).

[13]   26 U.S.C. § 461(h)(3)(A).

[14]   Id. § 461(h)(4).

the time of Giant Eagle's tax filing. Thus, the only issue on appeal is whether "the fact of liability" was fixed at year's end—that is, before the end of the tax year, had Giant Eagle become liable to pay the fuelperks! 10-cent discount to its customers who had purchased qualifying groceries with their Advantage Cards.

A.

Two seminal Supreme Court decisions frame our discussion of the "all events" test's fixed liability requirement. In its first decision applying the "all events" test after its codification, the Court held, in *United States v. Hughes Properties, Inc.,* that a casino operator was entitled to deduct the annual increase in its progressive jackpot payoff amounts, including for jackpots not won by year's end. While the Court acknowledged that there remained an "extremely remote and speculative possibility [ ] that the jackpot might never be won," it nonetheless concluded that the anticipated liability was "fixed" under Nevada law, which "forbade reducing the indicated payoff without paying the jackpot."

One year later, in *United States v. General Dynamics Corp.,* the Court disallowed deductions claimed by a commercial taxpayer on the basis of its obligation to reimburse employees for medical expenses incurred by year's end, but not yet submitted for reimbursement on an official claim form. The Court reasoned that because the taxpayer was "liable to pay for covered medical services *only* if properly documented claims forms were filed," "[t]he filing of the claim [was] thus a true condition precedent to liability on the part of the taxpayer." Though decided one year earlier, *Hughes Properties* expressly survives *General Dynamics.* Whereas the casino operator in *Hughes Properties* "could not escape" its "fixed liability for the jackpot . . . as a matter of state law," the *General Dynamics* Court emphasized that employees' "[m]ere receipt of services . . . does not, in our judgment, constitute the last link in the chain of events creating [employer] liability."

     * * *

[O]ur only reported decision on the subject [is] *Lukens Steel Co. v. Commissioner.* [In that case, which] predated codification of the "all events" test, we held that an accrual method taxpayer was entitled to deduct payments credited to a "contingent liability account," even though they "would not be paid out immediately or at a specified time." Critically, however, under the terms of a collective bargaining agreement, "[i]t was not possible for Lukens to cancel the contingent liability account without paying" the credited amounts. Because the taxpayer irrevocably committed to the payments during the tax year at issue, it was entitled to deduct corresponding future liabilities that "would be paid in a reasonable period of time."

B.

As in *Lukens Steel*, here we determine whether the taxpayer's anticipated liability was fixed at year's end with reference to contract law principles. Specifically, Giant Eagle characterizes its issuance of fuelperks! rewards as a unilateral contract formed at checkout, which conferred instant liability on the supermarket chain to its customers for the rewards they accrued.

Unlike bilateral contracts, which are premised on reciprocal promises, "unilateral contracts . . . involve only one promise and are formed when one party makes a promise in exchange for the other party's act or performance. Significantly, a unilateral contract is not formed and is, thus, unenforceable until such time as the offeree completes performance." A unilateral contract also differs from an unenforceable contingent gift in that a reasonable person would understand that she could accept the offer and reap the promised reward simply by performing the task specified. Thus, a Pennsylvania court held that a car dealership, advertising a discount on a future car purchase if a hole-in-one was made on the ninth hole of a local golf course, was obligated to honor its "offer" when a golfer finally aced the hole—despite the dealership's stated intention to end the promotion two days earlier. The court reasoned, "[i]t is the manifested intent of the offeror and not his subjective intent which determines the persons having the power to accept the offer." Because "the offeror's manifested intent, as it appeared from signs posted at the ninth tee, was that a hole-in-one would win the car," the dealer was liable in accordance with such reasonable expectations. So too might a Giant Eagle customer have reasonably presumed the redeemability of accumulated fuelperks! rewards, as provided by the well-publicized "Simple Program Guide".

The brochure distributed to Advantage Cardholders also included fine print providing, *inter alia*, that "discounted fuel cannot exceed 30 gallons and discounts must be used in full on one vehicle in one transaction"; "[t]he promotion is valid for a limited time and may end at any time without prior notice"; and "fuelperks! discounts expire 3 months after the last day of the month in which they're earned." But none of the published program parameters suggested that Giant Eagle reserved the right to retract rewards that customers had already accrued. Indeed, in the entire history of Giant Eagle's fuel rewards program, "[n]o such retroactive termination ever occurred, or was even contemplated."

Like the golfer who teed off with a promise of reward in mind, a customer anticipated the promised fuel discounts when deciding to shop at Giant Eagle in the first place—and thus deciding not to shop at a different store. Because she was then aware that she could apply the discounts as advertised if she spent fifty dollars on supermarket purchases using her Advantage Card, she was indeed a party to a unilateral contract with Giant Eagle. Liability therefore attached upon her performance, *i.e.,* at checkout.

For purposes of the "all events" test's fixed liability prong, it is irrelevant that neither the total *amount* of Giant Eagle's anticipated liability nor the identity of all the customers who eventually applied discounts toward gasoline purchases could be conclusively identified at year's end. And while there remained an "extremely remote and speculative possibility" that the amount of Giant Eagle's claimed deductions would overstate the value of the rewards its customers ultimately redeemed, Giant Eagle significantly mitigated that risk by tracking its customers' monthly redemption rates and offsetting the deductions accordingly to account for prospective non-redeemers. Giant Eagle amply demonstrated the existence—as of year's end—of both an absolute liability *and* a near-certainty that the liability would soon be discharged by payment. The chance of non-redemption had been calculated by Giant Eagle "with reasonable accuracy" as conceded by the Commissioner. The "all events" test demands no more. We hold, therefore, that following *Hughes Props.* and *Lukens Steel*, Giant Eagle was entitled to deduct fuelperks!-related liabilities incurred during the tax years at issue.

III.

By disallowing deductions claimed on the basis of established recurring expenses, the Tax Court effectively obliterated the distinction between two accounting methods expressly authorized by the Tax Code.[42]   The extent to which cash and accrual methods of accounting sometimes yield different deductions is a byproduct of the Tax Code's design. So long as a taxpayer consistently adheres to one accounting method, the Code is agnostic as to the benefit or hardship wrought by his selection.[43]

---

[42]   *See* 26 U.S.C. § 446(c)(2). The accrual method of accounting differs fundamentally from its cash counterpart. Whereas businesses that choose the latter method refrain from counting revenues until they are received and expenses until they are paid, those using the accrual method account for transactions when they occur, regardless of when the money, goods, or services actually change hands.

[43]   *See* 26 U.S.C. § 446(a), (b) (providing that the Treasury Department may only recalculate a taxpayer's liabilities without respect to the accounting method regularly used in keeping his books if "no method of accounting has been regularly used by the taxpayer, or if the method used does not clearly reflect income").

For the foregoing reasons, we will reverse the Tax Court's order sustaining the Commissioner's deficiency determinations and remand this case with instructions to grant judgment in favor of Giant Eagle on the ground that the claimed deductions are permissible under the "all events" test.

Hardiman, Circuit Judge, dissenting.

The Court reverses the Tax Court's order after finding that, at the close of the 2006 and 2007 taxable years for which Giant Eagle deducted anticipated fuelperks! expenses, "all events ha[d] occurred which determine[d] the fact" that it was liable to pay those expenses. 26 U.S.C. § 461(h)(4). Because I believe Giant Eagle's liabilities were not determined until fuelperks! were redeemed, I respectfully dissent.

I

The law applicable to this case is relatively clear. An accrual method taxpayer need not ascertain the *amount* of a liability, to *whom* it is owed, or *when* it will be paid in order for events to "determine the fact" of the liability and render it deductible. Instead, all that is required is that it became "fixed and absolute" in the taxable year for which the deduction is sought.

* * *

[T]he liabilities that accrued to Giant Eagle on account of its fuelperks! program were not absolute. The casino in *Hughes Properties* * * * and the steel company in *Lukens Steel* operated under a set of rules that offered no hope of escape from their fixed liabilities. In each case, those liabilities had to remain on their books until discharged by payment. Here, in contrast, Giant Eagle made each liability temporary by providing that "fuelperks! discounts expire 3 months after the last day of the month in which they're earned." If a shopper failed to redeem fuelperks! within that timeframe, the discounts were lost and Giant Eagle had no obligation to honor a belated attempt at redemption. After acknowledging this fact, the Majority offers reasons why we should nonetheless conclude that Giant Eagle faced "an absolute liability." After careful consideration of those reasons, I remain unconvinced.

* * *

Had Giant Eagle not included an expiration provision in its terms and conditions, I would be inclined to agree with my colleagues that the company incurred a fixed and absolute liability to each shopper at checkout. In that case, we would face the difficult task of determining whether historical redemption data and other evidence reveal more than "an extremely remote and speculative possibility" that any given shopper would fail to timely redeem discounts and how much bearing, if any, the answer to that question has on whether the company's liabilities were "determine[d] in fact." But the fact that the store did include an expiration provision—thereby conditioning its liability to each shopper upon fuelperks! redemption * * * within approximately 3 months' time—made "redemption" a condition precedent to the establishment of an absolute liability. Because that event had not occurred by the close of the 2006 or 2007 taxable years with respect to the deductions Giant Eagle claimed on accrued-but-not-yet-redeemed fuelperks!, I would hold that the "all events" test was not satisfied and those anticipated expenses were not deductible.

> * * *

Notes

1.   *All events test.* As the Giant Eagle court explained, an accrual method taxpayer must satisfy the all events test to claim a deduction in a given tax year. Specifically, the following three conditions must be satisfied for a deduction to be claimed: a) all the events have occurred that establish the fact of the liability, b) the amount of the liability can be determined with reasonable accuracy, and c) economic performance has occurred with respect to the liability. Only the first of the three requirements was at issue in the Giant Eagle case.

2.   *Economic performance requirement.* An "economic performance" requirement must be satisfied for an accrual method taxpayer to claim a deduction. (No analogous requirement exists for an accrual method taxpayer to report income.) The economic performance requirement was satisfied in the Giant Eagle case because of a special exception for "recurring items." See IRC § 461(h)(3). When this exception does not apply, the economic performance requirement often operates in a manner that delays the ability of an accrual method taxpayer to claim a deduction. The time when economic performance occurs in various contexts is delineated in IRC § 461(h)(2).

■ **PROBLEM 11-3.** *Accrual method of accounting.* Deduction Co., a manufacturer, relies on technology to conduct its business. Problems have developed with the technology Deduction Co. uses. Deduction Co. hires Income Co., a technology service and sales organization, to address Deduction Co.'s technology issues. Both Deduction Co. and Income Co. are accrual method taxpayers. Determine the year(s) in which Income Co. has gross income and Deduction Co. is allowed a deduction under each of the following alternative scenarios:

a)   Deduction Co. agrees to pay Income Co. $10,000 for its services. Income Co. performed all services in Year 1 and Deduction Co. pays Income Co. $10,000 in Year 2.

b)   Deduction Co. agrees to pay Income Co. $10,000 for its services. Income Co. performed all services in Year 1. Deduction Co. agrees that all services were performed but Deduction Co. is encountering financial problems and does not pay Income Co. in Years 1 or 2.

c)   Deduction Co. agrees to pay Income Co. $10,000 for its services. Income Co. performed all services in Year 1. Deduction Co. agrees that all services were performed but Deduction Co. has declared bankruptcy and it is apparent by the end of Year 1 that none of its creditors will ever be paid.

d)   Deduction Co. agrees to pay Income Co. 10% of the profits it earns in Years 2 and 3 for Income Co.'s services. Income Co. performed all services in Year 1. Deduction Co.'s profits have varied dramatically from year to year and it is impossible to predict the amount of profits it will earn in Years 2 and 3.

e)   Deduction Co. agrees to pay Income Co. $10,000 for its services. Income Co. claims it performed all the services in Year 1 but Deduction Co. maintains Income Co. did not perform all the services because Deduction Co. continues to have problems with its technology. Deduction Co. refuses to pay Income Co. until the technology problems are solved.

f)   Same as e) but Income Co. sues Deduction Co. to recover the $10,000.

g) Same as f). Income Co. wins at the trial court level but Deduction Co. files an appeal and is not compelled to pay Income Co. until the appeal is decided.

h) Same as g). Deduction Co. loses on appeal and pays Income Co. the $10,000. Deduction Co. then appeals the case to highest court to which an appeal will lie.

3. Change in Circumstances in Subsequent Tax Year

a. Surrender of Prior Year's Income

In rare cases, a taxpayer who properly included an economic benefit in gross income might be required to surrender that benefit in a later tax year. This section will explore whether, in these circumstances, the taxpayer is entitled to a refund of the tax paid on the surrendered benefit.

UNITED STATES v. LEWIS

Supreme Court of the United States, 1951
340 U.S. 590, 71 S.Ct. 522, 95 L.Ed. 560

Mr. Justice Black delivered the opinion of the Court.

Respondent Lewis brought this action in the Court of Claims seeking a refund of an alleged overpayment of his 1944 income tax. The facts found by the Court of Claims are: In his 1944 income tax return, respondent reported about $22,000 which he had received that year as an employee's bonus. As a result of subsequent litigation in a state court, however, it was decided that respondent's bonus had been improperly computed; under compulsion of the state court's judgment he returned approximately $11,000 to his employer. Until payment of the judgment in 1946, respondent had at all times claimed and used the full $22,000 unconditionally as his own, in the good faith though "mistaken" belief that he was entitled to the whole bonus.

On the foregoing facts the Government's position is that respondent's 1944 tax should not be recomputed, but that respondent should have deducted the $11,000 as a loss in his 1946 tax return. The Court of Claims, however,

* * * held that the excess bonus received "under a mistake of fact" was not income in 1944 and ordered a refund based on a recalculation of that year's tax. We granted certiorari because this holding conflicted with many decisions of the courts of appeals.

In the North American Oil case we said:

> If a taxpayer receives earnings under a claim of right and without restriction as to its disposition, he has received income which he is required to return, even though it may still be claimed that he is not entitled to retain the money, and even though he may still be adjudged liable to restore its equivalent.

Nothing in this language permits an exception merely because a taxpayer is "mistaken" as to the validity of his claim. * * *

Income taxes must be paid on income received (or accrued) during an annual accounting period. The "claim of right" interpretation of the tax laws has long been used to give finality to that period, and is now deeply rooted in the federal tax system. We see no reason why the Court should depart from this well-settled interpretation merely because it results in an advantage or disadvantage to a taxpayer.[1]   [Thus, respondent's 1944 tax should not be recomputed and respondent should have deducted the $11,000 as a loss in his 1946 tax return.]

Reversed.

Mr. Justice Douglas (dissenting).

The question in this case is not whether the bonus had to be included in 1944 income for purposes of the tax. Plainly it should have been because the taxpayer claimed it as of right. Some years later, however, it was judicially determined that he had no claim to the bonus. The question is whether he may then get back the tax which he paid on the money.

Many inequities are inherent in the income tax. We multiply them needlessly by nice distinctions which have no place in the practical administration of the law. If the refund were allowed, the integrity of the taxable year would not be violated. The tax would be paid when due; but the government would not be permitted to maintain the unconscionable position that it can keep the

---

[1]   It has been suggested that it would be more "equitable" to reopen respondent's 1944 tax return. While the suggestion might work to the advantage of this taxpayer, it could not be adopted as a general solution because, in many cases, the three-year statute of limitations would preclude recovery.

tax after it is shown that payment was made on money which was not income to the taxpayer.

 FOR DISCUSSION

Timing of adjustment. What difference does it make whether the repayment of the bonus was allowed as a deduction on the taxpayer's 1944 tax return (the year the bonus was received) or on the taxpayer's 1946 tax return (the year the bonus was repaid)?

When a taxpayer is compelled to surrender a benefit that was included in the taxpayer's gross income in a prior tax year, the Lewis decision limits the taxpayer's remedy to claiming a deduction in the year the item is returned. This remedy is inadequate if a lower tax rate applies to the taxpayer in the year the item is returned than the tax rate that applied in the earlier year when the income was reported. In these circumstances, the deduction allowed in the later tax year will yield less of a reduction in tax than the amount of tax paid on the item in the year the income was reported.

For example, if an individual reported $10,000 of income in Year 1 that was taxed at a rate of 30%, a tax of $3,000 would have been imposed in Year 1 ($10,000 × 30% = $3,000). If the individual was compelled to return the $10,000 in Year 4 and she was taxed at a rate of 20% in Year 4, deducting the $10,000 in Year 4 would reduce her tax by only $2,000 ($10,000 × 20% = $2,000). In this situation, the individual paid more tax when the item of income was received ($3,000) than the tax she recovered in the year the item was returned ($2,000). To remedy this inadequacy, Congress enacted IRC § 1341.

Primary Law: IRC § 1341

(a) If—

   (1) an item was included in gross income for a prior taxable year (or years) because it appeared that the taxpayer had an unrestricted right to such item;

   (2) a deduction is allowable for the taxable year because it was established after the close of such prior taxable year (or years) that the taxpayer did not have an unrestricted right to such item * * *; and

> (3)   the amount of such deduction exceeds $3,000,
>
> then the tax imposed by this chapter for the taxable year shall be the lesser of the following:
>
> (4)   the tax for the taxable year computed with such deduction; or
>
> (5)   an amount equal to—
>
>> (A)   the tax for the taxable year computed without such deduction, minus
>>
>> (B)   the decrease in tax under this chapter * * * for the prior taxable year (or years) which would result solely from the exclusion of such item * * * from gross income for such prior taxable year (or years).
>
> * * *

In Van Cleave v. United States, 718 F.2d 193, 195 (6th Cir. 1983), the court explained the origin and effect of IRC § 1341 as follows:

> Section 1341 was enacted by Congress to mitigate the sometimes harsh result of the application of the "claim of right" doctrine. Under the claim of right doctrine, a taxpayer must pay tax on an item in the year in which he receives it under a claim of right even if it is later determined that his right to the item was not absolute and he is required to return it. The taxpayer, however, is allowed to deduct the amount of the item from his income in the year of repayment. This result was held to be required because income and deductions are determined on an annual basis. But * * * it is possible for a taxpayer to benefit less from the deduction in the year of repayment than he would benefit if he had been able to deduct the amount repaid from his income in the year of receipt. This result of the claim of right doctrine could occur when * * * the taxpayer had been in a higher tax bracket in the year of receipt than he was in the year of repayment.
>
> Section 1341 allows the taxpayer to choose the more favorable alternative as follows: If the taxpayer included an item in gross income in one taxable year, and in a subsequent taxable year he becomes entitled

to a deduction because the item or a portion thereof is no longer subject to his unrestricted use, and the amount of the deduction is in excess of $3,000, the tax for the subsequent year is reduced by either the tax attributable to the deduction or the decrease in the tax for the prior year attributable to the removal of the item, whichever is greater. Under the rule of the Lewis case, the taxpayer is entitled to a deduction only in the year of repayment.

Notes

1.   *Section 1341 does not sanction an amended return.* Under no circumstances does IRC § 1341 allow the taxpayer to go back and amend the tax return on which the surrendered benefit was originally included in gross income. The provision merely allows the taxpayer to reduce the tax otherwise due in the year the benefit is surrendered. The reduction in tax in the year the benefit is surrendered equals the amount of tax that would have been saved *if* the recovery had been excluded from the earlier year's tax return. But no change is made to the earlier year's tax return.

2.   *Interest does not accrue from earlier tax year.* If a taxpayer who surrenders an economic benefit in a later tax year were permitted to amend the earlier year's return on which the benefit was included in gross income, an overpayment of tax in the earlier tax year would result. In these circumstances, the government would be required to pay the taxpayer interest dating from the earlier tax year. See IRC § 6611. Because the adjustments permitted by IRC § 1341 are confined to the tax return for the year in which the benefit is returned, no overpayment exists in the earlier tax year. Thus, the government is not obligated to pay interest to the taxpayer.

■ **PROBLEM 11-4.** *Surrender of economic benefit in subsequent tax year.* Jacalyn reported $120,000 of gross income in Year 1. In Year 3, Jacalyn was required to surrender $20,000 that she included in her Year 1 gross income. By including that $20,000 in her Year 1 gross income, her Year 1 Federal income tax liability was $5,000 higher than it otherwise would have been. Assume Jacalyn became entitled to a $20,000 deduction when she surrendered the $20,000.

a)   Which of the following is the proper way for Jacalyn to report the surrender of the $20,000 if deducting the $20,000 on her Year 3 tax return would cause her Year 3 Federal income tax liability to decline by $4,000?

   1)   deduct the $20,000 on her Year 1 tax return and claim a $5,000 refund for Year 1;

   2)   deduct the $20,000 on her Year 3 tax return and thereby reduce her Year 3 tax liability by $4,000; or

   3)   do not deduct the $20,000 on either tax return but reduce her Year 3 tax liability by $5,000 (the amount by which her Year 1 tax liability would have declined if she had not included the $20,000 in her Year 1 gross income).

b)   Same as a) except that deducting the $20,000 on her Year 3 tax return would cause her Year 3 Federal income tax liability to decline by $6,000?

   1)   deduct the $20,000 on her Year 1 tax return and claim a $5,000 refund for Year 1;

   2)   deduct the $20,000 on her Year 3 tax return and thereby reduce her Year 3 tax liability by $6,000; or

   3)   do not deduct the $20,000 on either tax return but reduce her Year 3 tax liability by $5,000 (the amount by which her Year 1 tax liability would have declined if she had not included the $20,000 in her Year 1 gross income).

b.   Recovery of Prior's Years Deduction

In rare cases, a taxpayer who properly deducted a disbursement from gross income in one tax year might recover the disbursement in a later tax year. This section will explore whether, in these circumstances, the taxpayer must include the recovery in gross income.

ALICE PHELAN SULLIVAN CORPORATION
v. UNITED STATES

United States Court of Claims, 1967
381 F.2d 399

COLLINS, JUDGE.

Plaintiff, a California corporation, brings this action to recover an alleged overpayment in its 1957 income tax. During that year, there was returned to taxpayer two parcels of realty, each of which it had previously donated and claimed as a charitable contribution deduction. The first donation had been made in 1939; the second, in 1940. Under the then applicable corporate tax rates, the deductions claimed ([$4,200] for 1939 and [$4,500] for 1940) yielded plaintiff an aggregate tax benefit of [$2,000].

Each conveyance had been made subject to the condition that the property be used either for a religious or for an educational purpose. In 1957, the donee decided not to use the gifts; they were therefore reconveyed to plaintiff. Upon audit of taxpayer's income tax return, it was found that the recovered property was not reflected in its 1957 gross income. The Commissioner of Internal Revenue disagreed with plaintiff's characterization of the recovery as a nontaxable return of capital. He viewed the transaction as giving rise to taxable income and therefore adjusted plaintiff's income by adding to it [$8,700]—the total of the charitable contribution deductions previously claimed and allowed. This addition to income, taxed at the 1957 corporate tax rate of 52 percent, resulted in a deficiency assessment of [$4,500]. After payment of the deficiency, plaintiff filed a claim for the refund of [$2,500], asserting this amount as overpayment on the theory that a correct assessment could demand no more than the return of the tax benefit originally enjoyed, i. e., [$2,000]. The claim was disallowed [by the Internal Revenue Service].

* * *

A transaction which returns to a taxpayer his own property cannot be considered as giving rise to "income"—at least where that term is confined to its traditional sense of "gain derived from capital, from labor, or from both combined." Eisner v. Macomber, 252 U.S. 189, 207, 40 S.Ct. 189, 64 L.Ed. 521 (1920). Yet the principle is well engrained in our tax law that the return or recovery of property that was once the subject of an income tax deduction must be treated as income in the year of its recovery. The only limitation upon that principle is the so-called "tax-benefit rule." This rule permits exclusion of the recovered item from income so long as its initial use as a deduction did not provide a tax saving. But where full tax use of a deduction was made and a tax saving thereby obtained, then the extent of saving is considered immaterial. The recovery is viewed as income to the full extent of the deduction previously allowed.[2]

Formerly the exclusive province of judge-made law, the tax-benefit concept now finds expression both in statute and administrative regulations. Section 111 of the Internal Revenue Code of 1954 accords tax-benefit treatment to the recovery of bad debts, prior taxes, and delinquency amounts. Treasury regulations have "broadened" the rule of exclusion by extending similar treatment to "all other losses, expenditures, and accruals made the basis of deductions from gross income for prior taxable years * * *." [Reg. § 1.111–1.]

Drawing our attention to the broad language of this regulation, the Government insists that the present recovery must find its place within the scope of the regulation and, as such, should be taxed in a manner consistent with the treatment provided for like items of recovery, i. e., that it be taxed at the rate prevailing in the year of recovery. We are compelled to agree.

* * *

Ever since Burnet v. Sanford & Brooks Co., 282 U.S. 359, 51 S.Ct. 150, 75 L.Ed. 383 (1931), the concept of accounting for items of income and expense on an annual basis has been accepted as the basic principle upon which our tax laws are structured.

It is the essence of any system of taxation that it should produce revenue ascertainable, and payable to the government, at regular intervals.

---

[2]   The rationale which supports the principle, as well as its limitation, is that the property, having once served to offset taxable income (i. e., as a tax deduction) should be treated, upon its recoupment, as the recovery of that which had been previously deducted. See Plumb, The Tax Benefit Rule Today, 57 Harv.L.Rev. 129, 131 n. 10 (1943).

Only by such a system is it practicable to produce a regular flow of income and apply methods of accounting, assessment, and collection capable of practical operation.

282 U.S. at 365, 51 S.Ct. at 152. To insure the vitality of the single-year concept, it is essential not only that annual income be ascertained without reference to losses experienced in an earlier accounting period, but also that income be taxed without reference to earlier tax rates. * * * [5]

Since taxpayer in this case did obtain full tax benefit from its earlier deductions, those deductions were properly classified as income upon recoupment and must be taxed as such. This can mean nothing less than the application of that tax rate which is in effect during the year in which the recovered item is recognized as a factor of income. We therefore sustain the Government's position and grant its motion for summary judgment. * * *

Notes

1.   *Tax benefit rule can apply to deductible personal expenses.* When a corporation like Alice Phelan Sullivan Corporation makes a charitable contribution, it is allowed as a deduction as an ordinary and necessary business expense under IRC § 162, subject to certain limitations. When an individual makes a charitable contribution in a personal capacity, it is deductible under IRC § 170, subject to certain limitations. In either case, the tax benefit rule applies in the same manner; namely, the recovery is taxed at the rate that applies to the taxpayer in the year of the recovery.

2.   *Tax benefit rule is a two-way street.* The tax rate that applied to the Alice Phelan Sullivan Corporation in the year the properties were returned to the taxpayer (1957) was *higher* than the tax rate that applied to the taxpayer in the years the deductions were claimed (1939 and 1940). As a result, the taxpayer

---

[5]   This opinion represents the views of the majority and complies with existing law and decisions. However, in the writer's personal opinion, it produces a harsh and inequitable result. Perhaps, it exemplifies a situation "where the letter of the law killeth; the spirit giveth life." The tax-benefit concept is an equitable doctrine which should be carried to an equitable conclusion. Since it is the declared public policy to encourage contributions to charitable and educational organizations, a donor, whose gift to such organizations is returned, should not be required to refund to the Government a greater amount than the tax benefit received when the deduction was made for the gift. Such a rule would avoid a penalty to the taxpayer and an unjust enrichment to the Government. However, the court cannot legislate and any change in the existing law rests within the wisdom and discretion of the Congress.

saved only $2,000 in tax when it claimed the deductions but paid $4,500 in tax when the recovery was reported as income. Therefore, the taxpayer incurred a *net cost* of $2,500.

By contrast, when the tax rate that applies to a taxpayer in the year of the recovery is *lower* than the tax rate that applied when the deduction was claimed, the taxpayer will enjoy a *net benefit* by saving more tax as a result of the deduction than the amount of tax triggered when the recovery occurs. For example, if a taxpayer deducts a $10,000 charitable contribution in a tax year when a 30% tax rate applies, the taxpayer will save $3,000 in tax. If the charitable contribution is then recovered in a later tax year when only a 20% tax rate applies to the taxpayer, only $2,000 of tax will result from the recovery. In these circumstances, the taxpayer will enjoy net tax savings of $1,000.

Hence, the fact that the tax rate in the year of the recovery is applied to the recovery will sometimes yield a net tax cost to the taxpayer (as in the Alice Phelan Sullivan Corporation case) and other times yield a net tax savings to the taxpayer (if the tax rate that applies in the year of the recovery is lower than the tax rate that applied in the year the deduction was claimed).

3.   *Recovery is excluded to the extent earlier deduction did not provide tax savings.* In the Alice Phelan Sullivan Corporation case, the court found that the taxpayer obtained "full tax benefits from its earlier deductions." To the extent that a potential deduction does not yield a tax benefit to a taxpayer, the recovery is excluded from gross income. For example, if the Alice Phelan Sullivan Corporation had not deducted the contributions it made in 1939 and 1940, it could have excluded the recovery of the property from gross income in 1957. See IRC § 111(a).

■   **PROBLEM 11-5.**   *Recovery of deductible disbursement in subsequent tax year.* In Year 1, David paid $13,000 in state income tax and no other deductible state or local taxes. Due to the annual $10,000 limit on the deduction of state and local income taxes (IRC § 164(b)(6)), David deducted only $10,000 of state income taxes on his Year 1 Federal tax return. In Year 2, David received a partial refund of the state income taxes David paid in Year 1.

a) How much of the state income tax refund must David include in gross income if the amount of the refund was—

1) $1,000?

2) $5,000?

b) Do the answers to a) change if David claimed the standard deduction in Year 1?

c) To the extent that part or all of the refund is taxable to David, which of the following is the proper way for David to report the recovery?

1) Include the taxable amount in his Year 2 gross income which will increase his Year 2 Federal income tax liability.

2) Reduce the deduction for state income claimed on his Year 1 tax return which will increase his Year 1 Federal income tax liability.

d) Do the answers in c) depend on which option leads to a greater increase in David's tax liability?

SYNTHESIS

The timing of income and deductions is important because of the time value of money. Specifically, one who possesses money can invest that money and earn a return on that money for the duration of the period in which the money is invested. Hence, most taxpayers normally desire to defer the payment of taxes as long as possible to maximize the amount of time they can earn a return on their tax dollars. Tax deferral is accomplished by deferring gross income and/ or accelerating deductions. Both of these actions reduce the taxpayer's current taxable income and, accordingly, the taxpayer's current tax liability. Deferring a tax liability enables the taxpayer to keep the dollars that would have been used to pay the tax invested and to earn a return on that investment.

The tax year in which a taxpayer must report gross income or claim a deduction normally depends on the tax accounting method used by the taxpayer. Most individuals use the cash method of accounting. As such, gross income is reported in the year payment is received and an allowed deduction is claimed in the year payment is made. Individuals who own a business are often required to use the accrual method of accounting. Under the accrual method, gross income is reported when all the events have occurred that fix the right to receive the income and the amount of the income can be determined with reasonable accuracy. Deductions are claimed under the accrual method in the taxable year in which all the events have occurred that establish the fact of the liability, the amount of the liability can be determined with reasonable accuracy, and economic performance has occurred with respect to the liability.

In rare cases, a taxpayer who properly included an economic benefit in gross income might be required to surrender that benefit in a later tax year. When this occurs, the taxpayer may claim a deduction in the year the item is returned or, if IRC § 1341 applies, reduce the tax in the year the item is returned by the amount of tax that would have been saved *if* the recovery had been excluded from the earlier year's tax return. Under no circumstances, however, may the taxpayer amend the earlier year's tax return. In other rare cases, a taxpayer who properly deducted a disbursement from gross income in one tax year might recover the disbursement in a later tax year. When this occurs, the taxpayer must include the recovery in gross income in the year of the recovery, unless no tax benefit was derived from the earlier year's deduction.

Test Your Knowledge: To assess your understanding of the material in this chapter, click here to take a quiz.

CHAPTER 12

Timing of Gains and Losses from Dealings in Property

Overview

Chapter 6 focused on the category of gross income designated "gains derived from dealings in property." See IRC § 61(a)(3). There, you learned that a mere increase in the value of property does not trigger gross income until a sale or exchange of the property (realization event) occurs. Once a realization event occurs, gain (or loss) is quantified by subtracting the adjusted basis of the transferred property from the amount realized. See IRC § 1001(a). As you will recall, the formula for quantifying potential § 61(a)(3) income is as follows:

Realization Event
    Amount Realized
    <u>– Adjusted Basis</u>
    Realized Gain (Realized Loss)

This Chapter focuses on the time when a realized gain or loss is reported on a tax return. Generally, a realized gain or loss is "recognized" in the year the realization event occurs. See IRC § 1001(c). This general rule of recognition means that a realized gain is normally reported as gross income on the tax return for the year in which the realization event occurs. A realized loss is also normally recognized in the year in which the realization event occurs.[1] Under certain circumstances, however, the recognition of part or all of a realized gain

---

[1] A loss recognized by an individual may be claimed as a deduction only if it is allowed under IRC § 165(c). See Chapter 10.

or loss may be deferred temporarily to a future tax year under a "deferred-recognition" provision of the Code. Alternatively, gain or loss may sometimes be deferred indefinitely under a "non-recognition" provision of the Code. This Chapter will explore certain deferred-recognition and non-recognition Code provisions.

A. Deferred Recognition of Gain—§ 453

When high-priced real estate or other property is sold, it is not unusual for the seller to allow the buyer to pay the purchase price in installments over a period of several years. When an individual sells property and at least one payment is to be received after the year in which the sale occurs, the transaction is labeled an "installment sale" under the Code. See IRC § 453(b). When an installment sale occurs, the seller must normally include the entire purchase price in her amount realized in the year of sale. If the amount realized exceeds the seller's adjusted basis in the transferred property, the seller realizes the entire gain in the year of sale. However, the realized gain is normally *not* taxed in its entirety in the year of sale. Rather, the "installment method" of reporting applies and a portion of the seller's gain is taxed as each payment is received. See IRC §§ 453(a), (c). The installment method supersedes the taxpayer's normal method of tax accounting. The application of the installment method differs depending on whether the deferred payments are fixed in amount, or contingent on future events.

Note

Imputed interest. When an installment sale occurs, the total purchase price is included in the seller's amount realized only if the buyer is obligated to pay the seller a market rate of interest on the deferred payments. If the buyer is not required to pay a market rate of interest, part of the purchase price is treated as interest for tax purposes ("imputed interest") and the seller's amount realized is reduced by the imputed interest. Imputed interest will be explored in Chapter 14.

 WORTH NOTING **Not applicable to losses.** The installment method does not apply when an installment sale results in a realized loss.

1.   Fixed Payment Installment Sales

Primary Law: IRC § 453

(a)   Except as otherwise provided in this section, income from an installment sale shall be taken into account for purposes of this title under the installment method.

(b)   For purposes of this section—

(1)   The term "installment sale" means a disposition of property where at least 1 payment is to be received after the close of the taxable year in which the disposition occurs.

* * *

(c)   For purposes of this section, the term "installment method" means a method under which the income recognized for any taxable year from a disposition is that proportion of the payments received in that year which the gross profit * * * bears to the total contract price.

* * *

When an installment sale occurs (i.e., at least one payment is to be received after the tax year in which the sale occurs) and the deferred payments are fixed in amount, the installment method of reporting essentially allocates the total realized gain proportionately among all the payments. The amount of gain attributed to each payment is recognized in the tax year in which the payment is received.

Technically, under the "installment method," the amount of gain to be recognized each year is "that proportion of the payments received in that year which the gross profit * * * bears to the total contract price." See IRC § 453(c). The ratio of the "gross profit" to the "total contract price" is referred to as the "gross profit ratio." See Reg. § 15A.453–1(b)(2)(i). To calculate the gross profit ratio, the following definitions must be kept in mind:

The "gross profit" is the "selling price" less the adjusted basis of the transferred property. See Reg. § 15A.453–1(b)(2)(v).

The "selling price" is the gross selling price without reduction to reflect any existing mortgage on the property. See Reg. § 15A.453–1(b)(2)(ii).

The "total contract price" is the "selling price" reduced by certain indebtedness assumed or taken subject to by the buyer. See Reg. § 15A.453–1(b)(2)(iii).

■ **EXAMPLE 12-A.** *Fixed-payment installment sale.* Abby owns a piece of land she purchased for $10,000. She sells the land in Year 1 for $100,000, payable as follows:

Year	Payment
Year 1	$10,000
Year 2	40,000
Year 3	50,000
Total Selling Price	$100,000

The buyer will also pay Abby a market rate of interest on the deferred payments.

The tax consequences of the sale to Abby are as follows:

Realization Event

Amount Realized	$100,000
Adjusted Basis	10,000
Realized Gain	$90,000

The realized gain represents the total income Abby must report from the transaction. In what tax year(s) does Abby report the $90,000 of realized gain?

Because the transaction is an installment sale (i.e., she receives at least one payment after the year in which the sale occurs), she recognizes the $90,000 gain under the installment method (rather than under her normal tax accounting method). Under the installment method, the portion of the $90,000 realized gain to be recognized each year is computed as follows:

Gross profit (selling price less adjusted basis): $90,000 = 90% (gross

Total contract price (selling price): $100,000 profit ratio)

Thus, 90% of each payment is recognized (reported as gross income) in the year received.

1. Year 1: 90% × $10,000 payment = $9,000 gain recognized
2. Year 2: 90% × $40,000 payment = $36,000 gain recognized
3. Year 3: 90% × $50,000 payment = $45,000 gain recognized
        Total $90,000 gain recognized

If not for the installment method, the entire $90,000 realized gain would be recognized in Year 1 and the tax due would likely exceed the $10,000 cash payment the taxpayer received in that year.

The following excerpt from Huff v. Commissioner, T.C. Memo. 1994–451, offers another illustration of the installment method:

[P]etitioner purchased [a retail store] in 1976 ***. Petitioner sold the store in December 1988 for [$36,000], and of that amount, petitioner received $6,000 in cash; a note was given for the [$30,000] balance. Petitioner's store had [an adjusted basis of $27,000]. ***

Respondent determined petitioner's reportable income on the sale using the installment sales method under section 453(a). Section 453(a) provides that income from an installment sale shall be taken into account under the installment method, except as otherwise provided. An installment sale means a disposition of property under terms where at least one payment is received in a tax year after the year in which the disposition takes place. Sec. 453(b)(1). The installment method requires a portion of payments received from an installment sale in a tax year to be included in gross income in the year received and permits the taxpayer to spread out the recognition of gain on the sale. Sec. 453(c). Generally, installment sales result in reportable income in an amount equal to the product of the amount received in the year of sale and the gross profit percentage. Sec. 453(a). The gross profit percentage is computed by dividing the gross profit (sale price less adjusted basis) by the total sale price. Sec. 453(c); Reg. sec. 15A.453–1(b). Respondent calculated petitioner's gross profit to be [$9,000] and the gross profit percentage to be [25] percent [$9,000 gross profit/$36,000 selling price]. Thus, after applying the gross profit percentage of [25] percent to the $6,000 cash received by petitioner in December 1988, respondent determined petitioner had a [recognized] gain in the amount of [$1,500] for taxable year 1988 on the sale of the retail store [$6,000 × 25% = $1,500]. In addition, petitioner received principal payments totaling [$30,000] in 1989 with respect to the sale of the store. When the gross profit percentage of [25] percent is applied to that amount, the resulting [recognized] gain is [$7,500] for 1989 [$30,000 × 25% = $7,500].

■ **PROBLEM 12-1.** *Fixed-payment installment sale.* Chase purchased a diamond for $80,000 several years ago. Chase sells the diamond in Year 1 for $200,000 payable as follows:

Year	Payments
Year 1	$20,000
Year 2	$40,000
Year 3	$40,000
Year 4	$100,000

The buyer will also pay Chase a market rate of interest on the deferred payments. How much gain will Chase recognize in each year?

FOR DISCUSSION

Time value of money. From an economic standpoint, is the installment method normally beneficial or detrimental to the taxpayer? Why?

Notes

1.   *Liquidity to pay tax.* The installment method helps to ensure that, when an installment sale occurs, the cash payments the seller receives each year will be sufficient to satisfy the seller's tax liability (i.e., the taxpayer will have

sufficient liquidity to pay the tax). In this regard, is IRC § 453 an aberrational provision? In other words, when an individual receives an economic benefit in a form other than cash, is the benefit normally not included in the individual's gross income in the year of receipt because there is no apparent source of cash to pay the resulting tax?

2.   *Sales of inventory.* The installment method does not apply to sales of inventory and other property held for sale to customers in the ordinary course of a trade or business. IRC § 453(b)(2). The question of whether a realized gain is recognized arises only in connection with IRC § 61(a)(3) income. Does the sale of inventory trigger IRC § 61(a)(3) income? See IRC § 61(a)(2).

3.   *Electing out of the installment method.* Although the opportunity to defer gain under the installment method is normally beneficial to taxpayers, use of the installment method is not mandatory. A taxpayer who makes an installment sale may "elect-out" of the installment method of reporting gain. See IRC § 453(d). When an installment sale with deferred fixed payments occurs and the seller elects out of the installment method, the entire realized gain will be recognized in the year of sale. Under what circumstances might a taxpayer wish to elect-out of the installment method?

4.   *Assumption of liabilities.* If an installment sale occurs and the buyer assumes certain liabilities of the seller, the contract price (i.e., the denominator of the gross profit percentage) is determined by subtracting the assumed liabilities from the selling price. See Reg. § 15A.453–1(b)(5) Example (2). Moreover, if the amount of liabilities assumed by the buyer exceeds the seller's adjusted basis in the transferred property, the difference is treated as a payment received by the seller in the year of sale. In this situation, the entire amount of each subsequent payment received by the seller is taxed as gain (i.e., the gross profit percentage is 100%). See Reg. § 15A.453–1(b)(5) Example (3).

2.   Contingent Payment Installment Sales

When income-producing property is to be sold, the seller and the buyer will sometimes resort to contingent, deferred payments to reach an agreement on price.

■ **EXAMPLE 12-B.** *Contingent payment installment sale.* In Year 1, Seller wants to sell a business for $5,000,000, but Buyer is only willing to pay $4,500,000. Seller expects the business to earn profits of $1,000,000 in each of Years 2 and 3, but Buyer expects a profit of only $500,000 in each of Years 2 and 3.

The parties can bridge the gap in price by agreeing to:

1)   an initial payment of $4,500,000, and

2)   contingent, deferred payments in Years 2 and 3 equal to 50% of the business's annual profits in excess of $500,000.

If Seller is correct and the business earns profits of $1,000,000 in Years 2 and 3, Seller will receive the $5,000,000 she sought:

Initial payment:	$4,500,000
Year 2 payment:	$250,000 [50% × ($1,000,000 – $500,000)]
Year 3 payment:	$250,000 [50% × ($1,000,000 – $500,000)]
Total:	$5,000,000

Alternatively, if Buyer is correct and the business earns only $500,000 of profits in Years 2 and 3, Buyer will pay only $4,500,000 because no contingent payments will be due [50% × ($500,000 – $500,000) = 0].

Initial payment:	$4,500,000
Year 2 payment:	0 [50% × ($500,000 – $500,000)]
Year 3 payment:	0 [50% × ($500,000 – $500,000)]
Total:	$4,500,000

Although the use of contingent payments can help parties reach an agreement on purchase price, the presence of contingent payments complicates the tax reporting. Questions surrounding the tax reporting of contingent payments arose long before IRC § 453 was enacted. The threshold issue was whether a contingent payment sale should be treated as a "closed" transaction or an "open" transaction. Closed transaction treatment requires reporting of the entire gain in the year of sale, regardless of when the deferred payments are scheduled to occur. By contrast, open transaction treatment enables the taxpayer to defer reporting any income until she receives payments in excess of her basis in the transferred property.

BURNET v. LOGAN

Supreme Court of the United States, 1931
283 U.S. 404, 51 S.Ct. 550, 75 L.Ed. 1143

[U]ntil March 11, 1916, respondent, Mrs. Logan, owned 250 of the 4,000 [shares of] stock of the Mahoning Ore & Steel Company, [that she had purchased for $200,000. Since 1895, the Mahoning Company has owned a mine from which it] has regularly taken large, but varying, quantities of iron ore.

On March 11, 1916, the owners of all the shares in [the Mahoning] Company sold them to Youngstown Sheet & Tube Company * * *.

For the shares so acquired, the Youngstown Company paid the [shareholders of the Mahoning Company] $2,200,000 in money, and agreed to pay annually thereafter for distribution among them 60 cents for each ton of ore [mined by the Mahoning Company. Because Mrs. Logan had owned 250 of the 4,000 outstanding shares of the Mahoning Company, she received the following:

250/4,000 (6.25%) of the $2,200,000 cash payment ($137,500), and

250/4,000 (6.25%) of the contingent payments made by the Youngstown Company with respect to the amount of ore mined each year.]

* * *

During 1917, 1918, 1919, and 1920 the Youngstown Company paid large sums under the agreement. Out of these respondent received on account of her 250 shares [a total of amount of roughly $35,000]. * * *

[Mrs. Logan's income tax returns] included no part of what she had obtained from * * * the Youngstown Company. She [regarded the transaction as an "open" transaction and] maintains that until the total amount actually received by her from the sale of her shares [exceeds her $200,000 basis in the Mahoning Company shares], no taxable income will arise from the transaction.[2] * * *

---

[2]   Editor's note: Based on the modified figures used in this casebook, Mrs. Logan received $137,500 cash in 1916 and payments totaling $35,000 from 1917–1920. Thus, she received a total of $172,500 prior to 1921. This amount was less than her $200,000 basis in the shares she sold.

* * *

The Commissioner ruled that the [sale should be taxed as a "closed" transaction]. The Commissioner [argued that the] obligation of the Youngstown Company to pay 60 cents per ton had a fair market value of [$2,000,000] on March 11, 1916; that this value should be treated as so much cash, and the sale of the stock regarded as a closed transaction [resulting in a taxable gain to Mrs. Logan in 1916.][3] His calculations, based upon estimates and assumptions, are too intricate for brief statement. He made deficiency assessments according to the view just stated, and the Board of Tax Appeals approved the result.

The Circuit Court of Appeals held that [the sale should be taxed as an "open" transaction because], in the circumstances, it was impossible to determine with fair certainty the market value of the agreement by the Youngstown Company to pay 60 cents per ton. Also that respondent was entitled to the return of [the basis in her shares] before she could be charged with any taxable income. As this had not in fact [occurred by the end of 1920], there was no taxable income.

We agree with the result reached by the Circuit Court of Appeals.

The 1916 transaction was a sale of stock * * * [T]he situation [does not] demand that an effort be made to place according to the best available data some approximate value upon the contract for future payments. * * * As annual payments on account of extracted ore come in, they can be readily apportioned first as return of capital and later as profit. The liability for income tax ultimately can be fairly determined without resort to mere estimates, assumptions, and speculation.

FOR DISCUSSION

Mrs. Logan's preference for open transaction treatment.

Why did Mrs. Logan prefer open transaction treatment rather than closed transaction treatment?

When the profit, if any, is actually realized, the taxpayer will be required to respond. The consideration for the sale was [$137,500] in cash and the promise

---

[3]   Editor's note: Based on the modified figures used in this casebook, Mrs. Logan's share of the $2,000,000 value the Commissioner attributed to the contingent payments equals $125,000 (250/4000 × $2,000,000). Thus, the Commissioner treated Mrs. Logan as realizing $262,500 in 1916 (the $137,500 payment of cash plus her $125,000 share of the estimated value of the contingent payments). As a result, the $262,500 Mrs. Logan realized in 1916 exceeded her $200,000 basis and resulted in a $62,500 taxable gain in 1916, the year she sold her Mahoning Company stock.

of future money payments wholly contingent upon facts and circumstances not possible to foretell with anything like fair certainty. The promise was in no proper sense equivalent to cash. It had no ascertainable fair market value. The transaction was not a "closed" one. Respondent might never recoup her capital investment from payments only conditionally promised. Prior to 1921, all receipts from the sale of her shares amounted to less than [her basis in the shares]. She properly demanded the return of her capital investment before assessment of any taxable profit based on conjecture.

* * *

The judgments below are affirmed.

NOTE

Valuation of contingent payments for estate tax purposes. Mrs. Logan's mother had also owned shares of the Mahoning Company and she died shortly after the Youngstown Company had acquired her stock. An estate tax was imposed on the value of all the property she owned at the time of her death. Among her assets was the right to contingent payments she received from the Youngstown Company which she bequeathed to her daughter. The value of the right to contingent payments for estate tax purposes was determined to be roughly $277,000. However, the Logan Court was not persuaded that the estate tax valuation should apply for income tax purposes, stating the following (at 283 U.S. 413–14):

> From her mother's estate, Mrs. Logan obtained the right to share in possible proceeds of a contract thereafter to pay indefinite sums. The value of this was assumed to be $277,164.50, and its transfer was so taxed. Some valuation—speculative or otherwise—was necessary in order to close the estate. It may never yield as much, it may yield more.

Under current law, IRC § 453 applies to contingent payment sales, unless the taxpayer elects out of the installment method. A "contingent payment sale" is defined by the regulations as—

a sale or other disposition in which the aggregate selling price cannot be determined by the close of the taxable year in which the sale or other disposition occurs.

Reg. § 15A.453–1(c)(1). Unlike a fixed payment installment sale, the deferred payments in a contingent payment sale depend on the occurrence of future events. Thus, the amount of the deferred payments that will ultimately materialize is unknown in the year of sale.

In a fixed payment installment sale, the "gross profit ratio" determines how much of each deferred payment must be recognized. See Reg. § 15A.453–1(b)(2)(i). It is impossible to calculate the gross profit ratio for a contingent payment sale because the amount of deferred payments that will ultimately materialize is unknown in the year of sale.[4] Consequently, when a contingent payment installment sale occurs, a special set of rules is employed to determine how much of each payment must be recognized when a payment is received. The Perlin case that follows introduces these rules.

PERLIN v. COMMISSIONER

United States Tax Court, 1993
T.C. Memo. 1993–79

Parker, Judge: * * *

Findings of Fact

    * * *

By letter dated June 6, 1983, * * * petitioner and Realtec memorialized their final agreement ["the Realtec Agreement"] for the acquisition by Realtec of petitioner's [income-producing real estate ("the Property")]. * * *

The consideration agreed to by petitioner and Realtec consisted of a [$750,000] cash payment [in 1984 and a] $250,000 Contingent Note [payable] 10 years after acquisition of the Property, [if, and only if, the Property's

---

[4]   Technically, it is impossible to calculate the "selling price" when the amount of deferred payments is unknown in the year of sale; and both the numerator and the denominator of the gross profit ratio are based on the "selling price." The numerator of the gross profit ratio is the "gross profit" which equals the *selling price* less the adjusted basis of the transferred property. See Reg. § 15A.453–1(b)(2)(v). The denominator of the gross profit ratio is the "total contract price" which equals the *selling price* reduced by certain indebtedness. See Reg. § 15A.453–1(b)(2)(iii).

market value 10 years after the acquisition is at least $2 million. Realtec also had the right to prepay the Contingent Note at any time.]

The Contingent Note was expressly made payable only if the development of the Property was successful. At the time of the Realtec Agreement, both petitioner and Realtec understood that there would be a risk of failure and that two developers of that land had previously failed.

* * *

Opinion

* * *

On their 1984 tax return, the individual petitioners reported the purchase price received pursuant to the Realtec Agreement as [$850,000], which consisted of [$750,000] cash received in 1984 * * * and the Contingent Note [which, according to the taxpayer, had an estimated value of only $100,000. By contrast, the Internal Revenue Service claimed the taxpayer should have reported a purchase price of $1,000,000, which consisted of the $750,000 cash payment and the Contingent Note which, according to the Internal Revenue Service, should have been included at its $250,000 face amount. The parties agree that the] transaction qualified for installment sale treatment.

An installment sale is a disposition of property where at least one payment is to be received after the close of the taxable year in which the disposition occurs. Sec. 453(b)(1). If a disposition qualifies as an installment sale, the installment method of accounting permits a taxpayer to defer recognition of gain (profit) on the disposition until the taxpayer actually receives the money. Thus, under the installment method, the taxpayer is able to recognize the gain on the installment sale over the period during which the installment payments are received, rather than be taxed on all of the gain in the year of sale.

Each payment received in an installment sale is treated in part as a nontaxable recovery of a portion of the taxpayer's basis in the property, and in part as a taxable * * * portion of the taxpayer's gain upon disposition. Sec. 453(c). The amount of each payment that must be reported as gain is determined by multiplying the total amount of payments received during the year by the gross profit percentage. Sec. 453(c). The gross profit percentage is the ratio of the gross profit (the selling price less the taxpayer's adjusted basis) to the total contract price (the selling price reduced by any qualifying indebtedness assumed or taken subject to by the buyer). Sec. 453(c).

The installment method of reporting gain also applies to sales with a contingent selling price. A contingent payment sale is defined as a sale or other disposition of property in which the aggregate selling price cannot be determined by the close of the taxable year in which the sale or disposition occurs. Reg. Sec. 15A.453–1(c)(1). Regulations provide rules for ratable basis recovery in transactions where the gross profit or the total contract price (or both) cannot be readily ascertained. Sec. 453(j)(2); Reg. sec. 15A.453–1(c). The regulations also provide special rules for determining gain from contingent payment sales and for allocating the taxpayer's basis to payments received and to be received.

The temporary regulations address three different contingent sale situations: (1) sales for which a maximum selling price is determinable, Reg. sec. 15A.453–1(c)(2); (2) sales for which a maximum selling price is not determinable but the time over which payments will be received is determinable, Reg. sec. 15A.453–1(c)(3); and (3) sales for which neither a maximum selling price nor a definite payment term is determinable, Reg. sec. 15A.453–1(c)(4).

The situation in this case falls within Reg. section 15A.453–1(c)(2) [sales for which a maximum selling price is determinable]. Under Reg. section 15A.453–1(c)(2)(i)(A),

> The stated maximum selling price shall be determined by assuming that all of the contingencies contemplated by the agreement are met or otherwise resolved in a manner that will maximize the selling price and accelerate payments to the earliest date or dates permitted under the agreement.

In computing the maximum selling price under Reg. section 15A.453–1(c)(2)(i)(A), petitioners argue that the face value of the Contingent Note should be reduced to reflect [the fact that no interest was to be paid by Realtec on the deferred contingent payment during the ten-year term of the Note. Thus, petitioners] contend that the $250,000 Contingent Note should [be valued at only $100,000 when computing the maximum selling price in the year of sale under the regulations]. Respondent, on the other hand, has determined that the full [$250,000] face value of the note should be included in the computation of the maximum selling price in the year of sale due to [Realtec's] right to prepay, at any time, the entire amount of the Contingent Note. [If Realtec prepaid the Note immediately after it was issued, no interest would accrue on the deferred contingent payment.]

We do not sustain respondent's interpretation of the operation of Reg. section 15A.453–1(c)(2)(i)(A). We do not think that the prepayment provision of the Contingent Note is a "contingency" as contemplated under Reg. section 15A.453–1(c)(2)(i)(A). A "contingency" exists when the enforceability of a right to the payment of an obligation depends upon the occurrence of some future event which may or may not occur. In this case, for example, petitioner's right to enforce the obligation of [Realtec] to pay $250,000 is contingent upon [the Property appreciating in value to $2,000,000], which may or may not occur. The prepayment clause, however, does not represent an event, the occurrence of which would give rise to an enforceable obligation. Petitioner cannot force [Realtec] to prepay the Contingent Note. Therefore, a prepayment cannot be viewed as a "contingency", the occurrence of which would give petitioner an enforceable right to payment. [Consequently, we agree with the taxpayer that the "maximum selling price" for purposes of allocating the taxpayer's basis in the transferred property to the payments the taxpayer received is $850,000, not $1,000,000.]

NOTES

1. *Indeterminable maximum selling price.* Sometimes, the terms of a contingent payment installment sale will render it impossible to determine the maximum selling price in the year of sale. For example, assume Allison owns all the stock of a corporation conducting a business and that she sells the stock for an initial payment of $1,000,000, and deferred contingent payments in Years 2 and 3 equal to 10% of the profits generated by the business in those two years. In this situation, the maximum selling price cannot be determined because the maximum amount of profits the business will generate in future years is unknown.

Although the maximum selling price is indeterminable, the maximum number of years in which payments may be received is known (three years in this example). In this situation, the taxpayer's basis in the transferred property is allocated in equal annual increments to the years in which payments may be received. See Reg. § 15A.453–1(c)(3). Thus, if Allison had a basis of $300,000 in the stock she sold, she could apply one-third of the basis ($100,000) to the $1,000,000 payment she received in the year of sale and would recognize a $900,000 gain. She could also apply one-third of the basis ($100,000) to the amount of any contingent payments she received in Year 2, and one-third of the basis ($100,000) to the amount of any contingent payments she received in Year 3.

In highly unusual cases, a contingent payment sale may occur where neither the stated maximum selling price nor the maximum number of years in which payments may be received are known. Here, the regulations provide that the taxpayer's basis in the transferred property is to be allocated in equal annual increments over a period of fifteen years beginning with the year of sale. See Reg. § 15A.453–1(c)(4).

2. *Electing out of the installment method.* When a contingent payment sale occurs and the taxpayer elects out of the installment method (IRC § 453(d)), the sale normally will be treated as a "closed" transaction. In this situation, the taxpayer will be compelled to recognize the entire realized gain in the year of sale. If, however, the taxpayer can demonstrate that the value of the right to contingent payments is unascertainable when the sale occurs, the sale will be treated as an "open" transaction. In this situation, the taxpayer can defer all gain until the payments received exceed the basis in the transferred proper-ty. Reg. § 15A.453–1(d)(2)(iii) limits the use of open transaction reporting as follows: "Only in those rare and extraordinary cases involving sales for a con-tingent payment obligation in which the fair market value of the obligation cannot reasonably be ascertained will the taxpayer be entitled to assert that the transaction is 'open'."

a) Why is the government antagonistic toward open transaction treatment?

b) What are the tax consequences to a taxpayer who sells property in a contingent payment transaction and elects out of the installment method if the contingent payment obligation in fact has an ascer-tainable value?

c) Why is it rare for a taxpayer to elect out of the installment method when a contingent payment sale occurs?

LOOK ONLINE For additional analysis of contingent payment sales, see Kwall, "Out With the Open-Transaction Doctrine: A New Theory for Taxing Contingent Payment Installment Sales," **81 North Carolina Law Review 977 (2003)**.

B. Non-Recognition of Gain and Loss

As a general rule, when property is sold or exchanged (i.e., a realization event occurs), any realized gain is immediately recognized (i.e., included in gross income). See IRC § 1001(c). Congress, however, has created certain narrow exceptions to this general rule. These exceptions, referred to as "non-recognition" rules, sanction indefinite deferral of realized gains. Unlike a statutory exclusion, which permanently eliminates potential income, a non-recognition rule normally merely defers gain. Most non-recognition rules also apply to realized losses, although this is not always the case.[5] Thus, whenever a realization event occurs, the following analysis should be employed:

Realization Event
　　Amount Realized
　　– Adjusted Basis
　　Realized Gain (Realized Loss)
　　Recognition? Yes, unless a non-recognition provisions applies.[6]

This Chapter will explore three non-recognition rules: IRC §§ 1031, 1033 and 1041.

---

[5]　See, e.g., IRC § 1033 that applies to gains, but not to losses.

[6]　When a loss is recognized, the loss must also be allowed for the taxpayer to claim a deduction. See IRC § 165(c), examined in Chapter 10.

1. Like-Kind Exchange of Business/Investment Property—§ 1031

Primary Law: IRC § 1031

(a) No gain or loss shall be recognized on the exchange of real property held for productive use in a trade or business or for investment if such real property is exchanged solely for real property of like kind which is to be held either for productive use in a trade or business or for investment.

* * *

a.   Like-Kind Property

KOCH v. COMMISSIONER

United States Tax Court, 1978
71 T.C. 54

FEATHERSTON, JUDGE:

* * *

FINDINGS OF FACT

* * *

OPINION

During 1973 and 1974, petitioners transferred the Glen Oaks Golf Club and the Chautauqua Subdivision to Imperial and U.S. Home, respectively, and received from those corporations 17 parcels of real estate which were subject to 99-year condominium leases. The parties have stipulated that both sets of properties were held either for productive use in a trade or business or for investment. They also agree that the transactions were exchanges of properties. The issue thus is narrowed to whether, within the meaning of section 1031(a), the real estate subject to the 99-year leases which petitioners received and the real estate not so encumbered which they transferred in the exchanges were properties of a "like kind."

Section 1031(a) provides as follows:

No gain or loss shall be recognized if property held for productive use in trade or business or for investment * * * is exchanged solely for property of a like kind to be held either for productive use in trade or business or for investment.

Petitioners contend that the long-term leases on the property which they received from Imperial and U.S. Home do not affect that property's fundamental character. Since they conveyed fee simple interests to Imperial and U.S. Home and in exchange received fee simple interests from those corporations, petitioners argue that the exchange involved properties of a like kind within the meaning of section 1031(a). Respondent maintains that * * * the exchanged properties were not of a "like kind" and, consequently, petitioners' gain is [recognized] under section 1001(c). * * * We hold for petitioner.

The basic reason for allowing nonrecognition of gain or loss on the exchange of like-kind property is that the taxpayer's economic situation after the exchange is fundamentally the same as it was before the transaction occurred. "(I)f the taxpayer's money is still tied up in the same kind of property as that in which it was originally invested, he is not allowed to compute and deduct his theoretical loss on the exchange, nor is he charged with a tax upon his theoretical profit." H. Rept. 704, 73d Cong., 2d Sess. (1934), 1939–1 C.B. (Part 2) 554, 564. The rules of section 1031 apply automatically; they are not elective. The underlying assumption of section 1031(a) is that the new property is substantially a continuation of the old investment still unliquidated.

Section 1.1031(a)–1(b), Income Tax Regs., explains that the words "like kind" as used in section 1031(a) have reference to "the nature or character of the property and not to its grade or quality." This means that "the distinction intended and made by the statute is a broad one between classes and characters of property, for instance, between real and personal property." The regulations contain illustrations of this broad distinction, stating that [the like kind requirement will be satisfied] if a taxpayer * * * exchanges city real estate for a ranch or farm, exchanges improved real estate for unimproved real estate, or * * * exchanges a leasehold of a fee with 30 years or more to run for unimproved real estate. Sec. 1.1031(a)–1(c), Income Tax Regs.

* * *

[S]ection 1031(a) requires a comparison of the exchanged properties to ascertain whether the nature and character of the transferred rights in and to the respective properties are substantially alike. In making this comparison, consideration must be given to the respective interests in the physical properties, the nature of the title conveyed, the rights of the parties, [and] the duration, nature or character of the properties as distinguished from their grade or quality. Significantly, as the standard for comparison, section 1031(a) refers to property of a like, not an identical, kind. The comparison should be directed to ascertaining whether the taxpayer, in making the exchange, has used his property to acquire a new kind of asset or has merely exchanged it for an asset of like nature or character.

In the instant case, petitioners exchanged improved real estate for improved real estate in 1973 and unimproved land for improved real estate in 1974. Quite clearly, apart from the long-term leases outstanding on the 17 parcels received by petitioners, the properties were of a like kind, and the only question is whether the leases disqualify the exchange. We do not think they do. When Imperial and U.S. Home granted the long-term leases, those corporations retained fee simple ownership of the 17 parcels. In 1973 and 1974, the corporations transferred their fee simple title of those 17 parcels to petitioners in exchange for the fee simple title of petitioners' properties. Both parties thus parted with their entire interests. The exchanged interests were perpetual in nature, and they thus meet the duration-of-the-rights test. Petitioners' money is still tied up in real property of the same class or character as they owned before the exchange. We conclude that the exchange was made of properties of a like kind.

＊ ＊ ＊

Quite true, as respondent argues, the long-term leases prevent petitioners from taking physical possession of the properties and using them for other purposes as long as the leases remain in effect. But section 1031(a) "was not intended to draw any distinction between parcels of real property however dissimilar they may be in location, in attributes and in capacities for profitable use." ＊ ＊ ＊

FOR DISCUSSION **Realization vs. recognition.** Did a realization event occur in Koch? Is recognition of any relevance in the absence of a realization event?

Under current law, real property is the only type of property that can satisfy § 1031. See IRC § 1031(a)(1). Prior to enactment of the Tax Cuts and Jobs Act of 2017, however, IRC § 1031 could apply to an exchange of like-kind personal property as well as real property. Now that exchanges of like-kind personal property are no longer eligible for nonrecognition treatment, certain types of businesses will incur greater tax liabilities. This change in the law is particularly problematic for professional sports teams that frequently trade player contracts and draft rights. The Internal Revenue Service has attempted to ease the tax burdens these teams would otherwise face by issuing Rev. Proc. 2019–18.

Revenue Procedure 2019–18

I.R.B. 2019–18

SECTION 1. PURPOSE

This revenue procedure provides a safe harbor for a professional sports team to treat certain personnel contracts and rights to draft players as having a zero value for determining gain or loss to be recognized for federal income tax purposes on the trade of a personnel contract or a draft pick that is within the scope of this revenue procedure.

SECTION 2. BACKGROUND

* * *

.02 Trades of player contracts, staff-member contracts, and draft picks.

(1) Professional sports teams (teams) generally engage the services of players and staff members, such as managers and coaches, through the use of employment contracts that provide agreed upon compensation to the employed individual in return for future performance of specified services for a defined period of time, usually longer than one year (personnel contract). During the term of a personnel contract, the value of that contract may fluctuate based on a variety of factors, including player performance, the changing needs of the team, the changing needs of other teams, a player's effect on fan attendance, and the number of years until a player becomes a free agent and is able to sign a contract to play for any team in a league. Other considerations affecting the value of a player contract include the size of the team's market (whether a smaller city or a major

urban population), the cost of player development, and the impact of injuries and slumps on player performance. * * * In addition to these unique factors, the market in which personnel contracts are traded is small and private. From time to time, teams trade one or more personnel contracts to other teams in exchange for one or more personnel contracts for the services of other personnel. Trades may include the transfer of a right to draft players in the league's player draft (draft pick) or a cash payment. Some trades involve only draft picks.

(2) In general, a team does not agree to a trade of one personnel contract (or set of personnel contracts) or a draft pick (or set of draft picks) unless the team believes that it is receiving something of equal or greater value to what it is giving up in light of the team's circumstances and priorities at the time. The exact value that a team places on the future performance of services by the personnel it is receiving in a trade is highly subjective and may be influenced by the team's specific needs at the time rather than by whether the compensation provided for under the contract may be viewed as at market value, over market value, or under market value. * * * As a result, although each team may believe it is receiving something of equal or greater value to what it is giving up in a trade of personnel contracts or draft picks in light of its particular circumstances and priorities at the time, it is unusually difficult to assign an objective monetary value to the personnel contracts or draft picks.

(3) In order to avoid highly subjective, complex, lengthy, and expensive disputes between professional sports teams and the IRS regarding the value of personnel contracts and draft picks for the purpose of determining the proper amount of gain or loss to be recognized for federal income tax purposes on the trade of one or more personnel contracts or draft picks, this revenue procedure provides a safe harbor permitting teams to treat the value of traded personnel contracts and draft picks as zero if certain conditions are satisfied.

SECTION 3. SCOPE

This revenue procedure applies to trades of personnel contracts and draft picks by professional sports teams (trades) that meet all of the following requirements:

.01 *All parties to trade must use safe harbor.* The parties to the trade that are subject to federal income tax in the United States must treat the trade on their respective federal income tax returns consistent with this revenue procedure;

* * *

SECTION 4. SAFE HARBOR

.01 *In general.* This revenue procedure provides a safe harbor for determining the amount of gain or loss to be recognized on a trade by a professional sports team of personnel contracts or draft picks. For a team making a trade of a personnel contract or draft pick within the scope of this revenue procedure, the value of the personnel contract or draft pick is treated as zero for purposes of this section 4.

.02 *Application of safe harbor.*

(1) *No gain or loss on a trade.* Except as provided in paragraph (5), below, for a professional sports team making a trade of a personnel contract or draft pick within the scope of this revenue procedure, because the contract value of each personnel contract or draft pick is treated as zero for purposes of this revenue procedure, no gain or loss is recognized on the trade for federal income tax purposes.

(2) *Receipt of cash in a trade, computing amount realized.* Under § 1001, a team receiving cash in a trade includes in amount realized the cash the team receives from another team in the trade. Under this revenue procedure, because the contract value of each personnel contract or draft pick is treated as zero for purposes of this revenue procedure, a team that does not receive cash in a trade has an amount realized of zero.

(3) *Providing cash in a trade, computing basis.* Under § 1012, a team providing cash to another team in a trade has a basis in the personnel contract or draft pick received equal to the cash the team provides in the trade. Under this revenue procedure, because the contract value of each personnel contract or draft pick is treated as zero for purposes of this revenue procedure, a team that provides no cash in the trade has a zero basis in the personnel contract or draft pick received in the trade.

(4) * * *

(5) *Trades of personnel contracts or draft picks, determining gain or loss.* Under § 1001 * * *, a team making a trade of a personnel contract or draft pick recognizes gain to the extent of the excess of the amount realized under section 4.02(2), over the unrecovered basis (if any) of the personnel contract or draft pick traded * * *. Under §§ 1001 [and] 165 * * *, a team making a trade of a personnel contract or draft pick recognizes a loss to the extent of the excess of the unrecovered basis of the personnel contract or draft pick traded, over the amount realized under section 4.02(2) * * *.

.03 *Limited applicability.* This revenue procedure applies only to trades of personnel contracts or draft picks among teams in professional sports leagues and has no application to transactions not described in this revenue procedure. In addition, this revenue procedure does not apply to trades of a team for another team or a sale of a team.

* * *

SECTION 5. EXAMPLES

The following examples illustrate the application of the safe harbor described in section 4 of this revenue procedure. Unless otherwise provided, the teams in the examples have a $0 basis in the player contracts being traded. * * *

Example 1. Trade with no cash. In 2018, Team A trades Player Contract 1 to Team B for Player Contract 2. The teams apply the safe harbor in this revenue procedure. Under section 4.02(1), neither Team A nor Team B has an amount realized or gain on the trade because neither team received cash in the trade. Under section 4.02(3), Team A has a $0 basis in Player Contract 2, and Team B has a $0 basis in Player Contract 1.

Example 2. One team provides cash in the trade. The facts are the same as in Example 1, except Team A trades Player Contract 1 and $10x to Team B for Player Contract 2. Under section 4.02(1), Team A has no amount realized or gain on the trade because Team A did not receive cash in the trade. Under section 4.02(2), Team B has a $10x amount realized on the trade because Team B received $10x from Team A in the trade. Under section 4.02(5), Team B must recognize $10x of gain, the excess of Team B's $10x amount realized over its $0 basis in the Player Contract 2 it traded. * * * Under section 4.02(3), Team A has a $10x basis in Player Contract 2, the amount of cash Team A provided to Team B in the trade. Team A's $10x basis is recovered through depreciation * * * over the life of Player Contract 2. Under section 4.02(3), Team B has a $0 basis in Player Contract 1 because Team B provided no cash to Team A in the trade.

Example 3. No cash in the trade, one team has an unrecovered basis.

(i) In 2019, Team C signs Player 3 to a contract (Player Contract 3) for 5 years. Under the terms of Player Contract 3, Team C pays Player 3 a $25x signing bonus in 2019. In each of 2019 and 2020, Team C takes a depreciation deduction * * * of $5x for the $25x it paid to Player 3. In 2021, Team C trades Player Contract 3 to Team D for Player Contract 4, and the teams apply the safe harbor in this revenue procedure.

(ii) Under section 4.02(1), neither Team C nor Team D has an amount realized or gain on the trade because neither team received cash in the trade. Because neither team provided cash in the trade, under section 4.02(3), each team has a $0 basis in the contract it received in the trade. Under section 4.02(5), Team C may deduct in 2021 a $15x loss under § 165 * * *, the excess of its unrecovered basis in Player Contract 3 over its amount realized of $0. * * *

FOR DISCUSSION

Receipt of property that is difficult to value. As a general matter, are taxpayers normally relieved from reporting gross income when they receive an economic benefit in the form of property that is difficult to value? Why do you think the Internal Revenue Service provided the relief delineated in Rev. Proc. 2019–18?

---

b.   Property Held for Business or Investment

For non-recognition treatment to be conferred by IRC § 1031, it is necessary, but not sufficient, for the real property transferred and the real property received to satisfy the like-kind requirement. In addition, the property transferred must have been "held for productive use in a trade or business or for investment" *and* the property received must be "held for productive use in a trade or business or for investment." The Adams case that follows focuses on the latter requirement.

ADAMS v. COMMISSIONER

United States Tax Court, 2013
T.C. Memo. 2013–7

MEMORANDUM FINDINGS OF FACT AND OPINION

MORRISON, JUDGE: * * *

FINDINGS OF FACT

[W]illiam Adams is a semiretired electrical engineer who resided in California * * *. We refer to him as Adams. We refer to his son, whose name is also William Adams, as Bill.

* * *

In 1963, Adams bought a house in San Francisco (San Francisco house) for $26,000. He and his family lived in the house until 1979, when they moved to Rohnert Park, California. Soon after moving to Rohnert Park, Adams rented the San Francisco house to an acquaintance. During the period that he rented out the house—1979 to 2003—Adams made various improvements to it, including upgrading the electrical service, installing a circuit for an electric range, installing three energy-efficient windows, installing carpet, painting the exterior, painting the kitchen, and patching and ultimately replacing the roof.

After the renter moved out in 2003, Adams decided to sell the San Francisco house. He consulted a real-estate broker to help him with the sale.

At the broker's suggestion, Adams engaged [in an exchange of properties] to reduce the income tax on the [transfer] of the San Francisco house. [In June 2004, Adams exchanged the San Francisco house for] a house in Eureka, California (Eureka house) * * *. Adams' son Bill, who had extensive homebuilding and home renovation experience, lived in Eureka. Adams thought buying a house in Eureka would be advantageous because Bill could manage its rental to a third party or even be the tenant himself. Adams chose the particular house because of its size; with five bedrooms, it suited Bill's large family.

The Eureka house was old, dilapidated, and moldy. It had been damaged by a previous squatter. Much work was required to make it livable.

Bill and his family began working on the Eureka house in July 2004. They worked an aggregate of 60 hours per week on the property during July, August, and September 2004. They repaired mold damage, replaced broken doors, fixed holes in walls, repaired rotten subflooring, prepared floors for new carpet installation, scrubbed and repaired surfaces for painting, painted the interior of the house, renovated the kitchen, replumbed the kitchen and laundry room for gas, replaced electrical fixtures and appliances, and performed landscaping. They exterminated rats and other pests and, on one occasion, even chased away a bear. Their efforts made the house livable. For July, August, and September 2004, Adams accepted the services performed by Bill and his family in lieu of monetary rent. (Adams did not reimburse them for the labor and out-of-pocket costs of the home improvements.) The three months of services were worth $3,600.

In October 2004, Bill and his family started living in the Eureka house and paying monetary rent. They paid $1,200 per month in October, November, and December 2004. They continued to pay rent of $1,200 per month * * *until they moved out in early 2008. Bill and his family also continued to maintain and conduct home improvement work on the Eureka house until they moved out. Similar houses in the neighborhood rented for a few hundred dollars more than $1,200 per month. However, the tenants did not maintain or conduct home improvement on the houses. In the meantime Adams continued to live in Rohnert Park, where he had moved in 1979.

* * *

OPINION

* * *

Adams argues that the [exchange] of the San Francisco house [for] the Eureka house was a valid section 1031 exchange that qualified for nonrecognition treatment. He claims that both the San Francisco house and the Eureka house were held "for productive use in a trade or business or for investment" within the meaning of section 1031. For the Eureka house in particular, Adams asserts that he charged fair market rent to Bill and his family, considering the condition of the house and the home-improvement work Bill and his family performed. * * *

* * *

The IRS argues that the [exchange] of the San Francisco house [for] the Eureka house did not qualify as a section 1031 exchange. The IRS claims that Adams acquired the Eureka house for personal purposes—i.e., "with the intention of letting his son and family live there at below market rent." Thus, the IRS claims, Adams must recognize gain [realized on the exchange]. * * *

Section 1031(a)(1) provides:

> No gain or loss shall be recognized on the exchange of property held for productive use in a trade or business or for investment if such property is exchanged solely for property of like kind which is to be held either for productive use in a trade or business or for investment.

[To qualify for nonrecognition treatment under section 1031, three requirements must be satisfied: (1) The transaction must be an exchange; (2) the exchange must involve like-kind properties; and (3) both the properties transferred and the properties received must be held either for productive use in a trade or business or for investment. Reg. Sec. 1.1031(a)–1(a) and (c). The parties do not question that the transaction at issue constitutes an exchange.

Furthermore, they agree that the two residences are like-kind properties. The controversy, therefore, centers on whether the Eureka house was held for investment.]

We find that Adams bought the Eureka house "for investment" within the meaning of section 1031(a)(1). In determining whether the taxpayer intended to hold the acquired property for investment in a section 1031 exchange, we consider the taxpayer's intent at the time of the exchange. The taxpayer's conduct before and after the exchange can inform our determination of the taxpayer's intent. Although Adams chose the Eureka house because Bill and his family lived in Eureka and the house suited Bill's large family, we do not believe Adams intended to charge Bill and his family below-market rent. Bill and his family paid rent of $1,200 per month from July to December 2004 and continued to pay rent of $1,200 per month * * * until they moved out in early 2008. The monthly rent of $1,200 was a fair rental value because Bill and his family assumed substantial responsibilities for renovating, maintaining, and repairing the Eureka house. Even though Adams stated that the rental of the Eureka house was a "gift" when pressed on cross-examination, we construe his testimony to mean that he wished to offer Bill reduced rent in exchange for working on the house.

We conclude that the [exchange] of the San Francisco house [for] the Eureka house constituted a valid section 1031 exchange of like-kind property to be held "for investment". * * *

 FOR DISCUSSION **Double or nothing?** When two taxpayers exchange like-kind properties, can one of the taxpayers satisfy § 1031 without the other taxpayer satisfying § 1031, or is it "double or nothing"?

---

c.   Deferral of Gain (or Loss) and Impact of "Boot"

IRC § 1031 is a non-recognition provision; it is not an exclusion. As such, gain or loss is normally deferred (not eliminated) when a taxpayer meets the requirements of the provision. To achieve this end, a taxpayer who exchanges real property in a transaction that qualifies under IRC § 1031(a) takes a basis in the property received equal to the taxpayer's basis in the property surrendered. See IRC § 1031(d).

WORTH NOTING

Exchanged basis property. When a taxpayer who exchanges property takes a basis in the property received that is determined by reference to the basis in the property surrendered, the property received is referred to as "exchanged basis property." See IRC § 7701(a)(44).

■ **EXAMPLE 12-C.** *Deferral of unrecognized gain.* Bob owns a parcel of land that he purchased for $400,000. Bob holds the land for investment. The land has a current fair market value of $500,000. Ellen owns a parcel of land that she purchased for $300,000 and has a current fair market value of $500,000. Bob transfers his land to Ellen in exchange for her land. Bob holds the land that Ellen transferred to him for investment. What are the tax consequences to Bob?

Bob has a realization event (the exchange of his land for Ellen's land)

Amount realized:	$500,000	(the value of Ellen's land)
Adjusted basis:	$400,000	(the purchase price of Bob's land)
Realized gain:	$100,000	
Recognized gain:	0	(IRC § 1031(a))

Basis in land Bob received: $400,000 (same as Bob's basis in land he transferred)

Bob's $100,000 realized gain is not recognized when he exchanges his land for Ellen's land. However, Bob takes a $400,000 basis in the land he received from Ellen (which has a $500,000 fair market value). Hence, the $100,000 gain Bob realizes on the exchange is merely deferred until he sells the land he received from Ellen (if he ultimately sells that land for $500,000). Can you think of any circumstances where Bob's $100,000 deferred gain could be diminished, or even eliminated, before he sells the land? See, e.g., IRC § 1014.

If two taxpayers wish to exchange like-kind properties, it is highly unlikely that the value of both properties will be exactly the same. If Property A and

Property B are "like-kind" but Property A has a value of $200,000 and Property B has a value of only $175,000, can IRC § 1031 still apply if the owner of Property B adds $25,000 of cash (often referred to as "*boot*") to equalize values? See IRC § 1031(b). How does the receipt of the $25,000 of cash impact the basis that the transferor of property takes in Property B? See IRC § 1031(d).

Primary Law: IRC § 1031

* * *

(b)   If an exchange would be within * * * subsection (a) * * * if it were not for the fact that the property received in the exchange consists not only of property permitted * * * to be received without the recognition of gain, but also of other property or money, then the gain, if any, to the recipient shall be recognized, but in an amount not in excess of the sum of such money and the fair market value of such other property.

* * *

(d)   If property was acquired on an exchange described in this section, * * * then the basis shall be the same as that of the property exchanged, decreased in the amount of any money received by the taxpayer and increased in the amount of gain * * * that was recognized on such exchange. * * *

■ **EXAMPLE 12-D.** *Impact of boot in like-kind exchange.* Bob owns a parcel of land that he purchased for $400,000. Bob holds the land for investment. The land has a current fair market value of $500,000. Ellen owns a parcel of land that she purchased for $300,000 and has a current fair market value of $460,000. (The facts are the same as Example 12-C except that Ellen's land has a fair market value of only $460,000.) Thus, Ellen must give Bob $40,000 of cash in addition to her land to equalize the value of each party's consideration. Bob holds the land that Ellen transferred to him for investment. What are the tax consequences to Bob?

b/c prop exchange had a lesser value than 500k prop

↑ transferring title

Bob has a realization event (the exchange of his land for Ellen's land and cash)

> Amount realized: $500,000 ($460,000 value of Ellen's land and $40,000)
>
> Adjusted basis: $400,000 (the purchase price of Bob's land)
> Realized gain: $100,000
> Recognized gain: $40,000 (lesser of realized gain or cash received)—§ 1031(b)

Bob's basis in Ellen's land—§ 1031(d)

> Exchanged basis $400,000 (basis in the land Bob transferred)
> Less: Money received   40,000
> Plus: Gain recognized   40,000
> Total $400,000

The answers to the following questions should help you understand why Bob takes a basis of $400,000 in the land he receives from Ellen.

1) How much unrealized gain existed in Bob's land before the exchange? *100K*

2) How much gain was recognized by Bob in the exchange? *40K*
   CG rate of 40k

3) How much of the gain Bob realized on the exchange was not recognized? *60K*

4) How much gain would Bob recognize if he sold the land he received from Ellen for $460,000 (its fair market value)?
   60K b/c value of land is 460k — if left at 500k, there's a built in loss

■ **PROBLEM 12-2.** *Impact of boot in like-kind exchange.* Same facts as Example 12-D, except that Ellen's land has a fair market value of only $360,000 at the time of the exchange. Thus, when Ellen transfers her land to Bob, she must add $140,000 of cash to acquire Bob's $500,000 property. What are the tax consequences of the exchange to Bob and to Ellen?

2. Involuntary Conversion—§ 1033

Primary Law: IRC § 1033

(a) If property (as a result of its destruction in whole or in part, theft, seizure, or requisition or condemnation or threat or imminence thereof) is compulsorily or involuntarily converted—

    (1) Into property similar or related in service or use to the property so converted, no gain shall be recognized.

    (2) Into money or into property not similar or related in service or use to the converted property, the gain (if any) shall be recognized except to the extent hereinafter provided in this paragraph:

        (A) If the taxpayer during the period specified in subparagraph (B), for the purpose of replacing the property so converted, purchases other property similar or related in service or use to the property so converted, * * * at the election of the taxpayer the gain shall be recognized only to the extent that the amount realized upon such conversion * * * exceeds the cost of such other property or such stock. * * *

        (B) The period referred to in subparagraph (A) shall be the period beginning with the date of the disposition of the converted property, or the earliest date of the threat or imminence of requisition or condemnation of the converted property, whichever is the earlier, and ending—

            (i) 2 years after the close of the first taxable year in which any part of the gain upon the conversion is realized * * *

DAVIS v. UNITED STATES

United States Court of Appeals, Ninth Circuit, 1979
589 F.2d 446

Wallace, Circuit Judge:

The government appeals the district court's judgment granting relief under the nonrecognition provisions of section 1033 of the Internal Revenue Code of 1954 and awarding an income tax refund. Although we rest our decision on a ground different from that relied upon by the district court, we affirm the judgment.

I

The Trustees of the Estate of James Campbell (taxpayer) have been in the business of leasing trust owned land since 1901. Taxpayer's holdings included both industrial property being developed for lease, and improved agricultural land leased for sugar cane cultivation and livestock grazing. Taxpayer also owned a sea fishery adjacent to its agricultural property.

The state of Hawaii condemned taxpayer's sea fishery and various portions of taxpayer's agricultural property. Taxpayer used the condemnation proceeds to build a storm drainage and water system, grade land, and excavate a roadway in Campbell Industrial Park (the Park), trust owned land taxpayer was developing for lease to industrial concerns.

The Internal Revenue Service did not consider these improvements to be replacement property under section 1033 and informed taxpayer that taxes would have to be paid on the condemnation proceeds. Taxpayer paid the additional taxes plus interest, in the amount of $106,050, filed a timely claim for refund, and upon denial of the claim, instituted this suit.

The district judge granted a refund. He found that, because Hawaii's historically plantation economy had changed to a mixed industrial, commercial, resort, and agricultural economy, little agricultural land in Hawaii was available for purchase, and no prospective agricultural tenants could be found who would be willing to pay the rent required to allow taxpayer a reasonable return on an investment in newly acquired agricultural land. Additionally, because Hawaii had a declared public policy of absorbing ownership of Hawaiian sea fisheries into the public domain, it was virtually impossible for taxpayer to reinvest in agricultural land with an adjacent sea fishery. The court further found that the risk attendant to taxpayer's investment in the Park was no different from the risk which would have been undertaken had taxpayer reinvested the condemnation proceeds in other agricultural property, that the cost to taxpayer of managing the industrial property was substantially the same as had been the cost of managing the condemned property, and that, since taxpayer did not provide substantial management services to either the industrial or agricultural tenants, the services provided at the Park were the same as those that taxpayer had provided to the agricultural tenants.

As a result, the district court held that, by investing the condemnation proceeds in the Park, taxpayer had maintained a substantial continuation of its prior commitment of capital. Believing, however, that the improvements were not of the "same general class" as the condemned agricultural land, the court held that the improvements did not qualify for nonrecognition of gain as "property similar or related in service or use" within the meaning of section 1033(a)(3)(A). [The district court nevertheless found for the taxpayer on other grounds and granted the refund.]

II

Pursuant to section 1033, gain realized because of the condemnation or other involuntary conversion of property is not recognized if the converted property is replaced by similar property within a specified time. Replacement property may qualify * * * under subsection (a) as property "similar or related in service or use" * * *. We hold that given taxpayer's substantial continuation of its prior commitment of capital, the district court erred in concluding that improvements to the Park were not similar or related in service or use to its prior investment in agricultural land. * * *

[Under section 1033(a),] we look to the taxpayer's relationship to his old and new investments.[5] Long ago, we established the proper analysis for determining the applicability of subsection (a).

> The test is a practical one. The trier of fact must determine from all
> the circumstances whether the taxpayer has achieved a sufficient

---

[5]   The Internal Revenue Service originally took the position that the statutory phrase, "similar or related in service or use" meant that the property acquired had to have a close "functional" similarity to the property converted. Under this test the physical characteristics and the end use of the converted and replacement properties had to be similar. We and several other courts of appeals, however, rejected this approach. The Service therefore reconsidered its position in regard to property held for investment, and now focuses attention on "the similarity in the relationship of the services or uses which the original and replacement properties have to the taxpayer-owner." Rev. Rul. 64–237, 1964–2 C.B. 319, 320. The tax court also adopted this test. * * *

continuity of investment to justify non-recognition of the gain, or whether the differences in the relationship of the taxpayer to the two investments are such as to compel the conclusion that he has taken advantage of the condemnation to alter the nature of his investment for his own purposes.

Filippini v. United States, 318 F.2d 841, 844–45 (9th Cir.).

Filippini requires that we consider a broad range of factors in determining whether a taxpayer has maintained a sufficient continuity of investment. When the taxpayer holds both the condemned and the replacement properties for the production of rental income, the inquiry specifically includes, among other things, "the extent and type of the lessor's management activity, the amount and kind of services rendered by him to the tenants, and the nature of his business risks connected with the properties." Filippini v. United States, supra, 318 F.2d at 845. We must also consider the more general factors that influence the choice of any investment the character of the particular properties and the market of which each is a part.

Applying this test to the facts in this case, we believe that taxpayer is entitled to relief under subsection (a). "(W)hether the acquired property is 'similar or related in service or use' to the condemned property turns upon whether in all the circumstances it represents a substantial continuation of the taxpayer's prior commitment of capital, or a departure from it." Id. at 844. The district judge found "that the improvements made by the (taxpayer) represent a substantial continuation of (its) prior commitment of capital." We agree. Although taxpayer invested the condemnation proceeds into its already owned industrial park rather than into agricultural land, taxpayer's relationship to its investments remained essentially the same. The district court found, and the government does not dispute, that the risk attendant to taxpayer's investment in the industrial park was not greater than the risk concomitant with an investment in agricultural land. Taxpayer's management also remained substantially the same, without great variance in cost or service. Moreover, given the change in the Hawaiian economy, reinvestment in agricultural property was unreasonable, and purchase of another sea fishery was virtually impossible. Thus, the district court did not err in concluding that taxpayer had substantially maintained a continuation of its prior commitment of capital.

The government argues, however, that our decision in Filippini requires that the replacement property be of the "same general class" as the condemned property before it can qualify under subsection (a). In Filippini, the taxpayer purchased urban property and erected an office building using money received from the condemnation of substantially rural property. The district court compared the characteristics and uses of the two properties and, after finding that the properties were dissimilar and not even of the "same general class," refused to allow nonrecognition of the taxpayer's gain. While we affirmed the district court's judgment, we specifically rejected resolution of the issue by simplistic talismanic rules. Instead we adopted the test referred to earlier which compares all of the circumstances surrounding the two investments. That taxpayer's condemned agricultural land is not of the "same general class" as its improvements to the Park is thus not determinative. Rather, taxpayer's relationship to the two investments controls.

The government also argues that the district court's determination regarding the continuation of taxpayer's prior commitment of capital is irrelevant because it pertains to taxpayer's relationship to the industrial park and not to the replacement property itself, i. e., the grading, excavation and other improvements to the Park. We reject the government's narrow construction of our test. The improvements to the Park have significance only as part of the Park, and their relationship to the taxpayer necessarily is a function of the investment in the industrial park as a whole. We therefore conclude that the district court's inquiry was not misdirected. As we have stated before, the purpose of section 1033 "is to relieve the taxpayer of unanticipated tax liability arising from involuntary conversion of his property * * *. The statute is to be liberally construed to accomplish this purpose." Filippini v. United States, supra, 318 F.2d at 844.

The record amply demonstrates that taxpayer's investment of the condemnation proceeds represents a sufficient continuity of taxpayer's original investment. The improvements were therefore similar or related in service or use to the prior investment, and taxpayer is entitled to relief under section 1033(a). On that basis, we affirm the judgment.

Notes

1.   *Comparing IRC § 1031 with IRC § 1033.* Do each of these two provisions apply automatically or must an election be made qualify for non-recognition treatment? Does each provision apply to gains and losses, or only to gains? Does each provision apply to realty and personalty, or only to realty? Does each provision apply to business, investment and personal use property; or only to business and investment property?

2.   *Similarity between old property and new property.* Nonrecognition treatment is often justified in cases where new property bears substantial similarity to the old property for which it substitutes. Compare the similarity standards employed by IRC § 1031 and IRC § 1033. Which standard is more stringent? Why is one standard more stringent than the other?

3.   *Conversion into money.* Nonrecognition rules normally do not apply when money, rather than replacement property, is received for the old property. Yet, IRC § 1033 permits money to be received provided the money is reinvested in replacement property within a specified time period. See IRC § 1033(a)(2). Why might the circumstances in which IRC § 1033 applies have caused Congress to allow the taxpayer to receive money without recognizing any gain?

WORTH NOTING

Nonrecognition rule vs. exclusion. IRC § 1033 confers nonrecognition treatment; it is not an exclusion. As such, gain is normally deferred (not eliminated) when the provision applies. To achieve this end, special basis rules are employed to preserve any unrecognized gain in the replacement property. See IRC § 1033(b).

3. Property Transfers Between Spouses and Former Spouses—§ 1041

Primary Law: IRC § 1041

(a) No gain or loss shall be recognized on a transfer of property from an individual to * * *—

   (1) a spouse, or

   (2) a former spouse, but only if the transfer is incident to the divorce.

(b) In the case of any transfer of property described in subsection (a)—

   (1) for purposes of this subtitle, the property shall be treated as acquired by the transferee by gift, and

   (2) the basis of the transferee in the property shall be the adjusted basis of the transferor.

(c) For purposes of subsection (a)(2), a transfer of property is incident to divorce if such transfer—

   (1) occurs within 1 year after the date the marriage ceases, or

   (2) is related to the cessation of the marriage.

* * *

LOUISE F. YOUNG v. COMMISSIONER

United States Court of Appeals, Fourth Circuit, 2001
240 F.3d 369

DIANA GRIBBON MOTZ, CIRCUIT JUDGE:

* * *

I.

Louise Young and John Young married in 1969 and divorced in 1988. The following year they entered into a Mutual Release and Acknowledgment of Settlement Agreement ("1989 Settlement Agreement") to resolve "their

Equitable Distribution [of] Property claim and all other claims arising out of the marital relationship." Pursuant to this agreement, Mr. Young delivered to Mrs. Young a promissory note for [$2.2] million, payable in five annual installments plus interest * * *.

In October 1990, Mr. Young defaulted on his obligations under the 1989 Settlement Agreement; the next month Mrs. Young brought a collection action in state court in North Carolina. On May 1, 1991, that court entered judgment for Mrs. Young * * *. Mr. and Mrs. Young [then] entered into a Settlement Agreement and Release ("1992 Agreement"), which provided that Mr. Young would transfer to Mrs. Young, in full settlement of his obligations, a 59-acre tract of land * * *. Mrs. Young [subsequently sold the land] for $2.2 million.

[M]r. Young did not report any gain from his transfer of the property * * * to satisfy his * * * $2.2 million obligation to Mrs. Young. [(Mr. Young had an adjusted basis of $200,000 in the property.)] Moreover, Mrs. Young reported no gain when she sold the property. Thus, the [$2 million of appreciation in the property] went untaxed * * *.

The Commissioner asserted deficiencies against both Mr. Young and Mrs. Young. Each then petitioned the Tax Court, which consolidated the two cases. [T]he Tax Court [invoked] 26 U.S.C. § 1041(a)(2) (1994), which provides that "[n]o gain or loss shall be recognized on a transfer of property . . . to . . . a former spouse, . . . if the transfer is incident to the divorce." [T]he Tax Court held that the 1992 property transfer was "incident to the divorce" [and] concluded that Mr. Young [recognized] no gain through his transfer of this property to his former spouse. Rather, according to the Tax Court, Mrs. Young took Mr. Young's adjusted basis in the land [per IRC § 1041(b)(2)] and should have recognized a taxable gain upon the subsequent sale of that property. * * *

[Mrs. Young appealed.]

II.

[S]ection 1041 provides that no taxable gain or loss results from a transfer of property to a former spouse if the transfer is "incident to the divorce." 26 U.S.C. § 1041(a)(2). Section 1041 further provides that "a transfer of property is incident to the divorce" if it is "related to the cessation of the marriage." 26 U.S.C. § 1041(c)(2). The statute does not further define the term "related to the cessation of the marriage," but temporary Treasury regulations provide some guidance. Those regulations extend a safe harbor to transfers made within six years of divorce if also "pursuant to a divorce or separation instrument, as defined in § 71(b)(2)." Temp. Treas. Reg. § 1.1041–1T(b). * * *

The Tax Court held that the 1992 transfer from Mr. Young to Mrs. Young was "related to the cessation of the marriage," thus [Mr. Young did not] recognize a gain or loss on the transfer, and Mrs. Young took the same basis in the land that the couple had when they were married. The court applied the regulatory safe harbor provision, but also found that the transfer" completed the division of marital property" and, regardless of the safe harbor provision, it "satisfied the statutory requirement that the transfer be 'related to the cessation of the marriage.'" Id. We agree with the Tax Court that the 1992 land transfer was "related to the cessation of the marriage," finding that it "effect[ed] the division of [marital] property." Temp. Treas. Reg. § 1.1041–1T(b).

* * *

[M]rs. Young challenges the Tax Court's finding and argues that the 1992 transfer did not "effect the division of [marital] property." In support of her contention, Mrs. Young notes that she was a judgment creditor when she entered into the 1992 Agreement. But the only status relevant for § 1041 purposes is "spouse" or "former spouse." Beyond her position as a former spouse, Mrs. Young's status makes no difference when determining whether the transfer is taxable; § 1041 looks to the character of and reason for the transfer, not to the status of the transferee as a creditor, lien-holder, devisee, trust beneficiary, or otherwise. * * *

* * *

Nor do we find Mrs. Young's "fairness" argument compelling. She points out that under the 1989 Settlement Agreement she was to receive [$2.2 million], but if forced to pay the capital gains tax she will receive a lesser amount. For this reason, she argues that application of § 1041 to the 59-acre transfer would "result in a radical and unfair re-division of the Young's [sic] marital property." But, this argument overlooks the fact that Mrs. Young agreed to accept the 59 acres in lieu of enforcing her judgment against Mr. Young and receiving a cash payment. For whatever reason—and the record is silent as to Mrs. Young's motivations—she chose not to follow the latter route. In addition, if Mrs. Young had agreed to accept land in 1989, as she ultimately did in 1992, the resulting transfer would unquestionably have "effect[ed] the division of [marital] property" and been within § 1041. That the transfer occurred three years later does not alter its "effect," or its treatment under § 1041.

The sole reason for the 1992 Agreement was to resolve the disputes that arose from the Youngs' divorce and subsequent property settlement. Had the Youngs reached this settlement at the time of their divorce, there is no question that this transaction would have fallen under § 1041. There is no reason for the holding to differ here where the same result occurred through two transactions instead of one.

The policy animating § 1041 is clear. Congress has chosen to "treat a husband and wife [and former husband and wife acting incident to divorce] as one economic unit, and to defer, but not eliminate, the recognition of any gain or loss on interspousal property transfers until the property is conveyed to a third party outside the economic unit." Thus, * * * no gain was [recognized] until Mrs. Young sold the 59 acres to a third party.

Indeed, holding otherwise would contradict the very purpose of § 1041. Congress enacted that statute to "correct the [ ] problems" caused by United States v. Davis, 370 U.S. 65 (1962), in which "[t]he Supreme Court ha[d] ruled that a transfer of appreciated property to a spouse (or former spouse) in exchange for the release of marital claims results in the recognition of gain to the transferor." H.R. Rep. No. 98–432, at 1491–92 (1984). Congress found this result "inappropriate," id., and thus amended the tax code in 1984 to add § 1041. Given this history, to impute a gain to Mr. Young on his transfer of "appreciated property . . . in exchange for the release of [Mrs. Young's] marital claims" would abrogate clear congressional policy.

The dissent's contention that the result we reach here is not supported by equitable considerations misses the point. Congress has already weighed the equities and established a policy that no gain or loss will be recognized on a transfer between former spouses incident to their divorce. Thus anytime former spouses transfer appreciated property incident to their divorce, the transferee spouse will bear the tax burden of the property's appreciated value after selling it and receiving the proceeds. Although this rule will undoubtedly work a hardship in some cases, the legislature has clearly set and codified this policy. We cannot disregard that choice to satisfy our own notions of equity.

In so concluding, we do not suggest that the boundaries defining when a transfer is "related to the cessation of the marriage" or made "to effect the division of [marital] property" are always clear. We cannot, however, on the facts of this case hold that Mr. Young's "interspousal property transfer" was a taxable event, when the purpose behind Mr. Young's transfer was to satisfy his obligations arising from the "cessation of the marriage." To do so would, we believe, contravene the language, purpose, and policy of § 1041 and the regulations promulgated pursuant thereto.

* * *

Therefore, the Tax Court's judgment is * * * affirmed.

Notes

1.   *Tax reporting by each party.* The Young court states that—

    a)   Mr. Young did not report gain when he transferred the property to Mrs. Young, and

    b)   Mrs. Young did not report gain when she sold the property.

Can you explain the reasoning underlying each party's position that he/she did not recognize any gain?

2.   *Counsel for Mrs. Young.* If you had represented Mrs. Young, how would you have advised her to structure the terms of the 1992 Settlement Agreement with Mr. Young?

3.   *Deferral of gain (or loss).* IRC § 1041 is a non-recognition provision; it is not an exclusion. As such, gain or loss is normally deferred (not eliminated) when a taxpayer transfers property to which the provision applies. To achieve this end, when property is transferred in a transaction that qualifies under IRC § 1041(a), the transferee's basis in the transferred property is equal to the adjusted basis of the transferor. See IRC § 1041(b)(2). Notwithstanding this transferred basis rule, under what circumstances could the deferred gain or loss in the transferred property be diminished, or even eliminated? See, e.g., IRC § 1014.

WORTH NOTING

Transferred basis property. When a transferee's basis in property is determined by reference to the basis of the transferor of the property, the property is referred to as "transferred basis property." See IRC § 7701(a)(43).

C. Exclusion of Gain on Sale of Residence—§ 121

As a general rule, when property is sold or exchanged (i.e., a realization event occurs), any realized gain is immediately recognized (i.e., included in gross income). See IRC § 1001(c). As you have seen, Congress has created certain narrow, non-recognition rules, that sanction indefinite deferral of realized gains. Unlike the non-recognition rules this book has explored, IRC § 121 is a statutory exclusion, which permanently eliminates the realized gains to which it applies.

Primary Law: IRC § 121

(a) Gross income shall not include gain from the sale or exchange of property if, during the 5-year period ending on the date of the sale or exchange, such property has been owned and used by the taxpayer as the taxpayer's principal residence for periods aggregating 2 years or more.

(b)

   (1) The amount of gain excluded from gross income under subsection (a) shall not exceed $250,000.

   (2) In the case of a husband and wife who make a joint return for the taxable year of the sale or exchange of the property—

   (A) Paragraph (1) shall be applied by substituting "$500,000" for "$250,000" if—

   (i) either spouse meets the ownership requirements of subsection (a) with respect to such property;

   (ii) both spouses meet the use requirements of subsection (a) with respect to such property; and

   (iii) neither spouse is ineligible for the benefits of subsection (a) with respect to such property by reason of paragraph (3).

   (3) Subsection (a) shall not apply to any sale or exchange by the taxpayer if, during the 2-year period ending on the

> date of such sale or exchange, there was any other sale or exchange by the taxpayer to which subsection (a) applied.
>
> * * *

GATES v. COMMISSIONER

United States Tax Court, 2010
135 T.C. 1

Marvel, Judge:

* * *

On December 14, 1984, petitioner David A. Gates (Mr. Gates) purchased the Summit Road property for $150,000. The Summit Road property included an 880-square-foot two-story building with a studio on the second level and living quarters on the first level (original house).

On August 12, 1989, Mr. Gates married petitioner Christine A. Gates. Petitioners resided in the original house for a period of at least 2 years from August 1996 to August 1998.

In 1996 petitioners decided to enlarge and remodel the original house, and they hired an architect. The architect advised petitioners that more stringent building and permit restrictions had been enacted since the original house was built.

Subsequently, petitioners demolished the original house and constructed a new three-bedroom house (new house) on the Summit Road property. The new house complied with the building and permit requirements existing in 1999. * * *

Petitioners never resided in the new house. On April 7, 2000, petitioners sold the new house for $1,100,000. The sale resulted in a $591,406 gain to petitioners.

* * *

On their 2000 [tax] return, petitioners did not report as income any of the $591,406 capital gain generated from the sale of the Summit Road property. Petitioners subsequently agreed that $91,406 of the gain should have been included in their gross income for 2000, but they asserted that the remaining gain of $500,000 was excludable from their income under section 121. On

September 9, 2005, respondent mailed petitioners a notice of deficiency for 2000 that increased petitioners' income by $500,000 and explained that petitioners had failed to establish that any of the gain on the sale of the Summit Road property was excludable under section 121.

Petitioners timely petitioned this Court seeking a redetermination of the deficiency and addition to tax. Petitioners assert that respondent erred in determining that they were not entitled to exclude $500,000 of the gain under section 121. * * *

     * * *

Gross income means all income from whatever source derived, unless excluded by law. See sec. 61(a); sec. 1.61–1(a), Income Tax Regs. Generally, gain realized on the sale of property is included in a taxpayer's income. Sec. 61(a)(3). Section 121(a), however, allows a taxpayer to exclude from income gain on the sale or exchange of property if the taxpayer has owned and used such property as his or her principal residence for at least 2 of the 5 years immediately preceding the sale. * * * The maximum exclusion is $500,000 for a husband and wife who file a joint return for the year of the sale or exchange. Sec. 121(b)(2). A married couple may claim the $500,000 exclusion on the sale or exchange of property they owned and used as their principal residence if either spouse meets the ownership requirement, both spouses meet the use requirement, and neither spouse claimed an exclusion under section 121(a) during the 2-year period before the sale or exchange. Sec. 121(b)(2)(A).

The issue presented arises from the fact that section 121(a) does not define two critical terms—"property" and "principal residence". Section 121(a) simply provides that gross income does not include gain from the sale or exchange of property if "such property" has been owned and used by the taxpayer "as the taxpayer's principal residence" for the required statutory period.

Respondent contends that petitioners did not sell property they had owned and used as their principal residence for the required statutory period because they never occupied the new house as their principal residence before they sold it. Respondent's argument interprets the term "property" to mean, or at least include, a dwelling that was owned and occupied by the taxpayer as his "principal residence" for at least 2 of the 5 years immediately preceding the sale. Respondent urges this Court to conclude that a qualifying sale under section 121(a) is one that includes the sale of a dwelling used by the taxpayer as his principal residence. Because petitioners never resided in the new house before its sale in 2000, respondent maintains that the new house was never petitioners' principal residence.

Predictably, petitioners disagree. Petitioners argue that any analysis of section 121(a) must recognize that the exclusion thereunder applies to the gain on the sale of *property* that was used as the taxpayer's principal residence. Petitioners' argument focuses on two facts—petitioners used the original house as their principal residence for the period required by section 121(a) and they sold the land on which the original house had been situated. Petitioners contend that the term "property" includes not only the dwelling but also the land on which the dwelling is situated. Petitioners seem to argue that the requirements of section 121(a) are satisfied if a taxpayer lived in any dwelling on the property for the required 2-year period even if that dwelling is not the dwelling that is sold. Petitioners contend that because they used the original house and the land on which it was situated as their principal residence for the required term, the Summit Road property qualifies as their principal residence and $500,000 of the gain generated by the sale of the property is excluded under section 121.

Because section 121 does not define the terms "property" and "principal residence", we must apply accepted principles of statutory construction to ascertain Congress' intent. It is a well-established rule of construction that if a statute does not define a term, the term is given its ordinary meaning. It is also well established that a court may look to sources such as dictionaries for assistance in determining the ordinary meaning of a term. We look to the legislative history to ascertain Congress' intent if the statute is ambiguous. Exclusions from income must be construed narrowly, and taxpayers must bring themselves within the clear scope of the exclusion.

* * *

[W]hen the dictionary definitions of "principal" and "residence" are combined, we conclude that "principal residence" may have two possible meanings. It can either mean the chief or primary *place* where a person lives or the chief or primary *dwelling* in which a person resides. Likewise, the term "property" as used in section 121(a) can refer more broadly to a parcel of real estate, or it can refer to the dwelling (and related curtilage) used as a taxpayer's principal residence.

Because there is more than one possible meaning for both the term "property" and the term "principal residence", we cannot conclude that the meaning of section 121(a) is clear and unambiguous. Section 121(a) is not explicit as to whether Congress intended section 121 to apply to a sale of property when the property sold does not include the dwelling that the taxpayer used as a principal residence for the period that section 121(a) requires. Because section 121(a) is ambiguous, we may examine the legislative history of section 121 and its predecessor provisions to ascertain Congress' intent regarding the proper tax treatment of principal residence sales.

    * * *

[T]he legislative history demonstrates that Congress intended the term "principal residence" to mean the primary dwelling or house that a taxpayer occupied as his principal residence. Nothing in the legislative history indicates that Congress intended section 121 to exclude gain on the sale of property that does not include a house or other structure used by the taxpayer as his principal place of abode. Although a principal residence may include land surrounding the dwelling, the legislative history supports a conclusion that Congress intended the section 121 exclusion to apply only if the dwelling the taxpayer sells was actually used as his principal residence for the period required by section 121(a).

The conclusion that we reach from an examination of the legislative history surrounding the enactment of section 121 is bolstered by and is consistent with regulations promulgated under the predecessor provisions of section 121. * * * Our conclusion regarding the meaning that Congress attaches to the terms "property" and "principal residence" in section 121(a) is also consistent with caselaw interpreting [the predecessor to section 121].

Although we recognize that petitioners would have satisfied the requirements under section 121 had they sold or exchanged the original house instead of tearing it down, we must apply the statute as written by Congress. Rules of statutory construction require that we narrowly construe exclusions from income. Under section 121(a) and its legislative history, we cannot conclude on the facts of this case that petitioners sold their principal residence. Accordingly, we hold that petitioners may not exclude from income under section 121(a) the gain realized on the sale of the Summit Road property.

    * * *

Colvin, Cohen, Gale, Thornton, Wherry, Gustafson, Paris, and Morrison, JJ., agree with this majority opinion.

    * * *

HALPERN, J., dissenting:

There is adequate ground for the majority's conclusion that, to qualify for the section 121 exclusion, the taxpayer must sell not only the land on which her principal residence is located but also the principal residence itself. Nevertheless, I think that there is also adequate ground for concluding that petitioners' sale of the new house qualified for that exclusion. * * *

The gain exclusion rule of section 121(a) applies if three conditions are met: (1) There must be a sale or exchange (without distinction, sale); (2) the sale must be of "property* * * owned and used by the taxpayer as the taxpayer's principal residence" (the property use condition), and (3) the property use condition must be satisfied for 2 out of the 5 years ending on the date of sale of the property (the temporal condition). The majority focuses on the second condition (the property use condition) and interprets the condition as being satisfied only if the property sold constitutes, at least in part, "a house or other structure used by the taxpayer as his principal place of abode." * * *

While the majority is correct that the Supreme Court has said that exclusions from income are to be narrowly construed, the Supreme Court has also said that, if the meaning of a tax provision liberalizing the law from motives of public policy is doubtful, then it should not be narrowly construed.

With that latter rule of construction in mind, consider a taxpayer whose longtime home is demolished by a natural disaster (a hurricane). The taxpayer lacks insurance. Nevertheless, she rebuilds on the same land (perhaps a bit further from the ocean) and lives in the rebuilt house for 18 months, and then she sells the house and land at a gain. Although the taxpayer satisfies the property use condition, I assume that, nevertheless, under the majority's analysis, she gets no exclusion because she fails the temporal condition; i.e., she has not lived in the rebuilt house for 2 or more of the last 5 years. I assume further that, if her house had been only damaged (and not demolished), and she repaired it, she would get an exclusion. That seems like an untenable distinction to me.

     * * *

The majority's interpretation of the property use condition naturally suggests that there is some recognizable difference between remodeling a house and demolishing and rebuilding the house. I assume the majority does not mean to suggest that any remodeling of a home (1) terminates the use of that home as the taxpayer's principal residence and (2) resets the temporal clock to zero time elapsed. If not, then is there some level of remodeling that does (1) terminate the use of the home as the taxpayer's principal residence and (2) set the temporal clock to zero? What about a taxpayer who, wanting a bigger house, demolishes the old house (but not the foundation) and constructs a larger (taller) house using the old foundation? Is that remodeling or rebuilding? What about keeping part of the foundation, and expanding horizontally? If that is remodeling, then there may be an easy way for the Court to reach a similar result in the case before us. The parties have stipulated an exhibit, a blueprint, that shows footprints of both the old and the new house. I have examined the exhibit, and the footprints overlap. Might we not conclude that part of the foundation of the old house was incorporated into the new, thus making the case a remodeling case and not a rebuilding case?

The majority's report will undoubtedly raise the kind of remodeling versus rebuilding questions that I have raised. I think that the better course would be to avoid provoking those questions.

* * *

I would treat the demolition and reconstruction of petitioners' house no differently from a renovation. * * *

WELLS, GOEKE, KROUPA, and HOLMES, JJ., agree with this dissent.

FOR DISCUSSION

Exclusion vs. non-recognition rule. IRC § 121 is an exclusion whereas IRC §§ 1031, 1033, and 1041 are non-recognition rules.

a) What is the difference between an exclusion and a non-recognition rule?

b) IRC § 121 applies to potential § 61(a)(3) income. Do any of the exclusions examined in prior chapters apply to potential § 61(a)(3) income?

■ **PROBLEM 12-3.** *Exclusion of gain on sale of principal residence.* Shanna and Andrew are married. In Year 1, they purchased the home in which they live for $400,000. What are the tax consequences to Shanna and Andrew if they sell the home in Year 5 for—

a) $750,000?

b) $950,000?

c) $350,000? See IRC § 165(c).

d) How do the above answers change if they moved out of the home at the beginning of Year 2 and rented it to tenants until they sold it?

SYNTHESIS

This Chapter addressed the timing of gains (and losses) derived from dealings in property. When property is sold or exchanged, gain is realized to the extent the amount realized exceeds the adjusted basis of the property (and loss is realized to the extent the adjusted basis of the property exceeds the amount realized). A realized gain is recognized, i.e., taxed in the year of sale, unless a deferred recognition provision, a non-recognition provision, or an exclusion applies. A realized loss may be claimed as a deduction only if it is both recognized and allowed as a deduction under IRC § 165.

When a taxpayer realizes a gain on the sale of property and at least one payment is to be made in a future tax year, IRC § 453 defers recognition of the realized gain until the payments are received by the seller. The gain is allocated among the current and deferred payments to ensure that the seller has sufficient funds with which to pay the tax.

When an exchange of like-kind real property occurs and certain other conditions are met, IRC § 1031 confers non-recognition treatment on the taxpayer's realized gain or loss. In this situation, the gain or loss is preserved in the substituted property because the seller's basis in the transferred property attaches to the property received in the exchange.

When property is destroyed or otherwise involuntarily converted into money, and replacement property similar or related in use is purchased within a specified time period, IRC § 1033 permits the taxpayer to elect not to recognize any realized gain. When this election is made, special basis rules are employed to preserve any unrecognized gain in the replacement property.

When property is transferred to a spouse, or to a former spouse incident to divorce, IRC § 1041 confers non-recognition treatment on the transferor's realized gain or loss. In this situation, the unrecognized gain or loss is preserved because the transferee spouse (or former spouse) takes a basis in the property equal to the basis of the transferor.

When a taxpayer sells a house that she owned and lived in for at least 2 of the 5 years prior to the sale, IRC § 121 allows the seller to exclude up to $500,000 of any realized gain (if she is married and files a joint return). Unlike the nonrecognition provisions examined in this chapter, which normally merely defer gain or loss, IRC § 121 *excludes* the gain, which means that the gain will never be taxed. It is highly unusual for a statutory exclusion to apply to a gain derived from dealings in property (IRC § 61(a)(3) income).

 Test Your Knowledge: To assess your understanding of the material in this chapter, click here to take a quiz.

CHAPTER 13

Special Deferral Rules

Overview

Congress has enacted targeted rules that defer certain types of gross income and deductions beyond the time that they would normally be reported under the taxpayer's tax accounting method. With regard to the deferral of gross income, this Chapter will examine IRC § 83 which defers income when certain restrictions are imposed on property received for the performance of services. As to the deferral of deductions, this Chapter will explore statutory restrictions on claiming deductions for passive activity losses (IRC § 469), net operating losses (IRC § 172), and excess business losses (IRC § 461(*l*)(1)).

A. Deferral of Income—§ 83

It is common for corporate employers to devise compensation packages for high-level employees that will motivate these employees to exert maximum efforts on behalf of the enterprise. Accordingly, an employer will often include an ownership interest (i.e., corporate stock) in the employee's compensation package to align the employee's economic interests with those of the employer. Rather than transferring unrestricted stock to employees, however, employers will often condition a grant of stock to an employee on continued employment for a specified period of time. This arrangement advances the employer's goal of motivating the employee to put forth future efforts, rather than rewarding the employee for past results.

For example, an employer might convey 1,000 shares of stock to a high-level employee on the condition that the employee must return the shares to the employer if the employee terminates employment within two years of the stock grant. Thus, unless the employee continues to perform services for two additional years, the stock will revert back to the employer. Stock that is granted conditionally on the performance of future services is referred to as "restricted stock." The tax treatment of restricted stock is governed by IRC § 83.

Pursuant to § 83(a), an employee is normally *not* required to report gross income at the time her employer issues restricted stock to her. Rather, her gross income is deferred until the restrictions imposed on the stock expire. When the restrictions expire, the employee must report gross income equal to the fair market value of the shares at that later time (as opposed to the fair market value of the shares when they were granted). In the language of the Code, an employee who receives restricted stock normally reports gross income at the time that her rights "are not subject to a substantial risk of forfeiture." IRC § 83(a). A "substantial risk of forfeiture" exists as long as the employee's ownership rights are "conditioned upon the future performance of substantial services." IRC § 83(c)(1).

Primary Law: IRC § 83

(a)   If, in connection with the performance of services, property is transferred to any person * * *, the excess of—

(1)   the fair market value of such property * * * at the first time the rights of the person having the beneficial interest in such property are transferable or are not subject to a substantial risk of forfeiture, whichever occurs earlier, over

(2)   the amount (if any) paid for such property,

shall be included in the gross income of the person who performed such services in the first taxable year in which the rights of the person having the beneficial interest in such property are transferable or are not subject to a substantial risk of forfeiture, whichever is applicable. * * *

* * *

(c) For purposes of this section—

    (1) The rights of a person in property are subject to a substantial risk of forfeiture if such person's rights to full enjoyment of such property are conditioned upon the future performance of substantial services by any individual.

    (2) The rights of a person in property are transferable only if the rights in such property of any transferee are not subject to a substantial risk of forfeiture.

* * *

WORTH NOTING

Risk of forfeiture vs. transferability. Technically, IRC § 83(a) requires an employee who receives restricted stock to report gross income *at the earlier of* the time that the stock is transferrable, or is not subject to a substantial risk of forfeiture. Per IRC § 83(c)(2), stock is "transferable only if the rights in such property *of any transferee* are not subject to a substantial risk of forfeiture." (Emphasis added.) Normally, an employee will not be permitted to transfer restricted stock and, even if a transfer is allowed, the restricted stock will retain its restricted status until the employee performs the required future services. Therefore, the substantial risk of forfeiture will normally expire before the stock is transferrable.

■ **EXAMPLE 13-A.** *Timing of income under § 83(a).* Yvonne is a key employee of Zanzibar Corp. On June 1, Year 1, she is awarded 1,000 shares of Zanzibar stock when the stock has a fair market value of $1 per share. However, if Yvonne leaves Zanzibar or is terminated before June 1, Year 4, the shares revert back to Zanzibar.

Pursuant to § 83(a), the restricted stock is not included in Yvonne's gross income in Year 1 because the shares are subject to a substantial risk of forfeiture. However, if she is still employed by Zanzibar on June 1, Year 4, Yvonne must include the then fair market value of the stock in her gross income in Year 4. If the stock has a fair market value of $100 per share on

June 1, Year 4, she must report $100,000 of gross income in Year 4 (1,000 shares × $100/share = $100,000). What type of gross income under § 61 does Yvonne derive?

Although deferral of gross income is normally desirable from a taxpayer's perspective due to the time value of money, Example 13-A illustrates that the deferral conferred by § 83(a) can be very costly in certain cases. Specifically, if the value of the restricted stock increases dramatically between the time the restricted stock is granted and the time that the restrictions terminate, the employee will have a much larger amount of income on which to pay tax. Under these circumstances, the employee would be better off paying an immediate tax on the small value of the restricted stock at the time of the grant, rather than deferring the tax on a much higher value until the restrictions lapse.

Recognizing that recipients of restricted stock might sometimes prefer to be taxed at the time the restricted shares are granted, Congress allows recipients of restricted stock to elect to be taxed on receipt of the restricted shares. See IRC § 83(b). Under § 83(b), a recipient of restricted stock may make an election within 30 days after the stock grant to forego the deferral conferred by § 83(a). Instead, the employee must include in gross income in the year the restricted stock is granted the value of the restricted stock at the time of the grant (less any amount the employee is required to pay for the restricted shares). See IRC § 83(b).

> **Primary Law:** IRC § 83
>
> (a)   * * *
>
> (b)   Election to include in gross income in year of transfer—
>
>   (1)   Any person who performs services in connection with which property is transferred to any person may elect to include in his gross income, for the taxable year in which such property is transferred, the excess of—
>
>   (A)   the fair market value of such property determined at the time of transfer * * *, over
>
>   (B)   the amount (if any) paid for such property.

If such election is made, subsection (a) shall not apply with respect to the transfer of such property, and if such property is subsequently forfeited, no deduction shall be allowed in respect of such forfeiture.

(2) An election under paragraph (1) with respect to any transfer of property shall be made in such manner as the Secretary prescribes and shall be made not later than 30 days after the date of such transfer. Such election may not be revoked except with the consent of the Secretary.

■ **EXAMPLE 13-B.** *Timing of income under § 83(b).* Yvonne is a key employee of Zanzibar Corp. On June 1, Year 1, she is awarded 1,000 shares of Zanzibar stock when the stock has a fair market value of $1 per share. However, if Yvonne leaves Zanzibar or is terminated before June 1, Year 4, the shares revert back to Zanzibar. Yvonne makes a § 83(b) election within 30 days after June 1, Year 1 (the date the restricted stock was granted). [Same facts as Example 13-A except that Yvonne makes a § 83(b) election.]

Pursuant to § 83(b), Yvonne must include the fair market value of the stock in her gross income in Year 1. Because the stock has a fair market value of only $1 per share on June 1, Year 1 (the date of grant), she must report only $1,000 of gross income in Year 1 (1,000 shares × $1/share = $1,000). If she is still employed by Zanzibar on June 1, Year 4, she will own the stock without restrictions but she will not derive any additional gross income until she sells the Zanzibar shares. If her employment terminates prior to June 1, Year 4, she must return the shares to her employer.

For the § 83(b) election to be advantageous to the taxpayer, two conditions must be met. First, the value of the stock must increase between the time of the grant and the time that the restrictions on the shares lapse. Otherwise, the election will merely accelerate income that otherwise would have been deferred under § 83(a) until the time that the restrictions lapse. Second, the employee must remain employed at least until the restrictions lapse. Otherwise, she will have reported gross income with respect to a benefit she will never receive by virtue of forfeiting the stock. Moreover, the statute explicitly states that the employee may *not* claim a deduction for the gross income she previously reported if she forfeits the shares. (See IRC § 83(b), second sentence.) Unfortunately, the taxpayer cannot be certain that either of these conditions will be met at the time she must make the § 83(b) election (within 30 days of the stock grant).

Making a § 83(b) election is generally a gamble due to the uncertainty at the time of the election as to whether the two conditions listed in the prior paragraph will be met. Sometimes, however, making the 83(b) election is a "no-brainer," as demonstrated by the Alves case that follows.

ALVES v. COMMISSIONER

United States Court of Appeals, Ninth Circuit, 1984
734 F.2d 478

Schroeder, Circuit Judge.

* * *

FACTS

General Digital Corporation (the company) was formed in April, 1970, to manufacture and market micro-electronic circuits. At its first meeting, the company's board of directors * * * voted to sell * * * shares of common stock to seven named individuals, including [Lawrence] Alves. All seven became company employees.

Alves joined the company as vice-president for finance and administration. As part of an employment and stock purchase agreement dated May 22, 1970, the company agreed to sell Alves [30,000] shares of common stock at ten cents per share "in order to raise capital for the Company's initial operations while at the same time providing the Employee with an additional interest in the Company * * *." 79 T.C. at 867. * * * The agreement divided Alves's shares into three categories: one-third were subject to repurchase by the company at ten cents per share if Alves left within four years; one-third were subject to repurchase [at ten cents per share] if he left the company within five years; and one-third were unrestricted. * * *

* * *

On July 1, 1974, when the restrictions on the four-year shares lapsed, [those shares] had a fair market value * * * of $6 per share [i.e., the fair market value of the 10,000 four-year shares increased from $1,000 (10,000 shares × $.10 per share = $1,000) to $60,000 (10,000 shares × $6 per share = $60,000)]. On March 24, 1975, the restrictions on the * * * five-year shares lapsed [when those shares had a] fair market value of $3.43 per share [i.e., the fair market value of the 10,000 five-year shares increased from $1,000 to $34,300].

[Alves] did not report [as gross income] the difference between the fair market value of the four and five-year shares when the restrictions ended, and the [$.10 per share] purchase price paid for the shares. The Commissioner treated the difference as ordinary income in 1974 and 1975, pursuant to section 83(a).

In proceedings before the Tax Court, the parties stipulated that: (1) General Digital's common stock had a fair market value of 10 cents per share on the date Alves entered into the employment and stock purchase agreement; (2) the stock restrictions were imposed to "provide some assurance that key personnel would remain with the company for a number of years;" (3) Alves did not make an election under section 83(b) when the restricted stock was received; * * * and [(4)] the four and five-year restricted shares were subject to a substantial risk of forfeiture until July 1, 1974, and March 24, 1975, respectively.

The Tax Court sustained the Commissioner's deficiency determination. It found as a matter of fact that the stock was transferred to Alves in connection with the performance of services for the company, and, as a matter of law, that section 83(a) applies even where the transferee paid full fair market value for the stock.

DISCUSSION

Resolution of the legal issue presented here requires an understanding of section 83's * * * operation. * * *

Section 83 [requires] the taxpayer either to elect to include the "excess" of the fair market value over the purchase price in the year the stock was transferred, or to be taxed upon the full amount of appreciation when the risk of forfeiture was removed. 26 U.S.C. Secs. 83(a), 83(b). By its terms, the statute applies when property is: (1) transferred "in connection with the performance of services;" (2) subject to a substantial risk of forfeiture; and (3) not disposed of in an arm's length transaction before the property becomes transferable or the risk of forfeiture is removed. In the present case, it is undisputed that the stock in question was subject to a substantial risk of forfeiture, that it was not disposed of before the restrictions lapsed, and that Alves made no section 83(b) election. Alves's contention is that because he paid full fair market value for the shares, they were issued as an investment, rather than "in connection with the performance of services."

The Tax Court concluded that Alves obtained the stock "in connection with the performance of services" as company vice-president. To the extent that this conclusion is a finding of fact, it is not clearly erroneous. Although payment of full fair market value may be one indication that stock was not transferred in connection with the performance of services, the record shows that [the company] issued stock only to its officers, directors, and employees * * *. Alves purchased the stock when he signed his employment agreement and the stock restrictions were linked explicitly to his tenure with the company. In addition, the parties stipulated that the restricted stock's purpose was to ensure that key personnel would remain with the company. Nothing in the record suggests that Alves could have purchased the stock had he not agreed to join the company.

Alves maintains that, as a matter of law, section 83(a) should not extend to purchases for full fair market value. He argues that "in connection with" means that the employee is receiving compensation for his performance of services. In the unusual situation where the employee pays the same amount for restricted and unrestricted stock, the restriction has no effect on value, and hence, Alves contends, there is no compensation.

The plain language of section 83(a) belies Alves's argument. The statute applies to all property transferred in connection with the performance of services. No reference is made to the term "compensation." Nor is there any statutory requirement that property have a fair market value in excess of the amount paid at the time of transfer. Indeed, if Congress intended section 83(a) to apply solely to restricted stock used to compensate employees, it could have used much narrower language. Instead, Congress made section 83(a) applicable to all restricted "property," not just stock; to property transferred to "any person," not just to employees; and to property transferred "in connection with . . . services" not just compensation for employment. * * *

    * * *

Alves suggests that the language of section 83(b) indicates that Congress meant for that section to apply only to bargain purchases and that section 83(a) should be interpreted in the same way. Section 83(b) allows taxpayers to elect to include as income in the year of transfer "the excess" of the full fair market value over the purchase price. Alves contends that a taxpayer who pays full fair market value would have "zero excess," and would fall outside the terms of section 83(b).

Section 83(b), however, is not a limitation upon section 83(a). Congress designed section 83(b) merely to add "flexibility," not to condition section 83(a) on the presence or absence of an "excess." Senate Report at 123.

Moreover, nothing in section 83(b) precludes a taxpayer who has paid full market value for restricted stock from making an 83(b) election. Treasury Regulations promulgated in 1978 and made retroactive to 1969 specifically provide that section 83(b) is available in situations of zero excess:

> If property is transferred . . . in connection with the performance of services, the person performing such services may elect to include in gross income under section 83(b) the excess (if any) of the fair market value of the property at the time of transfer . . . over the amount (if any) paid for such property . . . . The fact that the transferee has paid full value for the property transferred, realizing no bargain element in the transaction, does not preclude the use of the election as provided for in this section.

Reg. Sec. 1.83–2(a). These regulations are consistent with the broad language of section 83 * * *.

Alves last contends that * * * every taxpayer who pays full fair market value for restricted stock would, if well informed, choose the section 83(b) election to hedge against any appreciation. [Thus,] applying section 83(a) to the unfortunate taxpayer who made no election is simply a trap for the unwary. The tax laws often make an affirmative election necessary. Section 83(b) is but one example of a provision requiring taxpayers to act or suffer less attractive tax consequences. A taxpayer wishing to avoid treatment of appreciation as ordinary income must make an affirmative election under 83(b) in the year the stock was acquired.

[T]he decision of the Tax Court is affirmed.

FOR DISCUSSION

Section 83(a) vs. section 83(b). By refraining from making a § 83(b) election, how much gross income was Alves compelled to report with respect to the restricted stock and when was such income reportable? If Alves had made a timely § 83(b) election, how much gross income would he have been compelled to report with respect to the restricted stock and when would such income have been reportable?

■ **EXAMPLE 13-C.** *Sale of restricted shares after restrictions terminate.* To evaluate the tax treatment of restricted shares, three points in time must be considered:

1) the time of grant,

2) the time at which the restrictions lapse, and

3) the time when the employee sells the shares.

Assume the following:

1) in Year 1, 100 restricted shares are granted to an employee free of charge when the stock has a value of $1 per share,

2) in Year 3, the restrictions lapse when the stock has a value of $8 per share, and

3) in Year 5, employee sells the shares when the stock has a value of $10 per share.

The following tax consequences result:

	Under § 83(a) [no § 83(b) election]	§ 83(b) Election
Year 1	0 income	$100 of income[1]
Year 3	$800 of income[2]	0 income
Year 5	$200 of income[3]	$900 of income[4]
Total Income	$1,000 of income	$1,000 of income

---

[1]   100 shares ×$1 per share=$100. Because employee includes $100 in gross income, employee takes a basis of $100 in the restricted shares. IRC § 1012.

[2]   100 shares × $8 per share=$800. Because employee includes $800 in gross income, employee takes a basis of $800 in the restricted shares. IRC § 1012.

[3]   Sale is a realization event.

Amount Realized	$1,000 (100 shares × $10 per share)
Less: Adjusted Basis	800 (see fn 2)
Realized Gain	$200

[4]   Sale is a realization event.

Amount Realized	$1,000 (100 shares × $10 per share)
Less: Adjusted Basis	100 (see fn 1)
Realized Gain	$900

The employee is taxed on $1,000 of income in both cases. However, the § 83(b) election defers the majority of the income to the year of sale which benefits the taxpayer from a time value of money standpoint. Moreover, the employee derives a second significant benefit from deferring income to the year of sale. Specifically, any income triggered at the time of sale is likely to be characterized as "capital gain" and taxed at a much lower rate than the employee's other income. The characterization of certain income as capital gain and the lower tax rates that apply to such income will be explored in Chapter 16.

■ **PROBLEM 13-1.** *Restricted stock.* Morry is a key employee of Belvidere, Inc. and is awarded 1,000 shares of Belvidere stock on March 1, Year 1 at which time the fair market value of the shares is $2 per share. Morry must return the shares to Belvidere if he dies, becomes disabled, or terminates employment before March 1, Year 3. Morry pays nothing for the restricted stock. What are the tax consequences to Morry under § 83(a) and § 83(b) in a), b) and c)?

a) Morry's employment continues beyond March 1, Year 3. On March 1, Year 3, the value of Belvidere stock is $15 per share. Morry sells the Belvidere stock in Year 7 for $20 per share.

b) Morry's employment continues beyond March 1, Year 3. On March 1, Year 3, the value of Belvidere stock is $2 per share. Morry sells the Belvidere stock in Year 7 for $2 per share.

c) Morry is fired on February 15, Year 3.

Would a § 83(b) election have been beneficial or detrimental to Morry in a), b), and c)?

WORTH NOTING

Employee stock options. As an alternative to restricted stock, employers will sometimes grant employees options to acquire corporate stock at a discounted price. The employee is normally not taxed on receipt of these options. In the case of most stock options ("nonqualified options"), the employee is taxed when the option is exercised (i.e., when the employee acquires the underlying stock). The amount on which the employee is taxed is the difference between the value of the stock when the option is exercised and the price paid by the employee. If, however, the stock option meets the stringent requirements to qualify as an "incentive stock option" (IRC § 422(b)) and certain additional requirements are met (IRC § 422(a)), the employee is not taxed when the option is exercised (IRC § 421(a)). Rather, the tax is deferred until the employee sells the stock at which time the employee is taxed on the difference between the selling price of the stock and the price paid by the employee.

B. Deferral of Deductions

1. Passive Activity Losses—§ 469

In contrast to IRC § 83(a), which defers gross income on the receipt of restricted stock, IRC § 469 defers the deduction of certain trade or business expenses within the scope of IRC § 162. As noted above, IRC § 83(a) is not an exclusion; it merely defers gross income until the restrictions imposed on restricted stock terminate. Similarly, IRC § 469 is not a disallowance provision; it merely defers deductions to a future tax year. The deferral of gross income under § 83(a) temporarily reduces taxable income and the amount of taxes that must be paid, which normally benefits the taxpayer due to the time value of money. By contrast, the deferral of deductions under § 469 temporarily increases taxable income and the amount of taxes that must be paid, which is normally a detriment to the taxpayer due to the time value of money.

Section 469 defers deductions attributable to "passive activities." Congress enacted § 469 out of concern that taxpayers with large amounts of income generated by their labor (e.g., corporate executives, doctors and lawyers) would invest in other businesses to secure tax deductions. These extra deductions could be used by these taxpayers to offset the income generated by their labor and thereby reduce their taxable income and their current tax liability. These taxpayers had little time to devote to these tax saving investments because their primary occupations demanded virtually all of their time. Although these taxpayers hoped that their passive investments would someday generate an economic return, they benefited in the interim by using deductions from these investments to reduce their income tax liability.

By enacting § 469, Congress put a stop to this conduct by deferring deductions attributable to passive activities to the extent such deductions exceeded the gross income from those passive activities. In other words, after the enactment of § 469, a taxpayer could no longer use deductions from passive activities to offset the taxpayer's non-passive sources of income (i.e., the income generated as an executive or a professional, as well as other income from non-business activities such as interest and dividends). By virtue of § 469, the § 162 expenses attributable to a taxpayer's passive activities, that would normally be deductible in the current year under the taxpayer's method of tax accounting, can now be deducted only to the extent of the taxpayer's gross income from those passive activities. Any excess deductions from passive activities, referred to as the "passive activity loss," are deferred to future tax years. See IRC §§ 469(a)(1)(A), (b).

Primary Law: IRC § 469

(a)

    (1) [N]either—

        (A) the passive activity loss, nor,

        (B) the passive activity credit,

    for the taxable year shall be allowed.

    (b) [A]ny loss or credit from an activity which is disallowed under subsection (a) shall be treated as a deduction or credit allocable to such activity in the next taxable year.

(c)

    (1) The term "passive activity" means any activity—

        (A) which involves the conduct of any trade or business, and

>   (B) in which the taxpayer does not materially participate.
>
> (d)
>
>   (1) The term "passive activity loss" means the amount (if any) by which—
>
>   (A) the aggregate losses from all passive activities for the taxable year, exceeds
>
>   (B) the aggregate income from all passive activities for such year.
>
>   * * *
>
> (h)
>
>   (1) A taxpayer shall be treated as materially participating in an activity only if the taxpayer is involved in the operations of the activity on a basis which is—
>
>   (A) regular,
>
>   (B) continuous, and
>
>   (C) substantial.

The starting point for determining whether § 469 applies to a taxpayer is to identify the taxpayer's passive activities. A passive activity is any activity—

1)   which involves the conduct of a trade or business, and

2)   in which the taxpayer does *not* materially participate.

IRC § 469(c)(1). To "materially participate," a taxpayer must be involved in the operations of the activity in a manner that is regular, continuous, and substantial. IRC § 469(h)(1). The Leland case that follows explores the material participation standard.

LELAND v. COMMISSIONER

United States Tax Court, 2015
T.C. Memo. 2015–240

MEMORANDUM FINDINGS OF FACT AND OPINION

NEGA, JUDGE: * * *

FINDINGS OF FACT

* * *

Petitioner is an attorney practicing in the Jackson, Mississippi, metropolitan area. Petitioner is also trained as an electrical engineer. In 2004 petitioner purchased a 1,276-acre farm in Turkey, Texas. In 2005 petitioner entered into a crop share arrangement with Clinton Pigg, a farmer local to Turkey. In accordance with their arrangement, Mr. Pigg has complete responsibility for planting and harvesting crops, and petitioner has complete responsibility for maintaining the infrastructure of the farm.

Of the 1,276 acres, approximately 130 are irrigated and are used by Mr. Pigg for planting and harvesting crops. In 2009 Mr. Pigg spent six hours planting cotton on 120 acres. Before and after planting, he spent a total of three hours spraying the cotton field over the course of two sprayings. Mr. Pigg checked on the farm weekly over the course of 3.5 months, spending approximately 15–20 minutes at the farm each time. It took Mr. Pigg 16 hours to harvest all of the cotton planted in 2009. In total, Mr. Pigg worked 29–30 hours on the farm in 2009. In 2010 Mr. Pigg sprayed and planted 60 acres, spending approximately four hours in total on both tasks. The cotton did not develop in 2010, and Mr. Pigg subsequently abandoned the crop. Petitioner and Mr. Pigg talked twice monthly during 2009 and 2010, but there is no evidence in the record as to the time spent on their conversations.

Maintaining the 1,276-acre farm requires petitioner to perform a lot of long, hard work. Petitioner performs most of these tasks himself, but he sometimes has assistance from his son or a friend, Steve Coke. Aside from petitioner, Mr. Pigg, Mr. Coke, and petitioners' son, no individuals perform any tasks on the farm. Petitioner visits the farm several times each year in order to perform necessary tasks, commuting approximately 13–16 hours each way, including the time it takes to load equipment onto his trailer. The farm has approximately 6–8 miles of perimeter roads and 18–20 miles of interior roads that must be bush hogged and disced regularly in order to remain passable. A Bush Hog is a device that is pulled behind a tractor to cut vegetation and clear land. Discing involves churning and plowing soil to uproot any existing vegetation. Trees and brush that grow near the roads must be controlled through spraying and chopping down limbs that protrude onto the roadways. Because high winds can erode soil on the roads, wheat must be planted each fall to prevent erosion on the roads and on acreage that is not part of the 130 acres planted and harvested by Mr. Pigg. Almost all of the roads have fences running parallel that must be maintained.

Wild hogs are a continuing problem at the farm. They dig underneath fences to get to edible crops and have dug up and broken water lines on the farm. In a year before the tax years 2009 and 2010, wild hogs ate 250,000 pounds of peanuts that petitioner and Mr. Pigg had grown on the farm. As a result, petitioner has to spend significant time controlling the wild hog population, which he accomplishes through hunting and trapping. Petitioner usually hunts hogs for three hours each morning and afternoon while at the farm, for a total of six hours per day. In addition, he spends time building traps and baiting them with corn millet and Kool-Aid to lure hogs to a specific area, where he waits in a tripod stand with semiautomatic weapons in order to eradicate them.

Petitioner also must maintain farm equipment regularly. Parts on tractors, Bush Hogs, and water lines must be replaced. Tractor tires regularly go flat and must be repaired or replaced. When petitioner visits the farm, he stays in a small travel trailer that also requires some maintenance. Each time petitioner leaves, he cleans the floor of the trailer and drains the water lines and adds antifreeze to prevent them from freezing. Additionally, petitioner keeps an old truck at the property; each time he leaves, he disconnects the batteries on the truck and on any tractors that remain at the farm.

Petitioner did not keep contemporary records of time he spent at the farm in 2009 and 2010. However, he reconstructed his records in preparation for trial by reference to a calendar he keeps at his law practice and credit card receipts and invoices for various purchases related to the farm activity. Petitioner provided logs to the Court detailing time spent working at the farm. Petitioner also credibly testified as to his activities at the farm, including the hours he spent each day on various tasks, such as hunting hogs and rebuilding roads. According to his records, petitioner spent 359.9 hours in 2009 and 209.5 hours in 2010 on farm-related activities.

Respondent mailed petitioners a notice of deficiency on April 30, 2013, that determined deficiencies of $5,066 and $10,244 in petitioners' 2009 and 2010 Federal income tax, respectively. The deficiencies were attributable to respondent's limiting loss deductions from the farming activity under section 469. * * *

OPINION

* * *

Section 469(a)(1) limits the deductibility of losses from certain passive activities of individual taxpayers. Generally, a passive activity is any activity which involves the conduct of any trade or business and in which the taxpayer does not materially participate. Sec. 469(c)(1). A taxpayer is treated as materially participating in the activity only if the taxpayer is involved in the operations of the activity on a basis which is regular, continuous, and substantial. Sec. 469(h)(1).

The regulations provide seven exclusive tests for material participation in an activity. Sec. 1.469–5T(a), Temporary Income Tax Regs. An individual will be treated as materially participating in an activity for purposes of section 469 if and only if: (1) the individual participates in the activity for more than 500 hours during such year; (2) the individual's participation in the activity for the taxable year constitutes substantially all of the participation in such activity of all individuals (including individuals who are not owners of interests in the activity) for such year; (3) the individual participates in the activity for more than 100 hours during the taxable year, and such individual's participation in the activity for the taxable year is not less than the participation in the activity of any other individual (including individuals who are not owners of interests in the activity) for such year; (4) the activity is a significant participation activity for the taxable year, and the individual's aggregate participation in all significant participation activities during such year exceeds 500 hours; (5) the individual materially participated in the activity for any 5 taxable years (whether or not consecutive) during the 10 taxable years that immediately precede the taxable year; (6) the activity is a personal service activity, and the individual materially participated in the activity for any 3 taxable years (whether or not consecutive) preceding the taxable year; or (7) based on all of the facts and circumstances, the individual participates in the activity on a regular, continuous, and substantial basis during such year.

An individual may prove his or her participation in an activity by any reasonable means. Contemporaneous daily time reports, logs, or other similar documents are not required if the taxpayer is able to establish the extent of his participation by other reasonable means. Reasonable means may include, but are not limited to, the identification of services performed over a period of time and the approximate number of hours spent performing such services during such period, based on appointment books, calendars, or other narrative summaries. The phrase "reasonable means" is interpreted broadly, and temporary guidelines may not provide precise guidance. However, a post-event "ballpark guesstimate" will not suffice.

Petitioner's reconstructed logs, his receipts and invoices related to farm expenses, and his credible testimony are all reasonable means of calculating time spent on the farming activity during tax years 2009 and 2010. Petitioner's records and testimony establish that he spent 359.9 hours in 2009 and 209.5 hours in 2010 on farm-related activities. As noted, a taxpayer is treated as having materially participated in an activity if the taxpayer participates in the activity for more than 100 hours during the taxable year and the taxpayer's participation in the activity for the taxable year is not less than the participation of any other individual. Sec. 1.469–5T(a)(3), Temporary Income Tax Regs. We are satisfied that petitioner's participation was not less than the participation of any other individual, including Mr. Pigg, Mr. Coke, and petitioners' son, during tax years 2009 and 2010. Accordingly, petitioner materially participated in the farming activity during tax years 2009 and 2010, and the deductions attributable to that activity are not limited by section 469.

* * *

Notes

1. *Calculation of passive activity loss.* If a taxpayer does not materially participate in one or more activities, it must be determined whether the taxpayer has a passive activity loss for the year. To make this determination, the income and deductions from all the taxpayer's passive activities must be isolated from all the other income and deductions of the taxpayer, and a profit or loss must be computed for each passive activity. A loss from one passive activity may be offset by a profit from another passive activity in determining whether an overall passive activity loss exists. See IRC § 469(d)(1). If total losses from passive activities exceed total profits from passive activities, the excess is a passive activity loss that cannot be deducted in the current tax year. See IRC § 469(a)(1).

Instead, this amount is treated as a passive activity deduction in the following tax year and may be carried forward indefinitely until sufficient passive income is generated to claim the loss (deductions) attributable to the passive activity. See IRC § 469(b). By contrast, if total profits from passive activities exceed total losses from passive activities, no passive activity loss exists and § 469 has no impact on the taxpayer in that tax year.

■ **EXAMPLE 13-D.** *Calculation of passive activity loss.* Taxpayer owns two passive activities in Year 1 (PA 1 and PA 2). PA 1 generates gross income of $10,000 and deductions of $19,000 in Year 1. PA 2 generates $10,000 of gross income and $4,000 of deductions in Year 1. The $9,000 loss from PA 1 is offset by the $6,000 profit from PA 2 resulting in a passive activity loss in Year 1 of $3,000. Thus, $3,000 of deductions from PA1 may not be claimed by the taxpayer in Year 1; however, that $3,000 of deductions will be added to PA 1's actual Year 2 deductions.

---

2. *Excluding portfolio income from passive income.* Certain types of income and expenses may not be attributed to a passive activity. See IRC § 469(e)(1). For instance, gross income from interest and dividends are generally not treated as passive income. See IRC § 469(e)(1)(A)(i)(I). The income described by IRC § 469(e)(1)(A)(i)(I) is often referred to as "portfolio income."

■ **EXAMPLE 13-E.** *Exclusion of portfolio income.* Taxpayer owns one passive activity (PA). In Year 1, PA has § 61(a)(2) income of $50,000, interest income of $5,000, and § 162 deductions of $75,000. Taxpayer's Year 1 passive activity loss is $25,000 ($50,000 gross income minus $75,000 of deductions), not $20,000. The $5,000 of interest income earned by PA is excluded from the calculation of its passive income.

---

3. *Disposition of a passive activity.* When a taxpayer has a passive activity loss, the deferred deductions may be claimed in the first taxable year when the taxpayer has sufficient gross income from passive activities to absorb the

suspended deductions. If, however, the taxpayer sells the passive activity before sufficient passive income has been generated to cause the deferred deductions to be allowed, all the taxpayer's deferred deductions may be applied in the year of sale against any of the taxpayer's gross income. See IRC § 469(g)(1). In other words, when a passive activity is sold, the previously suspended deductions attributable to that passive activity are no longer treated as passive and, therefore, can be applied against *all* income of the taxpayer (including income from the taxpayer's main livelihood) in the year of sale.

■ **EXAMPLE 13-F.** *Disposition of passive activity.* Taxpayer owns one passive activity (PA). In Year 1, the passive activity generates $25,000 of gross income and $45,000 of deductions. The resulting $20,000 passive activity loss is treated as a passive deduction in Year 2. In Year 2, the passive activity generates $30,000 of gross income and $31,000 of passive deductions. No net passive income exists in Year 2 to absorb any of the $20,000 Year 1 passive activity loss. Thus, the $20,000 Year 1 passive activity loss, as well as the $1,000 Year 2 passive activity loss, are treated as passive deductions in Year 3. During Year 3 taxpayer sells PA to an unrelated party. As a result of the sale, the $21,000 of passive deductions that were carried from Years 1 and 2 to Year 3 are no longer treated as passive. Therefore, the taxpayer may deduct the $21,000 without restriction and apply those deductions against *any* gross income of the taxpayer, including gross income from the taxpayer's main livelihood.

---

4.   *Rental real estate.* The ownership of rental real estate is generally a per se passive activity (see IRC § 469(c)(2)). However, if an owner of rental real estate meets an "active participation" standard, up to $25,000 of deductions in excess of gross income from the rental real estate may be applied against other (non-passive) income of the owner. See IRC §§ 469(i)(1), (2). "Active participation" (IRC § 469(i)(6)) is a much easier standard to satisfy than "material participation" (IRC § 469(h)(1)).

Primary Law: IRC § 469(i)

(i)

    (1)   [S]ubsection (a) shall not apply to that portion of the passive activity loss * * * for any taxable year which is attributable to all rental real estate activities with respect to which [an] individual actively participated in such taxable year * * *.

    (2)   The aggregate amount to which paragraph (1) applies for any taxable year shall not exceed $25,000.

    (3)

        (A)   In the case of any taxpayer, the $25,000 amount under paragraph (2) shall be reduced (but not below zero) by 50 percent of the amount by which the adjusted gross income of the taxpayer for the taxable year exceeds $100,000. * * *

■ **EXAMPLE 13-G.** *Active participation rental real estate.* Taxpayer owns rental real estate and meets the active participation standard. In Year 1, Taxpayer has $75,000 of adjusted gross income. In Year 1, Taxpayer's rental real estate generates $50,000 of gross income and $85,000 of § 162 deductions. Normally, Taxpayer's passive activity loss would be $35,000 ($85,000 – $50,000). But this example involves rental real estate in which Taxpayer actively participates. Thus, the passive activity loss is only $10,000 because Taxpayer may treat up to $25,000 of deductions from rental real estate with respect to which Taxpayer actively participates as non-passive.

The $25,000 ceiling on the amount of excess deductions that may be treated as non-passive with respect to active participation rental real estate is lowered (or reduced to zero) for higher-income taxpayers. See IRC § 469(i)(3). Specifically, the $25,000 ceiling is "reduced (but not below zero) by 50% of the amount by which the adjusted gross income of the taxpayer for the taxable year exceeds $100,000." See IRC § 469(i)(3)(A). Thus the ceiling is zero for a taxpayer with adjusted gross income in excess of $150,000 (50% × ($150,000 − $100,000) = $25,000).

■ **EXAMPLE 13-H.** Same facts as Example 13-G except that Taxpayer had adjusted gross income of $175,000 in Year 1 (rather than $75,000). In this situation, the $25,000 ceiling under IRC § 469(i)(2) would be reduced to zero (because the taxpayer's adjusted gross income exceeds $150,000). Therefore, the taxpayer's passive activity loss would be $35,000 (the amount by which the $85,000 of deductions from the rental real estate exceeds the $50,000 of gross income).

■ **PROBLEM 13-2.** *Passive activity losses.* In Year 1, Associate is paid a $70,000 salary by law firm. Associate also earns $20,000 of interest and dividends. In addition, Associate owns a bar which has receipts of $50,000 and incurs ordinary and necessary business expenses of $90,000.

a) What is Associate's adjusted gross income in Year 1? See IRC § 469(h).

b) Assume that Associate does not "materially participate" in the bar. In addition, assume that Associate also owns a clothing store in which he does not materially participate which has receipts of $60,000 and incurs ordinary and necessary business expenses of $50,000 in Year 1.

    1) What is Associate's adjusted gross income in Year 1? See IRC § 469(d).

    2) If only $58,000 of the clothing store's receipts were from sales of clothes and the other $2,000 represented interest income, what is Associate's adjusted gross income in Year 1? See IRC § 469(e)(1).

c) How would your answer to a) change if Associate owned an apartment building, rather than a bar? See IRC § 469(i).

d) If Associate had a passive activity loss in a), when, if ever, would that loss be allowed? See IRC §§ 469(b), (g)(1).

IRC § 469(c)(7) creates an exception to the general rule that rental real estate is a per se passive activity (see IRC § 469(c)(2)). Pursuant to IRC § 469(c)(7), if an owner of rental real estate meets a statutory standard that is higher than that required to achieve material participation in non-real estate activities, IRC § 469 will not restrict any deductions attributable to the owner's real estate activities.

Primary Law: IRC § 469(c)

* * *

(2) Except as provided in paragraph (7), the term "passive activity" includes any rental activity.

* * *

(7)

    (A) If this paragraph applies to any taxpayer for a taxable year—

        (i) paragraph (2) shall not apply to any real estate activity of such taxpayer for such taxable year * * *

    (B) This paragraph shall apply to a taxpayer for a taxable year if—

        (i) more than one-half of the personal services performed in trades or businesses by such taxpayer during the taxable year are performed in real property trades or businesses in which the taxpayer materially participates, and

        (ii) such taxpayer performs more than 750 hours of services during the taxable year in real property trades or businesses in which the taxpayer materially participates.

    * * *

WORTH NOTING The case that follows is a Tax Court "summary opinion." A summary opinion is rendered in certain small tax cases in which the taxpayer has elected the more liberal procedures provided by IRC § 7463. Generally, only cases involving deficiencies of not more than $50,000 are eligible for this treatment. IRC §§ 7463(a), (e). Moreover, decisions entered in these cases, which generally involve questions of fact, rather than law, are not appealable and are not treated as precedent. IRC § 7463(b). Notwithstanding their limitations, summary opinions can serve as useful learning devices.

FRANCO v. COMMISSIONER

United States Tax Court, 2018
T.C. Summary Opinion 2018–9

GUY, SPECIAL TRIAL JUDGE: * * *

Background

I.   Mr. Franco's Background

Mr. Franco is a licensed architect, and he runs a small architectural business. During 2013 he spent 109 hours providing architectural services to the trust department at Wells Fargo Bank and about 540 hours providing similar services to Axis Construction Consulting (including time that he spent traveling).

II.   Rental Real Estate Activities

A. Rental Properties

During 2013 petitioners owned two rental properties in Burlingame, California. One of the properties, Edgehill Drive, was a "fourplex"—a single building containing four separate apartments. The other property, Bayswater Avenue, was a single-family home.

B. Management of the Properties

Mr. Franco managed the rental properties during the year in issue. Because his tenants were not attentive to trash disposal matters, Mr. Franco made weekly trips to the properties to ensure that trash bins were set out for collection, cleaned if necessary, and returned to their storage locations. He also performed minor repairs at the properties, coordinated more substantial repairs with a handyman, communicated with the tenants and collected and deposited rent, maintained insurance policies, purchased materials for the properties as needed, paid bills, and kept books and records of his expenses for tax accounting purposes.

Two of the four tenants at Edgehill Drive moved out in 2013. As a result, Mr. Franco spent additional time coordinating with them as they vacated the apartments, performed extra repair and maintenance work to ready the apartments for new tenants, placed advertisements listing the apartments for rent, and worked with new tenants as they signed leases and moved into the apartments.

Mr. Franco was late paying property taxes and insurance premiums on both rental properties during 2013. Consequently, he was obliged to spend time negotiating a property tax installment payment plan and had to work with his mortgage lender to eliminate redundant insurance coverage on the properties.

Mr. Franco produced an activity log listing the personal services that he performed in managing the rental properties during 2013 and the time that he spent providing those services. The activity log indicates that Mr. Franco devoted 765 and 372 hours to the management of Edgehill Drive and Bayswater Avenue, respectively.

* * *

III. Petitioners' 2013 Tax Return and Respondent's Determination

Petitioners timely filed a joint Form 1040, U.S. Individual Income Tax Return, for 2013. Mr. Franco reported gross receipts of [$100,000] from his architectural business on Schedule C, Profit or Loss From Business, offset by * * * $28,580 for contract labor. Petitioners also attached to their tax return a Schedule E, reporting gross rental income of $101,950 from the two properties, offset by expenses of $169,832, resulting in a net loss of $67,882 from the rental activity. * * *

Respondent acknowledged in the notice of deficiency that petitioners are entitled to deduct $25,000 of the $67,882 loss in accordance with the exception prescribed in section 469(i). Absent a further exception, however, respondent determined that the $42,882 balance of the loss deduction is disallowed under section 469.

Discussion

* * *

Taxpayers are allowed deductions for certain business and investment expenses under sections 162 and 212. Section 469(a)(1), however, generally disallows for the taxable year any deduction for passive activity losses and credits. A passive activity loss is defined as the excess of the aggregate losses from all passive activities for a taxable year over the aggregate income from all passive activities for that year. Sec. 469(d)(1). A passive activity is any activity that involves the conduct of a trade or business * * *, in which the taxpayer does not materially participate. Sec. 469(c)(1), (6)(B).

A rental activity generally is treated as a per se passive activity regardless of whether the taxpayer materially participates. Sec. 469(c)(2), (4). The term "rental activity" generally is defined as any activity where payments are principally for the use of tangible property. Sec. 469(j)(8).

Section 469(c)(7) provides special rules for taxpayers engaging in real property businesses. Section 469(c)(7)(A) and (B) provides that rental activities of a qualifying taxpayer in a real property trade or business (i.e., a real estate professional) are not per se passive activities under subsection (c)(2) for a taxable year and, if the taxpayer materially participates in the rental real estate activities, these activities are treated as nonpassive activities. Sec. 1.469–9(e)(1), Income Tax Regs.

* * *

A taxpayer qualifies as a real estate professional under section 469(c)(7)(B) if (i) more than one-half of personal services performed in trades or businesses by the taxpayer during such taxable year are performed in real property trades or businesses in which the taxpayer materially participates and (ii) such taxpayer performs more than 750 hours of services during the taxable year in real property trades or businesses in which the taxpayer materially participates.[8]

"Personal services" means any work performed by an individual in connection with a trade or business. Sec. 1.469–9(b)(4), Income Tax Regs. * * *

---

[8]   The term "real property trade or business" means any real property development, redevelopment, construction, reconstruction, acquisition, conversion, rental, operation, management, leasing, or brokerage trade or business. See sec. 469(c)(7)(C). Petitioners do not contend that Mr. Franco's work as an architect constitutes a real property trade or business.

The evidence that a taxpayer may use to establish the number of hours that he or she participates in a real property trade or business is described in section 1.469–5T(f)(4), Temporary Income Tax Regs., 53 Fed. Reg. 5727 (Feb. 25, 1988), as follows:

> The extent of an individual's participation in an activity may be established by any reasonable means. Contemporaneous daily time reports, logs, or similar documents are not required if the extent of such participation may be established by other reasonable means. Reasonable means for purposes of this paragraph may include but are not limited to the identification of services performed over a period of time and the approximate number of hours spent performing such services during such period, based on appointment books, calendars, or narrative summaries.

We have held that the regulations do not allow a post event "ballpark guesstimate".

Although Mr. Franco worked about 650 hours providing personal services as an architect in 2013, the record shows that he also spent more than 750 hours providing personal services in connection with the management of the rental properties. Mr. Franco offered credible testimony describing the time and effort that he devoted to both activities during the year in issue. His testimony was largely corroborated with objective evidence including a rental activity log, receipts for various rental-related expenditures, emails, and other business records. Considering all the facts and circumstances, Mr. Franco qualified as a real estate professional in 2013 and his rental real estate activities were regular, continuous, and substantial within the meaning of section 469(h)(1). It follows that the loss deduction in dispute is not disallowed under section 469.

* * *

■ **PROBLEM 13-3.** *Real property trade or business.* How much of Mr. Franco's $169,832 of rental expenses did he deduct on his 2013 tax return? How much of these expenses did the Internal Revenue Service allow him to deduct? In light of the court's decision, how much of the rental expenses were in fact deductible in 2013?

IN PRACTICE

Importance of maintaining contemporaneous, credible time logs. The Franco court relied on the time logs Mr. Franco maintained to document the hours he devoted to his real estate activities. In contrast, the taxpayers in Ballard and Pu v. Commissioner, T.C. Summary Opinion 2018–53, failed to persuade the court that their time logs demonstrated that they had devoted the requisite hours to their real estate activities to satisfy IRC § 469(c)(7). The Ballard and Pu court stated—

> Petitioners attempt to show that they were real estate professionals during the years at issue by relying on Mr. Ballard's * * * non-contemporaneous time logs for 2008 * * *. The 2008 time logs—one for Mr. Ballard and another for Ms. Pu—list 1,669 and 772 hours of personal time that they respectively purportedly spent relative to their residential rental properties. These logs, which Mr. Ballard created on recollection several years after the fact in connection with the audit of petitioners' returns for the years at issue, were duplicative, and the hours reflected therein were inflated. The log entries were short and did not state with any specificity how the time for each entry was spent. * * * We conclude that the 2008 time logs are not trustworthy and decline to rely on them to reach the result petitioners desire.

2. Net Operating Losses—§ 172

If the deductions generated by a business in which the owner materially participates exceed the business's gross income, the owner can apply the excess deductions against income the owner derives from other sources (e.g., interest and dividends).[5] If the taxpayer still has insufficient income to absorb all the business's deductions, the business deductions that remain represent a "net operating loss." See IRC § 172(c). A net operating loss may be applied against 80% of the taxpayer's taxable income in future years. See IRC § 172(a).

---

[5]   The amount of excess business losses that can be deducted in any year, however, is subject to a limitation discussed in the next section of this chapter. See IRC § 461(*l*).

IRC § 172 is intended to allow cyclical businesses to average "lean" years against "fat" years for purposes of computing tax liability. Because business cycles often exceed one year, it is necessary to relax the rigidity of the taxable year to achieve the goal of taxing businesses on their net income.

When a net operating loss arises, it can be applied against 80% of taxable income generated in the year after the loss was incurred. If the net operating loss exceeds 80% of taxable income in the year after the loss is incurred, the remaining net operating loss is applied to 80% of taxable income generated in each subsequent tax year until the entire net operating loss has been absorbed. A net operating loss applied to income in a tax year after the net operating loss was incurred is referred to as a "net operating loss carryover." IRC § 172(b)(1)(A)(ii).

Primary Law: IRC § 172

(a)   There shall be allowed as a deduction for the taxable year an amount equal to the lesser of—

   (1)   the aggregate of the net operating loss carryovers to such year * * *, or

   (2)   80 percent of the taxable income computed without regard to the deduction allowed by this section. * * *

(b)(1)

   (A)   Except as otherwise provided in this paragraph, a net operating loss for any taxable year—

      * * *

      (ii)   shall be a net operating loss carryover to each taxable year following the taxable year of the loss.

      * * *

(c)   For purposes of this section, the term "net operating loss" means the excess of the deductions allowed by this chapter over the gross income. Such excess shall be computed with the modifications specified in subsection (d).

* * *

■ **EXAMPLE 13-I.** *Application of net operating loss.* In Year 1, David incurs a net operating loss ("NOL") of $100,000. In Year 2, David has taxable income of $50,000 before applying the Year 1 NOL. David can apply the NOL against only $40,000 of his Year 2 income ($50,000 × 80% = $40,000) and can carry the remaining $60,000 of his NOL to Year 3.[6] If David has $200,000 of taxable income in Year 3, he can apply all $60,000 of his remaining NOL against his Year 3 income because $60,000 is less than 80% of his Year 3 income ($200,000 × 80% = $160,000).

■ **PROBLEM 13-4.** *Timing of net operating loss deduction.* Shanna owns a clothing store in which she materially participates. Shanna has the following income and expenses in Years 1–3:

	Year 1	Year 2	Year 3
Business Income	$190,000	$250,000	$300,000
Interest	5,000	5,000	5,000
Dividends	3,000	3,000	3,000
Royalties	2,000	2,000	2,000
Business Expenses	350,000	160,000	110,000

Assume, unrealistically, Shanna has no deductions in Years 1–3 other than her business expenses.

How much of Shanna's business expenses may she deduct in each year?

3. Limitation on Excess Business Losses—§ 461(*l*)

As a general rule, if the deductions generated by a business in which the owner materially participates exceed the business's gross income, the owner can apply the excess deductions against non-business income (e.g., interest and

---

[6] For purposes of applying the 80% limitation, taxable income is computed without regard to any allowable net operating loss deduction. See IRC § 172(a)(2). Thus, in any taxable year in which a net operating loss deduction is allowed, the taxpayer's actual taxable income will be less than the taxable income amount used to compute the 80% limitation.

dividends). However, IRC § 461(*l*) limits the amount of business deductions that may be applied against non-business income by disallowing any "excess business loss" of a taxpayer.[7] An "excess business loss" exists when a taxpayer's trade or business deductions exceed, in the aggregate, the taxpayer's gross income from those trades or businesses by more than $250,000 ($500,000 in the case of a taxpayer filing a joint return). IRC § 461(*l*)(3). Any disallowed excess business loss is treated as a net operating loss that may be carried to the following taxable year under IRC § 172. IRC § 461(*l*)(2). Therefore, a business owner with business deductions in excess of business income may only apply up to $250,000 ($500,000 if a joint return is filed) of the excess business deductions against non-business income.

Primary Law: IRC § 461(*l*)

(1)   In the case of taxable year of a taxpayer other than a corporation beginning * * * before January 1, 2026—

(A)   * * *

(B)   any excess business loss of the taxpayer for the taxable year shall not be allowed.

(2)   Any loss which is disallowed under paragraph (1) shall be treated as a net operating loss carryover to the following taxable year under section 172.

(3)

(A)   The term "excess business loss" means the excess (if any) of—

(i)   the aggregate deductions of the taxpayer for the taxable year which are attributable to trades or businesses of such taxpayer (determined without regard to whether or not such deductions are disallowed for such taxable year under paragraph (1)), over

---

[7]   The passive activity loss limitation of IRC § 469 applies before the excess business loss limitation of IRC § 461(*l*). IRC § 461(*l*)(6).

> (ii) the sum of—
>
>> (I)   the aggregate gross income or gain of such tax-payer for the taxable year which is attributable to such trades or businesses, plus
>>
>> (II) $250,000 (200 percent of such amount in the case of a joint return).
>
> * * *
>
> (6)   This subsection shall be applied after the application of section 469.

■ **EXAMPLE 13-J.**   *Excess business loss of taxpayer who files a joint return.* Ben, who files a joint return with his spouse, owns a clothing manu-facturing business in which he materially participates (i.e., IRC § 469 does not apply). In Year 1, Ben's business has the following amounts of income and deductions:

Business Income:	$1,000,000
– Business Deductions:	$1,800,000
Business Loss:	$800,000

Consequently, Ben has an "excess business loss" of $300,000 ($800,000 business loss exceeds the $500,000 IRC § 461(*l*)(3) threshold for allowed business losses of a taxpayer who files a joint return by $300,000). The $300,000 excess business loss is treated as a net operating loss that Ben can carry to Year 2 under IRC § 172. The extent to which the disallowed excess business loss impacts Ben's Year 1 tax liability depends on the amount of his non-business income. Consider each of the following al-ternative scenarios:

a)   *Ben has no non-business income in Year 1.* Ben's excess business loss does not impact his Year 1 tax liability if he has no non-business income. In this situation, his business deductions offset his business income resulting in no taxable income in Year 1. His $800,000 business loss is a net operating loss that he can carry to Year 2 under IRC § 172.

b) *Ben has $200,000 of non-business income in Year 1.* Ben's excess business loss still does not impact his Year 1 tax liability if he has only $200,000 of non-business income. Because Ben files a joint return, he can apply up to $500,000 of his business loss against non-business income before IRC § 461(*l*) bars him from applying any additional business loss against non-business income. Here, Ben has only $200,000 of non-business income so he can apply $200,000 of his business loss against his non-business income and thereby reduce his Year 1 taxable income to zero. The remaining $600,000 of his Year 1 business loss ($800,000 business loss less the $200,000 he applies to his Year 1 non-business income) is a net operating loss that he can carry to Year 2 under IRC § 172.

c) *Ben has $900,000 of non-business income in Year 1.* If Ben has more than $500,000 of non-business income in Year 1, IRC § 461(*l*) will impact his Year 1 tax liability because it precludes him from applying more than $500,000 of his Year 1 business loss against his non-business income. Thus, if he has $900,000 of non-business income in Year 1, he can apply only $500,000 of his Year 1 business loss against that income and he will be taxed on the remaining $400,000 of non-business income. His $300,000 excess business loss ($800,000 business loss less the $500,000 he applies to his Year 1 non-business income) is treated as a net operating loss that he can carry to Year 2 under IRC § 172. If IRC § 461(*l*) had not been enacted, Ben could have applied his entire $800,000 Year 1 business loss against his $900,000 of non-business income in which case he would have been taxed on only $100,000 of non-business income. Had he been allowed to apply his entire business loss against his non-business income, he would have had no net operating loss to carry to Year 2.

Limited duration. IRC § 461(*l*) applies only to taxable years beginning before January 1, 2026.

WORTH NOTING

■   **PROBLEM 13-5.**   *Excess business loss of taxpayer who does not file a joint return.* Charlotte, who does not file a joint return, owns a widget business and a candy store. She materially participates in both businesses (i.e., IRC § 469 does not apply). The widget business earns $200,000 of gross income and incurs $700,000 of expenses in Year 1. The candy store earns $300,000 of gross income and incurs $250,000 of expenses in Year 1. Charlotte does not file a joint return.

a)   What is the amount of Charlotte's excess business loss?

b)   To what extent does Charlotte's excess business loss impact her Year 1 income tax liability if her non-business income in Year 1 is—

1) $100,000?

2) $300,000?

SYNTHESIS

This Chapter explored several special tax deferral rules. Pursuant to IRC § 83, property received in connection with the performance of services is not included in gross income until the earlier of the time that the property is transferable, or not subject to a substantial risk of forfeiture. However, the recipient of such property may elect to include the value of the property in gross income upon receipt. Although this election accelerates income, it is often advisable for a taxpayer to make this election. By making the election, the taxpayer can defer tax on future appreciation in the value of the property until the taxpayer sells the property and also receive favorable capital gains treatment (a topic explored in Chapter 16) at the time of sale.

IRC § 469 defers certain otherwise allowable deductions from trades or businesses in which the taxpayer does not materially participate (passive activities). If the taxpayer's deductions from passive activities exceed the taxpayer's gross income from these activities, the excess deductions (which constitute a passive activity loss) are deferred. These deductions are deferred until the taxpayer generates excess gross income from passive activities (gross income that exceed deductions from these activities) or the taxpayer sells her ownership interest in the passive activity.

When a taxpayer materially participates in a trade or business with deductions in excess of gross income, the owner can apply the excess deductions against all other (non-business) income of the taxpayer, except to the extent an "excess business loss" exists (discussed below). If the taxpayer still has insufficient business and non-business income to absorb all the business's deductions, the business deductions that remain represent a "net operating loss" under IRC § 172. A net operating loss may be applied against 80% of the taxpayer's taxable income in future years until it is fully absorbed by such income.

When a taxpayer materially participates in a business that generates deductions in excess of gross income, IRC § 461(*l*) defers any "excess business loss." An "excess business loss" exists when a taxpayer's trade or business deductions exceed, in the aggregate, the taxpayer's gross income from those trades or businesses by more than $250,000 ($500,000 on a joint return). An excess business loss is treated as a net operating loss under IRC § 172.

Test Your Knowledge: To assess your understanding of the material in this chapter, click here to take a quiz.

CHAPTER 14

Imputation

Overview

Money has a time value; i.e., the possession of money for any period of time has value because the holder can invest the money and earn a return on that money during the time of possession. As such, the ability to use someone else's money without paying a market rate of interest to compensate that person for the time value of money yields an economic benefit to the holder of the money. In addition, the use of someone else's money without paying interest distorts the tax consequences of the arrangement.

To mitigate the tax distortions that result when a market rate of interest is not charged for borrowed money, Congress has enacted rules that impute interest to certain formal and informal loans. When a *formal* loan is made and the lender refrains from charging the borrower a market rate of interest, IRC § 7872 often creates a fictional payment of interest with potential tax consequences to both lender and borrower. Even in the absence of a formal loan, an element of foregone interest arguably exists any time a taxpayer must wait to receive money to which she is entitled without being compensated for the time value of money. With respect to these *informal* loans, Congress frequently imputes interest under a set of statutory rules referred to as the "original issue discount" (OID) rules which triggers tax consequences to both lender and borrower.

A. Below Market Loans—§ 7872

Assume Employer lends $10,000 to Employee but does not charge Employee any interest on the loan. If Employee borrowed the money from an unrelated lender, Employee would be charged a market rate of interest to compensate the lender for the time value of money. If the market interest rate is 5% per year, an unrelated lender would charge Employee $500 of interest per year (5% × $10,000 = $500). By borrowing the $10,000 from Employer instead of an unrelated lender, Employee derives a $500 benefit because she gains possession of the money without paying for its time value. Is the $500 benefit derived by Employee included in Employee's gross income?

DEAN v. COMMISSIONER

Tax Court of the United States, 1961
35 T.C. 1083

RAUM, JUDGE:

[This case raises] a single issue, * * * namely, whether petitioners realized taxable income to the extent of the alleged economic benefit derived from the interest-free use of funds which they had borrowed from a family corporation controlled by them. The facts have been stipulated.

* * *

The Commissioner * * * charged petitioners with income equal to interest at the [prime rate][1] with respect to loans which they had obtained upon non-interest-bearing notes from their controlled corporation, Nemours Corporation * * *. The theory * * * was that the petitioners realized income to the extent of the economic benefit derived from the free use of borrowed funds from Nemours * * *.

* * *

[P]etitioner J. Simpson Dean owed Nemours on non-interest bearing notes [approximately $300,000].

[P]etitioner Paulina duPont Dean owed Nemours on non-interest bearing notes [approximately $2,000,000].

* * *

---

[1]   Editor's note: The "prime rate" of interest is the rate that banks charge their most financially sound borrowers.

[I]nterest computed at the prime rate * * * for the taxable years [at issue totaled approximately $21,000 for J. Simpson Dean and $143,000 for Paulina duPont Dean.]

     * * *

In support of its present position, the Government relies primarily upon a series of cases holding that rent-free use of corporate property by a stockholder or officer may result in the realization of income. Charles A. Frueauff, 30 B.T.A. 449 (rent-free use of corporation's apartment); Reynard Corporation, 30 B.T.A. 451 (rent-free use of corporation's house); Percy M. Chandler, 41 B.T.A. 165, affirmed 119 F.2d 623 (C.A. 3) (rent-free use of corporation's apartment and lodge); Paulina duPont Dean, 9 T.C. 256 (rent-free use of corporation's house); Dean v. Commissioner, 187 F.2d 1019 (C.A. 3), affirming a Memorandum Opinion of this Court (rent-free use of corporation's house); Rodgers Dairy Co., 14 T.C. 66 (personal use of corporation's automobile). These cases bear a superficial resemblance to the present case, but reflection convinces us that they are not in point. In each of them a benefit was conferred upon the stockholder or officer in circumstances such that had the stockholder or officer undertaken to procure the same benefit by an expenditure of money such expenditure would not have been deductible by him. Here, on the other hand, had petitioners borrowed the funds in question on interest-bearing notes, their payment of interest would have been fully deductible by them under section 163. Not only would they not be charged with the additional income in controversy herein, but they would have a deduction equal to that very amount. We think this circumstance differentiates the various cases relied upon by the Commissioner, and perhaps explains why he has apparently never taken this position in any prior case.

[W]e think it to be * * * true that an interest-free loan results in no taxable gain to the borrower, and we hold that the Commissioner is not entitled to any increased deficiency based upon this issue.

Opper, J., concurring: The necessity is not apparent to me of deciding more * * * than that there can be no deficiency. If petitioners were in receipt of some kind of gross income, * * * the corresponding interest deduction would perhaps exactly offset and nullify it. But because that would mean that there is no deficiency, it would not necessarily follow that there was no gross income, as the present opinion, in my view, gratuitously holds. Certainly the statement that 'an interest-free loan results in no taxable gain to the borrower' is much too broad a generalization to make here.

* * *

This being apparently a case of first impression, the present result seems peculiarly unfortunate in deciding a point that need not be passed on. * * *

BRUCE, J., dissenting: I respectfully dissent from the opinion of the majority * * *. In my opinion the present case is not distinguishable in principle from * * * cases cited by the majority, wherein it was held that the rent-free use of corporate property by a stockholder or officer resulted in the realization of income. 'Interest' in the sense that it represents compensation paid for the use, forbearance, or detention of money, may be likened to 'rent' which is paid for the use of property.

I agree with Judge Opper in his concurring opinion that 'the statement that 'an interest-free loan results in no taxable gain to the borrower' is much too broad a generalization to make here.' [I]t is difficult to believe that the interest-free loan of in excess of $2 million * * * by a [corporation] to its majority stockholders * * * did not result in any economic benefit to the borrower.

* * *

WORTH NOTING When the events in the Dean case occurred, all interest was deductible. Under current law, the extent to which interest paid on borrowed funds is deductible depends on whether the loan proceeds were expended in a trade or business, an investment, or for personal purposes. See IRC § 163(h), explored in Chapter 10.

More than two decades after the Dean decision, Congress enacted IRC § 7872 which imputes interest to certain "below market loans." IRC § 7872 does not apply to all below market loans. For § 7872 to apply, the below market loan in question must be described in § 7872(c). Three of the main categories of below market loans to which IRC § 7872 applies are—

1) gift loans (IRC § 7872(c)(1)(A));

2) loans between an employer and an employee (IRC § 7872(c)(1)(B)); and

3) loans between a corporation and a shareholder of the corpora-
    tion (IRC § 7872(c)(1)(C)).

Primary Law: IRC § 7872

(a)

  (1) For purposes of this title, in the case of any below-market
      loan to which this section applies and which is a gift loan
      or a demand loan, the forgone interest shall be treated as—

      (A) transferred from lender to borrower, and

      (B) retransferred by the borrower to the lender as interest.

* * *

(c)

  (1) Except as otherwise provided * * *, this section shall apply
      to—

      (A) Any below-market loan which is a gift loan.

      (B) Any below-market loan directly or indirectly
           between—

           (i)   an employer and an employee * * *

           * * *

      (C) Any below-market loan directly or indirectly between
           a corporation and any shareholder of such corporation.

      (D) Any below-market loan 1 of the principal purposes of
           the interest arrangements of which is the avoidance
           of any Federal tax.

* * *

(c)

  (1) The term "below-market loan" means any loan if—

      (A) in the case of a demand loan, interest is payable on
           the loan at a rate less than the applicable Federal rate,
           * * *

      * * *

(2) The term "forgone interest" means, with respect to any period during which the loan is outstanding, the excess of—

(A) the amount of interest which would have been payable on the loan for the period if interest accrued on the loan at the applicable Federal rate * * *, over

(B) any interest payable on the loan properly allocable to such period.

(f) * * *

(3) The term "gift loan" means any below-market loan where the foregoing of interest is in the nature of a gift.

* * *

(5) The term "demand loan" means any loan which is payable in full at any time on the demand of the lender. * * *

(6) The term "term loan" means any loan which is not a demand loan.

* * *

■ **EXAMPLE 14-A.** *Below market loan between employer and employee.* Employer lends $10,000 to Employee but does not charge Employee any interest on the loan. The loan is payable whenever Employer demands repayment (a "demand loan"), rather than specifying a particular repayment date (a "term loan").[2] Assume the "applicable Federal rate" is 5% when the loan is made.[3] The loan is a "below market loan" because interest is payable at less than the applicable Federal rate. IRC § 7872(e)(1)(A). The annual amount of "forgone interest" is $500 (5% × $10,000 = $500). See IRC § 7872(e)(2).

---

[2]   IRC § 7872 applies to both below market demand loans and below market term loans. This Chapter focuses only on below market loans governed by IRC § 7872(a). It does not address the tax consequences of non-gift, term loans which are governed by IRC § 7872(b).

[3]   The "applicable Federal rate" is defined in § 7872(f)(2). It is essentially a market interest rate announced by the Internal Revenue Service each month and applies to below market loans made during that month.

Section 7872 applies to this below market loan because it is a loan "between an employer and an employee." See IRC § 7872(c)(1)(B)(i). Because § 7872 applies to the loan, the following two *fictional* transfers of the $500 of foregone interest are treated as occurring for tax purposes:

1) Employer is treated as transferring the $500 to Employee as a payment of compensation by Employer for services rendered by Employee (IRC § 7872(a)(1)(A)); and

2) Employee (borrower) is deemed to retransfer the $500 back to Employer (lender) as a payment of interest on the loan (IRC § 7872(a)(1)(B)).

Although both of the transfers created by § 7872(a) are fictional, each of the transfers triggers potential tax consequences to Employer and Employee.

1) The first fictional transfer triggers $500 of gross income to Employee (compensation for services rendered under IRC § 61(a)(1)) and a $500 deduction to Employer (an ordinary and necessary business expense under IRC § 162(a)(1), assuming the compensation is reasonable).

2) The second fictional transfer triggers $500 of gross income to Employer (interest income under IRC § 61(a)(4)) and a $500 deduction to Employee (but only if the interest expense is allowed as a deduction under IRC § 163(h)).

KTA-TATOR, INC. v. COMMISSIONER

United States Tax Court, 1997
108 T.C. 100

Foley, Judge:

* * *

Background

[P]etitioner provided various services within the coatings industry, including consulting, engineering, inspection, and lab analysis. Kenneth B. Tator is the president of petitioner, and he and his wife (the Tators) are its sole shareholders.

In 1991, the Tators began two construction projects. The first project involved the expansion of petitioner's Pittsburgh headquarters, which the Tators owned and leased to petitioner. The second project involved the construction of a new office building in Houston, Texas, which the Tators would own and lease to petitioner. Petitioner was authorized by its board of directors to loan funds to the Tators for construction, the purchase of land, and other business purposes. During the construction phase of the two projects, petitioner made over 100 advances of funds to the Tators. [T]he Tators used the advances to pay contractors and meet other expenses. The advances were not subject to written repayment terms. On the corporate balance sheets, petitioner reported the advances as loans to shareholders. Monthly and year-to-date totals were recorded in two accounts entitled "Mortgage Receivable—Pittsburgh" and "Mortgage Receivable—Houston".

The Houston project was completed in October of 1992, and the Pittsburgh project was completed in October of 1993. Upon the completion of each project, the Tators * * * began repaying the advances. The [repayment] schedule for each project delineated monthly payments over 20 years at an interest rate of 8 percent. The [repayment] schedule for the Houston project had a beginning principal balance of $400,218, while the [repayment] schedule for the Pittsburgh project had a beginning principal balance of $225,777.60.

On its 1992 and 1993 Federal income tax returns, petitioner did not report interest income from the advances. On September 27, 1995, respondent issued a notice of deficiency to petitioner. Respondent determined that petitioner, pursuant to section 7872, had unreported interest income of $30,718 for 1992 and $5,225 for 1993. Based on these amounts, respondent determined that petitioner was liable for deficiencies of $10,443 for 1992 and $1,828 for 1993.

Discussion

Section 7872 was enacted as part of the Deficit Reduction Act of 1984 (DEFRA). Section 7872 sets forth the income * * * tax treatment for certain categories of "below-market" loans (i.e., loans subject to a below-market interest rate). Section 7872 recharacterizes a below-market loan as an arms-length transaction in which the lender made a loan to the borrower in exchange for a note requiring the payment of interest at a statutory rate. As a result, the parties are treated as if the lender made a transfer of funds to the borrower, and the borrower used these funds to pay interest to the lender. The transfer to the borrower is treated as a gift, dividend, contribution of capital, payment of compensation, or other payment depending on the substance of the transaction. The interest payment is included in the lender's income and generally may be deducted by the borrower.

Section 7872 applies to a transaction that is: (1) A loan; (2) [a "below-market" loan]; and (3) described in one of several enumerated categories. Sec. 7872(c)(1)(C), (e)(1). The parties agree that the [first and] third requirement[s have] been met.

[I.] Below-Market Loan Requirement

To determine if the below-market loan requirement is satisfied, we must ascertain whether the loan is (1) a demand or term loan and (2) subject to a below-market interest rate. See sec. 7872(e)(1).

A.   Demand or Term Loan

Below-market loans fit into one of two categories: Demand loans and term loans. Sec. 7872(e)(1). A demand loan includes "any loan which is payable in full at any time on the demand of the lender." Sec. 7872(f)(5). A term loan is "any loan which is not a demand loan." Sec. 7872(f)(6).

The determination of whether a loan is payable in full at any time on the demand of the lender is a factual one. Loans between closely held corporations and their controlling shareholders are to be examined with special scrutiny. Petitioner made loans, without written repayment terms, to its only shareholders and had unfettered discretion to determine when the loans would be repaid. Therefore, the loans are demand loans.

* * *

[N]ext, we must determine whether petitioner's loans are subject to a below-market interest rate.

B.   Below-Market Interest Rate

A demand loan is a below-market loan if it is interest free or if interest is provided at a rate that is lower than the applicable Federal rate (AFR) * * *. Sec. 7872(e)(1)(A). If a demand loan is classified as a below-market loan, the lender has interest income (foregone interest) equal to the difference between (1) the interest that would have accrued on the loan using the AFR as the interest rate and (2) any actual interest payable on the loan. Sec. 7872(e)(2). The parties are treated as though, on the last day of each calendar year, the lender transferred an amount equal to the foregone interest to the borrower and the borrower repaid this amount as interest to the lender. Sec. 7872(a).

During the construction phase of each project, petitioner made loans to the Tators. Prior to the completion of construction and the preparation of the [repayment] schedules, the Tators did not pay interest on these loans. Therefore, we conclude that the loans are below-market demand loans.

Petitioner contends that even if the requirements of section 7872 are met, a temporary regulation provides that section 7872 is not applicable, because the loans' interest arrangements have no significant effect on any Federal tax liability of the lender or the borrower. See sec. 7872(i)(1)(C); sec. 1.7872–5T(b)(14), Temporary Income Tax Regs. To determine whether a loan lacks a significant tax effect, all facts and circumstances should be considered including the following factors: (1) Whether the items of income and deduction generated by the loan offset each other; (2) the amount of such items; (3) the cost to the taxpayer of complying with the provisions of section 7872 if such section were applied; and (4) any nontax reasons for deciding to structure the transaction as a below-market loan rather than a loan with interest at a rate equal to or greater than the applicable Federal rate and a payment by the lender to the borrower. Sec. 1.7872–5T(c)(3), Temporary Income Tax Regs.

Petitioner contends that if section 7872 applies, the Tators would be entitled to claim an interest expense deduction equal to the interest they are deemed to have paid petitioner, and as a result, the items of income and deduction offset each other. Implicit in this contention is the assumption that the temporary regulation permits the borrower's reduction in tax from the interest deduction to offset the lender's increase in tax from the interest income. Petitioner has misinterpreted the scope of the exception. Because section 7872(i)(1)(C) and the temporary regulation refer to the tax liability of the "lender *or* the borrower", the factors must be applied separately to each taxpayer.

The following example illustrates this point. In the case of a below-market demand loan from a corporation to a shareholder, the corporation is treated as transferring to the shareholder, and the shareholder is treated as paying to the corporation, an amount equal to the foregone interest. The deemed transfer from the corporation to the shareholder is treated as a distribution, which generally is taxed as a dividend to the shareholder. Secs. 61(a)(7), 301(c)(1). The shareholder generally may deduct the deemed interest payment to the corporation. H. Conf. Rept. 98–861, at 1013 (1984). The shareholder's income from the deemed dividend and the shareholder's deduction for the deemed payment of interest may offset each other within the meaning of the temporary regulation. The corporation, on the other hand, is subject to tax on the foregone interest but is not entitled to a deduction for the deemed distribution it made to the shareholder. Therefore, it has no deduction to offset the interest income from the loan. Similarly, petitioner has interest income but is not entitled to a deduction for the deemed distribution it made to the Tators. As a result, petitioner's reliance on the exception is misplaced.

Accordingly, we hold that petitioner, pursuant to section 7872, has interest income from below-market loans it made to its shareholders.

Notes

1. *Corporation-shareholder loans.* The KTA-TATOR case involved a below-market, demand loan made by a corporation to the shareholders who owned all the stock of the corporation. Section 7872 applies to such a loan. See IRC § 7872(c)(1)(C). Assume that the annual amount of foregone interest was $10,000. Because § 7872 applies, the following two *fictional* transfers of the foregone interest are treated as occurring for tax purposes:

    1) the corporation is treated as transferring the $10,000 to the shareholder as a dividend (IRC § 7872(a)(1)(A)); and

    2) the shareholder (borrower) is deemed to retransfer the $10,000 back to the corporation (lender) as a payment of interest on the loan (IRC § 7872(a)(1)(B)).

What are the tax consequences of the first fictional transfer to the shareholder and the corporation? What are the tax consequences of the second fictional transfer to the corporation and the shareholder?

2.   *Deductibility of imputed interest.* The KTA-TATOR court states the following: "The shareholder generally may deduct the deemed interest payment to the corporation." Under what circumstances may an individual deduct the deemed interest payment on a below market loan to which § 7872 applies under current law? See IRC § 163(h).

3.   *Employer-employee loans.* Review Example 14-A. The first fictional transfer in Example 14-A results in $500 of gross income to Employee and a $500 deduction to Employer (assuming the compensation is reasonable). The second fictional transfer results in $500 of gross income to Employer and a $500 deduction to Employee (assuming the interest expense is allowed as a deduction under IRC § 163(h)). If both of the fictional transfers in Example 14-A resulted in gross income for one taxpayer and a corresponding deduction for the other taxpayer, might the taxpayers argue that the loan should be exempt from the application of § 7872 because its terms have "no significant effect on any Federal tax liability of the lender or the borrower"? See IRC § 7872(i)(1)(C). The KTA-TATOR court rejected this argument in the case of a below market, *corporation-shareholder loan.* Might a court be more receptive to the argument in the case of a below market, *employer-employee loan*?

4.   *Gift loans.* Assume that Parent makes a no-interest, demand loan to Child and that the annual foregone interest is $2,000. IRC § 7872 likely applies to the loan because the loan is a "gift loan" unless Parent and Child are engaged in a commercial relationship (i.e., Child is Parent's employee). See IRC §§ 7872(c)(1)(A), (f)(3). In the case of a gift loan, the following two *fictional* transfers of the $2,000 of foregone interest are treated as occurring for tax purposes:

1)   the parent is treated as transferring the $2,000 to the child as a gift (IRC § 7872(a)(1)(A)); and

2)   the child (borrower) is deemed to retransfer the $2,000 back to the parent (lender) as a payment of interest on the loan (IRC § 7872(a)(1)(B)).

What are the tax consequences of the first fictional transfer to the child and the parent? What are the tax consequences of the second fictional transfer to the parent and the child? In the case of a below market, *gift loan* can it be argued that § 7872 has "no significant effect on any Federal tax liability of the lender or the borrower"?

WORTH NOTING
De minimus exceptions. IRC § 7872 normally applies only if the aggregate amount of loans between a borrower and a lender exceed $10,000. See IRC §§ 7872(c)(2), (3).

■ **PROBLEM 14-1.** *Below market loans.* Lender lends $100,000 to Borrower at an annual interest rate of 1%. The loan is a demand loan. The applicable Federal rate at the time the loan is made is 6%. What are the tax consequences to Lender and to Borrower under each of the following alternatives?

a) Lender is Borrower's uncle.

b) Lender is Borrower's employer.

c) Lender is a closely-held corporation (i.e., the stock of the corporation is owned by members of a family and/or a relatively small number of unrelated shareholders) and Borrower owns 10% of the stock of Lender. See Proposed Reg. § 1.7872–4(d)(2).

d) Lender and Borrower are unrelated parties.

e) In any of the above situations, might a compelling argument be made that § 7872 has "no significant effect on any Federal tax liability of the lender or the borrower"?

B. Original Issue Discount

Even in the absence of a formal loan, an element of foregone interest arguably exists any time a taxpayer must wait to receive money to which she is entitled without being compensated for the time value of money. For example, assume a landowner sells land to a buyer for $1,000,000 but the entire purchase price is to be paid three years after the date of the sale. Because the seller must wait three years to receive her money, the tax law causes a portion of the purchase price to be treated as interest under a set of statutory rules referred to as the "original issue discount" (OID) rules. See IRC §§ 1271–1275.

The OID rules are complex and apply to a wide range of transactions where a market rate of interest is not explicitly stated. The discussion in this Chapter merely illustrates the general effect of the OID rules in one common situation to which they apply; namely, the sale of property with deferred payments that do not provide for a market rate of interest. To enable students to appreciate the impact of the OID rules on the tax consequences of a deferred payment transaction, the following example will first delineate the tax consequences in the absence of the OID rules and then illustrate how the OID rules change the tax consequences.

■ **EXAMPLE 14-B.** *Original issue discount rules.* Rachel purchased a piece of land many years ago for $100,000. On January 1, Year 1, she sells the land to Jeremy for $1,000,000. The $1,000,000 is payable on January 1, Year 4. No interest is provided for in the agreement of sale.

A. Tax Consequences in Absence of OID Rules

Rachel

Realization Event at Time of Sale

Amount Realized	$1,000,000
Adjusted Basis	100,000
Realized Gain	$900,000

Recognition Deferred Until January 1, Year 4—See IRC § 453.

Summary:

	Gain From Sale	Interest Income
Year 1	0	0
Year 2	0	0
Year 3	0	0
Year 4	$900,000	0
Total	$900,000	0

Jeremy

Basis at Time of Purchase: $1,000,000—See IRC § 1012.

Summary:

	Interest Deduction
Year 1	0
Year 2	0
Year 3	0
Total	0

B. Present Value of Deferred Payment

For the sake of computational simplicity, assume that the market rate of interest is 10% on January 1, Year 1 (the date of sale). If the market interest rate is 10% and no interest is provided for in the sales agreement, the purported $1,000,000 purchase price to be paid in three years has a present value of approximately $750,000. In other words, the right to receive $1,000,000 in three years when the market interest rate is 10% is economically equivalent to the immediate receipt of $750,000. This conclusion can be demonstrated by considering how much money one would have at the end of three years if one deposited $750,000 at the beginning of the first year, earned a market interest rate (assumed to be 10% per year) on that deposit, and added the interest to the deposit (rather than withdrawing the interest from the account).

	Balance at Beg. of Year	Interest Earned (10%)	Balance at End of Year
Year 1	$750,000	$75,000	$825,000
Year 2	$825,000	$83,000 (rounded)	$908,000
Year 3	$908,000	$92,000 (rounded)	$1,000,000
Year 4	$1,000,000		

Because the present value of Rachel's deferred payment obligation is $750,000, the OID rules treat the purchase price of the land as being only $750,000. The remaining $250,000 is treated as interest that accrues over the three year period between the date of sale (January 1, Year 1) and the date of payment of the $1,000,000 (January 1, Year 4).

C. Tax Consequences of OID Rules

The mechanics for applying the OID rules are highly technical and beyond the scope of this casebook. The following illustrates the general concept and does not strive for technical accuracy.

Rachel

Realization Event at Time of Sale

Amount Realized	$750,000
Adjusted Basis	100,000
Realized Gain	$650,000

Recognition Deferred Until January 1, Year 4—See IRC § 453.

Summary:

	Gain From Sale	Interest Income
Year 1	0	$75,000
Year 2	0	$83,000
Year 3	0	$92,000
Year 4	$650,000	0
Total	$650,000	$250,000

Jeremy

Basis at Time of Purchase: $750,000—See IRC § 1012.

Summary:

	Interest Deduction
Year 1	$75,000
Year 2	$83,000
Year 3	$92,000
Total	$250,000

NOTES

1.   *Impact of OID rules on timing.* In Example 14-B, the seller (Rachel) derives $900,000 of total income, regardless of whether the OID rules apply. To the extent the OID rules reclassify purchase price as interest, however, her income is accelerated. Thus, without the OID rules, Rachel has $900,000 of income in Year 4. With the OID rules, $250,000 of that income is accelerated to Years 1–3 (even though Rachel receives no payments in those years). Conversely, the OID rules accelerate the buyer's (Jeremy's) deductions. Without the OID rules, Jeremy cannot deduct any part of his $1,000,000 basis in the land until he sells the land (because land is not eligible for depreciation as it is not a wasting asset). With the OID rules, however, $250,000 of deductions are accelerated to Years 1–3.

2.   *Impact of OID rules on characterization.* In addition to accelerating the seller's income, the OID rules often increase the rate of tax that applies to the amount of the seller's income that is treated as interest. Generally, the gain on the sale of the land in Example 14-B is likely to be characterized as "capital gain" and taxed at a much lower rate than the seller's other income, such as interest income. (The characterization of certain income as capital gain and the lower tax rates that apply to such income will be explored in Chapter 16.) Thus, not only do the OID rules accelerate the tax on $250,000 of the seller's income in Example 14-B, they are also likely to cause a higher rate of tax to be imposed on the accelerated income than would otherwise be the case.

3.   *Combined impact of OID rules on seller and buyer.* The portion of the purchase price that the OID rules treat as interest has opposite effects on the seller and the buyer. Specifically, any amount treated as interest is normally includible in income by the seller and deductible by the buyer in the same tax year. If both

seller and buyer pay tax at the same rate, the OID rules will not increase the total amount of tax revenue collected from seller and buyer. Nevertheless, the OID rules change the tax liability of each of the parties to reflect more accurately the economics of the arrangement.

SYNTHESIS

If a lender refrains from charging the borrower a market rate of interest, IRC § 7872 often applies. When IRC § 7872 applies to a below market demand loan or a gift loan, the provision creates two fictional transfers.

The first fictional transfer treats the foregone interest as being transferred from lender to borrower in the capacity that is causing the lender to bestow the benefit on the borrower. If the first fictional transfer constitutes a gift, it is excluded by the borrower and not deductible to the lender. If the first fictional transfer represents compensation for services, it constitutes gross income to the borrower under IRC § 61(a)(1) and may be deducted by the lender under IRC § 162(a)(1) to the extent the compensation is reasonable. If the first fictional transfer represents a dividend, it constitutes gross income to the borrower under IRC § 61(a)(7) but is not deductible to the lender.

Regardless of the capacity in which the first fictional transfer occurs, a second fictional transfer treats the amount of foregone interest as transferred from the borrower to the lender as a payment of interest. The second fictional transfer triggers gross income to the lender under IRC § 61(a)(4). It triggers a deduction to the borrower only if an actual payment of interest would satisfy IRC § 163(h).

In the absence of a formal loan, an element of foregone interest arguably exists any time a taxpayer must wait to receive money to which she is entitled without being compensated for the time value of money. A common example is when property is sold for deferred payments but a market rate of interest is not explicitly charged to the buyer. In these circumstances, the original issue discount rules treat part of the purchase price as interest, notwithstanding the absence of a formal loan.

 Test Your Knowledge: To assess your understanding of the material in this chapter, <u>click here</u> to take a quiz.

PART V

Impact of Tax Rates

Progressive Tax Rates

Overview

In a "flat rate" tax system, all income is taxed at the same rate. As such, no incentive exists to shift income from one taxpayer to another because the same amount of tax is imposed on every dollar of income, regardless of the taxpayer. The United States has utilized a "progressive rate" tax system since the advent of the modern income tax in 1913. Rather than applying a single rate of tax to all taxable income, a progressive rate system applies different tax rates to different levels of income. Specifically, a relatively low rate of tax is imposed on the lowest amounts of taxable income and progressively higher tax rates apply to larger amounts of taxable income. A progressive rate system creates an incentive for high-income taxpayers to shift income to related, lower-income taxpayers to reduce the amount of tax imposed on such income.

Chapter 15 will explore the following topics:

1) the application of progressive tax rates to unmarried individuals,

2) the impact of progressive tax rates on marriage,

3) the manner in which high-income taxpayers have attempted to shift income to related, lower income taxpayers, and

4) the mechanism Congress has employed to deter the shifting of income to children.

A. Application of Progressive Tax Rates to Unmarried Individuals—§ 1(j)(2)(C)

In 2018, the taxable income of unmarried individuals was taxed as follows pursuant to IRC § 1(j)(2)(C):

Taxable Income	Tax Rate
0–$9,525	10%
$9,526–$38,700	12%
$38,701–$82,500	22%
$82,501–$157,500	24%
$157,501–$200,000	32%
$200,001–$500,000	35%
$500,001 and above	37%

■ **EXAMPLE 15-A.** *Calculating tax liability of an unmarried individual.* In 2018, Marla had taxable income of $60,000. Based on the tax rates that applied to unmarried individuals in 2018, Marla's income tax liability can be determined as follows:

Tax on the first $9,525 of taxable income:	$9,525 × 10% =	$952.50
Tax on the next $29,175[1] of taxable income:	$29,175 × 12% =	$3,501.00
Tax on the next $21,300[2] of taxable income:	$21,300 × 22% =	$4,686.00
Total Tax		$9,139.50

To enable taxpayers to determine their income tax liability without performing multiple calculations, the Internal Revenue Service publishes tables each year that provide the cumulative total tax for all the different tax rates that apply to a given taxpayer. The following Tax Table applied to unmarried individuals in 2018 (IRC § 1(j)(2)(C)):

---

[1]   The second row of the table above Example 15-A indicates that taxable income ranging from $9,526–$38,700 is taxed at a 12% rate. Marla's taxable income ($60,000) exceeds $38,700. Thus, the amount of Marla's income taxed at 12% is $38,700 – $9,525 = $29,175.

[2]   The third row of the table above Example 15-A indicates that taxable income ranging from $38,701 to $82,500 is taxed at a 22% rate. Thus, Marla's taxable income above $38,700 is taxed at a 22% rate. Marla has $60,000 of taxable income. Therefore, the amount of Marla's income taxed at 22% is $60,000 – $38,700 = 21,300.

SECTION 1(j)(2)(C)—UNMARRIED INDIVIDUALS

If Taxable Income Is:	The Tax Is:
Not over $9,525	10% of taxable income
Over $9,525 but not over $38,700	$952.50, plus 12% of the excess over $9,525
Over $38,700 but not over $82,500	$4,453.50, plus 22% of the excess over $38,700
Over $82,500 but not over $157,500	$14,089.50, plus 24% of the excess over $82,500
Over $157,500 but not over $200,000	$32,089.50, plus 32% of the excess over $157,500
Over $200,000 but not over $500,000	$45,689.50, plus 35% of the excess over $200,000
Over $500,000	$150,689.50, plus 37% of the excess over $500,000

In light of this table, in Example 15-A, Marla's 2018 tax liability can be determined with a single calculation, rather than three calculations. One simply locates the row that applies to her total taxable income (the third row: Taxable Income "over $38,700 but not over $82,500") which indicates that her tax is "$4,453.50 plus 22% of the excess over $38,700." Thus, the following calculation determines her tax liability:

$$\$4,453.50 + [22\% \times (\$60,000 - \$38,700)] =$$
$$\$4,453.50 + [22\% \times (\$21,300)] =$$
$$\$4,453.50 + \$4,686 = \$9,139.50.$$

Not surprisingly, the calculation of Marla's tax liability using the Table in § 1(j)(2)(C) yields the same outcome (a tax liability of $9,139.50) as the three calculations in Example 15-A.

WORTH NOTING The rate table that applied to unmarried individuals in 2018 was delineated in the Tax Cuts and Jobs Act (P.L. 115–97). See IRC § 1(j)(2)(C). The range of income to which each tax rate applies is adjusted upward each year to account for the impact of inflation. See IRC § 1(f). The Treasury Department issues new tax tables each year to reflect the inflation adjustments. However, the Code is not amended each year to reflect the new rate schedules. Thus, this casebook will utilize the rate tables in effect in 2018 because the 2018 rate tables currently appear in the Code. See IRC § 1(j)(2). To compute the actual income tax liability of an individual in a given year, one must use the rate tables in effect for that year.

B. Impact of Progressive Tax Rates on Marriage—§ 1(j)(2)(A)

In the case of married individuals who file a joint tax return, the range of taxable income to which each income tax rate applies is different from the range for unmarried individuals. In 2018, the taxable income of unmarried individuals and married couples was taxed as follows:

Unmarried Individuals (§ 1(j)(2)(C))		Married Couples (Joint Return) (§ 1(j)(2)(A))	
Taxable Income	Tax Rate	Taxable Income	Tax Rate
0–$9,525	10%	0–$19,050	10%
$9,526–$38,700	12%	$19,051–$77,400	12%
$38,701–$82,500	22%	$77,401–$165,000	22%
$82,501–$157,500	24%	$165,001–$315,000	24%
$157,501–$200,000	32%	$315,001–$400,000	32%
$200,001–$500,000	35%	$400,001–$600,000	35%
$500,001 and above	37%	$600,001 and above	37%

Note that individuals who are married may *not* use the Tax Table for Unmarried Individuals after the marriage occurs.

WORTH NOTING   An option exists for each married individual to file a separate tax return and use a "Married, Filing Separate Returns" Tax Table. See IRC § 1(j)(2)(D). However, that option is rarely exercised because the "Married, Filing Separate Returns" Tax Table imposes greater tax burdens on most married couples than the "Married, Filing Joint Return" table.

As in the case of unmarried individuals, the Internal Revenue Service publishes a Table each year that provides the cumulative total tax for all applicable tax rates that apply to a married couple filing a joint return. The following Tax Table applied to most married couples in 2018 (IRC § 1(j)(2)(A)):[3]

---

[3]   The tax table that applied to married couples filing joint returns in 2018 was delineated in the Tax Cuts and Jobs Act (P.L. 115–97). See IRC § 1(j)(2)(A). The range of income to which each tax rate applies is adjusted upward each year to account for the impact of inflation. See IRC § 1(f). The Treasury Department issues new tax tables each year to reflect the inflation adjustments. The Code is not amended each year, however, to reflect the new rate schedules. Thus, this casebook will utilize the rate tables in effect in 2018 because the 2018 rate tables are currently reflected in the Code. To compute the actual income tax liability of an individual in a given year, one must use the rate tables in effect for that year.

SECTION 1(j)(2)(A)—MARRIED INDIVIDUALS FILING JOINT RETURNS

If Taxable Income Is:	The Tax Is:
Not over $19,050	10% the taxable income
Over $19,050 but not over $77,400	$1,905, plus 12% of the excess over $19,050
Over $77,400 but not over $165,000	$ 8,907, plus 22% of the excess over $77,400
Over $165,000 but not over $315,000	$28,179, plus 24% of the excess over $165,000
Over $315,000 but not over $400,000	$64,179, plus 32% of the excess over $315,000
Over $400,000 but not over $600,000	$91,379, plus 35% of the excess over $400,000
Over $600,000	$161,379, plus 37% of the excess over $600,000

Because different tax tables apply to unmarried individuals (IRC § 1(j)(2)(C)) and married individuals (IRC § 1(j)(2)(A)), marriage will sometimes *increase* the total tax liability of two formerly unmarried individuals (a "marriage penalty"). Other times, marriage will *decrease* the total tax liability of two formerly unmarried individuals (a "marriage bonus"). Whether marriage increases a couples' tax or decreases a couples' tax often depends on the total amount of income the couple earns, and whether the couple consists of two roughly equivalent income earners or one primary income earner.

■ **EXAMPLE 15-B.** *Tax liability of two, unmarried earners vs. a two-earner married couple.*

a) *Two, unmarried earners:* Nisa and her fiancé, Jordan are single individuals who live together. Each had taxable income of $150,000 in 2018. Nisa's 2018 income tax liability is computed using the fourth row of the Tax Table for Unmarried Individuals (IRC § 1(j)(2)(C)) as follows:

$14,089.50 + [24% × ($150,000 – $82,500)] =
$14,089.50 + [24% × $67,500] =
$14,089.50 + $16,200 = $30,289.50.

Because Jordan's taxable income was also $150,000 in 2018, his 2018 income tax liability is also $30,289.50. Their combined income tax liability for 2018 is **$60,579** ($30,289.50 × 2).

b) *Two-earner married couple:* If, instead of remaining single in 2018, Nisa and Jordan married before the end of 2018, their combined taxable income is $300,000. Their 2018 income tax liability is computed using the fourth row of the Tax Table for Married Individuals Filing Joint Returns (IRC § 1(j)(2)(A)) as follows:

$$\$28,179 + [24\% \times (\$300,000 - \$165,000)] =$$
$$\$28,179 + [24\% \times \$135,000] =$$
$$\$28,179 + \$32,400 = \mathbf{\$60,579}$$

If Nisa and Jordan married in 2018, their combined tax liability remains exactly the same: **$60,579**. Thus, there is no "marriage penalty" in this situation. As will be demonstrated in Problem 15-1, however, a marriage penalty would have existed if Nisa and Jordan had each earned more than $300,000 of income.

■ **EXAMPLE 15-C.** *Tax liability of one, unmarried earner vs. a one-earner married couple.*

a) *One single earner.* Lauren and her fiancé, Eric, are single individuals who live together. Lauren had taxable income of $300,000 in 2018. Lauren's 2018 income tax liability is computed using the sixth row of the Tax Table for Unmarried Individuals (IRC § 1(j)(2)(C)) as follows:

$$\$45,689.50 + [35\% \times (\$300,000 - \$200,000)] =$$
$$\$45,689.50 + [35\% \times \$100,000] =$$
$$\$45,689.50 + \$35,000 = \$80,689.50$$

Eric had no taxable income in 2018. Therefore, Lauren's and Eric's combined tax liability for 2018 is **$80,689.50**.

b) *One-earner married couple:* If, instead of remaining single in 2018, Lauren and Eric married before the end of 2018, their combined taxable income is $300,000, the same as Nisa and Jordan in part b) of Example 15-B. Thus, Lauren's and Eric's income tax liability if they married is **$60,579**.

If Lauren and Eric married in 2018, their combined tax liability would *decrease* from **$80,689.50** to **$60,579**. The $20,110.50 difference is their "marriage bonus."

■ **PROBLEM 15-1.** *Higher income couples: impact on marriage penalty and bonus.*

a) In Example 15-B, if Nisa and Jordan each had taxable income in 2018 of $500,000 (instead of $150,000), how much of a marriage penalty would they have incurred if they married in 2018?

b) In Example 15-C, if Lauren had taxable income in 2018 of $1,000,000 (instead of $300,000), how much of a marriage bonus would she and Eric have enjoyed if they married in 2018?

C. Assignment of Income

A progressive rate system imposes increasingly higher tax rates on incrementally higher levels of income. Such a system motivates high-income individuals to attempt to shift income and the corresponding tax burden to related, lower income individuals. The extent to which this objective can be achieved depends largely on whether the income in question is attributable to services performed by the high-income individual or property owned by that person.

1. Income from Services

LUCAS v. EARL

United States Supreme Court, 1930
281 U.S. 111, 50 S.Ct. 241, 74 L.Ed. 731

Mr. Justice Holmes delivered the opinion of the Court.

This case presents the question whether the respondent, Earl, could be taxed for the whole of the salary and attorney's fees earned by him in the years 1920 and 1921, or should be taxed for only a half of them in view of a contract with his wife which we shall mention. The Commissioner of Internal Revenue and the Board of Tax Appeals imposed a tax upon the whole, but their decision was reversed by the Circuit Court of Appeals. A writ of certiorari was granted by this court.

By the contract, made in 1901, Earl and his wife agreed

> that any property either of us now has or may hereafter acquire * * *
> in any way, either by earnings (including salaries, fees, etc.), or any
> rights by contract or otherwise, during the existence of our marriage,
> or which we or either of us may receive by gift, bequest, devise, or
> inheritance, and all the proceeds, issues, and profits of any and all
> such property shall be treated and considered, and hereby is declared
> to be received, held, taken, and owned by us as joint tenants, and not
> otherwise, with the right of survivorship.

The validity of the contract is not questioned, and we assume it to be unquestionable under the law of the State of California, in which the parties lived. Nevertheless we are of opinion that the Commissioner and Board of Tax Appeals were right.

The Revenue Act of 1918 * * * imposes a tax upon the net income of every individual including 'income derived from salaries, wages, or compensation for personal service * * * of whatever kind and in whatever form paid,' § 213(a). * * * A very forcible argument is presented to the effect that the statute seeks to tax only income beneficially received, and that taking the question more technically the salary and fees became the joint property of Earl and his wife on the very first instant on which they were received. We well might hesitate upon the latter proposition, because however the matter might stand between husband and wife he was the only party to the contracts by which the salary and fees were earned, and it is somewhat hard to say that the last step in the performance of those contracts could be taken by anyone but himself alone. But this case is not to be decided by attenuated subtleties. It turns on the import and reasonable construction of the taxing act. There is no doubt that the statute could tax salaries to those who earned them and provide that the tax could not be escaped by anticipatory arrangements and contracts however skillfully devised to prevent the salary when paid from vesting even for a second in the man who earned it. That seems to us the import of the statute before us and we think that no distinction can be taken according to the motives leading to the arrangement by which the fruits are attributed to a different tree from that on which they grew.

Judgment reversed.

Note

No joint returns. The Earl case was decided at a time when each married person filed a separate tax return using the same tax table that applied to unmarried individuals. Under current law, married individuals typically collectively file a joint return. When married individuals file a joint return, what incentive, if any, exists for one spouse to assign income to the other spouse?

 FOR DISCUSSION **Assignment of income from services.** In light of the Earl case, how likely is it that a taxpayer can shift the tax burden on income from services to a related taxpayer who does not perform the services?

COMMISSIONER v. GIANNINI

United States Court of Appeals, Ninth Circuit, 1942
129 F.2d 638

Stephens, Circuit Judge.

[T]he taxpayer * * * was a Director and President of Bancitaly Corporation from 1919 until its dissolution after the tax year in question. From 1919 to 1925 he performed the services of these offices without compensation, and on January 22, 1925, the Board of Directors authorized a committee of three to devise a plan to compensate him, he in the meantime to have the privilege of drawing upon the corporation for his current expenditures.

On April 19th, 1927, the committee reported and on June 27th, 1927, the Directors unanimously approved the report. It was:

> The committee * * * unanimously agreed to, and hereby do, recommend to the directors of the Bancitaly Corporation that Mr. A. P. Giannini, for his services as President of your Corporation, be given 5% of the net profits each year, with a guaranteed minimum of $100,000 per year, commencing January 1, 1927, in lieu of salary.

On November 20, 1927, * * * the salary account on the books of the corporation was debited with the amount of $445,704.20, being the equivalent of 5% of the corporation net profits from January 1, 1927, to July 22, 1927.

In 1927 after the taxpayer learned the amount of the profits from January to July of that year and that he would receive $445,704.20 as his 5% thereof, the taxpayer informed members of the Board of Directors of the corporation that he would not accept any further compensation for the year 1927, and suggested that the corporation do something worth while with the money. The finding of the Board in this respect is that the refusal was "definite" and "absolute", and there is ample evidence in the record to support such finding.

The corporation never credited to the taxpayer or his wife any portion of the 5% of the net profits for the year 1927, other than the $445,704.20 above referred to, nor did it set any part of the same aside for the use of the taxpayer or his wife. [O]n January 20, 1928, the Board of Directors of Bancitaly Corporation adopted a resolution reading in part as follows:

> Whereas, this Corporation is prepared now to pay to Mr. A. P. Giannini for his services as its President and General Manager five per cent (5%) of the net profits of this Corporation computed from July 23, 1927 to the close of business January 20, 1928, which five percent (5%) amounts to the sum of One Million Five Hundred Thousand Dollars ($1,500,000.00); and

> Whereas, Mr. A. P. Giannini refuses to accept any part of said sum but has indicated that if the Corporation is so minded he would find keen satisfaction in seeing it devote such a sum or any lesser adequate sum to the objects below enumerated or kindred purposes; and

> Whereas, we believe that this Corporation would do a great good and derive a great benefit from the establishment of a Foundation of Agricultural Economics at the University of California * * *;

> * * *

> Now, Therefore, Be it Resolved, by the Board of Directors of this Corporation, that the aforesaid sum of One Million Five Hundred Thousand Dollars ($1,500,000.00) * * * be donated to the Regents of the University of California for the purpose of establishing a Foundation of Agricultural Economics; and

Be it Further Resolved, that said donation be made in honor of Mr. A. P. Giannini, and that said Foundation shall be named after him; and

Be it Further Resolved, that a Committee consisting of James A. Bacigalupi, P. C. Hale and A. Pedrini be appointed to confer with the President of the University of California, for the purpose of discussing and determining upon the general scope of said Foundation, and with full power of settling all details in connection therewith; * * *.

In accordance with said resolution the Corporation in February, 1928, submitted a written offer of contribution to the Regents of the University of California, and the offer was accepted. * * *

The taxpayer and his wife in reporting their income for taxation purposes in 1928 did not report any portion of the [$1,500,000] paid to the Regents of the University of California by the Bancitaly Corporation as aforesaid, and it is the Commissioner's contention that one-half of said sum should be reported by each. * * *

The Commissioner's argument in support of the claimed deficiency may be summarized as follows: That actual receipt of money or property is not always necessary to constitute taxable income; that it is the "realization" of taxable income rather than actual receipt which gives rise to the tax; that a taxpayer "realizes" income when he directs the disposition thereof in a manner so that it reaches the object of his bounty; that in the instant case the taxpayer had a right to claim and receive the whole 5% of the corporation profit as compensation for his services; and that his waiver of that right with the suggestion that it be applied to some useful purpose was such a disposition thereof as to render the taxpayer taxable for income "realized" in the tax year in which the suggestion is carried out. * * * [I]t is stated by the Commissioner, "Insofar as the question of taxation is concerned it would not seem to make much difference whether he directed Bancitaly Corporation to pay his compensation to the University of California or whether he merely told his employer to keep it."

[W]e agree that the question of the effect of the taxpayer's unqualified refusal to take the compensation for his services is a question of law subject to review by this court. That question is the sole question presented by this appeal.

The taxpayer, on the other hand, urges that

A person has the right to refuse property proffered to him, and if he does so, absolutely and unconditionally, his refusal amounts to a renunciation of the proffered property, which, legally, is an abandonment of right to the property without a transfer of such right to another. Property which is renounced (i. e. abandoned) cannot be 'diverted' or 'assigned' by the renouncer, and cannot be taxed upon the theory that it was received.

* * *

[T]he findings of the Board, supported by the evidence, are to the effect that the taxpayer did not receive the money, and that he did not direct its disposition. All that he did was to unqualifiedly refuse to accept any further compensation for his services with the suggestion that the money be used for some worth while purpose. So far as the taxpayer was concerned, the corporation could have kept the money. All arrangements with the University of California regarding the donation to the Foundation were made by the corporation, the taxpayer participating therein only as an officer of the corporation.

In this circumstance we cannot say as a matter of law that the money was beneficially received by the taxpayer and therefore subject to the income tax provisions of the statute. * * * To support the Commissioner's argument we should have to hold that only one reasonable inference could be drawn from the evidence, which is that the donation is but a donation of the taxpayer masquerading as a creature of the corporation to save the true donors taxpayer and his wife some tax money. The circumstances do not support this contention. In our opinion the inferences drawn by the Board are more reasonable and comport with that presumption of verity that every act of a citizen of good repute should be able to claim and receive.

Affirmed.

Assignment of income from services. In light of the Giannini case, what conditions must be satisfied for an individual to avoid being taxed on income attributable to services performed by that individual? Does the Giannini case provide a viable method for shifting the tax burden on income from services to a related taxpayer who does not perform the services?

2.   Income from Property

The Earl and Giannini cases focused exclusively on income from services. Those cases did not consider whether the tax burden on income from property might be shifted to a related taxpayer. This question came before the Court in the Horst case, which follows.

HELVERING v. HORST

United States Supreme Court, 1940
311 U.S. 112, 61 S.Ct. 144, 85 L.Ed. 75

Mr. Justice Stone delivered the opinion of the Court.

The sole question for decision is whether the gift, during the donor's taxable year, of interest coupons detached from the bonds, delivered to the donee and later in the year paid at maturity, is the realization of income taxable to the donor.

In 1934 and 1935 respondent, the owner of negotiable bonds, detached from them negotiable interest coupons shortly before their due date and delivered them as a gift to his son who in the same year collected them at maturity. The Commissioner ruled that * * * the interest payments were taxable, in the years when paid, to the respondent donor who reported his income on the cash receipts basis. The circuit court of appeals reversed the order of the Board of Tax Appeals sustaining the tax. We granted certiorari because of the importance of the question in the administration of the revenue laws and because of an asserted conflict in principle of the decision below with that of Lucas v. Earl.

The court below thought that as the consideration for the coupons had passed to the obligor, the donor had, by the gift, parted with all control over them and their payment, and for that reason the case was distinguishable from Lucas v. Earl, where the assignment of compensation for services had preceded the rendition of the services, and where the income was held taxable to the donor.

The holder of a coupon bond is the owner of two independent and separable kinds of right. One is the right to demand and receive at maturity the principal amount of the bond representing capital investment. The other is the right to demand and receive interim payments of interest on the investment in the amounts and on the dates specified by the coupons. Together they are an obligation to pay principal and interest given in exchange for money or property which was presumably the consideration for the obligation of the bond. Here respondent, as owner of the bonds, had acquired the legal right to demand payment at maturity of the interest specified by the coupons and the power to command its payment to others which constituted an economic gain to him.

* * *

[T]he question here is, whether because one who in fact receives payment for services or interest payments is taxable only on his receipt of the payments, he can escape all tax by giving away his right to income in advance of payment. If the taxpayer procures payment directly to his creditors of the items of interest or earnings due him, see Old Colony Trust Co. v. Commissioner, or if he sets up a revocable trust with income payable to the objects of his bounty, Corliss v. Bowers, 281 U.S. 376, 50 S.Ct. 336, 74 L.Ed. 916, he does not escape taxation because he did not actually receive the money.

Underlying the reasoning in these cases is the thought that income is 'realized' by the assignor because he, who owns or controls the source of the income, also controls the disposition of that which he could have received himself and diverts the payment from himself to others as the means of procuring the satisfaction of his wants. The taxpayer has equally enjoyed the fruits of his labor or investment and obtained the satisfaction of his desires whether he collects and uses the income to procure those satisfactions, or whether he disposes of his right to collect it as the means of procuring them.

Although the donor here, by the transfer of the coupons, has precluded any possibility of his collecting them himself he has nevertheless, by his act, procured payment of the interest, as a valuable gift to a member of his family. Such a use of his economic gain, the right to receive income, to procure a satisfaction which can be obtained only by the expenditure of money or property, would seem to be the enjoyment of the income whether the satisfaction is the purchase of goods at the corner grocery, the payment of his debt there, or such non-material satisfactions as may result from the payment of a campaign or community chest contribution, or a gift to his favorite son. Even though he never receives the money he derives money's worth from the disposition of the coupons which he has used as money or money's worth in the procuring of a satisfaction which is procurable only by the expenditure of money or money's worth. The enjoyment of the economic benefit accruing to him by virtue of his acquisition of the coupons is realized as completely as it would have been if he had collected the interest in dollars and expended them for any of the purposes named.

In a real sense he has enjoyed compensation for money loaned or services rendered and not any the less so because it is his only reward for them. To say that one who has made a gift thus derived from interest or earnings paid to his donee has never enjoyed or realized the fruits of his investment or labor because he has assigned them instead of collecting them himself and then paying them over to the donee, is to affront common understanding and to deny the facts of common experience. Common understanding and experience are the touchstones for the interpretation of the revenue laws.

The power to dispose of income is the equivalent of ownership of it. The exercise of that power to procure the payment of income to another is the enjoyment and hence the realization of the income by him who exercises it. * * *

The dominant purpose of the revenue laws is the taxation of income to those who earn or otherwise create the right to receive it and enjoy the benefit of it when paid. The tax laid by the 1934 Revenue Act upon income 'derived from * * * wages, or compensation for personal service, of whatever kind and in whatever form paid * * *; also from interest * * *' therefore cannot fairly be interpreted as not applying to income derived from interest or compensation when he who is entitled to receive it makes use of his power to dispose of it in procuring satisfactions which he would otherwise procure only by the use of the money when received.

It is the statute which taxes the income to the donor although paid to his donee. Lucas v. Earl. [As in the Earl case, * * * the purpose of the statute to tax the income to him who earns, or creates and enjoys it [cannot] be escaped by 'anticipatory arrangements * * * however skillfully devised' to prevent the income from vesting even for a second in the donor.

Nor is it perceived that there is any adequate basis for distinguishing between the gift of interest coupons here and a gift of salary or commissions. The owner of a negotiable bond and of the investment which it represents, if not the lender, stands in the place of the lender. When, by the gift of the coupons, he has separated his right to interest payments from his investment and procured the payment of the interest to his donee, he has enjoyed the economic benefits of the income in the same manner and to the same extent as though the transfer were of earnings and in both cases the import of the statute is that the fruit is not to be attributed to a different tree from that on which it grew.

Reversed.

[Dissenting opinion of three justices omitted.]

NOTES

1.   *Assignment of income from property.* The Horst decision holds that the transfer of income from property does not shift the tax burden on that income. Rather, just as Lucas v. Earl held that income from services is necessarily taxed to the service performer, Horst holds that income from property is taxed to the owner of the underlying property.

2.   *Timing of assigned income.* Note that a *gratuitous* assignment of income from property does not accelerate the time at which the income is taxed. Although Horst remained the taxpayer with respect to the interest coupons when he transferred the coupons to his son, that income would not be taxed to Horst until the interest became payable. In other words, the interest income was not accelerated by the transfer of the interest coupons. By contrast, if Horst had *sold* the interest coupons to his son, he would have been taxed at the time the coupons were sold. See the Stranahan case in Chapter 11.

3.   *Transfer of ownership of income-producing property.* Could Horst have caused his son to be taxed on the interest coupons if Horst had transferred ownership of both the bonds *and* the interest coupons to his son?

IN SIGHTS **Economic consequences of transferring ownership of property to child.** Although parents might be tempted to reduce their income tax liability by transferring ownership of income-producing property to their children, many parents will be reluctant to put children in the position of owning high value property. A parent who is perfectly comfortable with an economic transfer of the *income* from property to a child might not be nearly as comfortable with a transfer of the *entire* property to the child. For example, if

Parent owned $100,000 of bonds that paid $5,000 of interest per year, Parent will normally be hesitant to transfer the $100,000 to the child to achieve the objective of shifting the tax liability on $5,000. Here again, economic considerations should always take priority over tax considerations.

When an individual creates a trust and transfers income-producing property to the trust, the trust is generally treated as a taxpaying entity and is taxed on its income at the rates set forth in IRC § 1(j)(2)(E) (Tax Table for Estates and Trusts). If, however, the person who created the trust (the "grantor") retains too much control over the trust property, the income of the trust will be taxed to the grantor. The Corliss and Clifford cases that follow illustrate this principle.

CORLISS v. BOWERS

Supreme Court of the United States, 1930
281 U.S. 376, 50 S.Ct. 336, 74 L.Ed. 916

Mr. Justice Holmes delivered the opinion of the Court.

This is a suit to recover the amount of an income tax paid by the plaintiff, the petitioner, under the Revenue Act of 1924. * * *

The question raised by the petitioner is whether the [predecessor to IRC § 676] can be applied constitutionally to him upon the following facts. In 1922 he transferred the fund from which arose the income in respect of which the petitioner was taxed, to trustees, in trust to pay the income to his wife for life with remainder over to their children. By the instrument creating the trust the petition reserved power "to modify or alter in any manner, or revoke in whole or in part, this indenture and the trusts then existing, and the estates and interests in property hereby created," etc. It is not necessary to quote more words because there can be no doubt that the petitioner fully reserved the power at any moment to abolish or change the trust at his will. The statute referred to provides that "where the grantor of a trust has, at any time during the taxable year, * * * the power to revest in himself title to any part of the corpus of the trust, then the income of such part of the trust for such taxable year shall be included in computing the net income of the grantor." There can be no doubt either that the statute purports to tax the plaintiff in this case. But the net income for 1924 was paid over to the petitioner's wife and the petitioner's argument is that however it might have been in different circumstances the income never was his and he cannot be taxed for it. The legal estate was in the trustee and the equitable interest in the wife.

But taxation is not so much concerned with the refinements of title as it is with actual command over the property taxed—the actual benefit for which the tax is paid. If a man directed his bank to pay over income as received to a servant or friend, until further orders, no one would doubt that he could be taxed upon the amounts so paid. It is answered that in that case he would have a title, whereas here he did not. But from the point of view of taxation there would be no difference. The title would merely mean a right to stop the payment before it took place. The same right existed here although it is not called a title but is called a power. The acquisition by the wife of the income became complete only when the plaintiff failed to exercise the power that he reserved. Still speaking with reference to taxation, if a man disposes of a fund in such a way that another is allowed to enjoy the income which it is in the power of the first to appropriate it does not matter whether the permission is given by assent or by failure to express dissent. The income that is subject to a man's unfettered command and that he is free to enjoy at his own opinion may be taxed to him as his income, whether he sees fit to enjoy it or not. * * *

Judgment affirmed.

WORTH NOTING

No joint returns. As in Earl, the Corliss case (and the Clifford case which follows) were decided at a time when each married person filed a separate tax return using the same tax table that applied to unmarried individuals. Under current law, married individuals typically collectively file a joint return. No incentive exists for one spouse to assign income to another spouse when the spouses file a joint return.

HELVERING v. CLIFFORD

Supreme Court of the United States, 1940
309 U.S. 331, 60 S.Ct. 554, 84 L.Ed. 788

Mr. Justice Douglas delivered the opinion of the Court.

In 1934 respondent declared himself trustee of certain securities which he owned. All net income from the trust was to be held for the "exclusive benefit" of respondent's wife. The trust was for a term of five years, except that it would terminate earlier on the death of either respondent or his wife. On termination of the trust the entire corpus was to go to respondent, while all "accrued or undistributed net income" and any proceeds from the investment of such net income" was to be treated as property owned absolutely by the wife. During the continuance of the trust respondent was to pay over to his wife the whole or such part of the net income as he in his "absolute discretion" might determine. And during that period he had full power (a) to exercise all voting powers incident to the trusteed shares of stock; (b) to "sell, exchange, mortgage, or pledge" any of the securities under the declaration of trust * * *; (c) to invest "any cash or money in the trust estate or any income therefrom" by loans, secured or unsecured, by deposits in banks, or by purchase of securities or other personal property * * *; (d) to collect all income; (e) to compromise, etc., any claims held by him as trustee; (f) to hold any property in the trust estate in the names of "other persons or in my own name as an individual" except as otherwise provided. * * * And finally it was provided that neither the principal nor any future or accrued income should be liable for the debts of the wife; and that the wife could not transfer, encumber, or anticipate any interest in the trust or any income therefrom prior to actual payment thereof to her.

It was stipulated that while the "tax effects" of this trust were considered by respondent they were not the "sole consideration" involved in his decision to set it up, as by this and other gifts he intended to give "security and economic independence" to his wife and children. It was also stipulated that respondent's wife had substantial income of her own from other sources; that there was no restriction on her use of the trust income, all of which income was placed in her personal checking account, intermingled with her other funds, and expended by her on herself, her children and relatives; that the trust was not designed to relieve respondent from liability for family or household expenses and that after execution of the trust he paid large sums from his personal funds for such purposes.

[D]uring the year 1934 all income from the trust was distributed to the wife who included it in her individual return for that year. The Commissioner, however, determined a deficiency in respondent's return for that year on the theory that income from the trust was taxable to him. The Board of Tax Appeals sustained that redetermination. The Circuit Court of Appeals reversed. We granted certiorari because of the importance to the revenue of the use of such short term trusts in the reduction of surtaxes.

Sec. 22[a] of the Revenue Act of 1934 includes among "gross income" all "gains, profits, and income derived * * * from professions, vocations, trades, businesses, commerce, or sales, or dealings in property, whether real or personal, growing out of the ownership or use of or interest in such property; also from interest, rent, dividends, securities, or the transaction of any business carried on for gain or profit, or gains or profits and income derived from any source whatever." The broad sweep of this language indicates the purpose of Congress to use the full measure of its taxing power within those definable categories. Hence our construction of the statute should be consonant with that purpose. Technical considerations, niceties of the law of trusts or conveyances, or the legal paraphernalia which inventive genius may construct as a refuge from surtaxes should not obscure the basic issue. That issue is whether the grantor after the trust has been established may still be treated, under this statutory scheme as the owner of the corpus. In absence of more precise standards or guides supplied by statute or appropriate regulations, the answer to that question must depend on an analysis of the terms of the trust and all the circumstances attendant on its creation and operation. And where the grantor is the trustee and the beneficiaries are members of his family group, special scrutiny of the arrangement is necessary lest what is in reality but one economic unit be multiplied into two or more by devices which, though valid under state law, are not conclusive so far as § 22(a) is concerned.

In this case we cannot conclude as a matter of law that respondent ceased to be the owner of the corpus after the trust was created. Rather, the short duration of the trust, the fact that the wife was the beneficiary, and the retention of control over the corpus by respondent all lead irresistibly to the conclusion that respondent continued to be the owner for purposes of § 22(a).

So far as his dominion and control were concerned it seems clear that the trust did not effect any substantial change. In substance his control over the corpus was in all essential respects the same after the trust was created, as before. The wide powers which he retained included for all practical purposes most of the control which he as an individual would have. * * * We have at best a temporary reallocation of income within an intimate family group. Since the income remains in the family and since the husband retains control over the investment, he has rather complete assurance that the trust will not effect any substantial change in his economic position. It is hard to imagine that respondent felt himself the poorer after this trust had been executed or, if he did, that it had any rational foundation in fact. For as a result of the terms of the trust and the intimacy of the familial relationship respondent retained the substance of full enjoyment of all the rights which previously he had in the property. That might not be true if only strictly legal rights were considered. But when the benefits flowing to him indirectly through the wife are added to the legal rights he retained, the aggregate may be said to be a fair equivalent of what he previously had. To exclude from the aggregate those indirect benefits would be to deprive § 22(a) of considerable vitality and to treat as immaterial what may be highly relevant considerations in the creation of such family trusts. For where the head of the household has income in excess of normal needs, it may well make but little difference to him (except income-tax-wise) where portions of that income are routed—so long as it stays in the family group. In those circumstances the all-important factor might be retention by him of control over the principal. With that control in his hands he would keep direct command over all that he needed to remain in substantially the same financial situation as before. Our point here is that no one fact is normally decisive but that all considerations and circumstances of the kind we have mentioned are relevant to the question of ownership and are appropriate foundations for findings on that issue. Thus, where, as in this case, the benefits directly or indirectly retained blend so imperceptibly with the normal concepts of full ownership, we cannot say that the triers of fact committed reversible error when they found that the husband was the owner of the corpus for the purposes of § 22(a). To hold otherwise would be to treat the wife as a complete stranger; to let mere formalism obscure the normal consequences of family solidarity; and to force concepts of ownership to be fashioned out of legal niceties which may have little or no significance in such household arrangements.

     * * *

The judgment of the Circuit Court of Appeals is reversed and that of the Board of Tax Appeals is affirmed.

It is so ordered.

* * *

WORTH NOTING

Statutory grantor trust rules. IRC §§ 673–677 now delineate the interests in, and powers over, trust property that will cause a grantor to be taxed on the income generated by that property.

D. Higher Tax Rates on Child's Unearned Income— §§ 1(g), (j)(4)

As the prior section demonstrated, an individual cannot shift the tax on income from property to another without transferring ownership of the underlying property. If the ownership of income-producing property is, in fact, transferred, the transferee will be taxed on all future income generated by the property. Hence, if a high-income parent or grandparent transfers ownership of income-producing property to a child or grandchild, all future income generated by that property will, in fact, be taxed to the child or grandchild. Prior to the enactment of IRC § 1(g), such a transfer could dramatically reduce the tax imposed on that income because the child or grandchild would normally have significantly less taxable income than the parent or grandparent. Consequently, the income generated by the transferred property would be taxed at the lower rates that apply to the child or grandchild.

IRC § 1(g) dramatically reduces the incentive to transfer ownership of income-producing property to a child or grandchild by significantly curtailing the ability to apply a child's tax rate to income from property. IRC § 1(g) generally applies to children under the age of 18 and, in certain circumstances, to students under the age of 24. See IRC § 1(g)(2). IRC § 1(g) does not modify the principle that income from property owned by a child is taxed to the child. However, IRC § 1(g) causes the bulk of the income generated by a child's property to be taxed at the rates that apply to estates and trusts. See IRC §§ 1(j)(4)(A), (B).

SECTION 1(j)(2)(E)—ESTATES AND TRUSTS[4]

If Taxable Income Is:	The Tax Is:
Not over $2,550	10% of taxable income
Over $2,550 but not over $9,150	$255, plus 24% of the excess over $2,550
Over $9,150 but not over $12,500	$1,839, plus 35% of the excess over $9,150
Over $12,500	$3,011.50, plus 37% of the excess over $12,500

■ **EXAMPLE 15-D.** *Tax on child's unearned income.* Prior to 2018, Parents transferred income-producing property to Child, who is under 18. The property generated $9,150 of taxable income in 2018. Child had no other income in 2018. What is Child's 2018 income tax liability?

In the absence of IRC § 1(g), Child's tax liability would be **$915**[5] (see IRC § 1(j)(2)(C)—Tax Table for Unmarried Individuals).

Under IRC § 1(g), as modified by IRC § 1(j)(4), income generated by property owned by Child is still taxed to Child. However, Child's tax is computed under the rate table that applies to estates and trusts. See IRC § 1(j)(2)(E) (Tax Table for Estates and Trusts). Hence, Child's tax liability is **$1,839**.[6] Therefore, IRC § 1(g) increases *Child's* 2018 tax liability by $924 (from $915 to $1,839).

---

[4]   The tax table that applied to estates and trusts in 2018 was delineated in the Tax Cuts and Jobs Act (P.L. 115–97). See IRC § 1(j)(2)(E). The range of income to which each tax rate applies is adjusted upward each year to account for the impact of inflation. See IRC § 1(f). The Treasury Department issues new tax tables each year to reflect the inflation adjustments. The Code is not amended each year, however, to reflect the new rate schedules. Thus, this casebook will utilize the rate tables in effect in 2018 because the 2018 rate tables are currently reflected in the Code. To compute the actual income tax liability of an individual in a given year, one must use the rate tables in effect for that year.

[5] $9,150 taxable income × 10% tax rate = $915.

[6]   See IRC § 1(j)(2)(E) (second row). Tax is $255 + [24% × ($9,150 – $2,550)] =
$255 + [24% × $6,600] =
$255 + $1,584 = $1,839.

This Example ignores the fact that IRC § 1(g) does not impact the tax rate that applies to roughly the first $2,000 of a child's unearned income. See Note 3, below.

Example 15-D reveals that IRC § 1(g) increases Child's tax liability on unearned income. Nevertheless, an incentive may still remain for high-income parents (or grandparents) to transfer ownership of income-producing property to a child to reduce the tax imposed on the income generated by the property. For instance, if Parents, in Example 15-D, had more than $600,000 of taxable income in 2018, they would have been taxed at a 37% rate on any additional income. See IRC § 1(j)(2)(A) (Tax Table for Married Individuals Filing Joint Return). Therefore, if Parents had retained ownership of the income-producing property owned by Child in Example 15-D, they would have been taxed on the $9,150 of income it generated at a rate of 37%. As a result, Parents would have incurred a tax liability of **$3,386** on the $9,150 of income.[7] By transferring ownership of the property to Child, Child is taxed on the $9,150 of income generated by the property but the tax liability of Child is only **$1,839**. Thus, because Child owned the property, the family saved more than $1,500 in tax, notwithstanding the application of IRC § 1(g).[8]

Little tax savings could be achieved by the family, however, to the extent unearned income greater than $9,150 was shifted from high-income Parents to Child. In 2018, the next $3,350 of unearned income (taxable income over $9,150 but not over $12,500) was taxed under IRC § 1(j)(2)(E) at 35%, versus 37% for Parents, yielding a potential tax savings of only $67.[9] Moreover, no tax motivation would have existed to shift unearned income in excess of $12,500 from high-income Parents to Child because unearned income in excess of $12,500 was taxed to Child under IRC § 1(j)(2)(E) at the same 37% tax rate that would otherwise have applied to Parents. Consequently, IRC § 1(g) (as modified by IRC § 1(j)(4)) dramatically reduces the income tax incentive that would otherwise exist for high-income parents and grandparents to transfer ownership of income-producing property to their children or grandchildren.

---

[7] $9,150 × 37% tax rate = $3,385.50.

[8] $3,386 (if taxed to Parents) – $1,839 (if taxed to Child) = $1,547.

[9] $3,350 × 35% = $1,172.50. $3,350 × 37% = $1,239.50. $1,239.50 – $1,172.50 = $67.00

Notes

1. *Earned income of a child.* The higher tax rates imposed by IRC § 1(j)(4)(B) apply only to a child's *unearned* income; those rates do not apply to the earned income of a child. See IRC §§ 1(j)(4)(B)(i)(I), (ii)(I), (iii)(I). Thus, small amounts of income earned by a child from babysitting or shoveling snow are taxed to the child under the table that applies to unmarried individuals (IRC § 1(j)(2)(C)), not the table that applies to estates and trusts (IRC § 1(j)(2)(E)). Similarly, large amounts of income earned by a child who stars in movies are also taxed to the child under the table that applies to unmarried individuals (IRC § 1(j)(2)(C)).

2. *No reduction in child's tax liability.* IRC § 1(g), as modified by IRC § 1(j)(4), will never reduce a child's tax liability. The "shall not be more than" language employed by the statute imposes ceilings on the amount of unearned income to which the rates below the highest (37%) tax rate may apply. See IRC §§ 1(j)(4)(B)(i), (ii), (iii). In no circumstances, however, will the statutory language expand the range of income to which the rates below the highest rate can apply. Thus, the child movie star who earns $1,000,000 from acting and $5,000 of unearned income will pay tax on the unearned income at the maximum rate of 37%.

WORTH NOTING

Limited duration. The current version of IRC § 1(g) applies only to taxable years beginning before January 1, 2026.

3. *Non-application of IRC § 1(g) to small amounts of unearned income.* IRC § 1(g) does not apply to every dollar of unearned income. Rather, it applies only to unearned income in excess of a threshold amount. See IRC §§ 1(g)(4)(A)(ii), (j)(4)(D). In recent years, the threshold amount has been approximately $2,000.[10] The vast majority of children do not have more than $2,000 of unearned income. Thus, IRC § 1(g) only applies to those children who own relatively large amounts of income-producing property.

---

[10] The actual threshold amount in 2018 was $2,100.

■ **EXAMPLE 15-E.** *Application of IRC § 1(g), as modified by IRC § 1(j)(4).* Child who is under age 18, owns income-producing property that generated $7,000 of income in 2018. Child also earned $2,500 for babysitting in 2018. What is Child's 2018 income tax liability? (To simplify the calculation, any standard deduction to which Child is entitled will be ignored and the threshold amount of unearned income not subject to IRC § 1(g) will be rounded to $2,000.)

Child had $9,500 of taxable income ($7,000 of unearned income and $2,500 of earned income) in 2018. In the absence of IRC § 1(g), Child would have had a 2018 tax liability of **$950** ($9,500 × 10% = $950). See IRC § 1(j)(2)(C).

As a result of IRC § 1(g), as modified by IRC § 1(j)(4)(B)(i), however, only $7,050 of Child's income is taxed at 10%. This amount is the sum of:

    1) "the earned taxable income" (IRC § 1(j)(4)(B)(i)(I)), and

    2) "the minimum taxable income for the 24% bracket in the table under paragraph (2)(E)" (IRC § 1(j)(4)(B)(i)(II).

As to 1), the "earned taxable income" is the taxable income ($9,500) reduced by the "net unearned income" ($7,000 unearned income – $2,000 rounded threshold amount (see Note 3)). Thus, the "earned taxable income" is **$4,500** ($9,500 – $5,000).

As to 2), "the minimum taxable income for the 24% bracket in the table under paragraph (2)(E)" is **$2,550**.

Thus, only $7,050 of the Child's income is taxed at the 10% rate ($4,500 + $2,550 = $7,050). The remaining $2,450 of unearned income is taxed at the 24% rate under IRC § 1(j)(2)(E).

Accordingly, Child's 2018 tax liability is as follows:

$$\begin{array}{rl} \$7,050 \times 10\% = & \$705 \\ + \$2,450 \times 24\% = & \underline{\$588} \\ \text{Total} & \mathbf{\$1,293} \end{array}$$

Consequently, IRC § 1(g), as modified by IRC § 1(j)(4)(B), **increased** Child's 2018 tax liability **from $950 to $1,293.**

■ **PROBLEM 15-2.** *Impact of IRC § 1(g), as modified by IRC § 1(j)(4), on child with high amount of earned income.* Same facts as Example 15-E, except that Child is a performer who earned $500,000 in 2018, rather than a babysitter who earned $2,500. What is Child's 2018 Federal income tax liability?

SYNTHESIS

A progressive rate system imposes increasingly higher tax rates on incrementally higher levels of an individual's income. Such a system motivates high-income taxpayers to attempt to shift income and the corresponding tax burden to related, lower income taxpayers. It is virtually impossible for a taxpayer to shift income derived from services because such income is taxed to the service performer. By contrast, income from property is taxed to the owner of the property. Thus, if a high-income taxpayer transfers ownership of property to a related, lower income taxpayer, future income generated by the property will be taxed to the lower income taxpayer. Of course, transferring ownership of property has significant economic implications—once the related taxpayer owns the property, the transferor cannot reclaim the property regardless of the future behavior of the transferee. Here again, economic considerations generally outweigh tax considerations.

Under current law, no tax incentive exists to transfer income-producing property to a spouse because married couples normally combine their income on a joint tax return. By contrast, children (and grandchildren) are treated as taxpayers separate from their parents (and grandparents). Thus, an incentive would normally exist for parents (and grandparents) to transfer income-producing property to their children (and grandchildren) to reduce the tax burden on future income from such property (subject, of course, to the economic implications of such a transfer). Congress, however, has severely constrained the tax savings that can be derived from this conduct by limiting the amount of a child's unearned income that will be taxed at the lower tax rates that apply to an unmarried individual.

 Test Your Knowledge: To assess your understanding of the material in this chapter, <u>click here</u> to take a quiz.

Characterization

Overview

All gross income is not taxed alike. Certain gains from dealings in property (IRC § 61(a)(3) income) may be characterized as "capital gains" and taxed at a lower tax rate than other income ("ordinary income"). Similarly, certain losses from dealings in property may be characterized as "capital losses" and, as a result, are subject to restrictions that do not apply to other deductions ("ordinary deductions"). Chapter 16 will address the following topics:

1) how capital gains and capital losses are taxed,

2) what conditions must be satisfied for a recognized gain to be characterized as a capital gain, or a recognized, allowed loss to be characterized as a capital loss,

3) how most dividend income is taxed at capital gains rates, and

4) how capital gains and other investment income of high-income taxpayers is subject to an additional 3.8% Medicare contribution tax.

A. Taxation of Capital Gains and Losses

Chapter 6 focused on "gains derived from dealings in property." See IRC § 61(a)(3). There, you learned that a mere increase in the value of property does not trigger gross income until a sale or exchange of the property (a "realization event") occurs. When a realization event occurs, potential § 61(a)(3) income is quantified as follows:

Realization Event
 Amount Realized
 <u>– Adjusted Basis</u>
 Realized Gain

In Chapter 12, you learned that a realized gain is recognized (taxed immediately), unless a deferred recognition or non-recognition provision applies. See IRC § 1001(c).

Not all realization events result in a realized gain. A realized loss occurs when property with an adjusted basis in excess of its value is sold or exchanged. A realized loss is recognized (potentially deductible), unless a non-recognition provision applies. See IRC § 1001(c). In addition to being recognized, a realized loss must be allowed as a deduction under IRC § 165(c) in order for an individual to deduct the loss.

With regard to both a recognized gain, and a recognized, allowed loss, the final step in the analysis is determining the "characterization" of the gain or loss. Specifically, is the gain (or loss) characterized as a capital gain (or a capital loss)? If not, it will be treated under the default rule as ordinary income (or an ordinary deduction).

IN SIGHTS

Adding characterization to § 61(a)(3) analysis.
Characterization is the final step in the unique analysis that applies to § 61(a)(3) income. Specifically, when "gain property" (i.e., property with a fair market value in excess of basis) is transferred, the following analysis should be employed:

Realization Event	(IRC § 1001(a))
Amount Realized	(IRC § 1001(b))
– Adjusted Basis	(IRC § 1016)
Realized *Gain*	
Recognition	(IRC § 1001(c))
Characterization	(IRC §§ 1221, 1222)

The same analysis applies to "loss property" (i.e., property with a basis in excess of fair market value); however, the loss must also be allowed as a deduction. Thus, the following analysis should be employed when loss property is transferred:

Realization Event	(IRC § 1001(a))
Amount Realized	(IRC § 1001(b))
− Adjusted Basis	(IRC § 1016)
Realized *Loss*	
Recognition	(IRC § 1001(c))
Allowance	(IRC § 165(c))
Characterization	(IRC §§ 1221, 1222)

Capital Gains. "Long-term" capital gains are gains recognized on the sale of certain assets *held for more than one-year.* See IRC § 1222(3). Long-term capital gains of high-income individuals are taxed at a maximum rate of 20%.[1] See IRC § 1(h)(1)(D).[2] "Short-term" capital gains recognized with respect to the sale of certain assets *held for a year or less* (see IRC § 1222(1)) are taxed at ordinary income rates.

■ **EXAMPLE 16-A.** *Long-term capital gains.* Anthony, an unmarried individual, has $500,000 of ordinary income, and $10,000 of capital gains recognized with respect to the sale of assets held for more than one-year. The long-term capital gains are taxed at a rate of 20%. If they were taxed instead as ordinary income, a 37% tax rate would apply because of the amount of Anthony's other (ordinary) income. See IRC § 1(j)(2)(C).

■ **EXAMPLE 16-B.** *Short-term capital gains.* Same facts as Example 16-A, except that the $10,000 of capital gains are recognized with respect to the sale of assets held for one-year or less. Because the capital gains are short-term, they are not eligible for the 20% tax rate. Instead, Anthony's capital gains are added to his other (ordinary) income and taxed at a rate of 37%. See IRC § 1(j)(2)(C).

Note

Justification for reduced tax rate on long-term capital gains. Commentators have advanced a myriad of justifications for the favorable tax treatment of long-term capital gains. Some have argued that taxing these gains at lower tax rates is appropriate because gain from the sale of a long-held asset "bunches" income that accrued over multiple years into a single year (the year of sale). If ordinary income rates applied to this type of a gain, it would be taxed at a higher marginal rate than if the gain were spread evenly over the years that the asset was owned. Thus, the lower capital gains rates are seen as compensating for this bunching of income into a single tax year.

Others have argued that taxing gains from long-held assets at ordinary income rates would intensify a "lock-in" effect, the phenomenon that any tax imposed on the sale of an asset will deter taxpayers from selling the asset. The lower tax rates that apply to long-term capital gains are seen as mitigating this lock-in effect.

Another popular argument in support of favorable tax treatment for long-term capital gains focuses on the fact that a portion of the gain realized on the sale of a long-held asset is attributable to inflation (i.e., price increases). Many believe that it is inappropriate to impose any tax on the portion of the gain attributable to inflation because that element does not reflect a true increase in the seller's purchasing power. Taxing the entire gain from such an asset at a reduced tax rate arguably compensates for the tax imposed on the portion of the gain attributable to inflation.

Others believe lower capital gains rates will induce taxpayers to make investments that stimulate the economy. Whether these arguments or others are sufficiently compelling to justify the lower tax rates that apply to long-term capital gains has long been a subject of spirited debate.

Holding Periods. To determine whether a capital gain is "long-term" or "short-term," the taxpayer's holding period must be measured. Generally, the holding period of an asset begins on the day *following* the date the asset is acquired and includes the day the asset is sold. See Rev. Rul. 66–7, 1966–1 C.B. 188.

■ **EXAMPLE 16-C.** *Holding period of an asset.* If Jordan purchases an asset on May 25 of Year 1, and recognizes a gain when he sells the asset on May 25 of Year 2, the gain would be a short-term gain. In this situation, his holding period begins on May *26* of Year 1 (the day *following* the date he acquires the asset) and includes May 25 of Year 2 (the day he sells the asset). Consequently, he holds the asset for exactly one year resulting in a short-term gain.

To have a long-term gain, the asset must be held for *more than* a year (i.e., at least one year and one day). If rather than selling the asset on May 25 of Year 2, Jordan waits one more day and sells the asset on May 26 of Year 2, his gain will be a long-term gain. In this situation, his holding period still begins on May 26 of Year 1 (the day following the date he acquires the asset) but it includes May 26 of Year 2 (the day he sells the asset). Consequently, he holds the asset for more than a year (in this case, a year and a day) resulting in a long-term gain.

Capital Losses. Just as gains recognized with respect to the sale of certain assets are characterized as capital gains, losses that are recognized and allowed with respect to the sale of certain assets are characterized as capital losses. Like capital gains, capital losses are divided into long-term capital losses (if the asset is held for more than a year) and short-term capital losses (if the asset is held for one year or less). See IRC §§ 1222(2), (4).

Capital Gains in Excess of Capital Losses. In any tax year in which an individual's capital gains exceed the individual's capital losses, the capital losses may be applied only against the capital gains (and not against the individual's ordinary income). Specifically, the 20% tax rate that applies to long-term capital gains of high-income individuals is imposed on the individual's "adjusted net capital gain." See IRC § 1(h)(1)(D). To determine an individual's adjusted net capital gain in a given tax year, her long-term capital gains for the year are reduced by her long-term capital losses. See IRC §§ 1222(7), (11). Her long-term capital gains will be further reduced by her short-term capital losses (to the extent that her short-term capital losses exceed her short-term capital gains). In other words, if an individual has short-term capital losses in excess of short-term capital gains, the excess short-term capital losses will reduce the individual's long-term capital gains to which the 20% tax rate would otherwise apply. See IRC §§ 1222(6), (11).

■ **EXAMPLE 16-D.** *Capital gains in excess of capital losses.* In Year 1, Sander has $20,000 of long-term capital gains and $15,000 of long-term capital losses. Sander has no short-term capital gains and no short-term capital losses. Because Sander's long-term capital gains exceed Sander's long-term capital losses by $5,000, only $5,000 of Sander's long-term capital gains is subject to a maximum tax rate of 20%.

If Sander also had $3,000 of short-term capital gains and $4,000 of short-term capital losses in Year 1, his short-term capital losses would exceed his short-term capital gains by $1,000. This excess $1,000 short-term capital loss would further reduce Sander's long-term capital gains so that only $4,000 of Sander's long-term capital gains would be subject to a maximum tax rate of 20% (rather than $5,000).

Capital Losses in Excess of Capital Gains. In any tax year in which an individual's capital losses exceed the individual's capital gains, the capital losses may only be deducted to the extent of the capital gains plus $3,000. See IRC § 1211(b). If an individual's capital losses exceed the individual's capital gains by more than $3,000, the additional capital losses are not allowed as a deduction in the current year. However, these unallowed capital losses may be carried to future years and allowed as a deduction if sufficient capital gains are recognized in future years to permit the deduction of the carried capital losses. See IRC § 1212(b).

■ **EXAMPLE 16-E.** *Capital losses in excess of capital gains.* In Year 1, Charlotte has capital gains of $20,000 and capital losses of $33,000. In Year 1, she can deduct only $23,000 of her capital losses ($20,000 of which are applied against her $20,000 of capital gains and the additional $3,000 of capital losses are applied against her ordinary income). The remaining $10,000 of Year 1 capital losses are carried to Year 2 and treated as capital losses incurred in Year 2.

In Year 2, Charlotte has $6,000 of capital gains and no capital losses, other than the $10,000 of capital losses carried over from Year 1. She can thus deduct $9,000 of capital losses in Year 2 ($6,000 of which are applied against her Year 2 capital gains and $3,000 of which are applied against her Year 2 ordinary income). The remaining $1,000 of Year 1 capital losses that she could not deduct in Year 2 are carried to Year 3 and treated as capital losses incurred in Year 3.

■ **PROBLEM 16-1.** *Capital gains in excess of capital losses.* In Year 1, Donna has $200,000 of long-term capital gains and $150,000 of long-term capital losses. Donna has no short-term capital gains or short-term capital losses. What amount of Donna's long-term capital losses may she deduct in Year 1, and how much of Donna's Year 1 income is subject to a maximum tax rate of 20%?

■ **PROBLEM 16-2.** *Capital losses in excess of capital gains.* Same facts as Problem 16-1, except that instead of having $150,000 of long-term capital losses, Donna has—

a) $202,000 of long-term capital losses, or

b) $250,000 of long-term capital losses.

■ **PROBLEM 16-3.** *Long-term capital gains versus short-term capital gains.* How do the answers to Problem 16-1 and Problem 16-2 change if, instead of having $200,000 of long-term capital gains, Donna has no long-term capital gains in Year 1 and $200,000 of short-term capital gains in that year.

B. Characterization as Capital Gain or Capital Loss

Two requirements normally must be satisfied for a gain (or loss) to be characterized as a capital gain (or a capital loss):

1)   property must be transferred in a transaction that constitutes a "sale or exchange," and

2)   the property transferred must be a "capital asset."

See IRC §§ 1222(1)–(4) (each definition requires "the sale or exchange" of a "capital asset").

1.   Sale or Exchange Requirement

A "sale or exchange" must occur for a gain or loss recognized with respect to the transfer of a capital asset to be characterized as a capital gain or a capital loss. It is normally easy to make this determination, although exceptional cases do exist.

KENAN v. COMMISSIONER

United States Court of Appeals, Second Circuit, 1940
114 F.2d 217

Before Swan, Augustus N. Hand, and Chase, Circuit Judges.

Augustus N. Hand, Circuit Judge.

The testatrix, Mrs. Bingham, died on July 27, 1917, leaving a will under which she placed her residuary estate in trust and provided in item "Seventh" that her trustees should pay a certain amount annually to her niece, Louise

Clisby Wise, until the latter reached the age of forty, "at which time or as soon thereafter as compatible with the interests of my estate they shall pay to her the sum of Five Million ($5,000,000.00) Dollars." The will provided in item "Eleventh" that the trustees, in the case of certain payments including that of the $5,000,000 under item "Seventh", should have the right "to substitute for the payment in money, payment in marketable securities of a value equal to the sum to be paid, the selection of the securities to be substituted in any instance, and the valuation of such securities to be done by the Trustees and their selection and valuation to be final."

Louise Clisby Wise became forty years of age on July 28, 1935. The trustees decided to pay her the $5,000,000 partly in cash and partly in securities. The greater part of the securities had been owned by the testator and transferred as part of her estate to the trustees; others had been purchased by the trustees. All had appreciated in value during the period for which they were held by the trustees, and the Commissioner determined that the distribution of the securities to the niece resulted in capital gains which were taxable to the trustees * * *. On this basis, the Commissioner determined a deficiency of $367,687.12 in the income tax for the year 1935.

The Board overruled the objections of the trustees to the imposition of any tax and * * * confirmed the original deficiency determination. The taxpayers contend that the decision of the Board was erroneous because they realized neither gain from the sale or exchange of capital assets nor income of any character by delivering the securities to the legatee pursuant to the permissive terms of the will. The Commissioner contends that gain was realized by the delivery of the securities * * *.

The amount of gain is to be determined under [the predecessor to IRC § 1001], which provides:

(a) Computation of gain or loss. The gain from the sale or other disposition of property shall be the excess of the amount realized therefrom over the adjusted basis * * *.

(b) Amount realized. The amount realized from the sale or other disposition of property shall be the sum of any money received plus the fair market value of the property (other than money) received.

* * *

In support of their petition the taxpayers contend that the delivery of the securities of the trust estate to the legatee was a donative disposition of property pursuant to the terms of the will, and that no gain was thereby realized. They argue that when they determined that the legacy should be one of securities, it became for all purposes a bequest of property, just as if the cash alternative had not been provided, and not taxable for the reason that no gain is realized on the transfer by a testamentary trustee of specific securities or other property bequeathed by will to a legatee.

We do not think that the situation here is the same as that of a legacy of specific property. The legatee was never in the position occupied by the recipient of specific securities under a will. She had a claim against the estate for $5,000,000, payable either in cash or securities of that value, but had no title or right to the securities, legal or equitable, until they were delivered to her by the trustees after the exercise of their option. She took none of the chances of a legatee of specific securities or of a share of a residue that the securities might appreciate or decline in value between the time of the death of the testator and the transfer to her by the trustees, but instead had at all times a claim for an unvarying amount in money or its equivalent.

        * * *

In the present case, the legatee had a claim which was a charge against the trust estate for $5,000,000 in cash or securities and the trustees had the power to determine whether the claim should be satisfied in one form or the other. The claim, though enforceable only in the alternative, was * * * a charge against the entire trust estate. If it were satisfied by a cash payment securities might have to be sold on which (if those actually delivered in specie were selected) a taxable gain would necessarily have been realized. Instead of making such a sale the trustees delivered the securities and exchanged them pro tanto for the general claim of the legatee, which was thereby satisfied.

It is said that this transaction was not such a "sale or other disposition" * * * because it was effectuated only by the will of the trustees and not * * * through a mutual agreement between trustee and legatee. [W]e are not inclined to limit thus the meaning of the words "other disposition" * * * or of "exchange" * * *. The word "exchange" does not necessarily have the connotation of a bilateral agreement which may be said to attach to the word "sale." * * *

The Board alluded to the fact that * * * the bequest was fixed at a definite amount in money, that * * * there was no bequest of specific securities * * *, that the rights of the legatee * * * were a charge upon the corpus of the trust, and that the trustees had to part either with $5,000,000 in cash or with securities worth that amount at the time of the transfer. It added that the increase in value of the securities was realized by the trust and benefited it to the full extent, since, except for the increase, it would have had to part with other property * * * Under circumstances like those here, where the legatee did not take securities designated by the will or an interest in the corpus which might be more or less at the time of the transfer than at the time of decedent's death, it seems to us that the trustees realized a gain by using these securities to settle a claim worth $5,000,000 * * *.

It seems reasonably clear that the property was not * * * "acquired by bequest * * * from the decedent." It follows that the fears of the taxpayers that double taxation of this appreciation will result because the legatee will take the basis of the decedent * * * are groundless. It is true that under [the predecessor to IRC § 1014] the basis for property "acquired by bequest, devise, or inheritance" is "the fair market value of such property at the time of such acquisition" and that * * * the date of acquisition has been defined as the date of death of the testator. But the holding of the present case is necessarily a determination that the property here acquired is acquired in an exchange and not "by bequest, devise or inheritance," * * *. The legatee's basis would seem to be the value of the claim surrendered in exchange for the securities * * *.

    * * *

We have already held that a taxable gain was realized by the delivery of the securities. It follows from the reasons that support that conclusion that the appreciation was a capital gain * * *.

    * * *

[I]f the trustees had sold the securities, they would be taxed at capital gain rates. Both the trustees and the Commissioner * * * draw the analogy between the transaction here and a sale, and no injustice is done to either by taxing the gain at the rates which would apply had a sale actually been made and the proceeds delivered to the legatee. * * *

    Orders affirmed.

NOTES

1.   *Realization event.* In Chapter 6, you learned that a realization event normally requires a transfer of property in exchange for a quantifiable benefit. Did the transaction in the Kenan case satisfy this definition of a realization event? Describe the taxpayer's amount realized.

2.   *Characterization.* Explain why the transaction in the Kenan case satisfied the sale or exchange requirement for capital gain characterization.

3.   *Double taxation.* Why did the Kenan court reject the taxpayer's concern that the gain taxed to the estate would also be taxed to the beneficiary when the beneficiary ultimately sold the property?

■   **PROBLEM 16-4.**   *Bequest of property vs. use of property to satisfy bequest.* When Milton died, he owned a parcel of land with a fair market value of $100,000. The fair market value of the land increased to $160,000 between the time of Milton's death and the time the estate distributed the land to Nina, a beneficiary of Milton's estate. What are the tax consequences to Milton's estate and to Nina if—

a)   Milton's Will provides for a specific bequest of the land to Nina?

b)   Milton's Will provides for a bequest of $160,000 to Nina and the executor of the estate transfers the land to Nina to satisfy that bequest?

GALVIN HUDSON v. COMMISSIONER

Tax Court of the United States, 1953
20 T.C. 734

The sole issue is whether the gain realized by petitioners from the settlement of a judgment, which they bought from the residuary legatees of an estate, is ordinary income or capital gain. * * *

FINDINGS OF FACT.

* * *

Petitioners, * * * Galvin Hudson is in the lumber and cooperage business, and Hillsman Taylor is a practicing attorney.

On November 23, 1929, Mary Mallory Harahan obtained a judgment against Howard Cole in the amount of $75,702.12 in the Supreme Court of the State of New York. This judgment will hereinafter be referred to as the Cole judgment.

On June 30, 1943, the petitioners purchased the Cole judgment from the residuary legatees of Mary Mallory Harahan's estate; each petitioner acquired a 50 per cent interest in the judgment. Their aggregate cost of the judgment was $11,004 * * *.

In May 1945 Howard Cole paid petitioners the sum of $21,150 as a full settlement of the judgment against him.

Each of the petitioners reported his profit on the settlement of the Cole judgment for income tax purposes as a long-term capital gain for 1945.

Respondent explained the adjustment to petitioners' net income as follows: It is held that the profits realized on the collection of a judgment from Mr. Howard Cole is taxable as ordinary income. * * *

OPINION.

JOHNSON, JUDGE:

Simply, the issue is whether the gain realized from the settlement of a judgment is ordinary income or capital gain when the settlement was made between the judgment debtor and the assignee or transferee of a prior judgment creditor. Petitioners contend that * * * the gain from the settlement of a judgment [is a capital gain]. Respondent has determined that the gain is ordinary income and taxable as such. There is no question about the bona fides of the transaction, nor is there any disagreement about the fact that the judgment, when entered and transferred, was property and a capital asset. The parties differ, however, on the question of whether there was a 'sale or exchange of a capital asset.' Petitioners, citing authority, define the word 'sale' as follows:

A sale is a contract whereby one acquires a property in the thing sold and the other parts with it for a valuable consideration * * * or a sale is generally understood to mean the transfer of property for money * * *.

Also, 'Sell in its ordinary sense means a transfer of property for a fixed price in money or its equivalent.'

We cannot see how there was a transfer of property, or how the judgment debtor acquired property as the result of the transaction wherein the judgment was settled. The most that can be said is that the judgment debtor paid a debt or extinguished a claim so as to preclude execution on the judgment outstanding against him. In a hypothetical case, if the judgment had been transferred to someone other than the judgment debtor, the property transferred would still be in existence after the transaction was completed. However, as it actually happened, when the judgment debtor settled the judgment, the claim arising from the judgment was extinguished without the transfer of any property or property right to the judgment debtor. In their day-to-day transactions, neither businessmen nor lawyers would call the settlement of a judgment a sale: we can see no reason to apply a strained interpretation to the transaction before us. When petitioners received the $21,150 in full settlement of the judgment, they did not recover the money as the result of any sale or exchange but only as a collection or settlement of the judgment.

It is well established that where the gain realized did not result from a sale or exchange of a capital asset, the gain is not [a capital gain]. * * *

    * * *

Notes

1.   *Realization event.* Did a realization event occur in Hudson? If not, what justification exists for offsetting the amount each taxpayer received by the taxpayer's basis in the judgment? If a realization event did occur, is it reasonable to conclude that no sale or exchange occurred for purposes of characterizing the gain that resulted from the realization event?

2.   *Sale of judgment to anyone else in the world.* If the taxpayer in Hudson had sold the judgment to anyone in the world other than the party against whom

the judgment was rendered, would the taxpayer's gain have been characterized as a capital gain?

3.   *Impact of IRC § 1271.* IRC § 1271(a)(1), enacted long after the Hudson case was decided, provides as follows:

> Amount received by the holder on retirement of any debt instrument shall be considered as amounts received in exchange therefor.

Does IRC § 1271(a)(1) overrule the holding of Hudson?

2.   Capital Asset Requirement—§ 1221

Primary Law: IRC § 1221

(a)   For purposes of this subtitle, the term "capital asset" means property held by the taxpayer (whether or not connected to his trade or business), but does not include—

* * *

In addition to the sale or exchange requirement, the transferred property must constitute a capital asset for the resulting gain or loss to be characterized as a capital gain or a capital loss. The term "capital asset" is broadly defined as "property held by the taxpayer" other than the eight exceptions listed in IRC §§ 1221(a)(1)–(8).

a.   Property vs. Income

The capital asset definition requires that "property" be transferred. As a threshold matter, it must be determined whether that which is being transferred constitutes "property" or merely represents a right to future income.

HORT v. COMMISSIONER

Supreme Court of the United States, 1941
313 U.S. 28, 61 S.Ct. 757, 85 L.Ed. 1168

Mr. Justice Murphy delivered the opinion of the Court.

We must determine whether the amount petitioner received as consideration for cancellation of a lease of realty in New York City was ordinary gross income * * *.

Petitioner acquired the property, a lot and ten-story office building, by devise from his father in 1928. * * * In 1927, * * * the Irving Trust Co. and petitioner's father executed a contract in which the latter agreed to lease the main floor and basement to the former for a term of fifteen years at an annual rental of $25,000 * * *.

In 1933, the Irving Trust Co. found it unprofitable to maintain a branch in petitioner's building. After some negotiations, petitioner and the Trust Co. agreed to cancel the lease in consideration of a payment to petitioner of $140,000. Petitioner did not include this amount in gross income in his income tax return for 1933. * * *

The Commissioner included the entire $140,000 in gross income * * * and assessed a deficiency. The Board of Tax Appeals affirmed. The Circuit Court of Appeals affirmed per curiam. [W]e granted certiorari * * *.

Petitioner apparently contends that the amount received for cancellation of the lease was capital [gain] rather than ordinary income * * *. We cannot agree.

The amount received by petitioner for cancellation of the lease must be included in his gross income [as ordinary income. The predecessor to IRC § 61] expressly defines gross income to include 'gains, profits, and income derived from * * * rent, * * * or gains or profits and income from any source whatever'. Plainly this definition reached the rent paid prior to cancellation just as it would have embraced subsequent payments if the lease had never been canceled. It would have included a prepayment of the discounted value of unmatured rental payments whether received at the inception of the lease or at any time thereafter. * * * That the amount petitioner received resulted from negotiations ending in cancellation of the lease rather than from a suit to enforce it cannot alter the fact that basically the payment was merely a substitute for the rent reserved in the lease. * * *

The consideration received for cancellation of the lease was not a return of capital. We assume that the lease was 'property', whatever that signifies abstractly. * * * Simply because the lease was 'property' the amount received for its cancellation was not a return of capital * * *. Where, as in this case, the disputed amount was essentially a substitute for rental payments * * *, it must be regarded as ordinary income, and it is immaterial that for some purposes the contract creating the right to such payments may be treated as 'property' or 'capital'.

    * * *

We conclude that petitioner must report as [ordinary] gross income the entire amount received for cancellation of the lease. The cancellation of the lease involved nothing more than relinquishment of the right to future rental payments in return for a present substitute payment and possession of the leased premises. * * *

The judgment of the Circuit Court of Appeals is affirmed.

FOR DISCUSSION

Leasehold interest. Is a leasehold interest a capital asset? See IRC § 1221(a). If a tenant were to sell a leasehold interest to a third party, would the tenant's gain be characterized as a capital gain? If so, why did the Supreme Court hold that Hort's income was ordinary income rather than capital gain?

METROPOLITAN BUILDING COMPANY
v. COMMISSIONER

United States Court of Appeals, Ninth Circuit, 1960
282 F.2d 592

Before Hamlin and Merrill, Circuit Judges, and Wollenberg, District Judge.

Merrill, Circuit Judge.

The question presented by this case involves the owner of real property, his lessee and a sublessee. The sublessee wished to enter into a desirable arrangement directly with the owner and to this end to eliminate the intervening interest of the lessee-sublessor. He paid a sum of money to the lessee, in consideration of which the lessee released to the owner, his lessor, all his right and interest under his lease.

The question presented is whether the sum so paid to the lessee is to be regarded entirely as the equivalent of rent owed to the lessee and taxable to the lessee as [ordinary] income or whether it is to be regarded entirely as a sale by the lessee of a capital asset and taxable as capital gain. The Commissioner of Internal Revenue ruled that the payment was the equivalent of rental and taxable as [ordinary] income.

At issue is the amount of tax from Metropolitan Building Company, the lessee, for the taxable year ending June 30, 1953. Following the ruling of the Commissioner, this proceeding was instituted in the Tax Court by Metropolitan for redetermination of deficiencies in income * * * taxes for that year. The Tax Court affirmed the ruling of the Commissioner. Metropolitan has petitioned this Court for review, contending that the payment in question should be held to be capital gain. We have concluded that petitioner is correct in its contention and that the judgment of the Tax Court must be reversed.

The University of Washington owns real estate comprising about four city blocks in the downtown area of Seattle. In 1907 it executed a lease upon this property [with petitioner Metropolitan Building Company] extending to November 1, 1954. * * *

On August 1, 1922, Metropolitan executed a sublease of the greater portion of one city block [with The Olympic, Inc.], extending to October 31, 1954, one day prior to the termination of the main lease. Under the terms of the sublease the sublessee was to construct a hotel upon the leased premises. Rental provided was $25,000.00 a year. * * * The Olympic Hotel was constructed upon the leased premises. * * *

During the year 1952, the University of Washington, as fee owner, was attempting to arrange a long-term disposition of the Olympic Hotel property for the period following the expiration of Metropolitan's lease in November, 1954. To this end the University invited proposals for the lease of the hotel, and a number of highly competitive proposals were submitted * * *.

The proposal made by The Olympic, Inc., offered, at no cost or expense to the University, to procure from Metropolitan a release to the University of all Metropolitan's right, title and interest in and to the Olympic Hotel property under its lease. Olympic then offered the University to take a new lease directly from it for a term of approximately twenty-two years commencing forthwith.

Under this proposal, additional rentals of $725,000.00 would accrue to the University during the period prior to November 1, 1954, which otherwise would not have been forthcoming.

The University was favorably disposed to this proposal and negotiations were undertaken with Metropolitan for the acquisition by the University of Metropolitan's leasehold interest. A letter was written on August 18, 1952, by the Board of Regents of the University to Metropolitan requesting Metropolitan to release to the University its leasehold rights with respect to the Olympic Hotel property. * * *

On September 8, 1952, an agreement was reached between Metropolitan and the State of Washington, acting through the Board of Regents of the University, whereby petitioner conveyed, quitclaimed, assigned and released to the State of Washington all of the right, title and interest of Metropolitan in and to that portion of the leasehold upon which the Olympic Hotel was located. For this assignment and transfer Metropolitan received from The Olympic, Inc., the sum of $137,000.00. The University then proceeded in accordance with its understanding to lease the property to The Olympic, Inc.

* * *

The Commissioner contends that [the $137,000] payment is taxable to Metropolitan as ordinary income. He relies upon Hort v. Commissioner, 1940, 313 U.S. 28, 31 * * *. In that case the petitioner owned a business building, a portion of which had been leased to the Irving Trust Company for a term of fifteen years at $25,000.00 a year. The Trust Company, finding it unprofitable to maintain a branch office at that location, paid the petitioner $140,000.00 for cancellation of the lease.

In that case the Trust Company did not acquire any interest of its lessor. It simply compromised and liquidated its rental obligation under the lease. The sum received by the lessor was in lieu of the rentals which the Trust Company otherwise was obligated to pay and was not compensation for acquisition of any interest of the lessor.

In the case before us, the sums paid to Metropolitan were not simply a discharge of Olympic's obligation to pay rental. They were paid for the purchase of Metropolitan's entire leasehold interest. The case is not one of a liquidation of a right to future income as is Hort, but rather it is one of a disposition of income-producing property itself. The giving up of a lease by a tenant fits the legal requirements of a sale or exchange * * * and a gain realized by the tenant on such a transaction is capital gain. * * *

In [Commissioner of Internal Revenue v. Golonsky, 3 Cir., 1952, 200 F.2d 72, 73] the court stated the problem of the case as follows:

> A tenant in possession of premises under a lease, upon receipt of payment by the landlord, and pursuant to an agreement made with the landlord, 'vacated and surrendered the premises' before the date at which the lease expired.

It was held that the proceeds of the transaction constituted capital gain.

The Commissioner would (and the Tax Court did) distinguish Golonsky upon the ground that in the instant case the consideration passed not from the lessor but from the sublessee, the very party obliged to pay rental to the recipient, and that such consideration represented the amount which the recipient felt it would otherwise have received under the sublease. Further, it is said, the value of the leasehold was fixed and limited by the rentals due under the sublease since the term of the sublease corresponded with that of the lease.

We are not impressed by this proposed distinction. The lease clearly had value over the amount of rentals due by virtue of the fact that its acquisition was of importance to Olympic. Irrespective of the method used by Metropolitan in arriving at the figure of $137,000.00, it is clear that Metropolitan did profit to some extent by the transaction. The Commissioner seems to concede that if the consideration had been paid by the University or if the lease had been assigned to a third party the transaction would have constituted a sale by the lessee.

It is not the person of the payor which controls the nature of the transaction in our view. Rather, it is the fact that the transaction constituted a bona fide transfer, for a legitimate business purpose, of the leasehold in its entirety. It did not constitute a release or transfer only of the right to future income under the sublease and the business purpose of the transaction would not have been met by such a release.

We conclude that the sum of $137,000.00, received by petitioner for release of its leasehold, must be held taxable as capital gain and not as ordinary income.

Reversed and remanded * * *.

Notes

1. *Payment by lessor.* The Metropolitan Building opinion states that the "Commissioner seems to concede that if the consideration had been paid by the University * * * the transaction would have constituted a sale by the lessee." In other words, if Metropolitan's *landlord* had paid Metropolitan to surrender its leasehold interest, it was clear to all parties that Metropolitan's gain would have been characterized as a capital gain. How is this fact pattern (i.e., a landlord paying a lessee to surrender the lessee's leasehold interest) distinguishable from the fact pattern in Hort?

2. *Payment by sublessee.* In the Metropolitan Building case, it was not the landlord who paid Metropolitan Building to surrender its leasehold interest. Rather, Metropolitan Building's lessee (Olympic) made the payment to its lessor (Metropolitan Building). The only difference between Hort and Metropolitan Building is that Metropolitan Building held only a leasehold interest in the underlying property. By contrast, the landlord in Hort held a fee interest in the property. Why did this factual difference result in ordinary income in Hort and capital gain in Metropolitan Building?

---

b.   Inventory Exception—§ 1221(a)(1)

Primary Law: IRC § 1221

(a)   For purposes of this subtitle, the term "capital asset" means property held by the taxpayer (whether or not connected to his trade or business), but does not include—

    (1)   stock in trade of the taxpayer or other property of a kind which would properly be included in the inventory of the taxpayer if on hand at the close of the taxable year, or property held by the taxpayer primarily for sale to customers in the ordinary course of his trade or business;

* * *

WORTH NOTING The reference to "stock in trade" in IRC § 1221(a)(1) does not refer to ownership interests issued by a corporation to its shareholders (i.e., corporate stock). Rather, it refers to goods kept on hand that a business sells to its customers (i.e., inventory).

A "capital asset" is broadly defined as "property held by the taxpayer" other than the eight exceptions listed in IRC §§ 1221(a)(1)–(8). Property is *not* a capital asset when any of the exceptions applies. The first exception involves property held by the taxpayer for sale to customers in the ordinary course of business. IRC § 1221(a)(1). As the Boree and Sugar Land cases that follow reveal, it can be difficult to determine whether this exception to capital asset treatment applies in cases involving the development of real estate.

BOREE v. COMMISSIONER

United States Court of Appeals, Eleventh Circuit, 2016
837 F.3d 1093

Before Martin and Jordan, Circuit Judges, and Coogler,* District Judge.

Coogler, District Judge:

* * *

BACKGROUND

In November 2002, Gregory Boree ("Mr. Boree"), a former logger, * * * doing business as Glen Forest, LLC ("Glen Forest"), acquired 1,892 acres of vacant real property * * * in Baker County, Florida. Glen Forest bought the property for $965 per acre, for a total of $3.2 million, and borrowed much of the funds needed to purchase it. In December 2002, Glen Forest sold one ten-acre parcel of the property to an individual purchaser.

In January 2003, Glen Forest submitted to the Baker County Planning and Zoning Department a conceptual map of a planned residential development

---

*   The Honorable L. Scott Coogler, United States District Judge for the Northern District of Alabama, sitting by designation.

called West Glen Estates, which would consist of more than 100 lots, to be developed and sold in multiple consecutive phases. The following month, the county adopted the proposal and rezoned the West Glen Estates property into ten-acre lots. * * * During 2003, Glen Forest sold approximately fifteen lots located around the perimeter of the West Glen Estates property.

* * *

During [2003 and 2004], Glen Forest engaged in a series of other development activities, including obtaining county approval of the first three phases of development of West Glen Estates, applying for an Environmental Resource Permit, * * * and constructing * * * an unpaved road on the property, at a cost of roughly $280,000. * * * Glen Forest did not have a sales office for West Glen Estates or hire a broker to sell lots, but it did place classified advertisements for the subdivision in local papers from time to time. During 2004, Glen Forest sold approximately twenty-six lots.

Beginning in late 2004, the Baker County Board of Commissioners adopted a series of land use restrictions that affected West Glen Estates. In October 2004, the board adopted a temporary one-year moratorium on the development of non-platted subdivisions. * * * In April 2005, it adopted a requirement that all roads within subdivisions be paved. West Glen Estates was a non-platted subdivision that contained multiple unpaved roads. Mr. Boree testified that complying with the requirement that Glen Forest pave internal roads in West Glen Estates would have cost roughly $7 million.

The Borees assert that in 2005, Glen Forest sold approximately eight lots. * * * Mr. Boree requested an exception for the "whole parcel" of his property to the April 2005 ordinance requiring that roads in subdivisions be paved, but he was unsuccessful.

After his request was denied, Mr. Boree hired a land-use lawyer to pursue a different strategy. His new strategy included a higher-density development plan for West Glen Estates that would justify having to bear the costs of paving the roads imposed by the county's requirements. * * * With his attorney's help, Mr. Boree prepared and submitted applications in May and June 2005 to rezone the West Glen Estates property to accommodate the denser "Planned Unit Development." * * * The attorney, on behalf of Mr. Boree, requested that the county adopt a new land use designation of "rural commercial," never before used in Baker County, for the proposed 10.8 acres of commercial property. The board ultimately adopted the new land use category.

In January 2006, the county adopted a requirement that developers pave certain public roads leading to their subdivisions. Mr. Boree testified that complying with the requirement that Glen Forest pave connecting county roads would have cost an additional $4.4 million. The Borees assert that they did not sell any lots in 2006.

Around that time, the Borees discovered that a successful Miami developer, Adrian Development ("Adrian"), was planning a large-scale development on a parcel of property adjoining the West Glen Estates property. In April 2006, Mr. Boree negotiated a real estate purchase agreement with Adrian, whereby Adrian would purchase nearly all of Mr. Boree's remaining unsold West Glen Estates property, totaling over 1,067 acres, for a price of no less than $9,000 per acre.

In June 2006, Mr. Boree's attorney again appeared before the county board on Mr. Boree's behalf at a public hearing on the rezoning action for the West Glen Estates Planned Unit Development. * * *

In August 2006, the county recommended approval of the West Glen Estates Planned Unit Development, on the condition that Glen Forest pave the private Braxton Road and certain other county roads that transected the property. However, in late September 2006, Glen Forest withdrew the Planned Unit Development proposal and indicated its intent to rezone the West Glen Estates property into 7.5-acre agricultural lots for a "residential subdivision."

On February 6, 2007, Adrian closed the purchase of the remaining West Glen Estates property consisting of 1,067.63 acres for $9,608,670, or roughly $9,500 per acre. The sales agreement referred to the property as "unimproved." * * * One week after the sale, Glen Forest withdrew its pending rezoning application from the county.

In all, between 2002 and 2006, Glen Forest sold approximately sixty lots comprising approximately 600 acres of its original 1,892 acres. During that time period, Glen Forest's only business activities involved sales and development related to the property. * * *

[T]he Borees * * * reported the gain ($8,578,636) from the sale to Adrian as a long-term capital gain, rather than as ordinary income, on their 2007 tax return.

On September 27, 2011, the Commissioner issued the Borees a deficiency notice * * * relating to their 2007 income tax return. Specifically, the Commissioner found that the Borees' income from selling the West Glen Estates property to Adrian should have been characterized as ordinary income, rather than as a capital gain, resulting in a $1,784,242 tax deficiency. * * *

On December 27, 2011, the Borees filed a petition with the Tax Court asking it to redetermine their tax liability * * *. During a two-day bench trial in 2013, the Borees testified that Mr. Boree purchased the West Glen Estates property intending primarily to hold it as an investment and that he sold perimeter lots only to make payments on the debt he incurred to purchase the property. [T]he Tax Court [found that documentary evidence revealed that Mr. Boree's] true intent was to develop the property for sale in the ordinary course of business. The Tax Court explained that the Borees "consistently treated Glen Forest as a business" by such activities as subdividing the West Glen Estates property, building a road, spending significant time and money on zoning activities, and continuing to pursue development activities after the board had adopted the moratoria on unpaved roads. The court added that the Borees consistently represented Glen Forest as a real estate business to the buyers of its property, to the county board, and on their 2005, 2006, and 2007 tax returns. It also noted that between 2002 and 2006, the Borees made frequent and substantial sales of property to customers in the ordinary course of business. * * * The court thus found that the Borees' "actions from the time Glen Forest acquired the [West Glen Estates] property, through the date of the Adrian transaction, reflect their intent to develop [that] property and sell subdivided lots to customers." The Tax Court thus concluded that the Borees were not entitled to capital gains treatment on their 2007 tax return. * * *

The Borees timely appealed.

* * *

[D]ISCUSSION

* * *

The I.R.C. distinguishes between ordinary income and capital gains. "Income representing proceeds from the sale or exchange of a capital asset that a taxpayer holds for over a year is considered a capital gain and is taxed at a favorable rate." *Long v. Comm'r*, 772 F.3d 670, 675 (11th Cir.2014). The purpose behind capital gain treatment is to "ameliorate the hardship of taxation of the entire gain in one year." *Comm'r v. Gillette Motor Transp., Inc.*, 364 U.S. 130, 134 (1960). However, "[o]ther income, or 'ordinary income,' is taxed at a higher rate." *Long*, 772 F.3d at 675. "[T]he term 'capital asset' means property held by the taxpayer (whether or not connected with his trade or business), but does not include . . . property held by the taxpayer primarily for sale to customers in the ordinary course of his trade or business." *Id.* (quoting I.R.C. § 1221(a)(1)). Because capital gains treatment "is an exception from the normal tax requirements of the Internal Revenue Code, the definition of a capital asset must be narrowly applied and its exclusions interpreted broadly." *Corn Prods. Ref. Co. v. Comm'r*, 350 U.S. 46, 52 (1955).

To determine whether property is a "capital asset" within the meaning of § 1221 of the I.R.C., the Fifth Circuit enumerated a list of factors:

> (1) the nature and purpose of the acquisition of the property and the duration of the ownership; (2) the extent and nature of the taxpayer's efforts to sell the property; (3) the number, extent, continuity and substantiality of the sales; (4) the extent of subdividing, developing, and advertising to increase sales; (5) the use of a business office for the sale of the property; (6) the character and degree of supervision or control exercised by the taxpayer over any representative selling the property; and (7) the time and effort the taxpayer habitually devoted to the sales.

United States v. Winthrop, 417 F.2d 905, 909–10 (5th Cir.1969). No factor or combination of factors is controlling. Rather, each case must be decided on its particular facts. Still, the "frequency and substantiality" of sales is the "most important" of these factors. This is because "the presence of frequent sales ordinarily belies the contention that property is being held 'for investment' rather than 'for sale.' "

Despite the Tax Court discussing several of the *Winthrop* factors in reaching the determination that the Borees' 2007 income was ordinary income, and not a capital gain, the Borees nonetheless raise several points on which they assert the court legally and factually erred.

1.   The Tax Court's consideration of the Borees' purpose in holding the property from the time it was acquired until the sale to Adrian in 2007

      * * *

In determining whether property is held for sale in the ordinary course of business within the meaning of § 1221(a)(1) of the I.R.C., considerations include (1) whether the taxpayer was engaged in a trade or business, and if so, what business; (2) whether the taxpayer was holding the property primarily for sale in that business; and (3) whether the sales contemplated by the taxpayer were 'ordinary' in the course of that business. There is no real dispute at this point that prior to the enactment of the county land use restrictions, Glen Forest held the West Glen Estates property for sale in the ordinary course of the business of developing a subdivision. * * *

According to the Borees, however, they abandoned all intent to develop the property after the paving requirements were imposed * * *.

[E]ven if we were to focus only on the Borees' intentions for the property after the land use restrictions were imposed in 2004 and 2005, their actions in the years 2004 through the sale in 2007 [reveal] their true intent to continue to develop the property. When compliance with the moratoria threatened to render the original West Glen Estates development plan unprofitable, Mr. Boree did not passively hold the property in hopes that he could sell it to a buyer at an attractive price, but instead first sought to obtain exceptions to the paving requirements so that his subdivision could proceed. When that was unsuccessful, he hired a land-use attorney and applied to rezone the property for a more densely zoned residential and commercial development that would fund his costs of complying with the new county paving requirements. Indeed, Mr. Boree was successful in persuading the county board to create a new land use designation of "rural commercial," never before used in the county, for part of the Planned Unit Development. * * * Such evidence of strategic and thorough involvement in pursuit of developing the property indicates that the Borees were holding the property for sale in the ordinary course of business right up until they sold it to Adrian, and not merely as an investment property. Not only that, but the Borees continued to sell, or attempt to sell, some lots to individuals after the land use restrictions were first imposed in 2004 * * *. Thus, the Tax Court's factual finding that the Borees "continued to pursue development activities after the board adopted the moratoriums and requirements" was not clearly erroneous.

2.   *The Tax Court's determination that the Borees did not segregate the property ultimately sold to Adrian*

The Borees' second argument is that the Tax Court essentially ignored Mr. Boree's testimony that he always segregated the interior acreage ultimately sold to Adrian from the perimeter lots that Glen Forest regularly sold to individuals, treating the former as an investment asset and the latter as inventory merely to generate funds to pay off his debt.

A taxpayer may hold some property for sale in the ordinary course of business and some for investment, but

> the burden is on the taxpayer to establish that the parcels held primarily for investment were segregated from other properties held primarily for sale. The mere lack of development activity with respect to parts of a large property does not sufficiently separate those parts from the whole to meet the taxpayer's burden.

Suburban Realty Co. v. United States, 615 F.2d 171, 185 (5th Cir. 1980). Whether a taxpayer segregated property for investment as opposed to inventory purposes would appear to be a question of fact, just as is the taxpayer's overall primary purpose for holding the property.

There was no error in the Tax Court's factual determination that the Borees "did not segregate the property sold to Adrian from the rest of the [West Glen Estates] property." The Borees argue that they never platted the large interior parcel and that the sales agreement with Adrian described it as "unimproved," but all of the maps and development plans for West Glen Estates that the Borees originally provided to the Baker County Board of Commissioners included all of the acreage, and nowhere set aside or separated out the acreage later sold to Adrian from the ten-acre lots that were sold to individuals over the years. * * * Early maps of the project envisioned the entire property divided into ten-acre lots, and Mr. Boree sought an exemption from the county paving requirements for the "whole parcel." Later, the plans for the Planned Unit Development encompassed the entire acreage, undermining Mr. Boree's argument that he changed his primary purpose in holding the property after the county required paving.

3.   The Tax Court's alleged failure to consider that the Borees' gain resulted solely from market appreciation

The Borees next argue that the Tax Court erred in failing to find dispositive the fact that their $8 million profit in 2007 was due to the property appreciating in value over a substantial period of time and was not reflective of any improvements made to the property or other efforts on the part of Glen Forest in conducting ordinary business activities. However, the Fifth Circuit rejected the notion that just because an increase in property value is attributable more to market appreciation than to improvements made to the property, that the taxpayer is automatically entitled to capital gains treatment. * * * The Borees' fortuitous sale of their property to Adrian in 2007 was not entitled to capital gains tax treatment simply because the property had appreciated in value, when the sale arose from their engaging in the ordinary course of the business of developing real estate.

* * *

As we do not find any of the Borees' arguments in support of reversal meritorious, the Tax Court's determination of their tax liability will be affirmed.

* * *

IN SIGHTS **Justification for § 1221(a)(1) exception.** The issue of characterization of a gain arises only in connection with § 61(a)(3) income ("gains derived from dealings in property"). All other classes of gross income under IRC § 61 are simply taxed as ordinary income. Income derived from inventory and property held for sale to customers in the ordinary course of business is *not* within the scope of IRC § 61(a)(3). Rather, such income is "gross income derived from business" under IRC § 61(a)(2). Thus, you should not be surprised that inventory and other property held for sale to customers in the ordinary course of business is excluded from the definition of a capital asset.

Although the Borees could not convince the court that the real estate in question was a capital asset, the taxpayers in the Sugar Land case were more fortunate.

SUGAR LAND RANCH DEVELOPMENT, LLC
v. COMMISSIONER

United States Tax Court, 2018
T.C. Memo. 2018–21

Thornton, Judge: * * *

FINDINGS OF FACT

[Sugar Land Ranch Development, LLC (SLRD)] was established as a Texas limited liability company on February 27, 1998. It was formed principally to acquire contiguous tracts of land in Sugar Land, Texas, just southwest of Houston, and to develop that land into single-family residential building lots and commercial tracts. On or about March 18, 1998, SLRD purchased approximately 883.5 acres. * * *

The property had formerly been an oil field and was west of, and adjacent to, the Riverstone Master-Planned Community (Riverstone Community), which was being developed by parties related to SLRD. SLRD's original plan was to clean up the property and subdivide it into residential units for inclusion in the Riverstone Community. To that end, between 1998 and 2008 SLRD capped oil wells, removed oil gathering lines, did some environmental cleanup, built a levee, and entered into a development agreement with the City of Sugar Land, Texas, which specified the rules that would apply to the property, should it be developed.

SLRD sold or otherwise disposed of relatively small portions of the property between 1998 and 2008. The 824.7 acres SLRD continued to own as of 2008 were contiguous * * *.

The land * * * consisted of four large parcels. The westernmost parcel * * * was eventually conveyed to the City of Sugar Land. The remaining three parcels (comprising * * * a total of approximately 580.2 acres) were sold to a major homebuilder, Taylor Morrison of Texas, Inc. (Taylor Morrison), in * * * 2012. We will refer to these parcels as TM-1, TM-2, and TM-3 (collectively, the TM parcels).

Late in 2008 the managers of SLRD—Larry Johnson and Lawrence Wong—decided that SLRD would not attempt to subdivide or otherwise develop the property it held. From their long experience in the real estate development business, they believed that SLRD would be unable to develop, subdivide, and sell residential and commercial lots from the property because of the effects of the subprime mortgage crisis on the local housing market and the scarcity or unavailability of financing for housing projects in the wake of the financial crisis. Instead, Messrs. Johnson and Wong decided that SLRD would hold the property as an investment until the market recovered enough to sell it off. These decisions were memorialized in a "Unanimous Consent" document dated December 16, 2008 (signed by Messrs. Johnson and Wong), as well as in an SLRD member resolution adopted on November 19, 2009, to further clarify SLRD's policy.

Between 2008 and 2012 the TM parcels "just sat there" (as Mr. Johnson credibly testified); that is, SLRD did not develop those parcels in any way. SLRD did not list the TM parcels with any brokers or otherwise market the parcels because SLRD's managers believed that there was no market for large tracts of land on account of the subprime mortgage crisis.

In 2011 Taylor Morrison approached SLRD about buying [the] TM parcels. SLRD sold [the TM parcels] to Taylor Morrison in [2012].

The TM-2 and TM-3 contracts each called for Taylor Morrison to pay a lump sum to SLRD in 2012 for the largely undeveloped TM-2 and TM-3 parcels. * * *

[T]he net gain at issue in this case represents * * * the lump-sum payments SLRD received in 2012 for the largely undeveloped TM-2 and TM-3 parcels. Respondent has not argued, nor does the record suggest, that the lump sums SLRD received in 2012 represent payment for anything other than the fair market value of the largely undeveloped TM-2 and TM-3 parcels.

After commencing the sale of the TM parcels, SLRD decided to close out its property holdings by conveying the remainder of its property to related parties * * * in four sales in 2012, 2013, 2014, and 2016. These parcels were * * * 86.9, 12.1, 32, and 2.2 acres, respectively. These parcels were ultimately included in the Riverstone Community and appear to have been developed by parties related to SLRD.

The record contains SLRD's Forms 1065, U.S. Return of Partnership Income, for 2005, 2006, and 2012. On these three returns, SLRD stated that its principal business activity was "Development" and that its principal product or service was "Real Estate". On its 2012 Form 1065 SLRD reported an $11,086,640 capital gain from its sale of the TM-2 parcel and a $1,569,393 capital loss from its sale of the TM-3 parcel. [No gain or loss was apparently realized on the TM-1 parcel.] [R]espondent determined that the aggregate net income from these two transactions should be taxed as ordinary income.

OPINION

* * *

The issue presented is whether SLRD's sales of the TM-2 and TM-3 parcels should be treated as giving rise to capital gains or ordinary income. A capital asset is "property held by the taxpayer (whether or not connected with his trade or business)" but excludes, among other things, "inventory" and "property held by the taxpayer primarily for sale to customers in the ordinary course of his trade or business". Sec. 1221(a)(1).

The Court of Appeals for the Fifth Circuit—the court to which this case is appealable * * *—has held that the three principal questions to be considered in deciding whether gain is capital in character are: (1) "[W]as taxpayer engaged in a trade or business, and, if so, what business?" (2) "[W]as taxpayer holding the property primarily for sale in that business?" And (3) "[W]ere the sales contemplated by taxpayer 'ordinary' in the course of that business?" Suburban Realty Co. v. United States, 615 F.2d 171, 178 (5th Cir. 1980).

The Court of Appeals for the Fifth Circuit has also indicated that various factors may be relevant to these inquiries: the frequency and substantiality of sales of property; the taxpayer's purpose in acquiring the property and the duration of ownership; the purpose for which the property was subsequently held; the extent of developing and improving the property to increase the sales revenue; the use of a business office for the sale of property; the extent to which the taxpayer used advertising, promotion, or other activities to increase sales; and the time and effort the taxpayer habitually devoted to the sales. Frequency and substantiality of sales is the most important factor.

I.   Capital Character of Net Gains From Sales

The parties agree that SLRD was formed to engage in real estate development—specifically, to acquire the property and develop it into single-family residential building lots and commercial tracts. The record supports this conclusion: SLRD's tax returns, the development agreement, SLRD's formation documents, and the testimony of Messrs. Johnson and Wong all clearly show that SLRD originally intended to be in the business of selling residential and commercial lots to customers.

But the evidence also clearly shows that in 2008 SLRD ceased to hold its property primarily for sale in that business and began to hold it only for investment. SLRD's partners decided not to develop the property any further, and they decided not to sell lots from those parcels. This conclusion is supported by the highly credible testimony of Messrs. Johnson and Wong and by the 2008 unanimous consent and the 2009 member resolution. In fact, from 2008 on SLRD did not develop or sell lots from those parcels (and the evidence does not suggest that SLRD ever sold even a single residential or commercial lot to a customer at any point in its existence). Respondent concedes that SLRD never subdivided the property.

More particularly, when the TM parcels were sold, they were not sold in the ordinary course of SLRD's business: SLRD did not market the parcels by advertising or other promotional activities. SLRD did not solicit purchasers for the TM parcels, nor does any evidence suggest that SLRD's managers or members devoted any time or effort to selling the property; Taylor Morrison approached SLRD. Most importantly, sale of the TM parcels was essentially a bulk sale of a single, large, and contiguous tract of land * * * to a single seller—clearly not a frequent occurrence in SLRD's ordinary business.

Because the Taylor Morrison parcels were held for investment and were not sold as part of the ordinary course of SLRD's business, we hold that net gains from the sales of TM-2 and TM-3 were capital in character.

II.   Respondent's Arguments

Respondent argues that the extent of development of the TM parcels shows that these properties were held primarily for sale in the ordinary course of SLRD's business. We are not persuaded. It is clear that from 1998 to sometime before 2008 SLRD developed the property to a certain extent. But it is also clear that in 2008 SLRD's managers decided not to develop those parcels into a subdivision and decided not to market the land as it ordinarily would have. As the Court of Appeals for the Fifth Circuit held in Suburban Realty, 615 F.2d at 184, a taxpayer is "entitled to show that its primary purpose changed to, or back to, 'for investment.' " SLRD has made such a showing. Any development activity that occurred before the marked change in purpose in 2008 * * * is largely irrelevant.

Respondent also argues that the frequency of sales, along with the nature and extent of SLRD's business, shows that gains from the sale of the TM parcels should be ordinary in character. But SLRD's sales were infrequent, and the extent of SLRD's business was extremely limited. After 2008 SLRD disposed of its entire property in just nine sales over eight years (not counting conveyances to the City of Sugar Land, for which SLRD received no consideration). Byram v. United States, 705 F.2d 1418, 1425 (5th Cir. 1983) (holding that although the taxpayer made 22 sales over a three-year period, the taxpayer did not hold the property for sale). Moreover, the TM parcels had not been developed into a subdivision when they were sold, and little or no development activity occurred on those parcels for at least three years before sale.

* * *

Next, respondent points out that, on its 2012 Form 1065, SLRD listed its principal business activity as "Development" and its principal product or service as "Real Estate". Although this circumstance may count against petitioners to some limited degree, we believe that these statements "are by no means conclusive of the issue." See Suburban Realty, 615 F.2d at 181. Considering the record as a whole, we are inclined to believe that these stock descriptions were inadvertently carried over from earlier returns.

Finally, on brief respondent asserts in passing that a stipulated schedule of SLRD's capitalized expenses shows that SLRD "continued to incur development expenses up until it sold the Taylor Morrison land." But the record as a whole clearly shows that the TM parcels were not developed between 2008 and the sale to Taylor Morrison, and respondent concedes that SLRD never subdivided the TM parcels (or any of its property). Also, most of the post-2008 expenditures on the schedule of capitalized expenditures are either consistent with investment intent or appear to have been incurred with respect to parcels other than the TM parcels. For these reasons we accord the listing of capitalized expenses little weight—certainly not enough to override the factors in SLRD's favor, such as the infrequency of sales by SLRD (which is the most important factor in our analysis, see Suburban Realty, 615 F.2d at 178).

Therefore, on the basis of all the evidence, we conclude that SLRD was not engaged in a development business after 2008 and held the TM-2 and TM-3 properties as investments. Accordingly, we hold that SLRD properly characterized the gains and losses from the sales of these properties as income from capital assets.

IN PRACTICE

Importance of form. The Sugar Land court relied on the 2008 unanimous consent and the 2009 member resolution in reaching the conclusion that the taxpayer ceased to hold its property primarily for sale to customers several years before the sale of the property (and then held the property for investment). The court's reliance on these items demonstrates how important it is for the taxpayer's counsel to contemporaneously document any change in the taxpayer's relation to its property. The taxpayer's counsel apparently did not communicate this change to the taxpayer's return preparer, however, in light of the incorrect description of the property that appeared on the 2012 tax return. Although the court was willing to overlook this inconsistency, its presence highlights that it is critical for a business lawyer to identify all parties whose actions could impact the client's tax position and take responsibility for keeping them informed of any changes to the status quo.

3. Property Used in a Trade or Business—§§ 1221(a)(2), 1231

Primary Law: IRC § 1221

(a) For purposes of this subtitle, the term "capital asset" means property held by the taxpayer (whether or not connected to his trade or business), but does not include—

* * *

(2) property, used in his trade or business, of a character which is subject to the allowance for depreciation provided in section 167, or real property used in his trade or business;

* * *

The definition of "capital asset" includes all property other than eight exceptions delineated in the statute. See IRC §§ 1221(a)(1)–(8). The preceding part of this Chapter examined the first exception to capital asset treatment for inventory or property held for sale to customers in the ordinary course of business. IRC § 1221(a)(1). This part will explore the second exception to capital asset treatment for—

1)   depreciable property used in a trade or business, and

2)   real property used in a trade or business.

IRC § 1221(a)(2).

Although counter-intuitive, the exclusion of property used in a trade or business from the capital asset definition actually can result in a more favorable tax treatment of gains and losses triggered by the sale of such property than capital asset treatment would yield. In the case of a capital asset, long-term gains are taxed at lower rates than ordinary income. However, capital losses are subject to restrictions on deductibility that do not apply to ordinary losses. By contrast, gains and losses from property used in a trade or business held for more than one year potentially enjoy the best of both worlds under IRC § 1231.

When property to which IRC § 1231 applies ("section 1231 property") is sold or exchanged in a transaction that results in a recognized gain, the gain is referred to as a "section 1231 gain." IRC § 1231(a)(3)(A)(i). When section 1231 property is sold or exchanged in a transaction that results in a recognized, allowed loss, the loss is referred to as a "section 1231 loss." IRC § 1231(a)(3)(B). If the taxpayer's section 1231 gains for the taxable year *exceed* her section 1231 losses for the taxable year, both the gains *and the losses* are treated as long-term capital gains and long-term capital losses. IRC § 1231(a)(1). By contrast, if the taxpayer's section 1231 gains for the taxable year *do not exceed* her section 1231 losses for the taxable year, both the gains and the losses are treated as ordinary income and ordinary losses. IRC § 1231(a)(2).

Primary Law: IRC § 1231

(a)

    (1) If—

        (A) the section 1231 gains for any taxable year, exceed

        (B) the section 1231 losses for such taxable year,

    such gains and losses shall be treated as long-term capital gains or long-term capital losses, as the case may be.

    (2) If—

        (A) the section 1231 gains for any taxable year, do not exceed

        (B) the section 1231 losses for such taxable year,

    such gains and losses shall not be treated as gains and losses from sales or exchanges of capital assets.

    (3) For purposes of this subsection—

        (A) The term "section 1231 gain" means—

            (i) any recognized gain on the sale or exchange of property used in the trade or business, * * *

        (B) The term "section 1231 loss" means any recognized loss from a sale or exchange * * * described in subparagraph (A).

    * * *

(b) For purposes of this section—

    (1) The term "property used in the trade or business" means property used in the trade or business, of a character which is subject to the allowance for depreciation provided in section 167, held for more than 1 year, and real property used in the trade or business, held for more than 1 year, which is not—

    * * *

WORTH NOTING

Section 1231 applies only to property held for more than one year. IRC § 1231 applies to property excluded from the definition of a capital asset under IRC § 1221(a)(2), provided the property was owned by the taxpayer for more than one year prior to its disposition. If such property is held for one-year or less, the property is neither a capital asset nor a § 1231 asset. As such, any gain or loss triggered on the sale of such property held for a year or less is an ordinary gain or an ordinary loss.

■ **EXAMPLE 16-F.** *Section 1231 gains and losses.* Jimmy purchased the following assets for use in his trade or business on November 1, Year 1:

	Purchase Price
Land Parcel 1:	$300,000
Land Parcel 2:	$400,000
Land Parcel 3:	$500,000

Jimmy sold the three parcels as follows:

	Date of Sale	Sales Price
Land Parcel 1:	October 15, Year 2	$370,000
Land Parcel 2:	February 1, Year 9	$900,000
Land Parcel 3:	December 1, Year 9	$200,000

Land Parcel 1: This parcel is not a capital asset (due to IRC § 1221(a)(2)) because it is "real property used in a trade or business." Moreover, the parcel is not a section 1231 asset because it was not owned by Jimmy for more than 1 year. Hence, assuming no non-recognition provision applies, Jimmy would recognize $70,000 of ordinary income in Year 2.

Land Parcels 2 and 3: These parcels are not capital assets (due to IRC § 1221(a)(2)) because they are "real property used in a trade or business." However, these assets qualify as section 1231 assets (due to IRC § 1231(b)(1)) because they are real property used in a trade or business held for more than 1 year.

Jimmy realizes a $500,000 gain on the sale of Parcel 2 which, if recognized, is a "section 1231 gain" (IRC § 1231(a)(3)(A)(i)).

Jimmy realizes a $300,000 loss on the sale of Parcel 3 which, if recognized and allowed, is a "section 1231 loss" (IRC § 1231(a)(3)(B)).

Assuming Jimmy has no other section 1231 gains or section 1231 losses in Year 9, his section 1231 gains for the year ($500,000) exceed his section 1231 losses for the year ($300,000). Thus, Jimmy's $500,000 section 1231 gain is characterized as a long-term capital gain and his $300,000 section 1231 loss is characterized as a long-term capital loss.

Alternative Fact: If Jimmy had sold Parcel 2 for $600,000 (rather than $900,000), Jimmy would have realized (and presumably recognized) a $200,000 section 1231 gain on the sale of Parcel 2. In this situation, Jimmy's section 1231 gains for the year ($200,000) would *not* exceed his section 1231 losses for the year ($300,000). Thus, Jimmy's $200,000 section 1231 gain would be characterized as ordinary income and his $300,000 section 1231 loss would be characterized as an ordinary loss.

Notes

1. *Matching character of each year's § 1231 gains and § 1231 losses.* When a taxpayer's section 1231 gains exceed his section 1231 losses for the taxable year, section 1231 does *not* treat the gains as capital and the losses as ordinary. In this situation, the gains are treated as capital gains and the losses are treated as capital losses. Conversely, when a taxpayer's section 1231 gains *do not* exceed her section 1231 losses for the taxable year, the gains are treated as ordinary income and the losses are treated as ordinary losses.

2. *Character of each year's § 1231 gains and § 1231 losses determined after year-end.* It is impossible to determine the character of a § 1231 gain or loss at the time a § 1231 asset is sold. Rather, the character of any § 1231 gain or loss will be unknown until all the § 1231 gains and losses for the year have been tabulated and a determination can be made whether the § 1231 gains exceed the § 1231 losses. Thus, taxpayers must wait until after year-end to determine the character of their § 1231 gains and losses.

3.   *Distinguishing "used" from "held for sale."* Like § 1221, § 1231 excludes from its scope inventory and property held for sale to customers in the ordinary course of a trade or business (IRC §§ 1231(b)(1)(A), (B)).[4] Distinguishing property *used* in a trade or business (a § 1231 asset) from property *held for sale to customers* in a trade or business (not a § 1231 asset) can be difficult, as the case that follows demonstrates.

LATIMER-LOONEY CHEVROLET, INC. v. COMMISSIONER

Tax Court of the United States, 1952
19 T.C. 120

FINDINGS OF FACT.

* * *

Petitioner operated under a franchise from General Motors Corporation for the sale of Chevrolet and Cadillac automobiles and Chevrolet trucks. * * *

* * *

Petitioner served a trade area which was roughly 12 miles in all directions from Kingsport, Tennessee. * * * All business and policy decisions of the petitioner were made by J. L. Latimer and R. F. Looney, the managers. The petitioner employed between 53 and 58 persons during the period here in question.

* * *

The * * * new cars and trucks sold by petitioner were received from the Chevrolet Division of General Motors under the General Motors Acceptance Corporation's 'floor plan.' A flat nominal charge was made by G.M.A.C. for each car handled by it and, in addition, interest was paid by the petitioner on all cars held without remittance of the purchase price for longer than five days after acquisition. * * * Under the 'floor plan' petitioner was required to keep the cars and trucks new. Actually the cars were serviced and delivered to customers immediately upon or within a few days after receipt. New cars were not driven at all by petitioner with the exception of driving necessary for the servicing and delivery of these cars to customers.

---

[4]   IRC § 1231 also excludes certain other types of property that were excluded from the definition of a capital asset. See IRC §§ 1221(a)(3), (a)(5); 1231(b)(1)(C), (D).

* * *

[Certain new cars were used by the dealership in conducting its business.] The decision to place cars in company use was made by the managers. As soon as a car was placed in company use it was covered with insurance for the exclusive benefit of the petitioner. License plates were procured for it in the petitioner's name and General Motors Acceptance Corporation was paid in full for the automobile. After these cars were paid for, neither G.M.A.C. nor Chevrolet Division of General Motors had any restrictions whatsoever on the use of the automobile. The decision to place the cars in company use was based on necessity and availability as determined by the petitioner's managers.

The record discloses that the 'company cars' here in issue were used by the petitioner for the following purposes:

(1)   To permit the managers and company representatives to travel for business purposes to cities such as Johnson City, Bristol, Louisville and Atlanta:

(2)   To facilitate collection of delinquent accounts;

(3)   To pick up and tow cars into the plant for repair and service and to deliver the same to customers much in the same manner as motorcycles are frequently used in larger cities;

(4)   For loan to customers urgently needing transportation when their cars were under repair or servicing;

(5)   To fill customers needs where there was a gap in delivery of a new car due to factory delay;

(6)   To transport salesmen who were buying and selling used cars and trucks, and to furnish transportation to salesmen employed in maintaining good will;

(7)   For business errands, e.g., picking up mail, making bank deposits, etc;

(8)   For participation in various civic functions sponsored by organizations such as the American Legion, the Shriners, Moose, etc.;

(9)   For travel in locating and purchasing used cars at auctions in distant areas

(10)   To participate in the American Automobile Association public school driver training program.

* * *

The decision to sell the company cars was made by the petitioner's managers. They were sold primarily on the basis of usage. All of them were sold somewhere between the 8,000 and 12,000 miles' level of usage. All were held * * * for more than one year. They were sold at this usage period because after this period of usage operating costs increased and the tires, appearance of the automobiles, batteries, and other functioning parts were still in good condition and there was little reconditioning or repair cost involved before sale. * * *

In its return for the fiscal year ended September 30, 1949, petitioner deducted $2,540.71 as depreciation on seventeen company cars. In its return for the 3-month period ended December 31, 1949, petitioner deducted $673.63 as depreciation on nine company cars. * * * During the fiscal year ended September 30, 1949, petitioner sold eight company cars and reported the gain in the amount of $5,054.28 as long-term capital gain in its income tax return. During the 3-month period ended December 31, 1949, the petitioner sold two company cars and reported the gain in the amount of $637.26 as long-term capital gain in its tax return. * * *

OPINION.

HILL, JUDGE:

The question for our determination is whether seventeen Chevrolet cars held by the petitioner were property used in its trade or business of a character defined in [the predecessor to IRC § 1231(b)], which is subject to the amounts for depreciation provided in [the predecessors to IRC §§ 167 and 168], or whether as maintained by the respondent they fall within the exceptions contained in [the predecessor to IRC §§ 1231(b)(1)(A) or (B)] as either (a) property of a kind which would be properly includible in the inventory of the taxpayer if on hand at the close of the taxable year, or (b) property held by the taxpayer primarily for sale to customers in the ordinary course of its trade or business.

Property of the kind sold by a taxpayer in his normal trade or business has been considered entitled to [the predecessor to IRC § 1231(a)] benefits when used in the trade or business of the taxpayer in the following cases: securities, Carl Marks & Co., 12 T.C. 1196; livestock, United States v. Bennett, 186 F.2d 407; housing, Nelson A. Farry, 13 T.C. 8; slot machines, A. Benetti Novelty Co., 13 T.C. 1072. These cases point out that it is not the nature of the property itself which is determinative of this case but rather the purpose for which the property is held.

[T]he seventeen cars here in controversy were purchased new from the Chevrolet Division of General Motors under the so called floor plan of financing provided by G.M.A.C., as were all new Chevrolet cars acquired by the petitioner. * * * Shortly after the acquisition the petitioner paid cash in full for the cars, insured them for its exclusive benefit, and purchased Tennessee license tags for the cars. Thereafter, they were used by the petitioner in its trade or business for the purposes outlined in our findings of fact. Once the petitioner had purchased the cars for its use and paid for them, the record shows that neither General Motors nor General Motors Acceptance Corporation, through which the petitioner secured its financing, placed any restrictions upon the petitioner's use of the automobiles. They were the petitioner's property and, as the respondent admits upon brief, the petitioner had a free hand as to how they should be used.

Respondent points to the fact that these automobiles were acquired new, that petitioner's business was the sale of new cars, that the petitioner maintained a new car inventory and held cars for sale to customers in the ordinary course of its business, and draws the conclusion that the petitioner's intention was to hold the cars here in controversy as 'demonstrators' for a period of temporary use and then sell them. From this, respondent reasons that the cars in controversy * * * never lost their inventory character and remained, even after the 8,000 or 12,000 miles of business use to which they were put by the petitioner, cars properly includible in the inventory and held for sale to customers in the ordinary course of the business.

The cars here were sold by the petitioner on the basis of usage when the cars had been used between 8,000 and 12,000 operative miles. The petitioner's managers had them sold for the reasons, as they testified, that after this period of use operation and renovation costs increased and that it was more profitable in their business judgment to dispose of the cars before further usage.

The respondent points to the fact that these cars were sold in the year after they ceased to be current models and argues that this points to an intention of the petitioner to hold the cars for such a temporary use so as not to affect the primary purpose for which they were purchased, that is, sale to customers in the ordinary course of the business. However, the evidence supports the petitioner. We are not in a position to substitute our business judgment for that of the petitioner's managers, men who are apparently well versed in the subject of automobile repairs and sales.

On the basis of the evidence as a whole, we conclude that the cars here in issue were held primarily for use in the petitioner's trade or business and, hence, are entitled to capital gains treatment under the [predecessor to IRC § 1231(a)] and depreciation under [the predecessor to IRC §§ 167 and 168].

Decision will be entered for the petitioner.

Revenue Ruling 75–538

1975–2 C.B. 34

* * *

The question presented concerns the treatment for Federal income tax purposes of motor vehicles held by a taxpayer engaged in the trade or business of selling motor vehicles.

Section 61(a) of the Internal Revenue Code of 1954 provides, in part, that gross income means all income from whatever source derived, including (but not limited to) gross income derived from business.

Section 1231 of the Code provides, in part, that gains and losses on sales or exchanges, or compulsory or involuntary conversion, of "property used in the trade or business" shall be treated as gains and losses from sales or exchanges of capital assets held for more than [one year] if the aggregate of such gains exceeds the aggregate of such losses. If the aggregate of such gains does not exceed the aggregate of such losses, such gains and losses shall not be treated as gains and losses from sales or exchanges of capital assets.

Section 1231(b)(1) of the Code defines the phrase "property used in the trade or business," in part, to mean depreciable property used in the trade or business, held for more than [one year], which is not property of a kind which would properly be includible in inventory if on hand at the close of the taxable year, or property held by the taxpayer primarily for sale to customers in the ordinary course of the taxpayer's trade or business.

Section 167(a) of the Code provides, in part, that there shall be allowed as a depreciation deduction a reasonable allowance for the exhaustion, wear and tear (including a reasonable allowance for obsolescence) of property used in the trade or business or held for the production of income.

Whether a motor vehicle is held by the taxpayer primarily for sale to customers in the ordinary course of the taxpayer's trade or business is a question of fact that must be determined from all of the facts and circumstances in each case.

A taxpayer engaged in the trade or business of selling motor vehicles is presumed to hold all such vehicles primarily for sale to customers in the ordinary course of the taxpayer's trade or business. To overcome this presumption, it must be clearly shown that the motor vehicle was actually devoted to use in the business of the dealer and that the dealer looks to consumption through use of the vehicle in the ordinary course of business operation to recover the dealer's cost. A vehicle is not property used in the business if it is merely used for demonstration purposes, or temporarily withdrawn from stock-in-trade or inventory for business use.

Income derived from the sale of a motor vehicle that constitutes property used in the trade or business qualifies for section 1231 treatment, except to the extent that the provisions of section 1245 of the Code are applicable. In addition, a depreciation deduction is allowable under section 167 with respect to any motor vehicle used in the trade or business of the taxpayer. * * *

FOR DISCUSSION

Property used in a trade or business vs. inventory.
Compare the standards employed by the Tax Court in Latimer-Looney Chevrolet to the standards employed by the Internal Revenue Service in 75–238 for determining whether vehicles owned by an automobile dealership are to be regarded as "used" in the taxpayer's trade or business, or as "held primarily for sale to customers" in the taxpayer's trade or business. Are the standards consistent or is one set of standards more stringent than the other?

NOTES

1. *Impact of prior section 1231 losses on future section 1231 gains.* If—

    1) a taxpayer's section 1231 losses exceed her section 1231 gains in any year, and

    2) in any of the next five years, the taxpayer's section 1231 gains exceed her section 1231 losses,

then part or all of the taxpayer's excess section 1231 gains in the later years will be characterized as ordinary income. See IRC § 1231(c).

■ **EXAMPLE 16-G.** *Impact of section 1231(c).*

Year 1: Taxpayer has $50,000 of section 1231 losses and no section 1231 gains. Because Taxpayer's section 1231 gains do not exceed her section 1231 losses in Year 1, Taxpayer's $50,000 of Year 1 losses will be characterized as ordinary losses.

Year 2: Taxpayer has $90,000 of section 1231 gains and $30,000 of section 1231 losses. In the absence of IRC § 1231(c), Taxpayer's section 1231 gains and losses would be characterized as capital gains and capital losses because Taxpayer's section 1231 gains exceed her section 1231 losses. However, because Taxpayer reported $50,000 of section 1231 losses as ordinary losses within the past five years, $50,000 of Taxpayer's section 1231 gains in Year 2 will be characterized as ordinary income under IRC § 1231(c). The remaining $40,000 of section 1231 gains exceeds the $30,000 of section 1231 losses. Thus, in Year 2, Taxpayer will report $50,000 of ordinary income, $40,000 of capital gains and $30,000 of capital losses.

---

2. *Impact of section 1245 on sale of depreciable personalty.* Rev. Rul. 75–238 concludes with the following statement:

Income derived from the sale of a motor vehicle that constitutes property used in the trade or business qualifies for section 1231 treatment, except to the extent that the provisions of section 1245 of the Code are applicable.

When depreciable personalty is sold in a transaction where gain is recognized, IRC § 1245 overrides other characterization rules (IRC §§ 1221, 1231). In this situation, the recognized gain is characterized as ordinary income to the extent the gain is attributable to prior depreciation deductions. The operation of section 1245 will be examined in the next part of this Chapter.

4. Recharacterization of Depreciable Property—§ 1245

As discussed in Chapter 6, the basis of property used in a trade or business, or held for the production of income, may be recovered through depreciation deductions over a statutorily specified number of years. See IRC §§ 167, 168.[5] When depreciable property is sold and the fair market value of the property exceeds its adjusted basis, gain will be realized. The resulting gain will be attributable, at least in part, to the depreciation deductions that reduced the basis of the property. If the property is sold for a price that exceeds its initial basis, the balance of the gain will be attributable to asset appreciation.

■ **EXAMPLE 16-H.** *Sources of gain on sale of depreciable personalty.* Lauren purchased depreciable personalty for $100,000, and $30,000 of depreciation deductions were allowed while she held the property. As such, her adjusted basis is $70,000 ($100,000 – $30,000 = $70,000). If she sold the property for $110,000, a $40,000 gain is realized and recognized ($110,000 – $70,000 = $40,000). $30,000 of the $40,000 gain is attributable to the depreciation deductions (i.e., the basis declined from $100,000 to $70,000 due to depreciation deductions so the first $30,000 of gain is attributable to those deductions). The remaining $10,000 of gain is attributable to appreciation (i.e., the increase in the value of the property from $100,000 to $110,000 while she held the property).

---

[5] The Tax Cuts and Jobs Act of 2017 permits taxpayers to deduct 100% of the adjusted basis of most new *and used* depreciable personalty (e.g., vehicles, machinery and equipment) placed in service before 2023. See IRC § 168(k). The deduction allowed by section 168(k) is referred to as "bonus depreciation."

When depreciable personalty is sold, any recognized gain attributable to depreciation is automatically treated as ordinary income. See IRC § 1245. Therefore, the first $30,000 of Lauren's gain is characterized as ordinary income under IRC § 1245. Only the $10,000 of gain attributable to the appreciation that occurred while she held the property is treated as a section 1231 gain.[6]

■ **EXAMPLE 16-I.** *Character of gain on sale of depreciable personalty.* Same facts as Example 16-H, but assume Lauren also has $7,000 of section 1231 losses in the year in the year she sold the depreciable personalty. As explained above, the first $30,000 of gain recognized on the sale of the depreciable personalty is ordinary income under IRC § 1245. The remaining $10,000 of gain is section 1231 gain. Because Lauren's $10,000 section 1231 gain exceeds her $7,000 section 1231 loss, the $10,000 gain is a long-term capital gain and the $7,000 loss is a long-term capital loss.

If Lauren had $17,000 of section 1231 losses (rather than $7,000 of such losses) in the year she sold the depreciable personalty, the first $30,000 of gain recognized on the sale of the depreciable personalty is still ordinary income under IRC § 1245 and the remaining $10,000 of gain is still section 1231 gain. Because her $10,000 section 1231 gain does not exceed her $17,000 section 1231 loss, the $10,000 gain is ordinary income and the $17,000 loss is an ordinary loss.

Note

Character of gain on sale of depreciable real estate. When depreciable real estate (e.g., a warehouse or a factory) is sold at a gain, at least a part of the gain is attributable to depreciation deductions for the same reason that at least part of any gain is attributable to depreciation deductions when depreciable personalty is sold. See Example 16-H. As discussed above, when depreciable personalty is

---

[6]   When depreciable property is sold to certain "related persons," the entire recognized gain is characterized as ordinary income. See IRC § 1239.

sold at a gain, the portion of the gain attributable to depreciation deductions is characterized as ordinary income. IRC § 1245. Section 1245 does not apply to depreciable real estate. Therefore, when depreciable real estate used in a trade or business is sold at a gain, the entire gain is a section 1231 gain. If the taxpayer's section 1231 gains exceed her section 1231 losses for the year in which the depreciable real estate is sold, the entire gain recognized with respect to the depreciable real estate will be characterized as capital gain. However, the portion of the gain attributable to depreciation of real estate is normally taxed at a rate of 25%, rather than the maximum capital gains rate of 20%. See IRC § 1(h)(1)(E).

■ **EXAMPLE 16-J.** *Character of gain on sale of depreciable real estate.* Grace purchased depreciable real estate for $100,000, and $30,000 of depreciation deductions were allowed while she held the property. Thus, her adjusted basis is $70,000 ($100,000 – $30,000 = $70,000). If she sold the property for $110,000, a $40,000 gain is realized and recognized ($110,000 – $70,000 = $40,000). $30,000 of the $40,000 gain is attributable to the depreciation deductions (i.e., the basis declined from $100,000 to $70,000 due to depreciation deductions so the first $30,000 of gain is attributable to those deductions). The remaining $10,000 of gain is attributable to appreciation because the value of the property increased from $100,000 to $110,000 while she held the property. Because the property Grace sold is depreciable *real estate,* not depreciable *personalty,* IRC § 1245 does not apply and the entire $40,000 gain is a section 1231 gain. Compare Example 16-H.

Assume Grace also has $7,000 of section 1231 losses in the year she sells the depreciable real estate. Because Grace's $40,000 of section 1231 gain exceeds her $7,000 of section 1231 losses, the $40,000 gain is a capital gain and the $7,000 loss is a capital loss. However, only $10,000 of the $40,000 gain on the sale of the depreciable real estate is taxed at a maximum capital gains rate of 20%. The $30,000 of gain attributable to the depreciation Grace was allowed with respect to the real estate is normally taxed at a 25% tax rate. See IRC § 1(h)(1)(E). Compare Example 16-I.

If Grace has $57,000 of section 1231 losses (rather than $7,000 of such losses) in the year she sells the depreciable real estate, her $40,000 section

1231 gain does not exceed her $57,000 of section 1231 losses. Thus, her $40,000 gain is ordinary income and her $57,000 loss is an ordinary loss.

---

5.   Sale of a Business

WILLIAMS v. McGOWAN

United States Court of Appeals, Second Circuit, 1945
152 F.2d 570

L. Hand, Circuit Judge.

* * *

Williams, the taxpayer * * * had for many years been engaged in the hardware business in the City of Corning, New York. * * * [In September of 1940,] Williams sold the business as a whole to the Corning Building Company for $63,926.28—its agreed value as of February 1, 1940 * * *. This value was made up of cash of about $8100, receivables of about $7000, fixtures of about $800, and a merchandise inventory of about [$48,000]. Upon this sale Williams suffered a loss upon his original [investment] and in his income tax return he entered [the loss as an ordinary loss rather than a capital loss]. [T]he Commissioner disallowed and recomputed the tax accordingly; Williams paid the deficiency and sued to recover it in this action. The only question is whether the business was "capital assets" under [the predecessor to IRC § 1221].

[W]e have to decide only whether upon the sale of a going business it is to be comminuted into its fragments, and these are to be separately matched against the definition in [the predecessor to IRC § 1221], or whether the whole business is to be treated as if it were a single piece of property.

Our law has been sparing in the creation of juristic entities * * *. [I]n this instance the [predecessor to section 1221] itself furnishes the answer. It starts in the broadest way by declaring that all "property" is "capital assets," and then makes [two] exceptions. The first is "stock in trade * * * or other property of a kind which would properly be included in the inventory" [and] "property held * * * primarily for sale to customers"; and [second], property "used in the trade or business of a character which is subject to * * * allowance for depreciation." In the face of this language, * * * by no possibility can a whole business be treated [as capital assets]. Congress plainly did mean to comminute the elements of a business; plainly it did not regard the whole as "capital assets."

As has already appeared, Williams transferred to the Corning Company "cash," "receivables," "fixtures" and a "merchandise inventory." "Fixtures" are not capital because they are subject to a depreciation allowance; the inventory, as we have just seen, is expressly excluded. * * * There can of course be no gain or loss in the transfer of cash * * *. The gain or loss upon every other item should be computed as an item in ordinary income [or loss].

Judgment reversed.

FRANK, CIRCUIT JUDGE (dissenting in part).

　　　* * *

[I] do not agree that we should ignore what the parties to the sale, Williams and the Corning Company, actually did. They did not arrange for a transfer to the buyer, as if in separate bundles, of the several ingredients of the business. They contracted for the sale of the entire business as a going concern. Here is what they said in their agreement:

> The party of the first part agrees to sell and the party of the second part agrees to buy, *all of the right, title and interest* of the said party of the first part *in and to the hardware business* now being conducted by the said party of the first part, *including* cash on hand and on deposit in the First National Bank & Trust Company of Corning in the A. F. Williams Hardware Store account, in accounts receivable, bills receivable, notes receivable, merchandise and fixtures, including two G.M. trucks, good will and all other assets of every kind and description used in and about said business. * * * Said party of the first part agrees not to engage in the hardware business within a radius of twenty-five miles from the City of Corning, New York, for a period of ten years from the 1st day of October 1940.

To carve up this transaction into distinct sales—of cash, receivables, fixtures, trucks, merchandise, and good will—is to do violence to the realities. I do not think Congress intended any such artificial result. * * * Where a business is sold as a unit, the whole is greater than its parts. Businessmen so recognize; so, too, I think, did Congress. Interpretation of our complicated tax statutes is seldom aided by saying that taxation is an eminently practical matter (or the like). But this is one instance where, it seems to me, the practical aspects of the matter should guide our guess as to what Congress meant. I believe Congress had those aspects in mind and was not thinking of the nice distinctions between Roman and Anglo-American legal theories about legal entities.

WORTH NOTING

Allocation of selling price among individual assets. As the Williams case demonstrates, when the assets of a business are sold, the purchase price is allocated among the individual assets based on the fair market value of each asset. A gain or loss is then computed with respect to each asset. If recognized, each gain or loss is characterized based on the nature of the asset that gave rise to the gain or the loss. Problem 16-5 tests your understanding of these principles.

■ **PROBLEM 16-5.** *Characterization of gains and losses under §§ 1221, 1231, and 1245.* Eric manufactures and sells widgets. His business consists of the following *tangible* assets:

	Adjusted Basis	Fair Market Value
Cash	$100,000	$100,000
Widgets	$150,000	$250,000
Equipment	$300,000	$350,000
Factory	$450,000	$400,000
Land	$200,000	$500,000
Total	$1,200,000	$1,600,000

Abby has agreed to buy Eric's business for $2,000,000. She is willing to pay $400,000 more than the value of the tangible assets ($1,600,000) because the business has $400,000 of intangible assets attributable to an excellent reputation in the community and a long history of profitability. Intangible assets of this nature are referred to as "goodwill."[7] The goodwill was self-created as it simply arose through the operation of the business; it was

---

[7]   Goodwill is an intangible asset representing that part of the value of a business attributable to the expectation that customers will continue to patronize the business because of its name, reputation or other factors.

not purchased. How much gain or loss does Eric recognize with respect to each tangible and intangible asset and how is each gain or loss characterized? Assume Eric originally purchased the equipment for $330,000.

---

6.   Termination of Contract—§ 1234A

Primary Law: IRC § 1234A

(a)   Gain or loss attributable to the cancellation, lapse, expiration, or other termination of—

(1)   a right or obligation * * * with respect to property which is (or on acquisition would be) a capital asset in the hands of the taxpayer * * *

shall be treated as gain or loss from the sale of a capital asset. * * *

CRI-LESLIE, LLC v. COMMISSIONER

United States Court of Appeals, Eleventh Circuit, 2018
882 F.3d 1026

Newsom, Circuit Judge:

More than 40 years ago, Judge Henry Friendly lamented that "[t]he problem with respect to the tax treatment of payments for the termination of contract rights having a property flavor is among the most frustrating in income tax law." *Sirbo Holdings, Inc. v. Comm'r*, 509 F.2d 1220, 1223 (2d Cir. 1975). Alas, not much has changed. This * * * case, arising in the same sphere, presents what appears to be a question of first impression: Is a taxpayer that contracts to sell property used in its trade or business entitled to treat as capital gain an advance deposit that it rightfully retains when its would-be buyer defaults and cancels the deal? Constrained by the Internal Revenue Code's plain (if somewhat peculiar) language, we hold that it is not.

I

The pertinent facts are undisputed. In 2005, CRI-Leslie, LLC paid $13.8 million to buy what was then called the Radisson Bay Harbor Hotel in Tampa, along with the hotel's restaurant—Crabby Bill's—and the prime waterfront property on which both sat. Although CRI-Leslie ultimately hoped to sell the property for a profit, it hired a third party to run the hotel and restaurant in the meantime.

Just more than a year later, CRI-Leslie reached an agreement to sell the property to another company for $39 million. Over the course of the next two years—during which CRI-Leslie (through its manager) continued to operate the hotel and restaurant—the parties amended the contract several times, eventually settling on a total purchase price of $39.2 million, $9.7 million of which was paid immediately to CRI-Leslie as a nonrefundable deposit and would thereafter be credited toward the purchase price at closing. Unfortunately, in 2008 CRI-Leslie's buyer defaulted on the agreement and forfeited the $9.7 million deposit.

On its 2008 tax return—at issue here—CRI-Leslie reported the $9.7 million as long-term capital gain. The IRS, though, later sent CRI-Leslie an "adjustment" for the 2008 tax year—rarely a good thing—in which it determined that CRI-Leslie had improperly reported the amount of the forfeited deposits as net long-term capital gain rather than ordinary income.

CRI-Leslie filed a petition for readjustment in the Tax Court, asserting that the Internal Revenue Code was meant to prescribe the same tax treatment for gains related to the disposition of "trade or business" property regardless of whether the property is successfully sold or (as here) the sale agreement is canceled. The IRS responded that the plain text of the governing Code provisions distinguishes between consummated and terminated sales of trade-or-business property, providing capital-gains treatment only for the former. The parties jointly submitted the case to the Tax Court for decision without trial, and that court agreed with the IRS, holding that under the Code's unambiguous language CRI-Leslie couldn't treat the forfeited deposit as capital gain.

CRI-Leslie filed this appeal, which presents a pure question of statutory interpretation that we review de novo.

II

We begin with a point of agreement. It is common ground that if the sale of the Radisson Bay Harbor had gone through as planned, the $9.7 million deposit—which per the contract's terms would have gone toward the purchase price—would have been taxed at the lower capital-gains rate. As relevant here, I.R.C. § 1231 states that "any recognized gain on the sale or exchange of property used in the trade or business" shall "be treated as long-term capital gains." I.R.C. § 1231(a)(1)–(3). Section 1231 goes on to specify that "[f]or purposes of this section," the "term 'property used in the trade or business' means property used in the trade or business, of a character which is subject to the allowance for depreciation provided in section 167, held for more than 1 year, and real property used in the trade or business, held for more than 1 year . . . ." *Id.* § 1231(b)(1). Helpfully, the parties have stipulated that the property at issue here is properly classified as "property used in [CRI-Leslie's] trade or business" within the meaning of Section 1231. Accordingly, it is undisputed that if CRI-Leslie had sold the property in 2008, the resulting income, including the $9.7 million at issue here, would have constituted Section 1231 gain and, as such, been taxed as long-term capital gain.

But of course the deal fell through, and CRI-Leslie didn't sell the Radisson. Accordingly, the tax treatment of CRI-Leslie's $9.7 million deposit isn't governed by Section 1231, but rather falls under a different Code provision titled "Gains or losses from certain terminations." I.R.C. § 1234A. In relevant part, Section 1234A provides as follows:

> Gain or loss attributable to the cancellation, lapse, expiration, or other termination of . . . a right or obligation . . . with respect to property which is (or on acquisition would be) a capital asset in the hands of the taxpayer . . . shall be treated as gain or loss from the sale of a capital asset.

Id. Stated simply, Section 1234A says that any gain or loss that results from the termination of an agreement to buy or sell property that is properly classified as a "capital asset" will, notwithstanding the termination, be treated as a gain or loss from a consummated sale. Section 1234A thereby ensures capital-gains treatment of income resulting from canceled property sales by relaxing the "sale or exchange" element of the Code's general definition of "[l]ong-term capital gain"—*i.e.,* "gain from the sale or exchange of a capital asset held for more than 1 year . . . ." I.R.C. § 1222(3). Critically here, though, Section 1234A applies *only* to property that is appropriately classified as a "capital asset." The statutory analysis here therefore turns on whether the Radisson Bay Harbor was a "capital asset" in CRI-Leslie's hands during the 2008 tax year.

A

As a matter of plain textual analysis, the answer to the question whether the Radisson was a "capital asset" couldn't be clearer. The Code itself defines the term "capital asset" in a way that expressly excludes the property here. As relevant for our purposes, I.R.C. § 1221(a)(2) states that "[f]or purposes of this subtitle"—*i.e.,* "Subtitle A," comprising all Code provisions related to "Income Taxes," notably including Section 1234A—"the term 'capital asset' means property held by the taxpayer (whether or not connected with his trade or business), *but does not include . . . property, used in his trade or business, of a character which is subject to the allowance for depreciation provided in section 167, or real property used in his trade or business.*" *Id.* § 1221(a)(2) (emphasis added).

If Section 1221(a)(2)'s definition of "capital asset" sounds familiar, that's because it mirrors almost precisely Section 1231(b)(1)'s definition of the term "property used in the trade or business," already examined. There is, however, a decisive difference, which cuts to the very heart of this case: Whereas Section 1231's definition, which applies to consummated sales of trade-or-business property, expressly *prescribes* capital-gains treatment of the resulting income, Section 1221's definition, which applies (via Section 1234A) to terminated sales of such property, expressly *proscribes* capital-gains treatment. Because CRI-Leslie's sale transaction fell through, the controlling question here is whether the Radisson Bay Harbor falls within the terms of Section 1221(a)(2)'s exclusion.

By express agreement of the parties, it does. As the Tax Court observed, CRI-Leslie and IRS have "stipulated that from the date that CRI-Leslie acquired the property in 2005 and through December 31, 2008, the property was real property used in CRI-Leslie's hotel and restaurant business within the meaning of section 1221(a)(2)." Accordingly, CRI-Leslie "concedes that the hotel property falls within this exclusion and so is not a capital asset as defined in section 1221."

Based on the Code's plain language, that concession is fatal. Tracing it back up the statutory chain leads inexorably to the conclusion that the hotel didn't qualify for capital-gains treatment on CRI-Leslie's 2008 return. If, as CRI-Leslie acknowledges, the hotel isn't a "capital asset" within the meaning of Section 1221, then Section 1234A's special rule, which treats property resulting from the termination of a contract for the sale of a "capital asset" as if it were derived from a consummated sale of that asset—and thus subject to capital-gains treatment under Section 1222(3)—simply doesn't apply. That's it. End of case.

B

Not so fast, CRI-Leslie insists. A plain-text reading of the Code, CRI-Leslie vigorously asserts, impermissibly yields a result that is "illogical, absurd, and directly contrary to the objective of § 1234A." Br. of Appellant at 34. Having carefully considered CRI-Leslie's arguments, we find no basis for disregarding the Code's clear language.

1

As for absurdity, CRI-Leslie asserts two incongruities. First, it notes that while all "agree that, had the sale of the [p]roperty been completed, the [d]eposit would have been . . . applied toward the purchase price and, thus, treated as capital gain" under Section 1231, under a plain-text reading of Sections 1221 and 1234A, "that same deposit must be treated as ordinary income because the parties terminated the [c]ontract rather than completing it." *Id.* That, CRI-Leslie says, makes no sense—especially here, given that it certainly wasn't CRI-Leslie's fault that the Radisson sale cratered. Second, CRI-Leslie complains that reading Section 1234A to exclude trade-or-business property "effectively penalize[s]" taxpayers "for operating a trade or business as opposed to being a passive investor in real property," in which case (as with a consummated transaction) any resulting income would merit capital-gains treatment. *Id.* at 35. Echoing the Tax Court's own admission, CRI-Leslie complains that such "disparate treatment" reflects "intellectual inconsistency." *Id.* at 34. For both reasons, CRI-Leslie insists that the only rational way to read the Code is "to give the termination of a contract the same tax treatment afforded a sale or exchange of the property underlying the contract in order to eliminate differing tax treatment of economically equivalent transactions." *Id.* at 15.

We cannot agree that enforcing the Code's plain language here produces a qualifyingly "absurd" result. The supposed anomalies that CRI-Leslie posits— between completed and canceled transactions, and between active managers and passive investors—may seem a little (or even more than a little) odd, but oddity is not absurdity. While "[t]here is an absurdity exception to the plain meaning rule," it is necessarily "very narrow," *United States v. Nix,* 438 F.3d 1284, 1286 (11th Cir. 2006), and applies only when a straightforward application of statutory text would compel a truly ridiculous * * * outcome. We are not in that ballpark here—particularly given that, when the sale fell through, CRI-Leslie got to keep not only the $9.7 million deposit (albeit at an ordinary-income tax rate) but also the Radisson Bay Harbor.

2

Moving beyond the supposed absurdities, CRI-Leslie insists that a plain-text reading of the Code's interlocking provisions actually "ignore[s] the clear purpose behind the enactment of § 1234A"—which CRI-Leslie says "was to ensure that taxpayers receive the same tax characterization of gain or loss whether the underlying property is sold or the contract to which the property is subject is terminated." Br. of Appellant at 5, 32. * * *

In fairness, CRI-Leslie's purposes-and-objectives argument is not without foundation, and it seems to have attracted some scholarly supporters. The problem with the view that Section 1234A should be understood to reach Section 1231 property is that *the Code's plain language flatly forecloses it.* As already explained, if an asset *is* Section-1231 property, then by definition—literally—it *is not* Section-1234A property. The reason, again, is that the definitions of "property used the trade or business" in Section 1231 and "capital asset" in Section 1234A (via Section 1221) are mutually exclusive. Both refer to "property used in [the taxpayer's] trade or business, of a character which is subject to the allowance for depreciation provided in section 167," and "real property used in [the taxpayer's] trade or business." I.R.C. §§ 1221(a)(2), 1231(b)(1). But while Section 1231 expressly prescribes capital-gains treatment of such income, *see id.* § 1231(a)(1)–(3), Section 1234A—through its use of the term "capital asset," which is defined in Section 1221(a)(2)—expressly forbids capital-gains treatment of the same property.

In a contest such as we have here, between clear statutory text and (even compelling) evidence of sub- or extra-textual "intent," the former must prevail. That is so for myriad well-established reasons that we needn't belabor but that, in view of the parties' contending arguments, we recap briefly. As a formal matter, it is of course only the statutory text (as relevant here, I.R.C. §§ 1221 and 1234A) that is "law" in the constitutional sense—that's all that was enacted through the bicameral legislative process and presented to the President for his signature. And as a practical matter, conscientious adherence to the statutory text best ensures that citizens have fair notice of the rules that govern their conduct, incentivizes Congress to write clear laws, and keeps courts within their proper lane.

* * *

So in the end, this case is actually pretty straightforward: Section 1234A provides for capital-gains treatment of income resulting from canceled sales only where the underlying property constitutes a "capital asset," and Section 1221 defines "capital asset" in a way that all agree excludes the property at issue here. Accordingly, CRI-Leslie is not entitled to treat its $9.7 million deposit as capital gain. Q.E.D.

III

Now it may well be, as CRI-Leslie asserts, that Congress really did mean for the amended Section 1234A to reach beyond "capital assets" as defined in Section 1221 to include Section-1231 property. Perhaps, that is, Congress just stubbed its toe between the hearing room and the House and Senate floors. Even so, it's not our place or prerogative to bandage the resulting wound. If Congress thinks that we've misapprehended its true intent—or, more accurately, that the language that it enacted in I.R.C. §§ 1221 and 1234A inaccurately reflects its true intent—then it can and should say so by amending the Code.

The judgment of the Tax Court is Affirmed.

FOR DISCUSSION

Alternative facts. What would the tax consequences of the $9.7 million forfeited deposit have been if, immediately after acquiring the hotel and restaurant, CRI-Leslie had shut down the property, rather than operating the hotel and restaurant until the property could be sold?

---

7.   Virtual Currency

IRS Notice 2014–21

2014–16 I.R.B. 938
April 14, 2014

SECTION 1. PURPOSE

This notice describes how existing general tax principles apply to transactions using virtual currency. The notice provides this guidance in the form of answers to frequently asked questions.

SECTION 2. BACKGROUND

The Internal Revenue Service (IRS) is aware that "virtual currency" may be used to pay for goods or services, or held for investment. Virtual currency is a digital representation of value that functions as a medium of exchange, a unit of account, and/or a store of value. In some environments, it operates like "real" currency—i.e., the coin and paper money of the United States or of any other country that is designated as legal tender, circulates, and is customarily used and accepted as a medium of exchange in the country of issuance—but it does not have legal tender status in any jurisdiction.

Virtual currency that has an equivalent value in real currency, or that acts as a substitute for real currency, is referred to as "convertible" virtual currency. Bitcoin is one example of a convertible virtual currency. Bitcoin can be digitally traded between users and can be purchased for, or exchanged into, U.S. dollars, Euros, and other real or virtual currencies. * * *

SECTION 3. SCOPE

In general, the sale or exchange of convertible virtual currency, or the use of convertible virtual currency to pay for goods or services in a real-world economy transaction, has tax consequences that may result in a tax liability. This notice addresses only the U.S. federal tax consequences of transactions in, or transactions that use, convertible virtual currency, and the term "virtual currency" as used in Section 4 refers only to convertible virtual currency. No inference should be drawn with respect to virtual currencies not described in this notice.

* * *

For purposes of the FAQs in this notice, the taxpayer's functional currency is assumed to be the U.S. dollar, the taxpayer is assumed to use the cash receipts and disbursements method of accounting and the taxpayer is assumed not to be under common control with any other party to a transaction.

SECTION 4. FREQUENTLY ASKED QUESTIONS

Q-1: How is virtual currency treated for federal tax purposes?

A-1: For federal tax purposes, virtual currency is treated as property. General tax principles applicable to property transactions apply to transactions using virtual currency.

* * *

Q-3: Must a taxpayer who receives virtual currency as payment for goods or services include in computing gross income the fair market value of the virtual currency?

A-3: Yes. A taxpayer who receives virtual currency as payment for goods or services must, in computing gross income, include the fair market value of the virtual currency, measured in U.S. dollars, as of the date that the virtual currency was received.

Q-4: What is the basis of virtual currency received as payment for goods or services in Q&A-3?

A-4: The basis of virtual currency that a taxpayer receives as payment for goods or services in Q&A-3 is the fair market value of the virtual currency in U.S. dollars as of the date of receipt.

Q-5: How is the fair market value of virtual currency determined?

A-5: For U.S. tax purposes, transactions using virtual currency must be reported in U.S. dollars. Therefore, taxpayers will be required to determine the fair market value of virtual currency in U.S. dollars as of the date of payment or receipt. If a virtual currency is listed on an exchange and the exchange rate is established by market supply and demand, the fair market value of the virtual currency is determined by converting the virtual currency into U.S. dollars * * * at the exchange rate, in a reasonable manner that is consistently applied.

Q-6: Does a taxpayer have gain or loss upon an exchange of virtual currency for other property?

A-6: Yes. If the fair market value of property received in exchange for virtual currency exceeds the taxpayer's adjusted basis of the virtual currency, the taxpayer has taxable gain. The taxpayer has a loss if the fair market value of the property received is less than the adjusted basis of the virtual currency.

Q-7: What type of gain or loss does a taxpayer realize on the sale or exchange of virtual currency?

A-7: The character of the gain or loss generally depends on whether the virtual currency is a capital asset in the hands of the taxpayer. A taxpayer generally realizes capital gain or loss on the sale or exchange of virtual currency that is a capital asset in the hands of the taxpayer. For example, stocks, bonds, and other investment property are generally capital assets. A taxpayer generally realizes ordinary gain or loss on the sale or exchange of virtual currency that is not a capital asset in the hands of the taxpayer. Inventory and other property held mainly for sale to customers in a trade or business are examples of property that is not a capital asset.

Q-8: Does a taxpayer who "mines" virtual currency (for example, uses computer resources to validate Bitcoin transactions and maintain the public Bitcoin transaction ledger) realize gross income upon receipt of the virtual currency resulting from those activities?

A-8: Yes, when a taxpayer successfully "mines" virtual currency, the fair market value of the virtual currency as of the date of receipt is includible in gross income.

IN PRACTICE

IRS compliance campaigns. In 2017, the Internal Revenue Service announced a group of compliance campaigns with the goal of "improving return selection, identifying issues representing a risk of non-compliance, and making the greatest use of limited resources." One of these compliance campaigns is directed at "noncompliance related to the use of virtual currency." See "IRS Announces the Identification and Selection of Five Large Business and International Compliance Campaigns," July 2, 2018 (one of the five campaigns focuses on virtual currency). The IRS has warned taxpayers with unreported virtual currency transactions "to correct their returns as soon as practical." Thus, virtual currency transactions are likely to attract a great deal of IRS attention in the future.

8. Impact of Prior Year's Transaction on Characterization

The Arrowsmith case, which follows, involves a corporation that transferred all of its assets to its shareholders, a transaction referred to as a "liquidation." For tax purposes, when a corporation liquidates, each shareholder is treated as selling her shares for the amount of money and the value of the property received by that shareholder from the corporation. See IRC § 331(a). The shareholder realizes and recognizes gain or loss equal to the difference between the value of what the shareholder receives and the shareholder's adjusted basis in the shareholder's stock. If the corporate stock is a capital asset, which is normally the case, the shareholder's gain or loss is characterized as capital gain or capital loss.

From an economic standpoint, a shareholder receiving property in a liquidation takes the property subject to the claims of the corporation's creditors, a status referred to as "transferee liability." See, e.g., IRC § 6901 (imposing transferee liability on shareholders with respect to the liquidating corporation's Federal tax liabilities). Although a shareholder is not normally liable for the corporation's obligations, those obligations do not disappear when the corporation liquidates. Rather, the shareholders become responsible for all the obligations of the liquidated corporation, but each shareholder's exposure is limited to the amount of money and the value of any property received by that shareholder in the liquidating distribution.

ARROWSMITH et al. v. COMMISSIONER

Supreme Court of the United States, 1952
344 U.S. 6, 73 S.Ct. 71, 97 L.Ed. 6

Mr. Justice Black delivered the opinion of the Court.

[In 1937, petitioners] decided to liquidate and divide the proceeds of a corporation in which they had equal stock ownership. Partial distributions made in 1937, 1938, and 1939 were followed by a final one in 1940. Petitioners reported the profits obtained from this transaction, classifying them as capital gains. They thereby paid less income tax than would have been required had the income been attributed to ordinary business transactions for profit. About the propriety of these 1937–1940 returns, there is no dispute. But in 1944 a judgment was rendered against the old corporation * * *. The two taxpayers were required to and did pay the judgment for the corporation, of whose assets they were transferees. Classifying the loss as an ordinary business one, each took a tax deduction for 100% of the amount paid. Treatment of the loss as a capital one would have allowed deduction of a much smaller amount. The Commissioner viewed the 1944 payment as part of the original liquidation transaction requiring classification as a capital loss, just as the taxpayers had treated the original dividends as capital gains. Disagreeing with the Commissioner the Tax Court classified the 1944 payment as an ordinary business loss. Disagreeing with the Tax Court the Court of Appeals reversed, treating the loss as "capital." This latter holding conflicts with the Third Circuit's holding in Commissioner of Internal Revenue v. Switlik. Because of this conflict, we granted certiorari.

[The predecessor to IRC § 1222] treats losses from sales or exchanges of capital assets as 'capital losses' and [the predecessor to IRC § 331] requires that liquidation distributions be treated as exchanges. The losses here fall squarely within the definition of 'capital losses' contained in these sections. Taxpayers were required to pay the judgment because of liability imposed on them as transferees of liquidation distribution assets. And it is plain that their liability as transferees was not based on any ordinary business transaction of theirs apart from the liquidation proceedings. It is not even denied that had this judgment been paid after liquidation, but during the year 1940, the losses would have been properly treated as capital ones. For payment during 1940 would simply have reduced the amount of capital gains taxpayers received during that year.

It is contended, however, that this payment which would have been a capital transaction in 1940 was transformed into an ordinary business transaction in 1944 because of the well-established principle that each taxable year is a separate unit for tax accounting purposes. United States v. Lewis, 340 U.S. 590; North American Oil Consolidated v. Burnet, 286 U.S. 417. But this principle is not breached by considering all the 1937–1944 liquidation transaction events in order properly to classify the nature of the 1944 loss for tax purposes. Such an examination is not an attempt to reopen and readjust the 1937 to 1940 tax returns, an action that would be inconsistent with the annual tax accounting principle.

* * *

Affirmed.

Mr. Justice Douglas, dissenting.

I agree with Mr. Justice JACKSON that these losses should be treated as ordinary, not capital, losses. There were no capital transactions in the year in which the losses were suffered. Those transactions occurred and were accounted for in earlier years in accord with the established principle that each year is a separate unit for tax accounting purposes. See United States v. Lewis, 340 U.S. 590. I have not felt, as my dissent in the Lewis case indicates, that the law made that an inexorable principle. But if it is the law, we should require observance of it—not merely by taxpayers but by the government as well. We should force each year to stand on its own footing, whoever may gain or lose from it in a particular case. We impeach that principle when we treat this year's losses as if they diminished last year's gains.

Mr. Justice Jackson, whom Mr. Justice Frankfurter joins, dissenting.

This problem arises only because the judgment was rendered in a taxable year subsequent to the liquidation.

Had the liability of the transferor-corporation been reduced to judgment during the taxable year in which liquidation occurred, or prior thereto, this problem, under the tax laws, would not arise. The amount of the judgment rendered against the corporation would have decreased the amount it had available for distribution which would have reduced the liquidating dividends proportionately and diminished the capital gains taxes assessed against the stockholders. Probably it would also have decreased the corporation's own taxable income.

Congress might have allowed, under such circumstances, tax returns of the prior year to be reopened or readjusted so as to give the same tax results as would have obtained had the liability become known prior to liquidation. Such a solution is foreclosed to us and the alternatives left are to regard the judgment liability fastened by operation of law on the transferee as an ordinary loss for the year of adjudication or to regard it as a capital loss for such year.

This Court simplifies the choice to one of reading the English language, and declares that the losses here come 'squarely within' the definition of capital losses contained within two sections of the Internal Revenue Code. What seems so clear to this Court was not seen at all by the Tax Court, in this case or in earlier consideration of the same issue * * *.

I find little aid in the choice of alternatives from arguments based on equities. One enables the taxpayer to deduct the amount of the judgment against his ordinary income which might be taxed as high as 87%, while if the liability had been assessed against the corporation prior to liquidation it would have reduced his capital gain which was taxable at only 25% (now 26%). The consequence may readily be characterized as a windfall (regarding a windfall as anything that is left to a taxpayer after the collector has finished with him).

On the other hand, adoption of the contrary alternative may penalize the taxpayer because * * * capital losses are deductible only against capital gains, plus [$3,000], a taxpayer having no net capital gains in the ensuing five years would have no opportunity to deduct anything beyond [$15,000].

Solicitude for the revenues is a plausible but treacherous basis upon which to decide a particular tax case. A victory may have implications which in future cases will cost the Treasury more than a defeat. This might be such a case, for anything I know. Suppose that subsequent to liquidation it is found that a corporation has undisclosed claims instead of liabilities and that under applicable state law they may be prosecuted for the benefit of the stockholders. The logic of the Court's decision here, if adhered to, would result in a lesser return to the Government than if the recoveries were considered ordinary income. Would it be so clear that this is a capital loss if the shoe were on the other foot?

Where the statute is so indecisive and the importance of a particular holding lies in its rational and harmonious relation to the general scheme of the tax law, I think great deference is due the twice-expressed judgment of the Tax Court. * * * I should reverse, in reliance upon the Tax Court's judgment more, perhaps, than my own.

NOTES

1. *Reconciling Arrowsmith with Lewis.* In the Lewis case (p. 383), the taxpayer was compelled to surrender a benefit years after the taxpayer had included the benefit in gross income under a claim of right. The Supreme Court did not permit the taxpayer to go back and amend the earlier year's tax return on which the benefit was reported as income. Instead, the taxpayer's remedy was limited to claiming a deduction in the tax year the benefit was surrendered. By contrast, in Arrowsmith, the Supreme Court looked back to the tax year in

which the shareholders received liquidating distributions to characterize losses the shareholders incurred in a later tax year when they satisfied obligations of the corporation. Can the two decisions be reconciled?

2.   *The coin has two sides.* If a corporation liquidated in Year 1 and, in Year 3, the shareholder's recovered an item of income owed to the corporation,

>   a)   must the shareholders report the recovered item as gross income?

>   b)   if so, in what tax year should the income be reported?

>   c)   should the income item be characterized as ordinary income or capital gain?

C. Dividend Income Taxed at Capital Gains Rates—§ 1(h)(11)

At this point, it appears that capital gain characterization is relevant only to gains derived from dealings in property under IRC § 61(a)(3). The question of characterization of gain arises when a realization event occurs and a gain is realized and recognized. That analysis applies only to § 61(a)(3) income. Consequently, it would be logical to conclude that all other types of gross income are taxed as ordinary income.

It is true that only § 61(a)(3) income can be *characterized* as capital gain. However, when an individual receives dividends from a corporation in which she owns stock, the dividends, which constitute income under IRC § 61(a)(7), are generally *taxed at capital gains rates*. See IRC § 1(h)(11). Hence, dividends received by an individual are generally taxed at a maximum rate of 20%.[8]

Although dividends are generally taxed at capital gains rates, dividends are *not* characterized as capital gains. See IRC § 1(h)(11)(A). This distinction is important in the case of an individual with capital losses from other transactions. An individual with capital losses can apply those losses against income characterized as capital gains, but cannot apply those losses against dividend income. See IRC §§ 1(h)(11), 1211(b).

---

[8]   An additional 3.8% Medicare contribution tax on unearned income is also imposed on dividends (and other investment income) of high-income taxpayers. See IRC § 1411, discussed in part D. of this Chapter.

■ **EXAMPLE 16-K.** *Dividends vs. capital gains.* In Year 1, Erin has $500,000 of ordinary income, $200,000 of capital losses, and $200,000 of qualified dividend income. Erin cannot apply her capital losses against the qualified dividend income because the qualified dividend income is not characterized as capital gains. However, she will be taxed at a rate of only 20% on the qualified dividend income because qualified dividends are taxed at capital gains rates. By contrast, if her dividend income were taxed at ordinary income rates, Erin would pay a tax of 37% on the dividend income due to the amount of her other ordinary income.

Assume that instead of receiving $200,000 of qualified dividend income in Year 1, Erin received $200,000 of § 61(a)(3) income characterized as capital gains. In this situation, Erin could apply her $200,000 of capital losses against the $200,000 of capital gains and pay no tax on the capital gains.

WORTH NOTING

For a dividend to be taxed at capital gains rates, it must constitute a "qualified dividend." IRC § 1(h)(11)(B). To constitute a qualified dividend, the shareholder receiving the dividend generally must have held the underlying stock for at least 61 days during the 120 day period beginning 60 days before the date the shares become "ex-dividend" (i.e., the date on which the shares no longer trade with the right to receive the most recently declared dividend). See IRC § 1(h)(11)(B)(iii)(I).

D. Surtax on Net Investment Income—§ 1411

Certain higher-income individuals are subject to an additional 3.8% Medicare contribution tax on their investment income. See IRC § 1411(a). Specifically, most married couples with adjusted gross income in excess of $250,000 (and single individuals with adjusted gross income in excess of $200,000) are subject to the tax. See IRC § 1411(b). The tax is normally imposed on "net investment income." IRC § 1411(a)(1).[9] Dividends, interest and capital gains, other than

---

[9]   If the taxpayer's adjusted gross income exceeds the $250,000 (or $200,000) threshold by a lesser amount than the taxpayer's net investment income, the tax is imposed on the lesser amount. See IRC § 1411(a)(2).

those derived from a trade or business, are included within the scope of net investment income. See IRC § 1411(c)(1).

In light of IRC § 1411, qualified dividends received by a high-income individual are taxed at a maximum capital gains rate of 20% and are also subject to the 3.8% Medicare contribution tax, for a total tax of 23.8%. The same tax burden is imposed on long-term capital gains. Interest earned by a high-income individual is taxed at ordinary income rates up to 37% and is also subject to the 3.8% Medicare contribution tax, for a total tax of up to 40.8%.

SYNTHESIS

When an individual recognizes a gain or a loss with respect to the sale of an asset, the gain or loss must be characterized. If a recognized gain is characterized as a capital gain and the asset with respect to which the gain was recognized was held for more than one year, a long-term capital gain results. The long-term capital gain is taxed at a maximum rate of 20% (plus a 3.8% Medicare contribution tax in the case of certain high-income individuals). By contrast, if an individual recognizes a loss that is allowed as a deduction and the loss is characterized as a capital loss, the individual may apply the capital loss (and any other capital losses during that year) only against capital gains recognized during that year (and up to $3,000 of ordinary income). Any excess capital losses may not be deducted during the year in which the loss was triggered. However, these excess capital losses may be carried forward to future years and applied against any excess capital gains (and up to $3,000 of ordinary income) in each future year until all the capital losses have been utilized.

A recognized gain or loss will be characterized as a capital gain or a capital loss if the gain or loss resulted from the sale or exchange of a capital asset. Almost all property constitutes a capital asset, other than inventory, depreciable property used in a trade or business, or real property used in a trade or business, and certain other narrow exceptions. Gain or loss resulting from the sale of inventory is always characterized as ordinary income or ordinary loss. By contrast, gain or loss resulting from the sale of depreciable property or real property used in a trade or business constitutes "section 1231" gain or loss if the property was held for more than one year. If the taxpayer's section 1231 gains for the year exceed the taxpayer's section 1231 losses, both the gains and the losses are taxed as long-term capital gains and long-term capital losses. By contrast, if the taxpayer's section 1231 gains for the year do not exceed the taxpayer's section 1231 losses, both the gains and the losses are treated as ordinary income or ordinary loss.

When the assets of a business are sold, the assets are not treated as a unit. Instead, the purchase price must be allocated among the individual assets of the business (based on the fair market value of each asset) and gain or loss must be computed with respect to each asset. Each gain or loss must then be characterized (based on the nature of the underlying asset) and reported accordingly by the seller of the business.

 Test Your Knowledge: To assess your understanding of the material in this chapter, **click here** to take a quiz.

PART VI

Alternative Minimum Tax

CHAPTER 17

Alternative Minimum Tax—§ 55

Overview

This casebook focuses on the determination of an individual's Federal income tax liability. It has examined in detail:

1)   the base on which the income tax is imposed (taxable income), and

2)   the rates delineated in IRC § 1 that are applied to that base.

The product of an individual's taxable income and the rates in IRC § 1 represents the individual's "regular tax." See IRC § 55(c)(1). Unfortunately, the determination of an individuals' regular tax is not the final step in determining an individual's Federal income tax liability. In addition, certain individuals will be liable for an "alternative minimum tax." IRC § 55. This Chapter will explore the alternative minimum tax.

A. Alternative Minimum Tax Rates

Like an individual's regular tax, the starting point for determining an individual's alternative minimum tax ("AMT") is identifying the base on which the tax is imposed and the tax rates that apply to that base. The rates of the AMT, and the base amounts in 2018 for most individuals to whom those rates applied, are as follows:

26% of the first $191,100 of the AMT base, and

28% of the AMT base in excess of $191,100.

See IRC §§ 55(b)(1)(A), (d)(3)(A), (B)(i).

WORTH NOTING

The dollar threshold at which the 26% rate ends and the 28% rate begins is adjusted annually for inflation. IRC § 55(d)(3). For 2018, that threshold was $191,100. See Rev. Proc. 2018–18, 2018–10 IRB 392 (section 3.10).

B. Alternative Minimum Tax Base

The AMT base is "alternative minimum taxable income" ("AMTI") less an exemption amount. See IRC § 55(b). AMTI is derived from the taxable income of the taxpayer for regular tax purposes. See IRC § 55(b)(2). To determine AMTI, various adjustments to the calculation of taxable income are made that expand the scope of gross income and curtail allowable deductions. For example, in computing AMTI, no standard deduction is allowed. See IRC § 56(b)(1)(E). These adjustments to taxable income will normally cause AMTI to exceed taxable income.

An "exemption amount" is subtracted from AMTI to arrive at the AMT tax base. See IRC § 55(d)(1). Congress temporarily increased the AMT exemption amount, beginning in 2018, from $84,500 to $109,400, for married individuals filing joint returns, and from $54,300 to $70,300, for most unmarried individuals. See IRC §§ 55(d)(1), (4)(A)(i). After 2018, these amounts are adjusted upward each year to account for the impact of inflation. See IRC §§ 55(d)(3)(A), (B)(ii). The increased exemption amounts are scheduled to revert back to their pre-2018 levels in 2026. See IRC § 55(d)(4)(A)(i).

Not all taxpayers enjoy the full AMT exemption amount. A taxpayer's AMT exemption amount is reduced (but not below zero) by an amount equal to 25% of the amount by which taxpayer's AMTI exceeds a certain "threshold amount." See IRC § 55(d)(2). Congress temporarily increased the threshold amount, beginning in 2018, by more than 500% for married individuals filing joint returns (from $160,900 to $1,000,000), and by more than 300% for most unmarried individuals (from $120,700 to $500,000). See IRC § 55(d)(4)(A)(ii). After 2018, these amounts will be adjusted upward each year to account for the impact of inflation. See IRC § 55(d)(4)(B). The 2018 increases in the threshold amount of AMTI at which a taxpayer's exemption amount begins to phaseout are scheduled to revert back to their pre-2018 levels in 2026. See IRC § 55(d)(4)(A)(ii).

WORTH NOTING The Code is not amended each year to reflect the new AMT exemption amounts and the new AMTI threshold amounts at which the AMT exemption begins to phase-out. These new amounts are simply announced by the Treasury Department. Thus, this casebook will utilize the exemption amounts and threshold amounts in effect in 2018 because those amounts appear in the Code. To compute the actual alternative minimum tax liability of a taxpayer in a given year, one must use the relevant exemption amount and threshold amount in effect for that year.

C.   Calculating the Alternative Minimum Tax

The taxpayer's AMTI less the exemption amount (if any) yields a "taxable excess." See IRC § 55(b)(1)(B). The tax rates in IRC § 55(b)(1)(A) are applied to the "taxable excess" to determine the individual's "tentative minimum tax." If the tentative minimum tax is greater than the individual's regular tax, the individual's AMT is the difference between the tentative minimum tax and the regular tax. See IRC § 55(a). In this situation, the individual must pay both the regular income tax and the AMT. If the tentative minimum tax is less than or equal to the individual's regular income tax, the individual has no AMT liability. In effect, the total amount of an individual's income tax liability in a given year is the greater of:

1)   the regular tax, or

2)   the tentative minimum tax.

■ **EXAMPLE 17-A.** *Impact of AMT on total tax liability.* Assume that Zelda, an unmarried individual, had taxable income (for purposes of the regular tax) of $500,000 and AMTI of $700,000 in 2018. What is Zelda's 2018 Federal income tax liability?

Zelda's 2018 "Regular Tax" (IRC § 1(j)(2)(C)—bottom row).   **$150,689.50**

Zelda's 2018 "AMT" (IRC § 55(a)).

"Exemption Amount" (IRC § 55(d)).

Exemption Amount for Unmarried Taxpayer in 2018	$70,300
– 25% of AMTI > $500,000	50,000[1]
Exemption Amount	$20,300

"Taxable Excess" (IRC § 55(b)(1)(B)).

AMTI	$700,000
– Exemption Amount	20,300
Taxable Excess	$679,700

"Tentative Minimum Tax" (IRC § 55(b)(1)(A)).

26% × $191,100	$49,686
+ 28% × ($679,700 – $191,100)	136,808
Tentative Minimum Tax	$186,494

"AMT" (IRC § 55(a)).

Tentative Minimum Tax	$186,494
– Regular Tax	$150,689.50
AMT	**$35,804.50**

Zelda's 2018 Federal Income Tax Liability.

Regular Tax	$150,689.50
+ AMT	$35,804.50
Federal Income Tax Liability	**$186,494**

---

[1]   [$700,000 (AMTI) – $500,000 (2018 threshold amount for unmarried individual)] × 25% = $200,000 × 25% = $50,000.

The AMT was originally enacted to preclude high-income individuals from exploiting the exclusions and deductions allowed by the regular income tax to minimize, or even eliminate, their Federal income tax liability. Prior to the recent, temporary increases to the exemption amounts and the threshold amounts (at which the exemption begins to phase-out), however, the AMT often applied to individuals with relatively low incomes.

KATZ v. COMMISSIONER

United States Tax Court, 2004
T.C. Memo. 2004–97

MEMORANDUM OPINION

Chabot, Judge.

　　* * *

Background

　　* * *

On petitioner's 2000 tax return, * * * petitioner showed adjusted gross income of $46,834.16 [and] itemized deductions of $54,275.81 * * *. Petitioner computed his taxable income as zero, and his tax liability as zero. * * * Respondent agrees that petitioner's "regular tax" (see sec. 55(c)) is zero [but determined that petitioner had an alternative minimum tax liability].

Discussion

Petitioner contends that the purpose of the alternative minimum tax provisions is to prevent high-income taxpayers from escaping all income tax liability by using exclusions, deductions, and credits. He maintains that "Obviously, the Petitioner did not have a significant level of economic income and all of his deductions * * * were deemed legitimate by the Respondent." Petitioner concludes that the "Congress did not intend the AMT to apply at [sic] low or middle-income taxpayers like the Petitioner."

Respondent contends that the statute subjects petitioner to the alternative minimum tax and that the legislative history does not leave room for any interpretation of the statute that would result in petitioner's not being subject to the alternative minimum tax.

We agree with respondent.

* * *

Section 55 imposes a tax—the alternative minimum tax—equal to the excess (if any) of the tentative minimum tax over the regular tax. Sec. 55(a). Petitioner's regular tax is zero, and so his alternative minimum tax is his full tentative minimum tax. Using Form 6251 (Alternative Minimum Tax—Individuals), respondent added back petitioner's appropriate itemized deductions to the amount by which petitioner's total itemized deductions exceeded his adjusted gross income. This operation resulted in petitioner's alternative minimum taxable income (sec. 55(b)(2)) being $38,707. From this amount, respondent subtracted petitioner's exemption amount. For 2000, * * * this was $22,500. Sec. 55(d)(1)[(B)].[2] This operation resulted in petitioner's "taxable excess" being $16,207. Sec. 55(b)(1)(A)(ii). To this amount respondent applied a 26-percent tax rate. Sec. 55(b)(1)(A)(i)(I). This operation resulted in petitioner's tentative minimum tax being $4,214, which * * * becomes petitioner's alternative minimum tax.

In its unanimous opinion in *Crooks v. Harrelson*, 282 U.S. 55, 60 (1930), the Supreme Court gave us the following advice as to tax statutes:

> Courts have sometimes exercised a high degree of ingenuity in the effort to find justification for wrenching from the words of a statute a meaning which literally they did not bear in order to escape consequences thought to be absurd or to entail great hardship. But an application of the principle so nearly approaches the boundary between the exercise of the judicial power and that of the legislative power as to call rather for great caution and circumspection in order to avoid usurpation of the latter. It is not enough merely that hard and objectionable or absurd consequences, which probably were not within the contemplation of the framers, are produced by an act of legislation. Laws enacted with good intention, when put to the test, frequently, and to the surprise of the law maker himself, turn out to be mischievous, absurd, or otherwise objectionable. But in such case the remedy lies with the law making authority, and not with the courts.

* * *

---

[2]   Editor's note: In 2018, the exemption amount for most unmarried individuals is $70,300. See IRC §§ 55(d)(1), (4)(A)(i).

The Congress did give some consideration to the treatment of lower-income people. The relevant relief that the Congress chose is embodied in section 55(d), which provides an exemption amount of $22,500 for petitioner for 2000. We are not free to alter this amount, or otherwise engage in "wrenching from the words of * * * [the] statute a meaning which literally they did not bear" (*Crooks v. Harrelson*, 282 U.S. at 60) in order to achieve the result petitioner seeks.

Petitioner must look to the Congress for relief.

An appropriate order will be issued * * * granting respondent's motion for summary judgment. * * *

WORTH NOTING

The reach of the alternative minimum tax has been significantly curtailed but only until 2026. In 2018, Congress significantly increased both the alternative minimum tax exemption amount and the threshold amount of AMTI at which the exemption amount begins to phase-out. As a result, the alternative minimum tax now applies to far fewer taxpayers and the problem illustrated in the Katz case should no longer exist. However, recent increases in the exemption amount and in the level of AMTI at which the exemption amount begins to phase-out are temporary; both are scheduled to expire after 2025. See IRC § 55(d)(4)(A). Unless the increased exemption amount and the increased threshold amount are extended, the alternative minimum tax will snare many more taxpayers beginning in 2026 and the problem illustrated in the Katz case will likely reappear.

SYNTHESIS

This Chapter reveals that determining a taxpayer's regular tax liability under IRC § 1 is necessary, but not sufficient, to determine the taxpayer's Federal income tax liability in a given year. In addition to the regular tax, the taxpayer's alternative minimum tax, if any, must be calculated. The taxpayer is *always* liable for the regular tax but will also be liable for the alternative minimum tax if the tentative minimum tax is greater than the regular tax. Hence, the final step in determining a taxpayer's Federal income tax liability for the taxable year is to determine whether the taxpayer has an alternative minimum tax liability.

In 2018, Congress modified the alternative minimum tax in a manner that greatly diminished its reach. These modifications are scheduled to expire in 2026, however, at which time the alternative minimum tax could once again apply to a large number of individuals.

 Test Your Knowledge: To assess your understanding of the material in this chapter, **click here** to take a quiz.

PART VII

Introduction to the Federal Income Taxation of Businesses

CHAPTER 18

Introduction to C Corporations, S Corporations, and Partnerships[1]

The basic personal income tax course normally explores the principle that the owner of property is taxed on any income generated by that property. Accordingly, if a collection of assets owned by an individual comprises a business (a "sole proprietorship"), all income generated by the business is taxed to that individual. State law does not treat the sole proprietorship as an entity that owns property separately from the individual entrepreneur. Similarly, Federal law does not treat the sole proprietorship as a separate entity for income tax purposes. If state law did treat the business as a separate entity, Federal tax law might also treat it as a separate entity, in which case income of the business might be taxed to the business entity, rather than to the individual proprietor.

In contrast to a sole proprietorship, individuals may create a business by pooling their resources (a state law partnership) or by utilizing a business form of statutory creation (a corporation or a limited liability company). When this occurs, state law normally treats the business as owning the property. Who does Federal tax law treat as the taxpayer under these circumstances? Does Federal law regard the business as separate from its owners and tax the business, itself, or does Federal law tax the income generated by the business directly to the individual owners? The answers to these questions depend on the legal form in which the business is conducted and on how that legal form is treated under Federal tax law.

---

[1]   This Chapter is a condensed version of Chapter 1 of Jeffrey L. Kwall, The Federal Income Taxation of Corporations, Partnerships, Limited Liability Companies and Their Owners, Foundation Press, 6th edition (2019).

A. The Business as an Entity Under State Law

For purposes of state law, a partnership exists when two or more individuals engage collectively in an activity with the expectation of generating profits. Under these circumstances, state law recognizes the partnership as the owner of the enterprise's assets. A partnership is a very flexible business form because it is a purely consensual arrangement. Any of the individual owners of the partnership (any "partner") may dissolve the partnership at any time and depart with her share of the assets of the enterprise (though generally not the specific assets that she contributed). Moreover, each partner is personally responsible for any partnership obligations that arise during the existence of the partnership.

A corporation is a more rigid arrangement than a partnership. Collective business activity alone does not create a corporation. Indeed, the presence of a corporation is not contingent upon a pooling of resources by more than one individual; a single individual can create a corporation. To have a corporation, the owner or owners of an enterprise must follow the specific state law requirements for creating that entity. Once the entity is created, the assets of the enterprise must be transferred (by assignment or deed) to the corporation. The corporation is recognized by state law as a legal entity separate from its owners ("shareholders"). State law provides that the corporation owns the assets of the enterprise and is solely responsible for any obligations of the enterprise. Absent a contractual agreement to the contrary, the shareholders are not personally responsible for obligations of the corporation. Thus, the shareholders of the corporation are exposed to corporate obligations only to the extent of their investment in the corporation. The shareholders merely own stock in the corporation, which represents legal ownership of the corporation and a stake in the corporation's assets and any future profits.

The limited liability company is an alternative business form of relatively recent origin now authorized in all states. Though a limited liability company resembles a corporation in many respects, it accommodates more flexible business arrangements. Like a corporation, a limited liability company can be created only by following the requirements of state law. The limited liability company is treated as a legal entity separate from its individual owners ("members") and is recognized as the owner of the enterprise's property. The members of a limited liability company, like the shareholders of a corporation, are exposed to obligations of the enterprise only to the extent of their investment in the limited liability company.

The fact that state law treats the partnership, the corporation and the limited liability company as the owner of the enterprise does not dictate that any party other than the individual partners, shareholders or members be taxed on the income of the enterprise. No partnership, corporation or limited liability company exists by itself. Rather, the existence of every enterprise conducted in these forms, irrespective of its magnitude, can be traced to individual partners, shareholders or members. Thus, all business income presumably could be taxed to the individual owners of the enterprise irrespective of the legal form in which the business is conducted.

If, at the end of each year, all business income was divided and distributed among the individual owners of the enterprise, it would be a relatively simple matter to tax that income to the individuals to whom it is attributable. Quite often, however, an enterprise retains the income it generates and reinvests this income to maintain or expand the enterprise. Under these circumstances, it is appealing, if not necessary, to accord some tax significance to the enterprise. At the very least, it is convenient to treat the enterprise as an accounting entity for tax purposes where income can be calculated and then be allocated among the individual owners. Alternatively, it may be desirable not only to calculate income at the enterprise level, but also to tax the enterprise on that income.

The Federal tax treatment of a business enterprise depends largely on the legal form in which the business is conducted. As a general rule, corporations are treated as taxpaying entities. In other words, the corporation pays tax on the enterprise's income. (The shareholders are also taxed, but not until the corporation's income is distributed to them.) Corporations treated as taxpaying entities are identified by the tax law as "C Corporations" because the taxation of these corporations is governed by Subchapter C (IRC §§ 301–385) of Chapter 1 of Subtitle A of the Internal Revenue Code.

In contrast to corporations, most state law partnerships and limited liability companies are treated simply as accounting entities. These enterprises are identified as "partnerships" by the tax law and are governed by Subchapter K (IRC §§ 701–777) of Chapter 1 of Subtitle A of the Internal Revenue Code. The income of an enterprise taxed as a partnership is computed by the enterprise, but that income is taxed directly to the individual owners of the enterprise. Certain corporations also may elect to be treated as accounting entities. Eligible corporations that so elect are identified by the tax law as "S Corporations" because the taxation of these corporations is governed by Subchapter S (IRC

§§ 1361–1378) of Chapter 1 of Subtitle A of the Internal Revenue Code. In recent years, S Corporations have significantly outnumbered C Corporations.[2]

B.　The Business as a Taxpaying Entity—the C Corporation

Since 1913, a corporate level tax has been imposed on the income of C Corporations. In addition to this corporate tax, the individual income tax is imposed on C Corporation income, but not until the corporation distributes its earnings to its shareholders (pays dividends). Therefore, the income of a C Corporation is taxed twice.

The fact that the income of C Corporations is taxed twice does not mean that twice as much tax is imposed on corporate income as on individual income derived from other sources. Rather, the total tax burden on corporate income depends largely upon the design of the corporate tax. The corporate tax could be designed to *substitute* for part or all of the tax that the individual owners would otherwise pay on the business's income. In this event, the corporate tax would merely serve as a mechanism for collecting the individual income tax on business profits that are not immediately distributed to the owners. Alternatively, the corporate tax could be designed to *supplement* the individual income tax on the owners' profits. In this case, some independent justification should exist for taxing corporate income more heavily than other forms of income.

Exhibit I compares the tax burden on corporate income distributed as dividends to the tax burden on individual income from other sources. Columns A and B list the maximum corporate tax rate and the maximum individual tax rate, respectively, over time. Column C shows the effective rate of the double tax on corporate income distributed as dividends. Column D compares the double tax on dividends to the single tax that applies to an individual's income from other sources.

---

[2]　The following is a rough estimate of the number of enterprises reporting to the Internal Revenue Service in 2015 as:

C Corporations	1,800,000	(17%)
S Corporations	4,700,000	(45%)
Partnerships	3,900,000	(38%)

Internal Revenue Service, Statistics of Income, http://www.irs.gov/statistics/soi-tax-stats-historical-table-21 (at 5-21-18).

EXHIBIT I[3]

Comparison of Double Tax on Dividends
with Single Tax on Other Income

Years	(A) Maximum Corporate Tax Rate	(B) Maximum Individual Tax Rate	(C) Double Tax on Dividends	(D) Column C As a % of Column B
1913–1915	1.00%	7.0%	6.94%	99%
1916	2.00%	15.0%	14.74%	98%
1917	6.00%	54.0%	53.00%	98%
1918	12.00%	77.0%	69.20%	90%
1919–1921	10.00%	73.0%	68.50%	94%
1922–1923	12.50%	58.0%	56.25%	97%
1924	12.50%	46.0%	47.50%	103%
1925	13.00%	25.0%	30.40%	122%
1926–1927	13.50%	25.0%	30.80%	123%
1928	12.00%	25.0%	29.60%	118%
1929	11.00%	24.0%	28.80%	120%
1930–1931	12.00%	25.0%	29.60%	118%
1932–1933	13.75%	63.0%	61.19%	97%
1934–1935	13.75%	63.0%	64.64%	103%
1936–1937	15.00%	79.0%	82.15%	104%
1938–1939	19.00%	79.0%	82.46%	104%
1940	22.10%	79.0%	83.64%	106%
1941	31.00%	81.0%	86.89%	107%
1942–1943	40.00%	88.0%	92.90%	106%
1944–1945	40.00%	94.0%	96.40%	103%
1946–1947	38.00%	86.4%	91.57%	106%
1948–1949	38.00%	82.1%	88.90%	108%

[3]   Derived from Jeffrey L. Kwall, "Subchapter G of the Internal Revenue Code: Crusade Without a Cause?,"
5 Virginia Tax Review 223 (1985).

Years	(A) Maximum Corporate Tax Rate	(B) Maximum Individual Tax Rate	(C) Double Tax on Dividends	(D) Column C As a % of Column B
1950	42.00%	84.4%	90.95%	108%
1951	50.75%	91.0%	95.57%	105%
1952–1953	52.00%	92.0%	96.16%	105%
1954–1963	52.00%	91.0%	93.76%	103%
1964	50.00%	77.0%	87.50%	114%
1965–1978	48.00%	70.0%	84.40%	121%
1979–1980	46.00%	70.0%	83.80%	120%
1981–1986	46.00%	50.0%	73.00%	146%
1987	40.00%	38.5%	63.10%	164%
1988–1990	34.00%	28.0%	52.48%	187%
1991–1992	34.00%	31.0%	54.46%	176%
1993–2000	35.00%	39.6%	60.74%	153%
2001	35.00%	39.1%	60.42%	155%
2002	35.00%	38.6%	60.09%	156%
2003–2012	35.00%	35.0%	44.75%	128%
2013–2017	35.00%	39.6%	50.47%	127%
2018–	21.00%	37.0%	39.80%	108%

As Exhibit I demonstrates, prior to the 1980s, the two taxes imposed on corporate income distributed as dividends (column (C)) did not cause corporate income to bear a significantly greater burden than other forms of individual income that were taxed only once (column (B)). The burden of the double tax on corporate income was moderated by the fact that corporate tax rates (column (A)) were significantly lower than individual tax rates (column (B)). Consequently, before the 1980s, the corporate tax did not cause corporate income distributed as dividends to bear a significantly higher tax burden than other forms of individual income.

By contrast, from 1981 until 2002, corporate income distributed as dividends (column (C)) bore a significantly greater tax burden than other forms of individual income (column (B)). That result stemmed primarily from the dramatically lower individual tax rates that prevailed during this period. By virtue of these lower rates, the tax burden on individual income other than dividends was much lower than in the past. Dividends, by contrast, continued to bear a large corporate tax in addition to the individual income tax. Congress offered no justification for taxing corporate income more heavily than other forms of income during this period.

In 2003, Congress reduced the tax burden on dividends by causing dividends received by individuals to be taxed at the lower tax rates that applied to capital gains. This change caused the tax burden on corporate income distributed as dividends (column (C)) relative to the tax burden on other forms of individual income (column (B)) to decline considerably.

In December 2017, Congress dramatically reduced the corporate tax rate to 21%, its lowest level since 1939. As a result, the two taxes now imposed on corporate income distributed as dividends (column (C)) do not cause such income to bear a significantly greater burden than other forms of individual income that are taxed only once (column (B)). In effect, the current relationship between the corporate tax rate (21%) and the maximum individual tax rate (37%) resembles the relationship that existed prior to the 1980s when corporate tax rates were significantly lower than individual tax rates. Unfortunately, the relationship between the corporate tax and the individual income tax has evolved over the past century in a largely haphazard fashion, rather than from a clear Congressional policy.

C. The Business as a Tax Accounting Entity—the S Corporation and the Partnership

The income of enterprises taxed as partnerships and S Corporations (collectively referred to as "pass-through entities") is not normally subject to the corporate tax or any other entity-level tax. Instead, the income of a pass-through entity is taxed directly to the owners of the enterprise. Although the pass-through entity, itself, does not pay taxes, the owners must often withdraw a sufficient amount of the business's earnings to satisfy their personal income tax liabilities attributable to the income of the pass-through entity.

Prior to the 1980s, when individual tax rates were very high, pass-through entities were generally disfavored tax regimes for profitable enterprises. Although the pass-through entity did not pay the corporate tax, its income was taxed to the owners of the enterprise, generally at much higher individual tax rates.[4] If the owners withdrew funds from the business to pay their personal income tax liabilities, the amount of earnings available to reinvest in the business was smaller than the amount of earnings available to a C Corporation with the same amount of income, because the C Corporation could reinvest its earnings after paying only the lower-rate corporate tax.

■ **EXAMPLE 18-A.** *Amount of earnings available to reinvest in pass-through entity versus C Corporation.* If the individual tax rate is 70% and the corporate tax rate is 40%, $100 of income earned by a pass-through entity generates $70 of tax liability to the owners. If the owners withdraw $70 to pay the tax they owe, only $30 remains for reinvestment in the business. By contrast, if the $100 is earned by a C Corporation, the corporation pays a tax of $40 and $60 remains to finance expansion of the business. While it is true that this $60 will someday be subjected to a second tax at the owner level, that future tax burden may not be of much concern to the owners of a growing enterprise with a great need for capital.

During the 1980s, individual tax rates declined considerably and have remained at lower levels since that time.[5] Moreover, until 2018, the maximum individual tax rate (Exhibit I, column (B)) remained fairly close to the corporate tax rate (Exhibit I, column (A)), which dramatically increased the appeal of the pass-through entity. During periods when the single tax on pass-through entity income (the individual income tax) is roughly equivalent to the first of the two taxes on C Corporation income (the corporate tax), the pass-through entity will normally be preferred. This preference exists because pass-through entity income will never bear the burden of the additional tax imposed on C Corporation income when dividends are paid.

In December 2017, Congress dramatically reduced the corporate tax rate from 35% to 21% (Exhibit I, column (A)). Consequently, the 37% maximum

---

[4] See Exhibit I, compare columns (A) and (B).

[5] See Exhibit I, column (B).

individual tax rate (Exhibit I, column (B)) now greatly exceeds the corporate tax rate. One might expect this condition to lead to a resurgence in the popularity of the C Corporation. However, when Congress reduced the corporate tax rate, it also enacted a provision allowing certain owners of pass-through entities a 20% deduction with respect to business income of the pass-through entity.[6] This deduction can significantly reduce the tax burden on pass-through entity income.

Under current law, the pass-through entity is still generally favored over the C Corporation by privately-owned businesses. Nevertheless, the choice of business form decision must be evaluated on a case-by-case basis because the C Corporation can sometimes minimize tax costs. The Chapters that follow will explore the factors that must be considered when advising the owners of a business on the optimal business form to utilize.

D. The Uniform Taxation of All Business Income—Preview of the Future?

Since the origin of the Federal income tax, the total tax burden on the income of C Corporations has frequently differed from the tax burden on pass-through entities.[7] When the income of a business subject to one tax regime is taxed more heavily than the same amount of income generated by a business subject to another tax regime, tax considerations will likely influence the choice of business form decision. When the tax law influences a business decision, economic inefficiencies may result.

To eliminate the distortions created by the different tax regimes that now exist, many analysts advocate the adoption of a tax system that imposes the same tax burden on the income of all businesses, irrespective of their legal form. The process for achieving this goal is referred to as "integration". In its purest form, integration entails repealing the corporate tax and taxing corporate income directly to the corporation's shareholders when it is earned. In effect, every business, regardless of its legal form, would be taxed as a pass-through entity. Less extreme versions of integration involve retaining the corporate tax but reducing or eliminating the shareholder tax on dividends.

---

[6]   See IRC § 199A which applies to taxable years beginning before January 1, 2026.

[7]   See Exhibit I, compare columns (B) and (C).

Many years ago, the Treasury Department issued a comprehensive report intended to serve as "a source document to begin the debate on the desirability of integration" and concluded that integration would be desirable. Although integration has not been adopted to date and is not currently on the legislative agenda, the following excerpts from the Treasury report provide a useful point of departure from which to begin the study of existing law.

Treasury Department Report, Integration of the Individual and Corporate Tax Systems

January 6, 1992

PART I: THE CASE FOR INTEGRATION

Current U.S. tax law treats corporations and their investors as separate taxable entities. Under this classical system of corporate income taxation, two levels of income tax are generally imposed on earnings from investments in corporate equity. First, corporate earnings are taxed at the corporate level. Second, if the corporation distributes earnings to shareholders, the earnings are taxed again at the shareholder level. In contrast, investors in business activities conducted in non-corporate form, such as sole proprietorships or partnerships, are generally taxed only once on the earnings, and this tax is imposed at the individual level. Corporate earnings distributed as interest to suppliers of debt capital also are taxed only once because interest is deductible by the corporation and generally taxed to lenders as ordinary income.

Despite its long history, considerable debate surrounds the role of the corporate income tax in the Federal tax structure. The central issue is whether corporate earnings should be taxed once rather than taxed both when earned and when distributed to shareholders. Integration of the individual and corporate income tax refers to the taxation of corporate income once. This Report discusses and evaluates several integration alternatives.

Despite their differences, the methods of integration studied in this Report reflect a common goal: where practical, fundamental economic considerations, rather than tax considerations, should guide business investment, organization and financial decisions. * * * Corporate integration can thus be regarded as a phase of tax reform in the United States, extending the goal of neutral taxation to the choice of business organization and financial policy.

The current two-tier system of corporate taxation discourages the use of the corporate form * * *. The two-tier tax also discourages new equity financing of corporate investment, encourages debt financing of such investment, distorts decisions with respect to the payment of dividends, and encourages corporations to distribute earnings in a manner designed to avoid the double-level tax.

These distortions have economic costs. The classical corporate tax system reduces the level of investment and interferes with the efficient allocation of resources. In addition, the tax bias against corporate equity can encourage corporations to increase debt financing beyond levels supported by nontax considerations, thereby increasing risks of financial distress and bankruptcy.

Historically, the corporation has been an important vehicle for economic growth in the United States, but the classical corporate tax system often perversely penalizes the corporate form of organization. With the increasing integration of international markets for products and capital, one must consider effects of the corporate tax system on the competitiveness of U.S. firms. Most of the major trading partners of the United States have revised their tax systems to provide for some integration of the corporate and individual tax systems.

* * *

The classical system of corporate taxation is inefficient because it creates differences in the taxation of alternative sources of income from capital. Under the classical system, a taxpayer conducting business in corporate form faces a different tax burden on equity financing than a taxpayer conducting the same business in noncorporate form. A corporation that raises capital in the form of equity faces a different tax burden than a corporation that raises the same amount of capital from debt. A similar disparity exists in the treatment of corporations that finance with retained earnings and those that pay dividends and finance with new equity. This Report provides evidence that these distortions impose significant economic costs, including reduced financial flexibility of corporations and an inefficient allocation of capital.

A traditional goal of integration proposals has been to tax corporate income only once at the tax rate of the shareholder to whom the income is attributed or distributed. Under the traditional approach, corporate income ideally would be taken into account when earned in determining each individual's economic income and would be taxed at each individual's marginal tax rate. * * *

[Alternatively, integration might be achieved] with a schedular system in which all corporate income is taxed at a uniform rate at the corporate level without regard to the tax rate of the corporate shareholder. * * *

* * *

We approach integration primarily as a means of reducing the distortions of the classical system and improving economic efficiency. This Report's emphasis on enhancing neutrality in the taxation of capital income can be summarized in [three] goals for the design of an integrated tax system:

> *Integration should make more uniform the taxation of investment across sectors of the economy.* The U.S. corporate system discourages investment in the corporate sector relative to investment in the noncorporate sector and owner-occupied housing. That is, current law results in too little capital in the corporate sector relative to that elsewhere in the economy. Integration seeks to reduce this distortion.

> *Integration should make more uniform the taxation of returns earned on alternative financial instruments particularly debt and equity.* The U.S. corporate tax system discourages corporations from financing investments with equity as opposed to debt. Such a system violates the goal of neutral taxation. Although equalizing the tax treatment of debt and equity need not be the overriding goal of integration, equal treatment follows from the goal of attaining neutral taxation of capital income.

> *Integration should distort as little as possible the choice between retaining and distributing earnings.* The U.S. corporate system discourages the payment of dividends and encourages corporations to retain earnings * * *.

* * *

Revenue concerns * * * may prevent integration from fully equalizing the taxation of alternative investments. Some integration proposals would reduce government revenue from income taxes. Lost tax revenue must be made up either by increasing other taxes or by reducing government spending. Replacement taxes may create distortions and alter the distribution of tax burdens.

* * *

Notes

1. *Taxing undistributed corporate profits.* Undistributed corporate profits normally increase the value of the stock of a corporation and thereby accrue to the benefit of the shareholders even before these earnings are distributed. Is the requirement that gains be realized before they are taxed an impediment to including corporate profits in the gross income of individual shareholders before the profits are distributed? See IRC § 1001(a). What arguments can be advanced for or against changing the tax law to include corporate income in the tax base of shareholders when that income is earned, regardless of whether it is distributed?

2. *Subsequent developments.* Although no formal integration proposal has been adopted to date, Congress has significantly modified the tax burden on the income of C Corporations and pass-through entities during the twenty-first century. In 2003, Congress reduced the tax burden on corporate income by taxing dividends at the lower rates that apply to an individual's capital gains. See IRC § 1(h)(11). In 2017, the tax burden on corporate income was further reduced as Congress cut the corporate tax rate from 35% to 21%. See IRC § 11(b). At the same time, Congress reduced the tax burden on pass-through entity income by allowing certain owners of pass-through entities a deduction equal to 20% of the pass-through entity's business income. See IRC § 199A. Whether Congress will someday take a comprehensive approach to equalizing the tax burden on all business income remains to be seen.

Test Your Knowledge: To assess your understanding of the material in this chapter, click here to take a quiz.

Review of Major Themes

A. Economic Considerations vs. Tax Considerations

1. Would you rather receive a dollar of gross income, or receive nothing?

You would rather receive $1 of gross income. Assume your tax rate is 40%. If you receive $1 of gross income, you keep $.60 ($1 received less $.40 of tax paid). But if you receive nothing, you keep nothing. It is preferable to keep $.60 relative to keeping nothing.

CONCLUSION: If two alternatives involve different economic outcomes (i.e., the receipt of $1 vs. the receipt of nothing), economic considerations are paramount to tax considerations. If taxes took priority, you would opt not to receive the dollar so you did not have to pay any tax. But since the alternative is receiving nothing, you are better off receiving the dollar, paying the tax, and keeping what remains.

2. Would you rather receive a dollar of gross income, or a dollar that is excluded from gross income?

You would rather receive $1 that is excluded from gross income. If you receive $1 of gross income and your tax rate is 40%, you will pay a tax of $.40 and you will keep $.60 ($1 received less $.40 of tax paid). But if the $1 you receive is excluded from gross income, you keep $1. It is preferable to keep $1 relative to keeping $.60.

CONCLUSION: If two alternatives involve identical economic outcomes (i.e., the receipt of $1), tax considerations are paramount.

3. Would you rather pay $1 that is allowed as a tax deduction, or pay nothing?

You would rather pay nothing. If the $1 you pay is allowed as a tax deduction and your tax rate is 40%, your net outlay will be $.60 ($1 minus the $.40 in tax savings you derive from the $1 deduction). If you pay nothing, your total outlay is zero. An outlay of zero is preferable to an outlay of $.60.

CONCLUSION: If two alternatives involve different economic outcomes (i.e., the payment of $1 vs. paying nothing), economic considerations are paramount to tax considerations. If taxes took priority, you would opt to pay the dollar because it triggers a deduction. But since the alternative is to pay nothing, you are better off paying nothing and foregoing the deduction than paying the dollar and deriving a deduction.

4. Would you rather pay a dollar that is allowed as a deduction, or pay a dollar that is not allowed as a deduction?

You would rather pay a dollar that is allowed as a deduction. If the $1 you pay is allowed as a deduction and your tax rate is 40%, you will save $.40 in tax (the deduction will cause the amount of your taxable income to fall by $1 which will cause your tax to fall by $.40). Thus, your total outlay is only $.60 (the dollar you pay minus the $.40 in tax savings you derive from the deduction). If the dollar you pay is not allowed as a deduction, your total outlay is $1. An outlay of $.60 is preferable to an outlay of $1.

CONCLUSION: If two alternatives involve identical economic outcomes (i.e., the payment of $1), tax considerations are paramount.

B. The Time Value of Money

Money has a time value. If I have $1,000 and I deposit the money in the bank, I will earn interest for the period of time the money is in the bank. Interest rates have deviated dramatically over the past few decades. In the early 1980s, it was not unheard of to earn 12% annual interest on a bank deposit. If I deposited my $1,000 then, I would have earned $120 a year of interest. For the past decade, interest rates have been very low. During this period, I would have been lucky to earn 1% annual interest on my $1,000—or $10 a year of interest.

Regardless of the level of interest rates, money will normally have a time value associated with it. Thus, from an economic standpoint, it is desirable to hold money as long as possible to maximize the return one can earn on money that one controls. As a result, taxpayers normally want to defer taxes as long as possible to maximize the interest they can earn on their money. By contrast, it is in the government's interest to collect taxes as soon as possible to avoid having to borrow money on which the government would have to pay interest.

This casebook demonstrated many instances where the tax law endeavors to mitigate the benefits taxpayers can enjoy from the time value of money. It also revealed instances where the tax law facilitates such enjoyment by taxpayers. The realization requirement is a feature of the law that facilitates tax deferral (by not taxing increases in the value of property until a sale occurs) and, therefore, the enjoyment of the time value of money by taxpayers.

C. The Realization Event Requirement

Assume I buy a parcel of land for $10,000. A few years later, the surrounding area is substantially improved and, as a result, the value of my land increases to $110,000. When am I taxed on the $100,000 increase in the value of the land?

Regardless of one's knowledge of the tax law, most people believe that I am not taxed on the increase in the value of my land until I sell it. That conclusion is, in fact, correct. As you have learned, however, the tax system of the United States is theoretically supposed to tax increases in wealth *as they occur.* So the fact that we wait to tax the landowner on the increase in the value of the land until the land is sold is actually a deviation from the norm.

Our tax system deviates from the underlying principle of taxing increases in wealth as they occur by imposing a "realization requirement." By virtue of the realization requirement, any increase in the value of property owned by a taxpayer is not taxed until the occurrence of a "realization event" (normally, a sale of the property).

The realization requirement has the effect of deferring income when a taxpayer's property increases in value before it is sold. In the absence of the realization requirement, increases in the value of property would be taxed as they occur. By virtue of the realization requirement, however, the tax on any increase in the value of property owned by a taxpayer is deferred until the property is sold. At first blush, deferral may seem insignificant. As long as the increase in the value of property is taxed at some point, why does it matter if the tax is imposed in the future as opposed to the present? But deferral is of course significant from an economic standpoint due to the time value of money.

WORTH NOTING

A few discrete Code provisions deviate from the realization requirement and tax asset appreciation as it occurs (referred to as economic accrual or "mark-to-market" treatment). See, e.g., IRC §§ 467, 475, 817A, 1271–5, 1296.

D. The Effect of Progressive Tax Rates

If all income were taxed at the same rate (a "flat rate" tax system), the government would be indifferent with regard to whom a given item of income was taxed. Under these circumstances, the government would collect the same amount of revenue regardless of the taxpayer. For more than a century, however, the United States has utilized a "progressive rate" tax system. This means that the rate of tax imposed on income increases when a taxpayer's income exceeds specified levels.

Under current law, income tax rates range from 0% to 37%. High-income taxpayers pay tax at higher rates than lower income taxpayers. As a result, high-income taxpayers have gone to great lengths to shift the tax burden on income to related, lower-rate taxpayers. Congress and the courts have endeavored to impede taxpayers from achieving this goal. As long as a progressive rate system is utilized, an incentive will exist to shift the tax burden from high-income taxpayers to related lower income taxpayers.

Index